Pathologies of the Modern Self

PSYCHOANALYTIC CROSSCURRENTS
General Editor: Leo Goldberger

THE DEATH OF DESIRE: A STUDY IN PSYCHOPATHOLOGY
by M. Guy Thompson

THE TALKING CURE: LITERARY REPRESENTATIONS OF PSYCHOANALYSIS
by Jeffrey Berman

NARCISSISM AND THE TEXT: STUDIES IN LITERATURE AND THE PSYCHOLOGY OF SELF
Lynne Layton and Barbara Ann Schapiro, *Editors*

THE LANGUAGE OF PSYCHOSIS
by Bent Rosenbaum and Harly Sonne

SEXUALITY AND MIND: THE ROLE OF THE FATHER AND THE MOTHER IN THE PSYCHE
by Janine Chasseguet-Smirgel

ART AND LIFE: ASPECTS OF MICHELANGELO
by Nathan Leites

PATHOLOGIES OF THE MODERN SELF: POSTMODERN STUDIES ON NARCISSISM, SCHIZOPHRENIA, AND DEPRESSION
David Michael Levin, *Editor*

PATHOLOGIES OF THE MODERN SELF

Postmodern Studies on Narcissism, Schizophrenia, and Depression

DAVID MICHAEL LEVIN
Editor

NEW YORK UNIVERSITY PRESS
New York *and* London

Manufactured in the United States of America

Library of Congress Cataloging-in-Publication Data

Pathologies of the modern self.

(Psychoanalytic crosscurrents)
Bibliography: p.
Includes index.
1. Self. 2. Narcissism. 3. Schizophrenia.
4. Depression, Mental. 5. Psychology, Pathological.
I. Levin, David Michael, 1939– . II. Series.
RC455.4.S42P38 1987 616.89 87-5464
ISBN 0-8147-5026-5

Contents

Foreword

The *Psychoanalytic Crosscurrents* series presents selected books and monographs that reveal the growing intellectual ferment within and across the boundaries of psychoanalysis.

Freud's theories and grand-scale speculative leaps have been found wanting, if not disturbing, from the very beginning and have led to a succession of derisive attacks, shifts in emphasis, revisions, modifications, and extensions. Despite the chronic and, at times, fierce debate that has characterized psychoanalysis, not only as a movement but also as a science, Freud's genius and transformational impact on the twentieth century have never been seriously questioned. Recently psychoanalytic thought has been subjected to dramatic reassessments under the sway of contemporary currents in the history of ideas, philosophy of science, epistemology, structuralism, critical theory, semantics, and semiology as well as in sociobiology, ethology, and neurocognitive science. Not only is Freud's place in intellectual history being meticulously scrutinized, his texts, too, are being carefully read, explicated, and debated within a variety of conceptual frameworks and sociopolitical contexts.

The legacy of Freud is perhaps most notably evident within the narrow confines of psychoanalysis itself, the "impossible profession" that has served as the central platform for the promulgation of official orthodoxy. But Freud's contributions—his original radical thrust—reach far beyond the parochial concerns of the clinical psychoanalyst as clinician. His writings touch on a wealth of issues, crossing traditional boundaries—be they situated in the biological, social, or humanistic spheres—that have profoundly altered our conception of the individual and society.

A rich and flowering literature, falling under the rubric of "applied psychoanalysis," came into being, reached its zenith many decades ago, and then almost vanished. Early contributors to this literature, in addition to Freud himself, came from a wide range of backgrounds both within and outside the medical/psychiatric field: many later became psychoanalysts themselves. These early efforts were characteristically reductionistic in their attempt to extrapolate from psychoanalytic theory (often the purely clinical theory) to explanations of phenomena lying at some distance from the clinical. Over the years, academic psychologists, educators, anthropologists, sociologists, political scientists, philosophers, jurists, literary critics, art historians, artists, and writers, among others (with or without formal psychoanalytic training) have joined in the proliferation of this literature.

The intent of the *Psychoanalytic Crosscurrents* series is to apply psychoanalytic ideas to topics that may lie beyond the narrowly clinical, but its essential conception and scope are quite different. The present series eschews the reductionistic tendency to be found in much traditional "applied psychoanalysis." It acknowledges not only the complexity of psychological phenomena but also the way in which they are embedded in social and scientific contexts that are constantly changing. It calls for a dialectical relationship to earlier theoretical views and conceptions rather than a mechanical repetition of Freud's dated thoughts. The series affirms the fact that contributions to and about psychoanalysis have come from many directions. It is designed as a forum for the multidisciplinary studies that intersect with psychoanalytic thought but without the requirement that psychoanalysis necessarily be the starting point or, indeed, the center focus. The criteria for inclusion in the series are that the work be significantly informed by psychoanalytic thought or that it be aimed at furthering our understanding of psychoanalysis in its broadest meaning as theory, practice, and sociocultural phenomenon; that it be of current topical interest and that it provide the critical reader with contemporary insights; and, above all, that it be high-quality scholarship, free of obsolete dogma, banalization, and empty jargon. The author's professional identity and particular theoretical orientation matter only to the extent that such facts may serve to frame the work for the reader, alerting him or her to inevitable biases of the author.

The Psychoanalytic Crosscurrents Series presents an array of works from the multidisciplinary domain in an attempt to capture the ferment of scholarly activities at the core as well as at the boundaries of psychoanalysis. The books and monographs are from a variety of sources: authors will be psychoanalysts—traditional, neo- and post-Freudian, existential, object-relational, Kohutian, Lacanian, etc.—social scientists with quantitative or qualitative orientations to psychoanalytic data, and scholars from the vast diversity of approaches and interests that make up the humanities. The series entertains works on critical comparisons of psychoanalytic theories and concepts as well as philosophical examinations of fundamental assumptions and epistemic claims that furnish the base for psychoanalytic hypotheses. It includes studies of psychoanalysis as literature (discourse and narrative theory) as well as the application of psychoanalytic studies of creativity and the arts. Works in the cognitive and the neurosciences will be included to the extent that they address some fundamental psychoanalytic tenet, such as the role of dreaming and other forms of unconscious mental processes.

It should be obvious that an exhaustive enumeration of the types of works that might fit into the *Psychoanalytic Crosscurrents* series is pointless. The studies comprise a lively and growing literature as a unique domain; books of this sort are frequently difficult to classify or catalog. Suffice it to say that the overriding aim of the editor of this series is to serve as a conduit for the identification of the outstanding yield of that emergent literature and to foster its further unhampered growth.

Leo Goldberger
Professor of Psychology
New York University

Acknowledgments

We are grateful to the following authors and publishers for granting us permission to quote from:

MINIMA MORALIA: REFLECTIONS FROM DAMAGED LIFE by Theodor Adorno. By permission of New Left Books, London, 1974; Verso Editions, 1978.

THE LIFE OF THE SELF: TOWARD A NEW PSYCHOLOGY by Robert Jay Lifton. Reprinted by permission of Basic Books, Inc., Publishers.

THE QUESTION CONCERNING TECHNOLOGY AND OTHER ESSAYS by Martin Heidegger and translated by William Lovitt. English language translation © 1977 by Harper & Row, Publishers, Inc.

THE END OF PHILOSOPHY by Martin Heidegger and translated by Joan Stambaugh. Copyright © 1973 in the English translation by Harper & Row, Publishers, Inc.

THE WILL TO POWER by Friedrich Nietzsche, edited with commentary by Walter Kaufmann, translated by Walter Kaufmann and R. J. Hollingdale. Copyright © 1968 by Random House, Inc.

THE CULTURE OF NARCISSISM by Christopher Lasch. Copyright © 1979 by W. W. Norton & Company, Inc. Quotes used by permission of W. W. Norton & Company, Inc.

DAWN AND DECLINE by Max Horkheimer. English translation copyright © 1978 by The Continuum Publishing Company. Reprinted by permission.

Contributors

JAMES BERNAUER is currently Associate Professor of philosophy at Boston College. After the completion of graduate degrees in theology and in the Psychiatry and Religion Program at Union Theological Seminary, he earned his doctorate in philosophy from the State University of New York, Stony Brook. He attended Foucault's courses in Paris, 1979 and 1980. His essays have been published in such journals as *Commonweal, International Philosophical Quarterly, Man and World,* and *Philosophy and Social Criticism.* A collection edited by him will be published in 1986 by Martinus Nijhoff: *Amor Mundi: Explorations in the Faith and Thought of Hannah Arendt.*

EUGENE T. GENDLIN is both philosopher (Ph.D., University of Chicago) and practicing psychotherapist. His philosophical work on experiential processes has had applications in psychotherapy research. In 1970, the Psychotherapy Division of the American Psychological Association gave him an award in recognition of this research. He was the founder and for some years the editor of a journal, *Psychotherapy: Theory, Research and Practice.* Professor Gendlin currently teaches Heidegger, Aristotle, Kant, theory construction, and psychotherapy at the University of Chicago. His publications include *Experiencing and the Creation of Meaning, Focusing, Let Your Body Interpret Your Dreams,* "Befindlichkeit: Heidegger and the Philosophy of Psychology" (*Review of Existential Psychology and Psychiatry,* 1978-1979), "Experiential Phenomenology," in Natanson (ed.), *Phenomenology and the Social Sciences,* and "Analysis," in the English translation of Heidegger's *What Is A Thing?*

JAMES M. GLASS is a Professor in the Department of Government and Politics at the University of Maryland, College Park. He also holds an appointment as Research Associate at The Sheppard and Enoch Pratt Hospital in Towson, Maryland. His recently published book on *Delusion* addresses the relationship between the clinical world of schizophrenics and issues in political theory and philosophy. He is currently working on a project that looks at the classical theory of asylum from the perspective of how patients experience their "holding" environment and how the community and its "public space" are involved in bringing the delusional self back to consensual reality.

STANISLAV GROF, M.D. (Charles University School of Medicine, Prague) and Ph.D. (Czechoslovakian Academy of Sciences), is a psychiatrist with an experience of almost thirty years of research into nonordinary states of consciousness induced by psychedelic substances and various nondrug techniques. He has held research positions at the Psychiatric Research Institute in Prague, Johns Hopkins University, and the Maryland Psychiatric Research Center, and was Assistant Professor of Psychiatry at the Henry Phipps Clinic. At present he is Scholar-in-Residence and a member of the Board of Trustees at the Esalen Institute, Big Sur, California. He is one of the founders and chief theoreticians of transpersonal psychology and founding president of the International Transpersonal Association. He is the author of *Realms of the Human Unconscious, The Human Encounter with Death, LSD Psychotherapy, Beyond Death,* and *Journeys Beyond the Brain.*

IRENE E. HARVEY recently received her doctorate in philosophy from York University, Toronto. She is currently Assistant Professor in the Department of Philosophy, Pennsylvania State University. In addition to a number of journal studies on Hegel, Derrida, Foucault and Lacan, she has written a book, *Derrida and the Economy of Difference.*

PAULA B. JOHNSON is currently in the Core Faculty at the California School of Professional Psychology, Los Angeles, where she has been teaching since 1980. She is the author of numerous articles in social psychology, writing especially on her research into social power, sex roles, health care systems, and community psychology. Together with four others, she wrote *Women and Sex Roles: A Social Psychological Perspective.*

JOEL KOVEL is a psychoanalyst who has taught at The New School for Social Research and, until recently, in the Department of Psychiatry at the Albert Einstein College of Medicine. His books include *White Racism: A Psychohistory; A Complete Guide to Therapy; The Age of Desire;* and most recently, *Against the State of Nuclear Terror.*

CISCO LASSITER received his B.S. in ecosystem management from Antioch University and holds an M.A. in anthropology, awarded by Humboldt State University. He is now living in northern California, where he experiments with ecology conservation on his own land and does freelance writing and photojournalism. His most recent work calls attention to the social and political problems confronting the Amerindian cultures, and he has reproted on the struggles of Indian people from California and Arizona to Nicaragua, taking on assignments from the Pacific News Service, *The San Francisco Examiner,* and *The Mendocino Grapevine.*

DAVID MICHAEL LEVIN is Professor of Philosophy in the Department of Philosophy, Northwestern University. He took his B.A. at Harvard and his Ph.D. at Columbia; he taught at the Massachusetts Institute of Technology before going to Northwestern. He has published extensively in phenomenological psychology and is the author of three books: *Reason and Evidence in Husserl's Phenomenology*, *The Body's Recollection of Being: Phenomenological Psychology and the Deconstruction of Nihilism,* and *The Opening of Vision: Nihilism and the Postmodern Situation.*

ROGER LEVIN is an experiential psychotherapist in private practice (offices in New York City and New Milford, Connecticut) who specializes in the psychology of illness. Working with cancer patients who have been subject to the traditional allopathic interventions, he uses experiential focusing, imagery processes and other awareness practices to provide a foundation for either alternative or adjunctive therapy. He is currently continuing the research he began at the New School for Social Research on the relationship between psychological states and degenerative illness. He was at one time associated with the New York City Feminist Center and the New York Center for Medical Consumers. Presently, he is staff psychologist at the New Milford (Connecticut) Visiting Nurses Association In-Home Hospice and resident psychotherapist for the South Kent School. He has worked closely with Eugene Gendlin and is frequently called upon to lecture on illness and healing and to teach focusing to psychotherapists and other health care professionals in New York City, Connecticut, and Massachusetts.

RICHARD F. MOLLICA, M.D. is Assistant Professor of Psychiatry at the Harvard Medical School and Massachusetts General Hospital. He was trained in psychiatry and psychiatric epidemiology at Yale University and holds a Masters degree from the Yale University Divinity School. Since 1978 he has been conducting research that continues the studies begun by Redlich and Hollingshead, and reported in their book on *Social Class and Mental Illness*. Since 1979 Dr. Mollica has served as consultant to the Italian Institute of Psychiatry in Rome, sitting on the National Research Council.

From 1979-1980 he was a Fulbright Professor in the Department of Sociology, University of Essex, England. He is the author of important papers on Antonio Gramsci and Franco Basaglia, published in an issue of the *International Journal of Mental Health* (Spring-Summer, 1985), which was devoted to "The Unfinished Revolution in Italian Psychiatry," and which he put together as Guest Editor. He organized and is Director of one of the first psychiatric clinics for Indo-Chinese refugees: the Indo-Chinese Psychiatry Clinic in Brighton, Massachusetts. The clinic treats individuals with multiple traumas, including homelessness and torture.

KENNETH S. POPE is currently in the clinical faculty of the Department of Psychology at the University of California, Los Angeles. He is the author of numerous journal articles and books and co-editor, with Jerome Singer, of a new journal, *Imagination, Cognition, and Personality.* Together with Singer he edited *The Stream of Consciousness: Scientific Investigations into the Flow of Human Experience* and *The Power of Human Imagination: New Methods of Psychotherapy.* From 1979-1981 Dr. Pope was Director of Psychological Services at the Gateways Hospital and Mental Health Center; in 1981 he served as clinical director of the San Fernando Valley Community Mental Health Centers, Inc. At present he is in private clinical practice and is associated with The Wellness Community in Santa Monica.

JENNIFER RADDEN, PH.D. teaches in the Department of Philosophy, University of Massachusetts, Boston. Professor Radden is the author of several published studies, including "Diseases as Excuses: Durham and the Insanity Plea" (*Philosophical Studies*), and a book, *Madness and Reason,* in which she examines moral and legal questions concerning "insanity."

ROBERT D. ROMANYSHYN is Chairman of the Department of Psychology at the University of Dallas. He also maintains an extensive private clinical practice in the Dallas region. Dr. Romanyshyn is the author of many journal studies and a recent book called *Psychological Life: From Science to Metaphor.* In both his writing and his clinical practice, Dr. Romanyshyn combines an early training in phenomenological psychology with subsequent training in Jungian analytical psychology.

JEFFREY SATINOVER, M.D., psychiatrist and Jungian analyst, is currently a Fellow of the Child Study Center at Yale University and is in private practice in Connecticut. He holds degrees from M.I.T., Harvard, the C.G. Jung Institute of Zurich, and the University of Texas. In 1975 he gave the William James Lectures in Psychology and Religion at Harvard University.

He has lectured extensively to psychiatric, psychoanalytic, and Jungian groups. His most recent article, "Jung's Lost Contribution to the Dilemma of Narcissism," will appear in the forthcoming issue of the *Journal of the American Psychoanalytic Association*.

NATHAN SCHWARTZ-SALANT holds a doctorate from the University of California, Berkeley and a diploma in analytical psychology from the C.G. Jung Institute of Zurich. He is currently in clinical practice and teaches at the C.G. Jung Institute in New York City. He is a founding editor of *Chiron,* a new review of Jungian psychology and author of numerous monographs and public lectures and of a book, *Narcissism and Character Transformation: The Psychology of Narcissistic Character Disorders*.

BRIAN J. WHALEN is currently a doctoral candidate in the Institute of Philosophic Studies at the University of Dallas. He has authored, together with his teacher, Robert Romanyshyn, an essay called "Word, World, and Soul: Language and Desire" (*Journal of Metaphor and Symbolic Activity*).

INTRODUCTION

DAVID MICHAEL LEVIN

These essays, written especially for this collection, are concerned with "cultural epidemiology." We hope they contribute to the living discourse of humanism, which has persisted in our Western civilization, despite many repressions, since the very beginnings of its critical self-consciousness. These studies take part in the discourse of our tradition precisely because they challenge orthodoxy. Humanism is a task, and its goal is the development of our individual and collective potential as human beings. It stands for a tradition of "caring" which keeps open for thought and action the most fundamental question of our lives: "Who *are* we?" Or, in other words, what is it to be a human being? Thinking that questions our understanding of madness and therefore also our consensually validated sense of reality is especially needed in our epoch, since the pervasiveness of technology in the modern world creates institutions that require total standardization and are increasingly capable of imposing conformity to unquestionable norms. These chapters are bound together by virtue of their recognition that a fateful struggle for power is now taking place around the modern Self; together they set in motion, each one in its own distinctive register, an open-ended debate on the *being* of this Self and the practices most conducive to its health and sanity: in a word, its well-being.

Like its historical ancestors, the modern Self is subject to pain, disease, and countless forms of suffering. But it is also subject to afflictions that are specific manifestations of its historical situation. Thus, there are historically distinctive pathologies to which the modern Self is now subject. These studies are concerned, accordingly, with the interpretation of modern psychopathology. The sense of "psychopathology" at work in these studies, however, is not the sense to which our medicine and medical psychiatry have increasingly reduced it: that is, a sense which, in the name of objective science, imposes on the Self's experience of suffering a standard of normality and conceals inimical investments of power behind theories and operations that offer little compassion and can cause immeasurable destruction. We are committed to a sense that harkens back to the original Greek. According to this etymology, the word "psychopathology" refers to the "speech," or logos, of the psyche: all the psyche's ways of hiding, manifesting, expressing, communicating, sharing and, in brief, living out its experience of worldly suffering *(pathein)*. However, the sense of "psychopathology" we have retrieved from the Greek is not merely different from the sense assumed by the "mental health industry." In truth, it brings to light a fundamental conflict and calls attention to the stakes. What is distinctive about our sense of pathology is that it simply acknowledges the presence of human suffering; it does not judge, diagnose, classify, punish or control. These studies are unified by their determination to protest the prevailing understanding of psychopathology, and even to question as vigorously as possible the very existence of psychopathology in the traditional sense.

The chapters that follow make a very rich collection because they originate in different disciplines: medicine, psychiatry, social and clinical psychology, Freudian and Jungian analysis, philosophy, political science and sociology. Many of them are methodically interdisciplinary. Despite their differences, though, each one undertakes a critical challenge to the authority of some dominant ideological interpretation and practice. They are also unified, as the reader will soon perceive, in relation to more substantive theoretical positions and by virtue of their keen awareness of the historical situation that conditions their own strategies of enquiry. They are all motivated by their concern to alleviate the suffering in psychiatric illness and they share the conviction that greater knowledge and understanding would be helpful.

For readers perplexed by the word *postmodern,* which appears in the subtitle of this book, I would like to provide a brief explanation. Following a major current usage, I am considering the modern world—modernity—to begin, for the most part, with the Renaissance. In other words, the modern world is separated from its preceding historical epoch by some very dramatic changes in thinking and living: the Copernican revolution, Newtonian physics, Cartesian epistemology and metaphysics, humanism and its political revolutions, and the beginning of the technological, industrial and commercial tranformations of society. Modernity ends, since it is, in part, a question of culturally shared consciousness, as people begin to realize that there is a critical distance that separates them from the thinking and living that they have inherited. The Holocaust, the Second World War, the bombing of Japan, and all the things, great and small, that have happened since, seem now to evoke this realization in growing numbers of thoughtful people.

But postmodern thinking also begins with a strong sense—articulated, however, only with difficulty—that we are living in a time of transition, a moment between two epochs: the known and the unknown. Postmodern thinking begins with a sense that the foundations of the world we inherited are crumbling, and that we are being called upon, being challenged in a historically unique way, to build a very different world for the future. Postmodern thinking problematizes what was once unquestionable: the paradigm of knowledge, truth, and reality that has dominated the whole of modern history. These studies are postmodern because of their challenges to the most fundamental assumptions of our psychiatric practices and institutions: assumptions that are deeply embedded in our culture as a whole.

I call these studies "postmodern" because they situate epidemic pathologies of the self in relation to the social practices and institutions, the lifeworld, of the modern epoch, and because, in different ways, they all take a critical stand in relation to modernity as a whole. Postmodern thinking begins whenever a shared sense of history begins to emerge among people: a sense that they are thinking on the edge of something that can be characterized as "the whole of modernity," an awareness that the sharing of a critical attitude in relation to that sensed whole—the sharing, for instance, of certain critical arguments against Western metaphysics and epistemology—is putting them at a distance from it. Consciousness, as Sartre frequently said, is always inherently negative, inherently critical: it is reflexive and changes its initial situation.

Being on the edge of modernity, postmodern thinking faces into the future. So there is also, in such thinking, a sense of new historical possibilities: in medicine, healing, psychiatry, community networks for health care, living. There are also, of course, enormous challenges and difficulties. The hegemony of the old paradigm is not easily replaced by something better. Practices, routines, and institutions are not easily transformed by critical thinking. The studies in this book confront this challenge by directing their critical thinking towards the complex of practices that engage the modern self and affect its pathologies.

Three configurations of suffering—three different pathologies–will be examined in this collection: depression, schizophrenia, and the so-called "narcissistic character disorder." There are specific reasons why these three have been selected. First they seem to have captured, more so than any other complex of pathologies, the attention of our most powerful disciplines of enquiry. Second, they have recently appeared, more than other pathologies, in the theoretical constructions of a surprising array of different disciplines: not only in psychology, psychiatry, and medicine, but also in philosophy, cultural critique, sociology, history, anthropology, political science, literature, and literary criticism. And third, they seem to be very closely interconnected and more vividly coherent as a grouping than the other pathologies we might have considered. Many schizophrenias, for example, tend to degenerate into irreversible catatonic depression, especially when isolated by institutional internment; and problems attributable to narcissistic personality often conceal the signs of deep depression. Moreover, according to Otto Fenichel *(The Psychoanalytic Theory of Neurosis)*, narcissistic "disorders" of a more extreme, or regressive, nature will often deteriorate, placing the suffering Self on the borderline of psychosis: schizoid modes of experience and behavior are not at all infrequent in what are called the "narcissistic character disorders." Finally, as Harold Searles pointed out in his paper on "Anxiety in Paranoia," schizophrenia of the "hebophrenic" mode will often involve delusions of omnipotence and immortality that resemble narcissistic pathology because they function "narcissistically" as gestures to defend the Self against even more serious disintegration. Likewise, as Searles argued in "The Psychodynamics of Vengefulness" *(Collected Papers on Schizophrenia and Other Related Subjects)*, there is a schizophrenic paranoia characterized by rage, envy, vengefulness and highly destructive aggression, which develops out of the anxiety over an ontologically fundamental loss and separation, and which serves as a kind of defense against the feelings of rage that develop when there is a massive repression and denial of such loss, separation, and grief.

The studies in this book are committed to the assumption that pathology is always metaphorical. But what, then, is the modernity, the historically distinctive character, of these three pathologies? What makes them pathologies characteristic of the modern Self? How are they connected to our historical existence? What do these patterns of suffering disclose and what do they have to tell us about the distinctive character of our epoch, our culture, our present society? These questions examine our civilization by looking at it through the eyes of those who are suffering within it most intensely. But, to reverse our direction in the circle, we must also attempt to understand psychopathology by encountering it in terms of a wider interpretation of our modern world. Thus we ask: how have the material and spiritual conditions of modern society influenced the presence of these particular pathologies? If it is true that the better we understand our society, our history, our culture, our political economy, the better we will understand the prevailing forms of suffering, then it is also true that the better we understand the individual experience of suffering, the better we will understand our civilization as a whole. The conception of this book began with these very basic but vexing questions. Reverberating throughout the book, they still remain as questions, for they cannot really be settled once and for all. As long as such questioning is kept alive, however, there is reason to hope that we may learn from the presence of the suffering in our midst.

The pathologies under consideration here are historically conditioned pathologies of the will, and more particularly of the "will to power." These pathologies develop out of particular dispositions that are characteristic of the individual will in modern times: pride, delusions of omnipotence, apathy, despair, dependencies, self-alienation, low self-esteem. And they are produced collectively in particular formations of the will to power: social and political institutions, dominant systems of discourse, symbolic rituals. Psychopathology is as much a question of political economy and conceptual paradigm hegemony as it is a question for biology, medicine, and psychiatry. Pathologies of the Self are pathologies of the individual will and are generated within it; but they are also pathologies collectively willed into being, produced by our institutions, customs, and practices.

Near the middle-nineteenth century, while the Cartesian and Newtonian world-view brought forth an industrial revolution that changed the world forever, a great poet, one who felt and thought more deeply than others the nihilism and suffering of his time, finally succumbed to a fatal madness. It was this young poet who told us that, "where danger is, grows/ The saving power also." Commenting on Hölderlin's words, on the danger of nihilism and the possibility of surviving it, Heidegger wrote this:

> In what respect does the saving power grow there also where the danger is? Where something grows, there it takes root, from thence it thrives. Both happen concealedly and quietly and in their own time. But according to the words of the poet, we have no right whatsoever to expect that there where the danger is we should be able to lay hold of the saving power immediately and without preparation. Therefore, . . . it is necessary, as a last step upon our way, to look with yet clearer eyes into the danger. ("The Question Concerning Technology").[1]

It will doubtless be said by many that, like the poet, Heidegger was primarily concerned about a danger threatening the human spirit. This is true. And yet, it also misses the point. For spiritual significance is present in every danger and every form of suffering. What this poet and this thinker are saying could therefore prove to be decisive for our understanding of all manifestations of pathology: not only the depressions, schizophrenias, and narcissistic "disorders" that will be the principal topics of this book, but also the diseases, the somatic disorders, that seem to speak to us somehow about our time. If cancer, for example, is a disease whose essential nature is in many ways produced by historical conditions, then it, too, is a growing danger: a site where the saving power may also grow. And if, in an important sense, nihilism is a cancer of the spirit, as the chapter on "Psychopathology in the Epoch of Nihilism" will argue, then what is a cancer in the body, if it is not—among other things, of course—the body's way of bearing and manifesting the present danger of nihilism? One of the studies in this book will therefore attempt to "look with yet clearer eyes" into the growing epidemiological danger, arguing that it is manifest psychologically through depression and somatically through the presence of cancer.

Before we survey the land to be mapped by the studies that follow, I should like to comment briefly on the meaning of "cultural epidemiology," the fundamental perception in terms of which this book as a whole is conceived. For me, these studies constitute a new discipline, a new field of thought and action—new, at least, in a certain hermeneutical sense, namely, that they are deliberately assembled as studies in cultural epidemiology and are explicitly conceptualized in that mode of perception. "Cultural epidemiology" may at first seem a surprising or even bewildering term, not only to those whose deepest assumptions have been the currently prevailing ground-rules of biology and medicine, but also to those whose thinking is steeped in our long tradition of humanism.

For humanism, as for science, "cultural" is a word that concerns only the things of "the mind," while "epidemiology" is a word that belongs to the science of medicine and the jurisdiction of public health: the one refers to symbolic systems; the other refers to the study of the distribution of disease over a population in time and space. Thus it might seem that epidemiology is not to be at all concerned with the study of cultural symbols, practices and institutions. But this understanding makes a set of assumptions that the studies in this book very seriously call in question: the old Cartesian dualisms of mind and body, Self and Other, individual and society.

Let us note to begin with that epidemiology is a field of study, a discourse, a social, cultural, historical activity; it takes place within society. The epidemics of diseases with which it is concerned are constructs of theory, action, and perception. Both the diseases themselves and their epidemics are historical happenings with far-reaching consequences, and therefore significance, for the populations they ravage. Diseases of the body can become epidemics that afflict the body politic. The assumed subject of epidemiological study can no longer be separated from questions traditionally reserved for humanism and the social sciences. But by the same token, we must begin to think of psychopathology in epidemiological terms.

If our well-being requires an integration of mind and body, spirit and flesh, then we also need to integrate the sciences of the body and of the mind. We need to effect this integration without reducing one to the other; and what integrates without reduction must consider the genuinely human, the social dimension. Psychosomatic medicine is certainly one auspicious beginning; but in the past it has ignored the epidemiological and symbolic dimensions of its subject, human beings and their afflictions, and has only recently begun to break away radically from the compromise with dualism it initially tried to keep. Now at last it has begun to incorporate the social meaning its subject brings forth.

Cultural epidemiology represents an important further development not only in psychosomatic medicine, but also in depth psychology; it overcomes the old disciplinary boundaries between medicine and psychology, psychology and the study of society that were established during the hegemony of mind-body dualism, and it integrates the knowledges gathered in many different disciplines—specifically including, for the first time, the interpretive fields of psychohistory and psychopolitics. As a discursive field, then, cultural epidemiology represents the ideal of a fateful intersection; the sciences of nature and the sciences of life can fruitfully collaborate with the disciplines of a critical humanism to interpret the condition of human suffering while acknowledging its speech and listening openly to its dangerous truth. Madness is madness, is suffering; but even madness is death only when its truth cannot be heard. Compassion begins when this truth and the pain it exacts can be freely shared.

Let me now briefly summarize each of these chapters, so that what they share and how they differ will be readily apparent.

Jeffrey Satinover's contribution, in chapter two, concerns "Science and the Fragile Self: The Rise of Narcissism, the Decline of God." Beginning with a broad overview of narcissistic character problems, the paper analyzes the psychology of narcissism on the basis of a theory incorporating elements of both psychoanalysis and Jungian psychology. At the center of narcissistic psychopathology, Satinover sees a normal human longing for relationship and ego-transcendence as well as for the extraordinary specialness of life, the beauty and magic embodied in the mythic image of the Divine Child. In order to understand the suffering involved in this psychology, Satinover then stands back and considers the history of Western culture in its modern epoch. Noting the nihilistic effects of modern science and the "death of God", he argues that culture has not developed new ways to meet the self's new historical needs, and that this is why narcissistic pathology has made its historical appearance. His paper leaves us with a question other chapters will address: Can we envision a new type of self, and what conditions would be necessary for its historical emergence?

In "The Dead Self in Borderline Personality Disorders," the chapter that follows, Nathan Schwartz-Salant reflects on his clinical experience with borderline personality disorders and argues that these disorders are symptomatic of a "dead self." He suggests a clinical interpretation which argues that the heart of this suffering is an inability to achieve wholeness and integration and to develop meaningful relationships: "the borderline process," he writes, "is characterized by denial, splitting and dissociation." The self on the borderline feels dead, empty, worthless, desperately alone. This condition is one clinicians are seeing very frequently today, and Schwartz-Salant speculates that it may be symptomatic of the fact that the borderline patient is precariously positioned in history, and is borderline in this sense, too: partly suffering the "death" of God and partly receptive to the powerful influences of a newly manifesting archetype. He therefore contends that a clinical understanding of the borderline personality which respects the archetypal dimensions of its suffering can shed light on the social and cultural significance of this prevalent pathology.

The topic of chapter four is "Cancer and the Self: How Illness Constellates Meaning." Taking seriously our common belief, intuitively compelling despite an insufficiency of experimental support, that depression and cancer are somehow meaningfully related and that cancer is not just a disease of the physical body, a matter of cells and tissues, but a meaningful existential condition, Roger Levin challenges our traditional metaphysics, our epistemology, and even our prevailing conception of rational methodology, and proposes a new way to see the phenomenon of cancer. Arguing that the meaningfulness of cancer, and therefore also the connection between cancer and depression, cannot be perceived in a science of causalities, Levin suggests that we must develop a phenomenological, hermeneutical discourse around the presence of illness.

Speaking in the context of such a discourse, he takes "cancer" to designate the experiencing processes lived by the embodied self. Thus, the body we need to understand and work with is not the body of traditional science, but rather a body in and for which the presence of cancer becomes an individuating and sometimes therapeutic question for the self—the self of "subtle" embodiment. By thinking of cancer in this way, as an embodied state of meaning, he adumbrates the possibility of answering epidemiological questions about cancer and depression that concern their historical significance: what they can tell us about ourselves, our environment, and the age in which we live. Levin's parting word is that "Cancer is an invitation to heal, to regain wholeness, an invitation to ourselves as emergent individuals and to our culture at large."

In the next chapter, Robert Romanyshyn and his research assistant, Brian Whalen, draw on the work of Heidegger and Jung to give us their thoughts on the social and cultural significance of depression in an essay called "Depression and the American Dream: The Struggle with Home." Listening to the stories of depressive patients, Romanyshyn and Whalen propose a connection between the prevalence of depression in contemporary American life and a constellation of archetypal themes frequently found in American literature: the self-made man, the drive to succeed, the will to conquer, life in the wilderness, the American frontier, homelessness and homecoming, alienation, uprootedness. The authors perceive in depression a pathology of the will in which the chthonic needs of the soul are forgotten, and they suggest that this is related to the ideology of willful individualism characteristic of the modern epoch. Through their retelling of clinical stories, the authors deepen and amplify the modern experience of depression, an experience, they argue, which is buried within the psychology of the prevailing American dream.

In the next chapter, "Relocation and Illness," Cisco Lassiter calls our attention to the sufferings of the Navajo people in consequence of our government's decision to relocate more than ten thousand of them. Lassiter argues that the premodern self cannot survive without access to the traditional sacred places, orientation by tribal landmarks, and rootedness in the earth. The world of the modern self is located in a Euclidean-Newtonian space, homogeneous, uniform, and continuous: a space without sacred places, where all places are essentially interchangeable, and where geometry forgets the spiritual meaning of the earth, the land, and the human need for home. The identity and well-being of the Navajo, a premodern self, depends on earth, ground, and place for an essential relationship to departed ancestors, cultural traditions, the world of the dead, gods, and time itself. Relocation means that the Navajos must abandon all this. Lassiter documents his charge that the relocation is their spiritual death, that it is causing a multitude of physical and emotional illnesses, tremendous pain and suffering, and many suicides and deaths. Arguing that this tragedy can be understood only through recognition of the distinctive spiritual needs of the premodern self, he asserts that this decision reflects the failure of modern society to understand the needs of this self. The modern self cannot easily see the pathogenesis of disease, psychiatric illness and "behavioral disorders" in such separation from earth, land, and place. But, if the analysis in chapter five is true, then even the modern self now shows signs of suffering from homelessness and rootlessness, conditions brought about by the prevailing "rational" organization, the prevailing geometry of human existence.

"Melancholy and Melancholia" is the title of Jennifer Radden's chapter. Radden sees two significant historical shifts is psychiatric nosology since the beginning of the "modern" world: first, a shift from conceptualizing "melancholy" as "unreason" to conceptualizing it as "melancholia" and hence as "madness"; and second, a shift from "melancholia" as "madness" to "depression" as a "disorder" open to medical treatment. She notes an epidemiological shift in the populations designated by these terms: a shift from the melancholy men of the sixteenth and seventeenth centuries to the clinically-depressed women of today. Radden argues that our present conceptualization is much more alienating, pathologizing, and inhumane than the earlier ones because the clinical diagnosis stigmatizes the "patient," isolating her from the matrix of normal everyday living. Consequently, she argues, the diagnosis has the effect of intensifying the kinds of experience that induce severe depressions. Working out the implications of her argument, Radden finally calls into question the validity as well as the compassion of the psychiatric (DSM-III) nosology, suggesting that it may be responsible for producing the condition it designates.

Eugene Gendlin's contribution is "A Philosophical Critique of the Concept of Narcissism: The Significance of the Awareness Movement." Gendlin begins by arguing that the concept of "narcissism" which appears today in the discourses of psychoanalysis (Freud, Lacan, Kohut) and political theory (Adorno, Marcuse, Foucault, Lasch) is seriously confused and self-defeating. He does not dispute the existence of narcissistic pathology, but he points out that the theoretical definition of "narcissism" gives the self only two possibilities: either normalization or regression. In other words, any changes in personality, in the forms of the social ego, which differ from the common and the normal can only be regressive. By the same token, even the most serious challenges to the authority and domination of the prevailing social forms of ego-strength can be regarded only as infantile and hence invalid. Thus, the concept of "narcissism" takes sides in an ideological struggle, since it strengthens the existing social roles, routines, and structures.

Observing that we are living in a time of significant—but also perplexing—social changes, Gendlin sees the traditional self, the "subjectivity" that first emerged at the beginning of the modern period and has evolved with changing social conditions in the time which followed, now giving way to many different kinds of self-experiencing. The traditional self, identified with the roles, routines, practices and institutions of modernity, is now challenged by widespread experimentation with these identifications. Many people today are unwilling to continue living within the limitations of the traditional forms or are compelled, because of disintegrating social institutions, to try out new ways of structuring their various identification processes. Many people are seriously thoughtful about ways to continue their psychological growth and have committed themselves to experimenting with new ways of living, new ways of working and being with others. It is principally to these people, rapidly increasing in number, that we owe the existence of what social commentators have called the "Awareness Movement."

Although the existence of this movement has been widely recognized, Gendlin believes that its fundamental significance has not been understood.

Many of the thinkers contributing to the contemporary discourse in psychoanalysis and critical social theory have defined the movement in terms of the phenomenon they conceptualize as "narcissism." They jump to this classification because they can see only a preoccupation with "inner" experiencing and are distressed by the instabilities they see in the forms of social bonding. The psychoanalytic thinkers can see little more than self-indulgence and regressive pathology, while the thinkers in political theory can see only an inwardness that withdraws from political responsibility and fails to perceive the external controls that have penetrated this false "inwardness."

Gendlin argues that conceptual confusion dominates from a concealed position both the psychoanalytic and the political critiques of contemporary culture, and that the confusion makes it impossible for them to see the current "Awareness Movement" with understanding. Despite all its shortcomings, failures, and even narcissistic pathology, the distinctive character of this movement is that it has problematized the traditional "self" and encouraged serious experimentation around the historical opportunity to develop, out of need, a genuinely different way of being.

In order to show this, Gendlin details the existence of different experiential processes and practices, on the basis of which he can define different dimensions of "self": a self that is *no* self in the sense of a substance or essence. Challenging the conceptions of the self that we associate with Cartesian and Kantian metaphysics as well as the portrait of the ego-centered social self that still dominates psychoanalysis, Gendlin suggests that instead of thinking in terms of the "self," we should think of different styles, patterns, and dimensions of experiencing—and of different types, styles, and dimensions of coherence. Thus he takes us beyond the dualisms of mind and body, reason and emotion, self and other, inner and outer that have so deeply pathologized the modern self. In particular, he demonstrates the possibility of what Foucault might have called a new historical "practice of the self." We profess to care about the individuation of the individual; but his demonstration shows us that we continue to think of "the self" in ways that impose conformity and do not promote new forms of "subjectivity." The "focusing" practice Gendlin details, using dialogues from psychotherapy interactions, makes us aware of experiential processes in which new forms of living, new forms of identity, are being worked out.

This in turn sets the stage for a philosophical debate with critical social theory. Gendlin argues, against Foucault, that the human body is a body of meaningful experience: not a totally preprogramed biological machine, not a chaos of drives, a body without any organizing capacities of its own and upon which society must therefore impose some basic order, but rather a rich, creative source of meaningful experience that can *talk back* to the body politic with an original intelligence. There is, then, a third alternative to the body programmed by biology and the body totally imprinted by social force. This is the experiential body whose speech and silence Gendlin examines. Moreover, in the creative speech of this body, he records the emergence of processes of individuation and self-development that bespeak social changes of far-reaching significance: changes drawing our lives into a time of transition—on the edge, perhaps, between the familiar world of modernity and something we might call postmodern.

In "Metaphysics and Schizophrenia: Analyzing the DSM-III," Irene Harvey proposes a radical critique of the psychiatric conceptualization of schizophrenia and of psychiatric practice—diagnosis and treatment—by exposing and questioning the (essentially Cartesian) metaphysics concealed within their operations. Harvey explores the extent to which the "observations" psychiatry makes are nothing but its unconscious projections. Harvey's contribution helps us to hear the modern self's experience in a fresh way, liberated from the nihilistic spell of our prevailing metaphysics.

Joel Kovel writes on "Schizophrenic Being and Technocratic Society." He undertakes a radical critique of the prevailing institutionalized interpretation of schizophrenia, giving particular attention to the fact that psychiatry today turns the one who is suffering into a helpless, useless patient and a well-defined subject for medical discourse. Kovel questions not only the reductive biologizing and medicalizing, but also the reductive psychology of ego-adaptation—the terms in which contemporary psychiatry attempts to meet the need in schizophrenic suffering. He argues that psychiatry tends to protect the social system, our prevailing culture and its norm of rationality, from any responsibility, any participation in the etiology of schizophrenia—and also, therefore, from any serious criticism that might be rooted in the schizophrenic experience of social life.

According to Kovel, our institutional channels for responding to schizophrenic suffering only render the mad doubly mad, since, in addition to struggling with an experience of reality at odds with the prevailing consensus, the "schizophrenic patient" must also struggle against the impossibility of communicating with health care professionals in terms of a paradigm of rationality, truth and reality that denies any sense, any phenomenological truth, in the schizophrenic's communication. This problem points to the need for psychiatric communities in which experienced meaning would be genuinely respected and human relationships could be formed on the basis of this respect.

In chapter eleven, James Bernauer's contribution, "Oedipus, Freud, Foucault: Fragments of an Archaeology of Psychoanalysis," speaks out against the appropriation and medicalization of schizophrenia and psychosis in general by "an arsenal of psychological-psychiatric categories"; he argues for a more open, responsive conversation with "madness." In particular, Bernauer opposes the reduction of "madness" to the ontological status of a disease and challenges the wisdom of banishing the social threat inherent in madness. He believes that schizophrenia is an experience of the world that can teach the "more fortunate" of us about ourselves. Above all schizophrenia is an experience of marginality and nonconformity from which we can learn about the effects of power on the truth of the self. The pathology and suffering about which he is ultimately most concerned is the massive conformism produced by a society too frightened of "madness" to heed the truth that speaks through its suffering.

In chapter-twelve, "Upside-Down Psychiatry: A Genealogy of Mental Health Services," Richard Mollica interprets the results of the follow-up study twenty-five years after the epidemiological research pioneered by Redlich and Hollingshead and reported in their book *Social Class and Mental Illness*. Redlich and Hollingshead questioned the impact of social class on psychiatric treatment, and convincingly demonstrated that, contrary to what our democratic ideology would have us believe, differences in social class make a real difference in diagnosis; in the form, duration, and quality of treatment; and finally, in the ultimate course of the illness, the outcome of psychiatric intervention. In the twenty-five-year follow-up, Mollica attempted to find answers to two basic questions: (1) What impact, if any, on psychiatric services did the earlier study have? And (2), when the old statistics are compared with the new, can it be said that any fundamentally "progressive" structural changes in the health care system have taken place? Since no significant "progress" could be observed, two more questions arose: (3) What accounts for this? And (4) What can be done to bring about the necessary changes?

Mollica finds much evidence that the system of psychiatric care in this country did, at least for a while, change and improve. Nevertheless, Mollica's research indicates that "the modern psychiatric system has now entered a state of confusion and disintegration." In his attempt to explain this, Mollica points out that public support for public mental health services has sharply diminished; he argues that, in a society divided into rich and poor, the transfer of patients from long-term in-patient care to short-term outpatient care inevitably disadvantages the poor, since this transfer of care generally takes place without the corresponding creation of a variety of community networks and infrastructures to provide supplementary outpatient support and assistance for those in need. Deinstitutionalization, he argues, must always be tied to the creation of alternative structures for living within the local communities.

Kenneth Pope and Paula Johnson articulate and address some of the current urgent questions that surround "Psychological and Psychiatric Diagnosis: Theoretical Foundations, Research, and Clinical Practice." In this chapter, the authors relentlessly question the prevailing system of clinical perception, diagnosis and treatment. Probing deeply, they expose some of the theoretical assumptions presently underlying our institutional responses to psychiatric illnesses: assumptions our social and cultural institutions mask and protect from radical challenge. The authors bring to light issues of authority and responsibility, care and compassion, the operations of intolerant and brutal power, not only in the diagnostic process and its consequences for therapy but even in the nosological categories themselves. In particular, they point out that diagnostic categories often function as instruments of oppression in the experience of women, blacks, and many poor people. The questions Pope and Johnson formulate point to concealed forms of control and manipulation that sacrifice the needs and concerns of those who call for help in order to maintain existing practices and institutions, perpetuate the vested interests of the mental health industry, and discredit all initiatives to practice structural (i.e., systematic) criticism.

In chapter fourteen, entitled "Schizophrenia and Rationality," James Glass looks at the relationship between reason and unconscious fantasy. Like Harvey, Kovel, and Bernauer, Glass argues that rationality is a social norm and thus a form of power; rationality is in the service of institutions that exclude or deny the meaningfulness of unconscious fantasy. As he shows, this has dangerous consequences, not only for individual lives but also for the functioning of political institutions. Glass contends that the "rational consensus" advocated by political contract theories ignores schizophrenic utterances as legitimate social commentary; rational consensus theories cannot perceive, in their allusions and references to power, a painful but deep understanding of the subversive truth that coercive power is concealed in the "rule of reason"—what appears in contemporary life in the guise of an unimpeachable "rationality" might itself be regarded as a form of social pathology.

Stanislav Grof contributes a study on "Psychodynamic Factors in Depression and Psychosis: Observations from Modern Consciousness Research." Grof contests the hegemony of modern psychiatry and psychoanalysis, which he thinks inhibits therapeutic sensitivity to the sufferings of many patients considered to be dangerously disturbed or "psychotic." According to Grof, experiences that psychiatry and psychoanalysis often diagnose in a strictly negative way as "pathological" (in the sense of "psychotic") should be understood more positively and more compassionately as spiritual emergencies, crises in the emerging of the self. Seemingly psychotic experiences are better understood as crises related to the person's efforts to break out of the standard ego-bounded identity: trials of the soul on its spiritual journey.

The modern self is nearing the frontier of a historically new spiritual existence. But modern psychiatry has not yet thrown off its obsolete paradigm and still retains its theoretical commitment to the truth of a reductive biological model. Grof argues that we must not abandon a newly emerging self to more or less incurable breakdown (psychosis): he suggests that, with a different understanding, we can facilitate and care for its spiritual breakthrough. It is time for a real paradigm shift, and Grof accordingly proposes a new theoretical model with profound therapeutic implications.

We are living in a time of transition, a time of momentous changes and exciting opportunities. We cannot see the world to come very clearly, but we live with a preponderant sense, today, that the modern world, the world that began with the Renaissance, is now drawing to a close, its most distinctive historical possibilities, its blessings and its curses, either exploited and exhausted or only now revealing their true character, as they profoundly alter the most basic conditions of planetary existence.

Times of epochal transition are always extremely difficult, but each transition of this kind is shadowed by its own most distinctive danger. The ultimate danger facing us today is nihilism. This nihilism, fitting the definition of an epidemic, has been incubating for a long time in the culture of modernity, feeding on a narcissism of the will, the splitting and fragmenting of things that should remain whole, and changes that have caused us spiritually painful separations and abandoned us to irremediable loss.

The pathologies in question here are distinctively characteristic of the modern self, and are not necessarily pathologies in a strictly clinical sense. All of us suffer in ways the descriptive interpretation of these pathologies would suggest. Some people are more favored by their biological constitutions and social circumstances (especially by their family and community), and either adapt to the madness of prevailing social conditions or find ways to live a life of creative difference, transforming the pathogenic conditions of the epoch into something more benevolent. Others are not so fortunate, and they can neither adjust to the madness of the world nor creatively resist and transform it: these people succumb to the pathology and find themselves in need of organized and skillful caring. It is in conjunction with the appearance of this need that the clinical practices and institutions characteristic of the modern world have come into being.

But it should be noted that most of the studies in this book do not simply take it for granted that "narcissism," "schizophrenia," and "depression" are terms of discourse which designate pathologies in a strictly clinical sense. Instead of making that assumption and proceeding to comment on their nature or hastening to recommend some new treatment technology, these essays take a step back and approach the presence of pathology more indirectly, beginning with a critique of the practices and institutions which surround these forms of suffering, and taking the time to examine very critically the metaphysics, epistemology, and normative assumptions in terms of which our modern practices and institutions have been legitimated. It is for this reason that I think these essays contribute to the formation of a postmodern discourse in cultural epidemiology, in which the patterns of suffering characteristic of modernity, together with our ways of responding and caring, can be perceived more clearly.

NOTES

1. Martin Heidegger, "The Question Concerning Technology," in William Lovitt, ed., *The Question Concerning Technology and Other Essays* (New York: Harper and Row, 1977), pp. 28–29.

OPENING CONVERSATION

(1) "Perhaps what is distinctive about this world-epoch consists in the closure of the dimension of the hale. Perhaps that is the sole malignancy *[Unheil]*." Heidegger, *Letter on Humanism*[1]

(2) "The fateful question of the human species seems to me to be whether and to what extent the cultural process in it will succeed in mastering the derangements of communal life caused by the human instinct of aggression and self-destruction. In this connection, perhaps the phase through which we are at this moment passing deserves special interest. Men have brought their powers of subduing forces of nature to such a pitch that by using them they could now very easily exterminate one another to the last man. They know this—hence arises a great part of their current unrest, their dejection, this mood of apprehension. And now it may be expected that the other of the two 'heavenly forces,' eternal eros, will put forth his strength so as to maintain himself alongside of his equally immortal adversary." Freud, *Civilization and Its Discontents*[2]

(3) "It is no longer the end of time and of the world which will show retrospectively that men were mad not to have been prepared for them; it is the tide of madness, its secret invasion, that shows that the world is near its final catastrophe; it is man's insanity that invokes and makes necessary the world's end." Foucault, *Madness and Civilization*.[3]

(4) "Dialectical reason is, when set against the dominant mode of reason, unreason: only in encompassing and canceling this mode does it become itself reasonable . . . The dialectic cannot stop short before the concepts of health and sickness, nor indeed before their siblings, reason and unreason. Once it has recognized the ruling universal order and its proportions as sick . . . then it can see as healing cells only what appears, by the standards of that order, as itself sick, eccentric, paranoia—indeed, 'mad'; and it is as true today as in the Middle Ages that only fools tell their master the truth. The dialectician's duty is thus to help this fool's truth to attain its own reason, without which it will certainly succumb to the abyss of the sickness implacably dictated by the healthy common sense of the rest." Adorno, *Minima Moralia*[4]

(5) ". . . [R]adical change in consciousness is the beginning, the first step in changing social existence: emergence of the new Subject." Marcuse, *An Essay on Liberation*.[5]

(6) "Much has still to be learnt about the psyche, and our special need today is liberation from outworn ideas which have seriously restricted our views of the psyche as a whole." Jung, "The State of Psychotherapy Today"[6]

(7) "It is part of the mechanism of domination to forbid recognition of the suffering it produces. . . ." Adorno, *Minima Moralia*[7]

(8) ". . . [S]wamped in madness, the world is made aware of its guilt." Foucault, *Madness and Civilization*[8]

(9) "It is from need and distress that new forms of existence arise. . . ." Jung, "The Spiritual Problem of Modern Man"[9]

(10) "Thinking conducts historical existence . . . into the realm of the upsurgence of the healing." Heidegger, *Letter on Humanism*[10]

(11) "With healing, evil appears all the more in the lighting of Being. The essence of evil does not consist in the mere baseness of human action but rather in the malice of rage. Both of these, however, the healing and the raging, can essentially occur only in Being, insofar as Being itself is what is contested." Heidegger, *Letter on Humanism*[11]

(12) "To healing Being first grants ascent into grace, to raging its compulsion to malignancy [*Unheil*]." Heidegger, *Letter on Humanism*[12]

(13) "We should not try to 'get rid' of a neurosis, but rather to experience what it means, what it has to teach, what its purpose is. We should even learn to be thankful for it, otherwise we pass it by and miss the opportunity of getting to know ourselves as we really are. A neurosis is truly removed only when it has removed the false attitude of the ego. We do not cure it—it cures us. A man is ill, but the illness is nature's attempt to heal him. . . . In this case, it is man's soul, his hope, his boldest flight, his finest adventure." Jung, "The State of Psychotherapy Today"[13]

(14) "In periods of decline such as the present, the higher truth lies in madness." Horkheimer, *Dawn and Decline*[14]

(15) "But only later did I understand the moral of this: sense can only endure in despair and extremity; it needs absurdity, in order not to fall victim to objective madness. . . . What would happiness be that was not measured by the immeasurable grief at what is? For the world is deeply ailing. He who cautiously adapts to it by this very act shares in its madness, while the eccentric alone would stand his ground and bid it rave no more. He alone could pause to think on the illusoriness of disaster, the 'unreality of despair,' and realize not merely that he is still alive but that there is still life." Adorno, *Minima Moralia*[15]

REFERENCES

1. Martin Heidegger, "Letter On Humanism," *Basic Writings,* ed., with introductions, David Farrell Krell (New York: Harper & Row, 1977), 230.
2. Sigmund Freud, *Civilization and Its Discontents,* trans. Joan Riviére (New York: W. W. Norton, 1962), 105.
3. Michel Foucault, *Madness and Civilization: A History of Insanity in the Age of Reason,* trans. Richard Howard (New York: Random House, Vintage Books, 1973), 17.
4. Theodor Adorno, *Minima Moralia: Reflections from Damaged Life,* trans. E. F. N. Jephcott (London: New Left Books, 1974; Verso Editions, 1978), 72–73.
5. Herbert Marcuse, *An Essay on Liberation* (Boston: Beacon Press, 1969), 53.
6. Carl Gustav Jung, "The State of Psychotherapy Today," in *Civilization in Transition,* trans. R. F. C. Hull (New York: Pantheon, 1964), 173.
7. Adorno, 63.
8. Foucault, 288.
9. Jung, "The Spiritual Problem of Modern Man," in *Civilization in Transition,* 92.
10. Heidegger, "Letter on Humanism," 237.
11. Ibid.
12. Ibid., 238.
13. Jung, "The State of Psychotherapy Today," 170.
14. Max Horkheimer, *Dawn and Decline: Notes 1926–1931 and 1950–1969* (New York: The Seabury Press, Continuum Books, 1978), 181.
15. Adorno, 200.

CHAPTER 1
PSYCHOPATHOLOGY IN THE EPOCH OF NIHILISM

David Michael Levin

I. HYPOTHESES AND QUERIES

Freud's meditation at the end of *Civilization and Its Discontents* raises the question of our survival. Will Eros win out? Or will the culture of death prevail? Our thinking takes place in a time of extreme danger and need. Can we avoid nuclear annihilation? In the name of a dream we call "civilization," we—or those over whom we exercise no control—are destroying our lakes, our forests, our rivers. We—or those whom our indifference encourages—are poisoning the oceans and plundering the riches of the earth. If we continue to destroy our environment, how can we survive? In the last analysis, we are destroying ourselves.

As Foucault understood, Nietzsche's prophetic announcement of the "death of God" must now be followed by an announcement of the "death of Man": not merely, then, as Nietzsche thought, the "self-overcoming" of human nature as it presently is, but rather (and much more frighteningly), the destruction of our faith in ourselves, our most basic sense of who we, as human beings, essentially are—and who we could become. Under these circumstances, it should not be surprising that our violence against the "humanity" in us rages everywhere: in the creation of hunger and starvation and famines that could have been averted; in the official tolerance of malnutrition among children; in endless civil wars and national struggles over freedom; in military invasions and conquests; in the ferocious and interminable hatreds that divide different races and religions; in crimes of the street and home; in the crowded misery of refugee camps;

in the plight of honest people willing to work, but unemployed and homeless in the midst of urban prosperity; in the courts of law, where the poor seldom find justice and the destitute cannot receive a hearing; in the brutality of our institutions for punishment; in the bureaucracies of our hospitals and clinics; in the corporate exploitation of human beings and in their indifference to our individual and collective welfare. . . . And wherever there is violence, there is also the *fear* of violence: a fear that could itself destroy us.

These are effects, symptoms of nihilism: nihilism as a sociopolitical and cultural reality. But if we consult our deepest sense of how as a whole these diverse actualities constitute a coherent historical reality, we may perhaps be prompted to question our present historical situation and to respond to its anguish, in a discourse brought into being through our attunement to the experience of nihilism.[1]

In the tradition of Nietzsche, Freud, and Heidegger, I shall continue the critical interpretation of our culture and its history. What I propose is an epidemiological interpretation of the modern epoch, attentive above all to the metaphysical significance of our suffering and affliction in the contemporary world. Although there are and always will be competing interpretations, I think that the interpretation developed in this essay could help us to work out a more deeply ontological understanding of ourselves and our world. (What makes this understanding "ontological" is its concern for our experiences of Being and Nothingness.) I believe, moreover, that the studies which follow provide compelling support for the ontological hypothesis at the very heart of my interpretation.

I propose what is in effect a new conceptual framework for our collective consideration of the psychopathology that seems increasingly to predominate in our world. By "psychopathology" I do not merely designate the human experience of suffering *(pathein)*. I want to include any comportment that only deepens or intensifies the inadequate way in which the psyche manifests its pain, its suffering, its affliction. Today, our experience with nihilism speaks of its suffering in a psychopathology whose most thought-provoking urgency the science of psychiatry can recognize only in terms of its institutionally validated categories: the narcissistic personality disorders, the schizophrenias, and the depressions. I want to draw a clearer, more deeply ontological understanding of the way in which the epidemic psychopathology distinctive to our time is a historical manifestation of a cancerous nihilism: the "negation" of Being working its slow destruction through the agency of the human will, the human ego. The pathology is pervasive and not limited to a few unfortunates. This understanding of our pathology is what I call my "ontological hypothesis."

Nihilism is a cancer of the spirit because, just as surely as cancer is the death of the body, it is a self-destructiveness that brings death to the spirit and our source of identity as human beings. Kierkegaard would have called it the "sickness unto death": a sickness that concerns the Self; a sickness in which the Self experiences itself as unwhole, split beyond consolation, and threatened with the spectres of a deepening and even more hellish disintegration. Although I agree with this analysis, I believe that, in order to understand nihilism better, we must understand not only the affliction of the spirit, but also the various sociopathies, and the diseases of the body—the epidemic historical presence of cancer, for instance. If we must, we will need to generate a field of discourse in which this kind of interpretation could be constructively articulated.

In terms of our traditional conceptual framework, this assertion makes a provocative correlation. In a discourse on psychopathology dominated by our traditional metaphysical categories, this reference to cancer will of course be denied—or else interpreted as a metaphorical truth. However, the claim I want to argue is that it refers to a psychological process of self-annihilation, the will to power with nothing to will, in the end, but its own desire for death. This way of thinking about disease does not really require a total break with the past; it is, in fact, historically connected with the contemporary discourse of psychosomatic medicine, a discourse in which I would claim for the reference a more literal significance. Thus I submit that there is a literal truth in this interpretation of nihilism: a truth that will in time become more apparent as we begin to recognize in the epidemic prevalence of our somatic pathologies the historical evidence for a nihilism that is not just a sickness of the modern Self, but is also a distinctive affliction of our historical embodiment. If the modern Self is not well, the body of history will carry its illness. As Adorno said, "The break in the line of life that indicates a lurking cancer is a fraud only in the place where it purports to be found, the individual's hand; where they refrain from diagnosis, in the collective, it would be correct."[2] I take this to be an indictment not only of occultism, which claims to read illness in the hand, but also more importantly of biologism, which refuses to see in cancer a symptom of social disorder, connected, for example, with the injustice of political conditions and with the body's way of bearing the fate of spiritual self-destruction.

Perhaps I can use an observation Adorno made of the Holocaust to illuminate the significance of cancer in the epoch of nihilism. Adorno suggested that "What is decisive is the absorption of biological destruction by conscious social will."[3] If we think of these words in reference to cancer, perhaps we can begin to confront the possibility that the historical significance of cancer—its uncanny nature as an epidemic of "biological destruction"—might require that we consider its relationship to "conscious social will." I submit that this possibility deserves further thought, since nihilism is inseparable from the will to power, and this will to power bears within itself a tremendously self-destructive energy. Epidemics that affect our embodiment are not just "medical" problems. They need social, political, and historical interpretation. Our interpretation will demonstrate the presence of a corresponding pathology in the body politic and help us to recognize in both these patterns a self-destructiveness deeply afflicting the very meaning of our spiritual being. Can we not discern, in the truth that now calls itself "the death of Man," the truth of cancer? Is there not an endogenous affliction of the body, an interior mortification of the flesh, that is somehow, grimly, an appropriate "external" manifestation of our spiritual condition at the present time? Adorno argued that "Only a humanity to whom death has become as indifferent as its members, that has itself died, can inflict it administratively on innumerable people."[4] But, if this makes sense in the political field of interpretation, we should also consider what epidemic pathology we might expect to find in a civilization whose present population has spiritually died, or died at least to the point where dying and surviving in the world are rapidly becoming matters of indifference. We must understand how nihilism works its way through us, for the possibility of some kind of healing always lies concealed, as Hölderlin says, within our experience of its destructiveness.

According to Nietzsche, ours is the epoch in which a nihilism already latent in our civilization from the beginning finally becomes manifest in an explicit psychopathology.[5] On the basis of this interpretation, Nietzsche set in motion a powerful critique of the history of Western philosophy and Western civilization in general, in which he attempted to demonstrate how such nihilism has appeared in and determined the course of our history.

Heidegger continued the critical project Nietzsche began: but the more deeply he struggled with it, the more he realized that Nietzsche's critique was shaped, despite its intended radicality and without his awareness, by undercurrents of nihilism already at work in the metaphysics of his time. As many scholars have noted, Nietzsche's concept of the "will to power" is not defined with sufficient clarity and precision; but if one of its meanings is exemplified paradigmatically in the history of a patriarchal culture that exalts willful mastery and domination, then Heidegger was surely right to argue that there is a sense in which Nietzsche's "cure" merely instantiates and reproduces the self-destructive character of the destructiveness in nihilism.[6]

In "Cultural Epidemiology," the next part of this chapter, we shall briefly consider some of the most basic methodological problems that confront our interpretive task. In particular, we must at least acknowledge that practical and epistemic difficulties challenge our attempt to formulate an epidemiological interpretation of our culture and its history. In Part Three we shall reflect on the phenomenon of nihilism. Through a reading, first of Nietzsche and then of Heidegger, I would like to clarify both the concept itself, what the latter has called the "essence," and also the historical experience of its actuality. This should enable us to discern within our metaphysics the historical connection between nihilism and the modern Self.

I will argue that nihilism essentially involves self-destruction, and that our understanding of this needs to be gathered from the different disciplines of knowledge and self-knowledge, in all of which we can perceive some inherently self-destructive process or pattern: in cellular biology, medicine, psychopathology, sociopolitical critique, and in the history of metaphysics, where the self-destructiveness of the modern Self is recognized in the inwardness of an empty, merely formal subjectivity. Western metaphysics, a tradition in which our civilization has repeatedly asked about what is—about beings and the Being of beings—must be understood as the product of an historically situated subject's reflective activity: a mirror, a projection, of the modern Self. Thus, the history of metaphysics is a discourse in which we will find reflected—and simultaneously both clarified and distorted—the deepest historical experience of this Self: its historically distinctive psychic and somatic pathology, interpreted ontologically in relation to the question of Being, the question of nihilism, which most deeply concerns the historical condition of its own being and ultimately of its very survival.

In the seventeenth century, near the beginning of the modern epoch, Cartesian metaphysics conceived of Being in the discourse of subjectivity.

Henceforth, in a world increasingly organized around science, capital investment, and technology, we would understand ourselves in terms of a scientific psychology of the ego and an ontology fixed on objects—the standard objects of property, security, and commodity exchangeability. I submit that the epidemic occurrences of psychopathology prevalent at this time belong to a configuration that appears only when it is recognized as a larger historical process. There is a nihilism slowly consuming our civilization and its essence is implicit, if we read between the lines, in the discourse of Western metaphysics. If in this discourse nihilism consists, as Heidegger suggested, in the fact that Being itself is what is contested, then we might surmise that in terms of the psychopathology of our time nihilism would consist in the fact that the very *being* of the Self is what is at stake. The self-destructiveness of nihilism becomes the growing destruction of the Self: a destructiveness in which the Self itself takes part, working against itself. It is not, I think, purely accidental that our metaphysical discourse about the ego has accompanied and at times proclaimed the social emergence of the "individual," our modern, rationalized form of subjectivity. Although this "regression" into subjectivity can seem at first to affirm and secure the Self, our historical experience now suggests that this is an "inflation" of the individual, granting the Self its dream of absolute sovereignty at the price of a metaphysical isolation, and that it is actually beyond all dialectical imagination self-defeating: an unconscious choice of self-destruction.

The essence of nihilism is being actualized in the historical self-destructiveness of the Self, which increasingly finds itself so thoroughly reduced to the "mere subjectivity" of an ego-logical existence and so profoundly isolated in its absolutely sovereign "individuality" that it can no longer trust itself to speak for the truth, the reality, of "its own" experience. The formations of psychopathology we shall be considering—narcissistic disorders, schizophrenias, depression—are merely the most extreme cases of a collective and archetypal madness—nihilism—at work in all of us. Nihilism is a cultural epidemic that defines the spirit of our epoch. Thus, our cases of psychopathology cannot be understood outside of an ontological field of interpretation in which we acknowledge our present historical experience of Being: our debilitating loss of conviction in the meaningfulness of living; our dreadful encounter with the possibility of nothingness. We must begin to see in this historical experience the evidence of our growing madness. What can we learn about this uncanny sickness that haunts the glorious achievements of our civilization?

In arguing for an interpretation of nihilism not only ontological but also epidemiological, I will first demonstrate through a reading of Descartes that some of the postures most characteristic of narcissistic disorders, schizophrenias, and depressions are symptomatically implicit in the subjectivism of his philosophy. Since the modern epoch may be said to begin with Descartes, the hermeneutical reading of Cartesian philosophy will assume a paradigmatic significance. If Cartesianism is at the beginning of modern philosophy, then the fact that there are psychopathological complexes hidden within its reflections suggests the possibility that narcissism, schizophrenia, and depression may be fundamental experiences for the whole of modern philosophy. Does the history of philosophy, and in particular the historical course of metaphysics since Descartes, reflect and in its own way encourage the unfolding of a specific psychopathology latent from the beginning in our civilization? With this question, the ontological issue becomes epidemiological, in the broad sense I want to spell out: here and in chapter sixteen.

When we diagnose our present historical psychopathology with concern for the ontological significance of our pain, need, suffering and affliction—that is, with concern for our experience of the meaningfulness of Being—can we discern anything in our experience to suggest the unconscious operation of a pattern that is unquestionably extremely destructive? The emergence and self-disclosing of nihilism has been traced, despite its inevitable self-concealment, within the history of metaphysics: it is in its essence, as Heidegger said (in a passage quoted in our "Opening Conversation"), a history in which Being itself is being contested. But is this phenomenon of nihilism restricted to its unfolding in the history of metaphysics? If it is not, we need to inquire into the concealed nature of our epidemics in psychopathology in order to retrieve the implicit metaphysics whose nihilism is at work within them and to bring to self-disclosure the contemporary experience with nihilism that cries out for ontological understanding.

Can we bring to light a pattern of nihilism, an implicit metaphysics, when we contemplate in historical terms—and that will mean epidemiological terms—the presence within our culture of a most thought-provoking pathology? What ultimately is at stake in current psychopathology is the *being* of the *Self,* i.e., its deepest dimension of integrity, wholeness and vitality; thus our questions should call attention to patterns in our living where the Self is suffering its most extreme self-destruction: loss of grounding, centeredness, balance, identity, wholeness, meaning, purpose, energy, heart, reality, and a sense of Being, of dimensionality. We need to consider the history of metaphysics in cultural, and more specifically, in epidemiological terms. We need to translate the "hermeneutics of suspicion" (Paul Ricoeur's method) into a diagnostic reading of our metaphysical discourse, bringing out an implicit psychopathology in the ego-logical conception of subjectivity that dominates the discourse of metaphysics. Can we retrieve in this way a concealed madness unconsciously at work in our metaphysics? What do the successively more radical critiques of Nietzsche and Heidegger suggest, if not a deepening psychopathology of the Self? In our abbreviated but subversive reading of Cartesian metaphysics, we will bring into relief the self-destructive, self-defeating gestures of thought and rationality, desperately struggling against the nihilistic effects of dualism within a discursive field dominated by the standard of objectivity and an image of the ego-subject. The pathology implicit in metaphysical reflection does after all speak; and what it speaks, when it masks its madness, is in the language of subjectivity: the language of the ego or the will.

Both Nietzsche and Heidegger argued for a critical interpretation that reads an underlying nihilism of the will into the metaphysics of subjectivity; and, just as Nietzsche supported this interpretation by calling attention to nihilism as the historical phenomenon we actually experience, so Heidegger spelled out the historical significance of his interpretation by pointing to the nihilism gradually revealed in our technology and its political economy.

Part Three will conclude with an interpretation that connects the nihilism in our technological economy with the nihilism that comes from, and in its turn destroys, the peculiar subjectivity of the modern Self. In "Technology and the Rise to Power of the Modern Self," we shall begin to construct a framework for interpreting how the same pathology of subjectivity that threatens to destroy the Self "from within" is also at work "outside" it in the nihilism of a technology whose will to power was made possible only because of this pathological Self. I submit that this nihilism is doubly destructive, destroying the Self from within (a deep ontological pathology in our experience of ourselves), while at the same time destroying it from outside: in the toxicity, stress, and commodification of our technological economy. The modern Self encounters a self-destruction for which its egoism, its own greed, insecurity and indifference, are responsible: it encounters in the world outside itself, as threats to its very survival, the objective effects of extreme subjectivity, its own historical pathology. Our extreme ego-logical subjectivity has become a mode of production, and the objective world it has produced is now subjecting the subject to the effects of nihilism hiding in its own objectifications. I shall argue that in our present technological economy the nihilism of the modern Self—its extreme subjectivity—can no longer conceal itself.

Reification, the institutionalization of objectivity, requires the most extreme subjectivization of individual experience. Consequently we are beginning to see, in this advanced phase of our technological economy, an alarming negation of the subject: a negation so extreme that the experience of the individual is now virtually emptied of all sense—dissolved, as it were, into nothingness. The final refuge of the subject, its "inner freedom," its "inwardness," what Kierkegaard called the Self's relation to itself, is rapidly becoming a horrible emptiness: existence bereaved, without a Self. Objectivity will rule unchallenged when the Self is finally dead.

II. CULTURAL EPIDEMIOLOGY

Near the end of *Civilization and Its Discontents,* Freud wrote that there is one question he "can hardly ignore." He puts it this way:

> If the evolution of civilization has such far-reaching similarity with the development of an individual, and if the same methods are employed in both, would not the diagnosis be justified that many systems of civilization—or epochs of it—possibly even the whole of humanity—have become "neurotic" under the pressure of the civilizing trends?

Here is the answer he gave:

> To analytic dissection of these neuroses, therapeutic recommendations might follow which could claim a great practical interest. I would not say that such an attempt to apply psychoanalysis to civilized society would be fanciful or doomed to fruitlessness. But it behoves us to be very careful, not to forget that after all we are dealing only with analogies, and that it is dangerous, not only with men but also with concepts, to drag them out of the region where they originated and have matured. The diagnosis of collective neuroses, moreover, will be confronted by a special difficulty. In the neurosis of an individual we can use as a starting point the contrast presented to us between the patient and his environment which we assume to be "normal." No such background as this would be available for any society similarly

> affected; it would have to be supplied in some other way. . . . In spite of all these difficulties, we may expect that one day someone will venture upon this research into the pathology of civilized communities.[7]

Freud's question is of the utmost importance, one that we must not be afraid to consider. It is the question that has set in motion not only this study of mine, but also the other studies gathered in this collection. I agree with Freud that the attempt to make a diagnosis of our civilization, our cultural life as a whole, is not inherently impossible or self-contradictory, although—and here, too, I am in agreement with him—we must of course be extremely careful in shifting our diagnostic methods and categories from individual psychopathology to cultural epidemiology. But the "special difficulty" to which he called our attention, namely the absence of some "objective" standard for measuring or determining cultural pathology and the absence of any conceptual contrast, is not as much of an obstacle as Freud seemed to suppose. There is another way: another way of conceptualizing the problem of "immanent critique," diagnosis "from within" the culture. After all, Freud himself, at the end of the textual passage, seemed able with relative ease to contemplate the actualization of this kind of project. His final conjecture makes no sense unless we assume that he believed the project to be theoretically, methodologically, and conceptually possible. Freud's conjecture implies that, for him, the epistemological problem was not like the problem in the ancient paradox of the Cretan liar, the paradox a Cretan logician is supposed to have generated when he uttered the statement that "All Cretans are liars." When the paradox is translated into our discourse on cultural epidemiology, we see clearly that this epistemological problem would be hopeless, impossible for us to resolve: If our entire civilization is mad, then we cannot protect the judgments we make about it from the suspicion of universal madness. Thus, even if our epidemiological indictment were to be true, there would be no way for us to know this: the diagnosis could or perhaps must be considered as just another manifestation of the prevailing psychopathology. Is the diagnosis that sees in our civilization the pervasive danger of nihilism itself a manifestation of this nihilism? Is the diagnosis a symptom of the hysteria surrounding the disease? Freud's text gives no warrant for such radical doubt. On the contrary, the text indicates that he was looking forward to the time when we could finally think about the task and its problem in a way that he could not. Answering my own two questions, I would say "No." The criterion, the test I have applied here, is actually implicit in the meaning of "nihilism" as we have defined it, and was already suggested by Nietzsche himself: Is our interpretation self-defeating or does it contribute to our self-affirmation, our affirmation of life?

In *Minima Moralia,* Adorno speculates that a psychoanalytic examination of today's "prototypical" culture "would show the sickness proper to the time to consist precisely in normality."[8] Perhaps Freud's most challenging difficulty was, as Adorno suggested, that he could never choose "between negating the renunciation of instinct as repression contrary to reality, and applauding it as sublimation beneficial to culture."[9] Adorno was convinced that what passes for "normality" is in truth a kind of madness, and that the "sickness of the normal" is "the same disastrous pattern" as the sickness of those whom "the normal" consider to be sick; only the pattern is "present, in a different way."[10]

Here, then, is another way to think about the question Freud posed: If our entire civilization is touched by madness, some individuals suffering its destructiveness more than others, then it could be supposed that those who are able to withstand it the most, or suffer it the least, might be in a position to attempt a provisional diagnosis. The extent of the madness would of course explain the failure of the diagnosis to achieve immediate and widespread acceptance.

In an "Epilogue" to his *Essays on Contemporary Events,* Jung spoke without hesitation of "mass psychoses," "psychic epidemics," "epidemics of madness."[11] Many people are beginning to see connections between diseases, individual psychology, and social context.[12] According to David Bakan, "a relationship between psychological disorder and various forms of sociocultural separation, alienation and disintegration has been indicated in a large number of studies."[13] Our sciences are beginning to recognize in the individual pathology they are seeing that they may be compelled to acknowledge the legitimacy of cultural diagnosis. Our psychic and somatic complaints now begin to present themselves as manifestations of "deeper disorder."[14] Suffering always has a historical dimension; but this suggests that it must be correlated very specifically with social structures, political institutions, and cultural ideology. As Illich argued in *Medical Nemesis: The Expropriation of Health,* "The character of the society shapes to some degree the personality of those who suffer. . . ."[15] If this is true, however, we must add that society shapes the way its people experience their suffering: how they will recognize, understand, and respond to it. "All disease is a socially created reality. Its meaning and the responses it has evoked have a history."[16]

One of the difficulties standing in the way of a historical and epidemiological interpretation is the impression that psychopathology has not fundamentally changed in the course of human history, and that there is nothing really distinctive in the pathology of our present historical situation. Adorno understood the political significance—the nihilistic effect—of this conviction: "Criticism of tendencies in modern society is automatically countered, before it is fully uttered, by the argument that things have always been like this."[17] Adorno's reply to this criticism is very blunt, but it carries a ring of truth, since it was spoken so directly from the heart of his experience: Things only appear to be the same when one looks at history from a distance and with "cold-hearted contemplation".[18] In an ideological climate that can recognize "objectivity" only in neutral scientific observation, we must understand that "What is constant is not an invariable quantity of suffering, but its progress towards hell. . . ."[19] In our hypothesis regarding cultural epidemiology, how are we concerned with the quantitative distribution of disease and psychopathology in specified cultural and historical populations? What do our numbers and statistics really mean? Are we referring only to actual case histories, or are we projecting by induction? Are we distinguishing and correlating prevalence and incidence? Is the correlation between pathology and culture a question of "content" or only of "occurrence"? Is this a question we should struggle to answer? These are important questions.[20] But before we are overwhelmed by them, we should pause to consider the cultural assumption that all "knowledge" of society is a "scientific" knowledge modelled after the physics of Newton and Descartes. Scientism recognizes nothing other than "objective" standards of acceptability and truth; it is estranged from and therefore denies standards of acceptability and truth that derive from deeply reflective personal experience.

Our sense of objectivity is troubled by the fact that epistemological principles and standards are different in different cultures and different historical epochs. How can we establish transcultural and transhistorical invariance? And if we cannot establish some invariance, how can we speak—as did Nietzsche, Heidegger, and Adorno—of historical change, historical decline and growing malignancy? How can we speak of historically distinctive epochs and epidemics? How can we comprehend the whole, when we are only a part of this very whole? (Freud's question, with which we began). Are we reduced to silence because an absolute standpoint, or an absolute standard of objectivity, is not imaginable? In *The Idea of A Critical Theory,* Raymond Geuss has argued that "Our standards of reflective acceptability and the social and cultural ideals in terms of which we criticize societies and ideologies are just part of our tradition and have no absolute foundation or transcendental warrant."[21] But does this relativity mean that we have no standards to trust? Is no "immanent critique" possible for us? Is our capacity to trust our own experience and perceptions now totally destroyed? Geuss pointed out that "For Adorno, we must start from wherever we happen to be historically and culturally, from a particular kind of frustration or suffering experienced by human agents in their attempt to realize some historically specific project of 'the good life' "[22] Critical theories of society are "true," he says, "only relative to this particular historical situation and [they] are bound to be superseded."[23] So "we must start from . . . a particular kind of frustration or suffering." We must in this sense trust our own experience. And yet, it is possible for us to experience suffering without understanding its causes. Moreover, because there is social control over "inner life," ideological delusion, i.e., "false consciousness," is always possible. We human beings are not always aware, and of course never fully and immediately aware, of our suffering: "It is the particular insidiousness of ideology that it turns human desires and aspirations against themselves and uses them to fuel repression. . . . Therefore, the critical theory must also show in what way the particular form of expression these needs and desires found is self-destructive. . . ."[24] I would offer a further conclusion. Critical theory must take on the task of disclosing the "inner" experiential connection between our epidemics of psychopathology and an epoch of nihilism. And where there is either no awareness or an awareness in need of self-understanding, critical theory must take on the task of developing that.[25] Somehow, the individual's "own" experience, "inner experience," must become a trustworthy ground for the epidemiological interpretation. If we do not trust our own experience, if we do not believe in the possibility of trust; if we do not have any faith in the truthfulness of the individual's experience, then we have succumbed to the self-destructiveness of nihilism. Critical theory is not utopian or transcendental; it acknowledges the difficulties, but refuses to despair. By contributing to the awakening and development of awareness, by training perception, critical theory answers Freud's question. Yes, there is another way to think the validity of our epidemiological interpretation.

Freud's formulation of the theoretical problem in cultural epidemiology informs us that critical theory cannot restrict itself to the facilitation of awareness. The more urgent, more fundamental task is to protect the reality of the individual's "own" experience, to demonstrate the possibility of trusting "inner experience"—to preserve "subjectivity" from self-destruction. In the modern epoch, the being of the Self is so thoroughly subjectivized that the individual no longer trusts or believes in the reality of "lived experience." Thus, even Sigmund Freud, the father of psychoanalysis, was so completely trained in the "objective method" of natural science that he betrayed the truth of experience without the slightest whisper of resistance. He simply assumed without question that the individual's reflective experience could not be an "authoritative" source of critical standards in the diagnosis of collective neuroses. What is the rational ground for Freud's assumption? When the goal of therapy is assumed to be nothing more than social adaptation, i.e., conformity, then it will seem that the statistical and normative senses of "normality" coincide. But facts are not values, and once their divergence is recognized as a theoretical possibility, the assumption of their equivalence must be continually questioned. Is the goal of therapy merely a process of adjustment? What is well-being? What is sanity? What is health? Once the two senses of "normality" are understood as separate, the "rational ground" for Freud's assumption loses its apparent unquestionability. Like critical theory, the discourse of cultural epidemiology constitutes itself around precisely this questioning of the basic assumption.

Are sheer numbers to determine normality? Even if we choose to define "normality" by reference to population statistics, we still need a rationally compelling argument to demonstrate why we should take those facts to dictate our ideals, our dreams, our hopes.

Freud's argument against cultural diagnosis makes sense only if we assume that the contrast between the patient and his environment involves a statistical standard of normality. If, contrary to this assumption, every standard of "normality" is inherently an ideal, a value, then where is the standard's "objectivity"? The "special difficulty" that Freud could see only in the diagnosis of culture—that there is no objective point of reference nor absolute standard—also contests the assumption of objectivity in the diagnosis of individual patients. Here Freud did not wish to acknowledge that same "difficulty."

It is strange that Freud, a master of inwardness, kept looking outside himself for an objective standard of truth. In his analytic practice Freud worked from his own sense of reality and sanity; he helped others by teaching them to trust and to work through their own individual sense of "how things were" for them. But when he began to contemplate the possibility of a pathology inherent in our present historical situation or in our civilization as a whole, Freud forgot himself. Is our inwardness completely determined by our cultural environment? Is our own individual experience nothing but a repetition of archaic patterns transmitted in the continuation of civilization? Are we merely the products of our time? Why must we look "outside" ourselves to find "objective" standards of culture. Cultures and their epidemics are "internalized." This "inner" experience can speak of its pathology, but only if we are willing to listen.

Until the nihilism in "subjectivity" and "objectivity" is in remission and healing, we must defend the distinction critical theory makes between a true and false subjectivity; we must accordingly protect the truth in subjectivity against its abolition. Because of his commitment to scientism, Freud could see only false subjectivity. But to see only the false is itself an expression of nihilism, because it reinforces the belief that the individual's experience of culture and the life of the spirit is totally dictated by existing social institutions. This belief is profoundly self-destructive. But if our "inner" and "reflective" experience is *not* totally determined by the cultural background, how can we argue that it is not acceptable as a ground for critical theory and cultural epidemiology? From the beginning of human history, disciplines of cultural self-criticism have existed—for that is what history is. This attests to the vitality of "inner experience" as an irrepressible source of critical judgment regarding the spiritual condition of its culture.

In the first chapter of his *Reflections on the Causes of Human Misery and upon Certain Proposals to Eliminate Them,* Barrington Moore pointed out that it has never been possible to achieve widespread consensus, even among the population of one social culture, regarding the true meaning of "happiness," the "good life" and a "just society." But he argued,

> Matters stand otherwise with misery and suffering. . . . If human beings find it difficult to agree upon the meaning and causes of happiness, they find it much easier to know when they are miserable. . . . In straightforward factual terms, it is also possible to recognize certain widely recurring causes of human suffering. . . .

He consequently suggested that

> [a] conception of the unitary nature of human suffering, unitary at least in comparison with human happiness, is helpful in resolving some

> of the vexing issues of the proper role that subjective evaluations and moral judgments may or ought to play in social analysis.[26]

Cultural epidemiology is a discourse of interpretation generated by our experience of social life; in particular, it concerns our experience and diagnostic conceptualization of pathology. Although as a culture we are deeply confused about the nature of happiness and may easily be deceived about its actuality, our experience of suffering and misery is a different matter. Moore was correct, I believe, in pointing to an important difference: it is relatively easy for us human beings to be deceived into thinking that we are "happy," or at least as "happy" as we could ever expect to be; but it is much less likely that we could be systematically deceived into thinking we are suffering and miserable, when in fact we "really" are satisfied and "happy."

Let us consider Heidegger's observation about human suffering. In *Being and Time,* he observed that "In its everydayness, the human being [Dasein] undergoes a dull "suffering," can sink away in the dullness of it, and evade it by seeking new ways in which its dispersion in its affairs may be further dispersed."[27] But he added at once that "In the moment of vision, indeed, and often just 'for the moment,' existence can even gain mastery over the "everyday" [i.e., over its "normal" condition of suffering], but it can never extinguish it." (Ibid. Bracketed words added.) In a later text, "Nihilism as Determined by the History of Being," Heidegger very clearly expressed his strong support for the methodological position our study will assume: "We hardly need to illustrate in detail the spreading violence of actual nihilism, which we all personally experience to a sufficient degree, even without an ivory-tower definition of its essence."[28] Indeed, elsewhere in that same text, Heidegger observed that "Both openly and tacitly, boundless suffering and measureless sorrow proclaim the condition of our world a needful one."[29] Heidegger believed that the attempt to formulate a diagnosis of our culture "from the inside" must first overcome an enormous difficulty. Considering why such an "extreme measure of suffering" has not yet brought about a "transformation,"[30] Heidegger argued that,

> Even the immense suffering which surrounds the earth is unable to waken a transformation, because it is only experienced as suffering, as passive, and thus as the opposite state of action, and thus experienced together with action in the same realm of being of the will to will.[31]

There is, in this suffering, an "extreme need", but in our "age of confusion, violence, and despair," its nature is concealed.[32] Nevertheless, Heidegger did believe that it is possible for critical thinking to cut through the ideological distortions, confusions and deceptions that seem unavoidable once we acknowledge cultural relativism.

Presumably, if we allow Heidegger the right to trust his own experience as a ground for the "diagnosis" of our culture, we must believe that our culture does not completely determine all possibilities for experience and understanding. To be sure, the source of our inner fragmentation remains concealed from us. Thus, despite the unspeakable suffering, there is a prevalent sense in which, as he said, "we feel no pain".[33] (In "Recollection in Metaphysics," Heidegger connected this numbness with the metaphysics of our technological culture.[34] According to his analysis, our culture, forgetful of Being, misrepresents the true dimensionality of our spiritual pain and suffering.) But even this does not actually *preclude* cultural diagnosis grounded in the individual's reflective experience. Heidegger only contended that the first task for cultural diagnosis must therefore consist in demonstrating the pain in our lack of need. What would demonstrate this painful need, if not a discourse capable of communicating its own contact with that dimension of our experience?

Horkheimer was perhaps right, therefore, in suggesting, as he said in *Dawn and Decline,* that "Teaching people the capacity for pleasure constitutes a decisive moment in the hopeless struggle against the dawning totalitarian epoch of the world."[35] But I suggest that teaching people how to tap into their capacity to work with their own experience is even more fundamental and decisive. With that kind of self-knowledge, people could begin to touch the "needfulness" within them and integrate their sense of that needfulness into an appropriate historical praxis. "Inner" truth will appear only when there is *trust* in our "inwardness," in the body of one's own experience: recognition of its initial value and validity as a standpoint and viewpoint for interpreting social and cultural "reality."

Freud was ambivalent toward "cultural diagnosis." His skepticism derived from a conviction that, since the culture in which we live and become human is the absolute horizon of meaningful interpretation, there can be no objective standard—and a fortiori, no standpoint—outside culture, by reference to which we might contemplate and critically diagnose or measure the well-being of our social culture. For Freud, it was possible to judge the well-being of an individual *within* our culture because the prevailing cultural norm is taken without question as the standard: a standard that requires conformity and adjustment to the "average" and calls that conformity a condition of sanity and healthiness.

But is the cultural standard to which Freud appealed in his work with individual "patients" any more "objective" than the diagnosis of a pathology pervasive in our society? Why are cultures of disease, of bacilli and viruses, "objective," while discourses about cultures of mental illness and spiritual emptiness are excluded from the realm of truth? From where does the authority of the psychiatric diagnosis derive, in the case of an individual "patient"? Freud used the word "patient" to call the one who came to him in distress. This word defeats the one in distress before any further communication takes place. It annihilates any hope of retrieving "from within" oneself some truth of value. This calling assumes in advance that the example of learning "from within oneself," which Socrates tried to teach Meno, the slave boy, cannot be put into practice within the clinical situation. And it assumes that the clinician is in a position of interpretive authority that requires the patient's submission and self-effacement. However, we may question Freud's self-proclaimed authority; and we may question the cultural standard that he assumed as a basis for the "scientific objectivity" of his clinical judgment. Thus, we reduce his claims for "objectivity" in the diagnosis of individuals to the "relativity" he perceived in cultural diagnosis.

The fact is that we are capable of thinking critically about how we "inwardly" experience our time, how we are affected by our culture. And this means that we can turn relativity—the fact that we live and think within culture—into a strength. We should not consent to Freud's foreclosure of the horizon of cultural interpretations; we must question his assumptions that the norms of culture could never provide a reasonable standard for psychiatry; and we must recognize the need to justify the goal of "adjustment" and "normalizing," in the light of more "revolutionary" historical visions of who we are and who we could become. We must acknowledge his failure to recognize that there are standpoints and viewpoints that speak the truth about our time from within the culture itself. Ironically, it was Freud himself who, without fully realizing the implications of his work, made it easier for us to question the goal of adjustment to the prevailing cultural norms. And he has this effect because the subject of his discourse is, despite its attachment to an egology, "inner experience" and its entrustment with a truth. Why, then, can we not draw out of this "inner experience" a truth that comes from our cultural interiority and speaks for that very reason with an understanding of the culture as a whole? Even if we accept the fact of cultural relativism, we must consider: Who could ever be in a more authoritative position to understand the suffering of an epoch than the people who are living within it?

If our standpoint cannot be standpointlessness, it is pointless to make that a standard for objective truth. And not only pointless: it is self-destructive and self-defeating, for by neglecting our own experience as a source of truth we subject ourselves to the sufferings of an imposed truth. In his work on Nietzsche and the problematic of nihilism, Heidegger held firm to his conviction that what alone matters is that the critical diagnosis of our culture articulate our own individual experience in a way that calls thoughtful attention to the historical situation and exposes a rich field of questions, answers, and practical opportunities.[36] Since our relativity is inevitable, the most rational response is that we make the best of it—always taking care, of course, to avoid absolutism in dogmatic claims for our limited and conditioned knowledge.

This, I think, is how we must contend with another difficult question—a problem Erich Fromm adumbrated in the opening chapters of *The Sane Society*.[37] To speak of a pathology of the Self that is distinctive of our time, we must be able to make a valid comparison. But, given our historical situatedness, how can we compare our present epoch with earlier ones? What do we know about the experience of Self and pathology in times long past? How can we claim to know and understand what is really distinctive in the pathology of our modern epoch and living present, unless we are able to know and understand other cultures and other historical times? How can we identify patterns of mental illness in our cultural worlds? Can we accomplish this epidemiological comparison from a timely position within our cultural world? I believe that the epidemiological analysis which follows will illuminate something of recognizable and unquestionable importance for our time.

Whether or not we are defeated by epistemological problems depends on our break with the traditional theory of truth. Our discourse is avowedly hermeneutical, and the truth to which it accedes is therefore not a matter of correctness, an adequate correspondence between our theory and a fixed, unalterable reality; rather, it is a matter of setting in motion a dialectical process of disclosure. Our discourse generates a field of interpretation within which something concealed comes to presence, lets itself be seen. The truth we seek is a truth "in the making."[38] The test of this truth focuses on the difference it makes: whether or not the interpretation is life-affirming, life-enhancing.

In closing Part Two, I would like to recall what Hegel said about "truth" in his *Phenomenology of Mind:* "The life of the mind only attains its truth when discovering itself in absolute desolation. The mind is not this power as a positive which turns away from the negative, . . . it is this power only when looking the negative in the face, dwelling upon it."[39] We do not have to let the relativism of truth defeat our need to understand ourselves in the culture of our time. Instead, as Nietzsche suggested, we can accept the epistemological challenge and see how much of truth we are strong enough to acknowledge:

> Let us, from now on, be on our guard against the hallowed philosophers' myth of a "pure, will-less, painless, timeless knower"; let us beware of the tentacles of such contradictory notions as "pure reason," "absolute knowledge," "absolute intelligence." All these concepts presuppose an eye such as no living being can imagine, an eye required to have no direction, to abrogate its active and interpretive powers—precisely those powers that alone make of seeing a seeing of *something*. All seeing is essentially perspectival, and so is all knowing. The more emotions we allow to speak in a given matter, the more different eyes we can put on in order to view a given spectacle, the more complete will be our conception of it, the greater our [so-called] "objectivity."[40]

Understanding this, we can use the relativism of our epidemiological interpretation to our advantage. We can turn a situation that has long appeared to be self-defeating into a source of strength. Since relativism derives from the fact that our understanding is necessarily situated, the acceptance of our relative situation could be the basis for a deeper understanding of our situation. What better understanding could there possibly be than one coming from the historical experience of being in this situation? Drawing words from our suffering, from our experience of the situation in which we actually find ourselves, we will begin to discern decisive opportunities for the affirmation of life.

III. NIHILISM: THE SELF AND ITS METAPHYSICAL REPRESENTATION

Nietzsche's Interpretation of Nihilism

Looking into the advent of nihilism, Nietzsche announced the "death" of God. His eyes had the look of madness. Sometime between November 1887 and March 1888, Nietzsche wrote:

> What I relate is the history of the next two centuries. I describe what is coming, what can no longer come differently: *the advent of nihilism.*

> This history can be related even now; for necessity itself is at work here. This future speaks even now in a hundred signs, this destiny announces itself everywhere; for this music of the future all ears are cocked even now. For some time now, our whole European culture has been moving as toward a catastrophe, with a tortured tension that is growing from decade to decade: restlessly, violently, headlong, like a river that wants to reach the end, that no longer reflects, that is afraid to reflect.[41]

Nietzsche thought he could see the roots of nihilism buried very deeply in the character of our civilization.[42] Thus he began to analyze the etiology—or, as he preferred to put it, the "genealogy"—of the distress:

> Skepticism regarding morality is what is decisive. The end of the moral interpretation of the world, which no longer has any sanction after it has tried to escape into some beyond, leads to nihilism. "Everything lacks meaning" (the untenability of one interpretation of the world, upon which a tremendous amount of energy has been lavished, awakens the suspicion that *all* interpretations of the world are false).[43]

In other words, as we human beings developed within our culture and became increasingly self-conscious, increasingly disposed toward self-examination, we have been compelled with a corresponding intensity and lucidity to recognize our own participation in the presence of value in our world. Curiously, however, we have not been strengthened and ennobled by this insight. On the contrary, we are distressed and troubled. The being of value has lost its distant, absolute authority, the "mystery" of its commanding appeal. If we are *needed* to maintain our values, then the essential value in values—the "origin" of their unquestionable authority—appears destroyed. Valuing, now experienced as "merely subjective," becomes totally meaningless: "Everything is false! Everything is permitted!"[44] Here Nietzsche could see the contradiction in the very core of the will: the will's insistence that it is alone responsible for the creating of values will inevitably destroy them. Thus Nietzsche suggested, with perhaps an implicit sense of hope, that "nihilism represents the ultimate logical conclusion of our great values and ideals—because we must experience nihilism before we can find out what value these 'values' really had."[45]

Nietzsche offered a brief account in psychological terms of the nihilistic cultural response to the fact that "civilization" had finally entered the historical stage of human self-development where, by a sudden turn in self-consciousness, our ancestors would bring to light a terribly difficult truth: the evidence of our existential participation in the presencing of value:

> Thus the belief in the absolute immorality of nature, in aim- and meaninglessness, is the psychologically necessary affect once the belief in God and an essentially [absolute] moral order becomes untenable. Nihilism appears at that point, not that the displeasure at existence has become greater than before but because one has come to mistrust any "meaning" in suffering, indeed in existence. One interpretation has collapsed; and because it was considered *the* [only] interpretation, it now seems as if there were no meaning at all in existence, as if everything were in vain.[46]

For Nietzsche, this "in vain" is precisely what "constitutes the character of present-day nihilism."[47] We should note in passing that the psychology characterized in this passage on cultural behavior could be psychoanalytically interpreted in terms of a narcissistic personality disorder: strong infantile dependency needs, deep separation anxieties and insecurities, incipient paranoia, and oscillation between stretches of depression and despair and temporary delusions of omnipotence. As Nietzsche said, "We understand the old and are far from strong enough for something new."[48] Even when we understand "that all the old ideals are hostile to life," we find ourselves unable to realize that despair is not called for, because we are not strong enough to complete the process of breaking away from the old interpretation of values.[49] For it is only within the framework of the old cultural interpretation that the end of transcendentalism will seem to spell the end of all meaningfulness.[50] In truth, this could be the beginning of a new phase in our "self-overcoming"—our emancipation, our development as human beings. "Overall insight: the ambiguous character of our modern world—the very same symptoms could point to decline and to strength."[51]

Sometime in 1887, Nietzsche wrote: "What does nihilism mean? That the highest values devaluate themselves. The aim is lacking; 'why' finds no answer."[52] Our faith in morality vanished; and since nothing replaced it, we have been overwhelmed by despair.[53] If Nietzsche was hopeful, that is because he thought of history as a dialectic: "Now that the shabby origin of these values is becoming clear, the universe seems to have lost value, seems 'meaningless'—but that is only a *transitional stage*."[54] Nietzsche was very clear-sighted when he diagnosed what is "pathological"; it is not to be found in "nihilism" as a passing stage of destruction, but rather only in "nihilism" as the self-destructive belief that the end of the Judaeo-Christian world-view spells the end of all possible moral values and all possible existential meaning.[55] The nihilism is not in destruction as such—for some things must be destroyed to give way to something different—but rather in our incapacitation, our self-defeat.

According to Nietzsche, "Values and their changes are related to increases in the power [i.e., capability and sense of capability] of those positing the values.[56] Thus, instead of passively suffering the disillusionment that constitutes the moment of self-consciousness (*anagnōrisis*) when we recognize our own part in the handing down of traditional cultural values, or alternatively rushing blindly into a fury of self-destructive activity, we are urged to embrace the advent of nihilism as "an ideal of the highest degree of powerfulness of the spirit, the over-richest life—partly destructive, partly ironic."[57]

In Note 22, Nietzsche wrote:

> Nihilism. It is *ambiguous:*
>
> A. Nihilism as a sign of increased power of the spirit: as *active* nihilism.
>
> B. Nihilism as decline and recession of the power of the spirit: as *passive* nihilism.[58]

In other words, we can either suffer nihilism in an existential passivity and resignation of will, or we can attempt to master it by taking an active part in the destructive process. In its most extreme forms, however, "as a violent force of destruction," we see that even this active nihilism must be tempered by soundness of judgment, for it certainly can be just as self-destructive as the passive form.[59] But perhaps Nietzsche's most profound insight is to be found in the note immediately following, where he recognized the possibility that nihilism could be experienced "as a normal condition."[60] As a deep cosmological understanding of impermanence, of the inseparability of destruction and growth and the continuity between being and non-being, life and death, this experience could potentially be extremely liberating. But the more likely understanding would passively accept the suffering in nihilism as our inevitable and normal fate.

In Note 12, dated some time between November 1887 and March 1888, Nietzsche tried to clarify the "psychology" on which this nihilism feeds.[61] Basically, what he proposed is that we are suffering from a loss of faith in ourselves—in our own value. We are suffering a deep collective depression following our realization that existence has no ultimate end, that no ultimate unity underlies the changes we see, and that there is no supernatural world to guarantee the truths by which we live.

Since, for Nietzsche, too much faith in the categories of reason contributes to a psychology that falls into nihilism, the overcoming of our collective depression calls for a renunciation of our rationalism.[62] This is not to say that Nietzsche advocated existential irrationalism, but rather than he envisioned a culture committed to ongoing experimentation in the spirit of a healthy skepticism.

In *The Genealogy of Morals,* Nietzsche related nihilism to a profound crisis growing in the culture—and cultural interpretation—of humanism; he outlined how nihilism, as a total and pervasive "contesting" of Being, effects its self-destructiveness within the very *being* of the human Self, and accordingly manifests, individually and collectively, a clinically recognizable pattern of psychopathology. Nietzsche showed the forms of suffering that contemporary psychoanalysis is just now beginning to "see" in epidemic proportions, which it interprets—counterproductively, I believe—under the classification of "narcissistic personality disorders."[63] We need to understand the social and cultural significance of these disorders. We need to understand them as historical manifestations of a nihilism that also takes place in the cultural and spiritual dimensions of human existence, where it feeds on a poisonous and debilitating crisis within the heart of humanism and consumes our narcissistic attention while cutting us off ever more decisively and fatefully from the being of the Self: from our humanity, and the very ground of our individuality. "This is Europe's true predicament: together with the fear of man, we have also lost the love of man, confidence in man, indeed, the will to be man. Now the sight of man makes us despondent. What is nihilism today if not that?"[64] In other words, "The real danger lies in our loathing of man and our pity of him. If these two emotions should one day join forces, they would beget the most sinister thing ever witnessed on earth: man's ultimate will, his will to nothingness, nihilism."[65] But Nietzsche was not at all without hope, for, as we might surmise from his embrace of the Principle of the Eternal Recurrence of the Same, he was a thinker who drew sustenance for his meditations from the cosmological "economy" of human existence: "Principle: There is an element of decay in everything that characterizes modern man; but close beside this sickness stand signs of an untested force and powerfulness of the soul."[66]

Two years later (1887), Nietzsche confided his "overall insight": that "every major growth is accompanied by a tremendous crumbling and passing away," and that our experience with nihilism is a "suffering of the transition."[67]

The text of Nietzsche's analysis disseminates a hermeneutical treasury of interpretations, letting itself be read simultaneously as a contribution to our current discourses on ecological changes and catastrophes; the epidemic significance of an increase in the presence of cancer; planetary crises as a result of unrestrained and uncontrollable technological growth; deep, unresolved conflicts between a growing, but increasingly egocentric "individualism" and the humanism that underlies our traditional, modern commitment to the growth of democratic institutions; and finally, a discourse on the Self and its sufferings, calling our attention to the dangers that threaten our continued historical growth as a culture of human beings. Nietzsche understood the "elemental" and "organic" necessity of "nihilism." But in this case, this understanding generated a thoughtful response, not a nihilistic resignation before Fate.

For Nietzsche, the actuality of nihilism was clear: according to its "essence," it is manifest as processes and patterns that are, in the end, profoundly self-destructive. Thus he spent many years of his life bringing into discourse the "symptoms of this self-destruction."[68] For the sake of brevity, I shall now merely classify and catalogue some of the more prominent symptoms and signs before we consider more recent contributions to this disorder: Adorno and Heidegger.

(1) *The physical dimension of human existence:* the domain of concern to biology and medicine. Here is what Nietzsche saw.[69] "Exhaustion" and general debility (231, p. 134; 44, p. 27; 54, p. 34). "Anemic constitution" (341, p. 187). "Forms of sickness" (50, p. 32). "Physiological and moral ills" (52, p. 32). "Pathology" (52, p. 32). "Sickness and habitual weakness" (47, p. 29). Problems of digestion and consumption (47, p. 29). "Chronic disease" (351, p. 192; 373, p. 200). "Sicknesses, especially those affecting nerves and head" (43, p. 27). Poor systemic immunocompetence, "the lack of strength to resist the danger of infections" (47, p. 29; 44, p. 27).

(2) *The emotive and motivational dimension of human existence:* a domain of concern to the social sciences and to the practice of psychotherapy. Here are some of the symptoms Nietzsche saw. "Adiaphoria": inertia, apathy, and indifference (45, p. 28). "Spiritual weariness" (55, p. 38; 64, p. 43). "Weakness of will" (46, p. 28). "Paralysis" (152, p. 95; 351, p. 191). "Anesthesia," numbness (47, p. 30). Flattened affect and dissociated consciousness (44, p. 27). "Drugged tranquility" (*Genealogy*, p. 172). "Hopeless despair" (55, p. 37). "Resignation" (55, p. 38). "Pessimism" (9–11,

p. 11; 195, p. 115; 297, p. 167; 701, p. 373; 765, p. 400; 852, p. 450; 853, p. 453). "Fatalism" (243, p. 140). "Narcotization" (59, p. 41; 55, p. 37; 29, p. 20; 43, p. 26; 728, p. 386). "Alcoholism," "intoxication," "poisoning" (48–49, p. 31; 55, p. 37). "The *deed of nihilism*, which is suicide" (247, p. 143). "Depersonalization" and "disintegration of the will" (44, p. 27). "Impoverished life" (701, p. 373). A will "turned against life" (*Genealogy*, p. 154). Agitated activity, "hustling" (33, p. 22). "Restlessness" (33, p. 22). A "nomadic" life, without any place to call "home" (59, p. 40). "Lostness" (30, p. 20). "Emptiness" (29, p. 20). "We are losing the center of gravity by virtue of which we lived" (30, p. 20). Suppressed vindictiveness and hatred, blocked aggressions (*Genealogy*, pp. 171–72). "Extreme irritability" (43, p. 27; 44, p. 27; 62, p. 42; 71, p. 47). Envy and "ressentiment" (350, p. 191; 351, p. 192; 373, p. 201; 579, p. 311; 765, p. 402; 1021, p. 529; 864, p. 461). "Hostility toward the senses," toward the body and its organismic needs (400, p. 216). "Rage against life" (461, p. 253). "Blind rage" (55, p. 35). Difficulty accepting temporality: change, impermanence, contingency, "becoming" (581, p. 312; 585, p. 316; 708, p. 377). Entanglement in a fixated point of view (470, p. 262; 616, p. 330). "Self-contempt" (401, p. 217). Lack of "self-esteem" (288, p. 162; 296, p. 166; 773, pp. 405–6). Lack of self-confidence (353, p. 194). Weak ego-structure, weak will-to-power, ineffectiveness, inability to act (362, p. 197; 364, p. 198). "Extreme pride and the humiliation of petty weakness *felt* in contrast" (29, p. 20). A sense of helplessness, as the sources of authority we depended on—first God and then Reason—can no longer compel and sustain us (20, p. 17). A desperate hedonism, which never seems to bring any deep or lasting satisfaction (35, p. 23). Clinical psychology should recognize immediately the material assembled in this catalogue, which Nietzsche himself interpreted in relation to the *actuality* of nihilism, as evidence of serious psychopathology; in particular, the catalogue presents an array of "symptoms" from which the experienced clinician could easily discern and abstract the three patterns of psychopathology which concern the studies in this collection.

Heidegger and Adorno: Nihilism and the History of Metaphysics

As Nietzsche worked out his "genealogical" critique of Western metaphysics, he gradually realized that this interpretation of its history portrays the unfolding of nihilism within our cultural life. The devastation of nihilism is implicit within our metaphysics, where it takes place as the reflective and projective manifestation of a pathology encoded into our culture as a whole. In *The Will to Power*, Nietzsche declared, "The history of philosophy is a secret raging against the pre-conditions of life, against the value feelings of life . . ."[70] Metaphysics is a field of discourse; as such, it is a cultural phenomenon: first because it is a "product" of culture; second because it clearly, if only implicitly, reflects the metaphysical beliefs in effect within that culture; and third, because this metaphysics circulates, in concealed, often subterranean and unconscious ways, within its own culture and tends to perpetuate the cultural pathology which generated it. Since our culture of nihilism is pathogenic, and our metaphysics is a discourse of reflection generated within this culture, we may undertake a theoretical critique of the history of metaphysics in order to clarify our understanding of the pathogenic metaphysics deeply concealed, despite its pervasiveness, within the present cultural world. In particular, both the lucid metaphysics brought to light in our reflective discourse and the concealed metaphysics constitutive of our world contribute to the formation of pathologies that are specifically destructive to the being of the Self and that therefore can be understood adequately only in terms of this being.

In "Metaphysics as History of Being," Heidegger made the following observation: "Thus 'culture' begins historically as the structure of humanity which is certain of itself and intent upon the assurance of itself."[71] In other words, "In that truth becomes the certainty of knowledge of humanity making sure of itself, that history begins which is called *the modern period* in the historical calculation of epochs."[72] Note that in these two rich textual passages Heidegger articulated an "ideological" critique of our culture and its history—more specifically, a critique directed at our "humanism," our cultural understanding of "the human," of ourselves as human beings. Moreover, he implicitly connected this critique to his ontological, and therefore radically critical, interpretation of the nihilism at work in the history of metaphysics and the history of Being.

In a text on Nietzsche's "announcement" of the "death" of God, Heidegger reflected at great length on the meaning of nihilism. He argued that it cannot be understood only by looking at signs and symptoms—its various effects. Nietzsche saw nihilism as a pathology of the will to power, but diagnosed the pathology as a "weakness" of the will. For Heidegger, this analysis is not entirely mistaken, but it gets lost in the historical effects and fails to see the essence. The essence, he argued, is the negation of Being: our experience of the nothingness of Being. Nihilism is indeed a pathology of the will to power. However, the essence of the pathology is not, as Nietzsche thought, in our weakness, our failure to take over the creative powers of the dead God, but rather in our reduction of Being to a phenomenon of the will. In other words, nihilism consists in the fact that Being is experienced as nothing but a manifestation of the will to power. Nihilism is therefore not just a question of the "death" of God. Since the "death" of God is an event that calls into question *all* our sources of meaning, what is at stake is nothing less than the essence, the dimensionality, of our being. For Heidegger, nihilism involves a pathology of the will to power because the triumph of this will consists in a destructive rage against the dimensionality of Being. Thus understood, nihilism is not only a phenomenon of Nietzsche's time, nor does it rage only in the present historical situation; rather, it constitutes the most fundamental movement in the history of the West.[73]

Since nihilism is the negation of Being, we cannot understand the *essence* of nihilism without reflecting in a critical and ontologically deep way on our discourse of metaphysics—on the history of this discourse. Since its beginnings in ancient Greece, metaphysics has been the field of discourse in which the most thoughtful among us have pondered the "Question of Being".[74] It is also the only discourse in which the *essence* of nihilism can be kept in critical focus, clearly distinguished from historical consequences, signs and symptoms.[75] Heidegger's lectures on nihilism warn us repeatedly not to confuse causes and effects. (Christendom itself, for example, could be a consequence of nihilism.) We must be constantly wary of this confusion surrounding the phenomenon of nihilism, because our attention, both here and in the other studies of this collection, will be drawn not only to the "essence" of nihilism as it appears in the texts of our metaphysics but also to the "actuality" of nihilism as it appears in the culture and economy of the world.

Keeping these fundamental points in mind, we shall now begin to concentrate our thinking on the story of the Self as it unravels within the history of metaphysics. Our goal is to demonstrate that the nihilism implicit in the history of metaphysics—implicit, that is, in the systematic occlusion and negation of the experience of Being that takes place within this discourse—is also at work in a violent and destructive way around the *being* of the human Self and in our way of understanding ourselves: who we are as human beings. We shall briefly lay out Heidegger's ontological analysis of the fate of the Self in a metaphysics completely determined by the logic of nihilism. But before we get entangled in that deep analysis, let us consider

Adorno's interpretation of the social and cultural actuality. Adorno is important at this point because he proposed a critical "sociological" diagnosis of how the spreading of nihilism *correlates* with the historical evidence of an increasingly devastating social and psychological pathology specifically affecting the very being of the modern Self. As he says, "He who wishes to know the truth about life in its immediacy must scrutinize its estranged form, the objective powers that determine individual existence even in its most hidden recesses."[76] The "subject" of metaphysical discourse appears in modern life as an individual Self who is subject to historically specific forms of disease, suffering, violence and madness, and whose fate is inextricably bound up with the destiny of a civilization that provides a culture for the nihilism consuming and destroying it: "Not only is the self entwined in society; it owes society its existence in the most literal sense. [Increasingly, today, all] its content comes from society, or at any rate its relation to the object. [But it] grows richer the more freely it develops and reflects this relation, while it is limited, impoverished and reduced by the separation and hardening that it lays claim to as an origin."[77] (Bracketed words added)

I said that, for Nietzsche, the actuality of nihilism is not only in destruction; it is also, and perhaps more primordially, in a movement of *self*-destruction: "the will to destruction as the will of a still deeper instinct, the instinct of self-destruction, the will for nothingness."[78] Adorno made an observation that resonates clearly with this insight: "If the individual whom death annihilates is himself [reduced to] nothing, bereft of self-command and of his own being [a sense of his own being], then the annihilating power [itself] becomes also nothing,"[79] at least insofar as we are so deadened and empty "within ourselves" that we can no longer feel or accurately perceive the true ontological self-destructiveness of this power—death, violence, nihilism.

For Adorno, nihilism is made manifest in the pervasive domination of "objectivity" and in the "dissolution of the subject."[80] This means above all a social isolation and estrangement that is profoundly destructive to our "inner life," our "inner experience," and our capacity to contribute both critical and creative energies to our society, even when the nihilism it feeds does not completely annihilate us as physical beings.

Because "inner experience," "inwardness," in brief, the Self, is extremely precious to Adorno, he took care to expose the nihilism in the self-destructive character of life surrounding the modern Self. His discourse on subjectivity lets us actualize our caring for the Self. This is what situates it within the tradition of humanism, because "humanism" is the history of practices in which the human Self is cared for. Critical theory is a guardian of this humanism, caring very deeply, in its praxis, for the flourishing of the Self. Consider, for example, Adorno's discussion of the "corruption" of "inwardness" and "genuineness" in a society slowly consumed by its nihilism.[81] Adorno sharply repudiated the recent celebration of "genuineness", calling it "a last bulwark of individualistic ethics" and "a reflection of industrial mass-production."[82] But the critique he spelled out clears the way for a different ethics and a different psychology. The question of authentic subjectivity is not at all abandoned. (As we shall see, the corruption of genuine inwardness, this historical form of not being true to oneself, can emerge in a complex syndrome of narcissistic personality disorders.)

Much of Adorno's focus is on individualism: different historical kinds and conceptions of individuality, different historical ways for the human being to be an individual:

> A connection is commonly drawn between the development of psychology [discourse concerning the *psyche,* the human Self] and the rise of the bourgeois individual, both in Antiquity and since the Renaissance. This ought not to obscure the contrary tendency also common to psychology and the bourgeois class, and which today has developed to the point of excluding all others: the suppression and dissolution of the very individual in whose service knowledge was related back to its subject. If all psychology since that of Protagoras has elevated man by conceiving him as the measure of all things, it has thereby also treated him from the first as an object, as material for analysis, and transferred to him, once he was included among them, the nullity of things.[83] (Bracketed words added)

Taking a position that echoes Heidegger's discussion of Protagoras in "The Age of the World Picture," Adorno argued that "The denial of objective truth by recourse to the subject implies the negation of the latter: no measure remains for the measure of all things; lapsing into contingency, he becomes untruth."[84] Nothing ensures that the human being will become and remain an object of social domination so much as the belief, encouraged by modern psychology, that we are, in essence, subjects and our experience is only inner or subjective.[85] This belief is nihilistic: it effectively denies our experience any claim to reality; and at the same time that it defeats the possibility of authentic subjectivity, it also takes away from us any objective basis for critically challenging the self-destructive conditions of an oppressive society.[86]

The laboring masses know of nihilism as they know a work-weary body and carry within themselves a heavy sense of despair, emptiness, and the violence of death. They know of nihilism as they know the deadness within them—and it makes them violent. But they also despair of transforming the institutions that maintain their oppression.[87]

The manual workers are not alone, however, in experiencing the actuality of nihilism. The class of their oppressors also suffers. Adorno argued that capitalism freed the individual, but created a society based on aggressive competition and destroyed the individual's sense of social interconnectedness.[88] Capitalism transformed the individual's emancipation into an "unbridled individualism" destructive to the self-development of the authentic individual.[89] The individual it promotes is a monster, a monadic ego without a soul. What are we, what is left of our humanity, when we are torn out of the social fabric and lose all sense of social responsibility? Nihilism is at work in this false understanding of the "individuality" of the individual.

Adorno saw very clearly the social pathology in the modern "individual." He saw in our false individualism, our extreme subjectification of the individual, the isolation and death that haunt the daily life of the modern Self.[90] His analysis suggests, I think, that we should question Nietzsche's assumption that nihilism is to be overcome through the will to power: the will to power, not as affirmation of life but rather as the narcissistic will to dominate and master. When the will to power is understood in this sense, the glorification of individualism gives support to nihilism. It also, as Adorno was astute enough to perceive, gives support to forces inimical to the humanization of the social order, without which the authentic Self cannot develop.[91]

Now that we have considered, with Adorno, the historical pathologizing of the modern Self, let us return to Heidegger and ponder the fate of subjectivity within the history of metaphysics. In "Recollection in Metaphysics," Heidegger asserted that

> . . . since Being claims human being for grounding its truth in beings, man is drawn into the history of Being, but always only with regard to the manner in which he takes his essence from the relation of Being to himself and, in accordance with this relation, loses his essence, neglects it, gives it up, grounds it, or squanders it.[92]

Always primary for Heidegger was the "Question of Being." Heidegger argued that it is time for our thinking to become "ontological" rather than merely "ontic." In other words, he insisted that we will not understand the nature of the pathology experienced by the modern Self unless we consider the question of its being: more specifically, its being in relation to Being as a whole, Being in its wholeness. Considered in this way, the essence of our modern psychopathology comes to light with painful clarity in the reflections on subjectivity which appear in the discourse of metaphysics dominating our culture. The essence—nihilism—conceals itself in a theory of the Self that not only cuts it off from the openness and wholeness of Being, but also obscures and in fact obstructs a deeply ontological understanding of the pathology generated in the historical reality this theory uncritically reflects. Because of its nihilism, negating the dimension of Being, the categories of metaphysics must deprive us of any deeply healing experience through the integration of our subjectivity into the wholeness of Being. The nihilism Heidegger located within the discursive history of metaphysics destroys our "recollection" of Being; thus it legitimates a "subjectifying" psychology that silences all ontological awareness and only deepens the suffering of the de-ontologized Self.

When Heidegger formulated his ontologically grounded critique of Western metaphysics, he emphasized that this metaphysics interprets *Dasein,* the human Self, as reducible to *ego-logical* subjectivity. In a word, we are to be conceived as beings of "will." Thus, in this second phase of argument, Heidegger disclosed a second way in which the distinctive pathologies of the modern Self are mirrored in our metaphysics and assumed to be "normal." Not only does our metaphysics cut us off from the possibility of a healing experience with Being in its wholeness, it also reduces the being of the Self to the being of a willful ego, an ego whose fulfillment is understood to consist—as Nietzsche repeatedly said—in domination and mastery. In the discourse we call "metaphysics," the Self is represented in a way that leaves it almost totally cut off from itself. This, of course, is precisely the work of nihilism.

While we must recognize that Heidegger's critical interpretation of nihilism in the history of metaphysics is quite indebted to the preparatory thinking of Nietzsche, we must also appreciate the profundity of Heidegger's disagreement with Nietzsche. Nietzsche saw clearly that in the epoch of nihilism our historically distinctive psychology "takes the form of self-destruction." We know that by this he understood "the will to destruction as the will of a still deeper instinct, the instinct of self-destruction, the will for nothingness."[93] But what he did not see and understand is the self-destructiveness that is inherent in the ego-logical will as such. Thus, when he forgot himself and identified the "will to power" with "active nihilism"—the will to master and dominate—rather than with an affirmation of life that is beyond both "active" and "passive" nihilism, he failed to realize that the psychological breeding ground for nihilism is to be found wherever the willful ego is installed in power. But this means that he failed to realize how the cure he prescribed for the affliction is like a poison, only feeding the culture in which nihilism is spreading and deepening our historical submission to psychopathology.

Heidegger wanted to argue, against Nietzsche, that

> When metaphysics thinks whatever is, in its being as the will to power, then it necessarily thinks it [nihilistically] as value-positing. It thinks everything within the sphere of values, of the authoritative force of value, of devaluing and revaluing. The metaphysics of the modern age begins with and has its essence in the fact that it seeks the unconditionally indubitable, the certain and the assured, certainty. It is a matter, according to the words of Descartes. . . . of bringing to a stand [i.e., into position before us] something that is firmly fixed and that remains. This standing, established as an object, is adequate to the essence, ruling from of old, of what is as the constantly presencing, which everywhere already underlies *(hypokeimenon, subiectum)*. Descartes also asks, as does Aristotle, concerning the *hypokeimenon*. [*Subiectum* is in fact a translation of this Greek term.] Inasmuch as Descartes seeks this *subiectum* along the path previously marked out by metaphysics, he, thinking truth as certainty, finds the *ego cogito* to be that which presences as fixed and constant. In this way, the *ego sum* is transformed into the *subiectum,* i.e., the subject becomes self-conscious. The subjectness of the subject is determined out of the sureness, the certainty, of that consciousness.[94] (Bracketed words added)

According to Heidegger, "There can be an object, in the sense of ob-ject, only where man becomes a subject, where the subject becomes the ego and the ego becomes the *ego cogito*. . . ."[95] In the standardized, mechanized world where "objectivity" rules, the Self will be increasingly subjected to the most extreme objectification, i.e., domination by the exigencies of an "objective" ordering of reality; the Self will also be subject to the most extreme subjectification—since, in the modern world, only the "objective" is real and the human being is reduced to the unreality of the ego. Expressing himself in words reminiscent of Adorno, Heidegger wrote:

> Certainly the modern age has, as a consequence of the liberation of man, introduced subjectivism and individualism. But it remains just

> as certain that no age before this one has produced a comparable objectivism and that in no age before this has the non-individual, in the form of the collective, come to acceptance as having worth. Essential here is the necessary interplay between subjectivism and objectivism. It is precisely this reciprocal conditioning of one by the other that points back to events more profound.[96]

Experiencing itself as a subject, the modern Self undergoes an essential change. This change brings with it, however, another, no less fateful: our understanding of, and our relation to, what is as a whole.[97] The modern epoch has been brought into being in part by a change that has taken place in our way of experiencing ourselves: as we become subjects, whatever in any way *is* must present itself as an object of representation, and the world as a whole is given the character of a picture.[98] Our historical subjectification—the process whereby we have become subjects—is at first our self-glorification: as subjects, we objectify the world and gain mastery over the whole of Being.[99]

According to Heidegger, the "fundamental event of the modern age"—the event decisive even for our own being—is "the conquest of the world as picture."[100] As the world becomes "picture," "representation," a "frontal ontology" takes over, reducing everything to the kind of being that can be positioned within "our" control.

The epoch of nihilism, then, is the epoch of the world picture *(Welt-Bild)*, the age of the narcissistic image, the mirror and the screen, in which man asserts himself as "representative" of "that which is"—that which is represented with the "character" of object: "That the world becomes picture is one and the same event with the event of man's becoming *subiectum* in the midst of that which is."[101] Subjectivity and objectivity are interdependent and coemergent: they arise simultaneously and in necessary correlation. That is why our extreme measure of objectivity can subject the subject to an extreme subjectification: a subjectivizing that it is required to accept, even though this utterly empties and destroys it.

But Heidegger believed that "Only where man is essentially *already* subject does there exist the possibility of his slipping into the abberation of subjectivism in the sense of individualism. But also, only where man *remains* subject does the positive struggle against individualism and for the community as the sphere of those goals that govern all achievement and usefulness have any meaning."[102] Heidegger believed, however, that our tradition of humanism, which he described as "the grounding event of modern history," cannot serve any longer as our guiding light. Humanism itself has contributed to the darkening of this epoch, since nihilism hides within its cultivation of subjectivity and objectivity. What is humanism? For Heidegger, *humanism* "designates that philosophical interpretation of man which explains and evaluates whatever is, in its entirety, from the standpoint of man and in relation to man".[103] Humanism proclaims man as "that particular being who gives the measure and draws up the guidelines for everything that is."[104] Humanism smiled as the world became an image and "man brought his life as *subiectum* into precedence over *other centers* of relationship. This means: whatever is, is considered to be in being only to the degree and to the extent that it is taken into and referred back to this life, i.e., is lived out [in accordance with the disposition of the subject]. . . ."[105] Although this interpretation of humanism impresses me as an accurate rendering of its present historical impact, I want to register my faith, here, in a deeper, more original understanding: one for which the essence of humanism must be a "caring for the Self" that would *resist* the destructiveness in the metaphysical reduction of our existential situation to a structure of subject and object. This is the spirit of humanism out of which Heidegger himself addressed us, writing, in *The Introduction to Metaphysics,* about the "spiritual decline of the earth."[106] Epidemic psychopathology makes its historical appearance in the context of this analysis. "What do we mean," he asked, "when we speak of a darkening of the world?" And he answered: "World is always world of the spirit. . . . Darkening of the world means emasculation of the spirit, the disintegration, wasting away, repression, and misinterpretation of the spirit."[107]

How does nihilism happen? In "The Age of the World Picture," Heidegger translated this question into a concern for the rise to power of the subjective ego within the history of Western metaphysics. And what he conjectured was that the conception of human being as *sub-iectum,* i.e., as an underlying source of reality, accompanied the claim of man to be a *fundamentum absolutum inconcussum veritatis:* an independent, self-supporting, unshakable foundation of truth.[108] It could perhaps be argued that this claim to ultimate authority—an authority that for centuries has been surrendered to God—expressed a virtually inevitable over-reaction, an exaggeration necessary for the establishment of the modern paradigm of scientific rationality and the awakening of self-consciousness in its distinctively modern sense. Nevertheless, I think we must concede Heidegger's point. Our evolution as free, rational, self-conscious agents has taken a decisively nihilistic turn: instead of enjoying an appropriate posture of self-affirmation, we have allowed ourselves to glorify "subjectivity" as a position of power; and we have succumbed to delusions of omnipotence, narcissistic fantasies, and an overwhelming need for greater certainty and greater security.[109]

For Heidegger, the nihilistic consequences that have appeared in the course of our historical self-affirmation make it imperative that, from our present standpoint, we reflect on the spirit of humanism and consider the possibility that our continued allegiance to the modern egological interpretation of "humanism" might actually betray its spirit, which is to care for the Self, the ongoing self-development of the human potential.[110]

An insatiable need for greater security and certainty is concealed within Cartesian subjectivity—separation from the world and complete self-absorption—just as it is concealed in the dogmatism of scientific objectivity. It is therefore important to remember, as Heidegger pointed out, that the ego's *cogitatio* derives from *co-agitatio:* "But the *co-agitatio* is already, in itself, *velle,* willing. In the subjectness of the subject, will comes to appearance as the essence of subjectness. Modern metaphysics, as the metaphysics of subjectness, thinks the Being of that which is in the sense of will."[111] Now, when Heidegger referred to "modern metaphysics," it was Nietzsche, most of all, whom he had in mind. Nietzsche unknowingly contributed to the spreading of nihilism because he inflated the willfulness in subjectivity to such an extent that he left no otherness, no exteriority. In order to possess certainty, the will to power, the will to master and dominate, devours everything; in order to gain security, the will to power hoards its objects. But these strategies "empty" the world of value and meaning. The emptiness which willfulness has created finally drives the subject to self-destruction.

I will briefly restate the steps of the argument up to this point, so that our new steps will be more comprehensible. According to Heidegger, our civilization has been built by a "drive" to master and extend the field of our domination. This drive, all too often identified and justified as a "need" constitutive of individualism, is reflected in the mirror of our metaphysics as an attempt to find the security of an absolutely certain, unquestionable kind of knowledge. The epistemological attempt eventually takes the form, in the metaphysical work of Descartes, of an ego-logical sub-ject, or *subiectum:* the being of the one who is thinking gets to be interpreted as having the kind of being we may characterize by speaking of an ultimate authoritative source, the *hypokeimenon*. The *hypokeimenon* is a thinking substance or subject: an *ego cogitans*. The *cogitatio,* however, is essentially a manifestation of the will: *coagitatio.* As such, it becomes an aggressive act of op-positional re-presentation, since that with which the *ego cogitans* concerns itself must become, for it, a permanently dominated ob-ject:

> That which is, is no longer that which presences; it is rather that which, in representing, is first set over against, that which stands fixedly over against, which has the character of object *[das Gegen-ständige]*. Representing is making-stand-over-against, an objectifying that goes forward and masters. In this way, representing drives everything together into the unity of that which is thus given the character of object. Representing is *coagitatio.*[112]

The *cogitatio* manifests its underlying nature as *coagitatio,* will in the sense of "commanding," because it is understood, from the very beginning, as a claim to knowledge possessing the sovereign authority of absolute and unconditional certainty:

> Every relation to something—willing, taking a point of view, being sensible of [something]—is already representing; it is *cogitans,* which we translate as "thinking." Therefore Descartes can cover all the modes of *voluntas* and of *affectus,* all *actiones* and *passiones,* with a designation that is at first surprising: *cogitatio*. In the *ego cogito sum,* the *cogitare* is understood in this essential and [historically] new sense. The *subiectum,* the fundamental certainty, is . . . the *me cogitare* = *me esse* that is at any time indubitably representable and represented.[113]

The concept of *subiectum* represents how we appeared to ourselves when, at the beginning of the modern epoch, we dared to think of ourselves as the only source and ultimate ground of certainty, and could thereby affirm ourselves, in opposition to God, as the ultimate authority.[114] In becoming a willful subject *(subiectum)* possessed of absolute certainty, the human being wills himself and elevates himself above all other beings, assuming the position of "master." (Our metaphysics mirrors the truth of our socially constructed reality, which is ruled over by the males and interpreted within their patriarchal culture.) From this dominant position, we have begun to act out our collective cultural phantasy of omnipotence as "lords of the earth": "As *subiectum,* man is the *co-agitatio* of the *ego.* Man founds and confirms himself as the authoritative measure for all standards of measure."[115]

As man "rises up into the subjectivity of his essence," however, the world changes into "object."[116] When Heidegger said that metaphysics "is an epoch in the history of Being itself" and added that "in its essence, metaphysics is nihilism,"[117] he was restating a point that we need to bear in mind when we consider the correlation between nihilism and our current psychopathology: "The history of Being begins, and indeed necessarily, with the forgetting of Being."[118] The "objectness" that is inseparable from and required by the domination of an ego-logical subject manifests precisely this ontological forgetfulness. Objectification takes place as we become more and more forgetful of Being in its depth and wholeness. Thus we create for ourselves an existential situation in which the ontological dimensions of our modern psychopathology are constituted. Heidegger observed that

> The fact that metaphysics is transformed into the psychology [of a willful subject determined to enjoy an absolutely unchallengeable knowledge] . . . testifies . . . to the essential event, which consists in a change in the beingness of what is. The *ousia* (beingness) of the *subiectum* changes into the subjectness of self-assertive self-consciousness, which now manifests its essence as the will to will.[119] (Bracketed words added)

As the Being of beings is "forgotten," we seek to transform everything, both people and things, into mere "objects" of use, "objects" at our disposal. We are driven to create a world of "fixed and constant" presences, a world of permanence and predictability.[120] Gradually, this driving need determines a lasting change in our character as human beings.[121] Our "forgetfulness" closes off—splits us off from—the dimensionality of our own being.

Since subject and object are interdependently co-emergent, the narcissistic subjectivizing that stimulated the will to power was necessarily accompanied by an increasing objectification. Objectification ensures greater certainty and is inherent in all forms of mastery and domination.[122] But the rule of this objectivity is also destructive to the life of the spirit. Heidegger's critical review of the historical unfolding of metaphysics demonstrates that only one of the many "essential possibilities" for the presencing of Being as our historical reality got to be actualized in our historical life.[123] For the modern world, the dimensionality of beings, i.e., the presencing of Being in its wholeness, is reduced to a reality experienced and understood entirely within the structure of subject and object, a reality completely determined in relation to the calculative willfulness of the individual ego.[124]

Who are we? Who is "Man"? Are we nothing but ego-logical centers of willing? Are we biologically programmed to be masters in domination?[125] When the nature of human being is finally experienced, interpreted, and historically actualized as an ego-logical subject, the will to power holds sway over Being as a whole. This, however, is nihilism: "The desolation of the earth begins as a process which is willed, but not known in its being, and also not knowable at the time when the being of truth defines itself as the certainty in which human representational thinking and producing first become sure of themselves."[126]

It is within the hermeneutical discourse of humanism that we need to give renewed critical thought to the ancient question, "Who are we?," which implicitly involves taking a stand with regard to our optimal capabilities for being, i.e., our health and well-being, and that we begin to question, from out of our present suffering and pathology, the metaphysics that has enthralled us. Such self-questioning is preparatory for an exertion of thought that Heidegger called the "recollection of Being":

> Recollection of the history of Being in metaphysics is a bestowal which explicitly and uniquely gives the relation of Being and man to awareness for our pondering. . . . Recollection of the history of Being entrusts historical humanity with the task of becoming aware that *the essence of man is released to the truth of Being* before any human dependency on powers and forces, predestination and tasks.[127]

Since our humanity, our very being, is now at stake in the growing desolation of nihilism, there can be for Heidegger only one physic, one healing remedy, one small but not insignificant hope: ". . . to glimpse the history of Being, even if this succeeds only in the form of an essential need which soundlessly and without consequences shakes everything true and real to the roots."[128] Living as we do in the very midst of nihilism on a planet where the oblivion of Being draws us into the deepest forgetfulness, our only hope must lie in the "recollection" of Being. For Heidegger, this recollection *must* be at the very heart of all efforts to "care" for the individual Self. All our psychopathologies must accordingly be understood as pathologies of the Self, and more specifically, pathologies of the "will to power," in relation to the wholeness of Being. Inasmuch as these pathologies come into being "because of" the Self's self-destructive confinement within the metaphysical structure of subject and object, the task of healing calls upon medicine and psychiatry to help us open up our historical life within that structure to the matrix of Being as a whole.

As Herbert Guenther has observed in *The Tantric View of Life,* ". . . in the difference that is set up between subject and object, all the torment that usually accompanies the rift in Being asserts itself."[129] There are many texts in which Heidegger, like Guenther, connected the suffering of our age with the dominance of subject and object, although his words are commonly read in a way that catches only their metaphysical significance and fails to recognize their potential importance for medicine and psychiatry. He observed, for example, that "Objectification blocks us off against the open. The more venturesome daring does not produce a defense."[130] (Two questions: To what extent is the structure of subject and object a defense generated by anxiety? In what way could Heidegger's words shed light on the character of allopathic medicine?) To see the point of his observation, consider our field of vision. The dimensionality of this field is intrinsically open. But our vision is normally not rooted, not grounded, in that openness of Being; typically, it is disconnected, dissociated, estranged. And when it is not properly grounded in this matrix of openness, we begin to suffer. Many diseases and psychopathologies may result. Thus we might keep in mind the mythopoetic wisdom attributed to Xenophanes:

> It is the whole that sees, the whole that thinks, the whole that hears.[131]

Was Xenophanes speaking only with the words of myth? His words communicated a wisdom that could be profoundly healing. Perhaps Merleau-Ponty sensed something of this ancient, but virtually abandoned metaphysical wisdom, for he wrote, in his *Phenomenology of Perception:* "We must rediscover, as anterior to the ideas of subject and object, the fact of my subjectivity and the nascent object, that primordial layer at which both things and ideas come into being."[132] Merleau-Ponty was attempting here to retrieve the unified and unifying matrix of Being: an open expanse for living within which, and from out of which, the ego-logical subject and its simultaneously co-emergent object arise.[133] If this retrieval is, as I believe, an essential contribution to the recollection of Being, then it is also a signpost on the way to health and well-being. All the more reason to ask ourselves, with Heidegger: "Why is it that we stubbornly resist considering even once whether the belonging-together of subject and object does not arise from something that first imparts their nature to both, the object and its objectivity, and the subject and its subjectivity, and hence is prior to the realm of their reciprocity?"[134] But we might also reflect on the pervasiveness of self-destructive attitudes and comportments; we must bear in mind that the culture of nihilism is simultaneously an "effect" of the ego-logical subject's estrangement from Being as a whole and also a "cause" of its continuation in this afflicted state. Because there is an ontological dimension to the metaphysical structures of subject/object and mind/body, the healing of disease and psychopathology must embrace the life of the Self as it opens its work to the recollection of Being.

Technology and Its Political Economy: The Rise to Power of the Modern Self

The modern Self lives in a political economy that has been shaped by and for the "progressive" expansion of industry and technology. At present, this technology is so pervasive and powerful that we cannot begin to interpret either the advent of nihilism or the historical forms of psychopathology afflicting us without understanding (1) that our technology is implicitly and inherently nihilistic; (2) that our technological economy, which now increasingly appears to generate at least as much suffering, harm and danger as it does riches, manifests a nihilism made possible by, and increasingly requiring, the will to power (willfulness as the patriarchal will to master, dominate and control) constitutive of an *ego-logical* form of subjectivity; (3) that the nihilism at work in our technology is in part a historical manifestation of the nihilism inherent in the ego-logical character of the modern Self; (4) that the self-destructiveness in our technological economy constitutes an essential and perhaps fateful culture for the current appearance of certain epidemic or historically distinctive patterns of psychopathology—of pain, disease, suffering, and morbidity; and (5) that, in accordance with the essence of nihilism, both the destructiveness in technology and the self-destructive pathologies characteristic of the Self prevailing today need to be interpreted in relation to the "Question of Being" in the history of metaphysics, since it is in the history of this discourse that we will see most clearly the virtually imperceptible withdrawal and oblivion of Being as a whole, Being in its wholeness.

We shall begin our interpretation with some acute observations from the notebook of Max Horkheimer. Sometime between 1966 and 1969, he wrote:

> *The Subject in Industrial Society:* In industrial society, indeed, with the beginning of modern science, the meaning of the dialectic of the subject changes. The more thinking seeks to grasp nature, the more it has to trace, reflect on, its workings. . . . The unfolding of subjects in a variety

> of directions, the autonomy of many individuals, their competition from which autonomy derived its justification, *was* beneficial to society in unharnassing science and technology. With the victory of technology, indeed with its progress, with men's control over nature, with their independence, their autonomy, autonomy regresses, negates itself. What is under way in the bourgeois era will be completed in the automatized world. As the subject is being realized, it vanishes.[135]

As the *being* of "the subject," i.e., the authentically individual Self, is reduced ontologically until its self-development is harnessed to the modes of productivity required by our technology, we see the unfolding of a history in which its comportment becomes increasingly violent and self-destructive. According to Horkheimer, the future of humanity, of civilization as we know it, now hangs in the balance.

> Today, Critical Theory must deal at least as much with what is justifiably called progress, i.e., technical progress, and with its effect on man and society. Critical Theory denounces the dissolution of spirit and soul, the victory of rationality, without simply negating it. It recognizes that injustice is identical with barbarism, but that justice is inseparable from that technological process which causes mankind's development into a sophisticated animal species that degrades spirit to the level it had attained in its childhood. Imagination, longing, love, artistic expression are becoming moments of infantilism. Not only the natural sciences but even psychoanalysis already testify to this today.[136]

Technology, a "production" of the will to power, seems more and more to be turning *against* this will and rendering it useless or impotent. (Here we may see the narcissistic disorder, cultural and individual, which functions, in its concealment, within the nihilism of technology.)

Horkheimer further connected the technological transformation of our society with a political economy increasingly drawn into the totalitarian organization of repressive institutions, which dominate and "normalize" the individual and in the end could nearly destroy our inner sense of (personal, social, and symbolic) reality by imposing its own stamp of meaning on our individual experience: "The destruction of inner life is the penalty man has to pay for having no respect for any life other than his own. The violence that is directed outward, and called technology, he is compelled to inflict on his own psyche."[137]

For Horkheimer, as for Heidegger, the pathology that can be correlated with the nihilistic tendencies inherent in our technological economy is not at all just "psychological"; nor is it to be understood by considering, in addition, our deeper "spiritual" condition. For both of them, the pathology is multi-dimensional and is manifest in diseases and afflictions of our historical embodiment: not only, we may surmise, in pathologies of the body as a material substrate or physical organism (e.g., cancers; cardiovascular diseases; diseases of the will, such as anorexia and bulimia; and a variety of neurological, metabolic, gastrointestinal, and nutritional diseases), but also in pathologies of the body as a "subjective" center of perceptual experience. Thus, in "The Turning," Heidegger asserted that "we do not yet hear, we whose hearing and seeing are perishing through radio and film under the rule of technology."[138] And Horkheimer likewise argued that "As their telescopes and microscopes, their tapes and radios become more sensitive, individuals become blinder, more hard of hearing, less responsive, and society more opaque, hopeless, its misdeeds . . . larger, more superhuman than ever before."[139]

For Heidegger, the nihilism in technology is mirrored in the history of metaphysics. There, perhaps, we can see with greater clarity how Being in its wholeness is increasingly abandoned to the reality of the ego, the will to power.[140] Thus, in his "Sketches for a History of Being as Metaphysics," he argued that "The completion of metaphysics sets beings in the abandonment of Being."[141] "The Overcoming of Metaphysics" sheds further light on this interpretation. Heidegger set out to show that "It is first the will which arranges itself everywhere in technology that devours the earth in the exhaustion and consumption and change of what is artificial."[142] With the reduction of Being as such and the consequent reduction of the human being to an ego-logical subject within metaphysics, history removes the last obscurities concealing the rise to power of a violent technological will. Metaphysics insists on confining "the subject" to a discursive and structural field that necessitates its opposition and antagonism to the "object" of its will. As metaphysics deepens its denial of Being and the "mortal" of antiquity is compressed into a being of will—a will, in the end, for self-destruction—the nihilism inherent in technology, perhaps the extinction of all life on this planet, emerges from its concealment. And we should not be surprised that this historical evolution has precipitated specific pathologies of the Self.

Heidegger's essay on "The Overcoming of Metaphysics" defines the matter for thought in the following general way:

> The will to will forces the calculation and arrangement of everything

> for itself as the basic forms of appearance, only, however, for the unconditionally protractible guarantee of itself.
>
> The basic form of appearance, in which the will to will arranges and calculates itself in the unhistorical element of the world of completed metaphysics, can be stringently called "technology." This name includes all the areas of being which equip the whole of beings: objectified nature, the business of culture, manufactured politics, and the gloss of ideals overlying everything. Thus, "technology" does not signify here the separate areas of the production and equipment of machines. The latter of course have a position of power, to be more closely defined, which is grounded in the precedence of matter as the supposedly elemental and primarily objective factor.
>
> The name "technology" is understood here in such an essential way that its meaning coincides with the term "completed metaphysics." It contains the recollection of *technē,* which is a fundamental condition of the essential development of metaphysics in general. At the same time, the name makes it possible for the planetary factor of the completion of metaphysics and its dominance to be thought without reference to historiographically demonstrable changes in nations and continents.[143]

For Heidegger, the nihilism that prevails in our modern technological economy could ultimately enslave us, even if it does not literally destroy our bodies. Thus, the kind of thinking that attempts to recollect Being in its wholeness contributes to our hopeful bearing and well-being. More specifically, though, it calls into question the prevalent dehumanizing interpretation of our humanity, our essential being:

> The essence of the history of Being of nihilism is the abandonment of Being, in that in it there occurs the self-release of Being into machination. This release takes man into unconditional service. . . .
>
> Hence not just any kind of humanity is suited to bring about unconditional nihilism in a historical manner. Hence a struggle is even necessary about the decision as to which kind of humanity is capable of the unconditional completion of nihilism.[144]

As Heidegger shifted his gaze from the discourse of metaphysics, he saw many signs of nihilism, the "ultimate abandonment of Being," in the world remade by technology.[145] In "Overcoming Metaphysics," the essay from which we have been quoting, the analysis moves very quickly from an interpretation of nihilism in the history of Being to an interpretation of nihilism in our planetary economy of escalating armament. This may at first seem far removed from the question that most immediately concerns us: how technology conceals within it a nihilism that was already at work in the metaphysics of subjectivity. But this text introduces problems that are important to the discourse around psychopathology, and not only to the critical discourse that interprets our planetary politics: traumas of separation and abandonment, ontological insecurity, paranoia, mechanisms of defense, passively received identity, delusions of omnipotence, and an insatiable need to master and control.

Taking a position close to Heidegger's, Adorno insisted that we will not understand the psychopathologies to which the modern Self is subjected in the nihilistic age of technology unless we recognize the truth of our enslavement in a cycle of productivity and consumption: our fate in an economy that requires passivity, docile bodies, productive efficiency and pervasive standardization. The will to power begins with an aggressive productivity and ends in a narcissistic absorption, consumed in its consuming, driven by an obsessive compulsion to fill the inner emptiness and purchase some peace: "The change in the relations of production depends largely on what takes place in the 'sphere of consumption,' the mere reflection of production and the caricature of true life: in the consciousness and unconsciousness of individuals."[146] Thus, "Even what *differs* from technology in man is now being incorporated into it as a kind of lubrication. Psychological differentiation, originally the outcome both of the division of labour that dissects man according to sectors of the production process and of freedom, is finally itself entering the service of production."[147] In particular, the economic ordering of daily life and the political control which technology imposes on us gradually invade the boundaries that were protecting our "inwardness," our inborn sense of reality. But this imposed ordering is the beginning of our "inner" death, the annihilation of the Self. The human being must, in Adorno's words,

> pay for his increasing inner organization with increasing disintegration. The consummation of the division of labour within the individual, his radical objectification, leads to his morbid scission. Hence the "psychotic character," the anthropological pre-condition of all totalitarian mass-movements. Precisely this transition from firm characteristics to push-button behaviour-patterns—though apparently enlivening—is an expression of the rising organic composition of man. Quick reactions, unballasted by a mediating constitution, do not restore spontaneity, but establish the person as a measuring instrument deployed and calibrated by a central authority.[148]

(Concerning an interpretive specification of "the rising organic composition of man" in relation to the epidemiology of cancer and to the pathogenic etiology of depressions, see the contribution to this anthology by Roger Levin.) What Adorno interpreted within the discourse of critical theory, Heidegger interpreted within the hermeneutical discourse of ontological recollection, which turns our attention to the historical beginning of an "elemental strife" between Being and Nothingness, the epoch when Being goes into its self-concealment in the raging madness of nihilism: "[The human being] remains left out of his essence for a long time, as one let into the insurrection of production within Being's realm. . . . Being lets powers arise, but also lets them sink into what is without essence, together with their impotence."[149] (We should note Heidegger's reference to "impotence," for this is a pathology that specifically afflicts the will to power. Note also that this "impotence" is a symptom that emerges in a time when technology has apparently "given" the will to power a reach and range of unprecedented mastery and control. We are living in a time when profound crises in the will to power are reverberating throughout our technological economy: crises, for example, in our will to productivity, in the regulation and control of our will to economic growth, the technological control of our world, and in many other manifestations of this will to power.)

Being, then, is reduced to a reality that, "as will to power, has made man into an instrument of making (production, effecting)."[150] In this way the will to power produces a technological economy that increasingly turns against it and reduces it to a mere instrument serving the uncontrollable logic of technology: "The Open [i.e., the presence of Being in a wholeness which embraces the unity and harmony of subject and object] becomes an object, and is thus twisted around toward the human being. *Over against* the world as the object, man stations himself and sets himself up as the one who deliberately pushes through all this producing."[151] (Bracketed words added) As producing and securing increasingly determine all relationships within the subject-object structure, they harness the will to power for the sake of a technology no longer under the control of the will to power that brought it forth. Technology becomes an economy of uncontrollable growth; it requires the destruction of this will at the very moment when the ego's dream of omnipotence would seem to be within reach of realization: "The will produces itself in the exclusiveness of its egotism as the will to power. But in the essence of power there is hidden the utmost abandonment of Being to beingness [i.e., to the being of subjects and objects]. Through this abandonment, beingness becomes mechanization. . . ."[152] (Bracketed words added) As Nietzsche virtually prophesized, the political economy within which technology prevails unchallenged will become a society that must transform its individuals into productive machines: "absolute obedience, machine-like activity."[153] Can there be a correlation between this historical abandonment of Being and the epidemiology of depressions in the modern world?

Nietzsche repeatedly failed to differentiate the will to power as affirmation of life from the will to power as drive to master and dominate for the sake of ontological security and egological aggrandizement; despite this, he also experienced a profound reverence for nature and could eloquently speak in *The Genealogy of Morals* of what he called, invoking the mythic and archetypal standards of antiquity, our *hybris:* "Our whole attitude toward nature, our violation of nature with the help of machines and the heedless ingenuity of technicians and engineers, is *hybris* . . ."[154]

Heidegger's caring for the earth was more consistent and his ontological understanding of the historical significance of the technological appropriation of the earth was deeper, more radical, and more subversive. First of all, Heidegger recognized the connection between the "spiritual decline of the earth" and its "economic exploitation."[155] But he also understood how we must correlate this with an interpretation of the historical fate of subjectivity, finally consumed by a nihilistic will to power: "The world changes into object. . . . The earth itself can show itself only as the object of assault, an assault that, in human willing, establishes itself as unconditional objectification. Nature appears everywhere . . . as the object of technology."[156] Heidegger saw the unambiguous signs of nihilism: he saw in our relationship to nature the intensity of our ontological insecurity, our anxieties, our aggressiveness, rage, and violence. He connected this distinctive pathology in our civilization to the "oblivion of Being" that has taken place in the historical discourse on metaphysics. A focus for this connection appears in his observations concerning our self-inflicted dehumanization as productive machines and laboring animals: "The decline occurs through the collapse of the world characterized by metaphysics, and at the same time through the desolation of the earth stemming from metaphysics. Collapse and desolation find their adequate occurrence in the fact that metaphysical man, the *animal rationale,* gets fixed as the laboring animal."[157]

Are we essentially "rational animals"? Is this how we should understand ourselves? And in any case what is, or ought to be, our "rationality"? What is, or ought to be, our "animality"? As "rational animals," we have imposed upon ourselves a technological rationalization that harnesses our animal nature to mechanical and ultimately self-destructive productivity: ". . . man, as *animal rationale*, here meant in the sense of the working being, must wander through the desert of the earth's desolation. . . ."[158] For Heidegger, "The still hidden truth of Being is withheld from metaphysical humanity. The laboring animal is left to the giddy whirl of its products so that it may tear itself to pieces and annihilate itself in empty nothingness."[159] Such was Heidegger's apocalyptic vision of the future—the historical truth—of our civilization.

What is the truth in which, and for which, we live? Who are we? When Heidegger took up these questions, he answered without hesitation: "certainty is the modern form of truth."[160] Thus he argued that this need for certainty, constancy and permanence, a need first reflected in the history of metaphysics in the methodic self-examination practiced by Descartes, is what most luminously displays the truth of our time: the truth that discloses the pathogenic character of the modern Self.[161]

Western metaphysics sought to inscribe within its discursive field of power the presence of an absolute being that would endure and would continue to satisfy our need for security and our attachment to something of permanence; similarly, our advanced technology, also under the rule of the ego, has set in motion a political economy that can virtually command the disposition of all worldly beings according to a totally inclusive plan.[162]

Perhaps it would be useful at this point to consider the wisdom in Buddhist psychology. It is ancient, but amazingly relevant. In particular I would like to consider the Tibetan tradition of scholarship and thought, which presently offers to the Western world a precious transmission of teachings concerned with (1) the analysis of ego process; (2) the diagnosis of its corporeal, emotional, social and spiritual pathologies; and (3) an interpretation of ego process in relation to its cultural and symbolical world.[163] Despite their great antiquity and their consequent historical and cultural distance, these teachings immediately clarify the existing understanding of our present situation; they seem able to comprehend within their deeply compassionate universality—and in that sense perhaps even to anticipate—the technological nihilism that afflicts our epoch.

The Buddhist analysis of our ego-logical life supplements Nietzsche's critique of the ego in metaphysics; it penetrates and unmasks the nihilistic work of the ego in the historical evolution of a technological economy. It helps us see that our technology is a potentiation of the same will to power prevalent in the tyrannical rule of the masculine ego in our psychological life, and that the destructiveness in our technology displays a pattern similar to and inseparable from the pattern of destructiveness set in motion by the "normal" ego.

Buddhist psychology has always been both rigorously phenomenological (as in the *Abhidharma* texts) and ferociously diagnostic, critical and deconstructive (as in Nagarjuna's *Mulamadhyamikakarika,* and in the texts which followed.)

Here, for example, is Tarthang Tulku's mirroring of what he called the "tyranny of the I":

> When the notion arises: "I am having this experience, this experience is mine: I see this object, this object relates to me," the "I" is taking possession of our bodies and our experience. It is reaching out to extend its dominion in all directions.
>
> Once ownership is established, the "ego/I/self" structure alters our perception of ourselves and our world to suit its own requirements for security. Like water bending beams of light, it shapes our concepts, views, and attitudes to protect itself against exposure and loss. The "I" requires stability and security, and fills us with fear when we are faced with reminders of *impermanence.*
>
> In direct contradiction to our own knowledge of impermanence, we consider everything touching on the "I"—our thoughts, feelings, emotions, bodies—as *solid, real, and enduring.* Change and impermanence become enemies to be fought, denied, or avoided. We become *divided against ourselves,* torn between our inner awareness and the everyday "reality" we create.
>
> Once we establish ourselves as a subject and take possession of our experience—exerting our will to control its outcome to our satisfaction—we set ourselves up for suffering. We make a contract with ourselves, committing ourselves to ignore the implications of impermanence in our lives. Since it is based on an illusion, this contract is inherently untenable; it can be sustained only through continual reinforcement and reassurances, and protected at the expense of our vital energy.[164]

It is inherent in the character of the ego that it constantly "craves attention, approval, reassurance, possessions, and power."[165] The ego cannot bear ambiguity, confusion, relativity and uncertainty; it needs to be in absolute control. Because it is, however, an inherently insecure way of being-in-the-world, the ego is extremely greedy and possessive; and yet, although it imposes its will on things, it somehow never escapes feeling "precarious" and "vulnerable."[166]

In the final analysis, we need to see the self-destructiveness that surrounds, invades, and eventually consumes the ego-logical Self:

> Fed by power and control, the "I" [ego] cares nothing for our inner well-being. It cuts us off from our real feelings and makes it impossible

> for us to see clearly what is beneficial for growth. . . . [Thus unrestrained,] the "I" tends to dominate an ever-widening territory. . . .
>
> Through the veil of self-centered concerns, we equate domination, dependency, and control with real caring and responsibility, and blind ourselves to the conflicts we are creating. . . .
>
> The ego's demand for domination conditions us to an attitude of ownership. . . . Much as the "I" takes possession of our bodies, thoughts, feelings, and emotions, it extends dominion to our possessions; it leads us to think of what we own as an extension of ourselves. . . .
>
> Extending its dominion to all forms of life, the "I" leads us to think [in the end] that the beings who share this planet with us are subject to our use and control.[167]

What limits of destructiveness will we not transgress for the sake of this use and control? Our delusions of omnipotence, a pathology of the will to power, are totalitarian and self-destructive. Then, indeed, we become the "subject": the beings who are subject to the terror of a total objectivity, and we conceal this hopeless dependency within a delusion of omnipotence that makes us believe we have the capacity to survive continued indifference to the industrial poisoning of our environment.

Our technology is poisoning the environment, yet we depend on this Nature to survive in good health. In this sense, our technology has become intensely destructive. It is necessary to understand that there is a deeper truth, here. Our technological economy is becoming increasingly self-destructive; we seem bent on destroying our world, and even ourselves. We need to recognize that our technological economy is *our own work*. And now this work of ours is destroying us. After years of greedy plundering, years of reckless industrialization and profitable commerce, years of attacking Nature and attempting to dominate it, we may have finally created an environment so highly toxic that our very bodily nature must submit to this brutal attack. We have brought forth a technology that is dangerously carcinogenic.

In the carcinogenic nature of our technological environment, we can begin to see that, because of the deep interconnectedness of all things, there must be a hidden connection between pathologies of the will and pathologies afflicting our embodiment. As Susan Sontag has noticed in her provocative but enormously confused discourse on *Illness as Metaphor,* there are certain diseases—epilepsy, in the Middle Ages, consumption in the nineteenth century, and cancer today—that become historical "tropes for new attitudes toward the self."[168] Thus, before we proceed to our clinical analysis of the pathologies affecting the modern Self, I will briefly delineate the cultural and historical significance of cancer in relation to (1) the modern Self and its pathologies and (2) the pathology of the will that has finally become manifest in the destructiveness of technology. I shall argue, against Sontag's attempt to deny disease all cultural and spiritual significance, that cancer is a particularly appropriate symbol for the nihilism of our time. I do not propose that we should come to the defense of superstition; nor do I wish to encourage metaphorical thinking at the expense of science. But I am extremely troubled by Sontag's attempt to discredit all efforts to interpret cancer as a phenomenon occurring within a specific world. Sontag's unwillingness to reflect on its social world, its political economy, and its cultural history seems to me misguided. Her position is a symptom of and an unwitting contribution to the growing nihilism in our epoch, since it reduces cancer to just one more totally meaningless event. Cancer is significant as an historical pattern of disease, because it correlates with a specifically modern pathology of the Self, viz., the rule of its technological economy.[169]

I suggest that there must be a significant historical correlation between certain epidemic pathologies of embodiment—such as cancer and arteriosclerosis—and certain prevalent pathologies of the modern Self, and that a decisive factor in our understanding of this correlation is our advanced technology. The principal elements in my interpretation are: (1) Certain diseases—cancer, for example—seem to be potentiated, if not in some sense caused, by an environmental toxicity directly produced by our technology. (2) This technology is a "product" of ego-logical activity—the will to power as the will to master and dominate, as aggression, appropriation, violence. (3) But the principal pathologies of the modern Self all seem to appear as pathologies of the will: as a *subjectification* that reduces the modern Self to an ego, and correspondingly, as a pervasive drive toward complete *objectification,* which denies this ego any value. (4) Thus there are pathologies of embodiment that refer us to a technology of objects produced by the very ego whose way of being is a pathology of the self-destructive will afflicting the life of the Self. (5) The Self, identifying itself with the egological will to power, has created a technology that is turning against it, destroying both the embodiment and the spirituality in the keeping of which it lives. (6) Epidemic diseases are not just, as Sontag seems to think, "common [rhetorical] figures" for social disorder.[170] In the case of certain cancers, the evidence appears to indict our technology. But it is this very same technology that has brought forth a political economy within which the modern Self experiences its self-destruction: anomie, depersonalization, homelessness, isolation, and uselessness—conditions of mind that may themselves, in fact, contribute to the pathogenesis.

Sontag has chronicled and criticized the use of cancer as a metaphor for the distinctive ills of the modern era. This, however, has only strengthened my conviction that there is a deep (perhaps deeply concealed) truth in the metaphorical discourse: a truth too deep for Sontag's rhetorical analysis to recognize. Cancer, she noted, is now thought to be a "pathology of energy," a "disease of the will."[171] At the very least, it is a disease of the *will* insofar as it can be traced back to the "pollution" of our technology. For the unhealthy stress from this pollution is a consequence of our industrial will to power, and this will to power is a will to dominate, control, and consume—in other words, an imbalanced and "diseased" will.

In this context, Sontag's analysis of the language commonly used to describe cancer takes on considerable force. There is no doubt that the common rhetoric evokes a specific "economic catastrophe": "that of unregulated, abnormal, incoherent growth. . . . Cancer cells, according to the textbook account, are cells that have shed the mechanism which "restrains" growth. . . . Cells without inhibitions, cancer cells will continue to grow and extend over each other in a "chaotic" fashion, destroying the body's normal cells, architecture, and functions."[172] Thus, as she acknowledged, the homology between cancer and our technologically directed political economy is much too striking to ignore:

> Early capitalism assumes the necessity of regulated spending, saving, accounting, discipline—*an economy that depends on the rational limitation of desire*. Tuberculosis is described in images that sum up the negative behavior of nineteenth-century *homo economicus:* consumption; wasting; squandering of vitality. Advanced capitalism requires expansion, speculatio, the creation of new needs (the problem of satisfaction and dissatisfaction); buying on credit; mobility—*an economy that depends on the irrational indulgence of desire*. Cancer is described in images that sum up the negative behavior of twentieth-century *homo economicus:* abnormal growth, repression of energy, that is, refusal to consume or spend.[173]

But was Sontag justified in maintaining that the homology is—or must continue to be—nothing more than a metaphor, a rhetorical trope? The description of cancer is very much like the description of our technological economy in at least one essential factor: they both call attention to a "pathology of the will to power," a pathology profoundly self-destructive. We have good reason to believe that the uncontrollable growth of cells characteristic of cancer is causally related to the uncontrollable growth of our technology in ways we do not yet understand and cannot yet experimentally explore, and that the industrial pollution of our environment, with the various physical and psychological stresses that follow, takes the homology out of the realm of fiction. We know now that the uncontrollable growth of our technology has generated great psychological stress, and that such stress can seriously weaken the body's immunological defenses. We also know that the poisoning of our air, ground water, and food supplies could put more stress on these defenses than they would be able to cope with.

Note also the words that both physicians and patients commonly use to describe the cancer and their ways of responding to it. As Sontag has pointed out,

> With the patient's body considered to be under attack ("invasion"), the only treatment is counterattack.
>
> The controlling metaphors in descriptions of cancer are, in fact, drawn not from economics but from the language of warfare: every physician and every attentive patient is familiar with, if perhaps inured to, this military terminology. Thus, cancer cells do not simply multiply; they are "invasive." ("Malignant tumors invade even when they grow very slowly," as one textbook puts it.) Cancer cells "colonize" from the original tumor to far sites in the body, first setting up tiny outposts ("micrometastases") whose presence is assumed, though they cannot be detected. Rarely are the body's "defenses" vigorous enough to obliterate a tumor that has established its own blood supply and consists of billions of destructive cells . . .[174]

Here too, the language points to characteristics of the modern will to power: characteristics we might want to correlate with the aggressiveness and violence of the kind of Self who succeeds in and dominates our technological economy: invasions and attacks, struggles, defenses, counterattacks, resistance, victory, defeat, destruction, survival.

Our way of seeing cancer is already itself nihilistic: a struggle of wills, a contest of power, a nearness to rage and violence. Similarly, allopathic medicine, our way of responding to its "wrathful" and "terrifying" presence and to the needs of those who are thus afflicted, displays a technological, metaphysically dualistic framework of interpretation. Our thinking is confined to a framework of mind-body dualism, in which the cancer is a terrifying "otherness," an enemy, an alien object to be aggressively treated and if possible utterly destroyed. We tolerate a framework that turns the still living, hopeful patient into a passive, docile, objective body. We subject the patient to aggressive surgical invasions of the body, combined with depersonalizing, dehumanizing regimes of medical and psychiatric "care." We operate within a framework that sees the cancer as nothing but a temporary challenge to the power of medical technology. We think in a framework that is itself profoundly self-destructive, since its "requirement of objectivity" denies us, precisely when we need it most, any possibility of understanding—any possibility, in fact, that we might experience something of significance in what is happening with us.

In a recent book, *The Body and Society,* a sociologist in the tradition of Max Weber and the Frankfurt School has argued persuasively that our technological "rationalization" of the body must be understood as "the final triumph of capitalist development."[175] But if this makes sense, perhaps we should consider the possibility that, just as schizophrenia may express the child's only viable way of coping with an intolerably pathogenic family, so may the course of cancer, if not also its onset, express the body's resistance to this technical "rationalization." In any case, there are grounds for speculating that cancer is a site where the destructive *effects* of this "rationalization" on the material environment of our corporeal existence are "fought out at the level of a micro-politics of deviance and disease. Because the body is the most potent metaphor of society, it is not surprising that disease is the most salient metaphor of structural crisis. All disease is disorder—metaphorically, literally, socially and politically."[176] The body has become an object of technical knowledge. But, since knowledge is power and power is knowledge, the body has inevitably become the site of struggles for power. We may perceive cancer in terms of endogenous struggles within the body; but we also need to see the conflicts that exist between the body and society, the body and its natural environment. The body today is extensively "medicalized," monitored, measured, regulated, increasingly controlled by our will to power, our will to enjoy a medically defined health. Considered more generally, this body is socially produced—and so, in a corresponding sense, are its pathologies: not only in that the body can be poisoned by an environment that society produces and persists in maintaining despite the weight of evidence, but also in that the perception of pathology is always a question of interpretation, and such interpretation is always dependent on submerged social, political, cultural and spiritual commitments. The classifications and diagnoses of clinical medicine are *not* scientific statements of fact referring to "real" disease entities; rather, they are theory-laden *representations* that interpret what is perceived within the space that constitutes our modern rupture with an ancient tradition of sacred and secular knowledges, practices, and institutions. In sum, they are the historical effects of power on knowledge: products of culture, symbols of our time, constructs of the "rational" discourse we call "medicine."

In this light, perhaps we can begin to understand the ideologically hidden connection between the presence of cancer in our present world and the prevailing character of our medical perception. If we were not as a society completely enthralled by the will to power, the will to master and control, would we still *perceive* in cancer the danger of uncontrollable growth? And if we were not as a society completely enthralled by the will to power, would we continue to fuel a technology that everywhere challenges our control and creates an environment increasingly inhospitable to our bodily well-being?

In an essay called "The Forecasting of the Future," Ortega y Gasset observed that

> If the essence of each generation is a particular type of sensibility, an organic capacity for certain deeply-rooted directions of thought, this means that each generation has its special vocation, its historical mission. . . . But generations, like individuals, sometimes fail in their vocation and leave their mission unachieved. . . . It is obvious that such dereliction of historical duty cannot go unpunished. The guilty generation drags out its existence in perpetual division against itself, its essential life shattered.[177]

Is cancer an epidemic historical manifestation of this "existence in perpetual division against itself"? Is it only a "figure of speech" in our cultural interpretations, or is it perhaps a pathology of the human body in which the technological nihilism at work in our body politic has figured in some decisive way?

Was Ortega suggesting that our time for "making" history may be past? To believe this would be to submit to the nihilism of a blind fate. I believe that our historical task is to understand ourselves in our historical world.

In *Knowledge of Freedom,* Tarthang Tulku formulated a Buddhist reply to the questions Ortega generates: "When we see the hidden dangers in a self-oriented viewpoint, and realize how it can distort our perspective in potentially self-destructive ways, we have an opportunity to consider other possibilities."[178] But he noted further, that "Because we see no viable alternatives, we shy away from the evidence that our problems are proliferating, threatening the welfare of the individual and society alike. . . . But we cannot completely ignore the symptoms of what seems to be a deep underlying distress."[179] This suggests a crucial distinction: "Although some people today tend to blame technology for our difficulties and seek solutions in returning to a simpler way of life, the knowledge that has given us so much that is useful is not inherently destructive. Our problems do not seem [to me] to be rooted in technology, but in our inability to balance this knowledge with a wider vision of human life."[180]

It is my hope that the studies brought together here will contribute to a "wider vision of human life." But I will be more than satisfied if the understanding of psychiatric illness that we achieve were to lighten the burden of suffering for even a few.

NOTES

1. For further reflections on the modern experience of nihilism, the reader is invited to consult my book, *The Body's Recollection of Being: Phenomenological Psychology and the Deconstruction of Nihilism* (London and Boston: Routledge & Kegan Paul, 1985).

2. Adorno, *Minima Moralia: Reflections from Damaged Life* (London: New Left Books, 1974; Verso ed., 1978), 241.

3. Ibid., 233. See also Samuel Epstein, *The Politics of Cancer* (New York: Doubleday, Anchor Books edition, 1979).

4. Ibid.

5. I insist that our psychological diagnosis does not exclude a correlative diagnosis in political terms. On the contrary, the epidemic psychopathology requires it. In the kind of political analysis I would like to encourage, the pathologies of the will that are characteristic of the ego-logical subject translate into a dialectic of domination and submission, a mastery that needs violence and recklessly gambles

with self-destruction. The extreme subjectivity of the metaphysical Self must be understood as the reflection of a political condition that favors the dictation of meaning: in other words, political domination. When the being of Self is reduced to "mere subjectivity," we cannot easily resist the political imposition of socialized, normalized meaning. The dictation of meaning, and thus the political violation of our experience, i.e., its control over our critical awareness, our sense of reality, are possible only when the Self has acquiesced in the metaphysical dualism that locks it away in an asylum of pure inwardness. It is precisely because of this connection between the psychological and the political manifestations of nihilism, a connection that I am making in terms of the Self, that Adorno, for example, could suggest a connection, in his *Minima Moralia* (p. 46) between conditions that favor totalitarianism and conditions that call for the suppression and repression of "homosexuality."

6. For an excellent discussion of the ambiguities in Nietzsche's conception of the will to power, see Ofelia Schutte, *Beyond Nihilism: Nietzsche Without Masks* (Chicago: University of Chicago, 1984).

7. Freud, *Civilization and Its Discontents* (New York: Doubleday, 1930), pp. 103–104.

8. Adorno, 58.

9. Ibid., 60.

10. Ibid.

11. Jung, "Epilogue to 'Essays on Contemporary Events,' " in *Civilization in Transition, The Collected Works of Carl G. Jung.* (Princeton: Princeton University Press, 1964), vol. 10, 233–35. Also see "The Fight with the Shadow," *Civilization in Transition,* 218–19.

12. David Bakan, *Disease, Pain and Sacrifice* (Boston: Beacon Press, 1971), 4.

13. Ibid., 9. There is now a large body of literature on correlations between physical and mental conditions, correlations between disease and social environment, correlations between psychopathology and social class, and correlations between disease, psychopathology and culture. See for example, Richard Totman, *The Social Causes of Illness* (New York: Pantheon, 1979); G. E. Moss, *Illness, Immunity, and Social Interaction* (New York: John Wiley, 1973); G. W. Brown and T. Harris, *The Social Origins of Depression: A Study of Psychiatric Disorder in Women* (London: Tavistock, 1978); Anthony F. Wallace, *Culture and Personality* (New York: Random House, 1961); F. Reicheman, ed., *Epidemiologic Studies in Psychosomatic Medicine* (New York: Karger, 1977); Marvin K. Opler, *Culture, Psychiatry, and Human Values* (Springfield, Illinois: Charles C. Thomas, 1956); Mervyn Susser, *Community Psychiatry; Epidemiologic and Social Themes* (New York: Random House, 1968); B. P. Dohrenwend and B. S. Dohrenwend, *Social Status and Psychological Disorder: A Causal Inquiry* (New York: Wiley, 1969); R. E. Faris and H. W. Dunham, *Mental Disorders in Urban Areas: An Ecological Study of Schizophrenia and Other Psychoses* (Chicago: University of Chicago, 1939); A. B. Hollingshead and F. G. Redlich, *Social Class and Mental Illness* (New York: Wiley, 1958); J. L. Halliday, *Psychosocial Medicine: A Study of the Sick Society* (New York: W. W. Norton, 1948); A. Mutter and M. Schleifer, "The role of psychological and social factors in the onset of somatic illness in children," *Psychosomatic Medicine* 28

(1966): 333–43; Harold G. Wolff, ed., *Life Stress and Bodily Disease* (Baltimore: Williams and Wilkins, 1950); Hans Selye, *The Stress of Life* (New York: McGraw-Hill, 1956); Herbert Goldhamer and Andrew W. Marshall, *Psychosis and Civilization* (Glencoe: The Free Press, 1953); Joseph W. Eaton and Robert J. Weil, *Culture and Mental Disorders* (Glencoe: The Free Press, 1955); and finally, Roy R. Grinker, J. Miller, M. Sabshin, R. Nunn, and June Nunnally, *The Phenomena of Depressions* (New York: Paul B. Hoeber, 1961.)

14. Bakan, 13.

15. Ivan Illich, *Medical Nemesis: The Expropriation of Health* (New York: Random House, Pantheon, 1976), 142. Our health is being expropriated, denied us, when the theoretical possibility of a deep *ontological* significance in our pathology is ideologically concealed from us. Adorno said: "The inner health of our time has been secured by blocking flight into illness without in the slightest altering its etiology." (*Minima Moralia,* 58.)

16. Illich, 166.

17. Adorno, 233.

18. Ibid., 235.

19. Ibid., 234.

20. For some discussions of the methodological problems in epidemiological interpretations, see Eric D. Wittkower and Jacob Fried, "Some Problems of Transcultural Psychiatry," in Marvin K. Opler, ed., *Culture and Mental Health* (New York: Macmillan, 1959), 489–500; Charles Savage, Alexander Leighton, and Dorothea Leighton, "The Problem of Cross-Cultural Identification of Psychiatric Disorders," in Jane M. Murphy and Alexander Leighton, eds., *Approaches to Cross-Cultural Psychiatry* (Ithaca: Cornell University, 1965); Donald Kennedy, "Key Issues in the Cross-Cultural Study of Mental Disorders," in Bert Kaplan, ed., *Studying Personality Cross-Culturally* (New York: Harper & Row, 1961), 405–426; Robert Sears, "Transcultural Variables and Conceptual Equivalence," in Kaplan, ed., *Studying Personality Cross-Culturally,* 445–456; and Mervyn Susser, *Causal Thinking in the Health Sciences: Concepts and Strategies of Epidemiology* (New York: Oxford University, 1973).

21. Raymond Geuss, *The Idea of A Critical Theory: Habermas and the Frankfurt School* (Cambridge, Cambridge University, 1981), 63.

22. Ibid.

23. Ibid.

24. Ibid., 88.

25. See, e.g., David Ingleby, ed., *Critical Psychiatry: The Politics of Mental Health* (New York: Pantheon, 1980.)

26. Barrington Moore, Jr., *Reflections on the Causes of Human Misery and Upon Certain Proposals to Eliminate Them* (Boston: Beacon Press, 1969), 1–2.

27. Martin Heidegger, *Being and Time* (New York: Harper & Row, 1962), 422.

28. Heidegger, *Nietzsche,* vol. 4: *Nihilism* (New York: Harper & Row, 1982), 229.

29. Ibid., 245.

30. Heidegger, "Overcoming Metaphysics," in *The End of Philosophy* (New York: Harper & Row, 1973), 110.

31. Ibid.

32. Ibid.

33. Heidegger, *What Is Called Thinking?* (New York: Harper & Row, 1968), 84.

34. Heidegger, "Recollection in Metaphysics," *The End of Philosophy,* 91.

35. Max Horkheimer, *Dawn and Decline* (New York: Seabury Press, 1978), 224.

36. Heidegger, *Neitzsche,* vol 2: *The Eternal Recurrence of the Same* (New York: Harper & Row, 1984), 99–102, 117–119, 190–91.

37. Erich Fromm, "Can A Society Be Sick?," in *The Sane Society* (New York and Toronto: Rinehart, 1955), 12–21.

38. See Heidegger's discussion of discourse (*legein* as *apophainesthai*); truth in the sense of alētheia (disclosure) and truth in the sense of correctness and correspondence; phenomenology (as the *legein* of *phainesthai*); and hermeneutics (*hermeneuein*) as the discourse in which an experience of truth as *alētheia* is valued, in *Being and Time,* 51–63.

39. Georg W. Hegel, *The Phenomenology of Mind* (London: Muirhead Library of Philosophy, 1966), 93.

40. Nietzsche, *The Genealogy of Morals* (New York: Doubleday, Anchor Books, 1956), 255.

41. Nietzsche, *The Will to Power* (New York: Random House, 1968), 3.

42. See ibid., 7.

43. Ibid.

44. Ibid., note 602, p. 326.

45. Ibid., note 4, p. 4.

46. Ibid., note 55, p. 35.

47. Ibid.

48. Ibid., note 56, p. 39.

49. See *The Will to Power,* Book 1, note 28, p. 19: "Main proposition. How *complete nihilism* is the necessary consequence of the ideals entertained hitherto./ Incomplete nihilism; its forms: we live in the midst of it./ Attempts to escape nihilism without reevaluating our values so far: they produce the opposite, make the problem more acute."

50. Ibid.

51. Ibid., note 110, p. 69.

52. Ibid., note 2, p. 9.

53. Ibid., note 3, p. 9.

54. Ibid., note 7, pp. 10–11.

55. Ibid., note 13, p. 14.

56. Ibid., note 14, p. 14.

57. Ibid.

58. Ibid., note 22, p. 17.

59. Ibid., note 23, p. 18.

60. Ibid., note 23, p. 17.

61. Ibid., note 12, pp. 12–13.

62. Ibid.

63. See the contribution to this collection of studies by Eugene T. Gendlin. It

is a radical critique of the concept of "narcissism" as it functions in discourses concerned with human development.

64. Nietzsche, *The Genealogy of Morals,* First Essay, note 12, p. 177.

65. Ibid., Third Essay, note 14, p. 258.

66. Nietzsche, *The Will to Power,* note 109, p. 68.

67. Ibid., note 112, p. 69.

68. Ibid., note 55, p. 37. Also see note 113, p. 70.

69. Except where explicitly indicated, all references in the catalogue are to paragraphs and their pages in Nietzsche, *The Will to Power.*

70. Nietzsche, *The Will to Power,* Book 2, note 461, p. 253.

71. Heidegger, "Metaphysics as History of Being," in *The End of Philosophy* (New York: Harper & Row, 1973), 22.

72. Ibid.

73. See Heidegger, "The Word of Nietzsche: 'God is dead,' " in *The Question Concerning Technology and Other Essays* (New York: Harper and Row, 1977), 62–63.

74. Ibid., 65.

75. Ibid.

76. Adorno, 15.

77. Ibid., 154.

78. Nietzsche, *The Will to Power,* note 55, p. 37.

79. Adorno, 232.

80. Ibid., 15–16.

81. Ibid., 154–155. Concerning the Self's "homelessness," see the contribution to this anthology by Robert Romanyshyn and Brian Whalen, "Depression and the American Dream: The Struggle with Home."

82. Adorno, 155.

83. Ibid., 63.

84. Ibid. Also see Martin Heidegger, "The Age of the World Picture," in *The Question Concerning Technology and Other Essays,* 115–154, and the essay on "Science and Reflection," 155–182 in the same collection.

85. Adorno, 63.

86. Ibid., 231.

87. Ibid.

88. Ibid., 149.

89. Ibid.

90. Ibid., 150.

91. Ibid., 152–3.

92. Heidegger, "Recollection in Metaphysics," in *The End of Philosophy,* 82.

93. Nietzsche, *The Will to Power,* Book 1, note 55, p. 37. In "The Word of Nietzsche," Heidegger wrote: "But if the thinking that thinks everything in terms of values is nihilism when thought in relation to Being itself, then even Nietszche's own experience of nihilism, i.e., that it is the devaluing of the highest values, is after all a nihilistic one." (105).

94. Heidegger, "The Word of Nietzsche," 82–83.

95. Heidegger, "Overcoming Metaphysics," 97.

96. Heidegger, "The Age of the World Picture," 128.
97. Ibid.
98. Ibid., 132.
99. Ibid.
100. Ibid., 134.
101. Ibid., 132.
102. Ibid., 133. Also see "The Word of Nietzsche," 68, where Heidegger spoke of "the unconditional domination of subjectivity."
103. Ibid.
104. Ibid., 134.
105. Ibid.
106. Heidegger, *Introduction to Metaphysics* (New York: Doubleday, 1961), 37.
107. Ibid. "Wasting away" is a phrase that connects what is happening today in our spiritual life with what is happening in the physical organisms we call "the human body."
108. Ibid., 148.
109. Ibid.
110. Ibid.
111. Heidegger, "The Word of Nietzsche," 88.
112. Heidegger, "The Age of the World Picture," 150.
113. Ibid.
114. Ibid. Also see "The Word of Nietzsche," 77.
115. Ibid.
116. Heidegger, "The Word of Nietzsche," 100.
117. Ibid., 110.
118. Ibid., 109.
119. Ibid., 79–80.
120. Ibid., 83–4. Also see Heidegger, "Metaphysics as History of Being," 4 and 29.
121. Heidegger, "Metaphysics as History of Being," 28.
122. See "The Word of Nietzsche," *op. cit.*, 75–90.
123. Ibid., 25.
124. Heidegger discusses these human being/ego and thing/object transformations in *Discourse on Thinking* (New York: Harper & Row, 1966), 78.
125. Heidegger, "Overcoming Metaphysics," 87.
126. Ibid., 110.
127. Heidegger, "Recollection in Metaphysics," 76.
128. Ibid., 83.
129. Herbert V. Guenther, *The Tantric View of Life* (Boulder: Shambhala Publishing, 1976), 93.
130. Heidegger, "What Are Poets For?" in *Poetry, Language, Thought* (New York: Harper & Row, 1971), 120.
131. See Kathleen Freeman, *Ancilla to the Pre-Socratic Philosophers* (Cambridge: Harvard University Press, 1978).
132. Merleau-Ponty, *Phenomenology of Perception* (London: Routledge & Kegan Paul, 1962), 219. Also see p. 430, same text.

133. The "primordial matrix" in which subject and object inhere and belong together is accessible through our reconnection to what Merleau-Ponty calls the "pre-personal" dimension of our embodiment—and of course only in virtue of a willingness to open our existence to participation in the "transpersonal" dimension, where the ontological interconnectedness among all beings, and even their "interpenetration" and "intertwining" can be directly experienced. For the argument that this access to the transpersonal dimension can be extremely healing for the Self as well as overwhelming and psychosis-making, see Stanislav Grof's contribution to this collection, "New Insights into the Nature and Dynamics of Depressions and Psychoses."

134. Heidegger, "Aletheia (Heraclitus, Fragment B16)," in *Early Greek Thinking* (New York: Harper & Row, 1975), 103.

135. Horkheimer, 229.

136. Ibid., 238–9.

137. Ibid., 161–162.

138. Heidegger, "The Turning," in *The Question Concerning Technology and Other Essays,* 48.

139. Horkheimer, 162.

140. Heidegger, "Sketches for a History of Being as Metaphysics," in *The End of Philosophy,* 63.

141. Ibid., 66–67.

142. Heidegger, "The Overcoming of Metaphysics," 109. Notice that some key words in this passage on nihilism in technology are words that also carry significance in the cultural discourse on cancer: "devours," "exhaustion," and "consumption." Is this accidental? Could the use of those words indicate that there is, within our culture, a "preontological understanding" of the connection between nihilism as technology and nihilism as cancer? See Roger Levin's paper on "Cancer and the Self," published in this collection of studies.

143. Heidegger, "The Overcoming of Metaphysics," 93.

144. Ibid., 103.

145. Ibid. Italics added. I have slightly modified the translation.

146. Adorno, 15.

147. Ibid., 230.

148. Ibid., 231.

149. Heidegger, "Recollection in Metaphysics," 76.

150. Heidegger, "Sketches for a History of Being as Metaphysics," in *The End of Philosophy,* 73.

151. Heidegger, "What Are Poets For?", in *Poetry, Language, Thought,* 110.

152. Heidegger, "Recollection in Metaphysics," 80.

153. Nietzsche, *The Will to Power,* Book 1, note 45, p. 28. Also see Heidegger's discussion of the "standardization" and "normalization" of humanity, in *The Introduction to Metaphysics* (New York: Doubleday, 1961), 31–37.

154. Nietzsche, *The Genealogy of Morals,* 248.

155. See Heidegger, *The Introduction to Metaphysics,* 31.

156. Heidegger, "The Word of Nietzsche," 100.

157. Heidegger, "The Overcoming of Metaphysics," 86.

158. Ibid., 85. On "rational animal," see also p. 87, same text.

159. Ibid., 87.

160. Heidegger, "The Word of Nietzsche," 83.

161. Heidegger, "Metaphysics as History of Being," 22.

162. See ibid., 4 and 29. Also see "Overcoming Metaphysics," 99 and 106; "The Question Concerning Technology," 6–18; and "The Age of the World Picture," 149.

163. See, for example, Tarthang Tulku, *Knowledge of Freedom* (Berkeley: Dharma Publishing, 1984), 70. Italics added.

164. Ibid., 318–19.

165. Ibid., 319.

166. Ibid.

167. Ibid., 320–22.

168. Susan Sontag, *Illness As Metaphor* (New York: Random House, Vintage Books, 1979), 27.

169. See Roger Levin's contribution, "Cancer and the Self," where the relation between cancer and the embodied Self will be interpreted in greater psychological depth and in the historical context of medical and biological knowledge.

170. Sontag, 58.

171. Ibid., 61.

172. Ibid., 62.

173. Ibid. Italics added.

174. Ibid., 63.

175. Bryan S. Turner, *The Body and Society: Explorations in Social Theory* (Oxford and New York: Basil Blackwell, 1984), 112. See also Lester S. King, *Medical Thinking: A Historical Preface* (Princeton: Princeton University, 1982).

176. Ibid., 114.

177. Jose Ortega y Gasset, "The Forecasting of the Future," in *The Modern Theme* (New York: W. W. Norton, 1933), 19.

178. Tarthang Tulku, *Knowledge of Freedom,* 74.

179. Ibid., 68.

180. Ibid.

CHAPTER 2

SCIENCE AND THE FRAGILE SELF: THE RISE OF NARCISSISM, THE DECLINE OF GOD

JEFFREY SATINOVER

"Man's reach must exceed his grasp,
else what's a heaven for?"

Robert Browning

INTRODUCTION

The accusation that we are a narcissistic society is not new. Replace "narcissistic" with "excessively selfish," and we recognize a critique that the religious of every age make of the surrounding secular culture, particularly when religion is in decline.

But religion is in decline, and convincing critiques of human character are now more apt to come from a psychological than religious point of view. Over the past thirty years, two opposing schools of psychoanalytic thought, the Freudian and the Jungian, have given increasing attention to this problem of excessive selfishness. Authors such as Lasch (1979) have taken from recent Freudian investigations, and applied to our culture, the pejorative term "narcissistic" and the notion that narcissism is now pandemic; in the Jungian world the same problem has been described and worried about as the spread of the *Puer Aeternus,* or eternal adolescent (Von Franz 1970).

The Freudians in general are disinterested in religion, and classical psychoanalysis, at home in the great American medical centers, is not easily assimilated by the religious. (There are exceptions—Meissner 1984.) The Jungians are very interested in religion, and the religious have at times used Jung's concepts to recast in psychological language truths whose ancient forms of expression have become unpalatable to modern tastes (Edinger 1972).

I shall argue in this chapter that there is an irreducible human need for religious forms of expression. If a suitable, which is to say metaphysical, realm is not available to channel this need, then unsuitable, mundane realms will be burdened with fulfilling it instead, including the realm of the all too limited human self. Thus, the human need for religion is directly linked to problematic narcissism. By "religion" I do not necessarily mean any of the established organized religions, nor simply a personal set of spiritual beliefs, but rather a set of metaphysical beliefs shared by a community membership that is implicitly defined by holding these beliefs.

Freudian conceptualizations of pathological narcissism provide an incisive clinical analysis of this defect of individual character. But to understand the role of narcissism in society, we will need to turn to a somewhat modified Jungian conceptualization of religion.

The first part of this chapter, "Puer Aeternus," is a clinical sketch of a widespread personality type[1] essentially the same as the "narcissist." I shall argue that the basis of the *Puer* is a problem with identity. Upon this seemingly simple premise I shall build a psychological model that enables us to understand why so many people today lead a life of eternal adolescence.

The second part of the chapter, "The Mirror of Faust," takes a more sociological, or group-psychological, view of the same problem. Here I shall describe what I see as the dominating long-term change in Western culture: the growth of scientific reason and the abdication of religious faith. I shall argue that this sweeping, historical, culture-wide and seemingly impersonal change has had a direct and specific impact on the nature of personal identity as we each experience it today. I shall argue that this change is the reason that the *Puer* syndrome has become so widespread.

PUER AETERNUS

Identity

For some twenty-five years now, the problem of the Puer Aeternus—the eternal adolescent—has been of growing interest and puzzlement to Jungian analysts. Interest in the Puer has tracked what appears to be a striking rise in the incidence of this kind of personality. It is a personality characterized on the one hand by a poor adjustment to quotidian demands, a failure to set stable goals, and a proclivity for intense but short-lived romantic attachments, yet on the other hand by noble idealism, a fertile romantic imagination, spiritual insight and frequently, too, by remarkable talent.

The thesis of this section is straightforward: at heart the Puer lacks a sense of identity. About this lack revolves the entire constellation of personality traits (with their behavioral consequences) that characterizes him.[2]

What is this "sense of identity"? Colloquially, it is simply the feeling that "I know who I am," even if I can't articulate it. When the Puer seeks treatment, the lack of a sense of identity may not be his presenting complaint, but sooner or later it comes to the fore.

"Identity" is a difficult word to define, no less in psychology than in philosophy. An important feature of both definitions is the quality of "sameness," "openness" or "repetition." (These are the etymologic roots of "identity.") From the perspective of psychology, an important aspect of the sense of identity is the subjective impression of being the same person from one moment to the next. Puer psychology is characterized by a widely fluctuating sense of who one is and of one's worth.

The sense of identity occupies a unique place in the psyche, and it has therefore only an ill-defined place in highly structured metapsychologies (be they Freudian or Jungian). Strictly speaking, "identity" is neither a content of consciousness (viz., a thought, an image, a sensory impression, an emotion etc.) nor an unconscious (or partly conscious) structure (the "anima," the "superego," etc.). One way to conceptualize the sense of identity is to think of it as an introspective apprehension of a coherent relationship prevailing among the various structures of the psyche. That is to say: when the psyche is functioning in a stable and harmonious fashion, when there *is* a relationship among its parts, a functional "openness" exists and is apperceived by the ego as the sense of identity. Another way to speak of such an orderly dynamic interaction prevailing among all the parts of the psyche is to say that the (Jungian, capital "S") "Self" is constellated (Jung 1923). What the ego apperceives is the (Freudian, small "s") self. (See Hartmann 1950, on the "self-representation.") This notion provides the basis for a working Jungian definition of identity closely akin to many psychoanalytic definitions of the "self" (small "s"): it is the effect in consciousness of the constellation of the Self.

The Self may be present but unaware, a kind of background condition to one's consciousness, silently exerting its effect. But the Self may also be absent, and this absence, too, exerts its effect. What, then, are the differences between these two states of the Self, as sensed introspectively? When the Self is constellated, introspection senses being a particular person and no other, with an irrational, unassailable sense of worth; when the Self is not constellated, this sense is absent.

Narcissism

Freud (1914) imported into psychoanalysis the use of "narcissism" from Ovid's version of the classical myth. Narcissus was a beautiful youth, himself a Puer Aeternus, who fell in love with his own reflection and so pined to death. Early psychoanalysis used the term "narcissism" to indicate an excessive self-absorption that reduces the capacity to relate to others.

Freud considered that all people begin life in a blissful state he called "primary narcissism." In this state no distinction between self and world exists, hence no painful tensions in the form of as-yet-unfulfilled desires of the subject for any object, and therefore no conscious experience of drive and frustration.

As the infant develops, it separates its psychic representation of itself (the "self") from its psychic representation of its surroundings ("objects"), and an inchoate sense of tension differentiates into the experience of need for others. As it grows, need puts pressure on the developing ego to acquire the skills necessary to fulfill the need, and so the ego adapts to object-reality. All the energy that in infancy was bound exclusively to the subject in this way slowly extends out and becomes bound up in the subject's pursuit of objects. The process is essential to normal development.

Freud (1914) originally described the core of neurosis as an interruption in this smooth transition from subject-bound to object-bound libido. He described this interruption as follows: The childhood libido reaches out, fascinated by the objects of its desire. But being as yet insufficiently adapted to succeed, it fails to attain its goal. These failures are inevitable. However, when the libido responds to this failure not through further differentiation of its adaptive capacity but by regressing, neurosis ensues. In regression the libido, to compensate for its failure in adaptation and for the consequent lack of gratification, seeks an alternate, easier form of gratification, one with which the ego is already familiar. The libido reactivates the memory of an earlier form of adaptation, and the ego gives up what it has gained in differentiation; it returns to the blissful state of narcissism now called "secondary narcissism."

In this broad view, the heart of neurosis is the habit of seeking gratification through self-stimulation and the turning away from work. It is the tendency to flee back to the garden of Eden whenever sweat on the brow is needed or strife is brewing between the sexes. The grandiose fantasy is preferred to the modest accomplishment; the brief idealized romance to a rocky long-term commitment.

Introversion

Jung's important modification to this idea is that the retreat to earlier forms of psychic life and behavior, to secondary narcissism, is not only or even primarily an alternate means of gratification. It is rather the necessary way that as yet unused *innate* modes of adaptation (like Lorenz's concept of innate releasing mechanisms—1963) are triggered. Thus, the retreat to the narcissistic state releases archetypal fantasies, and these fantasies are the representations in consciousness of inherited but as yet unused adaptive behaviors. The regression, therefore, is not simply or only unhealthy; it also sets into motion compensatory processes of the psyche whose purpose is rather enhanced adaptation and thus greater psychic health.

Early in his career, while he was still within the psychoanalytic fold, Jung equated narcissism and introversion. The generally held notion that introversion is per se pathological grows out of the early Freudian idea that narcissism is a substitute employed where adaptation to object-reality (extra-version) has failed. When he expanded Freud's conception, Jung renamed narcissism introversion and then treated the turning inward of libido away from objects and towards the self as a servant of psychological development rather than as an enemy to it.

If we were to abandon our description of introversion (narcissism) here, we would be left with the following: introversion, while not per se pathological, is nonetheless a function of the psyche that is called into play only under pathological circumstances. Jung went further. He presented (1921) the idea that introversion occurs not only in response to failures of extraversion, but rather that the habitual turning inward of attention to the self is a normal function of the psyche that, in some individuals, predominates over the habitual turning of attention outward to objects.

To summarize, narcissism or introversion can be: 1) a pathological state; 2) a compensatory response; 3) a normal feature of psychic life.

Point 3) also leads to the following corollary, consistent with a recent change in psychoanalytic attitudes toward narcissism, as exemplified in the works of Heinz Kohut (1971, 1977): there is such a thing as healthy narcissism. Narcissism, or introversion, is a needed function in all individuals. Like its opposite, adaptation to the outer world, there is such a thing as adaptation to one's inner world, and there are better and worse forms of such adaptation. Neuroses can develop that are narcissistic, not in the sense that the narcissism is a neurotic response to failures of external adaptation (an extreme version of which—the total loss of the sense of reality—was an early conceptualization of psychosis), but rather in the sense that they are failures to develop healthy introversion.

I consider this the case with the Puer Aeternus. The Puer's failure to adapt to external reality, as in his unrealistic romantic expectations and idealism, is not the primary problem. These features are a secondary consequence of the failure to develop a particular sort of narcissism, a failure of introverted adaptation. Treatment or exhortation that focuses on adaptation to external reality at best addresses a secondary symptom, leaving the core problem untouched. It is for this reason that most psychotherapeutic or psychoanalytic approaches to narcissism (be they Freudian or Jungian) are so largely ineffective. (It is a conventional bit of psychoanalytic clinical wisdom, for instance, that the most difficult patient to treat is a successful narcissist.)

Turn for a moment to the classical myth of Narcissus. Why is it that Narcissus falls in love with his reflection? Let us assume the truth of a general psychological principle, consistent with Plato's allegory of the spherical man: one falls in love with one's missing half, that which one lacks. What Narcissus lacks is an image of himself, and it is with this, therefore, that he falls in love. He is unconscious of himself, he does not know who he is, he lacks a sense of identity and so turns outward to gain that reflection of himself that he cannot achieve inwardly, alone.

A stable sense of identity requires the capacity to sense oneself, as it were, to reflect oneself. In other words, the central function of introversion, of healthy narcissism, is to maintain a stable sense of identity.

This may sound trivial. Can it really be that the richness of the inner world is nothing but a devise to ensure an identity? Consider Melville's comment in *Moby Dick*: ". . . . and still deeper the meaning of that story of Narcissus who, because he could not grasp the tormenting mild image he saw in the fountain, plunged into it and was drowned. But that same image we ourselves see in all rivers and oceans. It is the image of the ungraspable phantom of life; and this is the key to it all." (Melville, 1964, 26) The simple question of personal identity, "who am I?," pursued persistently and answered precisely enough, can lead, as the mystics assert, to the deepest waters of all.

The central function of introversion can be understood as if there were an insistent voice, just beyond hearing, which over and over poses the question, "Who am I?" The sense of identity is the sense that perhaps, out of the range of hearing and beyond articulation, there is nonetheless an answer.

Just as a long, healthy developing relationship with another person rests on an unspoken core of basic trust, so too, the lifelong relationship with oneself rests on the presence of this unspoken answer. Just as the lack of trust in a relationship with another will lead to severe disturbances in that relationship, the lack of a sense of answer to the question, "Who am I?" will lead, over years, to a disturbed relationship to oneself. Just as the person who cannot trust expends his energy in a fruitless repetitive effort to gain and regain assurance of loyalty, so too, does the person who lacks a sense of identity expend his energy, like Narcissus, in repeated seemingly selfish efforts to obtain what he lacks. Thus, the proper development of introversion rests on the deep-seated sense of having an identity. In the Puer, the lack of this sense disturbs his relation to himself as well as secondarily to others.

The Childhood Self and the Origin of the Puer

What events in early life lead to the Puer character? To answer, we need first to make a rough sketch of how the Self constellates in childhood and of the consequences in the emerging personality. The constellation of the Self catalyzes a coalescing of diverse and conflicting impulses to form a functional unity. This coming-together is the basis on which the ego, as executor of the personality, forms, and it is marked by greatly improved functioning. Later in life, a loss of the sense of identity is marked by a striking decrease in the autonomous capacities of the ego as it returns to a fragmented state similar to the one prevailing in childhood before the appearance of the Self.

An example: a woman recalled having awakened from a nap at the age of two-and-a-half with the abrupt realization of who she was and with the sudden certainty that *she* could decide for herself whether or not to take a nap. She called her parents into her room and announced that from that day hence she was no longer taking afternoon naps.

This early kind of experience of identity is marked by specific feelings, the outward signs of which parents may easily note in their children as they enter the stage of separation (Mahler 1975). These are feelings of specialness and importance, even of grandeur, omniscience and omnipotence: that is to say, of god-likeness. These feelings, though attributed to oneself in a personal way, may be better thought of as a "gift," the trace of the Self in consciousness.

At the developmental core of later, more modest, adult identity is therefore what we might call a necessary inflation. The child, as a normal consequence of the constellation of the Self, needs to experience a grandiose enlargement of his sense of who he is.[3] The childhood Self remains at the core of the later experience of identity by providing, beyond all rational argument and the mature experience of limitation, a deep belief in one's ultimate worth and value. The early experience of the Self provides the basis for later healthy introversion. The adult who in early life has experienced this sense of unity and grandeur knows that, in times of frustration and failure, he can always look inward and touch a sense of worthiness. The habit of so turning inward for restoration becomes the bedrock of self-sufficiency, of healthy narcissism.

In the ideal course of development, the effect of the childhood Self on the child's identity becomes greatly modified. In the time following its constellation he experiences himself as far more potent than he actually is. Imagination is at its peak and the child can play at being a king or queen, a warrior, a parent, an explorer or a villain, all with equal ease. In imagination the full range of what it means to be human is available to the child. No human capacity is too great or too mean to be embraced in the life of fantasy and play. But the child is also faced with the task of increasing adaptation to mundane reality, and in this his capacities are as undeveloped as the imaginative capacities of the childhood Self are rich.

As the child meets reality with his grandiose fantasies, frustration inevitably results. This frustration is necessary. If the child experiences it slowly, in small, well-timed doses, the fantasies of who he is will be modified and made smaller—but not entirely crushed. (See Kohut, 1971, on transmuting internalization.) Simultaneously, the capacities and functions of the ego, through exercise, will grow larger and more efficient. In late adolescence the child's idealizations of himself and the pressure to grandeur exerted by the Self will have shrunk to the point where they match his increased ability.

There are two broad pathways (and a third more specialized one) of misdirected development along which this process can be diverted towards a Puer outcome. First, the constellation of the Self may be obstructed (by the environment); second, although allowed to constellate, the Self may be protected from the frustrations of reality that modify and reduce the grandiose sense of identity it generates.

The Puer may result from a parental milieu in which a roughly eighteen-month to two-year-old child is immersed. This milieu habitually disrupts any sign of assertiveness, action or fantasies that carry the hallmark of specialness. The disruption of the normally inflated childhood Self, as it constellates, will again and again return the child to a preceding state that we may think of as *fragmented,* unless he can find a haven where his inflation is accepted—with a grandparent, an older friend, a therapist.

If the disruption remains consistently uncountered, the child will eventually internalize the parental disapproval of the childhood Self, and the child will himself adopt a cynically undermining stance towards his idealized image of himself. A harsh internal critic will insinuate itself whenever there arises a new idea, an enthusiasm, or a self-gratifying fantasy. Every hopeful response to the question, "Who am I?" will be cut off with, "Who do you think you are?" As an expression of the innate urge to development, the Self will nonetheless reconstellate. An internal vicious cycle will thereby be established. Each constellation of the Self, with its surge of youthful hope and grandiosity, will be washed out by an ebbtide of self-recrimination and refragmentation.

A cycle between states of grandeur in which the Self is constellated, and states of despair in which it is fragmented, is typical of Puer psychology. It is the source of the narcissist's exquisite sensitivity: if he himself refrains from delivering the blow that ushers in fragmentation, the least criticism from another will do it.

When reconstellated in the adult Puer, the Self is in its childhood form and thus especially liable to refragmentation. It has not been tempered by the immersion in reality, and it reacts as it does in a child. This sensitivity accounts for the essential similarity between children of insufficiently supportive parents and those of excessively supportive ones. (The essential similarity of both kinds of parent is their inability to titrate their responses to the child's needs.) In the latter case, the Self is allowed to constellate, but it remains insulated from the frustrations of real life that make identity less grandiose but more cohesive. The grandiose fantasies are not only accepted, but they are pushed (because of the parents' overinvestment in them.) If the child's sense of specialness is overstimulated, he is pushed to behave and accomplish beyond his age. Precociousness becomes the currency he exchanges for love and admiration.

In effect such a child becomes addicted to the childhood Self. He will later devote much of his life to seeking experiences that maintain or reestablish the sense of grandiosity, while avoiding the frustrations that diminish his sense of specialness.

Puers from each kind of upbringing strike others as narcissistic: the introversion of each is engaged (by social standards excessively engaged) in a ceaseless effort to maintain the experience of the childhood Self, and each will choose external circumstances—brief affairs, intense mental or physical exertion, creative performance, drugs—that enhance this experience. Both appear to others as inordinately sensitive, and both are liable to sudden radical shifts in self-esteem.

There is a third source of Puer psychology, a source which, as I will detail in the second part of this chapter, provides the link to a social analysis of the Puer syndrome: great talent. The fantasy of being gifted or creative, however, is also one of the most common self-definitions generated by the childhood Self. Yet it may occur as readily in a genuinely gifted individual as in a relatively ungifted one. There is a critical difference between actual ability and the need to consider oneself especially able.

Talent may produce Puer psychology in the following way. As in the ungifted, the constellated childhood Self produces fantasies of omnipotence and grandeur in the gifted child. But the gifted child meets with far fewer actual frustrations in his attempt to realize these fantasies than does the ungifted child or the very talented but socially disadvantaged child. His parents and others may, for good reason, stand in awe of him, and he may thus come to stand unweeningly in awe of himself. While listening to music many children (and adults for that matter) indulge in the pleasant omnipotent fantasy that they are the virtuoso. They have become the virtuoso effortlessly. For the musically gifted child, this grandiose fantasy is more nearly a reality.

The gifted child meets with less pressure to modify his grandiose self-image than does the ungifted child. His capacities meet his fantasies, and he is confirmed in a view of himself, not in late adolescence, but early on, when that view retains much of its original splendor. His parents, in their astonishment and pride, reflect back to him a true view, not the artificial inflation of the excessively supportive parent.

The development of the gifted child may parallel the development of the child in an overly supportive environment. He becomes prey to the essential Puer feature of unstable identity, because his identity rests upon a relatively untempered Self. His sense of identity retains a greater degree of liability, and the gifted child learns to stave off fragmentation by the exercise of his talent in front of an admiring public. It is therefore in the area of his creativity that he is both most grandiose and most sensitive. Criticism of a highly creative individual's creations ushers in fragmentation of his personality.

Puer Psychology in the Adult

The characteristic features of the Puer syndrome can be related to the preceding model. The most general, overarching feature of the model is that in the Puer, the sense of identity closely follows a cyclic constellation and fragmentation of the Self. Identity is not only weakly linked to actual achievements of the ego in the "real" world of others; rather, the world of others is experienced as "good" or "bad" depending on whether the events in this world precipitate a fragmentation or a renewed constellation of the Self.

We can examine two broad arenas from this perspective: (1) work (goals and achievements), and (2) love (personal relationships).

WORK

Two difficulties in the arena of work are typical for the Puer: failure to set stable, realistic goals, and fantasies of extraordinary specialness. The latter is a chief cause of the former.

A characteristic feature of the Puer is the experienced pressure of intense recurrent fantasies of grandeur. Translated into consciousness, these fantasies are a way of defining identity, based on the childhood Self. Depending on how modified they are by frustrating experience, the fantasies correspond more or less to the original image of the Self. (This original image will be discussed shortly.)

Fantasies common to today's culture include (in a spectrum of decreasing grandiosity and hence decreasing delusionality):

1. Messianic fantasies
2. Fantasies of spiritual election
3. Fantasies of genius
4. Fantasies of unusual creativity
5. The anticipation of fame or authority
6. The anticipation of wealth
7. The anticipation of success

If we keep in mind that the core of each fantasy remains the Self, we see that as the pressure exerted by the childhood Self decreases and realistic capacities increase, a point is reached where the fantasies cease being delusional and become realistic. Where this point is reached is determined both by nature and by circumstance.

It is often overlooked that these fantasies are not only gratifying, but also painful. (Hence, the Self engenders a conflict, a point to which I will return in the second half of the discussion.) The Puer experiences these fantasies as a call to action. To the degree that he has a genuine appreciation of reality and its limitations, he will experience the failure to live up to the call as an inner reproach that reinduces fragmentation and feelings of worthlessness. He knows that his fantasies are unrealistic, but he is unable to be satisfied with anything less. Thus, he is either forced to greater and greater efforts (often of an exhibitionistic nature where the feedback will be large and immediate) or he denies the pressure completely and so splits off entirely the wellsprings of his motivation (being "laid back"). He never gains any satisfaction from his actual achievements, since they never live up to the demands of the childhood Self.

If the talents of such individuals are sufficient, they may well follow a meteoric rise in a profession that keeps them before the approving reflection of the public: thus today's plethora of "superstars" and an increasingly widespread struggle for instant fame.

A special feature of the inner life of the Puer is frequent dreams of flying. These dreams may be generally thought of as an intrapsychic representation of the pressure to specialness and grandeur exerted by the childhood Self. The motif is a metaphor for the wish to rise above limitation and of the sense of specialness that a successful escape engenders. Thinking of the wish to fly in these terms may evoke a somewhat psychopathological attitude towards it. But the age-old dream of flight is also the prototypical expression of the will and ability to actually shed the restraints of mundane existence. As a guiding fantasy it expresses that power of man's ambitions that has created so many of his extraordinary accomplishments.

The Puer is thus exceptionally ambitious. His ambition may be for fame or for creativity or for spirituality, but whatever its specific aim, its hallmark is the degree to which the Puer is narcissistically dependent upon limitless success to stabilize his sense of himself. The painful discrepancy between ambition and ability (almost any level of actual ability) engenders a common Puer complaint, the failure to complete projects.

The beginning of any project is marked by fantasies of its grandeur and specialness and particularly by pleasant reveries of the grandeur and specialness of its creator. The project is thus embarked upon with a strong sense of identity, whose source is the reconstellated childhood Self. But as the work drags on, enthusiasm fades; completion nears and the project reveals itself as not bad, but also not so different from all the others like it. With the dawning of this realization, the reestablished sense of identity begins to crumble and depression sets in. Either the project is abandoned for a new one that reconstellates the Self, or the fragmentation is staved off by endlessly revising the work towards an impossibly high set of standards.

Alternatively, as completion approaches methods are devised to snatch a grandiose defeat from the jaws of banal victory. Barely to pass the crucial exam, but without any preparation, is a more prodigious feat than to turn in an excellent performance due to strenuous effort. The Puer prefers to be known, and to know himself, as brilliant if erratic, rather than as a successful drudge. He prefers his fantasied potentials to his actual capacities because the former better evokes the glory of the childhood Self.

In these and similar instances, the problem can be traced to the pressure exerted by the Self, and consequent fear of failure is guaranteed. The Puer may acknowledge this fear and its paralyzing effect. This is most easily seen in cases of stage fright, where the fear and paralysis are acute and intense. It is less easily seen in those instances such as the ten-year doctorate. What remains most difficult for the sufferer to appreciate fully is how the project must fail, no matter how great the actual success, for no real success can live up to the core fantasy of the childhood Self.

This core fantasy is the archetype of the divine child (Jung 1951). The individual whose personal sense of identity remains too closely bound to this image in its unmodified form can experience satisfaction from a concrete achievement only if it matches the grandeur of the archetype: it must have the qualities of greatness and absolute uniqueness, and above all it must be prodigiously *precocious*. This latter quality drives our enormous fascination with child prodigies: the prodigy is a living embodiment of the divine child.

Because he can never quite make this archetypal image real, the Puer lives with a persistent if vague sense of failure. Projecting it onto his surroundings, he therefore sees the world around him as failed. The time of glory was earlier, in his own or his culture's younger days. Nothing in his or his society's present, no new accomplishment, can ever quite repair the sense of defect, and so the past is tinged with nostalgia. This attitude strongly affects Puer aesthetics, which runs to camp tastes and antiquarianism.

LOVE

The basis of Puer relationships is this: the Puer seeks relationships that provide him the kind of self-reflection he is unable to provide himself. The Puer does not truly relate to others; he relates instead to a missing part of himself which he either sees in another or makes another enact. Objects function for the Puer primarily as an indirect means of introversion.

The Puer gains the self-reflection he needs in one of two ways. Either he directly gains great admiration from others, or he feels himself chosen by someone he admires greatly. In the first instance the Puer, in order to maintain a sense of identity based on the childhood Self, seeks an admirer who will reflect back to him his specialness and grandeur. More adaptive prototypes for this kind of relationship include the performer in the midst of his crowd and the master before his disciple(s). In both cases the "inferior" partner (the fan or disciple) is valued not because of who he is as a peer, but rather because he subserves a reflective function that preserves the superior partner's sense of specialness and the cohesion of his identity.

The relation that prevails between two such partners—in either a personal or a public setting—is often referred to as love, but if by love we mean a true perception of deep caring for the other, then it's really something else. The performer at the end of a great performance is washed by a tide of anonymous admiration, and moved, he cries out, "I love you all!" But the emotion he experiences is different. Its cognitive content might be something like, "I never feel more myself and at one with myself than when I am on stage and the audience is with me." It is the feeling of wholeness, of the unitary functioning of his entire being within the compass of his talent.[4] He is able to feel this because the audience is reflecting it back to him. He sees himself through their eyes and is pleased with what he sees. Alone, he is uncertain, self-critical and moody. He cannot accurately gauge his true capacity. One day he sees himself as great, the next day as mediocre. The audience response verifies his deepest wish and assuages his greatest fear. They tell him that he is who he hopes he is, but fears he is not, a star.

If the audience disapproves, the failure is felt not as just that of a day's efforts. It is a calamity. The disapproval precipitates a violent fragmentation of the childhood Self. Criticism of his creative efforts is criticism of his very being. When next he performs, it will be in search of the almost mystical union with the audience that will reconstellate the Self and enable him to sense once again its presence.

This pattern is nowhere more typical for the Puer than in the performing arts, which is why, I believe, these have become so attractive today, and also why the focus of modern performances has shifted so dramatically away from the quality of the performance and toward the personality of the performer. As I will elaborate in the second part of this chapter, the rise of the Puer and the progressive evolution of a cult of personality parallel a decline in the quality of culture.

Puers frequently appear to be dominated by an urgent *will to power*. But their need to control others is only symptomatic. What the Puer is actually trying to control is his own radically unstable sense of self-worth. His control over others does not matter per se—others barely exist for him anyway; it is rather his control of his identity, via others' admiration, that matters. When his companion fails to provide the needed reflection of the childhood Self, the Puer's warmth, charm and romantic expansiveness give way to coldness. But neither the warmth nor the coldness is truly directed at the other person. The warmth is rather an expression of contentment when the childhood Self is constellated; the coldness is the absence of a relation to himself when the Self fragments. The Puer turns cold suddenly and unexpectedly in response to what appears a trifle, because he reacts not objectively (consensually) to the other person, but to highly unstable inner states that are invisible to all but the most empathic partner.

Narcissus and his reflection are what many Puer dyads consist of. As a Puer may equally seek out a relationship in which he is the admirer, a dyadic relationship between two persons with complementary needs may become a means to stave off individual internal instability. The audience may serve a certain function for the performer's inner life, but the performer serves a reciprocal function for the audience.

Accompanying the constellation of the childhood Self is a great inner pressure to live up to its demands. In a gifted individual, these demands may on occasion come close to being met, and the pressure reduced, by concrete achievement. Such an individual will therefore seek out situations in which to be admired. For individuals who perceive themselves as more moderately gifted, the pressure from the Self is intolerable. The solution is then to be chosen as the special partner of someone idealized—the human partner of the divine twinship, the master's disciple, the star's fan, the normal hero-worship of adolescence.

Summary

Here, then, is a capsule description of the Self in the Puer.

1. The Self in its primordial—that is to say childhood—form is associated with certain typical states of emotions. These are best described in the psychoanalytic literature on narcissism and in the most integrated fashion by Kohut (1971, 1977).[5] They are characterized subjectively by a sense of: specialness; grandeur; omniscience; omnipotence; perfect self-fulfillment of need.
   Regression to this emotional state is a typical feature of adult existence as well, adaptive and normal in some circumstances, pathological in others. The exaltation that follows successful execution of a creative act is a prime instance of the normal arousal in an adult of this archaic emotional state.
2. The child in whom the Self is constellated or the adult who has not yet learned to inhibit or modify (in the light of reality) the impulses to which these emotions give rise not only feels special, grand, and powerful, but *acts* in accordance with these feelings, in a way that others perceive objectively as: self-centered; grandiose; all-knowing; authoritarian; self-satisfied.
3. The Self in the child or in the narcissistic personality—the eternal adolescent—is fragile. In shattering, this larger-than-life imago gives way to feelings of: envy; worthlessness; stupidity; frustrated rage; emptiness. These are the opposites of each of the feeling states associated with the intact, constellated Self.
4. Although frequently triggered by external, "narcissistically wounding" events, the sudden shift from the all-good feeling states associated with the constellated Self to the all-bad states associated with the shattered Self is a dynamism implicit to the psyche; the impossi-

ble expectations engendered by the constellated Self, in their failure to be met, themselves usher in the dreaded shattering. Specific external circumstances and the actions or reactions of others are the efficient causes but are not the source of this central dynamism. Although pairs of fundamental "opposites" play a large role in Jung's theory of innate archetypes (1954), the specific opposing archaic emotional states of the Self are best described in the Kleinian and object-relations literature (Kernberg 1975, 1976; Klein 1928, 1946; Volkan 1976). Their origin, however, is attributed more to the vicissitudes of nurture than to nature.

5. The constellated Self and shattered Self are intimately linked. Thus, although the Self in its unified form is a source of pleasure, it is also a source of dread. Narcissistic elation and narcissistic depression condition one another and are at root inseparable.
6. The Self, constellated and shattered, like other wished-for but feared contents of the unconscious, is commonly dealt with by projection. In projection it can be at once experienced and held at bay.
7. The Self is the center of initiative. More than the sum of an individual's learned reactions and adaptations, it is that which conceives and initiates wholly new thoughts and actions. It is the wellspring of individual uniqueness and creativity, the daimon or genius in the classical sense.
8. The most common attributes of the deity, especially of the child-god, as characterized by religious thought and mythology, correspond to the fundamental emotional states of the Self. The all-good emotions associated with the sense of specialness and omnipotence are features of the good god; their antitheses, envy and frustrated rage, of the evil one. With regard to the relation of personal selfhood to creativity, Coleridge said: "Imagination I hold to be a repetition in the finite mind of the eternal act of creation in the infinite I AM" (1817). Although comparisons of the self to the child-god appear in Kohut (1971), the Jungian literature presents the most extensive survey of the motif.

THE MIRROR OF FAUST

It is a commonplace of our self-seeking time to treat the establishment of a coherent sense of Self and of a stable identity as a quest. Selfhood and identity are seen as desirable attributes, and one must overcome obstacles in order to achieve them. A somewhat more sophisticated view is that the obstacles are internal and that the "quest" is rather more subtle and complicated than overcoming external obstacles.

Yet even this view is too romantic, for the basic difficulty in the achievement of selfhood lies in the fundamental ambivalence to which little more than lip service is generally paid. That the Self, on an abstract level of description, has both a dark and a light side means that on the level of immediate experience the emotions it engenders are both pleasurable and painful, at heart simultaneously. Selfhood is both desired and feared, though we rarely allow ourselves to acknowledge that we are not of one mind in our narcissistic quest. The so-called obstacles to the achievement of our desire are inseparable from the desire itself, as Narcissus painfully learned.

The root conflict to which Self gives rise is this: How does one seek and fulfill one's own unique capacity for character and self-expression without falling prey to narcissistic inflation and depression (that is, to hubris or despair)? How can an individual be unique and special, yet realistic within his limitations (including his fearsome mortality), and therefore related to others?

There is no arena in which this conflict becomes more acute than that of creative work. The creative individual is always caught between his true capacity for expression, on the one hand, and his narcissistic need to define himself as creative on the other. This need brings with it the fear that he is not creative; together, the need and fear engender those morbidly fascinating distortions of love and work that both characterize the eternal adolescent and fuel a romantic idealization of him (See Hillman 1982).

Indeed, the achievement of a stable identity is a lifelong quest, and many of man's grandest cultural efforts can be seen as directed toward this achievement. I do not believe that this perspective trivializes art by turning it into therapy. Remember Melville's (1851) observation that the "tormenting mild image" of Narcissus' self is "the key to it all." As the Neoplatonists first suggested, elevating the story of Narcissus to a grand allegory of the self-knowing mind exposes this central, narcissistic problem of human nature as the locus at which the creative impulse intersects with religion.

The Dilemma

Another way of stating the problem is this: Man's reach exceeds his grasp. He is possessed by an insatiable yearning that drives him onward. The goal of this yearning changes with the changing seasons of life, but each incarnation of the goal has in common with its predecessor that it is finally both ineffable and unattainable.

It may be, as Ferenczi (1913) was the first to propose, that all of man's higher questings—his drives toward physical, mental, or spiritual perfection—are symbolic. Therefore, they are hopeless, even though at times noble, expressions of our yearning for a dimly recalled state of perfection forever lost at birth. To this compelling but unsettling explanation there is a sophisticated teleological response—rationally pious, one might say—namely, that the reduction of man's adventurousness to nostalgia only reveals the clever means by which some higher spirit animates an otherwise mechanical organism and drives it to its goal.

But this response begs the question, "Whence come these putative goals?" About the idea of a goal-directed self, Arnold Richards reported Jacob Arlow as commenting (archly, one assumes), "Is it part of a divine scheme, the hand of the Lord moving in biology?"

At this point the dialectic breaks. The faithful feel called to arms; the skeptics simply feel embarrassed. This great question of goal-directedness in biological systems (or of spirit-directed will in human ones) need not be answered here. The fact remains that the drive toward the impossible is an observable condition of human nature, informing the impulse to create even those very theories which aim to prove that the impulse is reducible to mere molecular mechanics. In pushing a limited human being to strive beyond his limits, the Self, whatever its origin, is itself a source of conflict. This conflict may or may not be the ingenious instrument of some higher will. In any event, the attempt to satisfy the demands of the Self and thus solve the dilemma of selfhood has yielded much that is great in culture—and in psychopathology.

The Creative Individual

The truly gifted, creative individual, by virtue of his gifts, is at greater risk of developing narcissistic disturbances in his career and in his relationships than is the more modestly gifted individual.

The definitive adult self-image is a kind of compromise between the grandeur of the divine child and implacable reality. For the omnipotent childhood self, fulfillment of need is absolute and coextensive with the wish itself; for the adult, it is the mere consequence of work and thus frustratingly limited. But the highly gifted individual comes closer, in proportion to his gift, to fulfilling the conditions of the childhood self. His adult self-image more closely approximates the divine child and therefore remains both larger and more fragile than the norm. He lacks the capacity to accept his actual limited self.

Consider Mozart: he heard, he wished to play, and he played. By his own account the process of composition was truly, as Coleridge put it, "a repetition in the finite mind of the eternal act of creation in the infinite I AM" (Hutchings 1976, but see also Peter Shaffer's play *Amadeus*). In the world of music, he was the consummate genius, in the world at large, an ineffectual child.

Thus, the self-image of the gifted individual becomes inextricably entangled with the divine child. As a result of his gift, the dilemma of the Self becomes in him especially acute, and in its poignant clarity paradigmatic for us all.

The genius will seek at times to be the divine child (with far greater success than most); at times he will project it onto his mates (with greater intensity of need), who thereby become his muses. But in any event, his art becomes the arena in which he gives expression to his struggle; his admirers witness and reverberate with this struggle.

Direct and complete identification with the Self in its primordial form as the divine child leads to an impossible and ultimately psychotic existence (Satinover 1985). If the image is denied entirely, however, existence remains rational but impoverished and barren. Projection as a compromise, except in certain controlled circumstances (e.g., in performance and rituals), leads to unrealistic and unstable human relationships. How, then, may the Self be borne?

Religion

I believe that the great traditional solution to the dilemma of the Self is religion. I think that Freud (1927) was correct in asserting that at the heart of religion lies a kind of delusion. That people fashion their explicit images of God after their own parents is undeniable. The conclusion appears to follow that religious belief is, therefore, a kind of benign neurosis by which childish wishes for dependency are kept alive.

But Jung, other psychologists, and philosophers such as Ludwig Binswanger (1963) and Suzanne Langer (1965), were convinced—as Freud was not—that religious yearning is a human need (or capacity) analogous to, yet distinct from and therefore not solely derivative of, nostalgia for one's parents. Accordingly, Jung proceeded to reverse Freud's conclusion, asserting that the image of God (i.e., the "Self") exists a priori and is the true reality upon which is based (via projection, not simply subjective experience) our illusory ideas about our parents (e.g., as perfect or all powerful). In Jung's view the Self thereby becomes a kind of sophisticated psychological euphemism for God (and is generally treated as such in the Jungian movement).

As I see it, the truth lies somewhere in between. I do believe that the images of God and the patterns of religious myth and ritual, especially in organized—or "exoteric"—religion, reveal a displaced continuing fascination with one's parents; in a loose manner of speaking, these images and patterns express and channel oedipal conflicts and resolutions. But the *deeper* function of religion, as is more evident at each religion's mystical—or "esoteric"—core, relates to the Self. The exoteric form of the deity is colored by memories of the parents, but the ineffable esoteric divinity whom we imagine behind this form is, I believe, a projection of the Self onto a metaphysical screen.

I do not believe that, as Jung would have it (1917), the projection occurs because, a priori, things that have not yet become conscious are experienced first in projection. Rather, the projection occurs because the Self generates an intolerable conflict. The child, living an existence of relatively unfettered imagination and play, is, so to speak, the child god; the adult, confronting reality, must put away his childhood Self. Splitting off and consequent projection of the Self resolve this conflict between one's childhood and one's maturity.

When, as a solution to conflict, the Self is projected onto some object in the human realm (e.g., one's own person, another, or a human institution), this is a poor situation that rapidly fails. When the Self can be projected onto a metaphysical realm, however, and an unchallengeable compromise is thereby struck between acceptance and repudiation of the Self, human relations are preserved, and one may be freed from the Scylla and Charybdis of narcissistic inflation and depression. Creative initiative is in turn preserved by the attribution of that initiative to a Creator. A person may then remain an instrument of the Creator's will without suffering an inflation of human dimensions.

The price paid for the religious solution to narcissistic conflict is a degree of irrationality. This irrationality presents few problems so long as one's religious beliefs remain restricted to realms where reason cannot, or has yet to, reach. But when irrational, metaphysical claims begin to be made on the axioms of science, in the conduct of personal relations, or on the governance of state, as seems inevitable, then no matter how benign the initial claims, fanaticism is sure to follow.

Strictly speaking, then, religion is not a neurosis. Rather, if one accepts that the Self and the conflicts it engenders arise in the earliest, preoedipal (prephallic) phases of life, then one can think of religion as a kind of necessary psychosis. It becomes dangerously psychotic only when its visionary, symbolic characterizations of subjective reality are applied to objective reality. The corollary to this is that in general, mysticism, religious imagery, and the occult play a strikingly larger role in the fantasy life of narcissistic, borderline, and psychotic individuals (loosely: those with predominantly preoedipal personality organization) than among neurotics, for whom the great objects of (oedipal) concern are the parents.

Religion and Art

Via a common projective identification, I believe that the shared God-image that characterizes a culture over many centuries serves to bind, collectively, the otherwise intolerable conflict of the Self in each member of that culture. The striking prominence, from early history to the present, of various forms of dismembered and resurrecting gods (Frazer 1890) is evidence of the universality of narcissistic inflation and depression.

I have suggested that the creative individual suffers most acutely the narcissistic conflict engendered by the Self. This conflict is, therefore, a common motif in artistic work. Thus, during those ages when religious belief was vital, religion was the natural subject to which the artist turned. His oeuvre became the vehicle wherein he worked out the conflict both for himself and for his public. In the great art of the West, this has most commonly taken the form of representations of the life and passion of Christ. In addition, profound religious belief not only determines creative content but shapes the personality of the creator, controlling the fires that the creative identity specifically fuels. If one stands back and takes a long view of the development of art in the West, a reciprocal relation between religion and the artistic self emerges.

Before the end of the first millenium, the general world-view was theocentric. The artist was not the creator, only God could create; individuals were the humble instruments of His expression. Artists of that time probably conceived of their work in a way very different from today's artists. Consider the great cathedrals of Europe or the illuminated manuscripts.

The cathedrals reflected the effort of innumerable masons and stonecutters and in some instances were erected over three generations. The manuscripts were anonymous, sometimes the result of one man's efforts, but commonly the work of many. The beauty of this kind of creation eludes today's grasp, for it requires an attitude as inaccessible to modern man as would have been to medieval man the technology, or desire, that yields a photocopy or a skyscraper.

This attitude results from the deeply held belief that one's creative efforts are not truly one's own, but are rather the manifestations of the animating spirit of a Creator passing through one. With such an attitude it becomes possible to work with painstaking craftsmanship and in complete anonymity on a project the completion of which is not likely to occur in one's lifetime. Indeed, in this frame of mind, would it not be hubris to concern oneself with completing the work of God, let alone with stamping one's own signature on it?

Religion, as the projection of the Self onto a collectively shared God-image, diverted the narcissism of creative medieval man into channels of expression no longer available to us today. Narcissistic inflation and depression were experienced privately by the individual, in prayer and meditation, as nearness to or distance from God, and communally, in ritual, as the death and resurrection of Christ in the cycle of the year. Nature was not a metaphor for the inner self, as it has become for us (Leishman and Spencer 1968); rather, nature here below was both the creation and mirror of the spirit above.

Somewhere around the year 1000 A.D., the beginning of Faustian Culture [in Spengler's term (1932)], all of this began to change. In some quarters at least, religion began to give way to a fascination with alchemy and magic (i.e., to a belief that one need not suffer one's conditions, one could alter them) and there arose, correspondingly and slowly, the cult of personality. The locus of creativity shifted subtly from God the Creator to creative man.

In the course of the Renaissance, these germinal motifs reached full flower. The true man of the Renaissance was. . . . the Renaissance Man. The popular books of the time recounted miraculous stories about the prognostic signs of precocity and genius (Cicero, Pausanias, Pliny, de Voragine), and the great men seemed much concerned with demonstrating that they were just that. Even—or perhaps more accurately, in particular—Leonardo fell prey to this pressure, constructing a pseudo-memory that duplicated the form of one of these miraculous stories that, in infancy, predict future genius (Schapiro 1968).

During this time the dying and resurrecting God moved somewhat into the background as a romance of the classical past, and Neoplatonic theories about the mystic nature of the Self came to the fore (Kristeller, 1964).

In short, the medieval projection of the Self onto a God-image began to break down. Outstanding individuals, no longer anonymous, began to carry that projection instead, both for others and, more dangerously, for themselves. Eventually, in "The Marriage of Heaven and Hell," Blake (1793) would say, "The worship of God is: honouring his gifts in other men, each according to his genius, and loving the greatest men best. Those who envy or calumniate great men hate God, for there is no other God." Would it have been impertinent to ask of this great man where in his firmament of worship he placed himself?

An equally important component of this shift in attitude was the growth of scientific reason. As Francis Yates (1964, 1966) and other scholars of the Renaissance have argued, modern scientific thought was a direct outgrowth of Renaissance alchemy, magic, and Neoplatonic philosophy. The great success of science made a return to theogonic conceptions increasingly difficult. So long as the physical world remained entirely mysterious, a pious imagination could shape it into mythic forms both conducive to and a result of the projection of the Self. Thus, the Ptolemaic solar system mirrored medieval conceptions of the soul's layered, concentric depths in a way refuted by the Copernican structure.

Although scientific discovery has never really laid claim to metaphysical territory (indeed, cannot, as Kant argued in 1781), the psychological effect of its success has been as profound as if it had. As, step by step, the structure of the physical world was revealed to be independent of theologic conceptions of divine form, belief in those forms—a belief rooted in unconscious projection—waned. By undermining this projection, the growth of science directly solidified the cult of the individual.

The Enlightenment as the apotheosis of Western reason is frequently contrasted with Romanticism as a reaction against it. I understand the relationship between the two movements differently. Romanticism is rather the mate of Reason in just the way that Renaissance Neoplatonic theories of the semidivine Self complemented the rise of magic and early science in supporting a world-view with the individual at its center.

If the year 1000 represents the stone of individualism dropped into the still, anonymous waters of the medieval communal world-view, Renaissance Neoplatonism and magic represent the first, and the Enlightenment and Romanticism the second, of a set of waves widening over the centuries to encompass an ever larger circle of individual points of view and diffracting an originally theocentric attitude toward the thorough and unreflected deification of the Self. The hallmark of this attitude is not simply the emergence of the "great individual," but rather the emergence of the Faustian individual: at times great, but always concerned about being so. With Romanticism, this Renaissance concern became yet more widespread, epitomized in the apotheosis of the artist/poet/genius.

The mobilization of science, the third wave, destined in the modern era to become a massive assault, and the concomitant spread of literacy via the ever swifter reproduction of the written word, brought the revolution of selfhood to a vastly wider circle of individuals than was even remotely possible in the Renaissance. Although most of these new individualists clung consciously to a religious view of life whose origin lay at least fifteen hundred years in the past, the foundations of unknowing upon which rested this highly projective view of things had been unconsciously destroyed.

To summarize: religion was a solution to the problem of narcissistic inflation and depression. A relatively modest degree of rational, scientific understanding allowed for belief in an hypostasized metaphysical realm and for the communal projection of the individual Self onto a shared God-image. Faustian Culture—from the early Renaissance through Romanticism to the present age of psychology—has been characterized by parallel and mutually enhancing alterations in our understanding of both the inner and outer worlds. The subjective perception of the locus of autonomous creativity and initiative has shifted from God to the Self, and concomitantly, the outer world has grown increasingly subject to manipulation. The actual capacity for world creation and destruction has accordingly shifted from God to man.

Narcissistic inflation and depression, no longer effectively bound by an irrational belief in a dying and resurrecting God, thus have correspondingly become psychological obstructions to the capacity for love, work, and self-acceptance, while the dying and resurrecting, eternally youthful God has become a mere symbol of this problem.

The Faustian Pact

Since creative expression is the activity wherein both the autonomy and exaltation of the Self are most powerfully evoked, in a religious era religion is a natural subject of art as well as a form of general cultural expression.

With the breakdown of religion as a vehicle for the channeling of the Self and its associated dilemmas, these dilemmas, and the individual Self, become the new subjects. More specifically, the individual Self of the creator (which is often to say, his sense of self-importance) has become the subject of so much current work that craftsmanship and excellence may be wholly displaced, either because these are considered unnecessary and are ignored, or because attention is deliberately or unwittingly, often subtly, drawn toward the person of the creator (i.e., his cleverness) and away from the creation. (See the works of Norman Mailer in literature, the performances of Keith Jarret in music, the plethora of gurus in religion, etc.)

As Spengler proposed in *The Decline of the West* (1922), the story of Faust may be thought of as a great anti-myth of the West, not only for the Germanic peoples. The tragedy of a great culture (or individual) self-consciously pursuing greatness is paradigmatic for our time, and for us, the individuals who characterize it. The Faustian urge, today seen everywhere, is nowhere revealed more clearly than in the displacement of creative achievement by the personality of the creator.

Faust forsook salvation in pursuit of personal omniscience and grandeur. Ironically, the self-image he thereby sought to instate is that of the eternally youthful God he had forsaken. As a definition of the human Self, the divine Self becomes demonic: the very transformation from light into dark that, via hubris, Faust's mentor Lucifer has himself undergone.

The mythopoeic imagination of an era when the Self was still susceptible of projection onto a metaphysical realm conceived of the conflation of the limited human personality with the image of the divine, eternal child—a conflation supported by the growth of scientific knowledge—in the myth of Faust. In our era, therefore, it is the artist in particular [as Mann (1947) represented in his *Doktor Faustus*] or, more generally, the individual in pursuit of creative achievement, who enacts the narcissistic tragedy of Faust. As the Self is elevated to replace the absent God-image, culture declines into a mere advertisement for that inflated and fragile Self.

CONCLUSION

I do not know if I can do more than point to what seems to me a great dilemma of our time. I have no answers to propose, not even partial ones. I do not find satisfying any of the great twentieth-century secular superstitions—the worship of the state, of science, or of the psyche—and I find a return to the traditional projective formulations of an earlier age neither desirable nor, to an honest intelligence, possible. Nonetheless, it does seem to me that an unflinching examination of the conflict between our wishes and our limitations is possible. Perhaps out of that examination will arise some as yet unimagined synthesis that will carry us safely past the difficult end of this millenium.

NOTES

1. As a clinical description, it will be easy to think of this personality type as a (variant of a psychopathologic) disease entity, the "Narcissistic Character Disorder" (DSM III). But I think that in its acceptance of a "rigorous" modern descriptive nosology, psychiatry goes too far in reifying mere conveniences. It is incorrect to conceive of personality as fitting in a very useful way into nosologic boxes. Rather, there are narcissistic strains in every personality, indeed, at the very heart of personality per se, and therefore at the heart of each of us. These strains have always revealed themselves to a discerning eye, and to point at them is to point to the human condition. The important concerns ought rather to be, "In what form does this selfish strain show itself in an individual?" and "Does this form serve society or subvert it?" Nonetheless, because it is easier to grasp the concept of the *Puer Aeternus* if we think of him as a type, I shall describe him as if he exemplified a syndrome.

2. I use the masculine term Puer (vs. Puella) and the masculine pronoun, because Puer traits are more pronounced in men.

3. This concept differs from psychoanalytic conceptions of early grandiosity, omnipotence and omniscience in presuming an innate basis, and hence maturational requirement, for this early mental state. I do not see childhood grandiosity as a derivative of the experience of maternal need-gratification, but as part of what the child brings to the mother-child unit. The constellation of the Self can be thought of as biologically timed, though profoundly affected by the specifics of the environment. Its appearance drives the child into separation from the matrix of infancy, just as biological changes in puberty drive the adolescent from the family matrix.

4. This experience is a component of mature, object-related love as well and is a necessary part of all long-standing relationships, in much the same way that

the childhood Self remains at the core of trust and belief in oneself and one's goals. But just as the Self in the adult is modified by reality, so too, in adult love is the role of mutual admiration balanced by a deep respect for one's partner's worthiness in the face of recognized differences and limitations.

5. A remark in passing: the psychology of mystical practice is at heart a paradigm for narcissistic conflict. Mysticism can be thought of as aiming, under rigidly controlled circumstances, at a complete withdrawal of any projection of the Self, and via the ego's resulting "union with god," achieving the most direct solution to the problem. It is therefore fraught with all those dangers of narcissistic inflation and depression, but in psychotic proportion, that are now apparently a culture-wide phenomenon. Thus on the one hand, there are such statements of the great mystics as "I am god" (*Angelus Silesius:* Flitch 1932), and on the other, there is a frequency of religious delusion, including identification with God, among psychotics.

REFERENCES

Binswanger, L. (1926). Freud's conception of man in the light of anthropology. *Being in the World.* New York: Basic Books, 1963, 147–181.

Blake, W. (1793). A memorable fancy (plate 23). *The Marriage of Heaven and Hell. The Poetry and Prose of William Blake,* P. Erdman, ed. New York: Doubleday and Company, 1965.

Cicero. On Divination. *Loeb Library,* 1:xxxvi. Cambridge: Harvard University Press, 1927.

Coleridge, S. T. (1817). Biographia Litteraria. *Norton Anthology of English Literature.* New York: W. W. Norton, 1981.

Edinger, E. (1972). *Ego and Archetype.* New York: Putnam.

Freud, S. (1914). On Narcissism: An Introduction, *Standard Edition of the Complete Psychological Works of Sigmund Freud,* London: The Hogarth Press and the Institute of Psychoanalysis, 1964, vol. 14, 73–102.

Freud, S. (1927). The Future of An Illusion. *Standard Edition,* vol. 21, 5–56.

Ferenczi, S. (1913). Stages in the development of the sense of reality. *Sex in Psychoanalysis*. New York: Basic Books, 1950, 213–239.

Flitch, Jr. (1932). *Angelus Silesius: Selections from the Cherubinic Wanderer*. London: Cross and Watkins.

Frazer, J. G. (1890). *The Golden Bough: A Study in Comparative Religion*. London: Macmillan, two volumes.

Hartmann, H. (1950). Comments on the psychoanalytic theory of the ego. *The Psychoanalytic Study of the Child,* 5: 74–96.

Hutchings, A. (1976). *Mozart: The Man, The Musician*. London: Thames and Hudson.

Jung, Carl G. (1917). On the Psychology of the Unconscious. *The Collected Works of C. G. Jung,* Princeton: Princeton University Press, vol. 7, 3–122.

Jung, C. G. (1923). *Psychological Types. Collected Works,* vol. 6, 460–461.

Jung, C. G. (1951). The Psychology of the Child Archetype. *The Archetypes and the Collective Unconscious. Collected Works,* vol. 9, Part 1, 160–220.

Jung, C. G. (1954). Archetypes of the Collective Unconscious. *The Archetypes and the Collective Unconsicous*. Collected Works, vol. 9, Part 1, 3–141.

Kant, I. (1781). *Critique of Pure Reason*. New York: Doubleday, 1966.

Kernberg, O. (1975). *Borderline Conditions and Pathological Narcissism*. New York: Jason Aronson.

Kernberg, O. (1976). *Object-Relations Theory and Clinical Psychoanalysis*. New York: Jason Aronson.

Klein, M. (1928). Early stages of the oedipus conflict. *International Journal of Psychoanalysis,* 9:167–180.

Klein, M. (1946). Notes on some schizoid mechanisms. *International Journal of Psychoanalysis,* 27: 100.

Kohut, H. (1971). *The Analysis of the Self.* New York: International Universities Press.

Kohut,H. (1977). *The Restoration of the Self.* New York: International Universities Press.

Kristeller, P. (1964). *The Philosophy of Marsilio Ficino*. Gloucester, Massachussetts: Peter Smith.

Langer, S. (1965). *Philosophy in a New Key*. New York: Dover.

Lasch, C. (1979). *The Culture of Narcissism*. New York: W. W. Norton.

Leishman, J. B. and Spender, S. (1968). Introduction to *Duino Elegies,* by R. M. Rilke. London: Hogarth.

Lorenz, K. (1963). *On Aggression*. New York: Harcourt, Brace & World.

Mahler, M., Pine, F. and Bergman, A. (1975). *The Psychological Birth of the Human Infant.* New York: Basic Books.

Mann, T. (1947). *Doktor Faustus.* Stockholm: Bermann-Fischer Verlag.

Meissner, W. W. (1984). *Psychoanalysis and Religious Experience.* New Haven: Yale University Press.

Melville, H. (1851). *Moby Dick or, the Whale.* New York: Bobbs-Merrill, 1964.

Richards, A. (1982). The superordinate self in psychoanalytic theory and the self psychologies. *Journal of the American Psychoanalytic Association,* 30: 948.

Satinover, J. (1985). At the mercy of another: abandonment and restitution in psychosis and psychotic character. *Chiron, 1985.*

Schapiro, M. (1968). Leonardo and Freud: An art-historical study. *Renaissance Essays.* New York: Columbia University Press.

Spengler, O. (1932). Perspectives of World History. *Decline of the West,* vol. 2. New York: Alfred Knopf.

Volkan, V. (1976). *Primitive Internalized Object-Relations.* New York: International Universities Press; 57, 58.

Von Franz, M. L. (1970). *Puer Aeternus.* Zurich: Spring Publications.

Yates, F. (1964). *Giordano Bruno and the Hermetic Tradition.* London: Routledge & Kegan Paul.

Yates, F. (1966). *The Art of Memory.* London: Routledge & Kegan Paul.

CHAPTER 3
THE DEAD SELF IN BORDERLINE PERSONALITY DISORDERS

NATHAN SCHWARTZ-SALANT

INTRODUCTION

Everyone knows borderline personalities. The term *borderline* has become a buzz word. In clinical consultations of one therapist to another, the mention of the word brings a knowing grimace acknowledging how difficult "they", that is, borderline patients, are. Psychotherapists commiserate with one another over this "difficult patient." It is true that the borderline personality disorder creates exceptional problems in psychotherapy, not the least of which are intense negative reactions in the therapist, which may explain why therapists console one another over borderlines.

It would be useful to have a profile that would help to identify this personality structure, but to do so poses certain difficulties. It may be helpful to contrast this structure with the narcissistic character disorder, a much easier one to describe. By noting the narcissist's extreme self-absorption, poor empathy with others, grave inability to accept criticism, grandiosity and exhibitionistic needs, and other important features (Schwartz-Salant 1982, pp. 37f.), one can recognize him without great difficulty. The borderline disorder is more problematic to describe.

It has been suggested that idealization plays a crucial role in the formation of the narcissistic character (Masterson 1981, p. 13). Such a person has been the target of extremely lofty ideals and grandiosity from one or both parents. Through largely unconscious communications the child is given the "charge" to fulfill these unlived drives that actually are archaic forms of his parent's own failures in individuation. Being treated as if "he is the greatest" could alone create difficulties for a child who is, at the least, made to overachieve. But the matter is far worse. The narcissistic personality has also been simultaneously given a completely contradictory message that comes from the parental unconscious, the communication of envy: "You are wonderful and I hate you for it. You have it all and I despise you, for I don't have it" (*It* refers to the idealized qualities that are more consciously espoused). Consequently, the narcissistic character forms by using the idealization he has received to adapt to those values and to create an inner and outer barrier against the attack of envy. Called the narcissistic defense, this barrier makes for an oddly inpenetrable personality. Tragically, the possibly positive use of idealization is largely drained into defensive purposes, and the narcissistic character rarely achieves his highest potential. He becomes a "Jack of all trades and a master of none." Often this is the best of outcomes; usually the person with a narcissistic character doesn't approach what everyone expected from him and ultimately shows himself to be very mediocre. He tends to age badly, clinging to a past that all too clearly reveals its shallowness.

The borderline personality disorder does not have the cohesiveness and defensive capacity of the narcissistic character. His development is often said to have been characterized by environmental support for clinging and dependency, while his separation-individuation attempts met with withdrawal of maternal love and concern. The narcissistic character has also generally experienced withdrawal, but for the borderline personality it has often been more overt and extreme, and idealization has never been employed to any advantage. The mixture of envy and idealization seems to combine in the development of the narcissistic character to form a self that is fused with unconscious processes and especially scornful of eros and relatedness. It is difficult to know if this inner fusion state is a blessing or a curse, but in any event the borderline individual has little of its stability.

The borderline personality employs idealization solely to hide extremely negative qualities of himself and others. This so-called splitting defense is very unstable. The borderline personality is more unstable than the narcissistic character, who can employ idealization to control others, demanding to be idealized or forming a relatively stable idealized relationship to others. Instead, an idealization is offered at one time, and soon after it changes to the total opposite, feelings of abandonment and persecution.

(The shifts can be rapid, changing several times or more within an hour when the person is in an acute stage of distress.)

The narcissistic character is adapted, smooth, seductive, and socially adroit. The borderline character is the opposite, an outsider. He does not fit in. Life is like a continual game in which one wonders how bad "it" will be this time; "it" can be a simple encounter with friends, a new experience, an exam, nearly anything. Everyone else seems to fit in, to know "the rules", yet he can only gamble and hope that his awkward efforts will go unnoticed.

The narcissistic character can be said to be someone who, far too early in life, was called upon to become his potential, what he could be. He was valued for his innate talents and what these could produce, not for his actual being. His being, in fact, was hated through the devastating mechanism of envy. He became stuck in an incessant drive toward doing, a grandiose, driven life punctuated only by bouts of depression and regression (Kohut 1971, p. 97), that overtake him when his grandiose image is punctured by someone's emotional attack or simply by another's honesty about his realistic limitations. He often will quickly recover from these attacks.

The borderline personality can rarely press his potential into any coherent form, not even into the pale copies of "special" form that the narcissistic character can produce. The affects that temporarily enfeeble the narcissistic character seem to attack furiously the borderline's creativity. It would appear that he lives so close to persecutory energy-fields that he is left chronically open to psychic dismemberment. For those familiar with Egyptian mythology (Rundle Clark 1959) it is difficult not to think of Osiris' eternal struggle with the Devil, Seth. If the borderline personality has sufficient support systems, like an Isis to Osiris, he can often achieve depths not known to the narcissistic character. But if such depths are even marginally achieved, it is often a result of terrible suffering, not the least of which are somatizations in which organs are devoured so that the mind can marginally function. The better the quality of the mind, the more tormenting the suffering.

The narcissistic character uses people until he gets what he needs and then discards them like toilet paper, often taking several years to do so. The borderline personality goes through a far more rapid sequence. One day he represents everything as marvelous and one is treated as a fine, helpful and most supportive person. The next day, one may encounter the borderline individual in his "bad" state; the air feels tense; it is hard to breath; one tends to feel insecure. One may talk a lot, or else feel that it's hard to say anything. It isn't that one feels controlled, as with the narcissistic character, for there, if one recognizes what is happening it is possible just to settle in and wait for an opening to talk. Not so with the borderline. Instead one feels driven to do something, and if we look carefully, that act is generally to survive with a sense of identify. One may feel that he knows everything, or that he has an overall understanding of the situation. Yet one experiences these responses in a strange way: one feels mechanical, somewhat manic and compulsive, and very cut off from his bodily feelings. The tendency to know everything also happens with the narcissistic character, but there it can be a pleasant, high feeling. The person's idealization can affect one until he does actually know things he did not previously know, much as one can know things with an hallucinogenic drug. Such rarely is the case with the borderline personality. Instead, one tends to become inflated, inwardly God-like; all of this is designed to get rid of the person, to somehow undo one's awful feelings. From being very nice and helpful to him yesterday, one has suddenly, in his eyes, become quite awful today. And from experiencing a patient who yesterday could develop, the therapist is now faced with someone he dislikes and whose suitability for analysis he questions. At times like this he tends to think in terms of diagnosis and prognosis. When things are going well, that is when he allows himself to be duped by a seemingly positive relationship, he instead tends to muse about the inadequacy of diagnostics, about how his patient has qualities of spirit and courage that transcend the scientific reductionism of psychiatry.

In a sense it would be nice if things were just that unconsciously driven, flipping back and forth between opposites. Then borderline phenomenology could be grasped through some mechanistic theory. But such is not the case. Generally, if the therapist does not mistakenly attempt to protect himself by using developmental theories he will be often confused. For example, amidst the emotional assaults he may feel—intense experiences that may result in a temporary loss of his sense of identity, wholeness and eros—he also may tend to feel that the borderline person ("Who is borderline now?" is a question!) knows something. At first experienced as a vague uneasiness, this feeling makes him think he did err or somehow do harm. The patient may be totally unable to verbalize this, instead assaulting the therapist with an unpleasant energy field. The therapist becomes subject to the patient's scanning, a kind of imaginal sight that is peculiarly discomforting. His sight is like the Negative Eye Goddess (Rundle Clark

1959, p. 90f.) in ancient Egypt, who roamed the waters before creation, destroying everything she saw. The vision one becomes subject to is the patient's only hope for survival, a tool with which, if he believed himself, he could see the parts of one that actually mean him harm. The therapist wants to get away. Everyone wants to get away from borderlines, except when the person is in his "good" state. Then he can be very attractive, like a magnet, a resource, a mine of creativity. Not uncommonly, he aids many people in remarkable ways and can do nothing for himself. When he isn't feeling persecuted and persecuting, he can be charismatic, inventive, a link to the *numinosum,* the power of the gods and especially gods that the normal collective awareness has long since displaced.

To be sure, even when he is dispensing this good energy and knowledge, he may seem odd. But when he feels persecuted, and does not trust his own capacities for seeing, there will be no truly contacting him; he will seem very odd, a bit inhuman. In my notes after seeing such a patient I wrote:

> There is a strange, uncomfortable, somewhat inhuman feeling to her. It feels somewhat like having a dream with an archaic figure who speaks in stilted language from a distant century, yet carries a strong affect. She speaks to me in plain English, has definite affects, is suffering, and also seems inhuman, of a different species. Her words each carry a totality, as if each is part of a whole yet expressed in a strangely shallow manner. Alternatively, she has great depth and insight. But each moment is strained too full and also too empty. She seems an outcast, living on the fringes of the human, cast into a dark shadow of inhuman, archetypal processes and speaking through them as if she were partaking of a human dialogue. She seems a prince, a witch, a clown, a trickster. We are in a fairy tale world of abstract characters that then, quickly, turn back to flesh and blood reality. I am left feeling guilty for ever thinking otherwise.

With the narcissistic character we can often be superficial, just as long as we do not impose anything that disturbs his need to be the absolute center of attention. With the borderline character, such moments come back to haunt us. The person feels persecuted by any hint of falseness or inattention. A word or phrase can suddenly take over the session or prove to have destroyed an entire previous session that we thought was finally clarifying our analytical work, especially the nature of our interaction. It is not that we encounter a magical attitude in which a part is identified with the whole. That would be a clever way of reducing the person's behavior to pathology. Instead, the person is often being severely critical because he knows that if he allows the analyst's failures and mere slips to pass, even if these seem slight, he will only be adding to his inner demons that lie. His life seems to hang in the balance of a word.

There are times in which the borderline personality can be normal in the best sense. He can be humble, humane in caring for his and another's soul, and aware of suffering in ways that are beautiful and extremely touching. There is nothing to suggest that these characteristics are any less genuine than the others. In fact the converse may be the case. The so-called borderline personality may at times be more genuine than other "non-borderline" people, and his swings between all-goodness and all-persecutory states may be defenses against this soul-centered state, for to be this genuine has led to too much pain.

We get none of this with the narcissistic character. He is so cut off from his inner world as to make the notion of soul a totally meaningless romantic stupidity. But the soul is vulnerable, extremely sensitive to injury. The borderline individual knows the realm of soul, but he keeps it carefully hidden from view. One of the main devices used to hide it is despair.

Despair is the soul's calling card. It is what the soul presents, and if we shy away from that awful feeling of helplessness verging upon a void of hopelessness, the soul of the borderline patient quickly withdraws. The narcissistic character doesn't know what despair means. His defenses carefully screen out any traces of it. The borderline individual lives close to despair and close to a void from which death beckons as a deceptive ally. A drive toward death is always near. The borderline personality is constantly seduced towards giving in, not fighting any longer, resting. In his outer life this despair is manifest in a dreadful form. It seems that at times "anything goes." The best of situations can be thrown away overnight, as if a good start in some endeavor *must* be undermined. The person will often be as perplexed by this as anyone else. It seems that his or her first allegiance is to some inner death demon, a ghostly lover. At times some understanding of it all is focused through a belief in a past life in which some disastrous deeds were committed. The person believes he or she is suffering from this past. Such beliefs can be very serious. They may also readily fall apart when eventually recognized as exaggerated covers for early childhood fantasies. And then they return. One never knows if in some strange way they are true, used, abused, or some complex mixture.

On closer inspection, the attack we often feel in the presence of the borderline individual shows itself to be a test. We are being tested, and the strangeness of it all is that there is something to it, and something in it for us! The test is a very difficult initiatory motif, like the torture of Lucius in

Apuleius' novel *The Golden Ass* (Graves 1951). Often it takes the form of checking whether we think we have really seen the person, or if we foolishly believe that all is well because the previous analytical hour went rather smoothly. The goal of this testing often proves itself to be our greater consciousness, our awareness of parts of ourselves that we had, in narcissistic fashion, split off. The borderline individual is always forcing us into our dark alleys, and there is something important there for us as long as we do not reduce his attacks to, for example, mere defenses against fantasies of abandonment.

One of the mottoes accompanying a picture in the Rosarium Philosphorum entitled "Naked Truth" says: "He who would be initiated into this art and secret wisdom must put away the vice of arrogance, must be devout, righteous, deep-witted, humane towards his fellows, of a cheerful countenance and a happy disposition, and respectful withal. Likewise he must be an observer of the eternal secrets that are revealed to him. My son, above all I admonish thee to fear God..." (Jung 1946, para. 450) While certainly a moral statement, this is also a list of qualities that the narcissistic character fails to have. It is a litany against narcissism; the attacks we frequently feel from a borderline personality are often aimed at our narcissistically defended sectors. As long as these are intact we can create him only in our own image, thus yielding another layer of falseness that hides his despair.

The borderline state itself can be seen as a failed initiatory motif. But initiation into what and through what? Notions like initiation bring to bear the charge of delusion. But in fact, this person is showing us a door through which he and we may pass. He is stuck in its portals, in limbo between life and death, between personal experiences that are normal and strangely numinous ones that are uncanny. He is suspended in liminality. Essential for his passage is the ability to experience despair and maintain faith. But faith in what?

That again becomes a vexing issue. One can look at the borderline personality in so many different ways. The "all good" state can be seen as a defense against the "all bad" one, essentially as a defense against feeling abandoned. The locus of this devastating condition can be placed in early childhood, in so-called separation-rapprochement failures. But, it can also all be seen differently. That is another reason the borderline disorder is so hard to describe; what one believes depends upon what one sees. This sight is by no means uniform among psychotherapists. It is akin to a kind of vision of the unconscious, an insight and imaginal perception that few people can articulate in some conscious form.

The concept of the borderline personality has filled many volumes in barely twenty years. All of these describe observations of confusing behavior known for its welter of intense affects and provocation of the same in others, complicated hypotheses of inner psychic structures to account for the phenomenology, and attempts to see where things went wrong in terms of infant development. The literature is vast, mixed in terms of basic assumptions, nearly impossible for anyone to master. (It would probably be an undesirable task for anyone to attempt, for to do so means to submerge oneself in many systems of thought that will be alien to one's basic beliefs.)

From the literature on the borderline personality it would appear that we are dealing with an esoteric entity that can only be understood in terms of splitting defenses against abandonment depressions, constitutional defects or excesses of rage, massive denial defenses, incapacities for repression, fixation at primary process levels of thinking, incapacity for whole object relations or use of symbols, ruthlessness or incapacity for moral behavior, and so on. It becomes so technical and pseudo-scientific as to lose sight totally of the person suffering from the borderline condition. There is no mention of the soul of the borderline personality, nothing about the nature of his suffering, let alone of its purpose, except that of subduing his own omnipotence. That is a great battle cry of many clinicians. One wonders if such theorizing doesn't hide a secret sadism towards the patient: He deserves what he gets!

In practice, one often quickly gets intimations of a borderline personality. Although intimations are sufficient as a diagnosis, most clinicians are immediately alerted by experiencing exceedingly unpleasant sensations—edginess, defensiveness, bodily tightness, and often a desire to flee from the person as fast as possible. All of this is mixed in with a strange sense of fascination, with a wonderment about the intense affects in a person so devoid of a persona. It seems so inappropriate, yet also honest. The phenomenon is all so very human and so ugly, that it makes one wonder if this thing called borderline is not after all potentially a common structure in everyone, actualized in borderline personality disorders.

FUSION AND UNION

The difference between fusion and union is crucial for understanding borderline states. Fusion is characterized by a non-differentiation of processes occurring between two people. For example, psychic contents that belong to a patient can enter a therapist and vice versa, and he can find himself behaving as if the patient's psychic state were his own. He may lose sight of the difference between his process and the patient's, and his identity may become hazy. Or, he may become aware that a fusion state exists between his own and the patient's unconscious psyches. This awareness is crucial if fusion states are to have a creative outcome.

The following is a rather odd example, but it points out the subtlety of fusion states. A patient entered the consulting room and complained about having stepped on some gum that he had trouble cleaning off his shoe. During the ensuing hour I found myself alert to my own shoe, thinking about not touching it. This is unusual for me. I usually do not touch my shoe, and in the hour even though my shoe was far from my hand I still felt compelled not to touch it. Only after some time passed did it occur to me that the patient had talked about his shoe. Even after I recognized this the drive not to touch my shoe persisted. I then became aware of the fact that a fusion state was developing between us. In some way his psyche had entered me and I was quite captivated by it, especially while I was unaware of the fusion quality of our interaction.

The latent content of this interaction was masturbation. Several weeks after this fusion experience, his masturbatory compulsions came to light and could be discussed, leading to a significant behavioral change. Previously, masturbation had never been mentioned. It was as if he had entered me in his masturbatory act and there was a kind of creative mix-up and mirroring between our psyches.

Throughout I felt no coercion, little by way of a demand that I do something, or do nothing. A lack of coercion is often a signpost of a creative mixup of boundaries in fusion states. In this fusion experience I had a sense of containing him.

Fusion states may be used to control another person, especially to deny loss, separation, and persecutory affects. This is usually the case with borderline patients. For example, patients may complain that not knowing enough about the analyst's personal life makes it impossible to trust him. At this point the analyst may withdraw or else tend to talk about himself, the common reactions to a fusion demand. If he is aware of this state, he may come to an analytical position of understanding the patient's fusion demand and not act it out as, perhaps, a defense against abandonment.

Fusion can be far more complex and coercive than this example, as the following experience shows. After writing an article I was surprised to discover that a person with whom I had discussed several minor points was enraged with me. He insisted that I had stolen his ideas and that it should have at least been a joint publication. When he said this I felt bewildered, not knowing if he was joking. But it was soon clear that he was dead serious, telling me how specific things in the papers had come from him. At one point I realized that I had used a phrase that he had admired from another writer. Quickly I found myself tense and defensive, fearing that he was right. I was a thief! But then he said more, and gradually began to reveal that he had been interested in the topic for a long time, and had ideas on it that he had just never published. It was then clear to me (but certainly not to him) that he was accusing me of stealing ideas that he had never spoken about and ideas that were certainly very unclear and ill-formed in his mind. But to him, I was merely a scribe who had put a minor degree of clarity into his ideas. For a moment he had got inside me and filled me with an illusion that it was all his work, that I was an appendage who merely wrote out what he always knew.

This was a very uncomfortable encounter. I felt my insides violated and my sense of self temporarily lost as I was fused with his illusions. Only later could I recognize that he had had a minor psychotic episode, and for nearly a half hour I was quite overtaken by his arguments. During this time of my own identity diffusion, it also seemed that his survival was totally in my hands, and that if I did not appease him in some way he would go to pieces. Even though moments of clarity broke through to me (such as an awareness that I was being accused of stealing his unborn, hazy and unstated ideas), I still tended to fuse with him and to think about giving him some mention of thanks in the paper. The moments of clarity faded in and out, and, like the alchemical Mercurius, were very hard to grasp in a cohesive, fixed manner. It was all quite mad, but I gradually regained enough sanity to tell him we could continue to talk about it later. I was prepared for another agonizing battle for which I attempted to gird myself and not give an inch. When I next met him he had, in borderline fashion, completely forgotten about the incident, which he now regarded as a minor disagreement that had long since past.

The experience of union is significantly different from fusion. By union, I mean an interaction between two people in which both experience a particular change in energy flow between them, specifically a kinship quality (Jung 1946, para. 445), a sense of communitas (Turner 1974, p. 286). This quality is carried by Buber's notion of the I-Thou relationship, and it is a key affect of the experience of union.

States of union vary in intensity and quality. There are processes of union that take place mainly unconsciously, with neither person aware at the time that anything special has occurred, save perhaps through clues gained from dreams. Then there are experiences that are quite intense. These can take the form of a shared imaginal vision.

Like Jung, I often will use the Latin term *coniunctio* for union (1946), for this alerts one to what can be the non-ordinary nature of union, especially when it is not an unconscious event but an imaginal, shared experience. But while hidden and arcane, the *coniunctio* also turns out to be far less mysterious than it initially appears to be. In a sense it is a well kept secret. Many a person knows about it, yet only when it is seen with another person does he become aware of what he always knew. This paradoxical nature of the event is aptly captured by its relationship in alchemy to Mercurius, the arch trickster. (Jung 1953) Through his paradoxical medium, the *coniunctio* seems to appear and then vanish, and to come and go in wily ways. Not the least of these is captured in the all too common experience in which the *coniunctio* is strangely avoided, ignored, and even despised. Borderline patients suffer deeply from this fact and will complain that "people just won't do it."

Often, as in the following example, the *coniunctio* experience is something completely different from anything that has previously transpired between the two people. For example, a patient began the session speaking about her brother who always humiliated her, and then said, "Last time I experienced you as a Hades type of judge." She explained that when she inwardly begins to feel young and has the experience of her inner child, I am critical of this child, especially when she presents problems with relationships. I thought that I understood the Hades metaphor, for I frequently feel a rising-up of energies in me that want to penetrate her, and at times I want to "shove an interpretation down her throat."

While reflecting upon this, I spontaneously became aware that another element dominates her relationship with her brother: there is an incest link. I told her this intuition and she said that she could feel her sexual desires for her brother. This was a new experience. She then mentioned a man she disliked, saying that there was no sexuality in him, just detached sadism. I took this as a rejoinder to not withdraw from her.[1]

At this point something unusual happened. I experienced an erotic energy field; she also experienced it. As we both felt this energy, which seemed like something between us, my consciousness lowered a bit and, just as in active imagination, I saw a shimmering image, which extended into both of us, move upwards from where it was, near the ground. I told her this. She said, "Yes, I also see it, but I'm afraid of it." I continued to share what I saw and experienced. I saw the image between us as white; she saw a kind of fluid that had a center. She said she knew that if she descended into her body, it would be too intense, that she was afraid. She stated she now felt that I was her friend, that she felt an I-Thou relationship, and that she had never had such an experience before with anyone. She told me that she was afraid and felt herself slipping away. I responded that she needed only to embody more, to come down into her body. A feeling of timelessness pervaded; I didn't know if one minute or twenty had passed. She worried about next time. What would she do if this experience wasn't there again? She said she felt that I was extremely powerful, but for the first time this didn't frighten her because she also felt equality. A sense of kinship, a brother-sister feeling, was clear to both of us. There was a pull toward sexual enactment, towards physical union, but this tendency had its own inhibition, as if the energy field between us oscillated, separating and joining us in a kind of sine wave rhythm. This was clearest when we allowed our imagination to see the other. Withdrawal of imaginal sight tended to obscure awareness of the dynamics and the inhibitions within the experience. She recognized this experience as a *coniunctio* happening in the subtle body. This awareness is typical of the "gnosis-yielding" nature of the *coniunctio* experience.

The hour came to a close. A strong bond had been created by this union. Not only did it bring us closer in a way that felt like kin, like blood relationship, but it resulted in a transformation in her inner life. In the next session she told of a dream in which, for the first time she could ever recall, her brother was a positive figure, helping her to learn a subject with which she had always had difficulty. I have seen this kind of result many times. After the *coniunctio* experience, there is a transformation of inner sadistic anima or animus figures. Generally such experiences allow the analysis to go much deeper, often into realms of negative transference that had hitherto been split-off.

In borderline patients, psychic structure is split between fusion states and extreme distancing, so that little or no real contact is possible. The experience of union, the *coniunctio* is so vital just because it can unify these opposites.

But the *coniunctio* is more than an event: it is part of a process, one that is especially uncovered through the alchemical imagery of the *Rosarium*. The borderline individual suffers from aspects of this process in which union has degenerated towards fusion or towards a soulless distance, an I-it dyad. It is a state in which the Self as an inner male-female union, or as a "third thing" uniting two people, is lifeless; it leads to a chronic feeling of helplessness. The Self in this condition is incapable of creating order, identity, or purpose. Yet properly understanding this deadened state as part of a process can lead to the experience of its central mystery, the *coniunctio*.

BORDERLINE PERSONALITY DISORDERS REFLECTED THROUGH ALCHEMICAL SYMBOLISM

Borderline personalities have a critical problem with merging and the whole issue of contact with others, with union and non-union in various degrees of intensity. While on the surface we may seem to be in absolutely no contact at all, in the unconscious, we can be deeply fused. The extremity of these states characterizes the treatment of borderline personality disorders.

For example, a patient complains that I do not emotionally support her, that I fail to really see her as she is. No matter how much we work at this, the next session is filled with her rage and despair over how the previous session underscored the lack of my connection to her. She complains that she feels empty and cannot eat enough. Since beginning therapy with me she has gained twenty pounds and cannot take it off. She is gaining more. In hearing this, for the nth time, I recognize that I feel guilty. I see that I have always felt guilty when she speaks of her weight. I have been harboring the idea that if I did something other than what I was doing she would not be so fat. If I loved her more, somehow felt something *more*, she would not be so empty. I have deeply (and unconsciously) believed it is my fault that she is not emotionally filled up and physically thin.

All along she had referred to a past therapist whom she loved and who cared for her. There were difficulties and she had to leave treatment with him. But he cared. All along I felt his *caring ghost* and my inadequacy. Finally we recognized the nature of the idealization of him that had been operating, and the fact that she actually hated him for the way he had been like a vampire with her, stealing her energy and depending upon it for their emotional contact. She recognized that at least I did not do that. After the dissolution of this idealization I gradually realized how much I believed it was my fault that she was gaining weight. And I realized how much I hated her for what I felt was her demand that I do something about it. I told her this, and she realized that in some way she might have been making that demand. Futhermore, she recognized that she lives with a deep-seated belief that what is wrong in the therapy (and life in general) is her fault. She always complained that I made everything her fault. I only now began to recognize that I thought everything wrong in our work was my fault. We had been wedded together, unconsciously fused as two masochists, in this state tormenting each other. Our heads knew only a lack of contact; yet our bodies were filled with a strange kind of mutual tension that seemed imageless. Finally, a clarifying thought came: "It is all my fault." And we were both unconsciously and eagerly grasping the whole fault! No wonder we developed a hatred of one another. There had been a lack of union and instead an abundance of unconscious fusion and conscious distance. Our linkage could have been imaged as a hermaphrodite with one body and two heads. Our bodies carried our unconscious fusion (through the complex: "It's my fault"); our heads were separate, each with its own defensive thoughts. Boundaries were thus both extremely unclear and distant at the same time. Fortunately there was enough alliance between us to work this through, to see how we were fused through the same complex.

When Jung said that the transference is based upon a mutual unconsciousness of both the therapist and the patient (1946, para. 364), he could not have better described work with the borderline patient. The situation of unmediated fusion and distance is so very difficult because it is a terrible suffering. The borderline personality needs to have an experience of union with another in order to know how to reach or create an internal union for himself and vis-à-vis others.

It is inadequate only to analyze this situation reductively into causal factors from infancy.[2] As Jung said, "The understanding of the transference is to be sought not in its historical antecedents but in its purpose" (1916, p. 74). For this we need an archetypal backdrop or scale. This is especially so with borderline personalities because the affect storms are so intense and disorienting and the feelings engaged are so deep and often so unpleasant. We need a large orienting archetypal reference for guidance.

Alchemy served this guiding function for Jung[3] and it appears to me to be especially apt for the states we experience with borderline patients. The central issue for alchemy was the *coniunctio*, the experience of union that contains and transcends the opposites of fusion and distance. Alchemy's primary concern was the religious issue of the union of the mind and body through the linking medium of relation, the soul. The alchemical text that most fully addresses this issue is the *Rosarium Philosophorum,* also known as the *Rosary of the Philosophers* (McLean 1980). One form of the union of opposites (including those of mind and body) is represented there by the symbol of the hermaphrodite. Both its formation and transformation are concerns of the *Rosary of the Philosophers*. In treatment of the borderline personality we first meet the negative aspects of the hermaphrodite, fusion states and the denial of psychic connections, states that create a field in which compulsion tends to rule and the free play of imagination is nearly nonexistent. Development depends upon the evolution of such split and contradictory fusion-distance states into a genuine experience of union, the *coniunctio*. As a result positive aspects of the hermaphrodite may emerge as a shared Self symbol experienced in the space between two people, and also as a symbol of an individual, inner union (Schwartz-Salant 1984, p. 10).

In his essay on the "Psychology of the Transference" C. G. Jung explored a series of pictures from the sixteenth-century *Rosarium Philosophorum,* employing them as an Ariadne thread through the complexities of the transference (1946, para. 538). These pictures were originally a series of twenty woodcuts that were probably used for meditative purposes, like a rosary. Later, a Latin text was added, a collection of sayings from various alchemical authors (McLean p. 4). At times these sayings seem appropriate to the picture; at other times they seem to be quite random. My experience has been that the more I grasp the latent meaning in these images, the more the sayings are useful.

Jung argued that by reflecting on complex psychological phenomena with the help of pertinent material from past historical times we could gain a vantage point on issues such as the transference, an orientation that is otherwise not readily available (1946, para. 539). In a sense, one gains a reference point outside of material to which one is normally inextricably linked. Furthermore, he finds that this approach has the advantage of not reducing the experiences and libido that can emerge into personalistic forms, which he would consider a form of apotropaic magic (1954, para. 562). Also, the historical approach has the added advantage of envisioning a present-day, historically pertinent change in cultural structures, thus again avoiding the limitations of personalistic reductionism. In most psychoanalytic approaches this is the common method; differences lie only in the choice one makes from the diversity of theories of child development. Naturally, this sorts out in terms of various "schools of thought," viz.: classical Freudian-psychoanalytic models, object relations theorists (covering a spectrum of persuasions), Kleinians, Mahlerians, the London School of Analytical Psychology, rooted in Michael Fordham's work, and adherents of Erich Neumann's approach in Analytical Psychology, to mention only some theoretical options.

Jung's approach to complex issues such as the transference was different. In distinction to developmental orientations, he insisted upon orienting towards what he called the archetypal transference, and he sharply differentiated his emphasis from Freud's (1946, para. 382, n34). For the archetypal transference engages psychic energies and potential structures that may never have been previously constellated in the individual's life. Jung clearly stated that his essay is concerned with the emergence of unconscious contents and processes that may not necessarily arise in every analysis. That is, while he believed he was making headway into inquiring about the structures of the transference in general, the intensity and impersonal nature of the forms he employed from the *Rosarium Philosophorum* will not always appear. Instead, in a mild and often unconscious manner its central image, the *coniunctio,* will work its ordering and disordering ways upon the experiences of both people. But in other cases, the energies that gain imagery in the *Rosarium,* for example those Jung referred to as the "Anthropos" or a "shade of Hades" (1946 para. 418), do break into the conscious field vividly and may have a severely disruptive as well as a healing effect.

Such is one's experience with the borderline personality disorders. Several of the states depicted in the *Rosarium* are quickly *constellated* with the borderline patient: we can be immediately thrust into the arena of the archetypal transference. It is even suggested that the early manifestation of the intense libidinal and aggressive energies that characterize borderline states is itself diagnostic of this disorder. In cases in which a borderline disorder has been obscured, say by an obsessive-compulsive character structure, the emergence of the archetypal energies of the borderline level several years after the treatment has begun can feel quite sudden. One's experience is often that what has previously occurred in therapy was a carefully contrived cover-up.

While the picture series from the *Rosarium* has twenty woodcuts, in this essay I am concerned only with amplifying borderline states, and consequently I will refer mainly to numbers six and seven, and somewhat less to three, four and five.[4] The *Rosarium* images refer to a process whose central feature is the union of opposites, symbolized in alchemy by the King and Queen, Sol and Luna, to mention several from a host of other names. Their union represents a linking of mind and body. By "mind" is meant the world of spirit and its imagery, along with psychic structures. This domain of "mind" would be composed of conscious contents and what Jung called the psychic unconscious (1934–1939, Part 3, Lecture 8). It is difficult to know precisely what the alchemists meant by "body," but it surely includes the physical body, especially in its state in which character armoring must be dissolved. Through a heightened awareness of sensations, the body can become a focus of awareness of unconscious processes. This connection to the unconscious through the body was denoted by Jung as the somatic unconscious or the subtle body.

Figure 1. The Mercurial Fountain. (This appears as Figure 1 in the *Rosarium Philosophorum;* see Jung 1946, p. 205.)

Figure 2. King and Queen (This appears as Figure 2 in the *Rosarium Philosophorum;* see Jung 1946, p. 213.)

Figure 3. The Naked Truth. (This appears as Figure 3 in the *Rosarium Philosophorum;* see Jung 1946, p. 237.)

Figure 4. Immersion in the Bath. (This appears as Figure 4 in the *Rosarium Philosophorum;* see Jung 1946, p. 243.)

Figure 5. The Conjunction. (This appears as Figure 5 in the *Rosarium Philosophorum;* see Jung 1946, p. 249.)

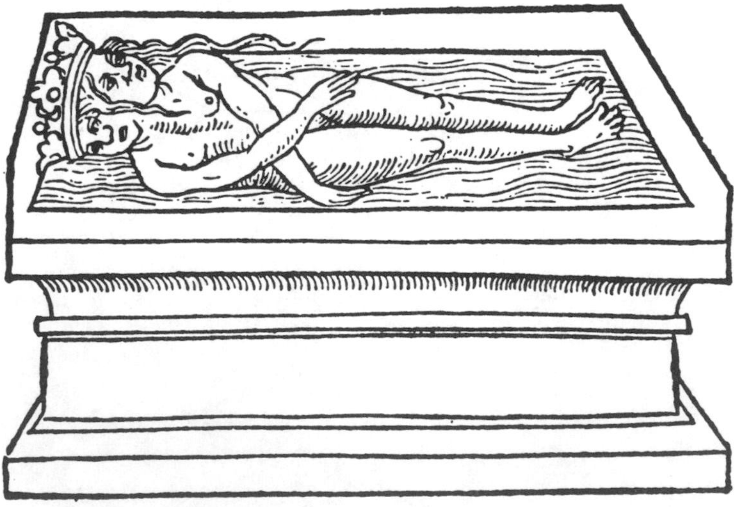

Figure 6. Death. (This appears as Figure 6 in the *Rosarium Philosophorum;* see Jung 1946, p. 259.)

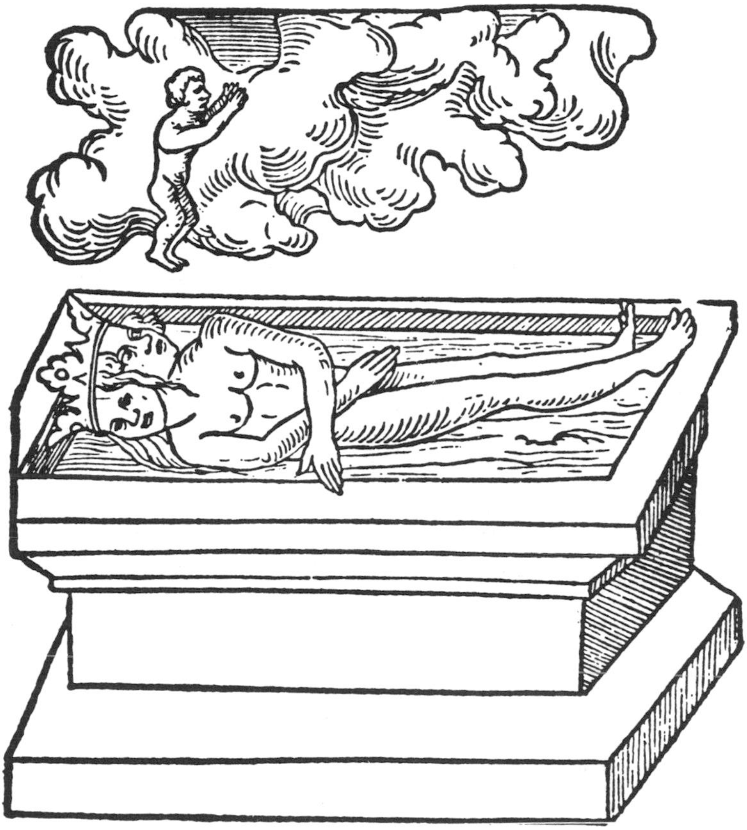

Figure 7. The Ascent of the Soul. (This appears as Figure 7 in the *Rosarium Philosophorum;* see Jung 1946, p. 269.)

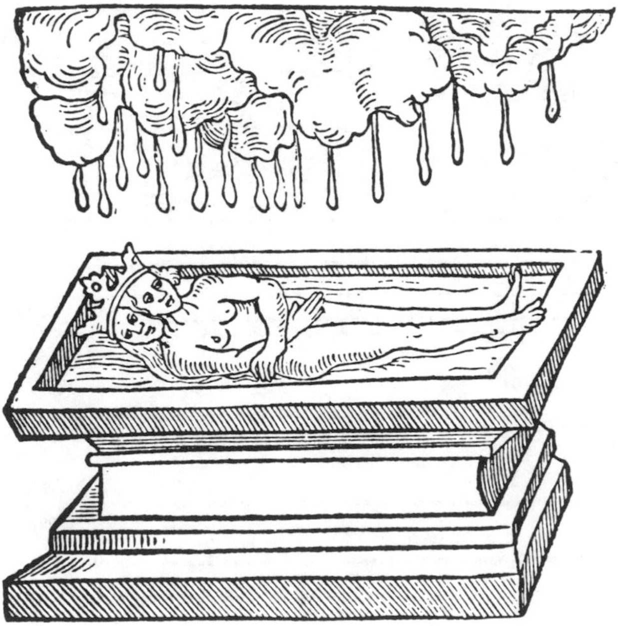

Figure 8. Purification. (This appears as Figure 8 in the *Rosarium Philosophorum;* see Jung 1946, p. 275.)

Figure 9. The Return of the Soul. (This appears as Figure 9 in the *Rosarium Philosophorum;* see Jung 1946, p. 285.)

Figure 10. The New Birth. (This appears as Figure 10 in the *Rosarium Philosophorum;* see Jung 1946, p. 307.)

The first picture of the *Rosarium,* the Mercurial Fountain, as Adam McLean has noted, represents a split between upper and lower realms of the soul (1980, p. 119), a mind-body split. This split represents the state of development of mankind, a result of the metaphysics that has prevailed in Western culture at least since Plato. But it is a state that is especially dominant in the borderline personality disorder, in which a chronic mind-body splitting exists. There one discovers body-images filled with hate and identified with anal-expulsiveness and mental images of mechanical structures that lie, that constantly undermine the truth one really *sees.* For example, imaginal perceptions that glimpse affective states beneath the persona-veneer of someone else may be dismissed as ridiculous fantasy, but this is because their possible truth is too awful to bear. More commonly, inner structures that lie prevent such perceptions from surfacing at all and instead, in an interaction with someone, the borderline individual is left with a vague and pervasive sense of dis-ease.

In alchemical ways of thinking, which I contend must be revived if we are to grasp the essence of borderline phenomenology, an interactive field would be thought of as existing between two people. That is to say, what is "in between" would not be considered empty, but on the contrary capable of manifesting energy with its own dynamics and phenomenology. To levels of ordinary perception, in which the imagination does not become an organ that perceives unconscious processes, this interactive field is not palpable. It would be omitted in thinking about human interactions. These would instead be thought of in terms of projections from one psyche to another along with the individual's conscious reflections. There would be no need for an "in-between" realm, let alone one that had its own properties. That would be considered to be a "mystical" notion without useful clinical relevance. In the previous example of union as contrasted with fusion, I described typical field dynamics while the *coniunctio* was its dominant archetypal constellation. I emphasized the field's sine wave rhythm as a crucial item that regulated the interaction. The field in itself is a factor in what both people experience, along with the psychic contents each person projects into it. The field cannot be reduced to their projections; both affect each other.

Generally, the field is itself in need of transformation, as are the individual psyches of the participants. The mutual transformation is described in the *Rosarium* woodcuts, one of many possible series to depict these stages. The alchemists gave numerous names to experiences of this field in its untransformed state, designations such as *the lion, the unicorn* and *the dragon.*

These referred to the field's compulsive, archaic nature, which tended to obscure any difference between concrete and symbolic reality, between inner, outer, and in-between. The analytical task when one chooses to approach psychotherapy from an alchemical perspective is—through imagination and conscious reflection—purifying this field and one's relationship to it over and over again. That is the "torture of the substances" the alchemists frequently mention.

The borderline personality is someone who is fused with the dark, disordering states of the transformation process, as imagined in the *Rosarium*. Consequently, he generally does not experience the central healing image of the *coniunctio*. This state of union is what he lacks and despairs of ever achieving. Instead, his energy and attention is conflicted, torn between split opposites, especially between polarities of fusion and distance, neither of which can be tolerated.

The central image of the *Rosarium,* the *coniunctio,* represents a state in which fusion and separation are united and transcended. As in the example I gave of union, this can be an experience between two people that is a shared vision. In the *Rosarium,* when picture five, " the Conjunction," is introduced, it is first denoted as "a vision" (McLean 1980, p.35). No other picture has this designation. We are dealing here with the healing capacity of vision, especially of vision that enters a liminal realm, that dimension of our experience whose essence is relatedness. This is a different quality of space and time from our normal experience. Categories of inside and outside are transcended. Vision and the experience of the energies of this other universe of experience is the essential issue.

A vision recorded by P. D. Ouspensky describes this world of relations.

> In trying to describe this strange world in which I saw myself, I must say that it resembled more than anything a world of very complicated mathematical relations . . . in which everything is connected, in which nothing exists separately, and in which at the same time the relations between things have a real existence apart from the things themselves; or possible "things" do not exist, and only "relations" exist. (quoted in Comfort 1984, p.19)

The alchemists knew that these liminal experiences are dangerous and difficult to achieve and that it is difficult to return from them to normal space-time existence. The waters of the Mercurial fountain are said to be healing but also "full of poison." (McLean 1980, 13). But it is the process of entrance and exit from liminality that transforms the compulsive and incestuous energies that are encountered. Hence, there can be several *coniunctio* states, each followed by the torment known in pictures six and seven. It is the phenomenology of these two pictures that is essential to borderline states. They indicate what the borderline personality suffers deeply in levels that, to the best of his ability, he has shut off from consciously experiencing.

These states constellate in treatment of the borderline personality. The imagery of "Death" and "Soul Loss" are responsible for the vexing phenomenology we meet with this patient. These are, to use a metaphor from hallucinogenic drug experiences, the "bad trip" without the *coniunctio*, the "good trip." Yet, if we can become aware of the fact that in treating the borderline personality we are actually thrust into a liminal space and its seeming confusions, and that this can be part of a process leading to a healthy experience of union, we can gain a different attitude towards what we experience with the patient. Fundamentally, this is an attitude based upon faith gained through seeing a *larger* background process. This faith must be sustained when vision is deadened by the *nigredo*, that "dark night of the soul" in which all meaning vanishes in despair and an emotional flood of once repressed impulses. We need not dispel despair and the torment of a lack of emotional contact through the apotropaic means of reductions to failed stages in infant development; rather we need a proper attitude that, however tentative and always unknowing, also retains a faith in a larger purpose.

What the *Rosarium* and associated alchemical wisdom teach us is that the extremely difficult stages associated with the *coniunctio* are functional. They are there as part of the transformation process which works through compulsiveness and unconsciousness and dissolves body-armoring. This suffering can lead not only to the awareness of a difference between inner and outer and to a mind-body union, but also to another "in between" realm that is characterized by relation.

People can engage relations as the experience of union in an intermediate realm. The transformation process needs the awareness of the individuals, yet it also has its own autonomy. Two people enter a realm in which they partake of energies and structures that cannot be fully integrated into space-time; they are of a far larger scale. It is our attitude that matters, the way we suffer these states with a patient, and especially the way we remain aware of the presence and absence of imaginal sight, the elixer that can kindle the awareness of an in-between realm amidst subject and object polarities and their confusions. That can allow the often sudden and mysterious experience of union to be freed from the death grip of despair.

PICTURES SIX AND SEVEN OF THE *ROSARIUM*: CORE EXPERIENCES WITH THE BORDERLINE PATIENT

In the *Rosarium*, picture seven represents an extremely dangerous state. The soul has left, and the pair, which in Jung's study represents the unconscious connection between two people or a dominant self-image in an individual, yields up a very negative field. Jung likened it to a schizophrenic dissociation (Jung 1946, para. 476). He found the alchemical saying that in the investigation of the work "not a few have perished," (para. 476) as here particularly apt.

This picture, as a representation of the interactive field between two people, is essentially characterized by non-union. It represents the shadow side or opposite of that phase in the process by which union, the *coniunctio*, forms and embodies. The alchemists regarded it as part of the process by which the body is transformed. Those that pass through this stage as a part of the coniunctio process do report a change in body-feeling. One is in the body in a different way. Embodied-life becomes a meaningful phrase, while prior to this process it was an intellectual curiosity. In a sense, picture seven, "The extraction or impregnation of the soul," (McLean 1980, p. 44) is nature's own Reichian therapist, breaking down body armor. "Destroy the bodies" is an ever-recurring motto in alchemy, especially found in Paracelsus; this stage refers to the dissolution of body-armoring so that a new mind-body image, based upon relationship, may incarnate.

Given the extremely difficult nature of this stage, it is all the more interesting that the alchemists regarded it as one in which the soul was not only extracted but was also impregnated, the picture being called the *impregnatio*. The idea is that there is purpose to the experience of an absolute loss of union, relation in any sense, inner or outer. The soul's capacity for experiencing psychological relation—the capacity for experiencing the energies and dynamics of an interactive field—is seen as renewed through the torment of non-union.

One of the quotes from alchemical authors that accompanies this picture is attributed to "Hermes", saying: "Take the brain . . . and grind it in most sharp vinegar, or in children's urine until it is obscured. This being done it liveth in putrefaction, and the thick clouds . . . are returned, and this being begun again as soon as I have written it, may again be mortified as before. . . . He therefore that maketh earth black shall come to his purpose and it shall go well with him." (McLean 1980, p. 45)

A borderline patient will commonly complain that the analyst does not understand him, is not in contact with him. In states such as those represented in picture seven this is especially easy for the analyst to deny. For the patient will be nearly possessed by his life experiences of being abandoned, and his link to the analyst will be severely distorted. It may verge here upon a transference psychosis in which the analyst *is* the abandoning parent. The *as-if* is nearly completely lost. Furthermore, this stage tends to activate a psychotic countertransference, in which the analyst loses contact with his patient and the process and instead treats him as an abandoning parent. Reality can be lost.

These facts make it all the more difficult to recognize that a lack of contact is not only what exists, but what must be seen as existing, allowed to be without judgement and without denial. I must emphasize that my experience, both in supervision of other analysts and in my own practice, suggests that treatment of the borderline patient tends to fail at this stage. Either the patient leaves treatment in an overwhelming despair about union, often stated as a sadness and pain over "not being seen," or the patient covers up with false-self. He says he has got a lot from therapy and it is time to leave. The latter is often the way borderline patients exit mental hospitals after "brief psychotic episodes." It can be many years later, if ever, that the person will again dare to enter the dangerous waters of unions that fail and linkages that are absent between people.

The last thing we generally think belongs in treatment is a *lack of union*. We tend to believe this is a result of poor empathy, countertransference reactions, negative therapeutic reactions, envy, and so forth. We tend to reduce absence to something else, to a resistence or attack of some kind. The problem is that once absence cannot be tolerated, once we are unable to live in a state characterized by non-union, then all these disruptive shadow qualities readily enter. Yet the primary fact, revealed by imagery such as the *Rosarium's* picture seven, can be put as follows: both people are not in the same psychological universe. They are in parallel or alternate universes. While bits of contact and understanding may exist, the dominant fact is that the patient will experience the therapist as if he is speaking to someone else. The therapist who thinks he is in contact, or who tries to be in contact, will always fail at this point. The patient knows this; often the therapist does not.

It is only when the therapist can acknowledge the state of non-union and feel the affects that accompany it, that some contact can emerge. Often this takes the form of a reemergence of the imagination, a dimly flickering sight that sees that difficult and obscure depths lie beneath what readily seems like denial and defense. Then it is possible to feel an affective contact and the awareness of just how out of contact one had been. But even now, an absence of union lurks about as a fact to be respected, valued, never to be taken lightly as something one has finally got past. Strangely, it is a field quality necessary for the *coniunctio* to become an embodied reality, rather than an ephemeral ghost.

CLINICAL NOTES WITH REFERENCE TO PICTURE SEVEN OF THE *ROSARIUM*: THE EXTRACTION OF THE SOUL

I think the notion of "grinding one's brain in sharp vinegar until it is obscured, and returning to thick clouds," the saying accompanying picture seven, was particularly apt for my experience with a patient. It also describes the patient's experience with me. Many of his nights and days were spent trying to think clearly, regaining inner mental links, trying to understand what was happening in therapy. His thought process, innately very superior, was commonly put out of commission, as was my own while I was with him and at times afterwards. I shall not be concealing my own countertransference reactions in the following notes. On the one hand I believe to do so is a disservice at best, and on the other hand my experience is that despite my reactions, *which denied that non-union existed,* we were both part of a process attempting to create union. In a sense, I was barely "reliable enough" in the process.

After two years of very difficult analytical work, this patient dreamed that he was gently embracing two women together; one was black and the other white. I understood this as a creative entrance into the depressive position, in which the "good" and "bad" mothers become the same person in an infant's mental representations. As in a creative entrance into the depressive position (Fordham 1967, p. 31f.), it was duly followed by reparation attempts that followed attacks upon the analysis. I also interpreted the black and white women whom he embraced together as an image of a combining state, something that I could now carry in projection because there had been sufficient reparation on my part of previous analytical errors. I thought that I had become reliable. This dream was followed by another in which he and another man, associated to me, were flying in a plane very close to the ground, gaining a view of the earth below. At first the other man was guiding the vehicle, and then the patient was taught to guide it himself. From this it seemed clear that finally the analysis was becoming one of mutual cooperation, perhaps even indicative of the potential emergence of a fruitful coital couple in the future. There is a container, and it is near the earth, thus having both spirit and a capacity for a mutually agreed upon overview. The latter had been sorely lacking in the prior two years, a condition that the patient suffered from terribly; he took great pains to make me understand how I was at least one if not the only cause of his great distress.

Soon after this dream I was surprised to find him again in a state of extreme agitation and doubt about me and the analysis. The key phrase here is "I was surprised," because there should have been no cause for surprise. This is one of the issues he accurately had with me, which, as he said, "drives me crazy." This in turn led as it generally did to an examination of "why I was driving him crazy," why I wanted to do such a thing to him. And, to use his metaphor, which I find unpleasantly apt, "why was I [again] operating in bad faith." But before such an examination could take place, quite a row occurred in which both he and I had doubts about the possibility of continuing the analysis.

In the session to which I refer, he arrived and, before sitting down, asked me a question about something I had previously said. I became very defensive. But my state was far more extreme than usual, and I lost sight of my defensiveness because I felt my body literally filled with an agitation that was dissolving in its affect. I can only describe this state as one in which I felt my insides to be under extreme attack of a global nature. (This is part of the state that I think is aptly described as "grinding up the brain . . ."). The attack was not pointedly at me from my patient, although I tried to see it in this manner; but it felt engulfing, with the result that I was anxious, inwardly shaking, and at the same time I found myself attempting to *act as if everything was okay*. I was denying the state of non-union. Clearly, here I was behaving in a borderline way. I had known this state with him before, but usually not so intensely. In previous times it was a reaction to the issue that gradually took on extreme seriousness in the analysis and to which I referred previously as one of "bad faith." I shall try to sketch out this "shadow history," for it is both necessary to understand the session I am describing, and also a good example of the destructive affects that the alchemists ascribed to his sulphur or to the trickster-like and lying qualities of Mercurius; here it is the falseness that a useful connection between us did exist.

I was slow to recognize my own unconsciousness of a desire *not* to have any form of union with him, and in retrospect I am chagrined and at the same time I marvel at the ingenuity of my tactics to avoid union. A subjective countertransference issue surely was present. But much more also existed here, a field quality, inherent to the process we were engaged in, in which non-union was the main fact. Rather than recognizing this for what it was, at times I denied it.

One way in which I avoided being in real contact with him was by being filled with the kind of anxiety and fear that I previously mentioned (a malignant energy field that seemed to be evoked by our mutual presence), and allowing him to take the lead in understanding. Clinically he manifested a vertical split in which one side of his personality was remarkably intact, clear-headed and psychologically adept, and next to it, in disparate fashion, was another personality constellation in which thinking easily failed, in which memory was confounded, and in which he was terribly vulnerable to being overwhelmed by despair at any hint of lying on my part, the chief lie being "I understand," or my behaving as if I were in a felt contact with him while in truth I was not.

We were in what I have called parallel universes, perhaps connected in numerous thoughts and at various moments, but in truth totally in different psychological universes. This is an essence of picture seven. At my worst I presented him with an extremely toxic double-bind, and I tended to hide this by choosing to see him as strong and adept, one of his vertical partitions. I lagged behind, found myself dulled, unable to think well, unimaginative, uncreative, leaden, a mixture of a Saturnian heavy authority and a compulsion to "know" when challenged. In any other case I had at the time I would have employed these countertransference reactions syntonically and unearthed the facts of his "other side" and its excess of chaos, its rootedness in despair and helplessness; I would have recognized that he needed me to be able to think with him if not for him. Here I *chose* not to. I just went along. At my best I recognized the state of non-union for what it was. This and his efforts saved the analysis.

I have emphasized that I "chose" non-union because I have no doubt that a choice was involved, although at the time I was unaware of this. But a choice to be immoral was involved, to lie about understanding, to lie especially about contact, about being in the same universe as he. I must emphasize the aptness, for me, of this metaphor, for the recognition of its truth was shocking. And all of this was occurring while my self-image was of someone who deeply wanted union, who held it in the highest esteem.

The sin of pride was not the least of my failings here. It is this kind of examination that is part of picture three, "Naked Truth." It runs throughout work with the borderline psyche.

It was against this background that I finally got hold of the analysis. I must emphasize that it was abundantly clear in all of this that transferential elements were involved: The way I was behaving was a representation of his own interaction with his mother, father, and with the parental couple that their psyche created, a couple in intense, antagonistic dis-union, out to do the other in through malicious envy. Everything I have described about bad faith and lies is a carbon copy of his experience of his parents; the state in which I would commonly find myself of being overwhelmed and barely holding on to my thoughts replicated how he felt with them while they continually denied his perceptions. Also, they represented behavior of which he was capable and which he indeed acted out over and over again in ways that were very distressing to him. But I can report only that I was also driven to behave in these ways, and while I can reduce this to a countertransference acting-out, which it was, and especially to countertransference resistance to experiencing despair, something else was involved. We were both part of a process that was not just a repetition of past histories but a creation in its own right.

This clinical material depicts some of the worst experiences with the borderline psyche, as imaged by picture seven of the *Rosarium*. It is impossible, I believe, adequately to sort out what is personally transferential and countertransferential from archetypal field dynamics that are constellated at this stage. What is certain, however, is that the analyst must get hold of the experience of non-union and must be capable of respecting it as a state that can be survived. The analysis will depend to large measure upon his capacity to repair his acting-out defenses against the pain of non-union and the despair it engenders.

PICTURE SIX, THE NIGREDO

Picture six from the *Rosarium*, the *nigredo*, is also extremely pertinent to borderline states. Jung took this stage to be a consequence of incest (1946, para. 468). But I have found that a core of despair also lies in this stage. Despair is associated with the experience or sensed absence of the *coniunctio*. This central image of union is first seen in picture five of the *Rosarium;* despair stems from a need to possess the union experience, as well as from a recollected history of lost unions. The latter may possibly begin with a trauma of loss at birth, which is later spoken about as a loss of God related to the age-old idea that a child is a "child of God." This initial trauma extends through the results of unions and losses as these occur in developmental phases such as the depressive position as described by M. Klein (Segal 1980, pp. 76–90), the separation-rapprochement subphase of individuation as described by M. Mahler (1980), and the Oedipal stage. But what is felt as a loss of God—as in the "death of God" in our nihilistic epoch—may be the key trauma in the borderline patient. One can get a hint of this at times through the strange quality of a rage at God, and through the despair over this loss, which dominates some borderline patients. This rage is an affect that does not seem to fit into reactions to personal loss, and it is usually kept a secret, for the person is wary of being viewed as crazy for having such feelings.

There is perhaps no emotion more difficult for the analyst treating borderline patients than despair. The borderline patient will often scan every moment, including those prior to the beginning of the therapy hour, for the therapist's optimistic ideas. The need to fill the analytical process with positive thoughts—usually as interpretations or amplifications or advice giving—notifies the patient that the therapist is not up to dealing with despair.

Furthermore, emotions such as fear and anxiety, which an analyst may experience in the face of the despair of the borderline patient, are apt to be solely his own subjective countertransference reactions. These are a very poor indicator of the patient's own process. For example, when the analyst feels anxious and even panicky, it often proves to be largely his own reaction, not a syntonic countertransference that can be used to infer the patient's split-off affects. In these instances the patient is often not panicky. He knows his despair only too well.

A borderline patient is usually an expert in despair. He is also expert in avoiding it through a myriad of splitting defenses. As he knows the depths of despair much better than do most analysts, he also despairs at having to be the analyst's teacher. Unfortunately this is not uncommon, and the envy that develops in the process can destroy the therapy endeavor. The patient does for the analyst what no one has ever done for him, a situation that is fertile ground for envy.

Despair seems to border on an objectless realm, a void, a chaos. But this can be deceptive. Despair also has a companion lurking in unseen regions. The object in the despairing state of the borderline patient consists in a vampire-like force. This creates a very strange object relationship, a very dangerous aspect of the process of the *coniunctio*. Often enough this object feels like a satanic force, cleverly convincing the person that there is no hope, that faith is yet untenable, and that it is best either to give up and just settle for things as they are, for falseness, or to die. Either of these two choices seems to satisfy this background influence.

"The *coniunctio* is a con-job," rages a patient, daring to wound my narcissism. "I don't believe in it," says another. Remarks such as these are extremely common after the *coniunctio* has been experienced. For then the greatest dangers evolve: abandonment by the analyst is now the greatest threat, the threat of an upsurge of despair that can be suicidal. We experience these levels with the borderline patient when no union has occurred; such is the intensity of fear which surrounds the *coniunctio*. For the latter state is an archetype, and the borderline patient is acutely sensitive to the potential of such processes in which despair is always near the union experience. Better not to try than to risk so much pain—that is an inner motto that dominates much of the life of the borderline personality.

Probably no image in modern life portrays the inner object or force in states of despair better than the vampire. In some legends, when the vampire looks in the mirror there is no image. He represents a psychic force that has absolutely no identity. He is in a sense the perfect shadow side of Narcissus, the psyche without a mirror, an identity-less force. The soul in despair is at the edge of being captured, lured by a vampire-like force. He is often lured into the night, when his previous terrors of emptiness were usually most intense, most in need of being filled by derangements of rituals that fill papers on perversions.

The rays of the sun, consciousness, kill the vampire. That is an apt image of how our consciousness can be destructive to the patient. For in our theories and unconscious ideas we are actually out to kill the possessing background force, but if we do this the patient can become disoriented and confused. Furthermore, our attempts at knowing deny despair and hence abandon him in his despair, for he is identified with it as a source of truth. The false self is all that can be saved in this way, perhaps even yielding a well-functioning ego that dies to itself at night or when it is alone. If we allow a further mythic reflection, we recall that the shadow side of Narcissus in his myths (from Pausanius) is Hades-Dionysos (*See* Schwartz-Salant 1982, pp. 140–143). And, Dionysos is the rapist-bridegroom of Persephone, who gains her power after her forceful descent and eventual ascent. The Persephone-like soul of the borderline individual lives this myth in its destructive form. Hades and Dionysos are dark enough, but they represent psychic aspects potentially life-giving through their capacity for imaginal penetration. Instead of these, the operative force is vampire-like, a Satanic representation of the underworldly powers.

The grave danger of such amplification is that it has a sense of knowledge about it. We begin to know something. And that is where any possibility of dealing with despair vanishes. For the essence of despair is that nothing works. Union feels like a fraud, and any focus upon it is more liable than anything to drive the person into a fusion state with a vampire-like force, to live in a constant schizoid depression, hidden in life by a false self.

A major reason analysts shy from despair is that entering this domain threatens a loss of identity. Mirrors don't work. (It should not go unmentioned, in this regard, that the distortions of mirroring are also avoided in despair; perhaps this is one of its major functions.) Consequently, there is often an unconscious mad scramble for some vantage point. Yet the essence of the despair is that there are no ideas, no thoughts that get one out of it. One can act out in various ways and temporarily escape despair, but thought, interpretation, action does not help. Despair is a chaotic void that destroys ideas, and when we approach despair our capacity to think quickly diminishes. Patients tell us that we have to ask the right questions, and in the right way. And they are right. If the patient is true to his despairing state, he cannot lead us, for instance through associations, without switching over to a competent, false self. This would destroy the healing endeavor.

There is no chance of maintaining a union of any stability, no possibility of the patient's gaining an inner or in-between couple that is creative if despair is sidestepped. A fruitful union, a coital couple that releases and engenders soul rather than a couple (comprised of the vampire-force and the person's true self) that sucks it dry, is impossible unless despair has been sufficiently plumbed. For despair is a haunting *nigredo* that will shred any union and thrust the person into the hands of its unconscious bridegroom, its vampire-like companion.

THE DEAD SELF

The imagery of pictures six and seven are of a dead couple. It represents the Self of the borderline patient, lying in a *nigredo,* a putrefaction that he tells us about with strange pervasions, unwashed bodies, repulsive mannerisms. The alchemical imagery tells us this is part of a larger, albeit often unseen and unfelt process. Healing depends upon linking up the dark, disordering aspect of the borderline process with its larger roots in the archetypal dynamics of the *coniunctio*. But one must begin with the borderline personality's *prima materia*, well characterized by the soulless and deathlike imagery of pictures six and seven, indeed by a dead Self.

The borderline process is characterized by denial, splitting and dissociation, whereby strands of past experiences of union engulfed in despair live side by side with states of non-union and deadness. These opposite states of mind (of union and non-union) rarely know each other. Generally, only the dark and disorienting condition of psychic deadness rules, a condition that the person desperately attempts to overcome. The alchemical imagery of the *Rosarium* shows us the archetypal process in which he is entangled. As always, when the conscious personality is involved in attempts to escape anxieties and to flee from the reality of the *numinosum*, the underlying archetypal process manifests its negative forms.

The borderline person is helpless to turn the archetypal process into a positive, life-giving form. He has aptly been called "the helpless patient." (Giovacchini 1979, p. 139). He suffers deeply from the states of inner deadness and the absence of a psychic connection. His Self is much like the pathetic Osiris of Egyptian myth, lying in the coils of the underworld serpent of Chaos, masochistically numb and inert and attacked if he attempts to rise up (Rundle Clark 1959, p. 167). In a spell from a coffin text his worshipers plead with Osiris (Rundle Clark 1959, p. 125):

> Ah Helpless One!
> Ah Helpless One Asleep!
> Osiris, let the Listless One arise!

As Osiris is constantly threatened by the devil Seth, a personification of M. Klein's "paranoid-schizoid position" and its persecutory anxieties, so too the Self of the borderline personality is constantly under the threat of dismemberment. States like the *nigredo* and soulless conditions of non-union can be a terrible yet safe territory; to leave it risks experiencing the pain of psychic dismemberment, total annihilation. If he complies with others and environmental demands, the borderline personality believes he can get by with a minimum of pain. But this is never satisfying, and death through suicide lurks as the consummate relief.

The borderline individual deeply hates himself. He has contempt for his impotence in changing anything and scampers about in cowardly fashion to avoid the awful, inner feelings of hating and being hated, a flight that only furthers his self-disgust and despair. Any of an analyst's tendencies toward withdrawal from his patient enacts the person's worst expectancies: no one will be present, especially no one will be there in the face of the awful feelings he carries, the rage, the hatred, and the fact that these are poor metaphors for that which constantly eats at him and informs him how bad things really are. Impulses to withdraw from him, however slight these may be, tell him of the abandonment he expects. And we always do abandon him—if only in our fantasies as we wish to be rid of toxic affects—an abandonment of which he is excruciatingly aware.

The borderline individual, unlike the schizoid personality who uses withdrawal as his main defense against the intrusions of other people, unlike the narcissistic character disorder who has a cohesiveness that allows him to nullify the effect of others, is caught in a ceaseless drama of desperately trying to make contact with other people. He is rarely satisfied with his death-like inner world and commonly attempts to awaken it in a very noisy way. A patient said, "I am finally able to be a 5, previously I was either a 0 or a 10. I had to have very strong feelings in order to feel alive. I had to feel very deeply about other people, to have very intense contempt or rage, or feel this about myself. Then I was alive. Now I am beginning to have more normal feelings, to hate my husband but also feel some care as well. Previously this was impossible. I had to start fights to feel alive. Anything that approached a 5 was too frightening. It meant I would feel dead."

Here is a clinical vignette of how a patient's inner deadness can manifest itself in analysis.

A patient says: "I feel dull, heavy." He speaks of being afraid, of living in fear most of his life. He mentions how remarkable it is to feel a moment of peace, a moment free of feeling attacked. "Last time," he says, "was the longest I was able to just be with you, make contact in a clean, open way." "Why," I ask, making use of what I believe to be an induced reaction, "are you so frightened now?" He says, "It's always there. I was attacked all the time in childhood, all the time by my brothers, mother and sisters, to say nothing of my father. It's just in me. I always feel attacked."

Why, I wonder to myself, am I feeling so leaden, heavy, blank, empty? I don't feel attacked, and not even uncomfortable. Just dense, heavy, and without a glimmer of any imagination. I don't seem able to open my mouth. It seems glued shut. Am I withholding, acting out something sadistic? Perhaps I am feeling his depression. That makes some sense, but it doesn't do much for me. I'm still heavy and blank. It feels like I've suddenly gained ten pounds. What's in this? What's going on?

I have said nothing. My patient begins to talk about his son and the son's problems. I feel drawn in a bit, not by him but by myself. It's something to talk about, something real, tangible, a problem to work with. I restrain myself and again wonder: why so leaden, dull, unimaginative? He seems fine, gaining in some way because I am like this. He is connecting now not only to his fears and even terror but also to a sense of joy. He looks alive and happy, and he speaks of his joy in life. But he also adds that his joy is terrifying, that it surely will bring on an attack. Perhaps, I wonder, my heavy, leaden state is just a cover for fear. Am I covering fear? His? My own? If so, fear of what? This inner dialogue lifts me up a bit, a slight sense of lightness begins to dawn.

Thirty minutes have passed in this way, there are twenty left. Will anything come of this session? What if I just remain dull? I am not too bothered by this, I think. It will just be what it is to be. I go back to the reflection: What am I afraid of? Am I now holding him off? Am I abandoning him out of fear of a too confusing merger? This reflection seems to yield more feelings of lightness or at least of less dullness and blankness. Little bits of imagination begin to flicker. I imagine I *see* bits of fear, imagine a kind of random motion in him or between us, an intense randomness like heat molecules. It is a dull, dim vision, but at least it is something. I can now talk about his fear, talk about it while I vaguely see it, talk about it but not as a defense against my discomfort. And then he says, "You know, I never have to see my parents again. It is my choice. I can make it!" When he says this he surprises himself; he is not sure where it came from, and he says "That feels like a moment of freedom, something much more radical than it sounds like." Now he speaks of his gratitude to me for not being like "them," like his parents and others who attacked him by unconsciously demanding that he save their lives and renew their dead relationship through killing off his own joy.

The interaction I have described recalls Winnicott's description of the process whereby a Self can come into existence.

"The subject says to the object: 'I destroyed you,' and the object is there to receive the communication. From now on the subject says: 'Hullo object!' 'I destroyed you.' 'I love you.' 'You have value for me because of your survival of my destruction of you.' 'While I am loving you I am all the time destroying you in (unconscious) *fantasy*' " (1971, p. 90).

The patient had known very little of such interactions. Instead, like all borderline patients his inner fantasy would have been: "I killed you (with my rage and joy that you wanted for yourself) and you stayed dead, and as I continued to (unconsciously) kill you, you acted as if I really meant to do just that. I could never use you, I always had to be too concerned for your survival. In the process I haven't survived. I am pathetic, helpless, dead."

To transform this state of deadness back into the archetypal process in which it must be imbedded as a felt reality, requires the recovery of the imagination, the capacity to play and most crucially to see. The borderline patient is someone who was prematurely thrust out of magical, mythopoetic space. He was forced to structure reality prematurely, and he became stuck between mythic realities and those of a rational world he fails to understand. He is in limbo between two ways of experiencing the world, and healing requires recapturing the earlier, mythopoetic world in its imaginal essence, rather than squeezing the ego into outer reality and repressing that previous world.

In his limbo state, energized by archetypes, the environment has a magical power. It rises up and strikes fear, its inanimate objects at times as real as live ones, and then it settles back, only to rise up again, encompass the person, and blur reality. Me-It doesn't exist in a stable way. A person describes this state: "*It* is always encroaching with *Its* power and being more real, the center I don't feel, and *Me* is always falling back into nonsubstantiality. Intermixed we mingle and neither has reality."

One must emphasize the numinous reality of other people for the borderline person. It is here that the archetypal realm is especially alive, always potentially intrusive. In people with less severe borderline constellations, or in whom this sector of personality is not aroused, this affect takes over and quickly fades away. Reality gets a bit fuzzy. In more severe cases it is a chronic situation, and fears abound that it will happen if it isn't already engulfing any sense of security. While fears of object loss and engulfment are more apparent, it is the numinosity of other people that accounts for the extreme fear of the borderline individual, distancing at all costs or frantically merging.

To be sure the project of the borderline person recapturing the earlier, imaginal world will be unsuccessful if the distortions of his ego, the splitting of the ego and the object world that severely distorts perceptions of what other people actually are doing to him, is not challenged. But this confrontation is shortsighted if we fail to understand the nature of the distortions involved. What we must consider is not only the observable fact that a hostile world, primarily represented by images of the mother linked to the child's experience of her as he attempted to negotiate the separation-rapprochment drama, has created his masochistic compliance along with a delusional creation of a "good" object world. It is not sufficient that we notice how these delusional creations of reality are a result of intense abandonment and persecutory anxieties. These items are true enough. But we can address the depth of the issues posed by the borderline patient, and especially the depth of his suffering and the essential contents of his personality that have been shut away, split off into a schizoid non-existence, only if we note that what the person has done is to stop seeing things as they are. Instead, imaginal sight has been either totally split off, or else captured by a negative version of seeing characterized by the destructive Eye of the Great Mother Goddess. In either form, the person has split off the kind of vision every child has. This vision sees a venomous hatred, a withholding smirk. It sees this as it sees the world.

This is not defensive projection. It is an imaginal act, and as described by Henry Corbin relative to mystical vision (1969, pp. 218ff.), a thrusting forth of one's own images into outer forms. It is an act of faith, unquestioned except perhaps for its oddness. "Mother is not really like that, yet that is how I see her." That is the real world of the child. It is a universe of vision, of a seeing that is highly developed in shamanic and other healing approaches. But its rudiments exist in childhoods where they are alive as a result of the child's closeness to the mythical or archetypal world. It is this seeing that is either cut off or else demonized because it is too awful to bear. It is too awful for the child to see what he meets as he ventures to create his world, to expand his consciousness. It is too awful to see the effects of his explorations in discovery of new events and in love, especially too awful to see how all of this resulted in his being hated, envied. And especially it is too awful to see how he is willfully deprived of the "containing" function of others that he desperately needs to transform the structure-dissolving disorder his own creativity has created.

This venture of recapturing the mythopoetic sense and its capacity for imaginal sight, cannot afford to overlook the actual reality distortions that afflict the borderline personality. Unless we deal with the way the world is split, for example into delusional "good" and "bad" objects, our attempts at reconnecting with an imaginal reality will only secretly inflate a person and reinforce a delusional approach to reality. Many a borderline individual secretly believed that he or she is a god or goddess, while the power and wisdom in the archetypes only afflict the person (and others), rather than providing support by encouraging an embodied life that respects the *numinosum*.

What can possibly contain all the richness of the borderline psyche without reducing it to so-called primary process thinking? How can the person's extra-sensory perception (ESP) be regained in a positive form as a link to the mystery of spirit and matter, rather than as an archaic fusion state that knows in trivial fashion what others are thinking, feeling, wearing? Must the borderline's incessant scanning of his environment for danger be seen only as a regressed state, a fixation at early infantile levels of perception? Can this sight be salvaged without reducing it to the curiosity of parental scene fantasies or to paranoid intrusions? How do we respect the borderline's life in transitional or liminal space without seeing it as archaic and something only to be outgrown?

How can we allow for the borderline's perplexing simultaneous display of fusion and separation without insisting that this is only a defense against abandonment? How can these rhythms be seen as goal oriented, not only as part of a delusionally created object world—while they are assuredly that too—but in essence as split opposites that might be joined in union? How can these opposites be led into their archetypal synthesis through that mystery that has captured minds for thousands of years and was driven underground only by the patriarchal ascent of the last two thousand, the mystery of the *coniunctio*? How can the regressive "all good object," be seen as a pathological form of the archetypal Feminine? How can the "all-good" splitting defense be seen through for what it is, a defense against these positive energies of love lest they lead not only to the *coniunctio* but also to attending dangers, to emotional flooding, mania, and a loss of control through sexual acting out? How can the split-off "totally rejecting object" be seen as this same Goddess in her fearful form ruling the threshold of the mysteries, where only those who would be willing to die (psychically) can pass? How can the borderline's delusional creations be both challenged and seen through as manifestations of the Feminine? How do we look toward healing without a patriarchal regression in which we glorify repression?

How do we help the borderline individual to embrace and make sense of his sexuality? How do we do better than understand his polymorphous perversity as only a sexualization of object relations, while they are assuredly also that? Must we merely wait for enough structure to be introjected so that repression can enter and Oedipal levels can be analyzed? We know this rarely works. It fails because the borderline individual is easily merged with sexual energies that our patriarchal culture has spent thousands of years repressing. Yet here they again flower. Of course in pathological form, but to what aim other than fusion states? These energies are the incestuous medium of union, the libido that was once embraced in antiquity as the God Dionysos, and known as well, as Jung said, as the Anthropos? How, then, are these energies to be embraced without flooding? In Egyptian terms, how is the wound in the thigh of Osiris, like the wound of the Fisher King of the Grail legend (Rundle Clark 1959, p. 161), to be healed?

Is the recovery of the capacity for repression and a degree of ego stability and reality functioning a good and a reasonable expectation in the treatment of borderline personalities? I do not think so. I believe that it betrays the borderline patient. The problem is that to some extent approaches rooted in developmental-object relations theories, which espouse such goals, can work. But, in actuality this is an Old Testament-like solution to the problem of the Negative Mother Goddess, the mythical image of the affect storms of terror, deception and destructive searing vision from which the patient suffers. It is a solution based upon exodus from the unconscious, a modern and I believe regressive replay of the ancient flight from Egypt and the exclusion of the Feminine Principle of existence. For it isn't primarily the mother who has abandoned the borderline individual, although that is surely an important and urgent issue, but it is the borderline personality who is in the vanguard of suffering the collective fact that the Feminine Principle has been abandoned by our scientific and patriarchal culture. Through such values, and in their proper use they are among the highest achievements of mankind, the Raging Eye of the Negative Mother Goddess is not tamed, it is attacked, and if possible destroyed. As a result it becomes, most assuredly, a Gorgonesque background that makes the unconscious itself a negative repository of envious affects and something to be outwitted if it cannot be repressed. Most pathetically, under this attack upon the rejected Feminine, we lose a central quality of the Eye, imaginal sight, the vision that best holds out healing possibilities for the borderline personality and our culture in general.

But an imaginal approach, one that orients to vision in the sense of actively grasping forms of interactive fields that greatly affect the conscious experience of two people, as if they were being dreamed, can function towards rekindling a positive archetypal process. Instead of being ruled only by images such as pictures six and seven of the *Rosarium*, the dead Self of the borderline patient may link with the larger mystery of union, the *coniunctio*.

The borderline patient may be at the leading edge of a new Self image for our historical-cultural time that bears witness to Nietzsche's pronouncement that "God is dead." Jung has shown how this refers to the death of the patriarchal God-image, and that a change that includes a Feminine aspect of God is in order. Furthermore, he has underscored how, among other ways, this quality shows itself through the *coniunctio,* perhaps the central image of the long repressed and ancient Feminine mysteries. The borderline patient may be showing us a new Self image in its struggles to become and in its failures. It is a Self image that roots in union, in an awareness of far greater realms than the fragments we know in consensually validated space-time life. This Self image depends upon an awareness of wholeness, and finds itself emerging nowadays in what the physicist David Bohm calls the implicate order, (1980) and what long ago Jung referred to as the pleroma, the archetypal field or matrix out of which the fragments we take to be reality fall into space-time life (1955, para. 662).

The dead Self of the borderline patient may thus be the dead Self of collective humanity, the Self that is dead to relatedness as the essence. It may represent what was left of the Feminine Self after the repressive power of the patriarchy. It is a state of Self in limbo, a condition that cannot be creatively encountered by social and economic conditions that heavily value linear discursive thinking and its technological gains. Generally, it cannot be met by the Cartesian spirit of the last three hundred years that has gone completely out of control. Rather, it is a state of Self that requires a fundamentally different attitude, one that revalues the Feminine and its archetypal processes upon which imaginal truth may be founded.

NOTES

1. This interaction and what follows could be easily decoded and reduced to the patient's unconscious messages to me. Thus, I could be the sadistic, humiliating brother, and rather than stay with this communication my "intuition" could be seen as a way of weakening the boundaries between us, sexualizing the transference,

and side-stepping her unconscious critique of "my destructive qualities." The patient's statement about the non-sexual man whom she hated could be seen as a comment to the point that I had seduced her and she was compliant. All of this could be seen to be in service of my refusal to see what I was really doing.

We know of such approaches in the work of Robert Lang and his followers. (See William Goodheart 1982). This point of view is extremely valuable, and if I were unaware of it what eventually transpired in the session could not have occurred. But to reduce this interaction—for example in the above manner—is to destroy the potential for union as a shared imaginal experience. There is a larger dimension of psychic reality involved that does not fit into the kind of Langian reductions I have outlined. I believe that the common experience among those following Lang's approach, that patient's tend to flee the analysis when the "frame is secured," is understandable in terms of the greater dimension of union. Among other things, "securing the frame" means that the analyst has stopped behaving in the way I would be accused of acting-out in this session. In a secured frame the patient feels a safe, open place in which anything can be expressed, free of intrusions by the analyst's unconscious, narcissistic needs. But when the analysis is "secure" in this sense, and the possibility for union does arise, it now occurs in a context that is devoid of symbolism and the imagination. The result is that the analyst has provided a "secure space" that is actually a coffin for the patient. And then those practicing this technique decry the fact that patients flee the secured frame out of a fear of death and madness.

In Jungian terms this approach is devoted to an unmasking of the shadow, but not without an awareness and respect for the greater knowledge of the unconscious. Hence it also can be said to include the Self and a quest for truth. This shows itself often in the religious fervor among the adherents of this method. But it fails to include the feminine, the *sine qua non* of Jungian approaches. In a male analyst this means a lack of anima, in a female analyst it means an alliance with the animus as an Apollonian quality, all to the exclusion of a feminine Self. As a consequence, "being right" overrides "being related," a situation that is anathema to the Feminine Principle.

2. This is not to say that a careful understanding of infantile developmental failures is not also essential. In the case I briefly described, after the fusion state had been disentangled a mild form of union and felt kinship emerged. In turn this led to the patient's trust so that a creative regression could be entered. This led to a deconstruction of her delusional idealizations, beginning in the first year of life, upon which her adult life had been precariously built.

Experiences of union, especially shared imaginal ones of the *coniunctio* as a "third thing" between two people, are the larger goal. It is something that can be further enhanced by reductive work. These are intertwined, union experiences allowing the trust through kinship for healing regressions, and the latter freeing up energies for deeper experiences of union. It is beyond the scope of this note to discuss this further but I wish only to mention that unless reductive work is done, the character armoring that defends early trauma will usually be too strong to allow the embodiment of the union experience. The result can be some mental unification but still a preponderance of mind-body splitting.

3. "We live today in a time of confusion and disintegration. Everything is in

the melting pot. As usual in such circumstances, unconscious contents thrust forward to the very borders of consciousness for the purpose of compensating the crisis in which it finds itself. It is therefore well worth our while to examine all such . . . phenomena (as alchemy) with the greatest care, however obscure they seem, with a view to discovering the seeds of new and potential orders. . . . What our world lacks is the *psychic connection:* and no clique, no community of interests, no political party, and no State will ever be able to replace this" (1946, para. 539).

4. I shall not go into any extensive criticism of the manner in which Jung employed these pictures. That would revolve about his use of only eleven of the twenty woodcuts, with the eleventh in the series, used to amplify the fifth, denoted by him as 5a (See Fabricius 1974). His criticism of the alchemical image of the hermaphrodite as a product of an immature mind (1946, para. 533) is peculiarly one-sided, something I have discussed elsewhere (1984, p. 6). Jung insisted that a more appropriate form of the goal would be a mandala or an image of the Total Man (1946, para. 535), yet this is exactly what picture 20 is! Thus, there are difficulties with his analysis. A more thorough criticism of Jung's approach to these pictures will be published. Here I wish basically to draw upon the useful nature of Jung's study, which definitely outweighs any criticism. Anyone entering the welter of alchemical imagery into which Jung brought order as no one before him or since has done, can only be extremely grateful for his efforts. He went first, now others may follow with his map. But I must also emphasize the metaphor that *the map is not the territory.* Jung's map, while an excellent first approximation, needs to be reworked, as will any study that uses these pictures.

REFERENCES

Bohm, D. 1980. *Wholeness and the Implicate Order.* London: Routledge & Kegan Paul.

Comfort, Alex. 1984. *Reality and Empathy.* Albany: State University of New York.

Corbin, Henry. 1969. *Creative Imagination in the Sufism of Ibn Arabi.* Translated by Ralph Manheim. Princeton: Princeton University Press.

Fabricius, J. 1971. The Individuation Process as Reflected by 'The rosary of the philosophers' (1550). *The Journal of Analytical Psychology*. Vol. 16, No. 1.

Fordham, Michael. 1967. *The Self and Autism*. London: William Heinemann Medical Books.

Giovacchini, Peter. 1979. *Treatment of Primitive Mental States*. New York: Jason Aronson.

Goodhart, W. 1982. Successful and Unsuccessful Interventions in Jungian Analysis: The Construction and Destruction of the Spellbinding Circle. *Chiron: A Review of Jungian Analysis*. 1984. Wilmette: Chiron Publications.

Graves, Robert. 1951. *The Golden Ass*. New York: Ferrar, Straus & Giroux.

Jung, C.G. 1916. The Transcendent Function. In *Collected Works,* vol. 8. Princeton: Princeton University Press, 1960.

Jung, C.G. 1934–39. *Psychological Analysis of Nietzche's Zarathustra*. Unpublished seminar notes. Recorded and mimeographed by Mary Foote. Privately distributed to Jung Institute libraries.

Jung, C.G. 1946. Psychology of the Transference. The Practice of Psychotherapy. In *Collected Works,* vol. 16. Princeton: Princeton University Press, 1954.

Jung, C.G. 1953. The Spirit Mercurius. In *Collected Works,* vol. 13. Princeton: Princeton University Press, 1967.

Jung, C.G. 1954. Answer to Job. In *Collected Works,* vol. 11. Princeton: Princeton University Press, 1958.

Jung, C.G. 1955. Mysterium Coniunctionis. In *Collected Works,* vol. 14. Princeton: Princeton University Press, 1963.

Kohut, Heinz. 1971. The Analysis of the Self. New York: International Universities Press.

Mahler, Margaret. 1980. Rapprochement Subphase of the Separation-Individuation Process. *Rapprochement*. Edited by Ruth Lax et. al. New York: Aronson.

Masterson, James. 1981. *The Narcissistic and Borderline Disorders*. New York: Brunner/Mazel.

McLean, Adam, editor. 1980. *The Rosary of the Philosophers*. Edinburgh: Magnum Opus Hermetic Sourceworks, Number 6.

Rundle Clark, R. T. 1959. *Myth and Symbol in Ancient Egypt*. London: Thames and Hudson.

Segal, Hanna. 1980. *Melanie Klein*. New York: Viking.

Schwartz-Salant, N. 1982. *Narcissism and Character Transformation*. Toronto: Inner City Books.

Schwartz-Salant, N. 1984. Archetypal Factors Underlying Sexual Acting-Out in the Transference/Countertransference Process. *Chiron*. Wilmette: Chiron Publications.

Turner, Victor. 1974. *Dramas, fields, and metaphors*. Ithaca, N.Y.: Cornell University.

Winnicott, D. W. 1971. *Playing and Reality*. London: Tavistock.

CHAPTER 4

CANCER AND THE SELF: HOW ILLNESS CONSTELLATES MEANING

ROGER LEVIN

> . . . all the diseases for which the issue of causation has been settled . . . have turned out to have a simple physical cause . . . and it is far from unlikely that something comparable will eventually be isolated for cancer . . . It is diseases thought to be multi-determined (that is, mysterious) that have the widest possibilities as metaphors for what is felt to be socially or morally wrong.
>
> (Sontag 1979)

> . . . the cancer that had most likely lain dormant in his body until then suddenly blossomed like a rose . . . the hopelessness pervading the entire country penetrated the soul to the body . . .
>
> (Kundera 1985)

> . . . each civilization has its own kind of pestilence and can control it only by reforming itself . . .
>
> (Dubos 1965)

Is cancer the pestilence of our time? Or is that kind of talk just ignorant superstition? Surely it seems we are in the midst of a cancer epidemic not solely attributable to the longevity of modern populations. With increasing frequency it strikes not just the elderly but the young as well. We all feel at risk, as if it were literally in the air. The probability of getting cancer, we often hear now, is about one-in-four over the average lifetime. These are pretty terrifying odds.

Our collective terror of cancer is partly the result of still prevalent, if not quite old-fashioned, beliefs about the inevitability of horrible, protracted suffering, brutish therapies and eventual death following a cancer diagnosis. Of course cancer is by no means always fatal, treatment is becoming little by little more humane, and some people even survive terminal prognoses. But the fear still lingers in the collective mind. I detect here evidence of a more shadowy foreboding, an inchoate sense of cancer's timeliness, its appropriateness to our social scene, as if an obscure historical logic were somehow involved. This is what Foucault (1975) has termed the historical individuality of pestilential disease in its time. Cancer apparently shares that feature with all great epidemics of the past. And therein lies one of cancer's more troubling aspects: to hope to avoid or survive cancer is, with evident circularity, to find oneself out of pace, beyond one's historical time. This is perhaps the root of the stoicism once very commonly observed, though probably less so nowadays, in cancer patients. So the sense of inevitability for us attaches not only to the course of cancer illness, but as well and less visibly to the logic of its occurrence.

Is cancer then uniquely modern? Collectively we seem to feel so. Images of wild, uncontrolled cell growth imaginatively capture the worst of technological society, as if a pact with the demons of progress can set the natural order of things out of balance. We pay for our collective hubris. Here in our mythologies of cancer the personal and historical collide and interpenetrate. We think depression and unexpressed anger occasion the visitation of cancer. We think it shameful and contagious. True to our positivistic moral traditions, we value optimism and stoutness of heart in our citizens. Even our New Age ethos teaches that decisiveness and positive thought heal cancer. The ideal cancer patient now is a successful player. I get the sense of a civilization believing itself to be held hostage to its own driven will to power, a will thought capable in the absence of due diligence of turning in on itself—sour and malignant—in a crisis of faith.

Cancer patients stand accused primarily of a failure of will. Small wonder they have been shunned and shamed in our recent history, hidden like a consummate obscenity from public view. Defeatism is a moral outrage, a form of treason in a production driven economy. So the damage is to be limited and contained. We still wage war on cancer with knives and poisons and ray guns—no measure is thought too severe, too disfiguring in the effort to purge the body politic. In the New Age of consumption driven postmodern enlightenment we are more inclined to rehabilitate cancer patients than punish them, less inclined to isolate and destroy. So, today we cajole. We infuse cancer with the power of good thoughts, optimism, and above all will power! Good health has become a new ritual of patriotism, a market place for the public display of secular faith in the power of will. To lose faith in progress, the triumph of rationality over chaos (this is the subtext of cancer in our time, the mythic surround) is to bring down on oneself the demons of an essentially destructive natural order.

But what bearing has this metaphoric vernacular on the problem of physical illness? Readers familiar with Sontag's by now famous line of argument will agree, I think, that for her the metaphoric vernacular around cancer is thoroughly spurious. Of course, all vernacular discourse about illness, even the concept and definition of illness itself, is socially embedded and hence captive of dominant moral/political/economic agendas. The militarization of allopathic medical culture in cancer management is certainly a case in point. The blaming of cancer patients for their illness is another. Even holistic approaches, presumed to be revolutionary, are often subtly captive of dominant ideologies, as I shall detail further on. Illness metaphors reveal as much as they obscure of social processes. It is a matter of how we read them.

Sontag's reading of the idiom is reactionary in two ways. First, insofar as it seeks to limit the legitimate exploration of cancer issues to the search for simple physical causes, it reinstates the hegemony of the orthodox Cartesian paradigm of embodiment. Disease in the dualistic orthodoxy is presumed to inhabit a purely material machinelike body distinctly separate from the mind, the seat of consciousness (Leder 1984). Disease is knowable as the simply physical through reductive analyses unencumbered by the complexity of subjective meanings. Second, in its outright dismissal of the mysteriousness of cancer as merely superstition, her reading forbids the possibility, much less necessity, of critical self-reflection at either the personal or social level. In effect, there is then nothing to know about cancer beyond the simply material. This position is anachronistic even by the standards of allopathic medical science.

To the contrary, cancer poses a significant epistemic challenge to our culture since it is, in fact, still quite mysterious. Cancer is neither controllable nor for the most part well understood. Idiomatic metaphors about cancer engage that mystery and attempt to formulate a relevant discourse about what cancer means for us in terms of both the social/productive organization of modern culture and the texture of our personal lives situated in that concrete historical context. The capture of that idiom by the apparatus of social control must be deconstructed. The most thoroughgoing deconstruction of the captive imaginings about cancer will necessarily depend upon an understanding of how the embodied individual experiences illness meanings authentically. This is no less a project than the penetration of the opaque objectivity of the simply material body of disease, the overthrow of the positivistic paradigm of embodiment that forms the principal ideologic superstructure of technologic culture.

There is an open question about the socially critical status of authentic personal meanings, especially since personal self-actualization in our consumer culture has become one of the locations for the deployment of desire in the market by the structures of social control. This is one of the central issues in the current critical discussion of the contemporary culture of narcissism. A working assumption for me in these pages is that bodily felt experiencing is inherently resistant to social capture, but the demonstration of this assumption lies well beyond the scope of this essay. Interested readers may wish to examine Gendlin, Chapter Eight, for a detailed discussion of this matter.

The task of this project is the deconstruction of cancer as a simply physical disease. I will develop instead the notion of cancer as an environment of bodily felt experiencing. Toward that end I will first look at the development of nineteenth century medical discourse about disease as it enshrines and then transcends the notion of simple physical causes. I will suggest a way of understanding the interpenetration of material and nonmaterial features of illness environment. I will then assess the adequacy of postmodern twentieth century medical discourses to comprehend the place of meaning in illness. I will propose a view of embodiment that is adequate to the task. Finally, I will close with some observations about the current status of holistic thinking about cancer in light of the recent paradigmatic shift in medical thinking and the popularity of elements of ancient sacred healing traditions.

Cancer is a staggeringly complex phenomenon for which there are not, and likely will not be, simple understandings. Currently allopathic medical opinion tends to regard cancer as not one but many separate diseases. While I suspect this is partly an artifact of incomplete knowledge and an atomistic classificatory schema, it nonetheless serves to underscore the extent of biologic variability encountered across the modern cancer phenomenon. Biologically suspect factors in the etiology of cancers are commonly thought to include: viral and fungal organisms, endogenous genetic/constitutional processes, exogenous environmental substances, and nutrition. Relatively little is still understood about how the interaction of these factors contributes to the appearance of symptomology. So the complexity is indeed great and cancer increasingly is viewed as multi-determined. In this atmosphere cancer research concentrates more and more on the regulatory environment of abnormal cell growth. Cancer medicine has moved steadily away from the language of first causes toward concepts of dynamically interactive fields. This brings medicine more in step with contemporary theoretical developments in physics, chemistry and biology which favor nonmechanically reductive models of reality (Capra 1983; Prigogine and Stengers 1984).

Paradoxically, the more adept modern hard-science technologies have become at penetrating deeper into the nexus of material reality the less convincing their mechanical/causal understanding. And this is certainly true of nineteenth-century bacteriologic science. Public health awareness prior to the development of the germ theory of pathogenic causes was dominated by attention to the cleanliness of the social environment (Starr 1982). Disease and moral condition were still conceptually interwoven. The origin of infectious disease was considered to reside in the moral dimension of community history. The representation of disease as a moral configuration was characteristic of the premodern social perspective (Turner 1984). With the advent of the microscope and the identification of microbial pathogens, interest in the social/moral environment of disease waned. In effect the moral discourse about disease, the language of environments, was appropriated and subsumed by the medical domain.

And yet this reduction of the moral dimension of disease to simple material causes was also ultimately responsible for the transcendence of material reductive paradigms in the postmodern era. Toward the close of the last century the technologically amplified vision of bacteriologic science revealed that the presence of pathogenic micro-organisms was a necessary but not sufficient cause of tuberculosis. Roughly 10 percent of those who were demonstrably in contact with the tubercle bacillus became actively symptomatic. The concept of host resistance or susceptibility to pathogenic agents, the concept of an internal disease environment capable of mediating the effect of simple physical causes, arose as a direct result of the technologic capacity to extend the visible dimension of material reality.

The concept of host resistance, however, did not gain currency nor reveal its revolutionary impact upon the metaphysics of disease until the latter half of the present century. This was contingent upon changing epidemiological patterns, economic conditions and modes of knowledge in advancing industrial societies. The success of bacteriologic science in controlling acute infectious epidemics disclosed beneath the veil of contagion a new domain of chronic, debilitative noncontagious diseases that could not be attributed to pathogenic agency. And it was here that the conceptualization of the patient as a host environment was to become a central heurism in the construction of disease models along the leading edge of postmodern allopathy.

The patient-as-host is a decisioning matrix at the convergence of social/historical, psychological and biological lines of force. The locus of disease consequently shifts from external invasive agents to the internal invitational climate of a concretely situated host. No longer a passive recepticle, like a culture dish, for implanted pathogens, the host body becomes the dwelling place of a conscious social actor. Social context and motivated responding become legitimate arenas for medical discourse.

While the medical subsumption of community morality under the supervision of bacteriologic science constituted a concentration of medical focus, a contraction of social concerns to matters of physical substance, the concept of host resistance widened the field of view. It now legitimately included nonmaterial dimensions.

The technology that made possible the ascendency of a material-reductive discourse about disease ultimately rendered that perspective theoretically obsolete. Sentimental faith in the language of simple physical causes, the language of nineteenth-century naturalistic modernism, is now out of step with the paradigmatic shift implicit in postmodern medical science. The opening of the field of disease recognizes that bodily disease is an appropriate occasion for simultaneous, interpenetrating theoretic speculations—political, philosophic, historical, psychological as well as physiological (Turner 1984; Foucault 1975). We are no longer confined to the timeless physical body of disease. We are now permitted to ask the sentient, historically situated body about environments and meanings of environments.

Thus, critical inquiry into the relationship between cancer and the organization of industrial culture finds legitimate expression not only in the metaphoric vernacular around the popular perception of cancer but increasingly in the medical literature as well. Empirical support comes from a variety of comparative epidemiologic sources. Cancer incidence across divergent cultures, populations within cultures, and geographic regions is known to vary widely (Winter 1979). Urban populations, for instance, tend toward higher cancer fatality than rural. And a similar differential in incidence has been systemically reported for nonindustrial people, for example, Tibetans pre- and postexile (Choedrak 1983) and North American Indians pre- and postcontact with whites (Hoffman 1928). Socioeconomic status effects, occupational hazards, life-style strains, diet, and environmental pollutants either singly or in combination have all been implicated at one time or another in the etiologic picture of cancer as an industrial phenomenon. And yet, while epidemiologic speculation about cancer incidence remains largely tentative and controversial in regard to specific hypotheses, it is nonetheless on the whole highly suggestive of industrial culture effects in cancer (Wilkins 1974).

So the mysteriousness of cancer is not a matter of some as yet unknown simple physical cause. It seems likely that how we live, the environments we create, and the meanings of those environments are important factors. And this, of course, echoes the deep traditional wisdoms about the interdependence of the material and nonmaterial aspects of existence. The elder statesman of traditional Tibetan medicine, when asked if he could account for the phenomenon of cancer, attributed it to "industrial manufacture and restlessness of mind" (Choedrak 1983). Despite the theoretic shifts in contemporary disease models this is still a difficult notion for our medical culture to grasp, that the material and spiritual worlds are a unified whole.

DISEASE AND THE SACRED

The irrationality of the metaphoric vernacular around cancer is what disturbs critics like Sontag the most. I have suggested above that this irrationality is valuable in so far as it challenges our culture's critical self-knowledge. I want to look now a bit more closely at how that works.

Disease that is perceived as uncontrollable, beyond the technologic range of our culture's medicine, will likely become the subject of a significant discourse framed in nonrational terms. Cancer is an example. Tuberculosis was in its time. But with the discovery of the pathogenic bacillus, tuberculosis for the most part ceased to carry those metaphoric meanings. This should not be construed as evidence for the spuriousness of metaphoric talk, but rather for a certain cultural smugness as newly captive disease loses it critical cutting edge, its authority to ask questions about how we understand ourselves and the world we inhabit. The value-free stance of naturalistic medicine silences such talk. It presumes that rationality exhausts the knowable.

But the hierarchies of understandings that mediate social action in human ecosystems are not capable of being fully rationalized (Rappaport 1970). Even highly sophisticated analytic models of complex natural systems are in general not sufficiently exhaustive to allow precise prediction of outcomes of many sorts of social action. There are innumerable instances of uncontrolled results of exhaustively analyzed technical operations in our contemporary experience—for example, petro-chemical interventions in our food chain.

Natural ecosystems are teleologically more complex and less coherently coupled than even the most elegant laboratory analogues. Complex living systems, unlike machine systems, continuously create order in the matrix of relationships among their elements that is not given by the elements themselves. Such systems are modulated and ordered through the operation of relationships only some of which are likely to be amenable to deterministic analysis. Natural systems are not totally visible to technologic scrutiny.

Technologic operations tend to presume, contrary to fact, that any segment of a complex system which may be isolated for the purposes of analysis may be in practice isolated from the whole. This central tendency of atomistic approaches contributes significantly to an ecological hubris, a lack of basic respect for not completely understood endogenous regulatory processes. This translates into technologically amplified insensitivities to the maladaptive effects of social actions, principally the degradation of the biotic environment. Rappaport (1970) warned therefore, that human activity must be informed by a large measure of respect for the living order which cannot be rendered causally transparent.

It is axiomatic that significant chunks of the collective belief systems of nontechnologic cultures can be naturalistically inaccurate without in any way impairing their adaptive capacity to regulate human activity in the natural world. People need not understand bacteriology, for example, to know that defecating in the public water supply is not a good idea. The religious fabric of cultural beliefs, for instance ritual relationships with the supernatural, will function in such cases to sustain an adaptive relationship with the environment. But it is not the dimension of material/causal facticity upon which religious beliefs rely for their adaptive value.

Rappaport rightly speculated that collective sacred understandings, grounded as they are in the commonality of nondiscursive personally felt experiences of organismic unity, provide a far better analogue of complex living ecosystems than analytic/technologic models. Thus, sacred discourse constellates the complex interrelatedness of living systems and empowers people to live adaptively in consonance with that wholeness. Sacred discourse is inherently mysterious as it leaps across the chasm of the inexplicable to the directly known.

My frank affection for disease metaphors, irrespective of their material facticity, has to do with an abiding sense that they are in our present positivistic climate one of the very last refuges of sacred discourse about illness. Disease, especially life-threatening disease, is the locus of collision for individual and collective, social and biological, material and nonmaterial, sacred and profane imperatives. Our metaphors struggle to comprehend the place of suffering and death, the possibilities for healing, in the complex scheme of things. Such matters are simply not subject to proof. And so our talk about them eschews the parsimonious logic of parts for the gestures that can embrace the whole.

In terms of the social/productive apparatus of technologic culture, the refusal to envision the wholeness of the living ecosystem in which we are inextricably embedded and to inform our actions with an appropriate respect for that intrinsically mysterious unity has encoded cancer directly into the organization of contemporary society. Carcinogenic potentials within the social body can be approached then as the cascades of ecologically maladaptive effects associated with the marginalization of sacred discourse in favor of atomistic, instrumental understandings of social process.

But the maladaptive effects of the marginalization of the sacred are not only a matter of external social/productive relations. My principal concern here is with our relation to ourselves and our capacity to constellate our own wholeness in a cultural context that utilizes the fragmentation of the individual self as an opportunistic strategy of the market economy. At the personal level cancer embodies this struggle of the self toward wholeness, the release of the self from the constraining identification with its objectified parts. Cancer is ultimately an invitation to journey to the interior of deeply, authentically personal meanings beyond the captive and conditioned partial self.

At this juncture I want to turn my attention to the two distinctive, though not wholly discontinuous, currents in twentieth century allopathy that have inquired about disease as an environment of personal meanings.

Both psychosomatic and behavioral medicine have contributed to the transition from the characteristically modern concern with specific causes to the postmodern conceptualization of a multidimensional interactive disease environment. Each, to the extent it has been captive of the reductionist ideologies of techological culture, has had to engage dialectically its own epistemological foundations in order to envision the new field of disease.

PSYCHOSOMATICS

Psychosomatic medicine at its prime during the third through fifth decades of this century set for itself the task of demonstrating psychological specificity in the siting and development of certain chronic degenerative diseases (Reiser 1975; Silverman 1968). The earliest systematic studies concentrated on detailed profiling of personalities in the chronically ill on a case by case basis (Dunbar 1935). While these first attempts were rich in clinical detail, they lacked theoretic coherence and ultimately contributed little to the understanding of specific disease etiologies. However, by the late 1930s psychosomatic medicine had acquired a determined theoretic perspective as the Chicago group around Franz Alexander pioneered the application of Freudian psychoanalytic concepts. Based on Freud's theory of neurosis, the essential pathogenic mechanism of degenerative illness was thought to be the innervation of organ systems associated with the damming of instinctual drive energies that a conflicted ego could not permit to be satisfied.

Since the formulation of neurotic innervation could not of itself account for specific symptomologies, a specificity hypothesis was added. The energy economies of psychosexual complexes were considered, then, to be symbolically encoded in target organ systems along a dimension of vegetative tonus (Alexander 1948). Thus, otherwise disparate illnesses, for example rheumatoid arthritis and hypertension, might be proximally classified. In this case, both conditions would exhibit the tonic quality of "constriction."

How drive energies got to be symbolically encoded at the level of the vegetative organs was the subject of unresolved debate throughout the history of psychosomatic medicine; it underscores the only marginal success research in the field had in coming to rest around the core project of mind-body unification. The debate had its origins in Freud's early distinction between actual neurosis and psychoneurosis (Freud 1929). The former included a variety of seemingly simple physical symptoms like headache, muscular cramping, or organ irritability. An absence of meaning, or what Freud termed "signification in the mind" characterized the actual neuroses. He considered them to be the result of unspecifiable metabolic toxins occasioned by sexual drive conflicts.

In contrast, the psychoneuroses were a class of symptomologies that arose as compensation or substitution around forbidden and repressed libidinal drives. Conversion, a subclass of psychoneurosis, involved the translation of such desires into a more or less transparent paralysis of the volitional body. Freud suggested in characteristically metaphoric style that the psychoneuroses formed around actual neuroses like an oyster pearl around a grain of sand. This implicit discontinuity between physical/metabolic mechanisms and epiphenomenal symbolic meanings was to haunt the steps of psychosomatic inquiry.

Franz Alexander, following Freud, defined a class of visceral neuroses that, unlike the compensatory meaning processes of conversion, functioned on the principle of direct metabolic innervation (Alexander 1939). The thrust of his argument was that while the volitional body seems capable of symbolization, the visceral body does not. This was at best a controversial view. Some researchers were more inclined toward the view that all psychosomatic illnesses, including those of the viscera, involved some kind of symbolic activity, if not strictly conversion.

In practice the whole field of psychosomatic medicine tended to frame the discussion of visceral disease against the backdrop of conversion. This in effect dichotomized the body of volition and the vegetative body, casting the latter as the true body, the dense body, the body alien to meaning. This was, of course, the traditional dualism of Cartesian orthodoxy somewhat in disguise.

With almost no exceptions analytic practitioners lent their attention to a relatively narrow range of diseases considered to be accessible to meaning. These came to be regarded as the psychosomatic diseases. Asthma, colitis, hypertension, migraine, rheumatoid arthritis, thyrotoxicosis, ulcers, and some skin conditions fell into this classification. These conditions presented themselves as concretely situated in their hosts' lives. While making the requisite theoretic genuflections to the notion that every disease is psychosomatic, the field nevertheless routinely defined itself as "bounded on one side by purely organic diseases and on the other by conversions" (Fenichel 1954, p. 307).

Conversion was uninteresting to psychosomatic medicine by virtue of the transparency of the volitional body. The bulk of diseases, however, was regarded as purely physical. They were unapproachable by virtue of their opacity, the density of the truly material body. Psychosomatic medicine bracketed beyond its field of view what it thought to be simply mind and simply body. What remained was neither transparent nor opaque but for the most part essentially murky in the no-man's-land between the dichotomized mind and body.

Psychosomatic medicine was a bit squeamish. It recoiled from the concrete body of disease, regarding it as base and dumb, without language. Psychosomatic discourse occurred at a certain remove from the newly visible body of disease disclosed in the modern development of pathological anatomy and its technological amplifications as Foucault (1975) detailed it. Rather, it preferred to converse in the abstract language of economies of desire and the structural configurations of psychosexual energies. It was principally a language of formal properties relevant to a very small range of primal mind-body interactions.

Thus, psychosomatic theory had little power to specify disease causes. Intrapsychic drive conflicts produced multilayered, complex and highly idiosyncratic interference patterns in the psychosexual personality that could be, in theory at least, teleologically unraveled through analytic dialogue to the point of origination. But this was not a causal/predictive strategy and could not be extended to populations. A persistent obstacle in this regard to the elaboration of predictive models was the demonstrable ubiquity of the standard, presumably determinant, conflictual drive elements even in healthy individuals lacking manifest organ symptomologies. Alexander resorted to calling the evident yet thoroughly elusive premorbid causative ingredients in individual disease incidence the "x-factor." Psychosomatic medicine failed in its own terms to specify disease causes.

But psychosomatic medicine was not a language of experienced meanings either. It valued the objective acumen of the analytic practitioner. As physical medicine was ushered into the modern era by the anatomical dissection of corpses the physician ceased to be a logician of correspondences and became the locus of sensory observation (Foucault 1975). But to the extent that experience became an essential ingredient of the medical encounter with disease, it was solely the experience of the skilled clinician, as neutral observer, that was enshrined. Psychosomatic medicine shared with physical medicine this naturalistic view of the medical context.

As far as the psychosomatic patient was concerned, the symbolic epiphenomenal meanings of the primal body were not so much experienced by as attributed to him or her. The objective of analytic dialogic disclosure was to bring the patient into rational proximity with the intricately prefigured irrational relations of desire. The patient as an experiencing self stood largely outside and subordinate to the formal properties of the system. The analytic diagnostician, rather than performing an examination as an act of direct perception, deciphered the essential, logically prior, order of the psychosexual economy through the patient's clues. The psychosomatic inquiry was basically a cryptographic project operated upon the patient as a somewhat incidental object. In this respect, the analyst, more logician of inferences than observer, was far closer to the premodern physician of classificatory medicine.

Characteristic of the premodern, preanatomical, medical perspective was the independence of disease from the concrete body (Foucault 1975). Definition and correspondences of formal elements had priority over the localization of disease in tissues and organs. Disease inhabited a categorical space above the body. In much the same way psychosomatic medicine remained aloof from both the body of experienced meaning and the body of disease. It resembled more a rarified nosology of primal desire than a deduction of specific psychological causes, despite its aspirations to predictive science.

And yet psychosomatic medicine was informed by a powerful mythopoetic intuition of the resonance of mind and body. It had the courage to project the space of desire onto the visceral body at the occasion of disease. And so it installed in the public domain the legitimacy, once and for all, of inquiry into the personal meaning of illness. Behavioral medicine was eventually to take that inquiry far from the confines of psychosexual concepts and nosological predilections.

BEHAVIORAL MEDICINE

Behavioral medicine emerged as an identifiably distinct approach to the mind-body problem in disease around the mid 1970s (Gentry 1984). Although some psychodynamically oriented research has carried over, particularly visible in the attempts to identify personality traits contributory to chronic illness, the culture-wide climate of naturalistic positivism finds itself quite at home in behavioral attitudes toward illness. Perhaps the failure of psychodynamic approaches to delineate a coherent causal/predictive strategy has accelerated the turn toward frankly positivistic constructs about meanings. At any rate, the most significant aspect of the multidisciplinary approach of behavioral medicine has been the explosive technologic expansion of insight into biophysiological substrates of animal and human behavior. Current behavioral perspectives survey a very broad field of biological and psychosocial contributory factors in disease.

Early work on the physiological substrates of behavior concentrated on defensive organic responses to stressful stimuli. Selye's (1950) conceptualization of a general adaptive response envisioned a unitary, nonspecific response to all stressors. But this unifying heurism, while attractive, has generally come to be regarded since then as too parsimonious to account adequately for the observed intricacy of interactions involving central nervous system structures, neurohumoral pathways, and organ systems. Research advances in neuroanatomy, immunology, and endocrinology have both allowed for and required far greater specificity with regard to the biophysiologic substrates of emotional states and behavioral responses to stress (see for example, Ader 1981).

Currently attention is focused on two neuroendocrine axes that function as the major chemical pathways of communication between the centers of the brain responsible for meaning processes and the rest of the body. Catecholamine pathways have been implicated in autonomic nervous system activation and thus in affective as well as visceral tonus. Corticosteroid pathways play a critical role in mediating immune responsiveness to disease processes.

While this new body of psycho/neuro/endocrinologic/immunologic literature is an impressive testimony to the intricacy of the relationships involved in disease mediation and the humbling incompleteness of knowledge about specific disease mechanisms, one conclusion is certainly in order. All physiologic systems, organ structures, and homeostatic processes in the human body, including perhaps most importantly immune functions traditionally thought to be autonomous, may be regarded as subject to the regulatory influence of central nervous system organizations of experienced meaning (Ader & Cohen 1984). The preponderance of scientific evidence—one source cites well over one thousand contributions to the literature in a recent six year period (Locke & Hornig-Rohan 1983)—now argues for a significant connection between mind and bodily disease.

Some researchers have begun to conceive of the neuroendocrine pathways as bi-directional vectors relating catecholamine activity to effort and relaxation and corticoid activity to depression and euphoria (Henry & Meehan 1981). In this way specific meaning states may be linked through neuroendocrine communication to specific disease susceptibility. Depression and suppression of immunocompetence is thought to be an exemplary case in point (Depue 1979).

But this is not only a powerful exposition of disease processes. Behavioral medicine has acquired almost unwittingly a heuristic tool for talking about wellness and extraordinary realities like yogic and shamanic ecstatic healing states.

While the expansion of scientific knowledge around molecular substrates of mind-body interaction has proceeded at break-neck pace, efforts to correlate psychosocial environment effects with disease onset have been generally disappointing. Animal experimentation throughout the 1970s consistently demonstrated a strong relationship between laboratory induced stress and lowered tumor resistance (see Riley 1975 for the classic study). This fueled interest in identifying epidemiologically premorbid human social stress factors, especially helplessness and depression. Results have been far from clear.

Studies of social support networks as factors in illness resistance have not achieved a strong consensus, though there is mild support for the hypothesis that social ties confer beneficial effects (Krantz & Glass 1984). The loss of a spouse is evidently a factor in increased cancer risk (Joseph & Syme 1982). But efforts to tally stressful life events in an arithmetic of illness susceptibility have proved confusing (Kasl 1983). Research into personality traits and coping styles as factors in disease incidence has produced divergent results (Lazarus 1982). The one notable exception in this last category is, of course, type "A" personality and coronary heart disease (Chesney & Rosenman 1983).

Dissatisfaction in the behavioral research community with many psychosocial studies has revolved around traditional methodological issues, especially retrospective design, which tends to confound cause and effect. But there are a few genuinely prospective studies that offer some corroborative evidence for the etiologic effect of psychosocial conditions (for example, Thomas et al 1979).

While the methodological criticisms are to be taken seriously and there is much to be gained from carefully controlled doubly prospective longitudinal study of well populations, there is an over-arching problem that has gone largely unaddressed. The conceptual apparatus of behavioral research is still very poorly equipped to explore the dimension of experienced meanings. I think this may account for many divergencies (perhaps corroborations as well) in research results.

Constrained by the positivistic bias of behavioral precepts to study objectively construable things, the literature has armed itself with static constructs about experience. These constructs refer basically to four classes of observable behavioral indicators: states, traits, styles and events. The quantity of stressful life events or social ties will be measured. Evidence for specific attitudes, stressful emotions or coping styles will be tallied. But the subjective meaning of these indicators to the individuals in the studied populations will not be adequately investigated. So we don't really know what the presence or absence of behavioral indicators means about illness and actually experienced meanings.

This is evident in the frequently heated ecclesiastical discussions in the literature of the formal properties, durations, quality and intensity of stress, in which little attention is given to the subjectively experienced meaning of presumedly stressful conditions. As an aside, it is interesting to note that in engineering terms 'stress' properly signifies the objectively measurable force applied externally to a mechanical system. 'Strain' signifies the impact of stress force. So the language of stress is actually twice removed from the dimension of human experiencing. It is not at all clear what the volumes of literature on psychosocial "stress" tell us realistically about humans; this is evident in the widely divergent findings.

We need to know not merely that certain events occur, attitudes are espoused or behaviors are performed. We need to know what they indicate about felt meanings, especially if we are to apply study results to therapeutic contexts for prevention and/or healing.

This sort of confusion in the behavioral literature results from the use of constructs that deal with attributed experiences rather than with directly felt experiencing. More than twenty years ago Gendlin (1962) distinguished between the construct "experience," which consists of all possible conceptual contents whether or not they are actually present in awareness, and the referent "experiencing," which points only to immediately felt data. Though routinely confounded in the literature, experiences as conceptual contents and experiencing as felt presence are not equivalent. Certainly, as every therapist knows, explicit conceptualizations of experience may or may not accurately reflect what is actually going on in a deeply felt way.

As Schutz (1967 p. 216) warned, "It is methodologically inadmissible to interpret a given series of acts objectively. . . .and then ascribe to them a subjective meaning." Yet this is what the behavioral literature does routinely out of a positivistic cynicism and insecurity about the reality or value of subjective experiencing.

In the wake of such methodological bias there have been frequent calls for the development of an interpretive science capable of researching subjective meaning processes from within but in a methodologically sound fashion. Gendlin (1962) observed, for instance, the relative ease with which direct reference to subjective experiencing may be integrated into positivistic research strategies both before and after operational steps without surrendering or altering such strategies. Thus, experiencing as such may even be quantified. More recently Rogers (1985) cited a number of well-developed heuristic, hermeneutic and phenomenological research approaches that all share a capacity for integrating nonreductionistic organization of experienced meanings into coherent investigative strategies. Nor has the recognition of the need for interpretive science been limited to humanistic social scientists. Thinkers on the leading edge of postmodern paradigmatic shifts in hard science frequently acknowledge the parallels between new acausal understandings of elemental physical reality and interpretive approaches to meaning in psychology (Prigogine & Stengers 1984).

THE VISIBLE AND NOT SO VISIBLE

Psychosomatic medicine occupied a place analogous to pre-anatomical classificatory physical medicine, which deciphered disease forms at considerable remove from the density of the concrete material body. Psychosomatics actually defined the legitimate field of interest in terms of its relative opacity. Much as, according to Foucault (1975), the development of pathological anatomy rendered the impenetrable density of physical disease finally visible even in the enclosed tissues of the individual body, behavioral medicine effected an equally dramatic and revolutionary descent into the psychosomatic body of disease meanings.

This penetration of the not so visible occurred simultaneously but with unequal clarity on two fronts: the technologic disclosure of molecular chemical substrates of behavior, the energic pathways linking the physiologic body with neurologic structures of meaning; and the broadening democratization of the field of meanings relevant to disease. The murky chasm between the mind and body of psychosomatic disease, conversed about in the hushed and rarified aristocratic formal language of desire, is revealed to be an energetic commerce of mind and body inputs languaged in an accessible vernacular of mechanical stresses.

On the face of it, the interactive mind-body field is now transparent not only to the scientific view but to the surveillance of the marketplace as well; witness the explosive expansion of the modern service sector devoted to the health of the "whole body". But this transparency may yet be deceiving. The descent of postquantum, postentropy elemental science into the subvisible interstices of the organization of matter deconstructed the traditional conceptual armamentarium of the knowledge of material reality. The organization of essential matter itself now resembles more the mysterious ineffability of mind than the solidity of machines (Prigogine & Stengers 1984). Bacteriologic science, I suggest, likewise installed and then ultimately overthrew the concept of simple physical causes in disease.

As the description of the material body of disease in naturalistic terms (now at the molecular and submolecular levels) seems to penetrate material density, the body as we know it becomes more elusive. The technologic instrumentation of neurobiology does not so much resolve the traditional discontinuity of the mind-body juncture into finer detail as radically dissolve it into the subtle energies of implicit, synchronic order, into pathways of communion.

At this new level of subtlety we lose not only the gross material body as we know it but the gross mind, the mind of mental and emotional contents. The projection of the structures of meaning onto the body of disease in behavioral medicine denies the dense body its absolute priority in disease, which had been a given of the naturalistic universe. Moreover, the neurohumoral gradient linking the physical body and the body of meaning discloses a range of interactions beyond the boundaries of pathology. The far reaches of extraordinary realities and capabilities fall within the disclosive range of a true biopsychology. This challenges not only the physical but also the mental realities into which our world is conventionally organized. Perhaps most significantly for behavioral research into the environments of meaning around illness, the infinitely fine differentiations of mind-body attunements implied by the neuroendocrine gradient far exceed the resolving power of our most sophisticated psychological vocabularies.

The boundaries of our familiar emotional states—anger, sadness and so on—begin to look crude and arbitrary. Emotional entities as such begin to lose their objective solidity as well. The revolutionary significance of the postmodern discovery of the pathways of embodied meaning is the dissolution of both psychic and physical entities as we customarily understand them into a fluid synchronic process. Paradoxically, at this historic juncture behavioral medicine finds itself conversing about human meanings in a curiously arcane and inadequate language of causal priorities among nonexistent entities quite as if the old verities which it itself exploded still stood.

THE SUBTLE BODY OF MEANING

Now we need to say a bit more concretely what this embodiment of meaning means in terms faithful to this new reality. Following Gendlin's (1962) philosophy of experiencing and the creation of meaning, we may distinguish abstract conceptual "experiences" from presently felt "experiencing." This is, in fact, an explication of the distinction between the psychic entities of the naturalistic metaphysics of psychology and the fluid process of embodiment implied by postmodern psychoneuroendocrinology.

"Experiencing" is the presence in awareness of bodily felt preconceptual wholes, implicit in which are an unlimited number of ways of symbolizing or making explicit aspects of this whole presence. Experiencing is always larger, richer, more complex than anything we can say about it, any way we at this particular moment refer to it. But we can gain access to the implicit preconceptual whole sense by letting the complexity emerge in explicit symbolizations that exactly fit the whole experiencing. This exact fit between explicit symbolizations and the flow of lived experiencing is the essence of the authentic self.

Since experiencing is implicit preconceptually, the fit of explicit symbolization to it can not be a relationship of logic. Yet as Gendlin discovered, it is hardly random. To Gendlin, experiencing—unlike the Cartesian stance, which radically separates the knower from the known—is an interactive unity in which the experiencing of meaning is never distinct from the situational context in which it occurs. As Gendlin expressed it, "How one feels is not some after-event coming on top of what happens, it is what happens" (Gendlin 1973, p. 324).

There is a purposive flow to experiencing, a temporal and valuative continuity in the sense that experiencing always wants to be carried forward. Every moment of experiencing implies still further specific situational relatedness, which will carry the meaning of the situation on. We know this quite concretely for ourselves in the way that, for example, with organismic imperatives only certain next steps will seem right. When we are hungry, eating constellates as the next step and then probably only certain foods will do at this moment, and so on. This is true not merely for such basically simple situations but for all experiencing. The felt continuity in experiencing, the rightness of fit of emergent symbolizations in the explication of implicit experiencing, is the defining characteristic of experiential process.

Experiencing is an organismic wholeness directly felt in the body. When experiencing proceeds in a way that is faithful to this organismic unity, a way Gendlin (1981) calls focusing, explicit symbolizations are allowed to fit, as they emerge step by step, the implicit whole felt sense rather than to be imposed upon it as a limitation of our self awareness; and the body consequently relaxes in distinctly pleasurable releases of held tension. Conversely, experiencing that identifies the self with objectified content conceptualizations and is thus stuck in symbolizations that do not really fit, that have not organismically emerged from the implicit whole felt sense, builds and holds tension in the body.

This latter condition, the various ways of not living in the embodied organismic experiencing of felt wholeness, is the definition of pathology for Gendlin. Thus, "the body forms any next behavior from all relevant aspects, but in troubles there is no way to live all aspects further . . . there is no way to act or speak so that all that is involved can be lived. Only on the plane of inward space and the forming of a felt sense is there a way for the body to produce a next step that takes everything relevant into account" (Gendlin 1974, p. 236).

In the absence of such felt whole sensing in the subtle energy body, we settle for socially captive discursive relations with ourselves and the world. We have ourselves as a collection of objectified entities: sensations, thoughts, feelings, concepts of self-reference that only inadequately carry the authentic whole meanings implicit in our bodily lived inner subjective space. Routinely we reject, ignore, tune out our ongoing experiencing that cannot readily be organized in the customary, socially consensual, objectified ways of construing our inner reality. Our rich sense of inherent connectedness, of our self with other, the world, the cosmos, and of our self most profoundly within the wholeness of our own lives is sacrificed to an atomized and thus diminished reality of thinly connected parts. We cling tenaciously to this construction of an objective universe of clearly bounded and separable entities.

This rather cynically mechanical view of reality conditions our relations to the nonmaterial dimension of feeling and spirit. We deny what cannot be mechanically construed and verified by essentially deterministic proofs. Even our feeling life is conducted this way as if it were a syllogistic exercise: this idea of me, and then that one, therefore I should feel/be this way and no other. So we expend enormous energy and effort constructing, defending and patching a reality of acceptable self-reflexive forms that do not permit the fresh and spontaneous creation of newly emergent modes of relatedness moment by moment in our intrinsically open and unconditioned ground of experiencing. It is this limitation of our self-experiencing to objectified self-concepts that keep us painfully stuck in our troubles, isolated from the rich and genuine contact with ourself and others that we desire.

Relaxing into an openness toward the deep currents of felt experiencing, we descend from the material body of static, determinate entities (things, ideas, emotions) into the subtle body of resonant energies. This is the place where we feel shifts in the subtle tensions of the energy body as we penetrate the static density of our concepts about our feelings into the infinitely richer whole felt experiencing. The subtle body speaks to us of realities for which there can be no proof, for it dwells beyond the logic of our causal certainties in a field of infinitely subtle relatedness. It is here in the subtle body that dreaming unfolds beyond the constraints of linear time and material space. And it is in the subtle body that spirit reveals itself as the unbounded continuity of all existence. And most importantly for our discussion here, it is in the subtle body that disease constellates as inherently meaningful self-process and symptoms transform from defects in the mechanically construed body into explicit signs of the emergent implicit self.

The subtle body of felt meaning is the body of true interiority and unconditioned subjectivity. While it is true that "bodies may be governed. . . .embodiment is the phenomenological basis of individuality" (Turner 1984, p. 251).

DISEASE AND MEANING: THE CANCER CONNECTION

Psychoneuroendocrinological research strongly implicates depression and hopelessness in the suppression of immunocompetence and hence in a decreased resistance to disease, in particular tumorogenicity. The mechanism principally indicated is increased corticosteroid activity, which when chronic tends to have deleterious effects on lymphatic tissues. While the state of current understandings still precludes any high degree of specificity with regard to depression and physiological correlates, a strong case has been made for depression as a final common pathway for a host of modern illnesses, cancer included (Depue 1979). Yet the epidemiological evidence for clinical depression as an etiological factor in particular cancers, while suggestive, is quite a bit less strong. It is hard to know what this means. It may signify that the artifactual parsimony of experimental conditions permits stronger findings than the "messy" conditions of real peoples' lives. This would argue in my view for the development of process-sensitive interpretive research methods rather than the static states/traits approach currently in vogue.

Further support for process-oriented research comes in the form of the major conundrum in the debate about the cancer-depression connection. It has to do with the issue of tumor latency. Conventional wisdom has it that tumors are commonly some thirty-to-forty years in the making. It is hard then to see how proximal life events, the loss of a spouse eighteen months prior to a cancer diagnosis, for example, might be causative. But the epidemiological literature, as I pointed out above, clearly points that way. It is commonly suggested in the literature that any observed depression in the vicinity of a cancer diagnosis may be an effect, not cause, of the cancer.

The puzzle intensifies when we consider the countless cases of cancer that commonly disregard prognostication of outcomes in both directions, for better or worse. William Boyd (1966), the eminent pathologist, was sufficiently moved by this phenomenon to collect clinical data on spontaneous, that is inexplicable, regressions in a variety of human cancers and to ruminate on the possible explanations. It seemed to him back then that far too little was known of the intricate cybernetics of cancer cell regulation to say anything conclusive about the temporal development of cancers. This is still largely the case today. But phenomenologically it seemed clear to Boyd that cancer growth was far more labile, both regressively and progressively, than it was customary to suppose.

This observation about clinically documented inexplicable regressions was buttressed by the high number (nearly 25 percent) of nonsymptomatic cancers unrelated to cause of death revealed in autopsy over the long course of Boyd's career. The presence of malignant tissue did not by itself seem to constitute disease, that is, illness in the sense one recognizes oneself to be sick.

Furthermore, Boyd was curious about the "phantom" ability of some cancers to disappear, sometimes quite rapidly, leaving paradoxical tissue evidence in support of their presumed existence. Boyd speculated that perhaps cancers can differentiate very quickly and become for all intents and purposes indistinguishable from normal surrounding tissue.

Overall, he was inclined toward the view that the phenomenology of cancer, if physicians did not arbitrarily exclude from their view these puzzling features for which there are not mechanical explanations, suggested it was not a "thing," an entity, but a process. The static histologic/morphologic snapshot used to diagnose and prognosticate could not, then, be expected to disclose the dimension of movement. In an analogous way, a high-speed snapshot of a ball thrown in the air would freeze the movement and then not reveal if the ball were on the way up or down.

Boyd did not hazard a guess about the relative weights of factors in the tumorogenic equation (genetics, toxins, psychic states, etc.). But there are some important speculations that may be drawn from his thinking. Cancer as a process-in-movement may not be reducible to cell morphologies, that is, momentary structural arrangements or contents. Cancer may be always present in the body as an interactive steady-state. This latter notion should not be confused with contemporary surveillance theory, which frames the discourse in terms of individual renegade cells. This steady-state may be highly labile and very sensitive to modulations of the whole body/mind system. In fact, the thresholds above which the process is perceived by the individual as disease symptomatic may vary as an aspect of the modulations.

Boyd did recommend as a result of his investigation into spontaneous remission that the medical community cease trying to kill cancer and instead concentrate on methods of inviting normal differentiation. Since in his view cancer was not an "it" there was nothing to kill but tissues that might be persuaded to differentiate normally. He suspected that the autopsy data argued for the possibility that a large number of people may live in balanced, non-ill relation to "cancer" for indefinite, perhaps extended, periods of time. One could wonder at this point whether the fine-comb approach in the technologic detection of cancers and the subsequent invasive treatment protocols does not in its own right account for a certain proportion of our high annual cancer fatality.

The ruminations above reinforce the central heurism of this paper: that cancer may best be thought of not as a disease entity but a relational process not separable from its subtle environmental context. In reducing cancer and life contexts to content entities and stripping them of their embedded contextual particularity, in assuming predictive lawfulness, the unfolding of individual process relationships as instances of unique and irreversible creativity is lost to our view. Contents are not, Gendlin (1974) reminded us, basic. They are created in the process of living, as aspects of that particular living. As a particular relational process moves forward through time, as it changes, so do the emergent contents. This particular movement is not repeatable. It can be grasped only as it unfolds its implicit order and only in ways that are respectful of the not fully knowable endogenous regulatory processes of the whole system. Cancer may be a good example of the kind of complex ecological process for which reductive discourse, the marginalization of the sacred respect for wholeness, is especially maladaptive at the individual level.

CASES

Let me cite a few representative cases from clinical practice to illustrate this point. These cases are not extraordinary; any clinician working with cancer patients in a way that respects and collaborates with embodied meaning process will have many similar stories to tell. But they are extraordinary because in some important respect each of them defies our customary understandings of how physical illness works. Those moments can only be comprehended as aspects of a contextual process in movement.

T. was a late middle-aged luminary in the human potential movement. He had a passionately conflicted marriage with a woman who at the time I met him had just died of breast cancer. In the course of their often violent fighting, which lasted right up to her death, she had on a number of occasions accused him of giving her the cancer. In the limousine on the way home from the cemetary he suddenly recalled her accusation and felt in some unclear way he could not quite get a hold of that she had been right. He sank into remorse, feeling the weight of their emotional symbiosis, which even death could not lift. On the ride home he developed a mild cough, but it persisted for weeks. Not too long after he was admitted to hospital for tests and an inoperable lung cancer was diagnosed. He engaged me at that point to help him out. In very short order, for he was experienced and adept at self-processing, a sense began to form of his thwarted but passionate desire to create as an artist and to live his life as he never had at the service of that desire. He decided to refuse the treatment offered—he was considered terminal anyway—and to spend his last days on a remote beach somewhere breathing the life of an artist and writing the novel of his dreams. He went south. A couple of years later, his novel complete, he died up north of a heart attack. There was no trace of his cancer.

M. was a vibrant young mother who at the time I first saw her had just begun chemotherapy following a mastectomy. Her prognosis was regarded as quite good. This was reinforced by the energetic optimism and spiritual immersion that characterized her life. She was a real fighter and a gentle inspiration to everyone who met her, especially the members of her liberal protestant church, who genuinely revered her. As we worked together over the course of a year a different picture surfaced. She had been raised in a stridently puritanical religious setting and despite all her efforts felt unable to break out from underneath the oppression of her family values, which hung over her like a pall. Through focusing inwardly on her bodily felt sense of an inchoate freedom deep within her she was finally able to give birth to a kinesthetic symbolization of it, a kind of dream dance that perfectly constellated her emergent free self. Though she worked with this transformative symbol during our sessions she became disturbed that she was unable to give her life on the outside that vital quality. Working with her bodily felt sensing of this new whole context, transformed as it was by the dance of life but still not free, she was able to find what was in the way. The newly awakened but still implicit sexual energies that vivified her dream dance were totally unacceptable to her. She was still captive of her nuclear family. The very next session she reported a nagging pain in her lower back which she thought was a strain. I encouraged her to focus on it. She felt the cancer was there somehow and that it was now systemic. Diagnostic work-ups later in the week proved her right. She became steadily worse and died not too long after, still an inspiration to her shocked and unsuspecting friends.

B. is a tradesman, at retirement age when I met him a few years back. He had come from a strict and serious background, accustomed to independence, competence and undiminished energy. But there was a side to him that just wanted to grow and smell the flowers. So he was experiencing some difficulty integrating his new life circumstances. Following some health problems he was diagnosed leukemic at a major cancer center. He was given a poor prognosis, about eighteen months with treatment. He was advised to begin transfusion immediately, with chemotherapy to follow soon. But he felt that if he accepted transfusion it would be the beginning of the end, the sure road to death, and he was not ready to die. So he refused. Instead, he started to explore nutritional healing on his own. But he had trouble settling on any one plan of the many he tried. Each one somehow did not quite fit. So little by little he put together his own program guided mainly by what felt right for him. It featured vitamins, especially 'C', which he took in megadoses. His history with psychological methods was similar. I never felt I succeeded in teaching him awareness work as I thought it should be done. But gradually I learned to trust his process, however it looked to me, and not interfere. His blood chemistry sometimes looks seriously leukemic, sometimes pretty healthy by normal standards. He always seems able to know implicitly when it is leukemic; it mirrors conflicts with his energies and expectations. The fluctuations continue. He is actively enjoying life several years now past the original terminal prognosis, without ever having any treatment.

N. was a bright and very caring middle-aged woman with grown children and a husband in the professions. Her marriage was unfulfilled. Her husband always seemed to her absorbed in his work and emotionally self-contained. Yet he leaned on her a lot. As a result her emotional needs went unmet. Their sexual life was by this time nonexistent. Her attempts at developing a career for herself once the kids were out of the house were verbally supported by her husband but, it seemed, shrewdly and passively undermined. Vacillating between staying in the marriage and leaving, she finally resolved to make a go of it. She determinedly planned activities the two of them could do together in the hopes of developing some emotional intimacy, but this strategy backfired. When they skied together he was competitive and much better at it; she usually felt worse after these events, alienated and resentful. One day on the slopes she fell, not badly, but it was a struggle to get up. Her husband, instead of being supportive, taunted and lectured about the proper way to fall and get up. She slumped back in the snow in a wave of despair and thought: I'll never do this again! Later that week a mild pain below her knee suggested to her that the fall had been perhaps worse than she thought. When it did not go away she saw a physician and a rare sarcoma was diagnosed. A very disabling surgery was performed, which saved her leg but left her lame. She completed a chemotherapy protocol and learned to walk on her leg despite the surgery. She was plucky and even taught herself how to use a brace to play tennis. At this time I began to work with her in group. She was generally reticent about her marital unhappiness and chose to concentrate on positive thinking. She seemed on the face of it to be doing well. But despite an optimistic prognosis, a couple of years after the initial diagnosis the cancer was found again around the knee and this time her leg was removed. Again, her recovery was nothing short of phenomenal. She attributed it to her indomitable spirit. But I felt her emotional life went largely unaddressed. She let fester a powerful romantic interest developed at the time of her first surgery without following it up. Her marriage continued to deteriorate beneath the surface. A few years elapsed during which she concentrated on learning to walk, keeping her spirits up and finding activities she could do. Her physicians finally informed her she was off the charts; she was cured. Within a year distant metastatic sites appeared. At this point her emotional life could no longer be contained. She made some efforts at trial separation, but they were half-hearted. As she grew weaker she fantasized leaving home and starting over, acknowledging to herself that in some way she had known all along that her unhappiness would probably kill her. She died a year and one-half or so after being declared officially cured.

These life stories are not principally stories of miraculous healing, though certainly such experiencing in the subtle body of meaning around cancers does genuinely, if rarely, occur. The range of meanings is as infinitely large and varied as the range of historic human possibilities itself. Thus, we do encounter in cancer patients not only simple modern naturalistic understandings of their disease process (the realization, for example, that the ionizing radiation of smoking has contributed to a lung cancer) but shamanic ones as well in which a frankly terminal cancer might present itself as a guided descent into esoteric knowledge through ritual dismemberment and miraculous rebirth. But a cautionary note is in order here, since our current cultural fascination with mystical healing can have a chilling and reifying effect upon the process of genuine self-knowledge around disease, as I shall elaborate further in a moment.

So here, in these cases, I have chosen to emphasize the more ordinary embeddedness of cancer in people's lives. While some cancer patients do present a classical picture of depression that seems on the face of it etiologic, it is also true that many do not. In fact, I am often struck by the seemingly robust psychological status of many patients I meet. From all indications N. fit what might be called the "fighter" profile so highly regarded these days. A spiritually engaged and upbeat woman with a health network of social support through her church, she tracked her cancer right off the charts. Her recovery from debilitating and demoralizing medical procedures was exemplary. And yet her life was stuck in a crucial respect and unfulfilled. The cancer spoke eloquently in her life of her courageous and extended struggle to understand her inner life and the tricky balance required to stand on her own in the context of relatedness to others.

For M., a similarly motivated fighter, her breast cancer constellated the difficulty she faced in accepting and living forward her deep sexual self. B.'s efforts to integrate his conflicted self-expectations with his available energies is mirrored in the fluid fluctuations of the leukemic process. The site of cancers speaks in this way directly to cancer patients about the critical arena in which the struggle for the wholeness of self is occurring.

Each of the above cases illustrates the remarkable synchronicity of the cancer process at the level of cells, organs and tissues with the felt meanings of the patients' lives. Often that synchronicity involves almost immediate shifts in the body of disease symptoms, sometimes apparently startling reversals in direction. M. was doing well when her inner work constellated her dream and its stuckness. The impasse was resolved in her death, which seemed more possible than carrying her sexual body forward.

For T., living out his heartfelt dream rid him of an incurable cancer. But he promptly died of heart failure. I am tempted to say his cancer was not a distinct illness but just one moment in his life-long struggle to find the heart for living. He succeeded and then stopped.

Death is an integral part of the process of living forward. Recently I saw an adolescent girl suffering with (not from) a horribly crippling and painful cancer. She continued to hold on despite all odds. Everyone around her marveled that she could live month after month in such a hopeless and weakened condition. Several hours after the birth of her sister's first child she died quietly. Not infrequently cancer patients predict with breathtakingly uncanny accuracy the moment of their deaths. Often the predictions seem to contradict the logic of their medical condition, but they are always meaningful in their lives.

Increasingly in clinical practice, if one keeps an open mind, the weight of such evidence argues that the symptoms of bodily disease and even death itself are not, as the mechanistic view would have it, discontinuities or dysfunctions. They are process continuities that arrive in a context of highly individual organismic meaningfulness. They are not extrinsic to life, things that happen to our patients. As with all contents of complex life processes, death is an intrinsic aspect of a particular living forward. Death, when it comes, is the meaningful next step in our patients' lives, no less authentic, no less right than a cure.

The scientific medical description of such intrinsic process continuities, despite the postmodern paradigmatic shift toward mind/body unity, is still inadequate to the task. Disease conditions that account for cancer onset and development are so complex as to elude deterministic specification. Minute variations along the biologic and psychologic dimensions will produce huge disease-outcome differences. In probabilistic terms we have no alternative but to describe such situations as essentially random. It is only just now that postmodern science is learning how to describe the irreversible, nonrandom emergence of order in such systems at the subvisible level of elemental matter. But we do know quite well how to describe disease-meaning systems in phenomenological terms respectful of the subtle synchronicity of the nondual bodymind.

CANCER IN THE NEW AGE

One passionate objection to this sort of thinking about cancer revolves around the fear that patients will be seduced into false hope for impossible cures and then blamed for their illness when the cure does not materialize. I have already argued that this concern may be rooted in sentimental attachment to naive naturalistic beliefs in the priority of the simply physical universe and that such beliefs are ideologically related to the moral agendas of the mechanisms of social control in our technological culture. But I do not wish to dismiss the matter out of hand. It is a more knotty issue than it might first appear.

Popular healing approaches rely for validation upon recent experimental evidence suggesting immune function may be subject to direct instruction by mental imaging (see, for example, Schneider et al. 1981). Study of cerebral laterality effects supports the view that activation of the right hemisphere through mental imaging may directly entrain neuroendocrine events that mediate depression and immunosuppression (Ley & Freeman 1984). And so it is then argued that imagery has the power to heal. In the New Age scripture this is the scientific basis of the efficacy of shamanic healing practices. This then sets up an all too facile equivalence basic to the subculture's view of itself between almost any contemporary imagery strategy and shamanism.

This way of thinking can be very problematic. Imaging instructions that produce desirable results in parsimonious experimental contexts are perhaps not so clearly efficacious when applied to illness situations in which both biologic and psychologic contexts are not nearly so simple. It is hard to be certain here, but my caution is based on the observation of many cancer patients for whom imaging instructions, even when performed correctly, seem not to do much. Cancer patients, after all, are immersed in dread of the disease and in a host of bad feelings, anxieties and physical sufferings from which imaging may momentarily distract them without touching anything deeply. Any potentially beneficial awareness practice may be used in that way to bypass rather than process and transform painful experience. So it is not enough just to give a set instruction. We have to know how it has concrete impact on experiential process in the particular individual.

The Cartesian bias of our technologic culture splits the body/mind into an intentional self-moving mind and a passive mechanical body. Both imaging instructors and cancer patients dwell at least to some extent within the constraints of this bias. As a result, imaging is often mutually construed as the application of positive/optimistic cognitive contents to a passive sick body. It is told to heal, or that it will. Of course, the body may fail at this extrinsic, content-specific task. This way of working may, indeed, set patients up for self blame.

I cannot emphasize too strongly that cancer therapists must respect and stay right with the emergent process of bodily felt meanings in individual patients in order to avoid further alienating them from a genuinely interior relation with themselves. In our thoroughly televised and media-captive culture we are all at sea in an ocean of disembodied images. I never assign cancer patients an imagery task to do with extrinsic imagery. I will work only with symbolizations, in whatever sensory modality, which have organismically emerged from the whole self. These symbolizations may then be elaborated or amplified in various exercizes, but only these symbolizations shift the subtle body energies and thus have the power to transform. Since process-emergent symbolization is not given to, but comes from, the cancer patient, it does not oppress, it releases.

Generally speaking, shamanic (and some yogic) systems differentiate power from knowledge. Awareness practices working at different levels of the subtle body generate many nonordinary energy states that may from a certain point of view be regarded as powers. But the generation of these states may or may not be treated as an end in itself. At the highest levels esoteric subtle body disciplines are methods to develop contentless presence in the unlimited ground of awareness. Too tight fixation on specific powers of the subtle body as ends in themselves can arrest the development of open awareness. This is what distinguishes a sorcerer from a knowledge-holder. One knowledgeable observer has cautioned that people from technologic cultures tend erroneously to deify the shamanic vision contents when it is not the visions themselves but the shaman's ecstatic in-dwelling in the divinely infinite that is the real point (Wasson 1980).

Our New Age culture tends to flatten and trivialize shamanic process by reducing it to imagery contents and technologies as ends. While our emulation of mystical healing rites seems to promise a resacralization of medical discourse, a retrenchment of what Turner (1984) identified as the central historic tendency of the modern secular order toward redeployment of moral stewardship from religious to medical institutions, the situation is somewhat contradictory.

The development in the modern era of the germ theory of disease established the dominance of scientific medical naturalism, which extracted from the social/moral organization a presumed value-free medical perspective which constituted "a second-order moral framework . . . masked by the language of disease" (Turner 1984, p. 214). The principal conceptual apparatus of this scientific ascendency was the bifurcation of the spiritual and natural orders. The disclosure in the scientific discourse of postmodern behavioral medicine of the neurohumoral synchronicity of mind and body threatens, as I have suggested, to dissolve that dualism. Without a doubt, the disclosure of the unitary subtle body, heretofore confined to the domain of spiritual disciplines, represents a potential respiritualization of the social perception of health.

And yet to the extent that this contemporary "spiritual" talk about health remains captive to a reductionist social agenda, it constitutes a further, veiled and hence deeper, degradation of the sacred. Currently our medical morality projects health as a life style. This is not to be confused with the ideal of the productive citizen of the industrial era. It is preeminently a consumer morality. We prefer fit, sexually attractive, stress-free, fun-loving citizens, the "hard bodies" of up-scale consumers who drive the postmodern economy. The marketing of hard bodies in all manner of self improvement has become itself an enormously invasive industry. With the expenditure of some few hundred dollars for a weekend workshop we are now even assured of becoming real shamans ourselves.

Our culture in this way sentimentalizes and simultaneously plunders ancient sacred traditions in the service of opportunistic economic imperatives. With the deployment of sex, health and wisdom as instruments of the consumer market we have more thoroughly objectified and commoditized body and spirit than at any previous time in human history. This systematic degradation of our phylogenetic wisdoms accumulated across the millenia of human history is a dangerously maladaptive trend. It threatens to lead us even further from the self-knowledge of organismic wholeness which is the sacred ground of all living systems.

CONCLUSION

Cancer may well be the pestilential challenge of our time that can awaken us to the need for critical self-reflection and reform. The atomized and specialized knowledges of our technological culture have imparted to us impressive powers to act upon the social and natural worlds. We have virtually banished infectious disease from the planet. And yet the reductionist focus of our specialized knowledges has left us powerless to comprehend the relationship of parts to the whole. This is reflected at every level of social organization. Our productive economy degrades the biotic environment at a scale the impact of which we can as yet barely comprehend. Our ascendant medical culture, just now beginning to imagine the synchronicity of the mind and body, still finds itself lacking the philosophic vision to conduct an exploration of disease as an aspect of meaningfully lived experience. The alternative medical discourse, while promising a respiritualization and revisioning of health, suffers itself the reductionist habit of confounding particular ideas and methods with the emergent process of the self. And cancer patients are themselves alienated from the wholeness of their physical/emotional lives, unable to carry essential aspects of their deep selves forward in meaningfully embodied ways.

Cancer constellates the basic human condition of relatedness. The physical devastation of cancer undermines the solid, immovable facticity of the discrete material body and our compelling notions of the bounded reality of things upon which we have come to rely. We penetrate the veil of objectivity that separates our self from others and parts of our own self from its intrinsic wholeness. We discover that the corporeal and spiritual, physical and emotional dimensions of existence are not separate but a single synchronous experiencing of the subtle embodied self, and that this inner felt synchronicity perfectly mirrors the vast interconnectedness of the living universe of which we are a part. Cancer is an invitation to heal—literally—to regain wholeness, an invitation extended to ourselves as emergent individuals and to our culture at large.

REFERENCES

Ader, R. ed., *Psychoneuroimmunology*. New York: Academic Press, 1981.

Ader, R. & Cohen N., "Behavior and the immune system," in Gentry, W. D. ed., *Handbook of Behavioral Medicine*. New York: Guilford Press, 1984.

Alexander, F., "Emotional factors in essential hypertension." *Psychosomatic Medicine,* vol. 1, 1939.

———"Present trends and the future outlook." Alexander, F. & French, T. M., eds., *Studies in Psychosomatic Medicine*. New York: Ronald Press, 1948.

Boyd, W., *The Spontaneous Regression of Cancer*. Springfield, Ill.: Charles C. Thomas, 1966.

Capra, F., *The Turning Point*. New York: Bantam, 1983.

Choedrak, T., First International Convention on Tibetan Medicine. Venice, Italy, April, 1983. Oral commentary.

Chesney, M. & Rosenman, R., "Specificity in stress models: examples drawn from type 'A' behavior", in Cooper, C. L., ed., *Stress Research: Issues for the Eighties*. New York: John Wiley, 1983.

Depue, R. A., ed., *The Psychobiology of the Depressive Disorders*. New York: Academic Press, 1979.

Dubos, R., *Man Adapting*. New Haven: Yale University, 1965.

Dunbar, F. H., *Emotions and Bodily Changes*. New York: Columbia University, 1935.

Fenichel, O., *The Collected Papers of Otto Fenichel,* second series. New York: W. W. Norton, 1954.

Foucault, M., *The Birth of the Clinic*. New York: Vintage Books, 1975.

Freud, S., "Ordinary neurosis," in *A General Introduction to Psychoanalysis*. New York: Simon & Schuster, 1929.

Gendlin, E. T., *Experiencing and the Creation of Meaning*. Glencoe: Free Press, 1962.

———"Experiential Psychotherapy," in Corsini, R. eds., *Current Psychotherapies*. Itasca, Ill.: Peacock, 1973.

———"Client-centered and experiential psychotherapy," in Wexler, D. & Rice, L., *Innovations in Client-centered Therapy*. New York: John Wiley, 1974.

———*Focusing*. New York: Bantam, 1981.

Gentry, W. D., "Behavioral medicine: a new research paradigm," in Gentry, W. D., ed., *Handbook of Behavioral Medicine*. New York: Guilford Press, 1984.

Henry, J. P. & Meehan, J., "Psychosocial stimuli, physiological specificity and cardiovascular disease." In Weiner, H. M. et al., eds., *Brain, Behavior and Bodily Disease*. New York: Raven Press, 1981.

Hoffman, F. L., *Cancer among North American Indians*. Prudential Press, 1928.

Joseph, J. G. & Syme, S. L., "Social connection and the etiology of cancer," in Cohen, J. et al., eds., *Psychosocial Aspects of Cancer*. New York: Raven Press, 1982.

Kasl, S. V., "Pursuing the link between stressful life experiences and disease: a time for reappraisal." in Cooper, C. L., ed., *Stress Research: Issues for the Eighties*. New York: John Wiley, 1983.

Krantz, D. S. & Glass, D. C., "Personality, behavior patterns and physical illness: conceptual and methodological issues," in Gentry, W. D., ed., *Handbook of Behavioral Medicine*. New York: Guilford Press, 1984.

Kundera, M., *The Unbearable Lightness of Being*. New York: Harper & Row, 1985.

Lazarus, R. S., "Stress and coping as factors in health and illness," in Cohen, J. et al., eds., *Psychosocial Aspects of Cancer*. New York: Raven Press, 1982.

Leder, D., "Medicine and paradigms of embodiment," *Journal of Medicine & Philosophy* (1984) 9: 29–43.

Ley, R. G. & Freeman, R. J., "Imagery, cerebral laterality and the healing process," in Sheikh, A., ed., *Imagination and Healing*. New York: Baywood Publishing, 1984.

Locke, S. & Hornig-Rohan, M., eds., *Mind and Immunity: Behavioral Immunology*. New York: Institute for the Advancement of Health, 1983.

Prigogine, I. & Stengers, I., *Order out of Chaos*. New York: Bantam, 1984.

Rappaport, R., "Sanctity and adaptation." *Io* (1970)7:46–71.

Reiser, M., ed., "Psychosomatic medicine," in *American Handbook of Psychiatry*, vol. 4. New York: Basic Books, 1975.

Riley, V., "Mouse mammary tumors: alteration of incidence as apparent function of stress," *Science* (1975)189:465–467.

Rogers, C., "Toward a more human science," *Journal of Humanistic Psycology* (1985)25, 4:7–24.

Schneider, J., et al., *Imagery and Neutrophil function: a Preliminary Report.* Michigan State University Department of Psychiatry, 1981.

Schutz, A., *The Phenomenology of the Social World.* Evanston, Ill.: Northwestern University, 1967.

Selye, H., "The physiology and pathology of exposure to stress: a treatise based on the concepts of the general adaptation syndrome and the diseases of adaptation," Montreal: Acta, 1950.

Silverman, S., *Psychological Aspects of Physical Symptoms.* New York: Appleton-Century-Crofts, 1968.

Sontag, S., *Illness as Metaphor.* New York: Vintage, 1979.

Starr, P., *The Social Transformation of American Medicine.* New York: Basic Books, 1982.

Thomas, C. B., et al., "Family attitudes reported in youth as potential predictors of cancer," *Psychosomatic Medicine* (1979)41:287–302.

Turner, B. S., *The Body and Society.* New York: Basil Blackwell, 1984.

Wasson, R. G., *The Wondrous Mushroom: Mycolatry in Mesoamerica.* New York: McGraw-Hill, 1980.

Wilkins, W. L., "Social stress and illness in industrial society," in Gunderson, E. K. E. & Rahe, R. H., eds., *Life Stress and Illness.* Springfield, Ill.: Charles C. Thomas, 1974.

Winter, R., *Cancer-causing Agents.* New York: Crown, 1979.

CHAPTER 5

DEPRESSION AND THE AMERICAN DREAM: THE STRUGGLE WITH HOME[1]

ROBERT D. ROMANYSHYN
AND
BRIAN J. WHALEN

INTRODUCTION

This chapter describes the pathology of depression in terms of the psychology that constellates the American dream. Beginning with a clinical case in Part One, we want to establish that depression tells a story about soul and the necessity of home. The depressive soul is the soul that has lost its home, and its suffering speech, its psychopathology, expresses the necessity of a return home. In Part Two we discuss this pathology in terms of the psychology of the American dream, showing how the struggle with home has been a pervasive problem for the American soul. Finally, Part Three considers several contemporary cultural expressions of the soul's necessity to return home. Throughout we take the position espoused in an earlier work[2] that soul incarnates itself as world, that the cultural world is the mirror of soul.

SOUL AND THE NECESSITY OF HOME: A CASE HISTORY

The following clinical case is meant to illustrate the psychopathology of depression. We are using psychopathology in its root sense—the logos or speech of the suffering soul. The case that follows exemplifies how this depression, or separation from home, is expressed on an individual level.

> B. E., a twenty-two-year-old white man, was seen on several occasions in a psychiatric hospital while in the midst of a prolonged depression. His chief complaint was that his parents did not love him or care about him. An only child, B. E. described how his mother was too preoccupied with her social clubs and did not concern herself with the welfare of the family. Likewise, his father's business interests keep him "too busy to spend time with the family." B. E. had sought comfort in a homosexual relationship, which he says "failed because I am not a homosexual; I just needed someone."
>
> Despite the problems in his family life, B. E. had done well in college and was close to completing a double degree. He had, in fact, one semester to complete and would then, as he says, "start to make decisions about my future." However, the fear of this prospect became too great for him and he fled from his home one day in the family car with no particular destination in mind. He says, "I could not face the decisions I had to make and because of this I had to flee from them."
>
> B. E. drove aimlessly for twenty-four hours and says he was surprised when he ended up in the driveway of his grandparents who live in Wyoming. He was glad to be at a place he had such fond memories of, a place he had visited when younger and one that was "a second home" to him. He was content to stay with his grandparents and did so for a short time, returning to his parents' house several days later.
>
> B. E. talked regretfully about how his parents treated him on his return home: "They had no idea that something may have been wrong with me." Instead, they viewed his odyssey as a "much needed vacation," not recognizing that it may have been a signal of a deeper problem.
>
> One week later B. E. left again in the family car, this time with a definite goal in mind: Indiana, the place of his birth. B. E. and his family had moved to Dallas when he was twelve years old. He talked nostalgically about Indiana, the place "where all my good friends and relatives live." On this trip he carried with him a loaded gun which was hidden in an empty guitar case. When his car broke down half-

> way through the trip B. E. said, "I became so frustrated that I wanted to kill myself." His suicide attempt failed when his gun misfired, and he subsequently "passed out" where local police found him lying on the side of the road.
>
> Upon his return to Dallas "things got progressively better." B. E. says he began to sense improvements in his relationship with his parents and felt better about himself. This improving situation broke down, however, on a night when B. E. spent the evening alone in the family home. While his parents were attending a dinner at a friend's house, B. E. found himself "very alone and lost." He says, "I felt as I always had—alone with no real home. I wanted to leave my house because I hated being there alone." B. E. left his house, drove out into the countryside, and swallowed sleeping pills and liquor he had taken from home. Before "passing out" he managed to call a friend who came and transported him to the hospital.

This brief case history alerts us to a central theme of depression: home as a psychological necessity. B. E.'s inability to face the prospect of making decisions about his life and career is related to his sense of having no ground, no nourishing source that would help to sustain his life. Without a sense of home as an image that supports him, he remains depressed. The blame he places on his parents, whether justified or not, reflects his experience of abandonment. That experience is dramatically enacted when B. E. finds himself to be suddenly alone in the family house. His flights from this house were attempts at recovering a home, the home of his past, a home that is given voice in his nostalgic musings about his grandparents' home and the place of his birth—Indiana. His literal attempts to return to these places echo the cry of a soul that has lost its connection with home and desperately searches for a reconnection with it.

HOME AND THE AMERICAN DREAM: A CULTURAL PSYCHOLOGY

In this section we move from individual case history to examples of how the pathology of depression has been a cultural story, incarnating itself in the American literary tradition and reflecting the fact that for the American soul the problem of home has been ever present. From the Puritan experience of being aliens in a strange land to Kerouac's examination of how the American psyche is always "on the road," there is a continuous sense that the American soul is not at home. The cultural examples that follow amplify this story of depression by showing the roots of this pathology and various expressions that have arisen from it.

The Myth of the New Jerusalem: Transforming the New World

The Puritan experience in the New World was an attempt to transform the native land into the "New Jerusalem." Because of their special covenant with God, it was the task of the Puritans to bring about the promised land on earth, to transform reality from its fallen state to something higher. This dream, imaged in John Winthrop's phrase, "we shall be as a city upon a hill,"[3] captured the imagination of the early settlers and meant that the land they encountered, "the palpable geography of the country, was of little importance as they projected instead a vision of a metaphysically transformed state that would characterize the New Jerusalem."[4] The Puritans were not at home in the New World; they had a distrust of the forest and its inhabitants, "the savage people, who are cruel, barbarous and most treacherous."[5]

Not at home in the New World, the Puritans believed that their true home was something to be made by industry and perseverance. An element of gnosticism characterizes this Puritan experience, for as Voegelin noted, gnosticism is "the experience of the world as an alien place into which man has strayed and from which he must find his way back home to the other world of his origin."[6] The Puritan's sense of estrangement from the world, however, did not prohibit an attempt at constructing the world of their origin, this New Jerusalem. This attempt puts man in the role of God: "he is a Gnostic who not will leave the transfiguration of the world to the grace of God beyond history but will do the work of God himself, right here and now, in history."[7] As Voegelin noted, such a man as this, one who "lives in the faith that a new truth and a new world begin with him, must be in a peculiar pneumopathological state."[8] This state is characterized by a "passion for destroying and making over things given,"[9] a fascination for the new and transformed. In the Puritan experience, then, gnosticism is an estrangement from the world *and* a belief in their power to recreate it.

Within this context of gnosticism the Puritan founding of the continent articulates a psychology of depression. As our case history illustrates, the depressed soul is not at home and searches for home. In the case of the Puritans this depression is hidden, however, beneath the confident persona that is to fabricate this home. The codes of the covenant unified their purpose and gave protection to the Puritan mind, to a psyche that was "in fear and without guidance, really lost in the world."[10]

Depression, then, lies at the roots of our history on this continent. For William Carlos Williams, "the nation was the offspring of the desire to huddle [and] protect,"[11] what Erikson called the "defensively sedentary pole of American experience."[12] The Puritan captivity narratives are a testament to the reality of this fear of the wild and untamed land; they reflect the experience of depression in the Puritan soul, the sense of being lost and far away from home.[13] But along with this fear came the promise of transforming the land, making it into the New Jerusalem, a promise that was given through scriptural prophecy. The Puritan view of history, as it is reflected in such works as Edward Johnson's *Wonder-working Providence,* holds that history is the unfolding of scriptural prophecy, a dramatic battle between the forces of good and evil. Their emigration to the New World, then, was equivalent "to the Exodus of Israel from Egypt . . . a period of trial which would make them worthy of entering a New Promised Land and a New Jerusalem."[14] It was their appointed task to win a victory over Satan, "subdue all the enemies of God,"[15] and deliver mankind to the promised land. This belief that human history had an everlasting importance gave the Puritans the strength to master the land and attempt to realize the dream of heaven on earth.

The Puritan interpretation of the Book of Revelation maintained that "the millennium was to be an earthly *utopia,* an age at the end of all history."[16] Because the promised land was to be realized *within* history as a transformation of the earth, the spiritual development of the Puritans coincided with alterations in the geography of the country. As Cecelia Tichi has shown, the Puritans assumed a "stewardship over God's created world" and asserted their dominion "by making a visible impress upon the natural world."[17] This impress was their way of legitimizing their "claim to America by manifestly improving it."[18] Thus, the "failure to make a civilizing impress upon the land . . . could cancel their self-defined interpreted rights to those lands."[19] The Puritans were faced, then, with either successfully transforming the American landscape and affirming their status as chosen redeemers, or else failing in their mastery of the wilderness and thus in their quest for spiritual fulfillment. This experience was the seed of a cultural psychology that for over three hundred years would assert its mastery over the land in search of spiritual fulfillment, a cultural psychology that would believe that we are "master organizers of the world . . . [a] chosen nation [who will] lead in the redemption of the world."[20]

As a "Redeemer Nation," a culture that believes in progress towards a utopian life on earth, we are a culture lost, far away from home. "Early New England rhetoric," Sacvan Berkovitch said, "provided a ready framework for inverting later secular values—human perfectability, technological progress, democracy, Christian socialism, or simply (and comprehensively) the American Way—into the mold of sacred teleology."[21] The rhetoric of the Puritans embodies a gnostic dream that takes us away from the maternal embrace of the land and keeps us looking toward a sacred future of our own making. The myth of making the earth over, of improving it from its fallen state and progressing toward a utopia, characterizes the American experience of relating to our continent "not as a 'motherland' in the soft, nostalgic sense of the 'old country,' " but instead "bitterly and in a remarkably unromantic and realistic way."[22] This Puritan inheritance has kept us forever looking forward to how we can realize our dreams, but at the expense of forgetting our home, mother earth.

Lucy Lockwood Hazard, in her classic work, *The Frontier in American Literature*,[23] traced the image of the American frontier from "the frontier of regional pioneering, which is primarily concerned with man's attempt to control nature" (the Puritan experience), to "the frontier of spiritual pioneering, which is primarily concerned with man's attempt to control himself" (xvii). This shift in the image of the frontier makes the frontier as landscape into an opportunity whereby man can transform *himself*. The Puritan mastery of the frontier, then, became a metaphor for the controlled transformation of the self. In the next section we take up this issue through a study of the figure of the self-made man.

Franklin and Gatsby: Archetypal Self-Made Men

Although Ben Franklin and Jay Gatsby make their appearance on the American scene roughly one hundred and seventy-five years apart, they are tied together in their enactment of the self-made man archetype. This connection is solidified in Gatsby's father's discovery, after his son's death, of a schedule of improvement that Gatsby had written in a book and hidden away in a drawer. The schedule, listing ways to "improve his mind"[24] and become successful, replicates Franklin's famous "Scheme of Employment for the Twenty-Four Hours of a Natural Day" that appears in his *Autobiography*.[25] Both of these documents reflect the ambition for greatness that these figures had, their attempt at realizing the American dream. This dream embodies the promise that one can create oneself, fashion one's personality in whatever way one wishes. In effect, the self-made man is the creator of his own home, the one who "makes his own place" in the world. In our literary tradition the appearance of this figure is vast, more notably showing its face in Emerson's doctrine of self-reliance, Whitman's *Song of Myself*, Melville's Ahab, and in James's American heroes who visit the shores of Europe.[26] But perhaps it is with Franklin and in Fitzgerald's Gatsby that the myth of the self-made man is most fully articulated.

In his *Autobiography* Franklin spelled out a doctrine "of how he invented, created himself; then of how he got ahead; and of how we may do likewise."[27] Through a set of numbered principles, suggested schedules, and success stories, the reader learns the ins and outs of the psychology of self-creation. This psychology knows no limits—one can become whomever he wishes. Franklin himself, says one critic, "invented a series of persons, each of whom he found it pleasant to project for a time."[28] He found no necessary connection to any one of these figures; the only continuous feature of his personality was his own power of reason. "So convenient a thing it is to be a *reasonable creature,*" Franklin told us, "since it enables one to find or make a reason for everything one has a mind to do."[29] With reason as his primary mode of relating to the world, Franklin became godlike, able to give birth to himself over and over again in a variety of forms, thereby effectively eliminating the necessity of any relation with the past. Franklin became his own father and mother, born of his own conception rather than placed within a tradition. Because his doctrine concerns itself with self-regeneration, Franklin made no mention of death: he intended only to teach us to "live life to the hilt, not to instruct [us] in the art of godly dying."[30]

Franklin's hubris involves not only a limitless and continuous self-creation and hence a denial of death, but also a simultaneous mastering of the land. John Callahan noted that through Franklin the myth "of the self-made man takes on a horrifying literal meaning" because "a man's worth . . . is determined by his material success."[31] Thus, "one symbolically [gives] birth to himself by becoming 'worth his weight in gold.' "[32] For Franklin and his generation this birth came at the expense of the Indians, a people to whom Franklin suggested giving rum to "extirpate these Savages in order to make room for Cultivators of the Earth."[33] Franklin saw the opportunity to regenerate his fortunes by "cultivating" the land—through laying waste to the wilderness and its inhabitants. This is the secularized version of the Puritan myth of the New Jerusalem. Man transforms the land in service of himself rather than in service of divine prophecy. Richard

Slotkin called this the "myth of regeneration through violence," a myth that, he said, "has become the structuring metaphor of the American experience."[34] For Franklin this meant meddling with the lightning—"not to realize it, but only to know how to run an engine with it."[35] His "practical wit" allowed him to master nature and in doing so to give birth to himself and to affirm his worth. His hands were always busy inventing, toying with nature, all the time "keeping the wilderness out with his wits."[36]

As the creator of his own personality, Franklin forgot home, how he was already placed and founded. As his friend Benjamin Vaughan told him in a letter Franklin included in the *Autobiography,* the one value of the book should be in showing that Franklin was "ashamed of no origin; a thing the more important as you prove how little necessary all origin is to happiness, virtue or greatness."[37] The self-made man would forget home, his heritage and origins, in order to create himself according to his own ideal. The tragic consequences of this forgetfulness are expressed in the figure of Jay Gatsby, a self-made man whose regenerative project is met with failure.

F. Scott Fitzgerald's novel *The Great Gatsby* presents the American dream as a style of personality embodied in the figure of Jay Gatsby. As Callahan noted, the desire of this personality, the continual striving to make its dream come true, relieves Gatsby from insecurity over his identity or continuity with his past.[38] Like Franklin, Gatsby has no need for origins: he is a "Mr. Nobody from Nowhere,"[39] "a man with a dim background" (p. 32). Also like Franklin, he fashions his personality according to his own desires, changing his identity from James Gatz to Jay Gatsby. But Gatsby's hubris runs deeper than Franklin's, for he does not simply dismiss the past, but seeks to recreate it according to his needs. When the narrator of the novel, Nick Carraway, confronts him about the impossibility of such a fantasy, Gatsby answers, "Can't repeat the past? . . . Why of course you can! . . . I'm going to fix everything just the way it was before" (p. 73). What Gatsby wishes to mend is his relationship with Daisy, a past love who has since married another man. Gatsby's enrollment in the army forced his separation from an event that Gatsby views as an "historical mistake." He therefore attempts to correct history and thereby fulfill "his Platonic conception of himself"[40]—an ideal that he has spent years in trying to fabricate.

Nick tells us at the end of the novel that the construction of this ideal meant transforming the "fresh, green breast of the new world" (p. 121). Fitzgerald's use of the metaphor of the land as a breast "that flowered once for Dutch sailors' eyes," and whose trees have now been uprooted to "make way for Gatsby's house" (p. 121), evokes Franklin and his "cultivating" the land for the sake of his own identity. Gatsby's dream evolves at the expense of the land not literally as Franklin's does, but symbolically, as a flight from his remaining within the nurturing care of mother, home, and tradition. Gatsby exhibits a "restlessness" (p. 42), giving Nick the sense that he was "never quite still," that "there was always a tapping foot somewhere or the impatient opening and closing of a hand" (p. 42). Both Gatsby and Franklin are "movers and shakers," not willing to remain rooted or tied down, but instead compelled to change their surroundings in order to regenerate themselves. Gatsby loses the possibility "for a transitory enchanted moment where [he could] hold his breath in the presence of the continent," and as a result be "compelled into an aesthetic contemplation . . . with something commensurate to his capacity for wonder" (p. 121). He is, like Franklin, a figure who remains one step ahead of himself, never slowing down in time to be claimed by the world, always seeking to anticipate what lies ahead.

Gatsby believes in the "orgiastic future that year by year recedes before (him)" (p. 121), forever in pursuit of the green light that flashes across the bay at the end of Daisy's dock. But when he finally meets Daisy, the incarnation of a lifetime of dreaming, she falls short of his expectations:

> Daisy tumbled short of his dreams—not through her own fault, but because of the colossal vitality of his illusion. It had gone beyond her, beyond everything. He had thrown himself into it all the time, decking it out with every bright feather that drifted his way. No amount of fire or freshness can challenge what a man will store up in his ghostly heart. (pp. 63-64)

Perhaps Gatsby did, as Nick suggests, feel at that moment that "he had lost the old warm world"—the green breast of mother earth that represents his origins and his collective past—"and paid a high price for living too long with a single dream" (p. 108). But his ultimate failure comes when the dream itself destroys him. We recall that Gatsby is murdered in retaliation for supposedly having killed a woman by striking her down with his car and driving away. But it is Daisy, unbeknown to the murderer, who was actually at the wheel of the car at the time, and it is she who bears the responsibility for Gatsby's death. Gatsby is literally killed by his dream, drained of life because of his blind commitment to an ideal vision of himself and the world. Like Oedipus, Gatsby's attempt at reconstructing the past leads him to fall victim to the past itself. His quest to regenerate himself and restore the love that he and Daisy once shared is undermined by the fact that he acts with no genuine connection to the past. He has no support, no ground for his action, except an illusive dream that urges him on.

Franklin's and Gatsby's forgetfulness of home as founding heritage, brought about by their obsession with creating their own reality, points to the irony of the American dream. The self-made man breaks free from the bonds of tradition and home only for the sake of *creating* an ideal home and thus weaving his own history. This figure denies the very thing he strives for, fleeing his historical roots in order to give birth to his own conception of himself. This soul's flight from home, from its origins and its past, characterizes the depressive soul. In Franklin's case this depression remains largely concealed beneath his confident persona, while with Gatsby it shows its face in his failure to fulfill his dream and in his death at the end of the novel. Through Gatsby, then, the underside of the archetype of the self-made man is given expression. In the next section this underside is further explored through three works by Hawthorne, who in addition suggested that relief from this dark world is gained through remembering one's origins, a task, however, that appears insoluble for the characters in his stories.

Hawthorne: The Dark Side of the American Dream and the Search for Origins

In his book, *Hawthorne as Myth-Maker,* Hugo McPherson compared Hawthorne to Freud and Jung because he saw "myths as narratives which reveal the deepest sources and patterns of human action."[41] Hawthorne's works are imaginative explorations of the unique characteristics and problems of the American soul. Most of these works reflect his "pervasive concern with the search for identity and place," where "Faustian characters all desire peace and an end to their continual searching and striving."[42] These characters rarely if ever discover their true identity. They are like Oedipus, who in the search for his origins—his father and his true home—is left homeless at the end of the play.[43] Hawthorne's imagery is dark, veiled, and gloomy, reflecting his sensitivity to the underside of the American soul. His characters live in this dark world, sometimes completely lost and despairing, at other times searching for a release from its grasp through discovering their origins.

"Young Goodman Brown," Hawthorne's most popular short story, is a tale about "the Puritan distrust of the forest."[44] The protagonist, Goodman Brown, wanders nightly among the gloomy trees of the forest despite protests from his wife, Faith. In characteristic style, Hawthorne left open the possibility that the action of the story may be a dream, highlighting the psychological significance of the forest by asking the reader to look at the wilderness as if it were a mixture of fantasy and reality. For Goodman Brown the forest is not a landscape of opportunity or a space where one asserts one's domination. Here we find the retelling of the Puritan fear of the forest, but with no will to transform it. Rather, his experience in the forest leaves him "a stern, a sad, a darkly meditative, a distrustful, if not desperate man."[45] His wanderings distress him and raise for him the problem of home, a problem which is reflected in the following passage: "Often, awakening suddenly at midnight, he shrank from the bosom of Faith, and at morning or eventide, when the family knelt down at prayer, he scowled, and muttered to himself, and gazed sternly at his wife, and turned away" (p. 255).

In turning away from his wife, Goodman Brown shows his loss of "faith" in home. Along with this loss of an appreciation for the necessity of home, he mysteriously assimilates the dark characteristics of the land. He becomes a lost and frightened soul, a soul that cries out in despair:

> The whole forest was peopled with frightful sounds—the creaking of the trees, the howling of wild beasts, and the yell of Indians; while sometimes the wind tolled like a distant church bell, and sometimes gave a broad roar around the traveler, as if all Nature were laughing at him in scorn. But he himself was the chief horror of the scene, and shrank not from its other horrors . . . Goodman Brown cried out, and his cry was lost to his own ear by its unison with the cry of the desert (p. 252).

The incarnation of the horrible forest in Goodman Brown's soul shows us how Hawthorne viewed the "wilderness myth as a tale of man's fall and degeneration."[46] The regenerative powers of the self-made man, alone on the frontier, are portrayed darkly here as characteristics of "a man of solitude . . . self-contained . . . without heirs and self-ending."[47] Young Goodman Brown, once an accepting and sanguine soul, is plunged into a perversely melancholic state. His soul's mimicry of the forest suggests a deep connection between psyche and land, soul and earth. Hawthorne showed us the dark side of this connection, the way in which the American soul is overwhelmed by the wilderness rather than able to assert the Puritan mastery over it or to find a place within its maternal embrace. This sense of being overwhelmed leaves Goodman Brown lost and despairing.

In *Dr. Grimshawe's Secret,* Hawthorne took up the theme of origins in attempting to work out "the true relation of America to its parent country,"[48] the theme to which Henry James later gave fullest expression. In this unfinished work, Hawthorne explored the psychology of the lost and despairing soul in search of its origins. Etherege, the hero of the novel, travels to England in order to research his ancestry, marry a beautiful maiden and assert his will over a wicked uncle. According to McPherson, Etherege "needs to assert his claim on English roots (for) England is really his spiritual home."[49] In a moving passage, he explains what it has been like to live in the New World, without roots or awareness of his origins:

> The current of my life runs darkly on, and I would be glad of any light on its future, or even its present course . . . I have tried to keep down this yearning [for roots], to stifle it, annihilate it, with making a position for myself, with being my own past; but I cannot overcome this horror of being a creature floating in the air, attached to nothing; ever this feeling that there is no reality in the life and fortunes, good or bad, of a being so unconnected. There is not even a grave, not a heap of dry bones, not a pinch of dust, with which I can claim connection, unless I find it here.[50]

Etherege's life is dark and depressing. But while Goodman Brown appears unaware of his degenerative state, Etherege takes steps to recover his true identity. He has a yearning, a desire for roots that will not go away. Etherege realizes that this desire cannot be fulfilled by enacting the figure of the self-made man—by "making a position" for himself—but that the fulfillment lies elsewhere, perhaps in the bones and dust of the dead who have come before him. Etherege longs for this return, for an understanding of his roots.

The issue of origins is deepened in Hawthorne's short story, "The New Adam and Eve." Here Hawthorne explored the myth of the American Adam and Eve, the young innocents who inhabit the American Garden of Eden.[51] At work in the story is a tension between earth and sky, the necessity of earth as home and the opportunity for escape. It is Adam who first expresses a sense that they do not belong to the earth and tells Eve that their home is elsewhere: ". . . surely we ought to dwell among those gold-tinged clouds or in the blue depths beyond them. I know not how nor when, but evidently we have strayed away from our home; for I see nothing hereabouts that seems to belong to us" (p. 329).

According to Adam, man's "allotted task is no other than to climb into the sky, which is so much more beautiful than earth" (p. 335). Adam's desire for flight is countered by Eve, who, with her "feminine instinct" and "happy influence" (p. 337), tells Adam that "it would be better to sit down quietly and look upward to the sky" (p. 335). The narrator of the story tells us that this suggestion, along with Adam's observation that "something drags us down in spite of our best efforts" (p. 329), serves as an important lesson, for it acknowledges the "necessity of keeping the beaten track of earth" (p. 329). As the first inhabitants of the earth and the innocent archetypal figures of the American psyche, Adam and Eve, despite Eve's "feminine instinct," lack an appreciation of this necessity. We are told that they can "live and be happy in the present" with "no reminiscences save dim fleeting visions of a preexistence" (p. 338). They are figures who "derive their being from no dead progenitors" (p. 338), and who thus awake each morning to make the world anew with no needed dependence on the past, "the beaten track of earth."

Hawthorne's Adam and Eve appear to be without origins or ancestry: "dust kindred to their own has never lain in the grave" (p. 338). Forgetful of their past, their defining lineage, they live out a psychology that is akin to the psychology of the self-made man. Like him, Adam and Eve exhibit an ambivalence toward home, to their life on earth and their connection with their ancestors. The narrator asks, "can death, in the midst of his old triumphs, make them sensible that they have taken up the heavy burden of that mortality which a whole species has laid down?" (p. 338) This suggests that death may remind one of one's origins, of one's ancestors who have died and been buried.

For this new Adam and Eve, the awareness of origins, of the history of man's mortality, leads to the recognition "that Time and the elements have an indefeasible claim upon their bodies" (p. 338). This awareness has two consequences. First, it reverses the psychology of the self-made man, the figure who continually fathers himself. Death destroys this psychology by imposing the limits of time onto this Promethean hubris. Second, the cognizance of death humiliates the self-made man. In destroying his project of self-creation it asks him to search beyond himself for another reason for his being. In a quite literal way it returns him to the earth, to the soil of the land, for men are dust and to dust they shall return. Death reconnects man to the earth. Earth becomes mother, our origin and our destiny. This connection with the land, as Kolodny has documented, was the "initial impulse to the New World landscape, not merely as an object of domination and exploitation, but as a material 'garden.' "[52] The earth as a garden from which we sprout and a container that we return to when we die potentially answers the question of origins for Adam and Eve. At the conclusion of the story, however, death is symbolized as "the butterfly soaring upward, or the bright angel beckoning them aloft" (p. 338). Finally, however, it is Eve who says that it does not "matter where we exist . . . for we shall always be together" (p. 338). This ending, ambiguous in the sense that neither the earth nor sky is affirmed as the soul's origin or destiny, perhaps reflects Hawthorne's sense that the question of the American soul's origins is an insoluble one.

The insolubility of this question of *home* as origin is especially clear in contemporary literature. In the next section we will explore one expression of this issue, the American epic *Death of a Salesman.*

Willy Loman: On the Road

Willy Loman, the protagonist in Arthur Miller's play *Death of a Salesman,* has been called "the quintessential American dreamer,"[53] a man who believes, as he himself tells us, that "the greatest things can happen" if only one can take advantage of the situation.[54] Willy is a salesman, and as his friend Charley tells Willy's sons, "a salesman [has] got to dream . . . it comes with the territory" (p. 138). Throughout the play it becomes apparent that Willy's dream has little basis in reality. He brags about his "important contacts" (p. 51), when it is likely that he has none at all. He tells a friend that "business is bad, murderous . . . but not for me" (p. 51), when we know that he is "tired to the death" (p. 13) and ready to quit his job. In short, Willy never stops believing in the dream of becoming prosperous and continually convinces himself that he has achieved some measure of success.

But Miller's play is not primarily about the persistence and promise of the American dream as much as it is about its bankruptcy. Willy remains unfulfilled, "on the road every week of [his] life" (p. 14), in search of this dream. The first scene of the play alerts us to the fact that this search no longer sustains Willy. When his wife asks him why he has returned unexpectedly from his sales trip, he answers, "I couldn't make it. I just couldn't make it . . . I suddenly couldn't drive anymore. The car kept going off the shoulder, y' know?" (p. 13) The breakdown of Willy's dream leaves him wondering about what has been truly valuable in his life. He suddenly becomes aware, after forty years on the road as a salesman, that he could have been anything he wanted to. His flashbacks often express his regret over opportunities missed, paths not taken, like following Charley's advice of moving to Alaska "where opportunity is tremendous" (p. 45), or becoming like his brother Ben, who walked into the jungle when he was seventeen and walked out when he was twenty-one and "by God, [he] was rich" (p. 52).

Willy's life on the road in pursuit of success raises for him the problem of home. He becomes regretfully aware of his neglect of home and his failure at raising his sons. He especially laments over his relationship with Biff, who was once "like a young god, Hercules" (p. 68), but who has "laid down and died like a hammer hit him" (p. 93) since discovering that his father had cheated on his mother while on a business trip. This event had "been trailing [Willy] like a ghost for . . . fifteen years" (p. 93), reminding him of his unfaithfulness toward home. But what makes Willy a tragic figure is his vain attempt at returning home through restoring the loving relationship he believes he and his sons once shared.

Willy wonders how he can "get back to all the great times," times "so full of light, and comradeship . . . and always some kind of good news coming up, always something nice coming up ahead" (p. 127). This longing for a lost home expresses the suffering Willy experiences in being disconnected from the loving bonds of home. Tragically, he tries to convince himself that these bonds still exist, but he is continually disappointed when his sons blame him for their troubles.

The figure of Willy Loman, then, remains forever on the road, unable to return home. Willy finds himself unconnected, wandering aimlessly along the highway, like Dean Moriarty of Jack Kerouac's novel *On the Road,* who says, "we gotta go and never stop going till we get there."[55] But when asked by Sal, the narrator of the novel, where it is they are going, he replies, "I don't know but we gotta go" (p. 196). For Sal and Dean home is everywhere, and thus *essentially* nowhere:

> Home in Missoula,
> Home in Truckee,
> Home in Opelousas,
> Ain't no home for me.

Home in old Medora,
Home in Wounded Knee,
Home in Ogallala,
Home I'll never be (p. 208).

Willy's full awareness that he cannot return home comes when he is having dinner with his sons. Here he seems to accept Biff's assertion that he has been a "fake, a phony little fake" (p. 121). After his sons abandon him at the restaurant, Willy symbolically relinquishes his dream by insisting on giving the waiter money, despite the fact that his sons have paid the bill: "Here—here's some more [money], I don't need it anymore" (p. 122). Willy throws his dream away, sending him into a frenzied attempt at trying to root himself somehow: "Oh, I'd better hurry. I've got to get some seeds. I've got to get some seeds right away. Nothing's planted. I don't have a thing in the ground" (p. 122).

Willy literally attempts to establish roots, something that is lasting and unchanging that will give him support. Without his dream to sustain him anymore he seeks for what is truly essential and necessary. But as the waiter mentions to him, "it may be too late now [to buy seeds]" (p. 122). Willy's wife observes that "not enough sun gets back there . . . nothing'll grow anymore" (p. 72). These predictions are proven true when Willy chooses suicide as the preferred alternative to being forever uprooted and away from home.

In choosing death Willy appears to resolve the problem of home and at the same time to fulfill his dream. His dream achieves immortality through his son Biff, who is to inherit twenty thousand dollars upon Willy's death and become the success that Willy always knew he could be. "I always knew," Willy says, "one way or another we were gonna make it, Biff and I" (p. 135). The problem of home is resolved because Willy becomes the good provider, someone whom Biff will "worship" (p. 135). Willy's suicide is, as Ben convinces him, "a perfect proposition all around" (p. 135), simultaneously fulfilling Willy's dream and returning him home in the role of the loving father.

But this fulfillment via suicide is really a failure of returning home from a life on the road. This failure is readily apparent in Willy's sons, who cannot leave home. The return home presupposes a leaving of it. One son, Happy, pronounces his support of his father's dream, saying "he [Willy] did not die in vain . . . He had a good dream. It's the only dream you can have—to come out number-one man. He fought it out here, and this is where I'm gonna win it for him" (p. 139). Biff, on the other hand, wants to escape his father's dream: "Will you let me go, for Christ's sake. Will you take that phony dream and burn it before something happens?" (p. 133) Both of Willy's sons are, in different ways, unable to leave home. While Willy cannot return home, his sons can never leave in order to make a return. Erikson took up this issue in his discussion of the sedentary and migratory poles of American consciousness.[56] The split between these poles appears throughout our history as the identification with either the world of the "work bench, writing desk, fireplace, and altar,"[57] or with the call of the frontier, a life on the road. Depression tells the story of the soul that lacks what Erikson called a "dynamic polarity" between these poles. This soul, like Willy, finds itself alone and apart from home and seeks a way to return. Or, like Biff and Happy, it drowns in the defensiveness and security of home. Depression, then, literalizes either home or frontier in the sense that the symbolic rhythm between these two realms is lost, resulting in a desire to return to a literal home that existed in the past (Willy), or in an attempt literally to escape the bonds of home (Biff), or, as in Happy's case, remaining at home to uphold to the letter the tradition that has trapped one.

Death of a Salesman is America's epic, dramatizing the polarization that lies at the root of the American psyche. It depicts the tragedy of forgetting that home is discovered only by leaving it, that the *heritage* of home is a *destiny*. In the final section we take up this issue of return, specifically in light of some contemporary cultural expressions of the American soul.

COMING HOME: SOME CULTURAL EXPRESSIONS OF RETURN

We have been suggesting in this essay that depression is a matter of home, and that home is a matter of the soul's landscape. Home is not a literal place or dwelling in the world; it is a way of taking up the world, a way of making the world into a home that transforms and preserves the world. In this respect home creation, the project of the self-made man, is also realized as a homecoming, a realization that one's heritage is one's destiny. Depression is the soul's realization that the givenness of one's home, including of course one's personal identity, is a reality yet to be made.

The figure of the self-made man incarnates the ambivalent response of the American soul to this necessity of remaking a home that is already made. In his hubris the self-made man would forget that his creation is already funded. Not only would he leave home, he would forget it. In the mastery of the wilderness, in the taming of the frontier, he would establish his inalienable right to build a New Jerusalem. To life and liberty he would also add the pursuit of happiness as such a right. Depression, the soul's call to remember what is forgotten in this pursuit, would by this measure be decidedly un-American. It would be a disturbing reminder that all human creation rests upon an inheritance, that a New Jerusalem is built only with the materials granted by a bountiful earth, materials not yet simply transformed as resources for consumption.

Three contemporary events indicate that the call of home exerts a powerful, albeit still ambivalent, claim on the American soul. In this last section we wish to discuss briefly these events as a way of indicating finally that depression, as a symptom of soul, is also a path of return. To hear the call of depression—to hear depression as a call, rather than only as a malady to be cured—is already to remember something of what we, disguised as the figure of the self-made man, have forgotten.

The first event is the mini-television series "Roots," adapted from and based upon Alex Haley's novel of the same name. When it first aired in 1977, it attracted one of the largest television audiences in history. The impact and the success of this event are in large measure due to its theme: the search for a cultural home, the necessity to discover the story of the founding father and to weave together the threads of a tale that bind the generations. Haley's story stirred the American soul. In the events it narrated and in the figures it portrayed, it showed us the face of the American dream.

It was, however a strange face, an unfamiliar face, a face not quite expected. "Roots" was a mirror, and when the figure of the self-made man, the carrier of the American dream, looked into the mirror, he saw reflected back to him the face of a black man. "Roots" presented the other face of the American dream. More precisely, it presented the issue of home and its loss as one belonging to an other face, and in so doing it allowed this issue a place in that dream.

The other face of the American dream is the face of the black man, the dark twin soul brother of the self-made man. Through that face the necessity of home-coming is transformed into an issue for the "other one," for the one who is a stranger. Through that face the figure of the self-made man, pursuing his dream of home-creation, can face the loss of home, for that loss has already been transformed into someone else's problem. The black face, the face of the stranger, is the only way the self-made man can face his depression, for that face as a symptom remembers *and* disguises what is forgotten. He, the other one, has lost his home. If that face is a reflection of the dark, denied twin of the self-made man, nevertheless it appears as an alien face. It is a face, therefore, that the self-made man can recognize because it is not his face. The face of the dark twin soul brother of the self-made man, that alien face, that face of depression is and is not the face of the American dream.

The second cultural event indicates even more directly that the other face of the American dream is an alien face. Stephen Spielberg's film "ET: The Extra Terrestrial" appeared in 1982, and like "Roots" it was one of the most successful films in history. The reason for its success is not difficult to understand, for it taps the same theme of home and its loss. But unlike "Roots" this issue is now a matter not of history but more of mythology. The figure of ET does not belong to the history of the American soul in the same way that Kunta Kinte, the African male made an American slave, does. On the contrary, ET is outside that history. Indeed he is otherworldly. The figure who faces us in the guise of ET is, therefore, already a more disguised expression of the American soul in its struggle with home. And more disguised, the figure of ET suggests that the problem of home and its loss has become even more intense in the years separating these two cultural events. Like a dream unheard, the symbols have become more insistent and more disguised.

We, self-made men struggling with home, are the alien, and the alien is us. When ET, so unlike us in his bodily appearances, says, "ET, phone home," we are moved and we become like him. We become like him because we recognize and share the depths of his request. Indeed we become like him, we identify with him, because he utters for us the same plea that gives voice to our plight. But the plight of a lost home has become so painful that we need to deny at the very moment of recognition that it is our *own* voice we hear. ET, this alien figure, makes the claim, and like the black face, ET's face is one that is *and* is not our own. "ET, phone home!" We can hear the request and we can simultaneously deny the anxiety of recognition. Home is his problem, the problem of an alien. Home is an alien problem.

The figure of the alien, of which ET is but one in a whole series of films from the "Star War" sagas to "Star Trek," brings us to the third cultural event that mirrors the American soul's struggle with home. The alien figure is not of this Earth, and in this respect he incarnates a figure who is estranged from the Earth. Today, humanity stands on the threshold of departing earth, and indeed space flight is already an initial realization of this departure. Is the alien figure, this figure of creative fantasy, the embodiment of the soul's wish to be apart from Earth as Hawthorne's Adam and Eve desire? And is it also the incarnation of the dread of soul estranged from Earth, from Mother Earth, from Earth as home? Do we see through the multiple figures of the alien the fulfillment of the dream of the self-made man, the dream whose fulfillment would finally leave home behind? Or do we see through these figures, especially through their more monstrous and inhuman forms, the anxiety over what we might become in forgetting the earth as home? Two recent films vividly depict this anxiety. "The Alien" and "The Thing" face us with the ultimate anxiety of losing home: in becoming estranged from the Earth as home, we no longer can recognize who we are.

The theme of space flight suggests that the psychology of the self-made man, the psychology of that figure who in this essay has incarnated the American dream, is part of the psychology of technology. As such, technology, especially through the event of space flight, reveals itself as a psychology concerned with the issue of home. If, as we have maintained in this essay, depression is the soul's response to a loss of home, then we would conclude by saying that depression is an appropriate psychological response to our historical condition in the age of advanced technology. As the other face of the American dream, as a reminder to the self-made man of what he would forget, depression is the call of home. In this respect it is a call we cannot afford to ignore, for technology as the realization of the American dream gives us the ultimate means of departing from and forgetting home. The very planet, Earth, that grounds and sustains every human psychology, is today endangered by the psychology of the self-made man. Nuclear annihilation is the other side, the dark side of the fantasy of escaping Earth via space flight, by a flight from Earth into space. Should we carry the psychology of the American dream forgetful of the Earth as home, we may very well realize a final destruction. In light of this possibility, the pathology of depression not only is an appropriate response to home loss, it is also necessary. Home is a psychological necessity, and depression, as a soulful reminder of home, is a path of return. It is a voice that we in the guise of the self-made man must begin to hear.

NOTES

1. I am indebted to Brian J. Whalen for his research into the literary tradition of the American dream, which forms a major part of this essay.—Robert D. Romanyshyn.

2. Robert D. Romanyshyn, *Psychological Life: From Science to Metaphor* (Austin: University of Texas Press, 1982).

3. John Winthrop, "A Model of Christian Charity," in *The American Puritans: Their Prose and Poetry,* Perry Miller, ed. (Garden City, New York: Anchor Books, 1956), 83.

4. Cecelia Tichi, *New World, New Earth: Environmental Reform in American Literature From the Puritans Through Whitman* (New Haven: Yale University, 1979), 5.

5. William Bradford, *Of Plymouth Plantation,* Samuel Eliot Morrison, ed. (New York: Modern Library, 1967), 26.

6. Eric Voegelin, *Science, Politics and Gnosticism* (Chicago: Henry Regnery, 1968), 9.

7. Eric Voegelin, *The New Science of Politics* (Chicago: University of Chicago, 1952), 147.

8. Ibid., 139.

9. M. E. Bradford, "A Writ of Fire and Sword: The Politics of Oliver Cromwell," *The Occasional Review* (Summer, 1975) 3:71.

10. William Carlos Williams, *In the American Grain* (New York: New Directions Paperbook, 1956), 67.

11. Ibid., 155.

12. Erik Erikson, *Childhood and Society,* 2nd ed. (New York: W. W. Norton, 1963), 293.

13. See, for example, "A Narrative of the Captivity and Restauration of Mrs. Mary Rowlandson" in *American Literature: The Makers and the Making,* Cleanth Brooks et al., eds. (New York: St. Martin's Press, 1973,), 45–50.

14. Richard Slotkin, *Regeneration Through Violence: The Mythology of the American Frontier, 1600–1860* (Middletown, Connecticut: Wesleyan University Press, 1973), 38.

15. Ernest Lee Tuveson, *Redeemer Nation: The Idea of America's Millennial Role* (1968); (Chicago: University of Chicago Press, 1980), 28.

16. Ibid., ix–x.

17. Tichi, 10.

18. Ibid.

19. Ibid., 11.

20. From a speech given at the turn of the century in the United States Senate by Albert J. Beveridge, a statesman-historian. Quoted in Tuveson, vii.

21. Sacvan Berkovitch, *The Puritan Origins of the American Self* (New Haven: Yale University Press, 1975), 136.

22. Erikson, 305.

23. Lucy Lockwood Hazard, *The Frontier in American Literature* (1927); (New York: Frederick Unger, 1967).

24. F. Scott Fitzgerald, *The Great Gatsby* (New York: Charles Scribner's Sons, 1925), 116.

25. Benjamin Franklin, "The Autobiography" in *The Norton Anthology of American Literature,* Ronald Gottesman, et al., eds. (New York: W. W. Norton, 1979), 355.

26. The figure of the self-made man also shows its face in our modern day "pop psychology," which supports this project of self-creation. The various "self-help" books that articulate this psychology are rooted in Franklin's *Autobiography.*

27. D. H. Lawrence, quoted in M. E. Bradford's *A Better Guide Than Reason: Studies in the American Revolution* (La Salle, Illinois: Sherwood Sugden, 1979), 138.

28. Ibid., 139. Professor Bradford's essay on Franklin ("Franklin and Jefferson: The Making and Binding of Self"), which appears in this work, provides an excellent critique of the psychology of the self-made man through contrasting him with his Southern antithesis.

29. Ibid.

30. Ibid., 138.

31. John Callahan, *The Illusions of a Nation: Myth and History in the Novels of F. Scott Fitzgerald* (Chicago: University of Illinois Press, 1972) 8.

32. Ibid.

33. Franklin, 353.

34. Slotkin, 5.

35. Williams, 155.

36. Ibid.

37. Quoted in Bradford, *A Better Guide,* 139.

38. Callahan, 5.

39. Fitzgerald, 86. Subsequent references to this work are included in our text.

40. Callahan, 65.

41. Hugo McPherson, *Hawthorne As Myth-Maker: A Study in Imagination* (Toronto: University of Toronto Press, 1969), 108.

42. Jac Tharpe, *Nathaniel Hawthorne: Identity and Knowledge* (Carbondale and Edwardsville: Southern Illinois University Press, 1967), 22.

43. Ibid.

44. R. W. B. Lewis, *The American Adam: Innocence, Tragedy, and Tradition in the Nineteenth Century* (Chicago: University of Chicago Press, 1955), 114.

45. *The Complete Short Stories of Nathaniel Hawthorne* (Garden City, New York: Doubleday, 1959), 225. Subsequent references to this work are included in our text.

46. Slotkin, 477.

47. Ibid.

48. McPherson, 195.

49. Ibid., 201.

50. Ibid.

51. For a fine discussion of the Adamic myth as it appears in nineteenth-century American literature, see the work by R. W. B. Lewis cited in note 44 above.

52. Annette Kolodny, *The Lay of the Land: Metaphor as Experience and History in American Life and Letters* (Chapel Hill: University of North Carolina Press, 1975), 5. See also Professor Kolodny's *The Land Before Her: Fantasy and Experience of the American Frontiers, 1630–1860* (Chapel Hill: University of North Carolina, 1984), for discussion of this feminine tradition of relating to the land as a garden rather than as a landscape to be dominated.

53. Michiko Kakutani, "Arthur Miller: View From Maturity Of a Life Tempered by Skepticism," *The New York Times,* 9 May 1984, p. 20, col. 1.

54. Arthur Miller, *Death of a Salesman* (New York: Penguin, 1980), p. 48. Subsequent references to this work are included in our text. The original edition was published by Viking in 1949.

55. Jack Kerouac, *On The Road* (New York: Signet, 1957), 196. Subsequent references to this work are included in our text.

56. Erikson, 285–325.

57. Ibid., 293.

CHAPTER 6
RELOCATION AND ILLNESS: THE PLIGHT OF THE NAVAJO

Cisco Lassiter

I

In what has been described as the largest forced civilian relocation since the internment of Japanese-Americans during World War II, the United States government is acting to remove more than ten thousand Navajos—or Dinéhs as they call themselves—from their ancestral homelands. As numerous studies have shown, the forced removal of indigenous peoples from their native lands invariably leads to mental and physical disabilities among relocatees. Predictably, psychopathological disorders have become widespread among Dinéhs faced with relocation. Yet the program continues.

The relocation is being carried out under the authority of the 1974 Navajo-Hopi Land Settlement Act (Public Law 93-531). The Land Settlement Act was passed by a largely uninformed Congress in order to end an alleged "land dispute" between the Dinéh and Hopi tribes over approximately 1.8 million acres of land in northeastern Arizona. But the fact is that, for hundreds of years, this land of stone, sage and sacred shrines had been shared by the Dinéh and Hopi peoples without major conflict. Until the passage of this act, even the U. S. government recognized the land as a Joint Use Area. Though the land, in the Dinéh way, could not be "owned" at all, the JUA "technically" belonged to both tribes.

Over the past century the JUA has come to be predominantly inhabited by the widely scattered, sheep-herding Dinéhs. The Hopis, who are traditionally sedentary farmers, have stayed for the most part near their ancient villages on the mesas. For them, the land on the JUA was primarily used only for hunting and gathering firewood. The Dinéhs originally began settling in the JUA in significant numbers when much of their own land was usurped by white settlers. Thousands of Dinéhs were imprisoned at Fort Sumner in 1864 in response to their active resistance to white encroachment. This action was the first mass relocation of the Dinéhs and is known historically as "the longest walk."

The Hopis, who are traditionally pacifists and did not resist white encroachment with violence, were allowed to remain on their land, although their territory was severely reduced. When the imprisoned Dinéhs were released in 1868, rather than fight a losing battle with the whites who had drifted onto their land, they moved toward the Dinéhs who had settled around the Hopis—in what later became the JUA.

The Dinéhs were fruitful. Their numbers increased dramatically over the past century, along with the size of their subsistence base. Thus began the tension over land use rights. Yet, according to traditionals of both tribes, the minor skirmishes between the Dinéhs and the Hopis over grazing rights on the JUA are not the real explanation for the government's decision to remove roughly ten thousand Dinéhs and one hundred Hopis from their land. The relocatees point out that the tribes have been intermarrying for hundreds of years and are invited to one another's ceremonies. Though they do have minor differences, they have come to believe that the real explanation for their removal is related to the wealth that lies hidden beneath their mother earth.

The Land Settlement Act changed the legal status of the Joint Use Area by authorizing the equal division of the land between the Dinéh and Hopi tribes. The law called for the construction of a barbed wire fence to demarcate the actual partition line and separate the Dinéh and Hopi inhabitants of the JUA. A "Navajo–Hopi Relocation Commission" was formed to administer the removal of the thousands who found themselves on the "wrong side of the fence." It is now becoming increasingly apparent that this relocation clears the way for white business interests to exploit the region's multi-billion dollar coal and mineral reserves.

II

This compulsory relocation is turning into a major sociocultural and psychopathological disaster. When relocatees move from the JUA, with their sheep, to other areas on the Dinéh reservation, the inhabitants already living there are subject to new social and environmental pressure. Many areas on the reservation are already overgrazed or maximally grazed. In addition, much of the existing reservation is inhabited by tightly knit extended family groups who have neither the resources nor the inclination to make room for relocatees. Thus the newcomers, especially those with sheep—the subsistence base of virtually the entire JUA—are often less than welcome. Tensions quickly arise. Yet being on the land *without* sheep forces relocatees, many of whom were previously self-sufficient, to resort to welfare and—far worse—to lose their sense of purpose and identity. This, in turn, has generated a multitude of mental and physical disorders.

Many Dinéhs have moved off the reservation into urban housing provided by the Relocation Commission, only to find themselves adrift in hostile border towns such as Flagstaff, Winslow and Gallup. Since those people are without any job skills other than raising sheep and in many cases lack even basic English language skills, their attempt to live in our cash economy has proven exceedingly stressful.

On the JUA, sheep are used for food, trade, credit and ceremonies. In town, things are different. Often, the only collateral available to relocatees who need a loan for the purchase of a car or even simply to meet the living expenses they never encountered while living on the reservation—property taxes, utility, water, garbage, and other bills—is the house that is provided as part of the relocation program's package of "benefits." But many families have lost their new homes to unscrupulous real estate and loan companies. Uncounted numbers of relocatees have fled back to the JUA, becoming "trespassers" on land that had been their peoples' for hundreds of years. Others, say relatives, have simply "vanished."

The psychophysiological stress directly attributable to relocation is apparent. The incidence of violence, crime, alcoholism, depression, suicide, sickness, and abject poverty has been abnormally high among relocatees (Scudder 1979, Topper 1979, Schoepfle 1980).

Martin Topper, a cultural anthropologist with the federal Indian Health Service, found that the Dinéhs facing relocation are utilizing mental health services at a rate eight times that of the Dinéhs not faced with relocation (1979). Topper also directly correlates several suicide attempts by residents of the JUA that occurred during the course of his twenty-five week study to the stress induced by the prospect of their relocation.

Thayer Scudder, a world authority on the effects of the forced removal of indigenous peoples from their ancestral lands, warned Congress to "consider very carefully the evidence that relocation will raise the death rate among those involved" (1979)—to no avail.

The Relocation Commission's own massive Report and Plan (1981) largely ignores Scudder's 1979 report on the projected impacts of the Dinéh relocation, referring to it only briefly in the following quote: "The results of over 25 studies around the world indicate, with no exceptions, that the execution of compulsory relocation among rural populations with strong ties to their land and homes is a traumatic experience for the majority of the relocatees." (Mander, p. 62)

The Relocation Commission's Report and Plan does however corroborate many of Scudder's predictions, noting that, as of 1981, 35 percent of the families already relocated had experienced "marked family instability, financial decline, major debts, mortgaging or selling their new home, had moved back to the reservation, had major health problems, significant depression, suicide, etc." (Mander, p. 62)

Examples of stress-induced psychopathological disorders are plainly evident both among relocatees and potential relocatees. One Dinéh elder who had been relocated to Flagstaff made a visit to the hogan where he was born and had lived his entire life—prior to relocation. When he arrived, he discovered that government workers had leveled his home with a bulldozer. That experience caused him to have a stroke.

The Relocation Commission has primarily emphasized improved (modern) housing, offering mobile or modular homes as replacements for the old hogans—the traditional polygonal Dinéh homes constructed of wooden poles and clay. But they haven't addressed the heart of the problem, which is not only a change of houses, but a change in the relocatees' entire way of life. The Dinéh feel that the spirit cannot survive in the cubic design of modern housing.

One male relocatee said: "We need a hogan to have singing ceremonies in. I was already told by a medicine man he can't perform in a square house. We also need a farm with a big enough place to store our corn and melons. We can't do it here. We are worse off now because we have to pay electricity bills and other expenses that we did not have before. And we had extra income from our livestock before relocation—now we have none." (Scudder 1979).

A number of relocatees, who initially were persuaded that a move away from their remote life on the JUA would be a positive step, now regret having accepted the promised "benefits." Said one relocatee: "There is nothing to live for. There is no land; there is no hogan; there is no sheep permit; there is no livestock. I'm not used to this world . . . I would have liked (at least) a small area of land like the one I had with a hogan on it . . ." (Schoepfle et al., 1979).

Another woman said: "I feel so lonely now, and sometimes I dream about herding sheep—I get sick often—I've been going to the hospital a lot. I feel like I'm in jail here." (Scudder 1979).

Recent research indicates that relocation is, and will continue to be, especially stressful for men and women over forty. This group in particular is lacking in education and maintains the strongest ties to their customary use areas and their livestock. Dinéh land, heritage and identity, all of which are defined by their customary use areas, are passed on to children primarily through the women. Many women relocatees are afraid that their children will lose their Dinéh identity and drift apart. Some worry about this constantly. One woman relocatee said: "It seems like the end for us here. Our future plan for our children is disrupted. We get very lonely after relocation. We ask ourselves why we relocated. Perhaps if we hadn't relocated, our daughter wouldn't have died."

But it is clearly not only the elders who suffer. Many young people, too, despite their acquisition of English language skills and their increased exposure to the dominant culture, are finding the changes difficult to cope with. Many have returned to the JUA after bouts with alcoholism, attempted suicide, imprisonment, and economic and cultural poverty. Those who have made it back to the land are considered the lucky ones, even given the uncertainty of their tenure there.

Many twenty-to-thirty-year-olds report that they are unable to raise their children properly, the way they themselves had been taught (i.e., on the land, with livestock, by way of example and practice). There has been a dramatic increase in alcoholism and mental health referrals among this age group too, since relocation began.

One young man said he could not think about marrying and having children of his own. He said he was too worried about his own parents' grandparents and siblings—who have thus far refused to move off the JUA and who have already had several confrontations with fence construction and stock reduction crews—to consider raising children of his own. He said that, without the aid of both the land and extended family, raising children properly would be impossible. This young man had returned to his family's land after two years of wandering through the urban centers of the southwest and California. "I spent most nights drunk in doorways, or in jail," he said. "I lost two years before I realized that all I needed was my family and the land." This story, or variations on the same theme, is heard time and again from young Dinéh who have been severed from the land and family.

Loss of memory, disorientation, an inability to concentrate, cases of partial paralysis, and especially, severe depression and physical deterioration, are all common forms of suffering—not only among a significant number of adult relocatees, but also among many *potential* relocatees as well. Depression and tension are also prevalent among the preteens, but very little research has been carried out on the impact of relocation on Dinéh children.

In his 1980 report on "The Human Impact of the Navajo-Hopi Land Dispute," Mark Schoepfle described conditions "of severe psychoneurotic and psychosomatic deterioration following severe personal and social trauma," and noted that "respondents indicated that, while they often visited the Indian Health Service hospitals for counseling, the only real solution would be the resumption of their original way of life."

These illnesses clearly demonstrate that Dinéh "psychopathology" cannot be understood only in psychological terms. We need to understand its origin in relation to social and political events. The causes of their psychiatric illnesses are not just "physical" or "psychological."

III

The suffering of the relocatees is rooted in their spiritual experience of life. Consequently, their illnesses cannot be understood, nor can they be "treated," without taking this experience into account. Dinéh psychology needs to be understood in terms of a premodern, primal self: a self-identity with needs that are distinctly different from those the modern self has recognized and produced.

Probably the most significant need of the premodern self is a sense of place. The modern self is expected and encouraged to be mobile, independent, and able to adapt to constant social and environmental change. For the modern self, all places are essentially the same: in the uniform, homogeneous space of a Euclidean-Newtonian grid, all places are essentially interchangeable. Our places, even our places for homes, are defined by objective measures. This relationship to places is perhaps epitomized by the image of the "rugged individual" in white American mythology. However, unlike the identity of the "self-made man," the Dinéh's identity is inextricably tied to its particular place on earth. Dinéh self-awareness—Dinéh identity and individuality—is grounded in the earth, the tribe, the community, the family, and the ecosystem—the Great Self. Without these connections, the primal self quickly begins to lose its bearings and disintegrate. Its very identity depends upon the continuation of a devotional connectedness to earth, ground, community, and ancestral place. The Dinéh sense of "home" is more closely tied up with their sense of who they are. In their experiential world, relocation *can* cause the death of the spirit.

The land of their ancestors, their ancestral dwelling-place, is the point of reference for everything that "takes place" in the Dinéh world. Their land is circumscribed by four sacred mountains, with one mountain lying in each of the Four Directions. The Dinéh believe that these mountains shield their people from dangers of the outside world.

Each Dinéh family has its own sacred location within the larger area, where all family prayers are made. Each family has a medicine bundle containing dirt from the four sacred mountains and sacred stones from the land, which are used as offerings during prayers in which an individual is instructed, through mythology and family legend, in the appropriate behavior for his particular stage in life.

Appropriate behavior means among other things appropriate thought, which in turn is evidenced by the presence of healthy children and livestock. Talismans are reminders and representatives of this good thought and are placed in the medicine bundle along with the sacred earth and prayer stones. Together, they make up the record of a sacred family history, a history in which the people and the land are one. Dinéh epistemology and psychology are based, from childhood through old age, on this complex system of prayers, mythology and offerings, all of which are deeply rooted in place (Mander 1981).

Paul Shepard, in his book *Nature and Madness,* elucidated the process by which premodern people such as the Dinéh internalize the local topography:

> Individual and tribal identity are built up in connection with widely separated places and the paths connecting them. Different places are successfully assimilated or internalized. They become distinct, though unconscious elements of the self, enhanced by mythology and ceremony, generating a network of deep emotional attachments that cements the personality. Throughout life those places have a role in the evocation of the self and group consciousness. They are mnemonic: integrated components of a sacred history and the remembered and unconsciously felt past. The whole of the region or home range becomes a heirophantic map, a repository of the first creation that parallels and overlies history. (Shepard 1982, p. 24)

The Dinéh's ancestral land is their most important source of cultural knowledge. Virtually all learning in traditional Dinéh culture is experiential; it occurs in the process of raising livestock and making prayers in a particular ancestral place. It involves becoming a part of that place. And that place serves as a point of reference for all else: memory, knowledge of the past, prayer, relationships, home, self, a vision of life. Closeness to the land and to their place on the land is their way of being grounded in tradition, in the traditional ground of their tribal ancestors. Their sense of history and even their sense of time itself are dependent on this closeness to their land. It is through their experience of the land that they stay in touch with their ancestors and with the gods of the place. Leaving the land means abandoning their ancestors and their gods. It means loss of orientation, and ultimately, loss of group identity, loss of self.

IV

The modern self views the external world as existing primarily to be manipulated and exploited for personal gain. For the Dinéh, however, as for most premodern peoples, there cannot be a whole, healthy self apart from the larger ecological community—the Great Self. To disrupt the balance of any part of the community is to hurt one's self. For the Dinéh, to take from the Earth without reciprocating, without having first become a part of the life of the place, is to disrupt a sacred balance and ultimately to grow ill.

Many JUA residents, and traditionals of both Dinéh and Hopi tribes, believe that after their removal, the land will be laid to waste by large-scale mining for coal and uranium: an irreversible destruction. The Dinéh have experienced the effects of being the inhabitants of what the government has called a "National Sacrifice Area." The mining is supposed to give this nation "energy independence." But the cost to the Dinéh people has been a dramatic increase in the rate of cancer—which is several times higher among Dinéh than the national average—and increases in other diseases also associated with the coal and uranium mining already in operation on the reservation. They know about groundwater contamination from the huge, still "hot" uranium tailing piles left uncovered by the banks of the rivers and stream beds. They already breathe air, near the Four Corners power plant on the Dinéh reservation, that is reported to have more particulate matter in it than the air in the Los Angeles basin. They have seen and/or experienced the mental and physical deterioration associated with being severed from their sacred land. And they now believe that the health of the Dinéh people—and the nurturing capacity of the land of which they are a part—have already suffered more than enough at the hands of energy developers and the U.S. government. They do not want to be part of the "National Sacrifice."

V

The fate of the Indian people removed from their ancestral lands has far-reaching implications for the future society we are preparing. We, too, are now finding ourselves increasingly vulnerable to the kind of "psychopathology" experienced by the Dinéh relocatees: homelessness, disorientation, rootlessness, alienation, loneliness, depression, and despair. In a society driven by the pursuit of an ever-increasing material standard of living, often at the expense of home, rootedness, and membership in the biotic community, these forms of suffering are probably inevitable. Many of the common illnesses of contemporary society suggest experiences which parallel the relocation of Dinéhs from their homeland. Can what remains of Dinéh culture be preserved in our future society? Cooperation and dialogue—each listening carefully to the other and learning from the other's experiences—are perhaps as essential for the survival of our society as for the survival of the Dinéhs. These apparently separate or even conflicting destinies are really one and the same.

What hope there is for the relocatees lies in what the rest of us in this country can learn from them. And what healing there is for us, for the modern self, could depend on our ability and willingness to learn from the traditions of Native Americans about a radically different way of living, being, and being well. This will require radical changes in our political economy and its social institutions. It will also require a profound change in our view of our position in Nature, as well as our remembership in the biotic community. These changes may be inspired by the spirit that survives even today, despite severe setbacks, among the Dinéh.

The plight of the Dinéh and the plight of all the other indigenous groups struggling to survive in the modern world should be a warning to us all. Our collective survival may well depend on the integration of their understanding of health and pathology, sanity and well-being. Unless we make this effort, it may not be only the society of the premodern (primal) self that is destroyed; it could also mean the end of our modern civilization.

Nabahe Keediinihii, a young Dinéh leader of the resistance movement in the Big Mountain area of the JUA and a well-respected member of his community, said to me: "The government and the energy companies may wipe us out in the end. We may not have the strength to fight any more after a while. But the struggle is not useless; because, even if we lose our land and disappear, the social, political, and environmental issues, over which we are also in conflict, will still be there, and it will be up to whomever is left to carry on the struggle."

REFERENCES

Mander, Jerry, "Kit Karson in a Three-Piece Suit," *Co-Evolution Quarterly,* Winter 1981.

Schoepfle, Mark, et al., *The Human Impact of the Navajo-Hopi Land Dispute: The Navajo View.* (Shiprock, Arizona: Navajo Community College, November 1980).

Scudder, Thayer, et al., *Expected Impacts of Compulsory Relocation on Navajos.* (Philadelphia: Institute for the Study of Human Issues, 1979).

Shepard, Paul, *Nature and Madness* (San Francisco: Sierra Club Books, 1983).

Topper, Martin, *"Mental Health Effects of Navajo Relocation in the Former Joint-Use Area,"* Report submitted March 7, 1979 to the Mental Health Branch Navajo Area Office, Indian Health Service. (Berkeley: University of California, 1979).

CHAPTER 7
MELANCHOLY AND MELANCHOLIA

JENNIFER RADDEN

Foucault's dense and brilliant "archaeological" analyses of the structures of insanity[1] reveal suggestions of a sixteenth- and seventeenth-century understanding of that condition as "unreason" *(déraison)*. The notion of insanity as unreason invites some interesting comparisons with its earlier medical understanding as madness *(folie)*, the ascendency of which Foucault so closely documented.

I shall draw these comparisons in relation to one particular kind of mental disturbance, excessive sadness or depression, looking at two categories of sufferer: the melancholy man of the sixteenth and seventeenth centuries and today's clinically depressed woman. By exploring Elizabethan melancholy and contemporary melancholia or depression, I shall assess some of Foucault's claims about the transformation by which, as he pictured it, unreason became madness.

I. UNREASON

On a superficial analysis, the history of madness during the last eight hundred years breaks where the medieval religious understanding gave rise to the secular, medical one that prevails today. In the former, madness was evil, caused by demonic possession and cured by the ministration of religious authorities; in the latter it came to be seen as akin to illness or disease—the unforseeable misfortune of a victim more pitiable than blameworthy.

But Foucault's analysis of the history of madness in the "Age of Reason" belies this superficial division, for it reveals ways of viewing madness that came between the end of the religious understanding of the medieval or "Gothic" period and the full flowering of the later medical one. The concept of "unreason" is introduced to describe one such conception: that which prevailed briefly in the sixteenth- and seventeenth-century period described by Foucault as "pre-Classical," only to disappear with the "Classical" experience of madness in the eighteenth century.[2]

Foucault described the concept of unreason as emerging with the emphasis on human reason and its powers that followed the Renaissance. He described the madhouse, where each form of madness "finds its proper place": "all this work of disorder, in perfect order pronounces, each in his turn, the Praise of Reason."[3] A state of unreason was seen as somehow especially hospitable to the entertainment of illusions. The illusory, said Foucault, is itself "the dramatic meaning of madness"[4] and in madness "equilibrium is established, but it masks that equilibrium beneath the cloud of illusion, beneath feigned disorder; the rigor of the architecture is concealed beneath the cunning arrangement of these disordered violences."[5] Yet in these very illusions of madness was thought to lie a truth more profound than that known to the sane. There was a secret delirium underlying the chaotic and manifest delirium of madness, a delirium that is "in a sense, pure reason, reason delivered of all the external tinsel of dementia . ."[6] The ordinary, unfrightening and human quality of madness was emphasized with a conception of the manifestations of madness as a failure of reason, since such failures were universally experienced. There came to be "no madman but that which is every man, since it is man who constitutes madness in the attachment he bears for himself and by the illusions he entertains. . . ."[7] The similarity between madness and other forms of "folly" was stressed, and with this stress came a concern with the manifestations of these failings that leaves out as insignificant the question of their moral status or causal explanation. The long series of follies, "stigmatizing vices and faults as in the past, no longer attribute them all to pride, to lack of charity, to neglect of Christian virtues,"[8] as they had done in the earlier period under the influence of a religious understanding of madness. Instead they came to be attributed to "a sort of great unreason for which nothing, in fact, is exactly responsible, but which involves everyone in a kind of secret complicity."[9] This concern with the manifestations of madness gives its unreasonableness a place as the defining characteristic of madness and provides the category through which it must be viewed. Unreason had, as Foucault put it, a nominal value: it "defined the locus of madness's possibility." Only ". . . in relation to unreason, and to it alone"[10] could madness be understood.

Many facets of the notion of madness as unreason can be derived from Foucault's references to the attitudes and ideas of the pre-Classical period, but I wish to concentrate on one suggestion: that madness and its sufferers were seen at that time as less divorced from everyday experience than they are today.

In general terms, one point made by Foucault seems undeniable. However it may have been regarded earlier, madness today is a remote and unfamiliar phenomenon that strikes fear, perplexity, suspicion and unease in the sane. Madness today is alienating. Moreover, some of this alienation seems to be attributable to the medical point of view from which it is standardly understood. True, the adoption of that point of view is associated with serious efforts to understand madness, with attempts to alleviate suffering and with the lifting of moral blame. But in other ways the medical analysis is guilty of ignoring and obscuring the sense of madness as a familiar and unpuzzling feature of ordinary human life. Identifying and controlling the "disease," for example, and so labeling and isolating its sufferer, introducing widespread institutionalized professionalism into the management of madness—these have increased our sense of the mad person as unlike ordinary sane people whose deviations—unreasonableness, strange ideas and excesses of feeling—we think of as like enough to our own weaknesses to be dealt with as normal human conditions.

Thus Foucault rightly attributed to the medical understanding a certain rarifying of madness. With the emergence of the medical point of view something was lost. *Déraison* (unreason) was transformed into *folie* (madness), as Foucault put it, and became what it is today: obscure, puzzling and remote from everyday human experience.

We shall now explore more closely the mechanics of that loss in the case of one kind of mental disorder—excessive sadness or despair. To do this, I wish to look at melancholy as it was understood in England during the period Foucault described as pre-Classical—Elizabethan times. Though only part of the "pre-Classical" period Foucault singled out is, strictly, Elizabethan (1558–1603), the term "Elizabethan melancholy" has come to connote the condition that gained prominence under that sovereign—and its influence in fact continued well into the eighteenth century. Moreover my emphasis on England is warranted by melancholy's other title, "the English malady."

II. ELIZABETHAN MELANCHOLY

In today's nomenclature, "depressive reaction" or "depressive episode" replace an earlier term, *melancholia*, which is to be found in the work of nineteenth-century nosologists and indeed in Freud. But although *melancholia* and *melancholy* are cognates, it cannot be concluded that the Elizabethan notion of melancholy to be explored here exactly corresponds to the contemporary one of clinical depression. The Elizabethans spoke of the disposition as melancholy and of the character as melancholic. But melancholia—the abnormal clinical condition—as we shall see, seems to be the product of a later age.

The last quarter of the sixteenth century saw what some scholars have judged an epidemic[11] of the condition known as melancholy, and it became the experience and concern of poets and scientists alike. Melancholy continued to be a concept and category of major significance both in England and on the Continent until the mid-eighteenth century,[12] but I shall restrict my discussion to the post-Renaissance period between the end of the sixteenth century and the middle of the seventeenth in order to remain in conformity with the "pre-Classical" era to which Foucault's analysis applies.

Melancholy is described, though never completely defined, in Burton's famous *Anatomy* published in 1626: where its main symptoms are listed as sadness and fear ("without a cause"), suspicion and jealousy, inconstancy, proneness to love and humourousness.[13] Sorrow and fear, particularly, Burton designates as melancholy's "true characters and inseparable companions."[14] And from an earlier scientific account, Timothy Bright's *Treatise on Melancholy* (1586),[15] comes the same emphasis on unwarranted black and apprehensive moods: those affected by melancholy "are in heaviness, sit comfortless, fear, doubt, despair and lament, when no cause requireth it."[16]

Reference here to the uncaused nature of the moods of despondency and apprehension that Bright and Burton and other commentators single out as primary features of melancholy seems to imply two things. Moods of melancholy are so pervasive as to be directed at or felt over no one particular thing. They were without objects, in Hume's terminology[17]—although they clearly have causes of one kind, as the humoral and other explanations Burton offers attest. And, more generally, they are at least unwarranted or unjustified in the sense of being disproportionate or inappropriate to their occasion.

In the literary tradition, the same moods of melancholy reveal themselves in feelings of sadness and apprehension, distress, misery and world weariness. "Come heavy sleep, the image of true death," the poet sings,

> And close up these my weary weeping eyes,
> Whose spring of tears doth stop my vital breath,
> And tears my hart with sorrows high swoln crys:
> Come and possess my tired thoughts-worne soule,
> That living dies, till thought on me be stoule.
>
> Come shadow my end: and shape of rest,
> Alied to death, child to this black fac't night,
> Come thou and charme these rebels in my brest,
> Whose waking fancies doth my mind affright.
> O come sweet sleepe, come or I die for ever,
> Come ere my last sleepe coms, or come never.
>
> Anon.[18]

The mood is dark,

> In darkness let me dwell, the ground shall sorrow be,
> The roofe Despaire to all cheerful light from me
>
> Anon.[19]

and suicide has charm,

> My thoughts hold mortal strife;
> I do detest my life,
> And with lamenting cries,
> Peace to my soul to bring,
> Oft call that prince which here doth monarchise:
> —But he, grim, grinning King,
> Who caitiffs scorns, and dost the blest surprise,
> Late having decked with beauty's rose his tomb,
> Distains to crop a weed, and will not come.
>
> William Drummond of Hawthornden[20]

A serious impediment to understanding the notion of melancholy during this period rests in its breadth and scope. Speaking of the varied symptoms of melancholy, Burton remarked that "Proteus himself is not so diverse; you may well make the Moon a new coat, as a true character of a melancholy man; as soon find the notion of a bird in the air as the heart of a melancholy man."[21] Moreover, present day commentaries[22] place emphasis on the varying meanings or interpretations intended by that commodious term. Not only does "melancholy" seem to have been extended to cover a broader spectrum of mental abnormalities than those that would today be classified as clinical depression. In addition melancholy traits were represented as ranging from despair and the black moods described by the poets to wit, wisdom and inspiration. And, finally, "melancholy" refers as much to a passing or long-term attribute of a normal person as to mental disturbance. To our contemporary minds, the concept of melancholy at that period is at first sight so broad as to be almost meaningless.

Let us look more closely at each of the areas of ambiguity introduced. First, melancholy seems sometimes to be used so broadly as to cover several different kinds of madness or derangement. One present day historian has gone so far as to conclude that " 'melancholy' was constantly used as a synonym for madness."[23] Burton, on the other hand, decried this equation with every form of madness, and "new and old writers who have spoken confusedly of [melancholy], confounding melancholy with madness . . . that will have madness no other than melancholy in extent, differing in degrees.[24] And despite the apparently disparate symptoms of melancholy cited even by Burton himself, there seem to run through these accounts two shared themes: blackness of mood and feeling, and a humoral explanation. We shall return to these unifying themes presently.

Second, the melancholy man was as likely a poet, rake or scholar as a madman. Alongside the tragic melancholic like Hamlet, in dramatic imagery, it has been pointed out, there stood the "fashionable melancholic."[25] There was "scarcely a man of distinction who was not either genuinely melancholy or at least considered as such by himself and others."[26] The figure of the melancholy man was fashionable and common, seen both in life and art. Characteristic poses and motifs, like the drooping head in Dürer's *Melancholia,* were associated with the condition in the stock melancholy characters of the stage and in painting.

The fashion of melancholy suggests there were compensations to this condition despite the subjective distress it brought. Melancholy was an object of interest and respect. The melancholic character, it has been said, "had something about it of sombre philosophical dignity, something of Byronic grandeur."[27] Moreover melancholy was associated with other esteemed traits. The melancholic man will suffer, for he is "morose, taciturn, waspish, misanthropic, solitary, fond of darkness . . . extremely wretched and [he] often longs for death."[28] But he is also, as Burton said, "of deep reach, excellent apprehension, judicious, wise and witty."[29] A person of melancholy mood or disposition was likely to be marked by his wit and wisdom—his wit and wisdom, indeed, may have occasioned his melancholy.[30]

Emphasis on the two sets of traits sketched here derives from one of two distinct traditions contributing to the Elizabethan notion of melancholy. Of these, the first, primarily medical in orientation and origin, was more concerned with melancholy as the sadness and despair of mental abnormality, while the second, which emphasized the link between sadness and wit and wisdom, was associated more with normal psychology, where intellectual pursuits were believed to increase a person's vulnerability to such despondency.

Stemming from Galen and Aristotle, respectively, each of these different traditions had been influential during the preceding Renaissance period. The early physician Galen described the effects of black bile as an unrelieved blackness of mood and demeanour. But to Aristotle, or more exactly to one of his disciples, is attributed the question, "Why is it that all those who become eminent in philosophy or politics or poetry or the arts are clearly of an atrabilious temperament and some of them to such an extent as to be affected by the diseases caused by black bile?"[31] Melancholy in the Aristotelian tradition is the world weariness of the sensitive and creative. In the words of one historian, "Renaissance physicians and psychologists, although they believed that melancholy is likely to produce blockish stupidity and absurd irrationality, do not question the Aristotelian dictum . . . in general they agree that there is a relationship between melancholy and mental capacity."[32] This same belief seems to have prevailed during the post-Renaissance period we are considering. Burton himself acknowledged it in suggesting that love of learning and overmuch study were causes of melancholy.

Finally, as the picture of the melancholy rake or scholar suggests, melancholy was attributed to ordinary people in the absence of any suggestion of mental disturbance. The term "melancholy" came to describe not merely a "melancholy habit" (Burton) in an otherwise sane person—a long-term character trait or disposition—but also what Burton described as a "transitory melancholy disposition." Momentary or short-lived moods of sadness, of the kind that must be seen as normal emotional responses, were also attributed to melancholy. Indeed, in everyday settings, according to one authority, there has occurred a shift in traditional usage. In the earlier Medieval period melancholy had referred solely to a long-term disposition, whether disturbed or normal. In the post-Medieval period at which we are looking, however, it tended more and more towards "the subjective and transitory meaning, until at length it was so overshadowed by the new 'poetic' conception that this last became the normal meaning in modern thought and speech."[33] Thus a man might be melancholy for a morning or a lifetime; moreover his lifelong melancholy might reflect either a normal but splenetic character or a serious mental abnormality.

Whether the various emphases considered here reflect, as present day authorities seem to suggest,[34] differing meanings or senses of the notion of melancholy; or whether, instead, we are dealing with a concept so loose as to have no present day equivalent, I shall discuss later. Let us first note two features of Elizabethan melancholy that may be appealed to in explaining the breadth and looseness of the notion: the humoral explanation apparently holding together each of the varying understandings of the condition, and the *feelings* associated with melancholy.[35]

Shared by all the different notions of melancholy is the causal principle appealed to in explaining them: black bile, described as "a heavy, viscid humour, so thick and adhesive that physicians have great difficulty evacuating it."[36] Other factors were also appealed to in explaining melancholy, e.g. divine and planetary intervention, but the humoral explanation seems to have been the most widely accepted. A balance of the four humors (bile, blood, choler and phlegm) was thought to determine a person's temperament. This tradition, which had influenced the understanding of health and illness alike since pre-Socratic times, allowed that a melancholic person had excessive black bile from the spleen. Thus wrote one contemporary physician, "If the spleneticke excrement surcharge the bodie, not only being purged by the help of the spleen, then are these purturbations far more outrageous, and hard to be mitigated . . . by persuasion."[37] Black bile proved a versatile explanation since variations in its condition according to temperature and viscosity accounted for a wide variation of effects, including the daily fluctuations in mood as well as more long-term states and dispositions.

In the case of melancholy, however, the humors provided causal explanations in a curious sense, since no bile ever was or would be black. Black bile, several authors have argued, was a kind of metaphor for the dark mood of melancholy rather than a reference to any actual substance. It was explained that there are associations among the notions of anger, darkness, blackness surging up with anger, and blackness as poisonous (thus *cholos* (anger) and *cholē* (bile) often overlap in poetic and literary usage): and "the black bile theory seems to have developed when subjective experience led to a search for causal agents that had some sort of intrinsic connection with the quality of the experience. If there is a black mood, there must be a black substance."[38]

We might conclude today that black bile was closer to a description than an explanation of melancholy.

Foucault hinted at a similar point in his discussion of melancholy when he insisted that it was "the phenomenology of melancholic experience"[39] which gave the concept of melancholy its coherence.

> A symbolic unity formed by the languor of the fluids, by the darkening of the animal spirits and the shadowy twilight they spread over the images of things, by the viscosity of the blood that laboriously trickles through the vessels, by the thickening of vapors that have become blackish, deleterious and acrid, by visceral functions that have become slow and somehow slimy—this unity, more a product of sensibility than of thought or theory, gives melancholia its characteristic stamp.[40]

Thus the apparently unifying function of the humoral explanations, Foucault seemed to suggest, is illusory.

This notion leads us to the second feature of melancholy apparently sufficient to unite the disparate manifestations to which it referred: the feelings associated with it. The purely affective qualities of melancholy—its phenomenology, in Foucault's phrase—may be appealed to directly in linking the conditions of the melancholy madman, the rake (albeit his affectations were self-induced and perhaps more perceived than real), and the sufferer from an isolated mood of sadness. The concept of melancholy was closely wedded to what Burton called its true characters and inseparable companions: sadness and fear without a cause. This may seem obvious, especially since in present day usage the faintly archaic "melancholy" means little beyond the subjective mood of sadness. But it is a point worth observing, nevertheless, as we shall see when we come to compare the Elizabethan notion with our contemporary concepts of clinical depression and melancholia.

III. MELANCHOLY AND MELANCHOLIA

Our contemporary notions offer some interesting comparisons with the earlier ideas of melancholy we have been considering. Most obvious is that where the all-encompassing "melancholy" spanned, several terms must now be distinguished. "Melancholy" remains, but now it is restricted to the sad or dejected frame of mind of a normal person: my melancholy may be dispositional or momentary, but it is always within the normal range of emotional responses. And in contrast, there is the term "melancholia," now itself somewhat outmoded, as we shall see, to cover the pathological or clinical dimensions of the condition. Thus Freud, in his famous 1917 paper "Mourning and Melancholia," characterized the mental features of the "melancholiac" or sufferer from melancholia, as "profoundly painful dejection, abrogation of interest in the outside world, loss of the capacity to love, inhibition of all activity, and a lowering of the self regarding feelings to a degree that finds utterance in self reproaches and self-revilings, and culminates in a delusional expectation of punishment."[41] We recognize a parallel between the feelings described here and those experienced in the earlier melancholy—even though "melancholy," by Freud's time, was a term already restricted in the way described above. Anyone may be melancholy, but only the mentally disturbed are described as melancholiacs or as suffering melancholia—just as, in a parallel case, anyone may be depressed, but only the mentally disturbed are said to be depressive.

For today, we also have the concept of depression both to describe the disposition or passing mood of sadness and despair of a normal person, and, with certain qualifications, to mark off clinical abnormality. Anyone may experience momentary depression. But the condition of depressive illness or depressive reaction affects those requiring treatment.

Thus today's term "melancholy" corresponds to "depression," and "melancholia" to depressive illness or reaction: the cognates of each term have been introduced to mark the distinction between ordinary sadness on the one hand, and pathological or clinical sadness on the other. These terminological distinctions, I shall argue, permit—and encourage—the class of those suffering melancholia or clinical depression to be set apart from the person who is merely depressed or melancholy. They seem to reflect—and abet—an attitudinal separation between these two groups apparently not as marked in the earlier period we have been considering.

We are familiar with the conditions of sadness, despair and dejection that affect ordinary people; they need no introduction. But contemporary clinical concepts of depression and melancholia require a closer examination. Let us consider the official nosology of the American Psychiatric Association, (DSM III) revised in 1980, which employs the terminology of the *depressive episode* to classify this kind of "affective disorder."[42]

Psychological states, both affective (moods and feelings) and cognitive (beliefs), as well as behavioral symptoms are introduced here: thus a major depressive episode is said to be marked by:

> A. the psychological 'dysphoric' mood, or loss of interest or pleasure in all or almost all normal activities or pastimes

and

> B. some of the following behavioral symptoms: poor appetite, insomnia, psycho-motor agitation or retardation, slowed thinking or indecisiveness, fatigue,

or psychological states,

> feelings of worthlessness or self-reproach or excessive guilt or wishes to be dead.

Confusingly, the notion of melancholia enters here as an adjunct to some but not all major depressive episodes of the kind just defined, but it is introduced as adding identical or closely similar symptoms:

> loss of pleasure, mood worse in the morning, psychomotor retardation or agitation, weight loss or insomnia

Thus it is left unclear what real difference, if any, marks the major depressive episode when accompanied by melancholia[43] and the major depressive episode without it.[44] The distinction seems to hint at the notion, implied for example in the concept of "masked depression," that there might be a depressive episode in the absence of any of the subjective feelings of sadness and dejection usually taken to be central to melancholia. But at least as it is formulated here, this extreme behaviorist interpretation cannot be adopted, since the subjective feelings described in item *A* above are presented as necessary conditions for the diagnosis (of major depressive episode)—as its broader status as an "Affective Disorder" would lead us to expect.

In a comparison of the melancholy of the earlier period with today's depressive conditions, one issue seems apparent. The same moods of sadness predominate subjectively: we seem to be dealing with the same kind of feelings. And this is true, also, of the contemporary category of normal depression. The sad feelings of the normal melancholy or depressed person parallel those of the sufferer from depressive reactions or illness. So it is by a matter of degree that the clinically depressed person not subject to grosser abnormalities of hallucination or delusion is distinguished, affectively, from the merely sad or disheartened or dejected one. The mood's relative persistence, pervasiveness and intensity alone mark the "pathology" of the former from the normal states of the latter. However, the contemporary concept of depressive episode as put forward in DSM III does suggest a lessening of emphasis on the subjective and particularly the affective side of this condition—despite its treatment of the presence of the feeling of "dysphoric mood" as a necessary diagnostic criterion. For there is now a strong emphasis on the assorted behavioral symptoms by which a clinician might detect the condition. While the patient's avowal of his or her feelings is presented as an essential ingredient in that diagnosis, the overall picture is as much of a behavioral disturbance as one of mood or "affect."

Some explanation of this trend towards a behavioristic analysis of depression may be found in the very subjective similarity between normal sadness and clinical depression, noted earlier. Emphasis on various cognitive and particularly the behavioral symptoms apparently better permit a sharp distinction to be drawn between the two categories. In a study of the factors distinguishing normal from clinical depression, it has been concluded that "The factors in social behaviour profile . . . which most clearly distinguish the severely depressed patient from the depressed normal one are: the extent to which self accusatory feelings are present; the level of 'helplessness', e.g. inability to make decisions; and, finally, the pace and tempo of his behaviour, i.e. overly retarded or overly agitated." Thus, "It is primarily the behavior . . . that distinguishes the two groups [normal people who are very depressed and those subsequently diagnosed as clinically ill], *not the central mood factor*. They can, in other words be equally sad, lonely—equally depressed in mood"[45] (emphasis added). So in order better to isolate, and thus, supposedly, to treat, those who are clinically depressed, it has become useful to clinicians to emphasize the nonaffective features of the condition.

The development of the notion of depression as a behavioral condition also goes some way to explain the widespread adoption of the term "depression" rather than "melancholia," which has occurred during this century. With the shift of emphasis away from the purely psychological towards behavioral and directly observable symptoms, the notion of depression gained currency and refinement. Thus *agitated depression*, marked by restless overactivity, came to be distinguished from *retarded depression,* where activity is slowed down or inhibited.[46]

Inviting this emphasis on observable symptoms at the expense of affective states, of course, was Freudian depth psychology. With the widespread acceptance of a psychoanalytic version of the unconscious state and early origins of depression, it was possible to account convincingly for the link between disparate behavioral symptoms.

The new terminology not only corresponds to an increasingly behavioristic emphasis in symptomatology; in addition, with its etymological suggestion of pressure and heaviness, the term "depression" conveys a physical and behavioral metaphor. We saw that "melancholy" suggested darkness, a purely psychological apprehension. But the weight and pressure upon the afflicted person conveyed by the term "depression" (Latin *deprimere*—to press down) carries images of physical as much as psychological burden and oppression.

Clinical depression, then, unlike the earlier melancholy, is characterized as much or more by certain behavioral manifestations as by the moods and feelings it involves: by a slowing or agitation of movement, by fatigue, loss of appetite and insomnia. And despite the etymology of "depression," remarked earlier, most of these manifestations do not have the symbolic power to reinforce and remind us of the mood underlying them. Loss of appetite, fatigue, insomnia and agitated movement do not as naturally seem to suggest dejection to an untrained observer—as the formalized melancholy gestures and motifs of the literature and painting of the seventeenth century, such as the drooping head.

Another difference between the earlier melancholy and today's clinical depression is that the latter is a women's complaint. One analysis has proposed that twice as many women as men suffer from depression in middle- and upper-class America[47]; other authorities suggest higher figures.[48] Our current image of the depression sufferer is, or ought to be—assuming those who complain of depression suffer accordingly—a woman. But although no comparable figures are available for the earlier period, the reverse seems true of melancholy.[49] While Dürer's series depicts a woman, the rakes, poets, scholars and artists who suffered melancholy were men, and the stage *melancholique* was standardly a male figure. And at least one sixteenth-century authority, the physician Weyer, explicitly noted that women's nature is less inclined to melancholy than men's.[50]

Moreover, it is presumably not unconnected with this change in gender association that contemporary clinical depression has lost its link with what was characterized earlier as the Aristotelian tradition: the notion that the other side of this mood of sadness and despair was intellectual depth, wisdom and learning, even genius. It is not today fashionable to affect the women's condition of depression, in the way that it was once to affect melancholy. Now depression is a scourge and an "illness"—something, in many circles, to be concealed and denied.

As the differences of terminology suggest, emphasis today is placed on the dissimilarities between normal states of sadness and melancholy and the clinical depression at the other end of the scale. The rationale for this has been introduced already and has some force. By being distinguished in this way, those who require treatment for their condition can more easily receive it. Where no sharp conceptual distinction permitted the separation of the clinically melancholy from the everyday, nonclinical melancholy sufferer, we might suppose the neglect of the former group. But nevertheless, this stress on the differences between the sufferer from clinical depression and the normal sad person invites the kind of alienation of the former that Foucault suggested.

Finally, it seems necessary to insert a corrective to the contemporary discussions of the earlier concept, with their emphasis on the disparity of meanings and traditions found in the commodious concept of melancholy. We seem to be asked to read the different emphases in the use of "melancholy"—its reference to normal states and dispositions as well as to the suffering of the mentally disturbed, and its Aristotelian and Galenic meanings, for example—as reflecting a term used ambiguously. But I suggest that the claimed ambiguity may be a twentieth-century misreading, revealing our contemporary dichotomy between normal states and the "affective disorder" of depression. The sense of "melancholy" that prevailed during the sixteenth and seventeenth centuries may, and perhaps ought, to be understood as univocal, even though it covered and connected both the more severe conditions on the one hand, and variations of normal, though splenetic character and mood on the other.

IV. THE ALIENATED DEPRESSIVE: A FEMINIST ANALYSIS

The contrast between the melancholy of the earlier period and today's two distinct notions of clinical and normal depression seems to provide added support for Foucault's contention: much that was ordinary and familiar about madness was lost with the emergence of medical structures. With emphasis on the behavior rather than the affect of depression, expressed in the new terminology, the element of feeling that seems to have united the various strands of the Elizabethan concept has relinquished its central place. And rather than an ordinary, familiar and everyday figure, the *depressive* of today is increasingly rendered remote and alien, her condition unrelated to ordinary experience.

Contemporary feminist analyses of female depression may be appealed to in order partly to explain two of the features of our present notion of clinical depression distinguished here: its apparent prevalence among female sufferers on the one hand, and its alienation from more ordinary states of sadness and despair on the other.

Let us avoid the question of how these feelings should be described and look instead at the explanation of why women might be expected to experience reactions of sadness and despair more frequently than men do in this society.

Theories as to why women are depressed appeal, either directly or indirectly, to their oppression. Thus, according to one authority, women are depressed because of their deprivation: "[They] are in mourning—for what they never had."[51]

At the simplest level this analysis attributes sadness as a reasonable response by women in patriarchal society to the lack of freedom, opportunity, self-expression, respect, and esteem.[52] A slightly more complex explanation attributes female sadness to male oppression by introducing the notion of internalized anger. The oppressed woman, according to this theory, is subject to feelings of anger and rage—both (a) those whose legitimate object should be her oppressors, and (b) those that are the internalized reflection of that hostility and contempt felt by her oppressor for her. In the face of this anger, her response is sorrow and self-loathing. Thus Greenspan appealed to each kind of anger. She spoke of the real cause of woman's depression as "an abiding, unconscious rage at our oppression which has found no legitimate outlet."[53] But she also introduces the notion of societal anger turned inward: "Internalization of oppression is the crux of women's depression and self-hate. It is as though every impulse of a depressed woman's consciousness is finely tuned to a view of herself that is in accord with that of the dominant culture's view of women as inferior."[54]

Here, then, is a theory sufficient to explain why, in today's society, more women than men might be prone to depression. But this is not adequate to account for all the differences between today's notion of depression and the earlier one we have been considering. As far as can be determined from the scant historical evidence, we saw that, in the Elizabethan period, melancholy was not distinguished as a woman's condition—rather, it was associated with men. Yet it must at least be questioned whether there was less oppression for women in that era. Why, then, might women be peculiarly susceptible to depression today?

The answer to this question lies, I suggest, in the trend by which contemporary depression is distinguished and set apart from ordinary everyday sadness and despair and treated as a separate clinical condition identified and defined in terms of its behavioral manifestations.

Evidence from the history of medicine suggests that women have long been subject to ideologically colored diagnoses and forms of treatment, and these have apparently differed extensively from period to period. But one theme remains constant: medicine's prime contribution to sexist ideology, as Ehrenreich and English put it, has been "to describe women as sick, and as potentially sickening to men."[55] To regard women as sick and requiring treatment was to wield a form of social control: it reflects sexist oppression exerted through the male dominated medical establishment.

Ehrenreich and English proposed the following historical analysis. Throughout early medicine, and well past the earlier Elizabethan period we have been considering, this emphasis on women as sick centered on women's bodily and, particularly, reproductive organs and functions. But nineteenth-century advances in physiology eventually precluded many of the obviously false theories supporting these accounts, for example the wandering uterus theory, which had held sway since ancient times. And the social control that Ehrenreich and English described as the "medical management of women" took an altered form by the end of the nineteenth century. Women's illness came to be seen as a psychic rather than bodily nature. The tendency of doctors to diagnose women's complaints as psychosomatic, it is argued, shows, ". . . that the medical view of women has not really shifted from 'sick' to 'well'; it has shifted from 'physically sick' to 'mentally sick'."[56] Today, these writers conclude, it is psychiatry rather than gynecology that upholds "the sexist tenets of women's fundamental defectiveness."[57]

Thus we see an explanation for the separation noted between ordinary moods experienced by normal people in response to everyday situations, on the one hand, and the "pathological" condition of clinical depression, on the other. Women's moods of sadness and despair are now the focus of this form of social control, women's responses have become "medicalized."

Whether or why women feel more sad and despairing in contemporary times than earlier is not something about which we can have any certainty. But it is now clearer why contemporary sadness and despair might have come to be regarded as illnesses and defects today in a way that they were not when they were the fashionable complaints of the Elizabethan rake or scholar.

I have shown here that the contrast between the unreason of Elizabethan melancholy and today's notion of clinical depression confirms Foucault's claims. That contrast has also illuminated ways in which earlier notions have been transformed with twentieth-century psychiatric thinking—a transformation that may be partly explained by appeal to contemporary feminist accounts of clinical depression.[58]

NOTES

1. *Madness and Civilization: A History of Insanity in the Age of Reason*. Translated by Richard Howard (Vintage Books, New York, 1973). First published as *Histoire de la Folie* (Libraire Plon, Paris, 1965). All page references are to the Howard translation and Vintage edition.

2. Before introducing Foucault's view one disclaimer is necessary. Nowhere in his work did Foucault systematically develop the thesis I am going to attribute to him, and what follows is an interpretation only.

3. Ibid., 36.

4. Ibid., 34.

5. Ibid., 34.
6. Ibid., 97.
7. Ibid., 26.
8. Ibid., 13.
9. Ibid., 13.
10. Ibid., 83.
11. Babb, L., *Sanity in Bedlam: A Study of Robert Burton's Anatomy of Melancholy* (The Michigan State University Press, East Lansing, 1959), 3.
12. See Moore, C. A., "The English Malady," in *Backgrounds of English Literature 1700–60* (University of Minnesota Press, Minneapolis, 1953), 179.

"No characteristic of English poetry in the mid-eighteenth century is more familiar . . . than the perpetual reference to melancholy. Statistically this deserves to be called the Age of Melancholy."

13. Burton, R., *The Anatomy of Melancholy* (J. E. Hodson, London, 1621, 11th Ed., 1806), 330.
14. Ibid., 149.
15. Bright, T., *A Treatise of Melancholy* (Thomas Vautrolier, London, 1586).
16. Ibid., 100.
17. Hume D., *A Treatise of Human Nature* (Selby Bigge, ed., Clarendon Press, Oxford, 1958), Book 2, Section 3.
18. Greenberg, N., ed., *An Anthology of Elizabethan Lute Songs, Madrigals and Rounds* (W. W. Norton, New York, 1955), 104.
19. Ibid., 121.
20. Gardner, H., ed., *The New Oxford Book of English Verse* (Clarendon Press, Oxford, 1972), 230.
21. Ibid., 469.
22. e. g. Skultans, V. *English Madness, Ideas on Insanity 1580–1890* (Routledge and Kegan Paul, London, 1979).
23. Klibansky, V., Saxl, F., and Panofsky, E., *Saturn and Melancholy* (Heffer & Sons, Cambridge, for Nelson, London, 1964), 218.
24. Ibid., 153.
25. Klibansky et al., 232.
26. Babb, L., "Melancholy and the Elizabethan Man of Letters," *The Huntington Library Quarterly* (1940–41) 4:261.
27. Babb, L., *Sanity in Bedlam,* 3.
28. Ibid., 3.
29. Ibid., 451.
30. See, for example, Robert Anton, *The Philosophers Satyrs* (London, 1616), 14: "Want makes the worthy *Artist* dull and sad, And *rare deserts,* most melancholy mad." and Babb, L., "Melancholy and the Elizabethan Man of Letters," 252: "Melancholy is the scholar's occupational disease."
31. Aristotle, *Problemata* xxxi, in W. D. Ross, ed., *Aristotle's Works* (Encyclopedia Brittanica, Chicago, 1955).
32. Babb, L., "Melancholy and the Elizabethan Man of Letters," 253.
33. Klibansky et al., 218.
34. e. g. Skultans, 19.

35. I do not wish to suggest that an essentialist analysis would be required here, but merely that, contrary to the implications of several modern commentators, evidence indicates that in this case one was available.

36. Babb, L., *The Elizabethan Malady: A Study of Melancholia in English Literature from 1580 to 1642* (Michigan State College Press, East Lansing, 1951), 54.

37. Bright, 109.

38. Simon, B., *Mind and Madness in Ancient Greece: The Classical Roots of Modern Psychiatry* (Cornell University Press, Ithaca, 1978), 236; also Kudlien, "Beginn des medizinischen Denkens," 77–99, and "Schwartzliche Organe," cited in Simon.

39. Foucault, 122.

40. Ibid., 124.

41. Freud, Sigmund, *Collected Papers* (Hogarth Press, London, 1957), 153.

42. Distinguished from the lesser Dysthymic Disorder or Depression Neurosis (300.40), only by severity or duration.

43. Axis 1, 296.23, American Psychiatric Association, *Diagnostic and Statistical Manual of Mental Disorders,* 3rd ed., American Psychiatric Association, Washington, D.C., 1981.

44. Axis 2, 296.22, American Psychiatric Association.

45. Katz, M. M., ed., "The Classification of Depression" in *Depression in the 1970s: Modern Theory and Research* (published in cooperation with Columbia University College of Physicians & Surgeons, Dept. of Psychiatry), Ronald R. Fieve, Amsterdam, 1971. See p. 6.

46. Other considerations also influenced the elimination of the term "melancholia." See Stainbrook, E., "A Cross Cultural Evaluation of Depressive Reaction," in Hoch, P., & Zubin, J., *Depression* (Grune & Stratton, New York, 1954).

47. Lehmann, H., "Epidemiology of Depressive Disorders" in M. Katz, ed., *Depression in the 1970s: Modern Theory and Research* (published in cooperation with Columbia University College of Physicians and Surgeons, Dept. of Psychiatry.)

48. For example, Chessler, P., *Women and Madness* (Avon, New York, 1972). See also the National Institute of Mental Health reference tables on Patients in Mental Health Facilities, reproduced by Chessler on pp. 42–43, where women diagnosed as psychotic depressive outnumbered men in general hospitals, 69 percent to 31 percent respectively; in outpatient clinics, 73 percent to 27 percent respectively; in private hospitals, 73 percent to 27 percent, and in state and county hospitals, 68 percent to 32 percent.

49. As has been noted (Skulkans, 81).

50. Though he goes on to observe that when subject to it they are more intensely affected. (From De praestigiis daemonum, 1563, quoted by Foucault, 120).

51. Chessler, 44.

52. See also Miller, J. B., *Toward a New Psychology of Women* (Beacon Press, Boston, 1976), 90–91.

53. Greenspan, M., *A New Approach to Women and Therapy* (McGraw Hill, New York, 1983), 300.

54. Ibid., 303.

55. Ehrenreich, B. & English, D., *Complaints and Disorders: The Sexual Politics of Sickness* (The Feminist Press, Old Westbury, New York, 1973), 5.

56. Ibid., 79.
57. Ibid., 79.
58. For help in writing this essay, I am grateful to Margaret Rhodes, Frank T. Keefe, Jane Roland Martin, Meredith Michaels and David M. Levin.

CHAPTER 8

A PHILOSOPHICAL CRITIQUE OF THE CONCEPT OF NARCISSISM: THE SIGNIFICANCE OF THE AWARENESS MOVEMENT

EUGENE T. GENDLIN

In this essay I examine and revise certain assumptions about the human body, language, and politics. These assumptions are implicit in the concept of "narcissism," in Freud's metapsychology, and in much of current discourse.

Today people generally are called "narcissistic," because of their preoccupation with "inner" processes. Bookstores offer walls of popular psychology. On subways and buses one hears psychologically sophisticated, introspective talk, with subtle distinctions and puzzlements. Twenty years ago such talk could be heard only in a therapist's office. Millions are involved in psychotherapy, self-help networks, ashrams, encounter groups, meditation, interpersonal training, and other experiential processes. Some have called all this the "Awareness Movement." One cannot simply approve, condemn, or ignore it all, but it is difficult to evaluate. We can say, for better or worse, that a major social change is taking place.

The change came partly from psychoanalysis and its descendants. During our century psychoanalysis influenced many fields. It opened the language, not only to forbidden topics like sex, but to whole reaches of human feeling and interaction. Much of what Freud found is now common parlance. People can discuss what could hardly be recognized in Freud's time.

People call their entry into the current change "getting in touch with my feelings." The phrase says that they look back on a time when they lived without sensing certain events they now sense, and prize. These so-called "feelings" are not simple emotions or desires, but complexities that give rise to new aspects of living, and create new troubles.

I. THE NARCISSISM CRITIQUE

Why the Critics Call the Awareness Movement "Narcissistic"

Most psychoanalytic thinkers can see little more than selfishness and self-indulgence in the current trends. They use the term "narcissism" to say that people's inner preoccupation interferes with their social bonding. The patterns of love and work have indeed become problematic for millions of people. Social change is a real problem.

Thinkers in political theory raise a second problem: they use the term "narcissism" to mark a withdrawal from political responsibility, and a failure to perceive the external social controls which "inwardness" masks, and only seems to avoid. To believe oneself inwardly free misses the point that many intimate feelings are socially programmed. I will discuss these two important problems—unstable bonding and unseen social control.

Traditional patterns of love, courting, and marriage have become less meaningful. Many people reject marriage in favor of less stable arrangements. The Census Bureau reports a "dramatic increase over the past fifteen years in the number of persons living alone. Households containing only one person jumped 90% since 1970."[1] The emphasis on intimacy makes for a quicker rejection when there is a lack of mutuality. People move from relationship to relationship. Millions are lonely and isolated. Those who do live in the old forms no longer identify fully with them.

Similarly, people continue in the old forms of work, but they are disaffected. *Inwardly,* they pursue other interests. Many are leaving the business world, and more would like to leave. The old forms have weakened, but most situations are, at least outwardly, unchanged; there are not very many new forms (and only a hint of a new *kind* of form).

The critics of the Awareness Movement point to a real problem. They see a disintegration. Not that they approve of the old social forms, but disintegration does not look hopeful to them. They see it as a falling back to something less ordered, and inherently asocial. In terms of the old social relations, this seems to be the case.

To call the currently common introspective complexity "narcissistic" implies that it is primitive and infantile, developmentally earlier than the ego. The fully developed person is supposed to identify with the ego. The ego derives from social reality. With a traditional ego one identifies oneself with the socially given roles and forms of bonding. Traditional individuals are said to feel that they *are* their roles, routines, and social identities. "Narcissism" is the only alternative. The critics assume that a failure to identify fully with the prevailing roles must be "narcissism," a regression to infantile experience, *less* ordered than the external forms, and *a*social.

We will ask whether regression is the only alternative to full identification with prevailing forms. Could new patterns arise from experiential processes? The critics consider that impossible. New forms cannot come from individual experience; that is deeply written in Freud's concepts. The individual consists of *externally given* forms. There are serious theoretical reasons for this view. Before I come to them, let me first show the poverty of this view. It has only this one concept, "narcissism," for anything and everything that is not the traditional ego.

The Narcissism-Critique Looks Only for the Old, Vanished Type of Person

The critics of the Awareness Movement see each change only in terms of what it is not. Their diagnosis of each new change is always the same: It is narcissism since it isn't the traditional ego.

The change in ego-identification since Freud's time has involved four well-known types. The first was the traditional type, people solidly identified with their roles—the "bourgeois ego." Adorno and Horkheimer criticized these people for believing that they were their own (subjective) source of strength, when it was actually the social system that formed their egos, and gave them their ego-strength. That blindness was called "false subjectivity."

After World War II, prosperity and consumerism weakened the family, which had been most important in traditional life. Social mobility and greater opportunities let parents do more living outside the family. Children spent their time with age-mates and TV. A second type of person emerged. But Adorno found this development worse than the previous bourgeois self. Now he thought he saw inner emptiness, people lost in a vacuous consumer culture, having an even shallower subjectivity, a selfish lack of family involvement, "narcissism."

The third type, the young people of 1968, rebelled against this very consumerism. They rejected social forms that felt vacuous to them, using the writings of Adorno, Horkheimer, and Marcuse as their texts. But Adorno considered this third type even worse, and he argued that their refusal to live in the social forms, their attempt at authenticity, could only be a delusion, a total narcissistic collapse of the ego.

Today a fourth type has appeared, but the students of Adorno can see only narcissism again. They call the current type "narcissistic" because conformity is now often merely outward, divided off from quite different inner concerns. People are now living and working in the old forms, again. On the one hand they do not rebel openly against the old forms. On the other hand, they do not fully identify themselves in them. They identify themselves with an inward complexity, even when there is no way to live from it.

But the previous, open rebellion was also called "narcissism," and the argument was that such a total refusal to live in the old forms could only be infantile and regressive. But, the type before that—the quiet "consumerism" of the postwar years—was called "narcissism" too.

With the concept of "narcissism" one ignores each new type, and looks only for the old ego-identification with the prevailing social forms. Anything different is always called "narcissism." It was true that the old ego was weakened with each new development. Parents were called "narcissistic" for being so involved in consumption. But when their children rejected consumerism, the same concept was applied, because the children could not tolerate the traditional forms at all. Now the outward conformity is also said to be narcissism, because it is not the old, full ego-identification with the social forms.

This critique lumps all the changes together. It knows only a traditional ego that exists in the prevailing social forms. What is not that, looks all the same. When these critics look out the window, they see only the same thing, no matter what comes by.

"Narcissism" is a catch-all category. Anything other than the ego is narcissism. Psychoanalytic theory was always odd in reducing so much valuable human experience to infantile regression. For example, the theory analyzed the greater intricacy and sensitivity of poetry as nothing more than regression. But poetry can exceed the ego. What it says about the world is not always unrealistic, regressive, less developed, less organized—"narcissistic." According to psychoanalytic theory, no experience can be realistic, adult, and interactional except through the ego. What is not the ego of the prevailing forms is *by definition* both primitive and autistic.

II. "UNCONSCIOUS PROGRAMMING"

What if some experiential processes are, on the face of them, more realistic and more intricate than the ego? What if they are not always autistic, but can include a better sense of interpersonal contact or its absence? What if they include more care for the intricacy of other people? Does such intricacy prove that there is an order other than that imposed by the prevailing social forms?

The greater order may simply be denied, if one continues to speak of experiential intricacy as "narcissistic" regression. But, the theory of "narcissism" leads some critics to a second answer: They grant the experienced intricacy, but explain it as stemming from past and present programming that is not being recognized. That is another version of the same critique. Again it is assumed that order must come from external sources. It is argued that experienced intricacy and relational sensitivity are only a *re*-discovery of the social order imposed by history upon the human body.

Human bodies are certainly social and cultural. Our long infancy and our language-brain attest to that. The human brain had its second great expansion *after* culture. Brain and body changed physically in the context of culture. Unquestionably, the body and experience are cultural. But this fact is mistakenly interpreted as *mere imposition* of social and political order. Upon what is this order imposed? External imposition assumes an original body without order, and without interaction. The ego is the extant social order, imposed upon a *purely individual, chaotic body consisting of mere autistic "desires."* Later I will question this theory of an unordered and asocial body.

The Two Versions of the Critique

Each version of the psychoanalytically based critique of the Awareness Movement points to a problem we will take up. Unstable interaction, regression, breakdown, and loss of "self" have indeed become more common. We must also recognize ingrained conformity even when it seems to originate from deep inside.

The two versions of the critique are often mixed together.[2] The current psychological processes are said to be regression, chaos, autism; then it is argued that their order and relational character merely reflect external repressive programming. We can see both lines of argument in the following quotations.

In contrast to the 1968 movement which demanded major social changes, the critics see in the current Awareness Movement:

> A loss of the project of structural change [in favor of a] strategy of withdrawal from society. [There are] . . . loose associations of people with a private, eclectic religiosity.[3]

The critic goes on to deprecate the inward processes, calling them *both* "narcissistic" *and* nothing more than a new external programming. The passage continues:

> [There are] psychologistic doctrines with a veneer of scientific ideology. [Four lines of "brand names" are listed.] These offer techniques for personal salvation and self-enhancing lifestyles based on the sacralization of the narcissistic self. That any public philosophy . . . could emerge from this is preposterous.[4]

The new processes are understood as external "techniques" imposed on "the narcissistic self." Foucault argues similarly:

> In the California cult of the self one is supposed to discover one's true self . . . thanks to psychological and psychoanalytic science which is supposed to tell you what your true self is.[5]

The critics of the Awareness Movement cannot imagine an inner emergence more ordered than external programming. The body has no order of its own. For Foucault the task of his "genealogy" was

> to expose a body totally imprinted by history and the process of history's destruction of the body.[6]

For Foucault there is not even a primitive "narcissistic" body left over. Aside from external programming there is nothing at all. For others there is a primitive narcissism. But all these thinkers assume that any intricate and relational experience can only reflect unconscious external programming.

Before we question that assumption, let us bring home to ourselves the real problem of unconscious programming. Let us grant how deeply programmed our bodies really are. However concerned we are with social change, we might create conformity if we are not aware of being programmed.

For example, people used to live on farms or in small towns, but by 1965 most of them led mobile urban lives. On farms a family works together all day; in cities we work separately with strangers all day, so that family life could not possibly have remained the same as on the farm. Socioeconomic arrangements structure the family and daily life; they affect the kind of individuals we can be.

The question of unconscious conformity applies also to our thinking about these matters. We cannot just call what we don't like "conformity," and what we like "a greater order in experience." Such a distinction would reflect our own programmed values.

Isn't it simply an illusion, if one seems to experience an inner individual freedom in an unchanged society? Since we are all *trained* to think of ourselves as individualists, this very illusion masks itself. We are stalled on the expressway at the same hour in our individual cars.

There is considerable reason to worry about such unconsciousness, because people do regard their psychological sophistication as "only inner" and unproblematic. Human beings are inherently interactional. We live and feel with, and at, others. Why, today, does "the real self" seem *only* inner?

The current split (inward freedom/outward conformity) accepts intricate experience as cut off from the environment. That split comes largely from helplessness, the impossibility of affecting external arrangements so that one could live from intricate experience. The self's new intricacy seems *only* inner because the external controls prevent it from being lived out. Therefore it can be lived only in private *self*-responding. But if the intricacy is accepted as *inherently* only something inner, then the social controls are accepted without having been noticed. What prevents one's outward efficacy is masked and unseen.

The rebellious movement of 1965–1972 was made possible by the wealth of the time. This movement disappeared, when the central banks of Western countries drastically reduced the money circulating in the economy. In the name of curing the (then very slight) inflation, economic policy since 1972 again and again "cut buying power," as it was officially called.

Jobs were made scarce. That stopped millions of young people from living as they liked, traveling about, working only when they wanted. Now there is unemployment. Unions are giving up their gains of sixty years. The change in the spirit of young people did not happen only as a result of changes inside them. Today students are quiet and concerned to ensure that their education will lead to a good job. "Relevance" otherwise is not so important to them. They are able to go along with the "educational" system. They can also tolerate meaningless jobs. But "inwardly" they are sophisticated about experiential processes.

The misunderstanding of experience as "only inner" reflects and masks the unchanged socioeconomic arrangements in which individuals must live. If we don't see the effects on us of the social arrangements in which we live, then we don't ask the genuine political questions that might lead to genuine structural changes.

The critics of the Awareness Movement are correct in arguing that considering intricacy as "only inner" hides the social controls that make it seem *only* inner. But they are wrong in thinking that the intricacy comes from those social conditions. Only its restriction to inwardness is due to social conditions. They prevent it from becoming externally real. Rather than rejecting the intricacy as an illusion, we must consider how it could change the social conditions. We must also consider why it has not, and why so many theorists have assumed so readily that it cannot. And if such change is possible, we must also ask how it is to be differentiated from mere unconscious conformity.

Some thinkers (Foucault, for example) have assumed that, except for imposed controls, the individual is only chaos. Freedom from control as such is therefore an illusion and a mystification. Others, critical theorists, like Marcuse, hold out for a liberating alternative, but search for it in a primitive, unrelational, narcissistic core. They have assumed that this hypothetical core is "the repressed." They all share the assumption I want to question: that, except for chaos or autistic drives, the individual is only what the power system imposes.

III. THE USUAL POLITICAL READING OF FREUD

Before we revise the assumption we have been discussing, we can learn much from Marcuse's refusal to revise it. Marcuse praised Freud for showing how the *social* order is built into the very structure of *individual* personality. The central part of Freud's individual, the ego, develops from the existing social order. Therefore no adult experience can transcend the social order. In *Eros and Civilization*, Marcuse argues that any modification of this theoretical plank would blind us to unconscious conformity and keep us from asking the political questions deeply enough. Marcuse writes:

> Freud demonstrated that constraint, repression, and renunciation are the stuff from which the "free personality" is made. . . . Psychoanalysis was a radically critical theory. . . . [But] its belief in the basic unchangeability of human nature *appeared* "reactionary". . . [therefore] revisions [like Erich Fromm's] began to gain momentum. (My italics).[7]

Such revisions must be superficial and conformist. They can only mask what Marcuse (with Freud) assumes, that individuals *are* the present society. Marcuse contended that,

> Whereas Freud, focusing on the vicissitudes of the primary instincts, discovered *society* in the most concealed layer of the genus and individual man, the revisionists attempt to free Freud's theory from its identification with present day society . . . to indicate the possibility of progress.[8]

According to Marcuse, what we might think of as "progress" is necessarily defined by standards that are still "compatible with the prevailing values."[9] To think we could change the prevailing values is to miss how deeply they have modified our instincts. The best we can do is to know that we cannot change this deep programming by our present day society. "Progress" is always in unconscious alliance with the controls implicit in the individual. Such "progress" is only quiescent "productivity," and hides the controls Freud brought to view.

People sometimes say that Freud should not be read so literally, when he says that any experienced opposition to the prevailing social forms can only be regression—narcissism. But it isn't a question of taking Freud too literally. This assumption inheres in most of the theories proposed during the last hundred years. It is not pedantic to take this assumption seriously. We can see how seriously Marcuse took it. He wanted to side with what society represses, and so he *championed* narcissism as the only alternative to imposed control. He called his own view "aesthetic narcissism." He assumed with Freud, that since myth and art exceed the social forms, they can only be narcissism. He looked to myth and art for an alternative to the given social order, but granted that it would be narcissism.

Marcuse did *not* say, as I say, that what is *called* "narcissism" (anything other than the imposed order) is much more, and very different from what the term implies. Rather, he assumed exactly what the term implies. He assumed with Freud, that the body consists only of autistic needs. "[The] instinctual needs . . . must be 'broken' so that the human being can function in interpersonal relations."[10] Marcuse said that narcissism is like sleep and death, a self-enclosed autism, selfishness, and autoeroticism. He assumed this about any experience that would not be social conformity. Therefore, his only hope was that "Narcissism may contain the germ of a different reality principle . . . transforming this world into a new mode of being."[11] He does not find that new reality, because he looked for it in the original body Freud posited. That concept of the body is too poor. The repressed drives are only chaotic and autistic. Behavior and interaction come only through the ego derived from the existing social norms. Therefore no adult experience can oppose the prevailing forms. Only *regression* can avoid unconscious conformity. Marcuse chose narcissism over unconscious conformity.

Unlike Adorno, Marcuse supported the 1968 movement: the young people's *experienced* rejection of common social behavior and their preference for *experiential* realness. By 1972 Marcuse's position had changed a little. In *Counter-Revolution and Revolt* he no longer calls nonconformist experience "narcissism." He sought, even more than before, *an experience of reality* from which society could be criticised: "a new sensibility."[12] But he never quite found it, because he continued to look for it only in myth and art.

Why look for an alternative to the imposed system in myth and in art? Since they exceed the ego, it was falsely assumed that myth and art are narcissistic and cannot be about this world. In an invented world a narcissistic regression could be enacted. It was falsely assumed that the real world is all of one piece, all formed by one common, imposed order. Reason was considered to be universal concepts, i.e., the commonalities that define classes. These commonalities were taken to be the meanings of all words. Commonalities were also the shared forms of social interaction, and "reality" was assumed to be socially defined. *One single imposed system was considered to encompass reason, commonalities, common language, social interaction, society, and reality.* If that is all one system of commonalities, an alternative can come only from what that system leaves over—autism in an *un*real world. That assumption has dominated Western thinking for a long time. It was still compelling for Marcuse.

When so much is granted to the system of commonality-categories, what can be left? Only Freud's chaotic, unrelational "primary" instincts. But my criticism of him, here, applies only to his *theory*. I must point out that even psychosis and "primary process" are not *described* as unrelational discharges. In the *Interpretation of Dreams* Freud describes "metaphorical," "condensational," "*over*determined" experience. Why is such experience put in a class with mere unordered drives? That comes about because all order is thought of as the categorial order. All that his order excludes falls together as having no order at all.

But, throughout recent centuries the nature of language has not been understood. Language is not a system of commonality-categories and fixed forms. It is more "condensational" and "metaphorical", and more intricate than it is "rational."

Similarly, interpersonal interaction has been misunderstood in Western thought. Like language, it involves more than commonality-patterns. Later we will see that the nonrational, noncategorical order is not necessarily asocial and not only a negation of order. Nor is it necessarily about an unreal world.

Recent thinking still assumes that all order and all interaction is externally programmed. For example, Deleuze and Guattari (1983)[13] argue that in order to overcome social control, a body would have to be "without organs", since it is through organs that it interacts with others. The assumption is that interaction is externally programmed; the body could be free only if it could give up all points of contact with other people. (The book has a laudatory preface by Foucault.)

We can honor Marcuse's and Deleuze's courage in siding with the body against the social controls. We should heed their warning that unconscious programming will be reinstated, if we don't penetrate the depth at which repression has modified the body. But let us study the body. Let us not assume that the body is as Freud hypothesized with his reductive model—unorganized, unrelational tensions. The body might have an order other than what repression has created. But if we find more, how can we know it is not just the result of external programming? We cannot drop that question.

Marcuse assumed that there could be only an aesthetic alternative in the world of myth and art. But now, throughout Western society, people are discovering a more intricate order—and not just in myth or art. Might Marcuse's search for a greater "sensibility" now succeed? Has *experience* now become a possible source of social criticism? To think theoretically about whether that is possible, we must first modify the assumption that covertly defines nonego experience as "narcissism."

The second question is important. It takes us beyond Marcuse: Even if there is an experiential order that is not imposed, can it be distinguished from unconscious conformity? I will propose a process-strategy with which that question can at least be studied.

Tracing the Assumption in Freud

To modify the assumption that "narcissism" is the only alternative to the ego, let us examine how Freud defined these two concepts. He defined the ego in relation to an "id" which has very little order, and no interaction at all. It consists in merely individual, chemical drives, tension-increases or decreases. It gets order only from interactions which are patterned by the existing society through the ego.

Freud's metapsychology has room only for this unordered id—and, of course, the ego. But elsewhere, Freud discussed many id-experiences which are neither of these. The complexities of "primary process" (as in psychosis), the overdetermined, "condensational," "metaphorical" character of dreams and pathology are much *more* organized than mere tensions, and much of their organization does not come from the ego.

This gap in the metapsychology has not been sufficiently noticed, because, in Western science, "metaphor" and "condensation" are evaluated in terms of the fixity of "rational" logic. From this viewpoint they have appeared primitive, and as derivative from logic. Although such experience is *more* intricate than logic, it has been considered to be less, and could therefore be safely ignored.

In Freud's metapsychology, the "metaphorical" and "condensational" intricacy of our experience does not appear at all. He wrote only of id and ego, and held that the "id" has no order and no environmental relations at all. He writes:

> The core of our being, then, is formed by the obscure *id,* which has *no relations with the outside world,* and is accessible even to our knowledge only through the medium of another agency of the mind. (My italics.)[14] He continues:
>
> The id, which is cut off from the external world, has its own world of perception. It detects . . . changes . . . in the tensions of its instinctual needs.[15]

> The ego is . . . a specifically differentiated portion of . . . the id . . . *the ego is an organized entity, whereas the id is not;* in fact, the ego is the organized part of the id. (My italics).[16]
>
> Starting from conscious experience, it [the ego] has brought under its influence ever larger regions and ever deeper layers of the id; and, in the persistence with which it maintains its dependence on the external world, it bears the indelible stamp of its origin, [as it might be "Made in Germany".][17]
>
> [The ego's] function is . . . to transform freely mobile energy into bound energy.[18]

Without the ego, the id has no connection to the environment, no modes of behavior, no channels of discharge. By repression and modification, one part of the id does develop such channels, and that part *is* the ego. The ego is formed under the influence of external reality—mostly social reality. Therefore there is no separate "social psychology":

> Social phenomena . . . may be contrasted with certain other processes described by us as "narcissistic," in which the satisfaction of the instincts is partially or totally withdrawn from the influence of other people. The contrast between social and narcissistic . . . falls wholly within the domain of individual psychology.[19]

Such passages leave individuals no experience other than autism with which to oppose the prevailing forms of interaction patterned by their society. It is true that Freud's work can be read in other ways. Here I am concerned, not with various readings of Freud, but with the reading that has been adopted by most philosophers and political thinkers. Using chiefly his metapsychology, they take from Freud the assumption that order and interaction must be externally imposed upon an inherently autistic body.

How did Freud come to assume this originally unordered, autistic body of mere "tensions"? And, where he discussed the "metaphorical" intricacy, why did he consider it only infantile regression?

IV. HOW THE ASSUMPTION AROSE

How could Freud have thought that the body contributes nothing to interactional behavior, except autistic tensions? There were two reasons.

The concept of a body without its own interactional order seems to follow from the observation of cultural variety. Traditional human behavior is culturally diverse. If one abstracts from the variety of behavior and interaction, there seems to be a *common* body without any behavior or interaction. I call this "the remnant body." It is only a theoretical fiction; no such body could ever have existed.

Animals behave and interact. Therefore Freud said that animals have an ego too. He assumed that behavior patterns are *imposed* on the animals, in other words, that they must *learn* all their behaviors and interactions. In this way he could maintain his hypothesis of an originally autistic body that senses only its individual energy-changes.

Today that view can no longer be held. The animal body is not just individual. Its interactions are not learned. Every animal species has been found to have complex *unlearned interaction patterns,* such as food-search, nest-building, mating dances, rearing the young, and so on. The autistic body of unorganized tension-desires is a fiction.

But suppose Freud had known these more recent findings of inherited interaction patterns. Might he not have argued that they are "imposed" through a "racial unconscious" that has programmed an originally selfish individual body? Such a body would have had to precede the existence of animals, since the animals we know all have complex, unlearned interaction patterns.

Human cultures did not create their interaction patterns. Culture could only have elaborated what was already the very complex behavioral order of the animal body. In humans we can no longer separate what is animal from what is culture, although the animal is ever with us. Of course, culture reforms it through and through, but never as its only organization. What repression "modifies" was never only simple drives, but already very highly organized interaction patterns. There never could have been an inherently unorganized, autistic, merely individual, tension-body. But this means that cultural, political and social forms cannot be thought of as imposed upon such a body. The relationship of social forms to the body is not that of a pattern imposed on simpler drives.

Animal patterns have been thought of as an inflexible biology, appealed to by reactionaries to argue for traditional patterns. Actually the various cultural patterns are always only *some* of the ways in which biological bodylife can be carried forward in more differentiated ways. The new intricacy can develop other, still more differentiated ways. Life-process is more intricately ordered than a set of patterns. It is not an order of forms, but an order that can always be carried further in new ways.

That nonego experience is not simpler than the ego-forms is shown in how psychoanalysts describe it. For example, they describe dreams and psychoses as *too complex* to fit the forms of reason and practice. They continue to say that the ego-forms are needed, but not to impose order on mere simple drives, rather *to simplify* the so-called "overdetermined" "metaphorical" complexity. Whereas in theory the social forms are said to give an order to *simpler* tensions, descriptively they are said to simplify the unmanageably complex "morass" of experience.

But let us untangle this. If the body were nothing but simple tensions, then ordering and channeling them would be a one-way imposition. On the other hand, if bodily experience is more complex than ego-forms, then other relations are possible between them. Ego-forms need not always just ignore the body's experiential complexity and impose an alien form on it. And, if an ordering of the body other than sheer imposition is possible, then it is conceivable that the direction of change could go the other way: the prevailing social forms could be modified by the body's more intricate experience too.

Freud may be read as intending more complex relations, but the philosophers' Freud assumes a simple scheme of imposition. An order exists before it is imposed. Then, when it is imposed, it remains the same, since what it is imposed upon has no order that could affect it in return. That is how commonality-categories were thought of. No feed-back. The so-called instances don't, in any way, change the commonality; they are supposedly subsumed by it. There are always only two participants in the process, the imposing and the imposed upon. Imposition is a simple dualism, and a simple type of process. But there are many other ways in which body and form can function. These are more complex kinds of processes. I will soon present some of these.

So long as the "metaphorical," "condensational," "overdetermined" order of the "id" was treated as if it were no order at all, order had to be thought of as the imposed kind.

The Source of the Assumption Before Freud

The assumption that order is always something imposed began with Western science. Before that time, naturalistic observations were catalogued, and many kinds of order and pattern were found. Modern science *imposes* its mathematical grids and records only the results of its own operations. At the beginning it was a dramatic, much-discussed idea that one could ignore everything in nature, and substitute mathematical relations. But as that method succeeded more and more, it became acceptable to say that there really isn't anything there but what we impose. It was Kant who most fully stated this reversal: the order of "nature" is only the order we impose. "Experience" consists of rational forms imposed on unordered bits of sensation. That states the full turnabout. The complexity of experience is made derivative from the imposed ordering forms.

The source of these rational forms was said to be the human mind, "the subject": "I"—not the "I" we introspect, but an underlying metaphysical source of unity and form. Since Kant, many thinkers have rejected this metaphysical subject as the source. They say that the imposed order comes, not from a metaphysical subject, but from "domination," from social and political power. This is not, however, the only way to reject metaphysics.

Marx rejected a metaphysical nature *without* assuming that human nature is the product of domination. Although now one kind of Marxism, it was not Marx's view that human nature simply is what is formed by the modes of production. In *Das Kapital* he said that human nature is *"crippled"* by capitalism. If human nature were only its product, there would be nothing to cripple. Moreover, Marx said that human nature is still "developing," and that it develops unevenly. He assumed no fixed or predetermined content, nor any metaphysical criterion. For him, human nature is an ongoing process of development, not a given order. He was very far from thinking that human nature *is* the order imposed by power and domination.[20]

More recently, the rejection of metaphysics has meant that human nature *is* whatever order the prevailing power imposes. This assumption did not come from Marx. Marcuse sees it in Freud, but Freud did not originate it. It was Nietzsche who rejected metaphysics only to embrace the assumption that human nature is imposed by domination. For him, organization can come only from domination.

It was a deadly assumption for those who sought a freeing social change. After Nietzsche, the Western hope for "free individuals" was viewed as mere "ideology"—inherently impossible. Individual experience was thought to have no role to play. What is not primitive in the individual was considered to be the creation of past domination. Only new domination—imposed social engineering—seemed possible to those who sought political "liberation."

The assumption I am tracing does not follow from rejecting a metaphysical source. On the contrary: *The assumption changes only the source, but retains the metaphysical notion of order as a form imposed on something unorganized.* One can reject *that* metaphysics too, rather than changing only the source and still assuming that human nature (and all order) is imposed (now by power) on a hypothetical, asocial substrate. One can agree with Marx that *human nature* is evolving. One need not assume that it *is* what power imposes, so that only some primitive core could possibly resist political conformity.

Positing an unorganized tension-body does not avoid metaphysical assumptions. It is itself an implausible assumption. I will show that we can think about the body (and language, social interaction, and politics) in other ways. We need not assume an orderless, autistic core on which order and interaction must be imposed.

The assumption is said to avoid a bifurcation: individual and society are said to be one thing, since the individual *is* the society programmed into the body. But the assumption bifurcates them after all: Society is the imposing; the individual is the imposed upon. The notion of *imposed form* splits them in two. First it postulates an animal body that was not originally social; then it tries to explain social interaction by imagining a social imposition. But it is not obvious that the body is inherently autistic, noninteractional. Social interaction is not necessarily something forced upon the body, as if only autistic, single-body discharge could be its original interest. Nor is an assumption that favors the other side of the dualism any more plausible: that mate, offspring, and community are the body's primitive interest, and that individuation must therefore be something imposed. Neither position avoids metaphysical assumptions. The problem is not in the rejection of metaphysics, but rather in the continuing metaphysical assumption that order is something imposed on something else.

V. INCLUDING EXPERIENTIAL INTRICACY IN PHILOSOPHY AND THEORY

We have seen one characteristic of an imposed order: it is not modified by what is already there. An imposed order ignores what it imposes upon. That soon leads to the claim that there never was any other order at all. If more complex order is actually found in experience, it is said to be wholly *derived* from the imposed order. As in the old metaphysics, the imposed order is thought of as a *more general* order of commonalities, such as: categories, conceptual distinctions, criteria, common practices, roles, rules, values—generalities. Current thinkers don't agree about which of these to champion, but experience is always said to be "derived"—which means: from a more general order. But can an order of generalities determine much more detailed experience?

When someone asks: "How can I tell if I'm really in love?" we smile. We know there is no such single criterion, principle, or *general* category, as if a situation were a mere particular, subsumed under it. On the contrary, the general words mean newly in and from this intricacy. And so it is also with questions like "Why do you like your work?" or "When are you really yourself?" Not only big things—little ones also have the same intricacy. For example, "Why did you move away, just now?" We give a simple reply to tell "the reason," but the intricacy cannot be subsumed under those category-words; rather, it lets them work, and changes them.

It is often pointed out that Marx's analyses of events (for instance, in *The Eighteenth Brumaire*) make use of much more detail and many more distinctions than his theory formally allows. But just this shows his rejection of underlying metaphysical principles. Practice does not consist of mere particulars subsumed under general categories. Experience is not just derived from underlying generalities.

People who have no experience of psychotherapy sometimes think that the patient's therapy process derives from the therapist's theory. That would be like deriving the world from a few generalities. Theory certainly has an influence; but experiencing is not derivative from simpler ordering principles.

Freud called the experiential process of psychoanalysis "working through." This, he said, is its most important part. He attributed most failures to the analyst's not knowing how to work with a process that cannot be derived from any theory. Freud knew that experiential intricacy is not derived from or subsumed under a theory. Experiential intricacy is not mere detail existing under general rubrics; it is not like the "unique" coloring of my cat, which still lets it be just a cat. The intricacy *changes* the generalities. But the intricacy he assumed in discussing "working through" could not arise, if the common categories were actually the only order.

Although it is obvious in any type of practice, this governing intricacy tends to disappear when we turn to philosophy and theory. Now "experience" is said to be *made* by the concepts. All experience does have implicit concepts, distinctions, values, rules, roles, schemes, interpretations, assumptions. A choice from among this string of words, as well as a word like "experience," also brings some scheme. *What* experience is, apart from ways of talking, cannot be said. Even mute experience has language implicit in it. So it can seem that the experiential intricacy is made entirely by assumptions, principles, schemes, criteria, values, and so on. But that conclusion is still the Kantian reversal—that it is only the *imposed* generalities that organize an unordered stuff of experience.

Experiential intricacy is historically earlier than generalities; it is not *made* by implicit ordering principles. Intricacy is older than human beings. Animals can sense complex situations, yet they lack general concepts. If one replies here that animal experience does include concepts (distinctions, differences) and argues that "concepts" include differences that are not generalities, then one grants my argument that generalities are not the only kind of order. Then experiential intricacy need not be *derived* from *generalities*.

Generalizations are a late human creation, later than the beginning of language. (And, of course, explanations of language come still later.) General concepts are now, of course, implicit in our language; but no situation and no speech is these *alone*. What concepts mean and do within this intricacy is not determined just by them. They are not just imposed, as if they alone were the order of a situation.

In ordinary life and praxis it is obvious that situations are not ordered only by generalities. Moreover, the generalities *function in many different ways*. Imposing a determinative order is only one kind of process. Admittedly, we cannot separate the intricacy from its implicit generalities. We can only observe the change-steps, when events and words don't happen according to the concepts, but change the concepts instead. Later I will discuss this strategy for studying change-steps.

So long as imposed generalities are considered to be the only order, a single system is said to include concepts, language, society, and the ego. Whatever is not that system is jumbled together as the pre-ego disorder.

VI. KOHUT'S "NARCISSISM" ADDS ONE DISTINCTION

We have seen that the psychoanalytic concept of "narcissism" merges everything that is not the imposed social system. In *The Analysis of the Self*, Heinz Kohut, an American psychoanalyst, revises psychoanalysis by marking out a distinction between psychosis and narcissism. Psychosis is thus no longer merged with all other nonego experience.[21]

How could even this one distinction have waited until so recently? It is because psychoanalytic theory is not subtle about "pre-Oedipal" experience. Most of its concepts concern the ego at the Oedipal stage. Nonego pathology was considered untreatable, and classified as "psychotic" or "schizoid." Kohut introduced one important distinction: he defined a range of people who *are* "treatable" despite the fact that their difficulties concern nonego experience rather than Oedipal issues. He classified these people as "narcissistic."

Kohut described "narcissistic" people as lacking inner experience. They must look to another person's reaction to gain any sense of themselves. They have few feelings and reactions. To help these people sense themselves, Kohut said one must hold a mirror up to them. Like Narcissus, in the myth, they have no inward access to themselves. They need an image held up to them, in order to have a sense of themselves. Only another person's perception of them enables them to feel anything inside.

Note that Kohut's narcissistic type is *the opposite* of the people in the Awareness Movement. The latter are called "narcissistic" because they are preoccupied with *so much* internal experience, that they seem to forgo outward, social concerns, and even the concern for how they look to others. Kohut's "narcissism" does *not* apply to them. Kohut's patients feel empty; they are compulsively social. They get some sense of self only through the reaction of others. That is the opposite of "too much" inner self-absorption.

Why, then, do critics of the Awareness Movement use the same term for those who have *more* interior experience than the old type of ego? It is because the theory has only two alternatives: either ego, or less than that. The theory does not allow for a *more* developed interiority than the ego's. Therefore, the term "narcissistic" is applied to more interior development as well as to the lack of interiority.

Even Kohut failed to distinguish the newer, oversensitive type (too much intricate interiority) from those who lack inward experience. How could *he* make such an error? In practice these two types of patients challenge a therapist differently. One of them has few early memories, no feelings to explore, and lacks any complexity. The other expresses very intricate experience, including pre-Oedipal memories. One gives the therapist very little to work with; the other requires an extremely exact understanding of many nuances that are far more specific than the common vocabulary. How could Kohut have put them both in the same category?

The answer is that, since the standard Oedipal material is not principally important in either type, he left them together. Before Kohut, orthodox psychoanalysts considered all neurosis as originating from Oedipal problems. All other troubles were untreatable, and were left without further distinctions at the margin of psychoanalytic discourse. Kohut opened psychoanalysis to the whole variety of human experience other than Oedipal problems. He did that by making one crucial distinction: *He showed that non-ego experience need not be (overt or latent) psychosis.* But other distinctions are needed: All nonego experience need not be narcissism, either. "Narcissism" means *less* inner experience than the traditional ego, but, until further distinctions are made, the term is applied also to those with *more* (and more intricately organized) experience than the ego's.

What the Term "Narcissism" Still Lumps Together

Psychoanalysis has had only one "pre-Oedipal" bin, into which to put the whole vast range of human experiential complexity. Therefore psychoanalysts struggle with the term "narcissistic" in all sorts of different applications:

- Mathematicians are said to be narcissistic because they spend so much of their time alone.[22]
- Poets and artists have always been termed "narcissistic" because their experience exceeds ego-forms.
- Spirituality is understood as a narcissistic return to mother-child fusion. (Freud called it the "oceanic feeling" and said he never felt it.)
- Any *experienced* rejection of social forms is considered necessarily narcissistic. Only an *intellectual* critique is supposed to be possible.

Narcissism theoretically merges:

- the deposited history of the human race in the unconscious
- the pre-linguistic infant, from womb to age 1
- the pre-Oedipal child, age 1–4
- primary process, psychosis
- "metaphor" (although psychotics have difficulty grasping metaphors)
- the complexity Freud called "the pathology of everyday life"
- the complexity of all experience, not only pathology

The theory requires that this whole gamut of human experiential complexity be considered "narcissistic." In practice, psychoanalysts don't apply the term in the same way to all these people. For example, when it is said of poets, it means they don't always repress primitive experience. It is argued that the poet's ego imposes *artistic form* on this experience. But that view is insufficient. One knows that poetry is more than a pattern with primitive content. Poets often bring a finer *content*—truer perceptions than the common social meanings. What are these?

Nonego experience does not consist of simple drives. It has variety and complexity. More importantly, it is not all regression. What concerns us most, here, is the possibility of *new* intricacy.

We will have to modify the terms. Kohut has added one distinction. What is other than ego is now *either* psychosis *or* narcissism. That still throws together everything but psychosis. To think about the current Awareness Movement, we need more distinctions. Before I supply them, let me examine how people have changed since the days of the Freudian ego.

VII. HOW MENTAL HEALTH HAS CHANGED

How did people live and feel a few generations ago, when the "strong ego" was still common? The majority rarely felt experiential intricacy. To Freud they seemed to *be* their social roles; they felt their identity in the abilities and inabilities of their social status and role-definition. They *identified* with their roles. It seemed that they *were* their religions, their nationalisms, and their assigned cultural places. Spiritual experience consisted of the services, rituals, and prescribed statements. Education was what an educated person would know. The right way to behave was the way of the group; others didn't know how to act. Originality was being odd, "different." Today it seems that "everybody has personality problems." But those earlier generations would not have believed that. One simply thought and acted normally. Inner complexity was crazy. They rarely felt uncategorizable intricacy.

In Jung's scheme such people are not the highest stage of human development. Jung's scheme has a further stage, called "interiorization" and "individuation." But, though younger than Freud, Jung reported that most of the people he knew were still identified with the ego. In that sense Freud's definition of the mature ego does fit traditional people: their "I" seems identified with the roles. Their feelings occurred within the structures. Nevertheless, even this ego could not have been merely imposed. It had to communicate with body-life to carry it forward.

Such people still exist all over the world. Only the urban middle class has changed, and is now much alike in all countries. But the traditional people had much that we would like to regain in some *new* way, as we develop on our new path. At least when we first meet them, they seem refreshingly spontaneous and healthy. They have solid family bonds. A man is a man and a woman a woman, no doubt about it. They love intensely and get mad easily. They are "emotionally free."

It was a mistake to think of this traditional ego as merely imposed. If the body really had been nothing but simple drives, the ego might have been externally imposed: a structure to organize the drives. But now we can see that the ego only elaborated an innate bodily order: the unlearned complexity and interactional organization of the animal body. In traditional people there is a high degree of bodily wholeness. The traditional ego did succeed in carrying that whole complexity forward. The traditional ego was not a merely imposed order.

There is a continuity from animal behavior through ego-patterns, to the new intricacy. But it is not a continuity of form. The order of the body is not patterns; it is an order of carrying forward. Carrying forward can always happen in new ways—but never in arbitrarily imposed ways. Only some patterns carry body-life forward. The processes of intricacy, too, can fail to find a way, although a new way is always possible.

Even in traditional people there *were* diverse and complex nonego processes. But I am not concerned with what was already there, but with *new* intricate experience. We can *not* say that today's new intricacy already existed in the past, somehow unconsciously, nor can we say that this intricacy exists covertly in traditional people today. We cannot read today's intricacy back into the past. It is a new, further development.

Traditional people cannot find this intricacy. Asked to explain a feeling, they are puzzled: They say: "Wouldn't any woman (or man, any father, etc.) feel just this way under these circumstances?" We soon see that their feelings occur only in the culturally defined contexts. Their feelings have no murky edges from which new steps come. These people are not aware of, and really do not have experiential complexities outside the given patterns. They have a wealth of inner experience, but it occurs only in the social forms.

Today, even when a middle-class individual has what seems like the old type of ego, there is a decisive difference. This ego does not now *function* as it did in traditional people. Rather, such a person will seem to be an empty shell, clinging to outward patterns. When we meet such people in middle-class life today, we assume they have *not yet* developed very far, and we hope they soon will. Psychoanalysts who see that type of ego today do not call it "strong." It does not do well in middle-class society today. That older type of ego no longer carries body-life forward very fully. But the concepts of psychoanalytic theory have not yet changed. If the ego is by definition an imposed order, then we cannot conceptualize the difference between its erstwhile whole-bodied carrying forward of body-life, and its present incapacity to do so.

Today, Freud's classical neuroses can be found only in backward, rural areas. The pathologies we find have changed, just as what is health has changed. A few generations ago the traditional ego *was* healthy; but it is not healthy now. That is because today it is not *functionally* the same as it was. This tells us something about how mental health can change. Why was the lack of intricate experience not pathological in previous times? Why did the lack of intricate experience allow for plenty of inward emotionality then, whereas today that lack makes one feel empty inside?

Emotions are not fixed things inside. There is no fixed catalogue of inner entities. They arise only in situations. They come in certain places in interactional events. The classical emotions—joy, sorrow, fear, anger, guilt, respect, triumph, shame, and dishonor—*can come* only in certain situational patterns, at certain points determined by the story plots. You cannot get angry whenever you like; someone has to *do* something that can make you angry. An emotion comes only in a story of events. Traditional society has roles and situations that are clear-cut stories. The traditional emotions exist only in their places in such stories. For example, anger erupts in one's body when, according to the role-identity, one isn't accorded one's due.

In our society the roles and satires are now partly unclear. How do women, men, parents, sons, daughters and daughters-in-law relate to each other? In many ways. Therefore, whole-hearted righteous anger does not come in our bodies so easily. Just when would it? The classical and classifiable emotions come more rarely today, because people are rarely in the traditional situations within which the human body made these emotions. Instead, we get a murky feeling that may include some rage, but does not chiefly consist of the well-known emotions.

The traditional stories are not sufficient to get us through a day. We have to define and structure much of every situation freshly, from moment to moment. The situations are more complex; we *make* them more complex. Did the change in social situations come from individual intricacy, or must we experience more intricately because the situations changed? Both, of course. Nor are there always just these two. The so-called "polarity" of individual and society greatly oversimplifies the many processes we must study. It is not the best, or the only distinction with which to begin.

Today we must let intricacy guide us, rather than the old clear roles and norms. These old forms still exist, but often as official demands, ideal models that we rarely fulfill. As expectations they are just one "social reality." But body-life is no longer carried forward by them. Our more complex and partly undefined situations are another "social reality."

The sociologist Giddens says that social rules exist as a tacit knowledge about how to act in different situations. He says that rules are "a tacit knowing how to go on" in almost any situation.[23] But now we must add: much of the time, each day, the rules don't work. They are insufficient to guide behavior. Then we have *a tacit not-knowing how to go on.*

At first what we experience is an unclear, complex blank. We are stuck. We don't know what to say or how to act. But tacit in the stuckness are *both the old rules and why they won't work just now.* Therefore we have to use that tacit sense to form the saying or the action freshly. Since the situations are subtle beyond the old role-patterns, *an unclear sense of the complexity* now comes in our bodies. And since we rarely live the old stories, the unclear complexity is sensed *instead* of the clear and simple emotions of our traditional culture: emotions such as anger, joy, respect, triumph, honor, or disgrace. Since these emotions rarely come, what inner experience *is* possible today? Intricate experience, however unclear it might be at first, is often the *only* kind.

Today, if one has not yet discovered the sensed intricacy, one senses nothing inside. In that case one is something like Kohut's type, lacking inner experience altogether. Then there are only "external" demand patterns. That is why the societywide discovery of intricate experience is so compelling. Once acquired, like westernization and middleclassness, no one wants to go back to the previous condition. And no one can. It shows that intricacy is a further development.

This development can not be "narcissism." Intricate experience must not be confused with the previously known types of nonego experience. If the traditional ego does not form, the old theory predicts only pathology and infantilism. Indeed, these *do* emerge, but in changed form. Intricate experience *does* include pathology, but it is mostly new in kind. Now that people are more than old ego patterns, some people are more selfish; others cannot manage even a little insensitivity to others in order to take care of themselves. Furthermore, intricate experience *does* include one's childhood experience, but not just as past. There is a direct sense of the role that the past plays *in* the present, and this role can also change. But we find much more than just these changed forms of what was there before. We find a *new* process which generates steps of altogether *new* intricacy. That process was not on the developmental continuum before.

VIII. ADDED DISTINCTIONS: KINDS OF EGO-STRENGTH

To revise the psychoanalytic theory so that we can use it to think about the new developments, we will differentiate some of the ways in which the ego *functions*. It should be noted, though, that even before the new experiential intricacy, the ego functioned in many different ways, and never only as an imposed order.

Traditionally, the ego functioned to elaborate the already complex body-life and (with partial repression) to carry it forward. In so far as it functioned this way, there was only ego-process, and *no nonego experience occurred at all*. This is our first kind of ego-strength.

But we saw that a whole range of nonego experience was always said to occur, but unconsciously. Therefore there always was a second kind of ego-strength, in which the ego functions as a kind of gatekeeper, only to keep other experience out of awareness. Loevinger says "The ego gates experience.[24] Thus *nonego experience does occur, but not in awareness*.

In a third type of ego-strength some nonego experience does enter awareness. In that case "ego-strength" consists of *conscious control* of the nonego experience. *Ego-strength as control becomes the capacity to follow socially prescribed judgments and actions, in spite of one's aware experience*.

These uses of the term "ego-strength" involve functionally different ordering processes. When I have characterized these three, which always existed, I will add two new kinds as well.

a) *Carrying body-life forward in ego's forms* so that no nonego experience occurs.

b) *Excluding, gating*. Nonego experience does occur, but not in awareness. (The so-called "pathology of everyday life" remains unconscious.)

c) *Controlling*. Nonego experience occurs in awareness, but it is denigrated as crazy and overpowered whenever it conflicts with the ego's social forms.

This is how the traditional ego functioned in relation to the nonego experience that was known to occur. In order to examine the new experiential intricacy, I must now add two more types of functioning:

d) *Choice*. Ego and intricate experience are both respected. One chooses when and how to move with either.

e) *A process of many steps of a certain kind, going on into the intricacy*. In the next section I will show these steps exactly. One does not remain in unresolved complexity forever. In this process a new kind of simplicity eventually arises, enabling speech and action. That is not the simplicity of a form; rather, a great deal of implicit intricacy is newly "jelled" in a new tacit knowing of what to say and do.

Orthodox psychoanalytic theory recognized only a) and b), and misunderstood both as mere imposition. In 1950 Ernst Kris added c). He called it "regression in the service of the ego." Conscious nonego experience is invited, but only the better to control it by imposing the ego order on it. The term "regression" means that nonego experience is only a return to infantile events and primary process. When we sense a new and realistic intricacy, rather than regression, it does not work well to deny or control it in the service of the ego. Many people still denigrate intricacy, or try to impose the old forms on it.[25]

Currently c) and d) are the most common types of process. People sometimes denigrate intricacy from the ego standpoint (c); but sometimes they respect it and choose to act from it (d).

The new ego-strength of type e) is not just one choice. Choice remains important; but now there are *many experiential steps*. Such steps are a very different kind of ordering process. In this type of process which I have called "focusing," fresh bodily sensed intricacy contributes to the coming of each step.[26] That is what I will now show.

IX. KINDS OF STEPS

Many kinds of nonego experience exist today, involving fantasy, imagery, and bodily experience. Most of them, however, are without the process of *steps* I will emphasize. Even without such steps, the openness to experience other than ego is a great development of the human being. Experiential openings that only poets and mystics once enjoyed, are now common. Just consider visual imagery. The old theory had held for two millennia that imagery can only rearrange previous external perceptions. Most people did not seem to know what millions now know: that there is a kind of imagery which is richer and not reducible to elements of external perception. But imagery is only one dimension. More important is the direct sensing of the body.

Many ways of sensing the body now allow it to reveal itself as much more organized, than the few bodily "reactions" people used to know. So-called "primitive" experiences are definitely included: not only the mythic type, but also, for example, that directly sensed, aggressive body-energy which has often been lacking in overly careful people. But, what differs from conventionality is not necessarily primitive. The new intricacy can also be found in any moment's experience. It is not primitive, not the "lower nature."

Intricate experience changes and moves through a process of *steps* (the process defined in (e) above.) I am about to present this process, called "focusing." If one is not familiar with the *change-steps* that come from intricate experience, one might misunderstand it as forms and patterns of the familiar kind, although more complex. It seems that way when an unclear "feeling" first opens and one discovers an intricacy. It seems as if it were a formed order. Then there seem to be two formed orders, ego and intricate experience. In any one moment there do seem to be these two, often in conflict. But one can go on; and with the next steps newly intricate forms will come. One realizes that there is a process-order, a form*ing* rather than a form*ed* type of order. *The order of intricate experience is a certain process of steps, not an already formed order that merely emerges.*

But how can one study an "order" that is not itself something formed? Wouldn't any study or description reduce it to the forms used to talk about it? Any formulation we might try out to characterize this forming order would render it as formed. We can study it, therefore, only as we examine the steps in which forms change, and new, more intricate patterns arise. It is in the steps that we will see experiencing as an "order" of its own, different in kind from a form.

We live *every* situation with the body—not only by simple emotions such as being glad, sad, scared, or angry, but with a complex kinesthetic sense in each situation. That sense is what gives rise to the steps.

I will now describe the steps of this currently still rare process of "focusing." The process begins in the implicitly complex body-sense which I earlier called "a tacit not-knowing how to go on." It is the bodily sense of a situation in which the usual sayings and doings won't work. I will show how, from that sense, *many little steps* may ensue. Each step is a change in that body-sense and also brings new thought about the situation. It is in the transitions that we can examine how forms change, and how new, more intricate forms can arise.

This "focusing" process[27] can occur in any setting. I will present excerpts from psychotherapy. But such steps can occur with any concern: personal problems, practical or intellectual work, artistic activity—anything.

People say what seems true, and then have an odd, unclear sense that what they said was not quite right. That "sense" is directly felt, but cannot easily be defined. Here is one woman's description.[28]

> It's like . . . that . . . I don't know quite how to say it. . . . It's like the feeling is there, but I can't quite put words on it. . . . [silence]. . . .

Then she sits silently with this . . ., stuck but not blank. The . . . . . cannot be defined, and yet it is enough to make one certain that what could be said would be wrong.

After a while of sitting with . . . . . she suddenly says:

> Yeah, [breath, whew] yeah.

Words follow. Then she checks again in silence.

> Is that right? . . . . . [It may turn out not to be.] Yeah, whew [breath], that's right.

Let me now present the whole excerpt from which I took these statements. I have put them in italics so that you can see where they occurred. Please note the role which each new silent . . . . . plays. A new step comes from each.

Note that the woman is actively interrogating, formulating, insisting on staying with an unclear sense until it opens. But she checks with the as yet undefinable body-sense in each silence. Note the progression from each silence to the next step.

> *Patient*: It's almost like . . . . . it kind of feels like . . . . . sitting here looking through a photo album. And each picture of me in there is one of my achievements . . . . . because I wasn't achieving for me. I was always achieving for . . . . . someone else so they'd think I was good enough . . . . .
>
> [Silence] . . . . . *It's like that I don't know quite how to say it . . . . . It's like the feeling is there, but I can't quite put words on it . . . . .*

[Silence] . . . . . *Yeah,* . . . . . It's . . . I've chosen this person [a prospective mate] as my challenge . . . knowing that I'd be defeated, knowing that this person wouldn't respond to me. So that I could kind of buy right back into the photo album being flipped through . . . . .

[Silence, checking inwardly] . . . . . Yeah. I think so. I think so because . . . . .

[Silence, checking inwardly] . . . . . Yes, this person feels inaccessible. Yet, not so inaccessible that it's not a total impossibility. So it's like I keep trying out my worth on him and keep coming up against, "yeah, I like you, but."

Therapist: "I like you but . . . . ." Always qualified.

Patient: That's how I felt when my mother "liked me," when we related. I like you but. . . . But there was always something missing. Some big flaw that was so awful, she couldn't quite love me because of it. . . . . .

[Silence] . . . . . It feels like such a hurt spot. [Begins to cry]

[Silence] . . . . . And, I always had to I always had to be a star or she wouldn't love me.

Note how her steps come from the silence, the body-sense, the . . . . . between each statement and the next.

I chose an example that can be construed as a "narcissistic wound." But that is not what makes her process-steps here. The narcissistic wound is what made her a conformist, *always* trying for further achievements, for a reward that would not come. It is these little change-steps that not only formulate this painful struggle to get an unreachable approval, but also enable her finally to reject that mode of living.

The hurt was there before, was then repressed, and is remembered now. But she says also that this unrealizable pattern *was* there all the time she conformed, although she neither saw nor rejected it. How the word *"was"* works here must be considered. She does not find that intricacy on her memory track of past conformity. It is formed for the first time in these process-steps, right here. Once formed, however, we can say it *was* already there in a way—in the way that this word "was" works here, in this very sentence. This retroactive "was" cannot be explained as if these intricate steps had actually occurred covertly, as an existing part of the old social form. More than what happened in the past is involved here. The steps are a new forming process.

Once the old form (as it functions today) is experienced *with* this intricacy, no psychoanalyst would advise her to try for this man, or to try to achieve any goal for what everyone would agree is a "wrong" motive, once the steps formulated it. In the old form, there was certainly such a thing as working for rewards. That has always been common; nothing new in that. What *is* new is her steps, which lets her find—in this way of "finding"—what can *then* be seen as obviously unsound. Generations ago, people did not usually experience what we are calling "the unclear body-sense." Therefore they couldn't take the steps that would enable them to differentiate how they experienced the old social forms. Intricate experience did not form. There were only clear emotions, like this woman's hurt. The old hurt is made again, here, but only in some respects is it as it was before. In the past no unclear bodily sense came with that hurt. Certainly the body did *in some way* include what we now say it "was." That *might* have led to an unclear sense which *might* then have been carried forward into intricate steps, but that did not happen.

This intricacy arises right in the steps. It is not dredged up from what was. Such steps do not uncover an already formed order; nor do they impose a formed order. We need to let our own word "order" work as these steps work. It is neither a finding of order, nor an imposing of order. The greater "order" of experiencing is not the formed patterns which result from the steps. It is *at least* the "order" of the steps. (I say "at least," because no one process should be taken as a model to think about all others.)

This process is distinguishable by its kind of steps. We do not distinguish it because we value the new content over the old one. Rather, her process had not been of this kind before. When she attempted impossible tasks, and performed for others, her thought and action *did not come in the kind of steps that are coming now*—from her own bodily feedback. This different process-mode *newly* constellates how she says she "was"—*lacking* in such feedback. *This kind of process is an experiencing-and-rejecting of the implicit control.*

Her old way, working for approval, was *less* intricate. It was the usual kind of process. Now this different kind of process brings more intricate content than the socially imposed order. You can recognize the difference in the mode of process.

Here is another woman talking about a prospective mate. Note how the silent "sense" corrects what she says. At each step the body's felt . . . . . "talks back" and reverses what she said.

> I've been holding him off. But he is really very special, and nobody's perfect. I'm impossibly demanding. It confuses me. . . . . .
>
> [Silence] . . . . . He says he cares about me, and I know he does, but I also doubt it. Uhm . . . . .
>
> [Silence] . . . . . [sigh] No, he cares. I don't doubt that. I see it in his eyes. When I pull back even a little, he looks so hurt. It's me, I have trouble letting someone care about me. . . . . .
>
> [Silence] . . . . . [sigh] It's not the caring, that gives me trouble. It's that when someone cares for me, then I have to get into *this* confusing feeling. . . . . .
>
> [Silence] . . . . . He says he cares about me and what I need. And he wants us to be together. But it seems like he doesn't want to see what's true, what isn't working in our relationship. And it is mostly this not wanting to see, which is what's not working. But if he doesn't care about that, then it seems like he doesn't really care about *me*-me. It's like he wants me, but only if I'm quiet and feel weird, like not-me. So he doesn't care about whether our connection is real or not. But it makes me feel crazy. Does it sound crazy to you?
>
> *Therapist:* Would it feel better if he said these things separately, something like: "*I want* you for me. *I try* to care about what's good for you, and I want to think I do. *I'm scared* of seeing anything about us, or about myself, that would get in the way?
>
> Yes, it would feel better if he said that.

Why does she feel confused and crazy? Isn't it because her perceptions exceed the usual social phrases? ("He doesn't want to see what isn't working. . . . . . And it is mostly his not wanting to see, which is what's not working." "He doesn't care about *me*-me.") That is more intricate than the usual social vocabulary. Isn't it also more realistic—a better predictor of what will happen in their marriage, if it does not change?

One might apply the term "depersonalization" to the experience of not-me. It is not a new phenomenon. But, traditional thinking would see only loss of a clear ego—narcissism. The process of forming newly intricate relational aspects would be missed. One would see only an incomplete ego-identity. Considered in terms of the theory of narcissism, an experience of "not-me" cannot indicate anything real; certainly it cannot be the formation of realistic aspects of interpersonal interaction.

From the standpoint of the "narcissism" theory one might say something like this: "If she had a 'healthy ego,' she would not lose her sense of identity in this interaction. She would not be enmeshed in this complexity. She would stand by her first statement, in which she imposed the common social form. She knows 'nobody's perfect.' If she cannot impose her ego's dictum and bond socially in the nonmutality, it must be ego-weakness. Her ego isn't strong enough to prevent not-me feelings."

Today, women are saying that the traditional woman's role *was* a demand for women to be "not-me." "If a man cares for me, I must be how he wants." We can now see that this is a case of social control; but until recently it was not experienced this way. In the past, people did not carry an unclear body-sense forward into these differentiations by means of intricate experiential process-steps. Now, however, they say all this "was" there before. They are right—in a way. But I must emphasize that the word "was" is working here in this new way. If such a body-sense had formed, and had been carried forward, the old form might sometimes have "turned out to be" what she finds here. But, what traditional people experienced was not this; nor was it any other intricate differentiation.

It would be difficult to argue that the woman's experienced intricacy is really symptomatic of her regression to an old type of nonego experience. Our excerpts should make clear that what she senses is her present situation.

Notice that many steps make up the experiencing-and-rejecting of this control, this pull, the "not-me" demand. Each step changes the content. Each such step arises from a bodily sensed . . . . ., her bodily sensed social reality.

One cannot design such steps. They come. They happen. All one can do deliberately is to *focus* attention on the body's sense of more than can be said. We could not have predicted the next step from the earlier steps. Each step makes sense retroactively, but only as we go back and *alter* what had seemed so true at the previous step. The . . . . . has *new* implicit speech which has not yet formed. In these two examples we have seen how language and situation are implicit in the body. And we have seen how one can sense the wrongness of what one says. Our examples also show that the *new* saying is not yet *in* the unclear sense—obviously not, since a *body-change* comes physically only when the saying forms.

X. INTRICACY AND PROCESS STRATEGY

But how can one study or speak about such steps and this ". . . . ." which cannot be said? In our excerpts people *did* speak in such steps also about such steps. We can distinguish the mode of process we have been discussing because we can clearly recognize the steps of the focusing process. The steps shown in these excerpts have, in fact, been reliably defined, recognized and studied. Researchers have shown that a standardized rating system, the EXP Scale, can measure the extent to which they happen in an interview.[29] That has been correlated with other variables.

Are such reliable marks not once again just *general* criteria? The process-indicators that the EXP Scale uses go *further* into intricacy than common phrases do. *Such characteristics are process criteria—they are themselves an intricacy*. But further intricacy could change, and add to, any description of intricate characteristics. "Process" says that experiential order is always open for further steps. That does not mean we always study steps as such. There are other experiential differentiations.

The steps cannot be described in the general terms currently available. There are no words or phrases in the common language for the intricacy we are discussing. The focusing process *can,* of course, be described, but only insofar as this very process lets our words work newly. I will soon discuss the character of language which enables words to do that.

The focusing steps are recognizably different from the steps involved in ordinary talk-continuity, logical inference, and event-reports (such as: then this happened, and then that happened). In our excerpts you saw that the sequence of focusing steps is *not* one of these familiar progressions. But you did not only notice what these steps are *not*. You also *followed* the progression they *did* make. Before I discuss how the focusing steps do "follow," let me list more continuities within which they *need not* remain:

The Steps Do Not Remain Within Logical Continuity

We examined steps that could not have been deduced from the preceding steps. They were not derived from any existing forms. Rather, each step retroactively changes the earlier form: the form from which one would otherwise want to deduce or explain it. From each step one looks back and changes what the preceding step meant. Only then does the new step follow from the preceding one.

They Need Not Stay Within Any Extant Situational Form

Process-steps change situations and make new intricacy. A situation can change what it is, and become more intricate than it "was." The change-steps can determine anew the role of any forms.

The Steps Do Not Occur Within The Continuity Of Any One Time-Model

Focusing steps make time more intricate. The word "was" works in a variety of ways. The use of "was" which we examined involved two pasts: When we *now* say what "was" implicit before, that is *another* past time, not the one we have on our linear memory-track behind us. But this dual-time model cannot be forced onto every progression of steps. The steps can make other time progressions, and are not determined by a time-scheme.

Some Unconscious Controls Can Be Overcome

We saw that such steps *may sometimes* exceed *some* internalized controls. We saw that an internalized control that had functioned in one kind of process could be experienced and rejected in steps of another kind (in our therapy excerpts, having to be a star and having to be not-me).

No "Unconscious" Continuity Explains Them

The steps are not determined by something that stays the same in "the unconscious," because they can change the unconscious as well. What is said to "emerge from the unconscious" *was not* there that way before. Only now, in a new sense of "was," can we say it was there before.

Such Steps Are Not Within The Continuity Of A Self-Known Agent

They *cannot* be explained by positing a self-thing whose content would determine the steps. These steps do not stay *within* how persons know themselves. Rather, the steps can *change* the self-known person. The "subject" is not defined or unified by a metaphysical or logical continuity.

XI. THE SELF AS EXPERIENTIAL RESPONSE PROCESSES

A person is not a Kantian object held together by an imposed unity. One form is not what makes a self. Why reduce the many intricate self-processes to the empty mathematical identity of *a* self? Why abstract *one* pattern and impose it on everything else? Why assume that "the self" must *be* as the Western assumption makes everything be: as held together by an imposed unity-form?

We reject not only the usual scheme: the self as a thing, entity, or object that is supposed to be the source and explanation of psychological content. We also reject the other general schemes proposed by some philosophers. For example, Heidegger offers a scheme of persons as *self-relatings* (my term for it). He says people relate to themselves mostly in the mode of self-avoidance. But they can *choose to be* what they *already are* and *have to be,* thereby *being in a further way*. Here the word "be" works in three different ways in a more complex pattern than the simple "is" of a brick. Like other philosophical schemes, Heidegger's does serve to undercut and correct the usual scheme of a self-thing. But it is again a scheme, and just one scheme.

We would follow Heidegger, if we said: "The self is a self-response process." But is it *a* process? We must at least say that the self is many kinds of self-response process*es*. Even Heidegger offers more than one. We *can* forcefully subsume the variety under these kinds, or under some other scheme of kinds. But there are many kinds, and many ways to formulate kinds. Nor is the self made only in *private* responding. Other people's responses can carry self-experiencing forward. Privacy and interaction are always implicit in each other: We respond to ourselves as persons involved in situations with others. Conversely, our interactions depend upon the private self-responses which each presumes in the other.

Some process-modes involve a newly found sense of self. Some are spontaneous, some calculated. Some involve reserve, boredom, withdrawal, depersonalization. There may be unconscious conformity, or, very differently, a calculated show of it in which the individual remains separate. There are many different differences in process types, and these determine what will actually result from some social process. What is lost in any general scheme is just those crucial differences in mode of process which make a sociological or psychological variable actually quite different in different instances.

But, is all one can say about "the self" just a characterization of steps? It is true that the *order* of the self is always *open* to further steps. Any differentiation can be studied as a kind of step, but much else about it can be studied. The kinds of steps is only one especially promising consideration. Rather than a scheme of things or steps, experiential differentiations *are* (make, find, have, work, step . . .) in their own intricate way. We let these words work newly in *this* "making," this "finding," in these "steps." We let them be their own ordering, rather than imposing a similar pattern to say what they are.

But should we not have a philosophical scheme, at least to ward off the effect of simpler and poorer schemes? I find that this purpose is better served by letting the steps which actually occurred stand, as themselves. An actual step can greatly exceed the patterns of a self that have been proposed.

For example, in one woman's excerpt I presented, is the *self* the "me" she refers to as "*me*-me"? Or is it the "not-me" way of being which she senses as false although there is a "pull" to be not-me? Or is her self perhaps rather the harried one who senses the one self as true and the other as false? Of course, any such answer would be foolish. It would break up her intricate pattern into several self-entities, each supposedly existing alone. We could go on multiplying such entities. There is also *the* "pull," and therefore a self that isn't strong enough to resist that pull. Which is that one? And is "not-me" her childhood self, or is it rather the adult self of the traditional man-woman pattern? Or "was" it always both, perhaps with the child-self remaining inside a woman's? Even this rough scheme of one self inside another is subtler than the attempt to define entities. And the multiplicity of entities is still better than the scheme of just one.

Why is anyone tempted to reduce this variety and intricacy to some single pattern? The temptation arises because of the belief that nothing exists without an imposed form of "unity." The variety seems to imply that there is no self, no person. Someone will ask: "Isn't each of us still *one* person?" Our answer would be: "Certainly—but not in every way." This answer is ambiguous because the oneness of a person is ambiguous *as a generality*. Here is a better answer: A person "is" and "is one" in many ways that are not in the mathematical unity-form. For example, a certain new way of being one does arise in the bodily processes I described. But that is only one of many ways of being one. Were you asking about the ways in which a person is one, and about other respects in which that isn't so? *These* can be studied.

XII. LANGUAGE AND THE BODY

How does language work in the process-steps I have presented? Can we discuss this question in language that works as it does in these steps?

Words change how they themselves work in these steps, and in talking about these steps. Since the steps of the focusing process violate logical continuity, we could say that they are *"discontinuous."* Then that word works very precisely to say this break in logical continuity. But since such steps make sense—we do follow them—we could also say that the steps are *continuous*. This opposite word works equally precisely in this kind of transition. But the two different words don't say the same thing. There is no "same thing" for the words to name. A word brings old uses into a new working. We follow this working without difficulty. But what sort of "following" is this? The word "follow" works newly, nonlogically, but in its own, very precise way. "Precise" works more precisely here than categories do. *This* "discontinuity," this "following," is made by these steps. Their possibility is in the nature of language!

Another striking characteristic of the focusing steps is the function of the bodily . . . . . Such silent sensing is *not without language*. There is implicit language in the . . . . ., since one can sense in this silence the wrongness of what has just been said. Obviously, the body-sense "knows the language." New phrasings may come from it. So, it must be appreciated that language is implicit in it.

The bodily . . . . . occurs not only in therapy. Pilots fly "by the seat of their pants." Poets and painters work from a bodily felt sense of what has not yet formed. Among business people it is well known that the best decisions are made by those who can size up a situation by the feel of it. Those who have this talent are admired as having "the business instinct." The use of the body's situational understanding is known in some way in every field of human activity. When there is a problem, we cannot just impose a solution. Since there is a problem, it is certain that the old forms did not suffice. Yet they are there, implicit in the bodily . . . . ., our sense of "stuckness" in the situation. When no new pattern comes to carry that "sense" into speech and action, we remain stuck. We fail to meet the situation. At such times it can *seem* as if the old forms were the only patterns of our bodies; now that *they* don't work, nothing does. But that murky physical discomfort is only the beginning. Soon something significant arises from it. After a few steps more intricacy arises, and may carry the "stuckness" forward into new speech and action. We must remember that this process involves more than one step. People often stop after the first step, and don't know that more steps can come.

All fresh thinking involves this. . . . . . We might have to read something over and over, till we say we "have it," we "get" the point. But then our further thinking is also a . . . . . To think theoretically about this . . . . . we must use it. No theoretical term can substitute for how theoretical terms change in the . . . . . We must let how it works be . . . . .

Where is this . . . . . ? It is in the body; it is a sentience of the body. *The body* can be thought of in this different, yet familiar way: After all, we meet most situations in life through kinesthetic body-sensing. We walk into a room and sense with our bodies—without verbal thoughts—who the persons sitting there are, and how we greet them. We can think very little of any event in explicit forms. When we find no way to act, when we are stuck, we sense that the body implies more than the known ways. Here the word "implying" draws a changed meaning from the function of the . . . . . in these sentences.

The Theoretical Question

Granting these common observations as well as the therapy excerpts, we must still ask the theoretical question: How can a physical body have *its own* implying and symbolizing? Can there be a bodily symbolizing other than the implicit concepts and social rules which are, of course, implicit in human situations, and are therefore learned by the body? But I have been saying that bodily process also symbolizes in a different way, not only in what I have called "generalities": concepts, distinctions, roles, rules. How is another symbolizing possible? Doesn't the very word "symbolizing" symbolize a generality—many particular cases brought under one category? Even if we let the word work freshly here for whatever happens in the focusing process, can we think theoretically about how the body could possibly function as it does, giving rise to new symbolization in the focusing steps?

If we assert that the body has a symbolizing of its own, are we making the old false assumption that "meanings" float somewhere, unspoken and unthought, as if words and symbols could come later, and only represent what were already meanings? But meanings are always the products of some kind of symbolizing. Meanings do not exist separately, so that they could merely be copied accurately—represented.

Indeed, the old notion of representational symbols applies neither to ordinary human practice nor to the body. A symbol is not a copy, not a stand-in for something; rather it changes what it symbolizes. That happens in most ordinary situations. Certain phrases or actions will change a situation. Other words or actions would change it differently. A situation *is* something that needs to be changed by some phrases or actions. We don't separate certain events out, and call them "a situation" unless some words or actions are called for. If we are puzzled about what to say or do, we don't know what the situation is. When at last we find what we can say or do in it, do we know what *the situation* "really was," all along? *It* was what required just this saying or doing. Our bodily implying, and the situation, are "symbolized" by this saying and doing, which says what the situation is—and changes the situation so as to "meet" it. So we are really very familiar with a use of symbols—indeed, it is the most common use—which changes something, while thereby saying what it was.

But the required acts are not determined by the situation, as if they could be deduced from it. Life would be easy if that were so. Rather, we often fail to meet a situation, because its *requiring* is so finely tuned, and so new, that we cannot come up with anything at all, to say or do. What is required may never have been said or done before in the history of the world.

The body's implying of speech and action is not limited to an existing repertory of actions and phrases. As we saw in the therapy excerpts, one can sense what is required even while one cannot yet phrase or do it. That is the body's . . . . . Since new phrases and actions *do* sometimes come, we see that the body can not only sense beyond its existing store of phrases and actions; it can also create new and more intricate phrases and courses of action than existed before. *In giving rise to new phrases it physically restructures the language that "was" implicit in the body.* One does not design new phrases or actions. They "come" physically—the body produces them if we attend to the body-sense of what cannot be said or done.

This functioning of words should not seem strange or incomprehensible. We need only discard the notion of an idealist world consisting of *separable* concepts, generalities, distinctions, differences, general category-names. These are not the only order of the world, nor of language. Language is "general" in an entirely different way; it does not consist of separable generalities. Words and phrases do not always have one "same" meaning in different uses. Separable generalities are a much later human development. Sometimes they *are* made to function with logical continuity. But in ordinary language and practice they do not function logically. They are changed and carried further by being part of another order, that of language in situations.

Notice that actions have the same role and function as words. Neither actions nor words merely describe or represent; rather they function to change something which, we later say, *was* the requiring of that change. If the ordinary use of words may be said to "symbolize," then action also symbolizes.

Even in an animal's physical life-process, actions have this symbolizing role. Body-tensions have been misunderstood as merely chemical. But they are also the calling for certain environmental behaviors. The so-called "tension" implies a certain behavior. When that behavior occurs, it is what the tension *was* (what the tension called for, what it implied). Animal behavior has this *symbolizing* role. The body *physically implies* its next interaction. When that interaction has happened, the body no longer implies it. When the cat first sees a mouse, its body tenses; every muscle implies jumping. When the cat has jumped, its body no longer implies jumping. The jumping *symbolizes* what the body *implied* before the jump. Hunger *implies* feeding, and feeding *symbolizes*—and changes—that hunger. An earlier and *wider* symbolizing exists, and it is richly elaborated by language.

The patterns of animal life seem endlessly repetitious. How, then, can I assert that the body can imply novel intricacy that has, as yet, never been formed? The answer is that the bodily implying, as a physical tension-event, does not contain *the formed events*. Nor does it contain their representation *as such*. Therefore the body's implying is not inherently limited to the repetitious form we usually see. The body's implying is not a form. Therefore, when an animal's body or environment change, we do sometimes see new behavior which has never been seen in that species. An ant crawls more intricately on a wooly rug. One may certainly argue that language is a very different symbolizing than animal behavior, but it does involve the role of the body which we have just discussed.

Elsewhere I have presented a theory of many modes of wider symbolization.[30] Body-process was always already a symbolizing that does not consist of separable generalities.

Since animal bodies imply interactions, culture and language did not create interaction. The cultures have only elaborated the bodily implying. Language does not consist of "encoded," stamped-in forms, which first organize experience. Language-acquisition used to be thought of as an encoding. In recent research that assumption is changing.[31] Complex mother-child interactions have been found from birth, even in infants born two months prematurely. In these interactions, the mother responds to already present complexity; she does not impose it.[32] At about one year, such organized interactions provide the complex contexts which are now said to be necessary for language-acquisition. In the field of language-acquisition, too, the long-ignored, nonconceptual order is returning. The animal, the body, the infant, the child, and language—these are found to have a more intricate *order* than had been believed.

We must pay attention to our own language in discussing "the body and language." The discussion of language must allow this reworking which is characteristic of language. Implicit speech and interaction are *lived on, further,* by the body, sometimes into actions and phrases that have never existed before in the history of the world. The word "order" can say this further forming, which is not just one form, or another.

The body can talk back in the silences. The phrases that form in these silences work in new ways, as a poet's phrases do. The words "body" and "talk" are in fact working newly right here. You know, from how the sentence is constructed, that "talking" works in a new way—since this talking happens in silences. Of course the word brings it old uses, but these are changed as the word works in the sentence. It is not a matter of my *announcing* that I want these words to work differently, while still using them in an old way. Rather, if you have followed these sentences, your body has already allowed these words to work in their new ways.

Words define themselves from their working—from the changes they make. Words don't work by definitions. New definitions can be devised only *after* words have newly worked. Definitions are important, but for something else. They are not this working. The words, "order," "body," "experiential," "intricacy," "language," "knows," "says," "sense," "situation," "step," "works," and "follows" all work as you have "followed" them here. Many other words can work newly to further characterize such steps. They can say more about how body, situations, and language are inherent in each other. How words work in this way can be said—if we let "work" and "say" work that way. We can study and say that "order."

The usual way of thinking can be turned right-side up: distinctions, categories, rules, roles—abstract commonalities are a later kind of order, never the only one. Language was and is not a categorial order. Nor is the order of language superimposed upon a passive, malleable body. A living body never consisted of fixed forms which could be wiped out and replaced by other fixed forms. The body's type of order is one that can always be carried further, and language does that. Language and culture do not abolish the animal. The complex body speaks the language, and can talk back to history—much more intricately than the extant forms.

XIII. A PROCESS VIEW OF UNCONSCIOUS PROGRAMMED CONTROL

Let us now return to the problem we postponed. The focusing steps do not always exceed all controls. In the following excerpt these steps failed to overcome an internalized control.[33]

> [Silence] . . . . . Like . . . like I feel almost like I'm trapped in my own self or something like that . . . . .
>
> [Silence] . . . . . It's hard to describe the feeling . . . . .
>
> [Silence] . . . . . Like that . . . that it's not going to get better. . . . And I guess, like you said, there doesn't seem to be a light at the end for me, and I can't see right now . . . or at least I can't see the light.
>
> *Therapist:* There's an element of. . . of. . . hopelessness. Perhaps that's too strong a word, but . . . you don't immediately see any hope of resolving this feeling.
>
> [Silence] . . . . . Well, it looks pretty hopeless to me right now . . . but then, when you said that what came to me was . . . I sort of had an angry place that. . . . Hopeless maybe, but I'm not helpless. That bugs me if someone thinks I'm helpless because . . . even though it does look hopeless right now . . . Like I've always been able to fight and work things out before . . . for myself . . . but if . . . . .
>
> [Silence] . . . . . there's . . . there's something real hurtful . . . . .
>
> [Long silence] . . . . . And, my reaction to that is that I just don't care (sobbing) . . . . .

This example shows that such process-steps can miss and merely reinstance some internalized programming. Isn't this an unrecognized, programmed feeling when she says: "That bugs me, when someone thinks I'm helpless"? Isn't this the controlling code speaking: "If you are helpless you must feel ashamed. Hide the fact. It is your own individual fault. What happens to you depends on you alone. Keep working. Take a job under any conditions." This code keeps people performing. Here we have seen that a political-economic injunction implicit in the experiential change process *may fail to be overcome* by the focusing steps.

Her reaction is not created only by the social code. Animals try to avoid helplessness, too. Value-codes are not just imposed on a formless body; they elaborate the already complex animal body. But the bodily order is not a set of fixed patterns. More than one social way can carry the body forward. To sense the bodily order does *not* mean obeying a given pattern, or just imposing another. Bodily sentient steps can bring new differentiations. It did not happen in this excerpt in regard to this code.

We have seen that process-steps *can* sometimes exceed internalized controls. The other people I cited exceeded a performance code (love that never comes for being a star, the pull to be how a man wants). But focusing steps do not always exceed *all* internalized controls. There is no such "all," since later steps can always determine what "was" such a code. But as we have just seen, a well-known code may be reinstanced, rather than overcome by the focusing process. That leads us to formulate the following question: *When do these process-steps change the internalized controls, rather than being dictated by the controls?* This question takes us to the heart of the political problem. We can consider politics in a different way, now that we have rejected concepts like "narcissism" and revised the assumption inherent in many other concepts, that the body cannot challenge or alter the forms imposed on it. If the body *can* alter them, rather than being controlled by them, when does it do so and when not?

How Can The Direction Of Change Be Made to Move From Experiential Process to the Larger System?

The question has several facets. It is not enough to avoid the dualism of society and individual. We must also ask about the causal direction. If that is not mentioned, the assertion of this unity is only a false comfort. We are made to feel that we have been included, when it is said that, "After all, the individuals and the society are one and the same system." In this joint system cause and effect might move in only one direction, as the old theory said. You and I are affected by the Federal Reserve Bank, since we and it constitute one and the same system together; but the Bank might be quite *un*affected by being in one and the same system with us. Although microsystems and macrosystems are interlocked, we must ask about the direction of change. How can change move *from* the experiential *to* the political?

Anything human is both social and individual; it is ordered in *many* systematic ways (not just by two large systems: individual and social.) We think of events as individual, or sexual, or economic, but sexuality can be changed by economic changes, and new sexual patterns change economics. Since the "laws" of change in these orders are so different, we are inclined to trace artistic changes in terms of aesthetics, and family changes in terms of family patterns—we study each within its seeming lawfulness. But we should not forget that anything concrete belongs to the other systems as well. The systems meet each other, not as separated entities, but as they are implicit in each event. A change in one system *will* change that event, and, as the event affects other events, the change *may* have an effect on the other systems. But that is not automatic. The change *may* go in both directions between two systems, but it may not! We must look each time and trace the reciprocal change, *if* there happens to be one.

For example, millions have currently lost their jobs. Most of them are helpless, and feel ashamed of being helpless. They know hardly anything about the Federal Reserve Bank and did not take part in its action to restrict the economy (1972–1986). Their sense of themselves does not in return affect the Federal Reserve Bank. Furthermore, the experiential process-steps I described can go on and on, without ever bringing up the Federal Reserve Bank. Personal process-steps do *not automatically* change the economic system, nor even increase one's understanding of that system. Therefore we need to study and collect the factors which make for a direction of change from experience to the structural system.

Five Factors That Determine the Direction of Change

1. Firstly, political and economic concepts have a necessary role. People need different concepts to interpret events such as the Fed's taking the money out of the economy to "cut demand." Most people don't know how the economy is controlled, or even that it *is* controlled. According to the now prevailing concepts the economy is an uncontrolled natural phenomenon like the weather. They don't think about how it is controlled anymore than they think about how the weather is controlled. Only with

political-economic concepts can *experience* give rise to the need for changes in how the structure now operates.

2. Secondly, how could experiential steps have any effect, considering the fixed job-structure within which everyone has to work? The bank directors can only perform their jobs, or yield them to others who will. The slots, that is to say, the structurally different roles and positions in which we all live and work, direct what can be done in the slots. From the highest to the lowest, each slot seems to have only its prestructured leeway. What, then, might be the role of the "focusing" process I have described? It is not only personal. Although each of our "slots" is *almost* totally structured, if one focuses on one's own next steps within the slot—*including* the limitations and seemingly fixed purposes—steps that change old forms *can* come. But this possibility is at first invisible. It is not already given in the slot. And, in any one slot, what can change, even in this way, may be painfully little. One is tempted to look only at broad issues, and to ignore one's own hard-to-find and hard-to-do novelty. But if we each do work at our own possible new differentiations, the collective degree of novelty can be considerable. A collaboration of many such individuals communicating with each other, especially in *vertically* connected slots, can open much more.

3. Thirdly, a genuinely political self-experience is possible. It is not only a question of jobs and money; our deepest self-responding also has political dimensions. There is a way to move *from* the "merely inner" psychology of self *to* a self-understanding within the larger system. We can learn from how the Women's Movement moved from what seemed to be only psychological issues to politically understood issues.

Decades ago most psychoanalysts would coerce an unhappily married woman to stay in her marriage. Whenever her intricate experience conflicted with the social pattern, it was given no validity. The analysts wanted a woman to be *aware* of her dissatisfaction ("regression in the service of the ego"), but then to control it. The analysts would not grant that her dissatisfaction could be *realistic* in her present life—or that she might act on it. They told her: "Most women manage the marriage pattern, so the trouble must be *in you*." That is the internal/external split: What exceeds the existing forms must be narcissistic. Reality is what is "external."

The Women's Movement rejected this invalidation of experience. Understanding how the dualism that divides "inner" from "outer" subjectivizes and invalidates the woman's experience of social reality, it was able to move *from* "inner" *to* "outer," that is to say *it brought about a change-direction from more intricate experience to society.*

Currently, a woman arguing about women's rights can tell a man: "I'm supposed to let you interrupt me, because you're a man. I was trained only to listen. I can't think of a comeback that fast. But that makes my point!" The same experienced inabilities which silenced her before and kept her *cut off* from the "external structural context, are now her *connections* to that context and the source of her challenge to it.

This way was first discovered by the Black Movement. A previously "shy" black person can now speak up for blacks. A different grammar is no longer an obstacle. The person says: "See? I don't talk 'right.' That's my point!" The awareness of "bad grammar" no longer prevents a black from being listened to. The difference in grammar is now a political way of understanding oneself. Thereby it connects the person to the structural context and becomes a channel of resistance.

Such self-understanding can be extended to everyone. We can all move in this way *from* some experienced need for change *to* an experientially implied social change. Suppose someone feels something of that sort, but lacks the solid conviction necessary to act entirely alone. The old training now says: "Why aren't you sure on your own? Shame on you for needing others to corroborate what you know." But this shaming inner voice is itself an example. To come to understand this code ("It all depends on you alone") *politically* is a recognizable type of process-step—and moves past the code. The dictum: "One should never need others" is experienced *as a control* which atomizes and isolates us, and prevents mutual action. One moves some steps past that code in the very act of sensing it in this experiential-political way. The steps are like those we saw in the therapy excerpts when a control becomes constellated and rejected in the same steps, but the steps include the political dimension.

Once you look for them in this way, you will find other internalized controls. For example: Does an unpaid bill make you more tense in your body than oncoming traffic? Can you stand it if your friends drive you to the airport, but not if they give you the money for a taxi? Do you feel ashamed about not earning as much as you "should?" Does your body pull itself in, as if to take up less space, when others are around? If any of these examples fits you, can you also understand your *self* within the larger system?

People differ in what they have developed. Therefore different steps are freeing for them. Are you good at pushing, winning, riding over others—and over that in you which longs to stop the constant tension? Would you like the peacefulness to look around you, to sense others, and to find your own creativity? If any of that fits, can you also understand this as more than an "only inner" peculiarity? The "inner" is never just inner. When you consider it "inner," you keep the tension within yourself and cut experience off from the social change it implies.

A great many people are currently leaving the business world. It's called "mid-life crisis." (But it includes many younger people.) They seek new professions—often psychology. Some blame themselves for not finding interesting new work. They say: "It's me. I should know what I want." Calling it "mid-life crisis" makes it "inner"—part of the individual lifecycle. "I should know what I want" says that you should want an already existing slot. But why accept the existing system of slots, rather than pursuing the flexibility and the new slots implied in your dissatisfaction with the existing fields? And, why learn to be an *ordinary* psychologist, when you are already an expert in the fascinating new field in psychology which is implicit in your experience—the study of what it is, about the business world, that can make it intolerable? The problem is not its tasks or contents. We must study *the characteristic type of experiential and interactional processes* which the business world now requires, and the *change in process-type* which is implicit, when people find the current type intolerable.

Political self-experience is not just negative. I do not speak negatively of the present society. The idea is not to turn against it, to stop loving it, but to sense how we live in it, and what we do to others. The privileged sector we live in is the hope and envy of the world. It has not made only emptiness and atrophy in people. Intricate experience is itself a development of this very society. Now that people are finding it, they assume that it always existed and explain the fact that they hadn't found it sooner by assuming that society must have repressed it before. Not so. It existed only in rare individuals. Its current development *was partly enabled by the conditions of this society:* its literacy, its relative openness, wealth, level of production, communication, sophistication, and its history of constantly evolving institutions. The current adult individual evolved in *this* society and now exceeds its routine forms and controls.

4. The *general* concept of "control" has its proper role in *specific* research. There is very little meaning to this question if the terms "control" and "development" are merely general concepts. The one condemns, the other lauds—everything. The difference is only the evaluative tone. Every social function can be described in either term: Education *develops* children into adults, that is to say, it seeks to *control* the type of people they become. Medicine has lengthened and improved life *by* governing everyone's daily habits and keeping the sick in medically controlled institutions. The de-

veloping is itself the controlling. Foucault was quite right when he said that the attempt to distinguish is only a mystification. Development is obviously a kind of control; one can know this without studying anything specific. But Foucault did not stop with this universal concept. He also studied specific historical records and detailed practices. But, in this *specific* study he was greatly helped by his *general* view that everything is control. It is interesting that the empty general concept made such a big difference when it was used together with the details. It enabled him to discover and perceive *specific* systematic controls where others have seen only accidents and exceptions. For example, how have generations of theorists thought about the unattractive aspects of the usual education—the locked routines, the constant grading, the ever-present, infantilizing authority patterns, and the great amount of useless content? These puzzling things were considered simply as accidents due to unenlightened administrators, byproducts that are not part of education as such. But in that view the greater part of what happens in education drops out as irrelevant. Only if, with Foucault, we consider that education is inherently control, can we perceive and study *these specific controls*—how they function to train individuals to be as their future jobs will require them to be. It is therefore an advantage to view specifics in terms of the general notion that every social function is inherently controlling. We can retain this advantage without being confused by the negative sound of that proposition. Control cannot be distinguished from development *in general*. Instead, we can study the details, especially the different kinds of processes. Then we can discover many important distinctions and a much greater variety than just control or development.

I seem to propose a *general* social theory that human individuals can exceed the social controls. But that is not what I propose. Rather, I assert that this happens only in certain recognizable kinds of processes, and that it does not happen in other, equally recognizable processes. We can study different kinds of processes and observe how controls function and how they are exceeded.

5. Different kinds of process give different, more specific meanings to sociological terms. For example, in one kind of control our response is prescribed. In a different kind, we devise our own new way, but in response to external events we did not control.

Depending on process-differences in intricate experience, seemingly similar social patterns can have very different results. In some processes we impose a pattern and life goes on within it. Other imposed patterns totally stop some part of living. These are different kinds of processes! Or, the imposed pattern works, but with puzzling symptoms. Some types of control make for violations in secret. Others prevent even the wish for a violation. Still other controls are explicit but resisted or disobeyed by almost everyone. These examples open up a gamut of unexplored process-differences. The focusing steps of intricate experience I described are one kind of process among many others. We can study process-differences.

A conceptual and experiential self-understanding within the slots and the specific controls is possible. I think I have shown that it can lead to a change-direction from experience to society—if political understanding and experiential intricacy can be joined. Let me now apply these points to evaluate the current situation.

XIV. OLD AND NEW INSTITUTIONS

There is now a hint of a really new kind of form: situations so structured that they make space, make room for the process of intricate further structuring.[34]

The old institutions are recognizing intricate experiencing. Many businesses, churches, and schools are moving toward including—*and also demanding!*—the individual's "creativity." A continuum of change spreads before us, with different institutions at various stages. Some corporations, churches, and schools still try to make the old way work. Others, including giant corporations, now demand that individuals *use* their intricate experience. Every year more companies and institutions change over. Now they *require* their employees to exceed the handed-down definitions. But, of course, only in certain ways. People must be "creative" in some ways in some situations, while keeping silent in others, as the unchanged hierarchy demands.

The invitation to create is often romanticized. Individual participation is invited. More decisions are made by lower echelons. Individuals perform better when they are involved in making some decisions. Work quality improves when people can act on what they notice as they work. "Creativity training" is now common in all industries. The employees must improve on their instructions. Meanwhile computers permanently record all their moves—a vastly heightened kind of external control.

The changes do not all remain within old bounds. It is simplistic to see only a misuse of intricacy to support a fundamentally unchanged structure. On the other hand, it must be understand that such experience does not automatically change the structure. There is neither just freeing nor just more control. *We must question and study the specifics, and especially the many kinds of experiential processes.*

Students must tell ideas of their own in class. Mere repetition is not acceptable. But the ideas must be appropriate. Is this freedom or control?

Sexuality is no longer just an official pattern. Each person must perceive and articulate feelings and needs more finely, so that sexual dissatisfactions and needs can be "worked out." Mere compliance is not acceptable from women, nor "slam, bam, thank you ma'am" from men. It brings a gamut of differences.

Women are now allowed—but also required—to have their own interests, and to act in the world. It gives some women the world. For others it means only that they *have* to work to earn enough for the family at the lowered standard of living. Or, they may feel there is something wrong with them if they devote themselves to the family: "Shame on me. My family is my life. I don't have my own thing." Is it a new freedom or a new compulsion? *The difference lies in the different manners of process.* For many women today freedom is their rejection of work opportunities in favor of their bodily desire to stay home with their children, or to let the baby sleep in bed with them, defying the demand to abandon their children.

What is control and what is freedom can be decided only from the manner of the process. Freedom is not the imposition of new roles instead of old ones. Rather, the increasing skill and differentiation of psychological processes is unquestionably a development of the human being. As was the case with mass literacy, it can be used for more control but is certain to develop people in other ways.

In 1968, the old forms were called "empty," but what would *not* be empty could not then be said. Today we speak of "empty forms" wherever something is still done as if there were no experiential intricacy. The "alternative institutions" of 1968 failed, partly because people could not get along with each other. They were willing to share everything, both property and feelings. But relations became intractably difficult. New social forms turned out to be impossible without inward and interactional sophistication. Skills in these regards were badly lacking. Precisely these skills are now developing.

Thirty million people belong to some new network or training program—in fact, new educational institutions. These institutions and experiments at the heart of the Awareness Movement arose *from* intricate experience and carry it forward at least as much as they impose on it. What they offer is not just imposed on experience. There is first the discovery of intricate experience. There are then also many process-differences, among them the ones I described in my excerpts. The current development is much more specific and different than an imposed order.

XV. CONCLUSION

After a long lapse in the history of philosophy, the non-metaphysical order of the body and language is returning to consideration. In philosophy it is still spoken of only negatively, as what *dis*organizes a supposed system of rules, roles, values, commonalities, similarities—generalities. Language had been explained as generalities, but how it works is not determined just by them. Generalities were also thought to be imposed on the human body as its only order. Indeed, all nature was thought to be just these.

The order of the body and language is more intricate, and not a formed order. It can be studied in transitions, the steps of various processes. It is best said in the more intricately working words. Rejecting metaphysical generalities does not close further study. It opens the study of intricacy.

Experiential intricacy can lead to new theoretical concepts. The uses of theory and logical consistency are not lost. But each such use always *also* enables other moves, in and from intricacy.

No one doubts that simpler generalities are implicit in language and situations, but they do not alone determine how they function and change. The greater intricacy of the body, language, and situations determines each time what concepts mean. It lets words work in new ways that are more intricate and precise than any preexisting forms.

Experiential and situational intricacy is not derived from generalities or subsumed *under* the generalities. They are not the order of language, and never were. Language has the order of experiential intricacy.

In the current Awareness Movement people find an experiential intricacy that was rarely had by the earlier, traditional type of person. It is new; neither primitive nor ordered only by prevailing ego-forms.

The so-called "self" also has the order of body and language. It is open for experiential steps that need not stay in a formed order. Many processes show the order, greater than any pattern, even an intricate one.

We are in the midst of a great development of persons and situations. The repressed, and the primitive, turn out to be more than had been thought, but experiential intricacy is new, not primitive. Its language can be spoken and can speak about itself. How the body functions in the languaging has to be considered. To call it "narcissism" exactly misses what is happening: Processes of new intricacy are moving beyond the "reality" assumed in the concepts of "ego" and "narcissism."

The term "narcissism" is reactionary. Its use denigrates the current social change, and opposes the far greater social change which experiential intricacy now implies—and may bring about.

NOTES

1. New York Times, 29 Nov. 1985.
2. *Telos* 44 (Summer 1980); *Telos* 59 (Spring 1984).
3. J. Casanova, "The Politics of Religious Revival," *Telos* 59 (Spring 1984).
4. Ibid.
5. Interview with Rabinow in Dreyfus and Rabinow, *Michel Foucault: Beyond Structuralism and Hermeneutics* (Chicago: University of Chicago Press, 1984), 216.
6. M. Foucault, "Nietzsche, Genealogy, History," in D. F. Bouchard, ed. *Language, Counter-Memory, Practice: Selected Essays* (Ithaca: Cornell University Press, 1977), 148.
7. H. Marcuse, *Eros and Civilization* (Boston: Beacon Press, 1974), 238–39.
8. Ibid., 240.
9. Ibid., 245.
10. Ibid., 274.
11. Ibid., 109.
12. H. Marcuse, *Counter-Revolution and Revolt.* (Boston: Beacon Press, 1972).
13. G. Deleuze and F. Guattari, *Anti-Oedipus: Capitalism and Schizophrenia* (Minneapolis: University of Minnesota Press, 1983).
14. S. Freud, *Outline of Psychoanalysis* (New York: Norton, 1949), 108.
15. Ibid., 109
16. S. Freud, *The Problem of Anxiety* (New York: Norton, 1936), 24.
17. S. Freud, *Outline of Psychoanalysis,* 108–10.
18. Ibid.

19. S. Freud, *Group Psychology and the Analysis of the Ego* (New York: Liveright, 1949), 2.

20. K. Marx, *Das Kapital,* vol. 1 (Frankfurt: Ullstein, 1969), 324.

21. H. Kohut, *The Analysis of the Self* (New York: International Universities Press, 1971), 16–23.

22. Fine and Fine, "The Mathematician as a Healthy Narcissist," in N. M. Coleman, ed., *The Narcissistic Condition* (New York: Human Sciences Press, 1979)

23. A. Giddens, *The Constitution of Society* (Berkeley: University of California Press, 1984).

24. J. Loevinger and R. Wessler, *Measuring Ego-Development* (San Francisco: Jossey-Bass, 1970).

25. E. Kris, "On Pre-conscious Mental Process," *Psychoanalytic Quarterly* 19 (1950): 540–60.

26. E. T. Gendlin, *Focusing* (New York: Bantam Books, 1981).

27. Ibid.

28. M. N. Hendricks, "Experiencing Level as a Therapeutic Variable," *Person-Centered Review* 1, no. 2 (May 1986): 141–62.

29. E. T. Gendlin, "A Theory of Personality Change," in J. Hart and T. Tomlinson, eds., *New Directions in Client-Centered Therapy* (Boston: Houghton-Mifflin, 1970); E. T. Gendlin, "Experiential Phenomenology," in M. Natanson, ed., *Phenomenology and the Social Sciences* (Evanston, Ill.: Northwestern University Press, 1973); E. T. Gendlin, "What Comes after Traditional Psychotherapy Research?," *American Psychologist* 41, no. 2 (February 1986); M. H. Klein, P. Mathieu-Coughlan and D. J. Kiesler, "The Experiencing Scales," in W. P. Pinsof and L. S. Greenberg, eds., *The Psychotherapeutic Process: A Research Handbook* (New York: Guilford, 1985).

30. E. T. Gendlin, *Experiencing and the Creation of Meaning* (New York: The Free Press, 1962); E. T. Gendlin, *Let Your Body Interpret Your Dreams* (Wilmette, Ill.: Chiron/Open Court, 1986).

31. M. H. Bickhard, *Cognition, Convention, and Communication* (New York: Praeger, 1980).

32. Z. F. Boukydes, "A Theory of Empathic Relations between Parents and Infants," *Focusing Folio* 4, no. 1 (1985): 3–28; M. P. Coyle "An Experiential Perspective on the Mother-Infant Relationship: The First Eight Months" (Ph.D. diss., Illinois School of Professional Psychology, 1986).

33. M. N. Hendricks, "Experiencing Level as a Therapeutic Variable," 141–62.

34. E. T. Gendlin, "Dwelling," in R. C. Scharff, ed., *Proceedings* of the Heidegger Conference, University of New Hampshire, 1983; E. T. Gendlin, "Some Notes on the Self," *Focusing Folio* 4, no. 4 (1985) 137–51; E. T. Gendlin, "Process Ethics and the Political Question," in A. Tymieniecka, ed., *Analecta Husserliana,* vol. 20 (Dordrecht: Reidel, 1986).

CHAPTER 9
SCHIZOPHRENIA AND METAPHYSICS: ANALYZING THE DSM–III

IRENE E. HARVEY

INTRODUCTION

In his report to the Congress of Rome in 1953, Jacques Lacan criticized the practice of psychoanalysis in the United States for its tendency towards simply adapting the individual to the social environment and hence becoming a type of "human engineering." As he said:

> In any case it appears incontestable that the conception of psychoanalysis in the U.S. has inclined towards the adaptation of the individual to the social environment, towards the quest for behavior patterns, and towards all the objectification implied in the notion of 'human relations.' And the indigenous term 'human engineering' strongly implies a privileged position of exclusion in relation to the human object.[1]

This criticism can equally well be applied, I suggest, to the current practice of psychiatry in the United States. The DSM–III (Diagnostic and Statistical Manual)[2] is the most recent attempt to standardize this practice and to formalize its terminology and classification of pathological symptoms and diagnoses.

This Manual reads as follows in its introductory pages under the heading of "Descriptive Approach":

> This approach can be said to be 'descriptive' in that the *definitions of the disorders* generally consist of *descriptions of the clinical features* of the disorders. These features are described at the *lowest order of inference necessary to describe* the characteristic features of the disorder. Frequently the order of inference is relatively low, and the characteristic features consist of *easily identifiable behavioral signs or symptoms,* such as disorientation, mood disturbance, or psychomotor agitation. (My emphasis)[3]

In all fairness to the task force that produced this manual, the next sentence following our quote admits to the necessity of "much higher orders of inference" when it comes to "Personality Disorders." My intention here is to analyze this orientation, which entails clinical observation on the one hand, and simple or "low level inference" descriptions of those observations on the other. This basically two-step process leads to a "reliable set" of criteria for diagnosis or what is called symptomatology. My task here in this analysis will be to consider one example of such "symptomatology" as outlined in the DSM–III in all its particularities of clinical observation and description and to show that: (1) there is a concept of normality presupposed in the description of symptoms; (2) there are philosophical schemas being applied to the "data" of clinical observation that are used seemingly unbeknown to the observers and that are questionable as foundations for the practice of analysis and its diagnostic procedures; and (3) the symptomatology imposes forms of the proper, correct and normal that do not cohere, do not synthesize, and entail a double bind for the patient/analysand, should the latter attempt to meet such demands and not be considered pathological or mentally "disordered."

I will consider here the symptomatology of schizophrenia and specifically the disturbances of the "form and content of thinking" that are said to characterize this pathology. My choice of this particular disorder is governed by Freud's occasional but revealing asides—marginal notes, one might call them—which often direct the reader to a parallel between philosophy and schizophrenia, particularly of the paranoid type.[4] His tone in these remarks will be shown by our analysis to be somewhat paradoxical, since there is evidently no such thing as philosophy in general. (Freud no doubt realized this despite his references to the same; he spoke of the multiple types of systems this field offered with no criterion to help one decide which to adopt.)[5] Yet there is a relatively unified tradition of metaphysics. This tradition, from Plato to Nietzsche (as Heidegger understood it)[6] or from Plato to Husserl, as Derrida[7] delimited it, characterizes

Being as presence, truth as Logos, time as a line, and is determined by an oppositional set of concepts whose closure is exemplified by Hegel's absolute system. I shall return to this notion of metaphysics, but for now I wish to point out that "schizophrenia," as "described" in the DSM–III, indicates a radical divergence from this tradition and is parallel to what Derrida has called its deconstruction. Far from being parallel to philosophy, as Freud claimed, the schizophrenic's form and content of thinking help to reveal the limits of that very tradition. Freud would no doubt have said that none of this can be shown empirically, but my point here is that what Freud (and a fortiori the practitioners of psychiatry, as made evident by the DSM–III) presupposed, in order to formulate his clinical hypotheses, is not derived from empirical observations, but from the unexamined tradition of metaphysics. Freud's own references to the possible relations of psychoanalysis and philosophy fall generally into two camps: on the one hand, philosophy has nothing to offer psychoanalysis and should be kept away from the clinical domain; on the other hand, psychoanalysis can do much to explain the "striking individuality" of the "men" who have developed "philosophical theories and systems." "In no other science does the personality of the scientific worker play anything like so large a part as in philosophy," Freud wrote. Further, "Psychoanalysis can indicate the subjective and individual motives behind philosophical theories which have ostensibly sprung from impartial logical work."[8] Although I do not disagree with Freud on these points, my claim here is that there is a philosophical blind spot—perhaps many—in the heart of analytic and psychiatric practice, in particular with respect to their symptomatology and diagnostic procedures.

A final note of caution or qualification, indeed disqualification, is perhaps warranted here since it may appear that I am criticizing from a philosophical and therefore nonclinical standpoint something that designates its own jurisdictional limits within the clinical situation and not the speculative. The DSM–III itself states in its final introductory pages, under the heading of "Cautions":

> The purpose of the DSM–III is to provide *clear descriptions of diagnostic categories* in order to *enable clinicians* and investigators to diagnose, to communicate about, study, and treat various mental disorders. *The use of this manual for non-clinical purposes,* such as determination of legal responsibility, competency or insanity, or justification for third-party payment, must be critically examined in each instance within the appropriate context. (My emphasis)[9]

In short, the frame of reference intended here is clinical, diagnostic and therapeutic. This assumption itself will be questioned in the following analysis, and I wish to point out that such framing of the limits is (a) not self-evident, (b) not so simple, and (c) not independent of "nonclinical," "nondiagnostic," and "nontherapeutic" issues, but rather that the assumptions made in this paragraph quoted above (concerning context, description, usage, intentionality, framing, limits, appropriateness) are themselves questionable in any context other than the simple pragmatics that Lacan's statement, quoted above, warns us against.

The symptomatology of schizophrenia in the DSM–III begins with a very general five-point description of the basic features of this disorder. The reader is informed in advance that both "Affective Disorders" and "Organic Mental Disorders" are not to be included in the category that this manual will define as "Schizophrenic Disorders." These five essential and general characteristics include the following: (1) "the presence of certain psychotic features during the active phase of the illness"; (2) "symptoms involving multiple psychological processes"; (3) "deterioration from a previous level of functioning"; (4) "onset before age 45"; and (5) "a duration of at least six months." Further, the manual insists that "at some phase of the illness, schizophrenia *always* involves delusions, hallucinations, or certain disturbances in the form of thought."[10] Our specific concern here is with these "disturbances in the form of thought" and their implied corrollary—undisturbed form(s) of thought.

Under the heading of elaboration, the manual tells us in greater detail what each of these five points signifies in analytic observation or clinical practice. In short, the ambiguities of the five points are systematically reduced in what follows. For instance, "deterioration" means that "concerning an earlier phase of the illness [one's behavior has deteriorated] in areas such as work, social relations, and self-care." Further, "family and friends often observe that the person is 'not the same'." The term "multiple psychological processes" used in part two above is amplified in the following way to include these dimensions:

(a) content and form of thought
(b) perception
(c) affect
(d) sense of self
(e) volition

(f) relation to external world
(g) psychomotor behavior[11]

The DSM–III next gives its reader the specific details, meanings or exemplifications of each of these seven categories. One should notice that the organization of the symptomatology here follows a hierarchical principle for science developed by Aristotle.[12] That is, it is a tree-like system of concepts moving from a general to ever-increasing specificity as one moves down the hierarchy. For instance:

TREE

tree$_1$	tree$_2$	tree$_3$	tree$_4$	tree$_n$
t_1 t_2 t_3 t_4	r_1 r_2 r_3	e_1 e_2 e_3	e_5 e_6 e_7	t_5 t_6

In the case of Schizophrenia, therefore, we find the same structure laid out in the manual verbally rather than schematically. The schema would appear as follows, however, had it been drawn:

SCHIZOPHRENIA

type$_1$	type$_2$	type$_3$	type$_4$	type$_n$
t_1 t_2 t_3	y_1 y_2 y_3	p_1 p_2 p_3	e_1 e_2 e_3	t_4 t_5 t_6

In this manner the concept of "schizophrenia" is articulated from within, levels of organizational specificity are sustained, and the most crucial details are situated in relation to all other elements in the concept. What is described there is a system—articulated from within and closed with respect to what it excludes or leaves outside. The DSM–III, true to this representational framework it uses (knowingly or not), does admit to having not addressed the issue of etiology. The origins, development and onset of the "disorders" are not the subject matter here. Hence, its pure "descriptions" have the appearance and the intention of being purely *synchronic, atemporal structures* that give the clinician a picture—indeed a photograph or a still life—of the illness. I suggest that the Aristotelian frame of reference used within the organization of the symptomatology is no accident here; and indeed there will be other Aristotelian foundations revealed within the DSM–III's notions of "disordered thinking" and its presuppositions about nondisordered or correct thinking procedures. Let us now turn to what the manual describes in subsection (a) "content and form of thought" of section (ii), elaboration of the concept and category in general, "schizophrenic disorders."[13]

The manual distinguishes between form and content of thought, but it does not discuss the basis for such a distinction. This is evidently presupposed as "self-evident." It is no accident, however, that "form and content" is a crucial distinction for Aristotle and for Plato before him. Forms were eternal for Plato, and content was the mere mental, particular and passing materialization and temporalization of those Forms.[14] Forms are essential; content is, in its specificity, accidental. The form of a thing, for Aristotle, also had the essential or eternal dimension within itself and the content had the mere temporal "stuff" of that form.[15] None of this is discussed by the DSM–III manual, of course, and none of this is simply empirical data, pure description in clinical observation; yet the distinction used—between form and content—is drawn from such classical sources. My point here is not simply to link the discourse used by the DSM–III to classical philosophy but to show that "pure description" at an empirical clinical level is simply not possible, and that whether or not one wishes it, intends it, desires it, philosophical (indeed speculative and sometimes transcendental) elements are used and presupposed not only in "clinical observation" itself but also in the DSM–III descriptions themselves.

Under "content of thought" one finds the following list of symptomatology in the manual: (1) "delusions that are often multiple, fragmented or bizarre *(patently absurd, with no possible basis in fact);* (2) persecutory delusions—i.e. others spying on me, spreading false rumors, planning harm; (3) delusions of reference–events or objects in the world are given particular and unusual significance—of a negative nature." (My emphasis)[16] Typical kinds of delusions are listed in addition, in order presumably to make the discussion less abstract and more concrete, less conceptual, more descriptive, and indeed less philosophical and more clinical (if one can still sustain such a distinction). Some of these kinds (species) of (the genus) "delusions" include:

(a) the belief or experience that one's thoughts, as they occur, are broadcast from one's head to the external world so that others can hear them (thought broadcasting);
(b) that thoughts that are *not one's own* are inserted into one's mind (thought insertion);
(c) that thoughts have been *removed* from one's head (thought withdrawal);
(d) that one's feelings, impulses, thoughts or actions are *not one's own* but are imposed by some external force. (My emphasis)[17]

Let us consider these "delusions" (or more precisely, these *descriptions* of delusions) in terms of what is said and, more importantly, what is *not* said but is presupposed. First, it should be noted that the term *delusion* is never defined, although it is exemplified. Indeed, "kinds of delusions that are common" are given to us in some detail, each with its apparent diagnostic label. Since the manual does not ask the question but presupposes a particular understanding—never formulated or thematized—let us begin with the question: what is a delusion? Given what has been said above, it must involve at least one of the following: (1) patent absurdity; (2) objects given particular or unusual significance; (3) illusory persecution. But what is "patently" absurd? Is this a type of absurdity or is this what makes absurdity absurd? Or, more precisely, is the patent on absurdity that it is *patently* absurd? That is, is the essence of absurdity to be patent, blatant or obvious? If this is so, as seems to be implied by the terminology used above, then what is absurd is so "self-evidently" or "obviously." Now, what creates the possibility of the self-evident or the obvious? That cats have nine lives is "patently absurd" for some and "patently obvious" for others. Who and what decides what is absurd? Consider Husserl's example of a nonsensical statement (patently absurd, perhaps): "green is or."[18] As Derrida has astutely demonstrated, this phrase is no longer nonsense once it is cited as an instance, or example, of nonsense.[19] That is, in itself, the collection of words is neither nonsense nor meaningful, but is prior to or withheld from such a distinction. Usage and context are the keys here, as in so many other instances of diagnostic possibilities. In abstraction, what is patently absurd cannot be decided. Indeed, maybe this was why Freud originally referred to the apparent similarity between the philosopher and the schizophrenic: for both, the abstract is taken for the concrete.[20] However, the clinician does not diagnose absurdity; this is presupposed, preunderstood, and never analyzed as such. It is part of the "normal" repertoire of the nonschizophrenic, by definition. Parenthetically, however, the manual continues to term "patent absurdity" that which "has no possible basis in fact." This, too, is in itself certainly neither identical to nor synonymous with the absurd, or else absurdity can no longer be considered part of the symptomatology of the "schizophrenically disordered"—lest many more normals be diagnosed as "schizophrenic."

The point here is that literature, for instance, can be understood as having "no possible basis in fact." "Fairy tales," and indeed Santa Claus, certainly have "no possible basis in fact"; yet they are nonetheless real, part of a particular *Weltanschauung* (contextualized absurdity, perhaps), and hence are not said to be a schizophrenic's delusion. Yet perhaps, if one made up one's own version of Santa Claus, saw him in the summertime climbing trees in Central Park, one might then be able without equivocation to say that this is a schizophrenic delusion, wherein one is seeking for a patent absurdity that has no basis in fact. Our point here, however, is to understand the contextually and philosophically loaded terms that are used in such descriptions and to attempt to document in precise terms why they are not self-evident or patent. Indeed, the patent is limited in time, space, culture, and metaphysics, as we shall see.

The particularity of significance given to objects is also at the very least questionable in terms of its diagnostic value. Who does not endow objects in his world with particular and unusual significance? Who does not establish connotations, memorabilia and affective relations of an idiosyncratic nature with "objects" in the world? This is my favorite and special pen, the writer says; this is my lucky cap, the baseball player says; this is not my day or this is my unlucky table, the gambler says, after having lost his fortune. Are such activities abnormal? Are such activities signs of delusions—attributing particular and unusual significance to events or objects in the world? The crucial term here in the symptomatological system of concepts is "unusual." Once again, as with "patent" absurdity, we have brought in an implicit standard or standardizing normativity that typifies what Lacan, in our opening quote, was concerned with in American psychoanalysis: namely, the construction or reconstruction of the individual to fit into a society that demands conformity, mass identification, and social stereotyping. It is in terms such as *unusual*, *peculiar*, and its obverse, *patent,* that such hidden agendas of analysis make their appearance—even, or perhaps especially, in the manual.

Before we leave the category of "delusions," there is one other significant and questionable element we must address here. This is the notion of "one's own" thoughts, feelings, impulses and actions. As opposed to the schizophrenic, the implied notion of normality here includes the following: (1) that one's own thoughts stay within one's own head (and are not broadcast to others so that they can hear them); (2) that *only* one's own thoughts are to be found in one's own head, or at least that thoughts that are not one's own are not inserted into one's mind; (3) that thoughts are not removed from one's head; and (4) that one's thoughts, feelings, impulses or actions are in one's own head and not imposed by some external force. We need not go to an extreme and take as our example the world that Orwell depicted—nor, for that matter, Russia or contemporary Poland—when we consider the question of the meaning of "one's own" in such a "normal" drama. First, what is "one's own?" What is the "ownness" of one's self? What is my very own, as we say outside the clinic? More specifically, what is my very own thought? It would seem that one's own thoughts are one's own as opposed to being someone else's or as opposed to being forced (imposed) upon one "from the outside."

We should perhaps restrain ourselves from sociological reflections at this juncture; but it is rather well-documented that one's own thoughts are an effect, a product and a result of the society in which one lives—not in the sense of some metaphysical determinism, but in terms of the constraints on possibilities for living. If I am thinking about what I wish to eat for lunch, in New Orleans, the possibilities may well include crayfish, oysters and red beans or gumbo soup. If I am a Laplander living near the fjords of Norway, and I am considering what to eat for lunch, such ideas and thoughts would evidently be "patently absurd," and if I had them, as a Lap, one might be tempted to conclude that they are not my own, but imposed. Indeed I, as the subject in question, might be tempted to think this. The point is that what is properly "my own" in each case—whether in New Orleans or in Lapland—is a standardized, culturally and socially conditioned "ownness" that I either accept or reject. The irony is that what would most be "my own" would be essentially *other than mine* in either case.

It is not my intention, however, to argue for the cultural relativity of psychoanalysis; nor am I concerned to mark its judgments as sociologically dependent. These analyses and objections have long since been made, although the DSM–III makes no mention of them.[21] My aim is rather to demonstrate, by way of an *argumentum ad absurdum,* that the descriptions used here are "self-evident" only within a particular horizon of understanding—indeed, a particular type of normalization, standardization, or socialization. One might even call it "prejudice," to use Gadamer's sense of the term.[22] By "prejudice," however, I mean a larger category than irrational preference. Rather, we might call it the presuppositions of a metaphysical tradition that began with Plato and Aristotle. With respect to our particular issue at hand, I want to argue that one's ownness and one's self-understanding, presupposing as they do, a sense of having *one's own* thoughts, feelings, impulses and actions, are in themselves perhaps the greatest metaphysically founded delusion of our time. The Cartesian *Cogito,* with its self-certainty, lurks within such a notion and implies the effacement of real connections between the subject (here described by inversion as being in possession of itself) and other subjects (or intersubjectivity); thus, it also occludes the social, political, and historical context and the *Weltanschauung* in which one lives and thinks.[23] Indeed, the Western tradition of metaphysics, which animates not only our language but also the "form and content" of our thoughts, feelings, actions and impulses, is very much in evidence in this symptomatology.

Derrida has outlined a deconstruction of this *ownness (Eigentlichkeit,* the proper, *le propre*) in *Of Grammatology;* he has shown in dramatic detail that what one thinks of normally as "one's own" is radically decentered and displaced from such a capture by the subjective agent.[24] The truth of the ownness is, first, that it is itself a delusion, a systematic metaphysical prejudice; and second, that one who realizes that his thoughts are indeed not his own (simply) is recognizing the often unconscious but nonetheless actual interconnectedness of the subject and his or her traditions. Lacan has also attempted to show that, after Freud (although notably not in the United States, where the DSM–III is authoritative), the Cartesian *cogito,* including its sense of itself, is no longer tenable.[25] The truth of the self is in fact that it does *not* govern itself, in fact that it *does* have thoughts, impulses, actions and feelings that are not only not always conscious, but are in no way one's *own;* that in fact, intention, purpose, and the theories of the subject based on self-certainty can no longer be seen as guidelines, fundamental grounds, or as normative, but rather must be understood as effects, products, and results, and not as origins. From the DSM–III one might well conclude that since this sense of the subject not having its own thoughts characterizes schizophrenia, it would be the clinician's task to restore this sense of self—the Cartesian one—so that the subject would in the end believe that his thoughts were his *own.* What we have here is an adherence by the most modern clinical establishment to a seventeenth-century notion of what the self and its sense of itself ought to be. Far from mere description, then, we have a prescription embedded within the clinical "observations" and empirical data. Indeed, beyond this we have a cultural, historical, and more significantly, a metaphysical myth that animates the direction of the diagnosis, treatment and cure of the schizophrenic.

Returning to the manual, and more specifically, to the category of "content of thought," one reads the following additional descriptive information: (1) "*overvalued* ideas may occur" or (2) "*markedly illogical* thinking (i.e. thinking that contains *clear internal contradictions* or in which conclusions are reached that are *clearly erroneous,* given the initial premises." (My emphasis)[26]

Presumably an "overvalued idea" that may occur in the schizophrenic disorder is "over" with respect to what the norm designates as appropriate. This symptom would seem to be consistent with that mentioned earlier, wherein some object or event is given "particular and unusual significance" with respect to an implied but unstated norm as well. How can an idea, however, be *overvalued,* surcharged, taxed or inflated affectively? This question is not addressed, nor is the issue clarified with respect to precisely what an idea would be if it were overly valued. The manual assumes it is possible to attribute to the idea a norm, a balance of the right amount of value—not too much and not too little. But the problem is, how can the same idea have the same value (the correct value, the appropriate and nonextreme valuation) given to it for different persons and different situations? For instance, the idea of "catching the next streetcar" may well be a mere convenience for the tourist who could equally well walk a few blocks or wait for the next one, but it would with good reason be of great importance and urgency for the person about to be late for work for the third day in a row. The idea of "catching the streetcar" then has no appropriate coefficient of value that could be rightly attached to it. Even if one reduces the differences in the example to two people, both of whom are about to be late for work for the third day in a row, there is still a reasonable possibility that the value of that idea will be very different for them. My point here is that the clinician's diagnosis that "overvalued ideas may occur" is in no respect merely a matter of observation and description. "Overvalued" is a judgment that requires a standard which, I suggest, is not only not formulated or made explicit in the manual, but is not possible to formulate a priori. Human life and emotions are not that calculable except in terms, as Lacan among others has pointed out, of "human engineering."

The last symptom under "content of thought" entails the idea of "markedly illogical thinking," which the clinician is said to be able to observe. The clarification given for this "illogicality" is as follows: "thinking that contains clear internal contradictions or in which conclusions are reached that are clearly erroneous, given the initial premises."[27]

The clinician's vision of the symptoms involves a more serious and questionable assumption, although a Cartesian criterion has been invoked for authorization. The "clear" is "the evident" or "the patently obvious," which we have discussed and criticized earlier. The "clarity" of a vision is a testament, therefore, neither to the truth of that vision nor to its objectivity. Rather, the converse is more accurate. Clarity of vision is a result of particular assumptions and presuppositions that, though effaced from the consciousness of the "seer," play a performative and constitutive role in "what" is (to be) seen. The crucial assumption in the view that "markedly illogical thinking" is to be treated as a symptom involves its violation of a fundamental Aristotelian law called the Law of Noncontradiction.[28] This law, I might add, originally had the purpose and function of sorting out for the philosopher which statements, claims and judgments could be said to have the possibility of truth and which, in fact, were structurally erroneous. Indeed, our manual uses the same frame of reference to indicate that "markedly illogical thinking" violates syllogistic structures of good argumentation, or, as the manual states, "the conclusions reached . . . are clearly erroneous given the initial premises." This raises some questions concerning the omnijurisdiction not only of Aristotle's law but also of the logocentric structure of thinking demanded of the "nonschizophrenic." Surely, all thought need not and in fact does not adhere to the law of noncontradiction. Surely, truth is not always the ultimate value in discourse, communication or thinking. Surely, one can think in "markedly illogical" ways and not have the symptoms of schizophrenia. For example, reveries, literary and artistic endeavors, creativity, and most conversations have little to do with the law of noncontradiction. I suggest, then, not only that this symptomatology is questionable but also that its corollary, the demand for logocentric (truth oriented), syllogistic, logical, and noncontradictory "thinking," is a prejudice adopted naively from Aristotle and the tradition of Western metaphysics, which, to be sure, makes the same demands on thought.

It is not simply a matter here of pointing out the Aristotelian biases of the manual, although this is also of some significance, but rather of indicating that "normality" is not simply Aristotelian in thought structures nor Cartesian in subject structure. Furthermore, the fact that these are the "hidden" dictates of the "descriptions" outlined in the DSM–III is not an innocent or chance connection. "Normality" has its history just as madness does, and it is a result or a product, not a pure natural origin that might fall into madness—or, in this case, into schizophrenia. If "normal" or markedly logical thinking were to be enforced as the standard (and, after all, we know of manuals that do standardize clinical practice and tell the clinical eye what "symptoms" to look for in the patient and how to classify them as "observable"), then our society, as represented by its clinical practitioners, would indeed be systematically destroying the literary, creative, imaginative, and nonlogical, nonmeans/end, non-techné-dominated thinking patterns of its members.

We are still orienting ourselves according to a norm coming from Aristotle; even now, this norm usurps all domains of thought. Thus, we live in a time marked by what Heidegger termed the end of philosophy and the predominance of technorational, scientific, calculative, indeed logical structures characteristic of the mid to late twentieth century.[29] The persistence of the Aristotelian norm is documented in the manual, if we look to its presuppositions in the formulation of schizophrenic symptomatology.

So far, we have dealt only with the "content of thought" as it is outlined in the DSM–III for the symptomatology of schizophrenia. It is now time to consider the "form of thought." One should note, however, that the latter notion of "markedly illogical thinking" seems to be particularly concerned with the structure of that thinking, not its "content" as such. Hence the issue revolves around the relation of the premises to the conclusions and particular violations the schizophrenic is said to make in attempting (supposedly) to organize his thoughts in this manner. This would seem to indicate a formal quality, and not one of content, although the manual suggests the reverse.

With respect to "form" the manual states that "loosening of associations" is a crucial element in the schizophrenic's thought patterns. For instance:

> The most common example of this [disturbances in the form of thought] is *loosening of associations,* in which *ideas shift from one subject to another completely unrelated or obliquely related subject* without the speaker showing any awareness that the topics are unconnected. *Statements that lack a meaningful relationship* may be juxtaposed, or the individual may shift idiosyncratically from one frame of reference to another. When *loosening of associations* is severe, *incoherence* may occur, that is, speech may become *incomprehensible.*[30] (My emphasis)

There are some interesting prescriptions invoked once again in this "description" of symptoms. First, let us consider the idea of subjects being "completely unrelated" or "obliquely related" to each other. Which subjects in themselves fit within either of these categories? Is the idea of a baseball park completely unrelated to a funeral? a wedding? a war? a parade? Which two ideas are more closely related or most distantly related than others? How can one tell? My point is that ideas themselves are not more or less related to each other; ideas or "subjects" (the term used in the manual) can all equally well be interrelated at various levels of intimacy and distance. The ideas of a cup and coffee beans are not in themselves related to each other. Rather, due to our particular cultural, social, historical penchant for brewing those beans to make a black drink we usually pour into a cup, the ideas "cup" and "coffee beans" have been related. Hence, the "completely unrelated" ideas or subjects that the clinician claims to be able to see in the schizophrenic are ideas that our particular traditions, culture, social standards, and so on, do not happen to relate. That is to say, the schizophrenic makes unusual and particular connections; but it is not a question of loosening associations—unless one is reduced to a one-word utterance, and even this is not so simply placed in such a category. Once again, the unusual and the particular (idiosyncratic) elements appear to be those that are in fact condemning the would-be schizophrenic. This is also perhaps the rationale behind Freud's own wariness of philosophers who do "the same thing"—make unusual and particular connections of ideas or connect what must appear to the layman as ideas with no or only oblique relations to one another.

The manual also indicates that these statements (of the schizophrenic) that "lack a meaningful relationship may be juxtaposed." This leads to incoherence or even incomprehensibility. Now, if the issue of subjects in themselves as essentially connected has been problematized, it should be equally clear that statements themselves do not either have or not have "meaningful relationships." This sounds distinctly anthropomorphic, and it is worthy of note that Nietzsche once defined truth as a "mobile army of metaphors, metonyms, and anthropomorphisms."[31] The main issue here, however, concerns the connection between coherence and comprehension; thus, indeed, it is intelligibility that is actually at stake. The schizophrenic's speech is supposedly unintelligible, since he makes unusual (idiosyncratic) connections or (from the normal standpoint) juxtaposes things/subjects that "lack a meaningful relationship"; he thus loses the clinician or the auditor in the bargain. In short, the schizophrenic's speech indicates a "loosening of associations" with reality (ours) and the creation of his own other world in which he lives, has delusions, and speaks—sometimes to himself and sometimes to the delusional, fictitious characters who inhabit that other world. I am not denying the reality of such symptoms, cases or tragedies of human life, when they are truly that; but I do insist that the symptomatology itself is a loose connection to this actual world of the schizophrenic, and further, that the symptomatology is loosely connected to that from which it claims to dissociate itself.

That incoherence is brought together with its "logical conclusion"—incomprehensibility—involves a number of complex assumptions concerning the nature of language, intentionality, thought, intelligibility, and communication. What would it be for statements not to be juxtaposed, but rather to cohere, and thus, in this frame of reference, be "comprehensible"? When are two statements not juxtaposed? Or better, when do two statements cohere? The hidden directive here is the term "logically," although it is not explicitly mentioned. Two statements, such as the "premises" and "conclusions" mentioned above in the manual, are appropriately connected—they cohere and are not merely juxtaposed—when one "follows" from the other. Once again, logocentrism forms the foundation, here, for normality—and indeed, for intelligibility.

The clinicians are in good company, whether or not they are aware of that, since Gadamer has stated that in hermeneutics, the study of interpretation and the understanding of texts, the criterion for a reading, indeed a good reading, is that all the parts of the text fit into a unified whole and all the pieces (the statements) cohere.[32] In short, the reader forms a Gestalt of the text as a whole—if it has been interpreted correctly. Now, if we adhere to such criteria even for an instant, we will appreciate that this model can equally well either support or condemn what the clinicians in the manual are describing. Either they are at fault in not being good interpreters of the "schizophrenic's" speech, or the "schizophrenic's" speech has violated the "laws" of comprehensibility, so that no one could piece it together or make sense out of it. No doubt clinicians would prefer the second possibility. However, the issue is more complex yet. More recent work in the study of textuality, notably that done by Jacques Derrida, has shown that Gadamerian hermeneutics involves a set of presuppositions that allow for a premature closure in textual interpretation, and that such assumptions are themselves questionable.[33] The coherence of a text is no longer the goal of interpretation and understanding; the reduction of multiplicity and diversity to unity is no longer considered a legitimate strategy; and the collapsing of levels of the text is no longer a viable method of enclosing a unified, coherent, logical message. Rather, texts are more complex and have a multiplicity of dimensions, the reduction of which is simply a prejudice based on logocentrism, indeed often on Aristotelian presuppositions. Any text entails juxtaposed levels, unintended aspects (beyond mere slips of the pen and tongue), hidden agendas, unthought and implicit but governing dimensions, and so on.

The "schizophrenic's" speech, then, is quite possibly an exemplar with respect to what in "normal" speech is effaced, or what the "normal" set of logical statements (whose conclusions follow without apparent contradictions from their premises) attempts to exclude, efface or bury. As Derrida has shown with his strategy of deconstruction, these elements are not lost, and the traces always remain to be unearthed and unravelled.

The manual continues, under the heading "form of schizophrenic thought," with the following: "There may be poverty of content of speech, in which speech is adequate in amount but conveys little information because it is vague, overly abstract or overly concrete, repetitious or stereotyped.[34] (My emphasis) Before we analyze this claim in detail we should consider a "loose connection" made in the manual here. The heading is "form of thought" and yet the description deals exclusively with speech. How does one move from *thoughts* to *speech* so readily? Is there an isomorphism between thought and speech? Evidently this is presupposed, since the terms are used synonymously. On what basis, however, can such a claim be substantiated? Once again, let us consider Aristotle. "Spoken words are symbols of mental experience and written words are the symbols of words spoken."[35] In addition, Aristotle claimed that thought and speech are externally related to each other, which paradoxically is what allows speech to represent thoughts completely and purely. Speech does not contaminate thought with its own forms; it is rather kept at a safe distance. (Is this juxtaposition?) Yet the mapping is perfect. It is thus not a question of isomorphism, but of a complete elasticity on the one hand, and an absolutely formal or constituted entity on the other. Speech represents thought without remainder in such a model; and it represents thoughts that are designed or intended to be spoken. There is no place for slippage here; the unintended is not said in Aristotle's model.

The manual's reliance on the Aristotelian model is called into question if we accept some of the more recent work on language, speech, and their relations to intention. This work has shown (a) that thought does not simply exist ready-made, in advance of its being said or written; (b) that language is constitutive for thought, and not its mere vehicle; and (c) that speech always says more, not the same and not less, than what is consciously thought.[36] Thus, at the very least, the usage in the manual makes an assumption of synonymy between its terms for the thinking of the schizophrenic and its terms for the speech of this thought that is highly questionable.

To return to the text at hand, we must address once again the term "overly," that quality of speech named "adequate"; the purpose imposed on speech that values it only as a medium for "conveying information"; and the problems associated with "repetition" and "stereotypical" speech. First, let us consider the value of conveying information. Is this the purpose of speech? Is this *always* the purpose of speech? Clearly not; yet the manual implies that this is indeed a central demand and presupposition of good and normal speech. To send information from one person to another—presumably. It is evident that speech often entails a performative purpose—to *do* something rather than to *say* something, for instance.[37] Yet this is not taken into account in the list of "symptoms" presented in the DSM–III. Speech is also very often used for the purpose of establishing or sustaining a relationship to someone, and not for the purpose of telling that person something or sending information as such. In short, we have Shannon and Weaver's model of communication at work in our manual, overshadowing all other ideas about the purpose and usage of speech.[38] A mechanical model for speech is imposed not only on the schizophrenic "abnormality" or disorder (an interesting metaphor as well), but also, by inversion, on the supposed sense of normality. Good, normal speech says something to someone about something, as Ricoeur has shown.[39] However, the other aspects of speech—those that are more affective, organizational and performative, for instance—are therein at least devalued, if not excluded, in favor of a logocentric and mechanical, rather than specifically human dimension.

"Adequacy" is an interesting choice of vocabulary. Good speech should be "adequate"—not too much and not too little—and should therefore convey neither too much nor too little information, but just the right, appropriate, balanced, medium amount. What assumptions are guiding such claims? Aristotle once again is in the background, this time with reference to his *Ethics*.[40] How did he obtain what is good, just, and true—indeed, the norm of the proper, the appropriate—by way of the mean? All extremes are vicious, he said, and virtue is the middle path. Not too much and not too little, but just the right amount. Our manual certainly adheres to this, but with little justification other than an age-old and indeed powerful prejudice. What is "adequacy"? How much is enough? How much is too little? Sometimes, whatever one says is not enough, and often, anything is too much. Who decides what is adequate? Evidently this too is a generalized standard that clinicians at least can simply observe, perceive and record. The issue here is indeed one of ethics: the imposition of standards of normality. As we shall see, the manual suggests that a schizophrenic feels not only that his thoughts, feelings, impulses and actions are not his own, but also that someone or something else is controlling these. This is evidently not a delusion, although earlier we found it classified in such a category. Now we find that the proper behavior, indeed "adequate" speech—not too much and not too little—is demanded of the schizophrenic in order for him to be considered normal (by implication) or at least to avoid being classified as a "schizophrenic." How can the manual reject "idiosyncratic connections" in speech, on the one hand, and *also* demand that one reject the idea that one is not totally in control of oneself? The manual demands tight, coherent connections of thoughts (which are essentially metaphysically structured thereby) and yet insists that one be one's *own* proper self. Furthermore, the manual insists that the normal person (at least the non-schizophrenic) should not disobey the law of non-contradiction; yet it seems that these very conflicting demands made by the manual themselves violate this same law.

The manual itself also has a category within the diagnostic symptomatology of schizophrenia that posits the *proper sense of self* of the "normal person." As it says: "The sense of self that gives the normal person a *feeling* of individuality, uniqueness, and self-direction is frequently disturbed. This is sometimes referred to as a loss of ego boundaries and is frequently manifested by extreme perplexity about one's own identity and the meaning of existence."[41] (My emphasis) The all-too-evident traditional philosophical focus on the questions of identity and the "meaning of existence" will not concern us here, since it would seem that the manual is not addressing the articulation and analysis of such issues (as philosophy aims to do), but focuses rather on the "extreme perplexity" with regard to them. However, the "normal" prescription does concern us, especially with reference to the earlier diagnostic categorizations for schizophrenia; in particular, those concerning: (1) the diagnosis of idiosyncratic connections/disconnections, made on the basis of an assumed separation between the "form" and the "content" of the "schizophrenic's" thought/speech; and (2) the "misguided notion that someone else, or something other than one's own self, is controlling one's thoughts, feelings, impulses, and/or actions." Hence, we have the "normal" designated as having a sense of self that gives one a feeling of individuality, uniqueness, and self-direction. The manual speaks of "feeling," rather than of a "knowledge" or an "idea," and this is revealing, especially since what one gives oneself to feel (as the manual puts it) are qualities of the personality that were abandoned, or at least condemned, as being typical characteristics within the diagnosis of "schizophrenia." More precisely, what is in evidence at this juncture is the belief that the normal person should feel that he is his own proper self—individual, unique and self-directed–and at the origin of his own proper activity: being in possession of oneself.

What is interesting about this is that what is called for is supposed to be a *feeling*. One should have these feelings, but they must in fact be *false*. More precisely, if one is *too* individualistic, unique, and self-directed, one is likely to fall within the symptomatology of schizophrenia; furthermore, if one feels that nothing is his *own proper self*—with respect to ideas, feelings, actions—and that all is controlled by "external forces," then too one is likely to fall into the symptomatology.

The norm here described is thus the "middle path" between too much ("overly") and too little individuality, uniqueness and self-direction. But it is impossible to designate the middle without setting down extremes and without affecting a quantitative linearization of our being-in-the-world as a self. Furthermore, this all revolves around the issue of one's feeling about oneself. Put in other terms, what this means is that the self-image is fundamentally an Aristotelian formula based on a continuum with two extremes. Aside from the issue of knowing how much is enough, appropriate and normal in this category (which is essentially a socio-political-economic and historical one), the self-image proposed here, the persona of the person or self, has no origin. From whence do such feelings arise, and how are they destroyed? The manual is not concerned with etiology, however; that is not its task. Yet the next sentence describes what the nonnormal sense of self feels like: "This is sometimes referred to as a loss of ego boundaries."[42] For the moment, let us ask what may appear as a most naive question: What *is* an "ego boundary"? A boundary separating/linking it to/from what or whom? We hardly need to invoke the name of Descartes, whose understanding of the self as "cogito" formulated precisely such distinctions. Indeed, the individual in this sense comes into existence in Western thinking with the work of Descartes. What we today would call "ego boundaries" were first drawn in the seventeenth-century—not before. What is described by the manual is not simply a self-enclosed ego, an individual, with a sense of his own uniqueness and self-direction, but a fundamentally ideological and metaphysical notion that has its own delusional consequences. Lacan was eager to point out that it is extremely difficult, if not impossible, to distinguish collective psychosis from what is called normality.[43] Derrida has suggested that Western metaphysics is a type, or perhaps *the* type, of "white mythology".[44] What the DSM–III points towards in its foundations, as well as in its explicit normative claims regarding "the proper sense of self," is the evidence in clinical practice for the very claims that many thinkers, Derrida and Lacan, for example, have made questionable in other contexts.

For both Lacan and Derrida, the ontology of the self must be radically decentered. The ideas of normality, of madness, of mythos as opposed to rationality, and of a self that would be identical to itself, have all been placed in question. The origin of the normality of normality is no doubt not simply a sociological, cultural, or historical one. Neither is it exclusively metaphysical. But it is all of these, and perhaps more besides. Thus, from our point of view, Lacan's dilemma concerning "collective psychosis" and Derrida's concerning the role of metaphysics, not only in textuality but also in everyday life, have been exemplified by the DSM–III. We need only to consider its attempts to secure a standardized symptomatology and a diagnostic system of interpretation based, as it says, on "neutral" clinical observation and mere "description." Let us return, now, to our more detailed analysis, bearing in mind that these other issues, as represented by Derrida and Lacan, are framing our interpretation.

A brief mention of the category of "volition" seems in order here. Following the "sense of self" category, the manual states:

> Nearly always, there is some disturbance in *self-initiated, goal-directed activity*, which may grossly impair work or other role functioning. This may take the form of inadequate interest or drive or inability to follow a course of action to its logical conclusion. Pronounced ambivalence regarding alternative courses of action can lead to near cessation of goal-directed activity. (My emphasis)[45]

Once again, we have the issues of self-initiation and the goal-directedness of one's actions brought into the portrait of normality, albeit more obliquely here. The interesting problem that is raised, however, concerns the goal of this goal-directed activity. It is no accident that "work" and one's "role functioning" are mentioned as instances or foci of the effects of this "disrupted behavior." This symptomology is taken to suggest a norm of proper activity for the normal self. Let us consider this norm, implicit in the prescriptions. Action that is goal-oriented requires, according to the manual, that one have adequacy of interest and drive, as well as the ability to follow that act to its logical conclusions. But what is the "logical conclusion" of an action? How is action submitted to the syllogistic grid of premises and conclusions? Is an action ever finished as a logical argument can be finished? What, for example, is the logical conclusion of a walk in the park? To return home again afterwards? To enjoy it as one is walking? To recall the event later as a memory? To make it all the way through the park or around it? To meet someone, unexpectedly, in the park? Not to make it all the way around the park?

These questions obviously have no abstract answers. Neither does the question of the "logical" outcome of an activity, except in circumstances where a particular task is to be performed: the typical work place, for example, where the task is already set for one by someone else, where a deadline is given, and the task must be completed by the "worker" within the specified time and in a particular way. Then the work will be done and the goal of the activity, or indeed its logical conclusion, will be reached.

All contractual employment follows such a structure in its organization of labor. Nothing about these premises, or how to get the job done, is unusual or noteworthy, except in the context of this manual and the other diagnostic symptomatology. Recall what we have noted with regard to the sense of self—the feeling of one's self that the "normal" ought to have. Uniqueness, individuality, self-initiated activity—or at least some feeling for what they involve—these things are prescribed. Now, we have the self-initiated, goal-directed activity modeled or exemplified by the work place and—what is more significant—by a situation in which such uniqueness, individuality, and self-initiation of activity (to say nothing of the idiosyncratic connections of thoughts and ideas) are completely ruled out. If one were actually to submit to the manual's idea of normality—what it calls our "sense of self"—one would lose one's job. For this sense is in serious conflict with the manual's concept of normality in regard to what it (quaintly) calls "volition." Once again the manual designates a double bind situation for the normal in its implicit, yet nonetheless powerful prescriptions of normality.

My point here is that the feelings—the sense of self—demanded in section (d) must be illusory, if the volition described in section (e) is to be taken into consideration. That is, the feeling that one is "one's own boss" (to keep to the labor metaphorics here), that one is a unique, irreplaceable individual different from others, and that one is initiating one's own activity (choosing one's tasks, goals, etc.) must be felt but never realized in fact. Indeed, if one feels that one is "one's own boss," one's own proper self, this cannot but be illusory. However, nothing of this dimension is mentioned in the manual. It does not refer us directly to the normal, since it does not claim to be the textbook on normality. We grant this assumption, but the intentions of the task force, their logical conclusions, and the aims of the project are overdetermined—to say the least.

The manual's diagnostic framework for establishing the symptomatology of schizophrenia relies on an implicit but powerful prescriptive, normative, metaphysical foundation that is never examined. Indeed, it is even openly rejected at the outset as having no place in this endeavor. The goal of the manual is therefore not reached. The goal-directed activity does not reach its logical (intended) conclusion. Furthermore, the manual generates a paradoxical conflict between criteria for the ascription of normality, since the level of conscious intention exhibited in texts in general is parallel to that of the place of the "feelings" of uniqueness, individuality, and self-direction considered to be so essential to the implied category of normality.

The illusions of intentionality—that one always says, does, and effects more than and other than what one simply "had in mind"—are not addressed by the manual in terms of this particular category of "volition"; nor are they addressed in its own structure and by its own explicit intentions. The irony is that this very lack of address thematically invokes this excess or slippage all the more clearly in the "role" of the foundational, formative, prescriptive and limiting presuppositions upon which the entire edifice has been built "above ground."

This area of slippage is not simply what Freud referred to as slips of the pen or tongue. Rather, it is the condition of the possibility of such slips. The excess of intentionality is more precisely illustrated by the work of Derrida—in what he has called "deconstruction." What I have been trying to show here is that: (1) the DSM–III has not taken this slippage into account within its category of "volition," and (2) the DSM–III itself exhibits this slippage between its intentions and its realization, between what it claims *en droit* and what it does *en fait*.

I have sought in my analysis to deconstruct the DSM–III and to show its reliance, at least within the symptomatology of schizophrenia, on the tradition of Western metaphysics. The manual, however, far from taking its philosophical presuppositions into account, critically examining them, or even acknowledging their presence, openly denies and rejects all but "low level" inferences based on "clinical observation." The role of "observation" in scientific and, a fortiori, medical-therapeutic practice has been subjected to scrutiny by the hermeneutic tradition. But I suggest that this is not enough. To have presuppositions that are unacknowledged is unavoidable at the ontological level; but to have metaphysically prescribed, authorized, grounded and organized frameworks in which a diagnosis and recommendations for treatment are practiced in the name of a noncoercive and indeed liberating "rationality" seems very questionable.

To avoid metaphysics completely is not the solution. But on the other hand, to embrace Western metaphysics and impose its standards of normality without awareness and without questioning is surely a form of blindness within a profession that takes pride in the emancipatory power of its insight.

NOTES

1. Lacan, Jacques, *Ecrits,* trans. Alan Sheridan (New York: W. W. Norton, 1977), "Function and Field of Speech and Language," 38.

2. *Diagnostic and Statistical Manual of Mental Disorders,* (3rd ed.), (Washington, D.C., American Psychiatric Association, 1980). Hereafter referred to as DSM–III.

3. *Ibid., 7.*

4. See Freud, Sigmund, *The Complete Psychological Works of Sigmund Freud,* Standard Edition, trans. James Strachey (Toronto: Hogarth Press, 1961), vol. 13, 73. Also see vol. 17, 261, where Freud said: "the *delusions of paranoics have an unpalatable external similarity and internal kinship to the systems of our philosophers.* It is impossible to escape the conclusion that these patients are, in an asocial fashion, making the very attempts at solving their conflicts and appeasing their pressing needs which, when those attempts are carried out in a fashion that is acceptable to the majority, are known as poetry, religion, and *philosophy.*" [my emphasis]

5. Freud, *Standard Edition,* vol. 22, 160–1.

6. Heidegger, Martin, *An Introduction to Metaphysics,* trans. Ralph Manheim (New Haven: Yale University, 1959).

7. For more on Derrida's notion of metaphysics see my article "Derrida and the Concept of Metaphysics" in *Research in Phenomonology,* vol. 13 (1983): 113–149.

8. Freud, *Standard Edition,* vol. 13, 179. In addition, Freud stated, "the fact that a theory is psychologically determined does not in the least invalidate its scientific truth." See also, *S.E.,* vol. 11, 185; vol. 15, 20.

9. *DSM–III,* 12.

10. *DSM–III,* 181.

11. *DSM–III,* 182.

12. Aristotle, *The Basics Works of Aristotle,* trans. Richard McKeon (New York: Random House, 1941). In the *Physics,* he explained this framework of analysis in the following way: (p. 218) "Now what is for us plain and obvious at first is rather confused masses, the elements and principles of which become known to us later by analysis. Then we must advance *from generalities to particulars;* for it is a whole that is best known to sense-perception, and a generality is a kind of whole, comprehending many things within it, like parts. Much the same thing happens in the relation of the name to the formula. A name, e.g. 'round,' means vaguely a sort of whole: its definition analyses this into its particular senses. Similarly a child begins by calling all men "father" and all women "mother," but later on distinguishes each of them."

13. *DSM–III,* 182.

14. Plato, *Collected Dialogues,* ed. Edith Hamilton and Huntington Cairns (Princeton: Princeton University, 1961). See on "Forms," Parmenides, 1326; Sophist, 254c; Timeaus, 51c. On "essences" see Sophist, 247b; Timeaus, 37d; Republic 9, 585c.

15. Aristotle, Metaphysica, 681–926.

16. DSM–III, 182.

17. Ibid., 19.

18. Husserl, Edmund, *Logical Investigations,* vol. 1, trans. J. N. Findlay (London: Routledge and Kegan Paul, 1970), 293. As he said: "A meaningless expression is therefore, properly speaking, no expression at all: it is at best something that claims or seems to be an expression, though, more closely considered, it is not one at all. Here belong articulate, wordlike sounding patterns such as 'Abracadabra,' and also combinations of genuine expressions to which no unified meaning corresponds, though their outer form seems to pretend to such a meaning, e.g. 'Green is or'."

19. Derrida, Jacques, *Margins of Philosophy,* trans. Barbara Johnson (Chicago: Chicago University), 319-20. Derrida said: "But even 'green is or' still signifies an *example of agrammaticality.* This is the possibility on which I wish to insist: the possibility of extraction and of citational grafting which belongs to the structure of every mark spoken or written, and which constitutes every mark as writing even before and outside every horizon of semiolinguistic communication; as writing, that is, as a possibility of functioning cut off, at a certain point, from its 'original' meaning and from its belonging to a saturable and constraining context."

20. Freud, Standard Edition, vol. 14, 204. Freud said, in particular, "When we think in abstractions there is a danger that we may neglect the relations of words to unconscious thing-presentations, and it must be confessed that *the expression and content of our philosophizing then begins to acquire an unwelcome resemblance to the mode of operation of schizophrenics.* We may, on the other hand, attempt a characterization of the *schizophrenic's mode of thought* by saying that he treats concrete things as though they were abstract." [my emphasis]

21. For example see Thomas Szasz, *The Myth of Mental Illness* (New York: Harper and Row, 1974).

22. For more on this see Hans-Georg Gadamer, *Truth and Method* (London: Sheed and Ward, 1975), in particular, 245–274.

23. Descartes develops this notion most notably in *Discourse on Method* and *The Meditations,* translated F. E. Sutcliffe (Harmondsworth: Penguin Books, 1968).

24. Derrida, *Of Grammatology,* trans. G. C. Spivak (Baltimore: Johns Hopkins University Press, 1974), in particular, 70.

25. Lacan, 292–326.

26. *DSM–III,* 182.

27. Ibid. 28.

28. Aristotle, "De Interpretatione," 40–65.

29. Heidegger, *Martin Heidegger–Basic Writings,* trans. David Farrell Krell (New York: Harper and Row, 1977), "The End of Philosophy and the Task of Thinking," 369–93.

30. *DSM–III,* 183.

31. Nietzsche, Friedrich, *The Complete Works of Friedrich Nietzsche,* ed. Oscar Levy (New York: Gordon Press, 1974), vol. 2., "On Truth and Falsity in their Ultramoral Sense," 180.

32. See Gadamer, 258, 417.

33. For instance see Derrida's *On Grammatology* and *Margins of Philosophy.*

34. *DSM–III,* 182.

35. Aristotle, 40.

36. For instance, see Derrida, *Speech and Phenomena,* trans. David B. Allison (Evanston: Northwestern University, 1973). See also Merleau-Ponty's work on language as constitutive in *Prose of the World,* trans. John O'Neill (Evanston: Northwestern University, 1973). In addition, see Heidegger's work on language, especially in *On the Way to Language,* trans. Peter D. Hartz (San Francisco, Harper and Row, 1971).

37. For more on the distinction between performatives and constatives, see J. L. Austin, *How to do things with Words* (Cambridge: Harvard University Press, 1962).

38. Claude E. Shannon and Warren Weaver, *The Mathematical Theory of Communication* (Urbana: University of Illinois, 1949).

39. Ricoeur, Paul, *Hermeneutics and the Human Sciences,* ed. and trans. John B. Thompson (Cambridge: Cambridge University, 1981), in particular, 168.

40. Aristotle, 927–1112.

41. *DSM–III,* 183.

42. Ibid., 43.

43. Lacan, 216.

44. Derrida, *Margins of Philosophy,* "White Mythology," 207–273.

45. *DSM–III,* 183.

CHAPTER 10

SCHIZOPHRENIC BEING AND TECHNOCRATIC SOCIETY

JOEL KOVEL

Some years ago, a psychiatrist named John Gunderson decided to poll a group of experts on schizophrenia with the aim of arriving at a composite definition of the puzzling condition. The result is worth quoting:

> Schizophrenia is a disorder of ego functioning caused by developmental, parent-child experience (which may include biological–constitutional elements) which results in an inability to separate out and maintain accurate internal representations of the outside real world. This inability, in turn, causes the production of restitutional symptoms (delusions, hallucinations) which are most prominent when the individual is confronted with the stresses of developing independent, mature, trusting adult relationships.[1]

Let us take up the chief points of this definition–which I imagine would be agreed upon as a fairly typical representation of prevailing medical-psychiatric, psychoanalytic and psychological opinion—one by one.

• "*Schizophrenia is a disorder. . . .*" To claim that schizophrenia is a disorder means that it is a discrete, identifiable and classifiable thing in the world, and that it has the attributes of a disease. It is characteristic of diseases (and disorders) that persons *have* them in certain parts of their organism, for example, the liver or the brain. The individual himself is not diseased, but suffers—i.e., becomes ill—from the effects of the disease, which is, so to speak, elsewhere. DSM–III, the official guide to contemporary psychiatric practice, makes the point very clearly. "A common misconception is that a classification of mental disorders classifies individuals, when actually what is being classified are disorders individuals have. For this reason, the test of DSM–III avoids the use of such phrases as 'a schizophrenic' or 'an alcoholic,' and instead uses the more accurate, but admittedly more wordy 'an individual with Schizophrenia' or 'an individual with Alcohol Dependency'."[2]

Although psychiatry will freely admit that the etiologies and pathogeneses of disorders are pretty much unknown, so that the notion in fact tells us very little, the practical effects of being raised to the conceptual level of a disease give a certain grandeur. Note how schizophrenia and alcoholism attain the status of upper-case proper nouns in the lexicon of DSM–III. Having an elaborate code number attached helps as well (schizophrenia gets to be 295.xx; alcoholism, 303.9x., the x's being further qualifiers). By speaking of disorders, psychiatry intends to zero in on the Disease. In this scheme of things, disease is an objective essence beneath the level of mere appearance or illness. Illness is a messy, informal concept, shot through with distortion, bias and social judgment. However, according to medical science, disease is the pure, real thing-in-itself. So potent is the contemporary, medicine-fed idea of disease that it takes on, fetishistically, the attributes of a person—and not just an ordinary person, but one of superhuman and terroristic proportions, a kind of nemesis stalking the individual. Watch out, AIDS will get you . . . or cancer . . . or schizophrenia.

Undoubtedly, psychiatry feels that it should abstract the essence-disorder, schizophrenia, away from the person, in order to isolate the relevant factors, pathways, even pathogens, and thus eventually to come up with a cure for the dread affliction. This is the classically Cartesian maneuver. It undoubtedly led to considerable mastery over conditions such as tuberculosis, and it has allowed some light to be shed on cancer. In the case of schizophrenia research, however, despite ardent promotion in recent years for the increased medicalization of its approach, psychiatry has been unable to demonstrate the fertility that characterizes a robust science. Studies of schizoprenia seem to circle around aimlessly without convergence or a sense of opening onto widening horizons. Even the supposedly secure hypotheses concerning the inheritability of schizophrenia[3] have recently been shown to be remarkably porous, through the rigorous critique of Lewontin, Rose, and Kamin, among others.[4] The point is not ours to elaborate here, but it appears impossible to factor out any kind of biological essence underlying schizophrenic manifestations. The trouble is only compounded with the qualification that schizophrenia is a "group of disorders," or by the plea that psychiatry needs more time, the "mind" being so much more complicated than the "body."

Psychiatry should take its cue from Manfred Bleuler, son of Eugen, who coined the term in 1911, and a man who has spent over six decades studying the problem: "It is wishful thinking that . . . schizophrenia is a specific disease, and that, therefore, it is bound to have one definite specific origin. We have never found any such."[5] And it should go further: schizophrenia is no disease at all—which does not mean, however, that it does not exist, or exists only as a "myth" or a set of social labels. There are other forms of existence.

• *". . . of ego functioning. . . ."* Here we have the all-purpose organ of "psy" discourse.[6] In order for there to be a dis-ease-order, something that persons suffer from, there has to be a location where this takes place. Enter the ego, a favored concoction, abstracted from the person and given life as the seat of orderly functioning. This ego is a frozen "I," the praxis of the individual taken out of time and given weight and substance. The ego *works:* it represses the rest of the person, the lazy, formless id; it gets us to the office and sees to it that the checkbook is kept balanced; it calculates self-interest and so knows when to lie and when to tell the truth; and, to be sure, it endears itself to the psy establishment by "testing reality."

Schizophrenics—that is, individuals with schizophrenia—do not, however, work. Their repression is terrible, contents of the dread id spilling over all the time; they quintessentially fail to reproduce, much less expand, the collective social product; they take awful care of themselves; and, as we shall see in a little more detail below, they fail to test reality. All this is so.

But if there is no disease, then why should there be an "organ," the ego, where the disease would have been? No one has ever seen an ego, weighed it, felt its pulse, or experienced desire related to it. We appreciate egoic qualities at all only when desire infuses the "I" in narcissism. The ego-concept produced by the mental health establishment, however, is abstracted from narcissism: it is not the subject, or self, but a construction of "psy" rationalization. Ego is an "organoid," mechanical notion that there is, in the strong substantive working sense, mind-as-object, with coherent, discrete properties. The substantive Ego is an object, moreover, for psychology, psychiatry and psychoanalysis, i.e. a technical figment. Is this not a kind of delusion, notwithstanding the impressive rationalizations by means of which the psy professions have managed to give the ego a semblance of reality? The Ego-machine is supposed to work all the time for the glory of the System, so much so that those who fail to measure up to snuff, like the schizophrenics, find themselves afflicted with the seal of a Disorder. For where there is an organ, there can also be organic malfunction.

• "*. . . caused by developmental, parental-child experience (which may include biological-constitutional elements) . . .*" This is an attempt to take into account the nature-nurture problem at the lowest common denominator, that of the family and the "constitution." Either the source is with mommy and daddy (generally the former, who turns into that contemporary harpy, the Schizophrenogenic Mother); or it lies in genetic programming, hence, the past rigidly projected forward: a Fate beyond human agency. Or, with a bow in the direction of the dialectic, through some "interaction" of the two levels. Again, this is consistent with the basic assumption: the being or personhood of the schizophrenic is not itself involved; it rather suffers extrinsic assault from a system outside itself, that either of the family or DNA.

There is no possibility in this framework for the living experience of the person itself to engender and contain the form of being known as schizophrenic. The schizophrenic is cursed, and not responsible for his Disorder. The causes are always in the past, or outside of history, residing either in nature or a family "system" whose essential properties are biological. No participation in society except that mediated by mommy-daddy is admitted, nor any encounter with nature lying outside the net of the prevailing scientific rationalization. In short, anything transcendent is excluded. The concept of schizophrenia is caught in a web of technocratic discourse, reduced and explained away as the product of bad genes or bad mommy. Meanwhile actual schizophrenic persons live in a world ruptured from this one. They are on another plane; and the language of their delusions represents the effort to relate this plane, and the suffering and violence of living on it, to the mundane world. Thus a transcendent motion is suggested in the delusional experience of schizophrenia; this often appears in frankly religious form, but it often has some historical referent: to nuclear weapons, nerve gas, persecution by the CIA, and so forth. To the privileged technocratic discourse, however, such utterances are utterly incomprehensible. The schizophrenic, then, is seen as doubly mad: mad in his break from reality and mad because the expression of that break has no point of mediation with the normal channels of scientific causation.

• "*. . . which results in an inability to separate out and maintain accurate internal representations of the real external world.*" Here we have the famous defect in "reality testing." How wonderful it is that psy science should have settled with one blow what had otherwise been a fairly vexing problem, namely, the relation between mind and reality. A few nagging details remain unresolved, such as the fact that even the furthest-gone psychotics usually know where door knobs are and when one has to use them to get from one room to another; or that no two human beings can ever consensually agree on external reality, except at the most trivial level (where door knobs are); or that "external reality" is not external anyhow, being constructed out of human practical and intersubjective activity. Psy science doesn't have to bother itself about matters of this kind, since it knows with utmost confidence just what reality is. To anybody who doubts, which is to say, thinks, however, the question of the schizophrenic's grasp of reality is not so simple—precisely because the normal grasp of reality is not so simple. Of only one thing can we be certain: that the schizophrenics' apprehension of reality is profoundly different from that of normal people. Whatever the merit or cause of their view of the universe, it is a radically estranged vision—not just distinct from the ordinary, but discontinuous with it.

We are, it seems, left with radical estrangement as the only valid datum about schizophrenic experience—that, and a sensitivity to the mischief latent in seemingly innocuous turns of phrase like "disorder" and "ego." Thus the twofold alienation of the schizophrenic: alienated in itself from consensual, everyday reality; and hyperalienated from the relevant objectifying discourse. The place of objectifying discourse in the practice of science is an ambiguous one under any conditions. Here, however, where the problem itself is the extreme alienation of the subject, an alienation so severe that a living person experiences the organism as a machine or an inert mass, objectification takes on truly monstrous proportions. Indeed we are left wondering whether the theme of dehumanization or mechanization that looms so large in schizophrenic speech is not in some way a product of this hyperalienation—and a mirroring of the technocracy in command of the mental health establishment. I would not know how to test adequately this proposition. However, the impression is strong that the nature of schizophrenia varies from culture to culture—and that the disturbance takes on especially severe, dehumanized proportions in societies dominated by the "new class" of technical experts—the technocratic societies of the industrialized world (including, to be sure, "really existing" socialist societies).

Radical estrangement, or alienation, is not an ultimate datum, and to postulate it as the essential feature of schizophrenia does not mean a retreat into obscurantism or mysticism. Alienation is a real form of existence. It is a type of "existence-gone-wrong," just as disease is a type of existence-gone-wrong. Both are abstractions corresponding to ways in which life goes awry. The disease concept is serviceable if one is describing, for example, a case of acute dysentery ensuing upon a visit to Mexico; while the alienation concept is serviceable to describe a range of estrangements, from the famous account of Marx about the alienation of labor[7], to the representation in fiction of alienated everyday life in late capitalist society, and to be sure, of schizophrenia. All alienations are different from each other, and the differences can be accounted for in a real way, which one can call "scientific," if one likes. But they are all alienations—estrangements within a historical manifold. Marx or Samuel Beckett can tell us more about schizophrenia than any medical text, even though neither Marx nor Beckett described schizophrenia as such.

Thus schizophrenia is a form of relationship to the self, and not an objectifiable entity. Every attempt to define schizophrenia substantively has failed and seems doomed to fail. What this means practically is that propositions along the lines of "X *has* schizophrenia" are without meaning, for schizophrenia is not something one "has," the way one has a disordered thyroid gland or a sprained ankle. It is rather something one "is," that is to say, a mode of being. Schizophrenia, in other words, is an ontological condition. It therefore makes sense to talk of "schizophrenics" (so long as it is kept in mind that the term includes the weight of being called so by this society), no matter how it may offend the sensibilities of the editors of DSM–III. Schizophrenia cannot be disjoined from the person, for it is of the person's whole being. This means that it is a real occurrence involving that person, and not, for example, something concocted out of labels or linguistic convention; but it is real as an altered configuration of the subject-object dialectic that constitutes personhood. Schizophrenia involves the entire organism, the soma-psyche, with all its relations through nature and history, and it vanishes once it is reduced to any of its elements.

Hence the hopeless dilemma of the mental health establishment. For the notion of mode of being is written off the map of professional training, since professionalism requires the segmenting of the unity of being into fiefdoms according to economic interest: the psyche for the psychologist, the brain for the neurologist, the family for the family-studies expert, and so forth. Such is the way of technocratic society.

What can be said of what transpires in the kind of event known as the schizophrenic mode of being? The most direct and simple way of putting it is this: something happens that cannot be named and that ruptures the experienced place of a person in the universe. This something is very violent and very awful. Being unnamable, it can only be suggested, and the words that suggest it are the words of poetry or the spirit. Schizophrenia is a kind of black hole of experience, a moment of fantastic density that sucks beings into its vortex. The center of schizophrenia is annihilation: the person becoming schizophrenic remains materially present and conscious, but ceases to be. The heart pumps; the liver secretes; the retina fires off its signals to the cortex, and the cortex relays them onwards . . . but the Subject in whom this is happening is in the process of disintegrating and creating schizophrenia out of the ruins.

Schizophrenia may resemble, but it does not overlap with religion or art. The reason for this follows from the fact that existence everywhere has destructive and creative moments. In everyday life, the amplitude of these moments is dampened; stability ensues, and little seems to happen. In moments of artistic creation or spiritual engagement, the amplitude of both moments is magnified, although creativity prevails. The world is destroyed, but then remade. Moreover, the new, transcendent product is associable, it can be communicated to others, makes sense to them, and lifts them out of their ordinary condition. In schizophrenia, by contrast, the moment of destruction is amplified out of proportion to that of creation. The result is annihilation without corresponding production or association. Or rather, what is left for the creative powers is not the building of new objects in the world (a poem being an object in the world, as would be a shared rite of passage), but the desperate restitution of the shattered subject.

If there is a place where we agree most fully with the composite definition of Gunderson, it is this: Everything we know of schizophrenic symptomatology can be understood as restitution—mending the lesion in subjectivity. Hallucinated voices fill the void. Delusions of persecution people the inner world with the Otherness of the self in the absolute conviction that to be Other is better than to be nonexistent. Or the catatonic enters into a statued immobility, freezing being into the presently occupied zone of space-time. It is always the same: I am ceasing to exist, the me-ness that circumscribes the elemental sense of what it is to live a life is going, if not already gone, something unspeakably violent is transpiring (a so-called "World-destruction fantasy" is considered pathognomonic of schizophrenia)—and as I cease to exist for myself, a bounded creature moving within a world of other creatures, I find parts of my scattered self in the world, while parts of the world come to occupy spaces of nonbeing within the self. The result—always malignant and often absurd—is a restituted, schizophrenic form of being, gained through an act of survival that simply happens to destroy the world to regain the self. A new subject-object configuration arises in which parts of the self are deployed as objects and parts of objects are taken into the self. This configuration enters into relations with the already existing, consensual subject-object structure of normality, as a result of which it achieves a certain stability—a stability won, however, through radical rejection of the everyday world. Whatever brings the configuration closer to the everyday, therefore, also increases the anxiety of annihilation—hence the absolute discontinuity between schizophrenia and normal existence. We should not think of a spectrum between the one and the other, but rather of a series of quantum leaps, tending toward a permanent core of radical alterity. This core can be masked over by mimicking normality; or it can fade away; or it can progress to take over the whole of being. But insofar as it exists, schizophrenic alienation is discontinuous with other forms of experience—including other forms of alienation. The outcome, to be sure, fails to "test reality." But the loss is not of the capacity to discern what is in fact going on in material exteriority (such an actual loss occurring, for example, through a neurological lesion). It is rather of the capacity to shepherd one's being, to sustain identity, to maintain a locus of subjectivity.

Even that shibboleth of medical psychiatry, the notorious "thought disorder," becomes intelligible—if not translatable—in terms of a response to schizophrenic annihilation. The schizophrenic's inability to use language syntactically has long been recognized as a cardinal sign of the condition. Setting aside the reification inherent in the notion of "disorder" (which characteristically abstracts and essentializes thought from being), the fact remains that schizophrenia is more clearly identified by an inability to communicate experience through language than by any other feature. There are various kinds of disturbances characteristic of schizophrenic language, which may be roughly summed up in terms such as neologism (creating idiosyncratic words), derailment (sudden shifts in frames of reference), poverty of speech (extending to blocking or a sudden absence of speech/thought), or various forms of logical violation. Practically, this results in either an inability to understand, or more subtly, the impossibility of recalling or reproducing, what the schizophrenic says. Since there is no organic deficit in speech, nor any cultural or intellectual impediment, the whole business is thoroughly puzzling.

It becomes more comprehensible, though, if the puzzle is transferred to the domain of being. For language is predicated on intersubjectivity. Speech links subjectivities together. It requires therefore mutual recognition that self and other exist. Speech-acts articulate an already existing field of intersubjectivity. This seems to be an irreducible ontological capacity. It can be transmitted through the eyes, whether or not individuals speak the same language or are of the same culture.

In schizophrenia, however, the radical alterity to which I have just referred succeeds in rupturing intersubjective boundedness. Mutual recognition is missing between the schizophrenic and the other. And this loss is decisive for the social relatedness of the condition. Since the schizophrenic has lost his end of the subjective mooring of being, linguistic communication cannot proceed. The schizophrenic does not talk to you, because she is not present to do so. You—the interlocuter—being part of the world, are to some extent replaced with parts of the self and to some extent inserted within the restituted self. As you are not there to be talked to, the basic function of language becomes superfluous. The coherent framework within which speech events take place has been replaced. The chaotic language which results merely mirrors chaotic being.

That schizophrenics talk like philosophers gone mad, and that what they say reveals the same ontological concerns that have occupied humanity since it became conscious—these facts should not be dismissed as incidental. Schizophrenia is not, as the psychological establishment holds, a disturbance of attention or arousal; nor is it some occult biochemical abnormality in the brain; nor even a response to maddening conditions—though all of these aspects are drawn into the process. It is a collapse of being—and the catastrophic reconstruction of subjectivity which results.

Can we explain this collapse? I should think not, although we may be able to account for some of the conditions under which it might begin, as well as for other conditions—which would not necessarily be the same—under which it might expand and become irreversible. We could say, for example, that whatever weakened the ontological foundations of the self *predisposed* to schizophrenia; that whatever interrupted the intersubjective moorings of the person could *precipitate* schizophrenia; and that whatever sustained alienation (thereby preserving the intersubjective rupture and through it, the subjective one) might *maintain* schizophrenia. And we could identify under these various rubrics a wide range of occurrences (including genetic disposition); moreover, we could even specify possible interactions between such occurrences, in other words, "loadings" of various factors that would increase the possibility of schizophrenic experience for a given individual, or tend to make any such experience, should it occur, relatively malignant.[8]

We would never, however, explain schizophrenia itself through any of these means. I do not mean to assert that there is some mysterious leap into being that eludes all but the philosophically initiated. I am simply proposing that the problem of schizophrenia is no less baffling than the problem of existence itself. Nonbeing is no more mysterious an affair than being. Whatever gives us subjectivity—the self-consciousness of being, or its interiority—can, by breaking down, take this gift away.

We can add this, though: that the terror or violence associated with this event is absolute, so that people who undergo the schizophrenic experience will exchange anything—the most absurd delusion, the most extreme form of mutilation—in order to achieve subjectivity. And this as well: that as being is collectively determined, so is schizophrenic nonbeing. The "break" that distinguishes actual schizophrenia from the kind of facultative reversibility of the shaman, the artist, and the visionary,[9] is a disintegration of subjectivity past the point of its connection to the fabric of intersubjectivity. It is then that the schizophrenic loses the world as well as the self, and having lost it, puts himself in the exceedingly dangerous position of allowing the break to become permanent through a repopulation of intersubjectivity with purely internal relations. Hence the state of radical rejection known as "autism," rightly viewed by traditional students of schizophrenia, beginning with Eugen Bleuler, as the *sine qua non* of the condition.

Autism defines the social relations of schizophrenia as negative. The fear of nonbeing is displaced onto a horror of being with others. Annihilation is exported, so to speak, to the surround, which then must be avoided. Because restituted subjectivity is deemed secure only on condition that it avoid relations with the remainder of the human world, schizophrenic existence becomes a fortified island in a sea of emptiness. To the extent, moreover, that the environment matches this motion of withdrawal, the schizoidal process accelerates and may take on an irreversible character. Mutual recognition is a *sine qua non* of intersubjectivity—and intersubjectivity is the essential condition of a truly human, sociated way of being. The schizophrenic flees in terror from recognizing the other and the community. It is up to others and the community, therefore, to provide the missing threads of recognition. In practice, this means an openness to the transcendent implications of schizophrenic experience. This requires an openness to the transcendent possibilities inherent to human experience itself.

We have already noted that schizophrenia and spirituality have a close yet complex relationship. Indeed, the boundary between schizophrenic autism and certain extreme spiritual states may be impossible to draw, inasmuch as they both share a tendency toward absolute rejection of the world. Today, spiritual extremism is considered *prima facie* irrational and even pathological. This is, however, more a measure of the estrangement of our age than of human reality. The image of humans as practical, gregarious and productive—Aristotle's political animal or Marx's *Homo laborans*—is true but not complete. We are also spiritual creatures, given to acts of transcendence. Obviously there comes a point when spiritual quests pass over into psychosis. This does not mean, however, that the questors were crazy to begin with, or that they cease being spiritual even at their most extreme. It would be more accurate to say that a spiritual venture becomes elaborated in a psychotic way. The "holy fools" who went off into the desert, there to sit perched on pedestals for decades, might have been objects of derision for an Edward Gibbon, but they were also expressing a presence in human nature. As insects have a tropism toward the light, so do we have the urge, perhaps only potentially, to go beyond desire toward confrontation with ontological ultimates. In all periods, some have lived according to this urge. No doubt many of this sort ended up in pretty bad shape. But it is logically impossible to decide a priori whether any disturbance was the cause or effect of the withdrawal. In other words, a schizophrenic break, itself mediated by terror and the annihilation of the self, can end up in the same pathway as an initially more benign spiritual journey that loses its way and goes to pieces in isolation and the "dark night of the soul." More to the point, we must conclude that there is an authentically transcendent component embedded from the beginning in the withdrawal of schizophrenics from reality, and that this is a point of potential contact—if someone in the environment can reach out to it. If a schizophrenic says, for example, that his skull has been invaded by extraterrestrial aliens, it may be validly interpreted (given the principle that world and self are reshuffled in schizophrenic subjectivity) that he has been moving away from the ordinary plane of existence, that he experiences this as a disastrous loss to his state of being, and that it would be better if someone could accompany him on his journey. The language by means of which this is expressed is only a "thought disorder" from the reference-point of the prevailing technocracy, which cannot recognize itself in schizophrenic speech, and so deems it irrational and puts it in the garbage pail. From a reference point open, however, to radical existential possibilities, the same speech takes on transcendent qualities. It is, we might say, nonrational rather than irrational, and it expresses the motion to reconnect nonbeing with being. To the extent that rationality inheres in the opposition of means to ends, transcendent discourse is, in this sense, rational—it becomes the only one available to express the shattering of being, even if the tone is catastrophic rather than ecstatic.

In any event, even if the schizophrenic motion toward transcendence is crushed under the intense hostility and inner violence intrinsic to the condition, the extremity of its displacement away from the compact norm has never failed to excite awe—except, of course, as seen through the eyes of the psy professions. This is because technocracy and transcendence are mutually exclusive. The former does not occur except through suppression of the latter, which is necessary to break the world down into discrete, technically manageable and, above all, self-contained problem areas. Thus, generally speaking, there is no one in a technocratic environment to reach out to the schizophrenic.

Even without the opacity of the psy establishment, schizophrenia would appear a massive negation of sociality. The lesion in intersubjectivity ensures that all social relations become disrupted. The schizophrenic break, and the resulting autism, does not mean that the schizophrenic cares nothing for others—as, for example, some of the original psychoanalytic formulations held in claiming that schizophrenics could not be analyzed because the transference was unattainable. It means rather that they care impossibly, in a way that utterly negates the independent existence of the other, some part of whom has been absorbed into the reconstructed self, and the rest jettisoned or destroyed, as need be. The schizophrenic's relations to others are therefore outside the social contract in the most radical sense imaginable. This is another way of saying that the schizophrenic's social relations are marked by very poor economic and political adaptation. In a word, they are not able to work productively.

However, this incapacity takes on greatly different meanings from one society to the next. Clearly, a system such as ours, dominated by the logic of the commodity, is going to be a peculiarly bad place to have schizophrenic experience. If one follows closely the argument of Foucault,[10] it is possible to observe that the radical differentiation of the insane from the rest of the misfits—indeed, even the formal conceptualization of insanity as a diseased rather than a potentially transcendent state—began with the realization that the labor of psychotics could not be a source of surplus value in the emergent capitalist economy. It is this defect above all that defines the present extreme marginality of schizophrenics, and the nearly total loss of appreciation for their insights into existential possibilities.

For all its wealth and power, capitalist society turns out to be one of the worst settings possible in which to be schizophrenic. In the terms described above, it conspires to predispose, precipitate, and maintain the condition in its most malignant form. Fragmentary and chaotic family experience, intrusion by the administered consciousness of the mass media, lack of an organic community—all these features of late capitalist life contribute to a weakened sense of self and to the dissolution of intersubjective relations. What Marcuse referred to as the prevailing mode of the reality principle under late capitalism, namely, the performance principle,[11] succinctly accounts for the difficulty faced by the individual slipping into schizophrenia. For the only behaviors to be rewarded are those that succeed in reproducing the commodity: the good worker, the good consumer, the efficient, productive and agreeable person who gets along.

I do not think we are able to make any claims as to whether late capitalist society contains people who are more genetically predisposed to schizophrenia, or whose very early infantile relations build into them a special predeliction for late schizophrenic experience. However, it would seem that those who begin to slide in a schizoidal way will find little in the way of spontaneous help under present conditions of everyday life. Observers from De Toqueville onward have noted the intolerance of American society—as pure a culture of capitalist relations as the world has ever seen—for deviance and eccentricity. The isolated, lonely preschizophrenic individuals are quite unlikely to find any recognition or toleration of their predicament under these circumstances. And as their condition worsens to the point where they are unable to produce in the workplace—after all, the only real source of value under capitalism—a vicious cycle of mutual nonrecognition takes over.

The hopelessness of the schizophrenics' predicament in our advanced economy is only partially suggested by their diminished contribution to surplus value. For they are equally useless as consumers, given the attenuated desire resulting from the schizophrenics' preoccupations with ontological survival. Indeed, the sole usefulness of the schizophrenic to capitalist society is that of being the occasion for the disease itself. Here the true significance of the disease-concept finally comes into view. For while illnesses are merely sources of disability, diseases, being discrete countable objects (remember the code numbers of DSM–III), are suitable raw material for the industries of mental health. The schizophrenic, then, may be said to be the crude ore, who, under the guiding genius of medical-psychiatry, is transmuted into a case of a disease that can then be worked over for the reproduction of the new system itself. If this seems a somewhat cynical view to take of a gigantic operation supposedly devoted to human service, consider the wretched condition of the mentally ill in our society in proportion to the staggering investment in the apparatus that is supposed to take care of them. And think of this in relation to the fact that the overall adaptation of schizophrenic people is better in poorer, preindustrial societies with miniscule investments in mental health facilities than it is at the center of medical-psychiatric progress.

Of course schizophrenics are even today not without advocates. There are those who would defend them from the hyperalienation of the mental health industries, and those who see emancipatory possibilities in the very extremity of their alienation. These latter critics see in schizophrenic sensibility, which more than any other resists socialization, the last redoubt of freedom. Thus Deleuze and Guattari (the latter with clinical experience), in their *Anti-Oedipus: Capitalism and Schizophrenia*[12] have pressed forward with truly heroic energy to the conclusion that it is the "schizo" and his "desiring machine" with its "uncodable flows," who presents the key to our salvation. *Anti-Oedipus* has the unmistakable advantage over the work of Laing—which it otherwise follows—of taking social structure seriously. Unhappily, the ontology with which its arguments are laboriously advanced is so twisted out of shape that it itself qualifies for delusional status. For in order to prime the "schizo" for his emancipatory role, the authors somehow neglect to put schizophrenia in a real light, denying the terror of annihilation and the autism that ensues upon the break. Despite their attention to the radical implications of the condition (and many sharp insights into the repressiveness of the psychoanalytic establishment), Deleuze and Guattari are forced by their need to locate emancipatory possibilities deep within the subject to assume a kind of continuity between schizophrenia and normal experience. But this is exactly what does not obtain, as we have discussed above. The schizophrenic does not reach toward, but repels the normal. Yes, there is an amazing uncodable flow to the schizophrenic's inner world—but it occurs at the price of desociation, and all the "schizoanalysis" in the world won't put this Humpty-Dumpty together again.

In fact, one might turn the argument around. The schizophrenic reveals not emancipation but the negative of emancipation: not unfree but anti-free. The critical negativity within being—that capacity to refuse the given world while remaining one's self—is demolished and transposed to the zone of nonbeing, where self as well as world are refused, broken-down, then commingled into the autistic configuration. Now, it remains true that the negative is truer to transcendent being than is the inertia of normality, and in this important sense, schizophrenia tells us more about radical existential possibilities—including emancipation—than does the flaccid despair of normal adaptation. But we appreciate this only if we recognize just how far the schizophrenic has fallen—that he shows us the contours of transcendant possibilities precisely by being so removed from them, as a pointillist image takes shape only from afar. So far as schizophrenic autism is removed from the everyday, to that degree has it lost the capacity of transforming material reality (including collective human reality) and with it, the only real possibility for emancipation. Schizophrenia, in fact, is hell.

One does not save the schizophrenic, or use the schizophrenic to save us. The only question is whether care can be given. And the tragic irony is the relative simplicity of caring for schizophrenia, coupled with the ever-receding possibility that this care can be given under present circumstances. To claim that caring for schizophrenia is simple is not the same as saying it is easy to carry out or that anything along the lines of a cure can be offered. It is rather to take one's cue from the ontological structure outlined above. If the key determinant of the outcome of schizophrenia is the extent to which the rupture in subjectivity induces a rupture in intersubjectivity (with the consequent autism), then it follows that the best the helping environment can do is to provide conditions that minimize intersubjective damage and permit healing powers—which remain flickering in even the seemingly hopeless cases—to assert themselves. This is no more, and no less, than offering the schizophrenic an authentic human presence. To be more exact, one has to provide a climate of recognition, in which the entity of "thought disorder" withers away, and where schizophrenic experience is not Other to a dominant technocratic rationalization. The psychotherapies are practices that have arisen in late capitalist society to tend to such a need as it emerged in the general populace. The common denominator of all psychotherapy (more or less compromised in actuality, to be sure) has been to provide a safe place for recognition, acceptance and overcoming the self-alienation of neurosis. In the instance of schizophrenia, however, the globality of the disturbance demands that the same principles be extended to a whole environment, rather than be sequestered in a few privileged hours of therapy. In any case, and for this very reason, the psychotherapy of schizophrenia has been a pretty dubious business.

There was a time when depth psychotherapy seemed to be the answer for schizophrenia. This possibility faded when it became clear how fantastically difficult it was to reach the chronically psychotic person—and it was apparently obliterated when the advent of phenothiazine drugs introduced a vastly more cost-efficient means of normalizing schizophrenic behavior. Given the congruence of this with the ideological needs of the mental health establishment (whose meal ticket is the drug industry), the hegemony of drug treatment was swiftly established and looks secure for the foreseeable future.

However, the fact that drugs work should be critically examined, that is, in terms of the totality of relations of schizophrenia. Such a critique has got to go beyond the problem of drug toxicity—which is a major issue, it may be added—to consider just what it means for something to "work." Drugs work, to be sure, but by numbing subjectivity—numbing it to the pain and terror of schizophrenic experience, so that a restitution can be effected at a less autistic level; and numbing it to the misery and alienation of the environment, so that the schizophrenic can "adapt" without being crushed by a crushing reality. To adapt here means to accept twisting and stunting, as trees on windswept mountaintops survive. Now we can see why studies have shown that schizophrenics did better when treated with drugs than with psychotherapy. Why shouldn't they, when the environment in both cases was the superalienation of the mental health industry? What is the good of good depth psychotherapy, which heightens consciousness, if to be conscious means exposure to the pain of technocratic dehumanization?

No, the real test is not drugs versus psychotherapy, but a human versus an inhuman environment. The former necessarily excludes the lobotomizing routine of drug therapy; nor does it provide a few hours in the week of "insight" therapy, with the rest given over to the miasma of hospital existence. It provides rather a continuous field of presence: of "being-there-for" the psychotic individual, an acceptance, a protection, even an enveloping—without intrusion or inconsistency.[13] This is as simple and as difficult a thing as can be imagined. Yet virtually nothing in the entire field of psy training prepares one for it. It will not cure schizophrenia—nothing can—but it will provide the best circumstances for schizophrenics to heal themselves, to reclaim their own being. And it can be done—and can be demonstrated within the accepted framework of scientific proof to be a superior mode of treatment to the existing drug-centered medical-psychiatric approach. Not by Laing's Kingsley Hall, which got the idea going and then foundered, but by less grandiose and more reliable successors such as Mosher and Carpenter.[14]

It is hardly necessary to point out that ventures of this kind remain marginal when they are not simply squashed. Mosher's Soteria House, for example, proved that a drug-free, nonmedical treatment environment worked better for acute psychosis and was far cheaper to boot. It should have been encouraged—in a rational society. In the present society, however, it was perceived as a threat to the medical-pharmaceutical-insurance-government power structure, and was eliminated. The lesson is clear: one can as soon develop a viable human environment for the treatment of schizophrenia in the midst of this society, as viable worker cooperatives, free schools, personal relationships unstained by sexual hatred, or indeed—and this is the main point—an authentic community. In every instance the system intervenes to bring things back to its own functioning. But the community is the main point. When Maxwell Jones coined the felicitous phrase, "therapeutic community" back in the fifties,[15] he was drawing attention—whether consciously or not is beside the point—to the prime relation between communality and so-called mental illness. The dissolution of community creates the isolated Subject, prone to ruptures in subjectivity and intersubjectivity. From its basis and origin in the differentiated unity of primitive society, subjectivity has undergone a "progressive" atomization and conflictual intensification with the intrusion, first of the state, then of the capitalist market, into the organic relationship between self, others and nature.[16] The result is the isolated, deeply problematic subject of today—and the technocracy that mirrors that self's fragmentation. If "underdeveloped" countries do better in the care of schizophrenia than we, it is for the elementary reason that our historical development was won through the destruction of community. In the poorest parts of the earth, people have a place to be and comprehensible others to be with; rituals that make sense to them; and a sense of the sacred, reinforced by collective life, that enables them to recognize the transcendent moment in schizophrenic experience and therefore to allow schizophrenics to accept themselves, thus permitting the process of healing. For us, living under the blessing/curse of rationalization, artificial communities have to be constructed. These communalities are restitutive, just as schizophrenic being is restitutive, within the interstices of a massified society. One such, which may be the closest we have to a communality that is primitive, would be the elementary association outlined above for the care of schizophrenia (and other severe forms of madness). Here restitution genuinely restores the wholeness of shattered existence. However, given the irrelevence of madness for the efficient running of the megamachine, it is no surprise that this membrane is only slightly less fragile than the subjectivity it is designed to protect. With the first economic storm it gets swept away.

Though it seems likely that better social relations—especially as they devolve upon early childhood—can reduce its incidence and severity, I cannot imagine the elimination of schizophrenia within the terms of the human condition. No conceivable society, in other words, can deny the vulnerability of our existence. But schizophrenia is one thing, and schizophrenics another. If no social transformation can fully protect us against the former, only a social transformation can begin to do justice to the latter. We do not need to absolutize. It is not a question of social revolution or nothing (which practically speaking, means nothing). We may rather learn to envision—and build—zones of relative emancipation, at times in the interstices of a contradictory society, at times relatively outside. More than a good treatment environment is demanded, for such an environment can function only to the degree it gets support from its own surround, and to the extent that it can send partially mended selves back into families, work-places and communalities that provide a degree of recognition for the otherness and transcendence intrinsic to schizophrenia. At the far end of this process lies utopia. In between is a zone of continual struggle. And that is where the work lies.

NOTES

1. J. Gunderson and L. Mosher, eds., *Psychotherapy of Schizophrenia* (New York; Aronson, 1975), xix.
2. Diagnostic and Statistical Manual of Mental Disorders (3rd ed. Washington, American Psychiatric Association, 1980), 6.
3. Which culminated in the adoptive studies of Kety, Rosenthal and colleagues; cf. Rosenthal, D. and Kety, S., eds., *The Transmission of Schizophrenia* (Oxford: Pergamon, 1968).
4. R. C. Lewontin, S. Rose, and L. Kamin, *Not in Our Genes* (New York: Pantheon, 1984).

5. Manfred Bleuler, "What is Schizophrenia?" *Schizophrenia Bulletin,* vol. 10, no. 1 (1984) p. 8.

6. For the definitive discussion of the rise of this phenonmenon, see Françoise Castel and Robert Castel, *The Psychiatric Society* (New York: Columbia University, 1982). See also my "The American Mental Health Industry," in David Ingleby, ed., *Critical Psychiatry* (New York: Pantheon, 1980), 73–101.

7. K. Marx, *Economic and Philosophical Manuscripts.* In *Early Writings,* ed. T. B. Bottomore (New York: McGraw-Hill, 1964).

8. S. Shapiro's *Contemporary Theories of Schizophrenia* (New York: McGraw-Hill, 1980) contains a reasonably complete compendium of what has been learned of these factors, without once committing itself to an understanding of what schizophrenia is.

9. Jane Murphy, "Psychiatric Labeling in Cross-Cultural Perspective," *Science,* 191: (1976) 1019–1028.

10. M. Foucault, *Madness and Civilization* (New York: Pantheon, 1965).

11. H. Marcuse, *Eros and Civilization* (New York: Random House, 1955).

12. Gilles Deleuze and Felix Guattari, *Anti-Oedipus: Capitalism and Schizophrenia* (Minneapolis: University of Minnesota, 1983).

13. This is not the place to take up the entire matter, but it may be noted that good air, good diet, feasible unalienated work, and so forth, are also essential, if slightly less so than the human environment.

14. For the relevant literature, see L. Mosher, J. Gunderson, "Group, Family, Milieu and Community Support Systems Treatment for Schizophrenia," in L. Bellak, ed., *Disorders of the Schizophrenic Syndrome* (New York: Basic Books, 1979).

15. Jones, M., *The Therapeutic Community: A New Treatment Method in Psychiatry* (New York, Basic Books, 1953).

16. Kovel, J. "Mind and State in Ancient Greece," *Dialectical Anthropology* 5 (1981): 305–316.

CHAPTER 11

OEDIPUS, FREUD, FOUCAULT: FRAGMENTS OF AN ARCHAEOLOGY OF PSYCHOANALYSIS

James Bernauer

For Michel Foucault, any adequate understanding of extreme human states such as psychosis will occur only after our culture has resumed its interrupted dialogue with madness. His partiality for the term 'madness' rather than psychosis or schizophrenia already announces his attempt to free a region of experience which finds itself most often colonized today by an arsenal of psychological-psychiatric categories. Madness is that constantly changing region of human experience which defies any regulating intentionality; which speaks in the language of the fantastic and the passionate; which dwells not merely in historical time but also in a violent, timeless stream of subversion, flooding the secure banks of all that is positively known about the order of the self and world. The most durable of Foucault's ambitions was to make a dialogue with that madness possible, for what is at stake in its continued suspension is our own intelligibility, our capacity for accurate self-knowledge and, thus, for effective care of the self. We can distinguish two directions in his effort to restore us to a conversation and struggle with madness.

The first was his historical investigation of madness in the modern age, *Folie et déraison: Histoire de la folie à l'âge classique*.[1] This volume delineated the complex, heterogeneous forces from which there arose our culture's refusal to acknowledge, as anything other than a dangerously mad absence of a reason that ought to be present, a wide range of personal behavior and belief that did not conform to a rationalistic understanding of human reality and its proper conduct. Two moments stood out in his account of the silencing of madness. The first was the confinement of those thought mad that characterized the seventeenth and eighteenth centuries. Although the age of reason kept those who were perceived as lacking reason out of hearing distance, the memory and scandal of madness was not totally eliminated, for the ugly fortresses in which the mad were originally enclosed testified to that period's continuing fear of its otherness. For Foucault, it was only with the nineteenth century's invention of the benevolent asylum, in which the person thought insane is awarded the status of a child, that the subversive speech of madness is rendered impotent. The doctor's diagnosis of mental illness begins a "monologue of reason about madness" and announces the appearance of a psychology and psychiatry whose principal themes will emerge from the child-like reality the asylum itself creates: the "relations of freedom to the compulsions, the phenomena of regression and the infantile structure of behavior, aggression and guilt."[2] These three themes proclaim not the intellectual mastery but the banishment of the experience of madness into the figure of the mentally ill person, whose incapacity for knowledge and care of the self invites the performance of these tasks by others. The banishment was never complete, however, for certain witnesses to the premodern dialogue with madness endured. In the texts of such writers as Nietzsche and Roussel and in the dossiers of countless unfortunates who seemed to pass their lives outside of the division between reason and absence of reason, madness emigrated into the chaotic region of libraries and archives where it waited—and waits—for rediscovery.[3]

If the reduction of madness to the empty, inauthentic speech of mental illness provoked Foucault's initial archaeological investigation, another more subtle danger to a renewed dialogue with madness has lurked throughout his writings, namely, Freud and psychoanalysis. For Foucault, Freud's greatest achievement was beyond dispute. His work brings the "violence of a return," for in place of the asylum's cult of observation, he returned to madness at the level of its language, a discourse so radically different from everyday speech.[4] Freud was the "first to undertake the radical erasure of the division between . . . the normal and the pathological, the comprehensible and the incommunicable, the significant and the non-significant." Freud's accomplishment and, thus, his "scandal" for psychology and psychiatry was his challenge to their anthropology, their grasp of human reality as a "homo psychologicus" who was positive in his self-consciousness.[5] Freud's achievement is seriously flawed, however, and cannot establish adequate foundations for self-knowledge and thus for a renewed dialogue with madness. In an effort to identify a dimension in Foucault's thought that is of assistance in approaching the difficult question of psychosis, I wish to focus upon the scattered fragments of his "archaeology of psychoanalysis" and its critique of Freudian claims to a knowledge of the self.[6]

I shall begin with an image of such self-knowledge, Freud's interpretation of Sophocles's *Oedipus*. For Freud, Oedipus's search for the truth "can be likened to the work of a psychoanalysis."[7] One relentlessly pursues the truth of one's identity that is hidden far from one's conscious awareness and that shows itself as tied to the dimension of sexuality. The story possesses perennial appeal because we recognize ourselves in Oedipus. As Freud pointed out: "His destiny moves us—because the oracle laid the same curse upon us before our birth as upon him."[8] Perhaps the myth would possess an equally intense attraction for Foucault because it exhibits so well his portrayal of the tragic destiny of the modern individual. Like Oedipus, one is under the obligation to seek the secret truth of oneself; it is a truth that is found through speech, one's own and that of authorized others (priest, scientist, government health official, and so forth). With the revelation of the truth of one's sexual desire, the self is regarded as discovered and the State is protected from the anarchy of restless identities.[9] Within the perspective of Foucault's political analysis of modern self-knowledge, I wish to claim that Freud's interpretation of the Oedipus myth as an image for psychoanalysis indicates that his thought is still part of the modern anthropological configuration; this configuration envisioned man in terms of a Cartesian subjectivity and rationality and led to the reduction of madness to mental illness.

Much of Foucault's work has been dedicated to the study of how modern man came to be born as a subject and to the analysis of the human sciences that articulate his positive reality.[10] For Foucault, the emergence of man and the forms of his self-consciousness are unintelligible apart from an understanding of modernity's political crisis. Following the collapse of feudalism, the division of Christendom, and the undermining of traditional conceptions of sovereignty, the paramount problem requiring solution was how political and social order could be established and justified. A new art of government was the modern period's resolution of this crisis. The justification for the exercise of authority was sought in its ability to follow a system of empirical truths regarding man in fostering and administering the life and happiness of a society.[11] The assumption of such responsibility put into operation a vast project of discipline in the interest of achieving a population capable of both knowing itself and governing itself. These disciplines are interdependent as modes of power, articulating knowledge and forms of knowledge, and exercising power. Modern culture could achieve the well-being and self-governance that were its objectives only by establishing clear norms for conduct that entailed procedures for successfully correcting departures from those standards, as in the case of those who were regarded as mentally ill or criminal. These norms and the disciplines for their achievement were justified by a careful examination of the daily life and habits of the population (birth and death rates, fiscal and health policies, educational and occupational aptitudes, and so forth). The other side of this social technology is a technology of the self, which produces a human individuality that is able to be carefully observed and described in written documentation: everyone becomes a case.[12] This modern ceremony of anthropological objectification is the epistemological space for personal individuality to be described and, if necessary, corrected. It is one of the openings for the development of the human sciences. While there can be no question of a monocausal theory, Foucault has restored the significance of the broadly political dimension, the modern period's need and manner of social governance, as crucial for comprehending the specific style of our culture's knowledge of the self and the network of power-knowledge relations in which Freudian analysis may appear. We can gain a more concrete appreciation for his approach by looking at how Foucault dealt with three central elements in Freudian psychoanalysis: the unconscious, the role of sexuality, and the functioning of the medical model.

1. The Unconscious. In his work, *The Order of Things*, Foucault examined the foundations for modernity's constitution of man as an "empirico-transcendental" doublet, the difficult object of knowledge as well as the presumed sovereign subject of knowing.[13] Man appears in a specific epistemological domain as the being who lives, produces and speaks or who must practice governance of the life process, the exchange of wealth, and the discourses of knowledge. Three disciplines become privileged in modern man's positive knowledge of himself: economics, biology, philology. Each of these empirical domains has its own proper history—the internal

laws that describe the various ways of life's adaptation to an environment, the modes of development in economic production, the modifications in language. The character of modern man's finitude is proclaimed through these three domains: he is the organism living under the sentence of death, the figure condemned to exist by the sweat of his brow, a process of thinking forced to lodge itself in the density of language. At the same time, however, he is not identical with life, labor, or language, but is dispersed within these empirical domains, which possess histories alien to and independent of him. It is this dispersion that establishes a specifically modern opaqueness at the heart of self-knowledge.

> How can man *be* that life whose web, pulsations, and buried energy constantly exceed the experience that he is immediately given of them? How can he *be* that labour whose laws and demands are imposed upon him like some alien system? How can he be the subject of a language that for thousands of years has been formed without him, a language whose organization escapes him, whose meaning sleeps an almost invincible sleep in the words he momentarily activates by means of discourse, and within which he is obliged, from the very outset, to lodge his speech and thought, as though they were doing no more than animate, for a brief period, one segment of that web of innumerable possibilities?[14]

Psychoanlysis occupies a privileged position in modern thought because it explores but is also defined by this opaqueness or unconsciousness generated in modernity's articulation of man as living, laboring, speaking. The themes of Death, Desire, and Law, in which one's psychoanalytic search for intelligibility takes place, are born together with and remain dependent upon modern knowledge's drawing of man in these three great regions of life, labor, speech. In exploring these psychoanalytical regions, modern Western culture is brought back to the foundations for its own self-knowledge and, thus, as Foucault pointed out, "pivots on the work of Freud, though without, for all that, leaving its fundamental arrangement."[15]

2. The central role that sexuality plays in the psychoanalytic image of the person is the second of those elements that indicate Freudian thought's coherence with the modern network of knowledge-power. The first volume of Foucault's *History of Sexuality* has sketched the context in which sexuality and its liberation or repression become defining features of modern self-identity. In contrast to the popular conception of a long history of sexual repression that has only recently been challenged, Foucault claimed that the nineteenth and twentieth centuries produced an explosion of discourses

concerned with sexuality, a proliferation of pathological forms of unorthodox sexualities, and a multiplication of institutional sites for their study. Indeed, rather than repressing sexuality, the modern period has engaged in a threefold sexual production: first, the very creation of sexuality as a reality and meaning for us, including the sexualization of children's experience;[16] secondly, the constitution of a science of sexuality that aims at establishing the truth of sexual experience by global study of the population and analytic study of the individual—what we take sexuality to be is correlative to this *scientia sexualis*;[17] thirdly, this sexuality was attached to the question of personal identity and came to function as the "seismograph of our subjectivity." We "demand that it tell us our truth, or rather, the deeply buried truth of that truth about ourselves which we think we possess in our immediate consciousness."[18] Within our order of governance, this fabrication of sexuality serves a crucial function. It provides our culture's disciplinary power with innumerable points of access and intervention into the life of individual and social bodies, while at the same time disarming potential criticism of such extensive intrusion. It accomplishes this by inscribing sexuality within the space of repression. For disciplinary power to function with the ease that it does, its pervasiveness must be hidden beneath a web of a limited and clearly identified series of repressions. The extent of its exercise is tied to the perception of power as a mere limit placed on people's desire, "leaving a measure of freedom—however slight—intact." "Power as a pure limit set on freedom is, at least in our society, the general form of its acceptability."[19]

Freud's psychoanalysis obviously operates within this modern regime of sexuality and even intensifies it. It gives support to the conception of sex as a stubborn drive, constantly at war with repressive powers; psychoanalysis, therefore, obscures the positive function of power as productive of what we take the sexual realm and its themes to be. And, for Foucault, this is the case whether the psychoanalytic approach is according to a theory of instincts or in terms of how the law itself constitutes the nature of sexual desire.[20] In addition, psychoanalysis unifies the system of the family with the modern sphere of sexuality by placing the incest desire at the center of the individual's sexual life. Freud cooperated in constituting the family as a privileged target for political governance in that he transformed it into the "germ of all the misfortunes of sex."[21] Finally, psychoanalysis provides one of the most striking examples in the modern transformation of medieval pastoral power. It has taken over the techniques of confessional practice, and thus places the individual under the obligation to manifest truth to another in a situation of dependence and through the action of speech, which is invested with a special virtue of verification. Charged with responsibility for the lifting of psychical repression, the self's task of truth is tied to the challenging of taboos, and thus, in Foucault's view, has its search for personal freedom all too often diverted into a quest for illusory sexual liberations.[22]

3. The medical model is a third factor that exhibits Freud's anthropological modernity. We know Freud's wish: in writing to Oskar Pfister, he pointed to a secret link between *The Question of Lay Analysis* and *The Future of an Illusion*: "In the former I wish to protect analysis from the doctors and in the latter from the priests."[23] In fact, he seems to have accomplished a union of the two professions, what he called "*lay* curers of souls" or a "secular pastoral worker."[24] Although Freud took over some religious techniques for the production of subjectivity, it is the medical model that triumphs in psychoanalysis. While he admitted that psychoanalysis "had its original on medical soil," Freud hoped that it could be readily transplanted.[25] Consistent with this, Bettelheim has recently claimed that the idea of psychoanalysis as the treatment and cure of mental illness is but an unfortunate metaphor in which the body merely stands for the soul.[26] For Foucault, such a claim misunderstands the place of both the body and medicine in modern experience. With respect to the body, it is important to recognize that the modern technology of the self has involved an intricate technology of the body. Calculated methods for disciplining it—its gestures, movements, attitudes, and so on—have been elaborated in a variety of institutions (the school, hospital, prison, factory, army). What this technology has produced is Man-the-Machine, which is not just a metaphysical concept but a physical reality. In the modern period, this body has been identified with the self to an unprecedented degree. Knowledge of the self is coupled to a medical and scientific reading of the body, a reading made possible by its machine status.[27]

In order to understand the dominant position of the medical model, however, one must consider another factor even more important than the disciplining of the body. For Foucault, modern knowledge of the truth of one's self is rooted in a certain type of medical perception. His study, *The Birth of the Clinic*, argued that clinical medicine was the first science of the individual. Integral to this science was the role of death as constitutive of one's individuality and unique intelligibility, a status that was the precondition for the extraordinary importance given by historians to pathological anatomy in the development of a science of medicine. Death and disease broke from metaphysical understandings and became essential elements in the identity of the person. The idea of a disease attacking life and destroying it is replaced by the conception that death is embodied in the living bodies of individuals. It is not because diseases attack him that man dies; it is because he will die that he is susceptible to disease. Created here is the crucially significant notion of a "pathological life," which can be carefully charted and analyzed in terms of an individual's existence.[28] But death is the essential truth of human life, and any inquiry into the meaning of individual life is guaranteed to meet that medical perception that holds up to man the "face of his finitude" but also promises to exorcise it through certain techniques.[29] The medical component is clear in questions of sexuality, but if Foucault was correct, all knowledge of the modern finite, bound-to-death self is oriented, by its object, to aim at a truth that aspires to function as cure. This would explain why Freud, who could demystify so many of the asylum's major structures—its constant silence, observation, condemnation—could not eliminate the place occupied by the doctor upon whom these structures are concentrated: the trained observer whose silence is judgment.[30] It is the very knowledge of our finite, individual selves that invites a medical paradigm and accounts for the fact that, in our culture, Freud and medical thought have come to take on philosophical significance.[31] In its reflection on the modern experience of being human, philosophy encounters a reality in large part produced by medical understandings. Likewise, the controversies that swirl around the relationship between medicine and psychoanalysis are native and permanent to Freudian thought to the extent of its modernity.

Foucault's critique of Freud, for whose thought and therapy he certainly had no replacement, may seem extremely unhelpful to those who are concerned with the question of psychosis, especially to those who must deal with the undeniable suffering of those diagnosed as psychotic. My remarks may seem a long-winded prelude to yet another raising of the antipsychiatry banner. Certainly, Foucault did share a superficial resemblance with this movement and its commitment to political-historical analysis of our therapeutic culture and institutions. Nevertheless, to conceive his archaeology as a simple antipsychiatry or antipsychoanalysis would be to miss the specificity of Foucault's thought and to misunderstand the dilemma in which his investigations wish to place us.[32] The emphasis certainly must be put there; the fragments of his archaeology of psychoanalysis, like all of his archaeologies, aim at making us aware of our options within the current historical moment. Foucault's attempt to make us aware of the need for dialogue with the voices of madness and to clear away some of the conceptional rigidity blocking such conversation is not, by any means, a celebration of psychosis. Detaching psychosis from a psychiatric or psychoanalytic model will not transform it into freedom or creativity. Within our social system, those identified as psychotic are always more or less victims who display for us the specter of a very particular fate: the loss of the modern possession of self, which places one in a situation of marginality within our culture and which exposes one to a wide range of disciplinary interventions in one's day to day life. Psychoanalysis itself testifies to this meaning of psychosis as loss of the modern self by frequently placing it beyond its own capacity to reach and heal. This outcome should be expected if, as Foucault has argued, psychoanalysis operates strictly within the framework of a modern fabrication of the self.[33] The plight of the psychotic's loss of self serves as a warning of what might occur to one who no longer follows modernity's path of self-development and self-knowledge, that task of binding ourselves to a positive nature that a specific technology of the self has fabricated and on which it has conferred a truth status. Our interminable examination of the unconscious, our identification with sexuality, our pursuit of an exorcism for death—each of these is a way to make us at home with our selves. The failure or refusal to bind oneself to this positive nature as an identity places one, at best, in a situation of jeopardy within our culture or targets one as mentally ill, with all that comes in the wake of such a status. Psychosis represents a rupturing of bonds with modern identity, but in such a way as to be confined in a place of silent exteriority to our culture. If the loss of the modern self poses frightening consequences, adherence to it is no less risky.

To embrace the modern system of undertaking and shaping the self is to make oneself subject to a series of norms dictating one's identity and exiling one's uniqueness. It is the choice to live in what Foucault called the "carceral archipelago": "The judges of normality are present everywhere. We are in the society of the teacher-judge, the doctor-judge, the 'social worker'-judge, the educator-judge; it is on them that the universal reign of the normative is based; and each individual, wherever he may find himself, subjects to it his body, his gestures, his behavior, his aptitudes, his achievements."[34] And, as Foucault's most recent work emphasized, this is not a tragedy just of individual lives. Arrogant in its knowledge and secure in the legitimacy for its power that such knowledge confers, modern political practice culminates in the atomic situation. The commitment to a knowledgeable governance exercised on life itself leads to the possibility of conceiving of a nuclear holocaust as a strategy for guaranteeing the biological survival of a national population. "But what might be called a society's 'threshold of modernity' has been reached when the life of the species is wagered on its own political strategies."[35] Although the nuclear situation is novel, the attitudes toward power and knowledge in the modern period, which have made it possible, are at least as ancient as the authority to define who we are, to determine our formation, and to separate the mad from the normal.

If neither loss of nor adherence to the modern self is a suitable alternative in contemporary life, what is? Foucault implicitly suggested two possible strategies. First is an engagement in the movement of renouncing the modern self.[36] I stress that it is a movement of renunciation because it must be considered as a series of always specific rejections of particular effects resulting from our current technology of self; it is not a simple act of overthrowing the Father or whatever else is perceived as functioning in his place. One of the specifically modern features of psychosis, as opposed to earlier historical forms of madness, may well be that its withdrawal from a shared world proceeds from a very modern sense of power as fundamentally repressive, and therefore of resistance to it as an issue of either-or, total Refusal or total Submission. The devastating entrapment by this type of reaction is one of the most important of the insights provided by the plight of modern psychotics. The second strategy is to abandon the modern will to know the truth of personal identity and acknowledge the self as a region of sameness and otherness that emerges from creative response to the particular historical situation of one's life. The abandonment of oneself as a truth and an identity, able to be deciphered by the human sciences and to be directed by their technologies, places one on a journey with no promise of a safe destination at its end. But this seems a mere recognition of the precarious condition of being human and historical. Foucault's work reminds us, in this age of technologies for the self, of the risk entailed by the human condition.

Looked at once again, perhaps the Oedipus legend still has the power to speak to us, but for reasons quite different from those that Freud put forward. A Foucauldian understanding of the power-knowledge technology, which has produced ourselves and the forms of self-analysis we employ, wrenches each of us from the positive truth we seem to be, an act that is comparable to the violence of a parricide or the unnaturalness of incest.[37] Oedipus's supposed discovery of his identity is, in fact, a revelation of how he has been fashioned as a visible, intelligible object for others. In him we glimpse the refusing blindness to all that is so clear and natural about our modern self, which follows bringing to light the historically contingent manner of that self's birth. For Foucault, such blindness is less ignorant and dangerous than the arrogance of modern self-knowledge. It is in the region of this renewed darkness about ourselves that a genuine dialogue with madness may take place; it will be a dialogue engaged in for the sake of a fresh encounter with the enigmatic otherness that is part of ourselves and that modernity attempted to stigmatize, silence, or cure. Foucault's contribution to facilitating that dialogue is an analysis that seeks to locate our questions about ourselves in the particular historical-political field within which they arise. This inquiry bears an essential affinity to that of Oedipus himself inasmuch as his name can be taken literally to mean "know where."[38] It is only in grasping from which historical situation our taken-for-granted questions about ourselves come that we will have the chance to encounter ourselves in our full complexity and answer the question of Oedipus: "Who begat me?" In assisting the achievement of that knowledge, Foucault's blinding archaeology of psychoanalysis leaves us with the hope that, as Oedipus at Colonus came to recognize, the "blind man's words will be instinct with sight."[39] Into ourselves. Into our madness.

NOTES

1. *Folie et déraison: Histoire de la folîe à l'âge classique* (Paris: Plon, 1961), trans., in greatly abridged form, by Richard Howard as *Madness and Civilization* (New York: Mentor, 1967).

2. *Madness and Civilization*, x; Foucault, *Mental Illness and Psychology*, trans. by Alan Sheridan (New York: Harper and Row, 1976), 73.

3. In addition to Foucault's study *Raymond Roussel* (Paris: Gallimard, 1963), cf. the articles on literature collected in his *Language, Counter-Memory, Practice: Selected Essays and Interviews,* ed. by Donald Bouchard and trans. by him and Sherry Simon (Ithaca: Cornell University Press, 1977), and Foucault's "The Life of Infamous Men" in *Power, Truth, Strategy,* ed. by Meaghan Morris and Paul Patton (Sydney, Australia: Feral Publications, 1979), 76–91.

4. *Madness and Civilization,* 162; cf. Foucault's "La folie, l'absence d'oeuvre," *La Table Ronde* (May, 1964), republished as appendix to 1972 edition of *Histoire de la folie,* 575–582.

5. Foucault, *The Order of Things: An Archaeology of the Human Sciences* (New York: Pantheon, 1971, original French, 1966), 361; "La recherche scientifique et la psychologie" in *Des chercheurs francais s'interrogent,* ed. by Jean-Edouard Morère (Paris: PUF, 1957), 195–196; *Mental Illness and Psychology,* 87.

6. Foucault, *The History of Sexuality, Vol. 1: An Introduction,* trans. by Robert Hurley (New York: Pantheon, original French, 1976), 130.

7. S. Freud, *The Interpretation of Dreams* (1901); English translation published in *The Standard Edition,* vol. 4, ed. by James Strachey (London: Hogarth, 1973), 262.

8. Ibid.

9. In three lectures at the Collège de France (Jan. 16, 23, 30, 1980), Foucault suggested the political approach to the analysis of the Oedipus legend that I mention here. In the first volume of his history of sexuality, Foucault has drawn attention to how nineteenth-century western governments committed themselves, as a requirement for national direction and growth of the State, to a detailed study and regulation of sexual matters. In the already vast recent literature on the development of sexuality as a political issue, two articles may be especially recommended. Cf. George Mosse, "Nationalism and Respectability: Normal and Abnormal Sexuality in the Nineteenth Century," and Sterling Fishman's "The History of Childhood Sexuality," both in *Journal of Contemporary History* 17 (1982): 221–246 and 269–283.

10. Foucault, *The Order of Things,* 387.

11. On this theme and its difference from premodern forms of governance, cf. *The History of Sexuality,* vol. 1, 135–159; "Governmentality," trans. by Rosi Braidotti, *Ideology and Consciousness* 6 (Autumn, 1979): 5–21; "The Subject and Power," trans. by Leslie Sawyer, *Critical Inquiry* 8 (Summer, 1982): 777–795.

12. Foucault, *Discipline and Punish: The Birth of the Prison,* trans. by Alan Sheridan (New York: Pantheon, 1977, original French 1975), 170–194.

13. Foucault, *The Order of Things,* chapters 8–10.

14. Ibid., 323.

15. Ibid., 361.

16. Cf. Foucault, *The History of Sexuality I,* 104–105.

17. Cf. Ibid., 68.

18. Foucault, "Sexuality and Solitude," *London Review of Books* (May 21–June 3, 1981), 5; *The History of Sexuality I,* 70.

19. Foucault, *History of Sexuality,* vol. 1, 86.

20. Ibid., 82–83.

21. Ibid., cf. 103–114.

22. Ibid., 130. On the theme of pastoral power, cf. Foucault's "Omnes et Singulatim: Towards a Criticism of 'Political Reason'" in R. Aron et al., *The Tanner Lectures on Human Values II* (Salt Lake City: University of Utah Press, 1981), 225–254.

23. S. Freud and Oskar Pfister, *Psychoanalysis and Faith: The Letters of Sigmund Freud and Oskar Pfister,* ed. by Heinrich Meng and Ernest Freud, trans. by Eric Mosbacher (New York: Basic Books, 1963), 126.

24. Ibid. and "Postscript" to "The Question of Lay Analysis" in *The Standard Edition,* ed. by James Strachey (London: Hogarth Press, 1973), vol. 12, 255.

25. "Introduction to Pfister's *The Psycho-Analytic Method*" (1913) in *The Standard Edition,* vol. 12, 329.

26. Bruno Bettelheim, "Freud and the Soul," *The New Yorker* (March 1, 1982): 67–68.

27. Cf. Foucault, *Discipline and Punish,* 3–31, 135–169; and Foucault, *Power/Knowledge: Selected Interviews and Other Writings 1972–1977,* ed. by Colin Gordon (New York: Pantheon, 1980), 59.

28. Foucault, *The Birth of the Clinic: An Archaeology of Medical Perception,* trans. by A.M. Sheridan Smith (New York: Vintage, 1973, original French 1963), 153.

29. Ibid., 198.

30. Cf. Foucault, *Madness and Civilization,* 216–222.

31. Foucault, *The Birth of the Clinic,* 199.

32. It is quite common to place Foucault in the antipsychiatry movement (for the most recent example of this tendency, cf. Frank Cioffi, "Honours for Craziness," *London Review of Books* 4,1 [June 17–30, 1982]: 10). To some extent, this identification is due to R. D. Laing's launching of *Madness and Civilization* for English speaking readers (see his "The Invention of Madness" in *The New Statesman* 73 [June 16, 1967]: 843) and the fact that Foucault was obviously doing a critique of psychiatric categories and practices. Foucault argued that antipsychiatry is intrinsic to the power-knowledge network that gives birth to psychiatry itself (cf. "Histoire des systèmes de pensée" in *Annuaire du Collège de France* 74 [1974]: 293–300). For Foucault, much of antipsychiatry's criticism emerges from within a humanistic perspective, as for example, Szasz's concentration upon the power of the State (cf. Foucault's "Sorcellerie et folie" in *Le Monde* 9720 [April 23, 1976]: 18). In *Power/Knowledge,* Foucault's desire to disassociate himself from the movement is clear: "Why should an archaeology of psychiatry function as an 'antipsychiatry', when an archaeology of biology does not function as an antibiology?" (192) Although it is directed to the work of Robert Castel, Peter Miller's "The Territory of the Psychiatrist" is a very helpful consideration of the issues separating antipsychiatry from approaches such as Foucault's (*Ideology and Consciousness* 7 [Autumn, 1980]: 63–105).

33. Cf. Foucault, *The Order of Things,* 375–376.

34. Foucault, *Discipline and Punish,* 304.

35. Foucault, *History of Sexuality* I, 143.

36. My formulations here, as in much of the previous paragraph, are based upon lectures by Foucault at Dartmouth College (Nov. 17 & 24, 1980) and at the University of Toronto (May 31–June 14, 1982).

37. In this interpretation, I rely upon that of Nietzsche in his *The Birth of Tragedy,* trans. by Francis Golffing (New York: Doubleday-Anchor, 1956), 61.

38. For this interpretation, cf. Charles Segal, *Tragedy and Civilization: An Interpretation of Sophocles* (Cambridge: Harvard University Press, 1981), 223–224.

39. "Oedipus the King," line 437 and "Oedipus at Colonus," line 74, both trans. by F. Storr in *Sophocles* I (Cambridge, MA: Harvard University Press, 1912).

CHAPTER 12

UPSIDE-DOWN PSYCHIATRY: A GENEALOGY OF MENTAL HEALTH SERVICES

RICHARD F. MOLLICA

INTRODUCTION

Kingsley Davis' essay "Mental Hygiene and the Class Structure" (1) anticipated by more than twenty years the classic Hollingshead and Redlich study, *Social Class and Mental Illness* (1958) (2).

In 1938, Kingsley Davis analyzed the failure of the mental hygiene movement and the traditional mental health system to recognize the association between social values and treatment. He stated:

> Mental hygiene hides its adherence behind a scientific facade, but the ethical premises reveal themselves on every hand, partly through a blindness to scientifically relevant facts . . . In so far as the mental hygienist retains his ethical system, he misses a complete scientific analysis of his subject and hence fails to use the best technological means to his applied-science goal. But if he forswears his ethical beliefs, he is alienated from the movement and suffers the strictures of an outraged society. Actually, the mental hygienist will continue to ignore the dilemma. He will continue to be unconscious of his basic preconceptions at the same time that he keeps on professing objective knowledge. He will regard his lack of preventive success as an accident, a lag, and not as an intrinsic destiny. All because his social function is not that of a scientist but that of a practicing moralist in a scientific, mobile world (1).

According to Davis, the mental hygienists of the 1930s were unable to recognize the realities of psychiatric practice because of their adherence to a value system that created the illusion that social factors are not an important influence on diagnosis or treatment. In contrast, *Social Class and Mental Illness* was the first empirical study to reveal the major class differences in psychiatric care. These findings produced an important long-term impact on the delivery of mental health services to lower-class patients.

Over the past twenty-five-years, psychiatric care to the poor has improved dramatically. American society has experienced an enormous expansion in inpatient and outpatient services; private and public dollars spent on mental health services; and the types and numbers of psychiatric practitioners (3). Yet in spite of these noteworthy achievements, American mental health policy is currently questioning its ability to maintain its commitment to serve the seriously disturbed and disadvantaged. In fact, in spite of enormous advances in the scientific study of mental disorders, as well as the greater availability of effective psychiatric programs over the past half century, publicly supported mental health services are in serious disarray (4). Most state and federally supported programs (including the community mental health centers) are suffering from serious financial cut-backs and are under increasing political attack despite their many remarkable achievements (5).

Declining social interest in mental health programs, however, does not correspond to declining mental health needs. A recent report (6) of the National Academy of Sciences to the Federal Alcohol, Drug Abuse and Mental Health Administration (ADAMHA) states that at any given time epidemiologic evidence has demonstrated that 15 percent of the U.S. population is experiencing a diagnosable mental illness. The most common severe disorders are schizophrenia and depression. About 1 percent of the population will experience a schizophrenic episode sometime during their lives; about 300,000 episodes occur yearly. An additional nine to sixteen million individuals are suffering from depression; fewer than a third will receive any form of treatment. Suicide, homicide and violent deaths are leading causes of death among the young, especially young minority males. And special subgroups of the mentally ill (e.g. the "homeless," the "chronic patient," and political "refugees") continue to make demands for services on society's shrinking mental health budgets and resource-poor facilities.

The contradiction between the declining social support of mental health services and the actual need for these services suggests a serious discontinuity in psychiatric trends and social goals. Why is there a noticeable decline in publicly supported mental health care in spite of the well recognized and documented high rates of untreated psychiatric illness? Furthermore, is the class structure in mental health care (originally revealed by Hollingshead and Redlich) the *Filum Ariadne* that organizes the psychiatric system?

This chapter will answer these questions by elucidating the realities of modern psychiatric practice. Specific psychopathologies and the subjective experience of these disorders will not be discussed. It is recognized, however, that the disruption of social life that occurs with most serious mental illness cannot be separated from those personal and social resources utilized by the individual to reestablish his social role as well as to minimize disability. This investigation of psychiatric services, therefore, can indirectly contribute to a better understanding of specific mental disorders by elucidating those social attitudes and values that restrict the individual's ability to gain "help" and "healing."

This chapter will reveal the sources of the current contradictions in the mental health system by using an empirical approach developed by Michel Foucault. Foucault called his approach a "genealogy" (7). Whereas Foucault's earlier methodological strategy, which he called "archaeology," questioned the foundations, the *archai*, of the dominance inherent in epistemological foundationalism, his "genealogy" is a methodological strategy that problematizes the authority and legitimacy of the prevailing institutions of power; it focuses a radical challenge to the prevailing social organization of power by examining the historically contingent formation of existing arrangements and the distribution of power in social practices. Psychiatry, for Foucault, is a social practice. Like all social practices, it is constituted by power and serves as a "setting" through which power is exercised and invested. Psychiatry is also a "discursive formation." It is a "formation" because it has a history: how it came into being as a practice in the economy of power. And it is "discursive" because it not only came into being, but is also reproduced, through the medium of language. Psychiatry is "discursive" because psychiatric power is principally exercised through various forms of language: interviews, therapy sessions, consultations, reports, histories, policy decisions, clinical studies, theoretical research, legal documents, documents which set the professional standards for certification, and forms of communication that contribute to the public debate on mental health, the social need for psychiatric care, and the best ways to achieve this care.

Foucault's genealogy offers a new approach to mental health research. Yet, realization that the tasks and treatment practices of psychiatry are closely associated with the values and problems of society is not unique and had already received considerable historical and sociological attention in psychiatry prior to Foucault's major mental health treatise, *Madness and Civilization* (8). What is new and interesting about Foucault's method is his emphasis on the "discursive" meaning of concrete practices, i.e., that concrete practices serve as a "mirror" to society's world-view. Three epidemiological studies focusing on the cultural meaning of changing psychiatric diagnosis over time illustrate this point.

In their research on patient diagnosis at the New York State Psychiatric Institute between 1932 and 1956, Kursansky, Deming and Gurland (9) tried to determine if a sharp rise in the number of patients with a diagnosis of schizophrenia reflected temporal changes in the kinds of patients admitted, or shifts in the diagnostic concepts used by clinicians at the hospital. Morrison (10) studied temporal changes at the Iowa State Psychopathic Hospital (1920–1966) in the shifting use of the diagnostic subtypes of schizophrenia. He found that although the total number of schizophrenics in the hospital remained constant, the shift in diagnosis from catatonic and hebephrenic schizophrenia to chronic undifferentiated schizophrenia was dramatic; Blum (11) revealed major diagnostic trends in the diagnosis of depression at a single New Haven facility over three time periods (1954, 1965, 1974) that were not due to a true increase in presenting symptomology.

Social Class and Mental Illness and its twenty-five year follow-up, entitled "Trends in Mental Health" (12), provide a unique opportunity for conducting a genealogy of mental health services. These two large-scale epidemiological surveys, conducted in the same geographic region over two time periods, provide the empirical evidence necessary for elucidating those cultural and social factors that are generating the major contradictions in the modern psychiatric system. New strategies, called "upside-down" psychiatry, will also be presented in this paper, as a response to the prevailing trends in psychiatric care. These trends are alarming, because they suggest an even further decline in the availability and quality of the care being offered to society's most psychiatrically disabled individuals.

GENEALOGY: A METHOD OF EMPIRICAL INVESTIGATION

The method of investigation used in this chapter will be called "genealogy," following Foucault. It is best described in his philosophical treatise,

The Order of Things (13). Foucault began his discussion by pointing out the arbitrary nature of the scientific systems of classification.

> This book first arose out of a passage in Borges, out of the laughter that shattered, as I read the passage, all the familiar landmarks of my thought–*our* thought, the thought that bears the stamp of our age and our geography–breaking up all the ordered surfaces and all the planes with which we are accustomed to tame the wild profusion of existing things, and continuing long afterwards to disturb and threaten with collapse our age-old distinction between the Same and the Other. This passage quotes a "certain Chinese encyclopedia" in which it is written that "animals are divided into: (a) belonging to the Emperor, (b) embalmed, (c) tame, (d) sucking pigs, (e) sirens, (f) fabulous, (g) stray dogs, (h) included in the present classification, (i) frenzied, (j) innumerable, (k) drawn with a very fine camelhair brush, (l) et cetera, (m) having just broken the water pitcher, (n) that from a long way off look like flies." In the wonderment of this taxonomy, the thing we apprehend in one great leap, the thing that, by means of the fable, is demonstrated as the exotic charm of another system of thought, is the limitation of our own, the stark impossibility of thinking that. (Preface, XV)

Foucault began his genealogical investigations with a recognition of their "horizon." By "horizon," he meant the value system within every culture and historical period that is reflected in its categories, practices, routines, and rules. "Thus within every culture," he wrote, "between the use of what one might call the ordering codes and reflections upon order itself, there is the pure experience of order and its modes of being." (13) Foucault was interested in exploring this space. His examination leads to a concept of order: "Order is, at one and the same time, that which is given in things as their inner law, the hidden network that determines the way they confront one another, and also that which has no existence except in the grid created by a glance, an examination, a language (13).

Foucault stated that the interest of his investigations is in revealing the "positive unconsciousness of science," i.e., those epistemological levels of theory that give the scientific approach its methods, but that at the same time generate assumptions that elude the consciousness of the scientist, although they are still part of the scientific discourse. The goal of Foucault's genealogy, therefore, is to manifest the entire field of complex social forces and their contradictory relationships, which permit certain historical forms of social behavior, institutions, language, and so forth, to exist. These historical forms he called "discursive formations." As previously mentioned, what is most significant about Foucault's concept of discursive formations is that it focuses attention on concrete practices, which can be empirically elucidated. In addition, it demonstrates that these practices are complex and historically influenced (although not necessarily historically determined), (14, 15, 16, 17) and that they often produce socially contradictory and competing results. Foucault's methodology rethinks the old questions: what do social practices mean and why do they occur?

For Foucault, although social practices reveal the historical foundations of their society, these practices are not easily understood. For example, neither policy planners, patients nor psychiatrists can readily explain the abysmal conditions that exist in our nation's public mental hospitals. Furthermore, the intelligibility of these practices has little to do with either the intentions of the actors or with the consensually legitimated structural regularities of the practices. Also, rules do not determine practices; nor do rules simply follow from practices. Foucault's descriptions of concrete practices are, therefore, not descriptions of events devoid of all content; nor transparent signs through which hidden meanings can be readily detected; nor reflections of sociological or psychohistorical principles and/or trends. All elements—rules, regulations, practices and routines–are part of the complex web that makes up a discursive formation; i.e., empirical phenomena situated within a field of complex social forces. For example, some of the factors that constitute psychiatry's discursive formation are its professionalism, its scientific orientation and medical model, a private versus public dichotomy in financing, and involuntary commitment laws.

Foucault's critical method, as described in this section, has been important in focusing and interpreting my research in psychiatric epidemiology. It has generated four insights useful in assessing the meaning of psychiatric practice.

1. Every public policy decision in psychiatry has built into it a deep and often invisible structural contradiction. For example, a decision to build community shelters for homeless former hospital mental patients might serve these individuals while simultaneously outraging the local community because of the presence of "undesirable" vagrants. Contradictions in public policy are unavoidable. Competing self-interests always exist. What is essential, therefore, is not the avoidance of conflict, but the recognition and anticipation of contradictions. It is more courageous to make "open" choices in accordance with this understanding.

2. Concrete practices reveal the patient's "symbolic" relationships with society. Foucault never took for granted the obviousness of basic social categories. Practices reveal the individual's power and status within an institution, organization or social structure irrespective of the claims that are made in regard to these practices and/or individuals. In addition, changes in practices must be evaluated by whether or not they reflect genuine changes within the system's social structure, i.e., look out for "old wine in new bottles."
3. *Positionality* describes the process by which individuals are "assigned" or "positioned" into various social settings. For example, positionality describes how psychiatric facilities "categorize" patients, thereby defining their clinical relationship to the staff and the institution. This process determines the type and intensity of care received by patients, and it ultimately affects the outcome of treatment.
4. Psychiatry is a discursive function.

These four insights are used in the genealogical analysis that follows.

THE TRENDS IN MENTAL HEALTH PROJECT: A TWENTY-FIVE YEAR FOLLOW-UP TO SOCIAL CLASS AND MENTAL ILLNESS

In 1975, Fritz Redlich initiated in south-central Connecticut a twenty-five-year follow-up to the original study conducted in that region, *Social Class and Mental Illness*. This work was one of the first empirical studies to demonstrate the relationship between social class and the delivery of mental health services. Shortly after the follow-up was initiated by Redlich in 1975, I became the director of this project, which was entitled "Trends in Mental Health" (12). In this project we have been involved in reexamining the relationship between the social characteristics of psychiatry patients and the treatment they receive; we have also been studying the major trends in American psychiatry since 1950. The major objective of the "Trends in Mental Health" project was to determine if, twenty-five years after the original study, social class continued to have a major impact on the delivery of psychiatric care.

The results of the "Trends" project are based upon two large patient surveys conducted on all patients receiving psychiatric treatment in south-central Connecticut in 1975 and 1978 (18–23). The empirical results of this work can provide a genealogy of mental health services, since its investigative approach roughly conforms to the techniques used by Foucault and outlined above. First, the original Hollingshead and Redlich study introduced a radical "otherness" by focusing on the most neglected and undesirable segment of psychiatric practice—the state mental hospital and the lower-class patient. In fact, Hollingshead and Redlich empirically tested a hypothesis relating social class to treatment that their critics claimed was already well-known, and furthermore, an insignificant question unworthy of clarification. The long-term impact of *Social Class and Mental Illness* on mental health services did not substantiate the initial objections of these critics. Second, the "Trends in Mental Health" project continued the original study's approach by not assuming that "progress" in mental health care for lower-class patients had been achieved. This assumption, in fact, was widely accepted by the psychiatric establishment in the late 1970s. Third, the "Trends" project carefully examined the modern practices of psychiatric care by assuming that the basic relationship between class and treatment may have remained unchanged in spite of the introduction of new treatment strategies, i.e., "old wine in new bottles." An interpretation of the empirical findings of the "Trends" project can be used to construct a genealogy of modern psychiatric care.

THE FINDINGS OF THE TRENDS IN MENTAL HEALTH PROJECT

Figure 1 demonstrates the service delivery pattern for south-central Connecticut (12,21) Prior to 1950, the state mental hospital dominated all psychiatric treatment. In 1950, this facility accounted for 66.7 percent of all patient-care episodes and was essentially the only source of psychiatric care for the lower-class patient; publicly supported outpatient treatments did not exist. In 1975, different patterns of care existed. The state mental hospital had diminished its resident population by over 60 percent and accounted for only 23 percent of all patient-care episodes. In contrast, public outpatient care (primarily provided by the regional community mental health center (CMHC)) had expanded from 8.0 percent of all patient care episodes in 1950 to 33 percent in 1975.

National data (24) revealed findings similar to those found by the "Trends" project in south-central Connecticut. Over the past twenty-five years, there has been a significant shift away from private and publicly supported inpatient treatment. These dramatic changes in the service de-

Approximate Percentage of Total Patient Population by In-patient and Out-patient Facility, 1900, 1950, 1975, South Central Connecticut

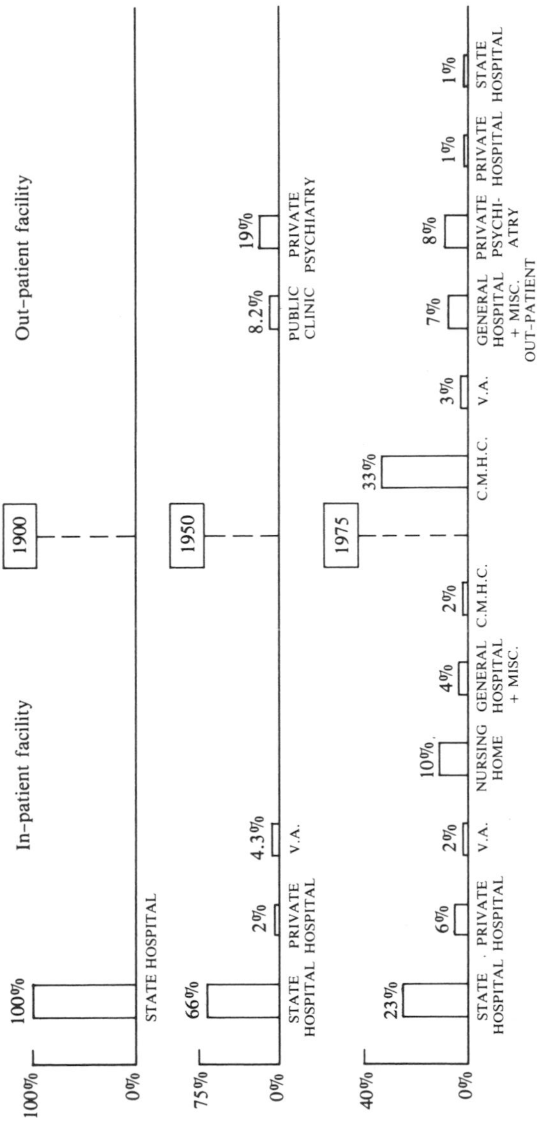

Note: V.A. = Veteran's Administration hospital

C. M. H. C. = Community Mental Health Center

FIGURE 1

livery system began in the early 1960s and were partially motivated by the sociological findings of Goffman (25), Hollingshead and Redlich (2), the enthusiasm of a young psychiatric profession, and the political sympathies of President John F. Kennedy (26). The 1960 Congressional Commission "Action for Mental Health" (27), initiated, under Kennedy's direction, a major mental health reform, the Community Mental Health Movement. This movement was directed by the Federal government to shift mental health care away from the state mental hospitals to publicly supported outpatient community mental health centers. Since its beginning, hundreds of CMHCs have been established throughout the United States. As demonstrated in Figure 1, the original goal of the CMHC movement has been partially accomplished in south-central Connecticut. Concurrently, private inpatient and outpatient facilities have also expanded in size and in the diversity of psychiatric institutions and practitioners available to the private patient. This proliferation in treatment institutions is reflected as well in the expansion in the numbers and in the diversity of service providers (3,28). In 1950, psychiatrists were virtually the only providers of active treatment in any mental health setting. For example, in 1950 in south-central Connecticut the patient-psychiatrist ratio was 8:1 for private hospitals and 168:1 for the state mental hospital. By contrast, in 1975 the state hospital had reduced its patient-psychiatrist ratio to 57:1 while the ratios in private hospitals remained essentially unchanged. Furthermore, while in 1950 both public and private outpatient treatment was provided exclusively by psychiatrists, by 1975 there were many different types of psychiatric professionals and paraprofessionals engaged in outpatient psychiatric settings. The "Trends in Mental Health" project, for example, revealed that in 1975 psychiatrists, psychologists, social workers and clergy counselors were all delivering privately supported outpatient psychotherapy. In contrast, nonprofessional mental health workers were providing psychiatric care at the CMHC along with other professionals, and were the primary and regular providers of treatment on all state mental hospital inpatient units. Psychiatrists were primarily used as consultants at the state mental hospitals.

The "Trends in Mental Health" project has demonstrated, in one geographical region, the enormous growth in services and practitioners that has occurred throughout the United States over the past twenty-five years. Yet, have these changes also influenced the type and quality of care assigned patients? In reviewing the history of modern American psychiatry, one sees clearly that there have always existed certain categories of psychiatric patients who have been either neglected or treated poorly by psychiatric institutions (29–31). When Hollingshead and Redlich conducted their original study in 1950, they focused primarily on the impact of social class on psychiatric treatment. Their analysis did not consider the influence in treatment of other patient/social characteristics. For example, they did not consider that, in addition to the influence of class, gender and race could also affect the delivery of treatment. What they basically wanted to discover was whether or not social class had any impact on where, how and for how long a patient was treated.

Hollingshead and Redlich's original findings are well known. In 1950, for neurotic patients in outpatient treatment, the lower the social class of the patient the greater the use of organic treatments as opposed to psychotherapy, the fewer the number of clinic visits, and the shorter the length of the therapy hour. One important correlation was the relationship between social class and the professional level of assigned therapist. Upper-class patients received fully trained psychiatrists; middle-class patients received treatment from medical students. Analysis of the treatment of patients with psychotic illnesses revealed similar trends. Lower-class patients used the state mental hospital exclusively and received organic treatment and custodial care. Psychotic patients of higher social classes used private hospitals and received psychotherapy; even within the state hospital, social class differences influenced treatment. Middle- to lower-class patients received significantly less custodial care than the lowest classes of patients within the same facility. The relationship between social class and inpatient treatment was probably the most startling and impressive finding of the Hollingshead and Redlich study. For psychotic patients, the lower the class of the patient the longer the hospitalization. In fact, the average length of inpatient hospitalization for upper-class schizophrenic patients was five years less than that for lower-class patients. In addition, while upper-class patients tended to move "in and out" of the hospital, lower-class patients had long, continuous and uninterrupted hospitalizations. In other words, once a lower-class patient was admitted to the state mental hospital, he remained there.

During the 1960s, many additional studies provided further evidence supporting Hollingshead and Redlich's findings. (32) A summary of these results include:

1. Treatment assignment and psychiatric diagnosis is less related to presenting symptoms than to socio-economic status; lower-class patients are generally perceived by staff as "sicker" and as having a worse prognosis than higher classes of patients;

2. Lower-class patients are less likely to be assigned to individual psychotherapy than patients of higher social class. They are more likely to be offered organic treatment (e.g. ECT, drugs) and be placed in medical clinics;
3. When admitted to psychiatric treatment, lower-class patients generally receive less experienced therapists, briefer treatment sessions, shorter lengths of treatment, and have a higher attrition rate than patients of higher social class.

The "Trends in Mental Health" project highlighted a number of important class-related changes in treatment. Public psychiatry reduced its dependency on the state hospital by shifting away from long-term custodial care to short-term inpatient and public outpatient treatment. This process was accomplished by discharging patients from the state hospitals and limiting admissions to these facilities, i.e., "deinstitutionalization." However, considerable evidence has surfaced that the "deinstitutionalization" of patients from the state mental hospitals has created serious problems for these patients. (5,33) Psychotic patients have been found living in "flophouses" under abysmal conditions. Many of these patients have replaced their isolation in the state mental hospital with the isolation of living in a hostile and unaccepting community; some are "homeless." In addition, all evidence has revealed that, although the state mental hospitals have decreased their resident population by two-thirds, admission rates to these facilities have quadrupled since 1950. A significant proportion of chronic patients are involved in the "revolving door" syndrome. (34) In addition, the state mental hospital partially diminished its resident population by discharging large numbers of elderly patients into nursing homes. In our survey of the medical records of the elderly at the state mental hospital in south-central Connecticut, it was impossible to determine what had happened to these patients once they had been discharged. It can only be assumed that the majority are in nursing home institutions where they are receiving little if any psychiatric treatment. Despite recognition of the fact that there have been many controversial and poorly conceived programs, deinstitutionalization remains an important aspect of the new reformed psychiatric system.

The "Trends" project also revealed that, in spite of an enormous proliferation in psychiatric inpatient services in the region, social class remained a major predictor of the locus of inpatient care (22). Individuals with major psychiatric disorders from the lower classes were still primarily receiving their treatment at the same mental hospital. For example, blacks from the region utilized this facility exclusively. The treatment implications of these findings are significant, since the state mental hospitals are poorly funded and publicly neglected institutions. In addition, deinstitutionalization and the shift of higher classes of patients to private inpatient facilities have contributed to a pooling of the most socially disabled patients in the public inpatient units. This "creaming" effect has essentially overloaded the state facilities with the most socially disabled patients with no hope of receiving effective treatment.

In contrast, lower-class patients are primarily receiving their outpatient services at the regional CMHC (18,19,21). Yet this introduction of publicly supported outpatient care has not totally eliminated the impact of social class on psychiatric care. Our survey of the regional CMHC demonstrated that although lower-class and minority patients were admitted to the CMHC in fairly high numbers (comparable to their relative proportion within the community), these same groups were found stratified on the CMHC's categorical treatment units as compared to its psychotherapy unit (21,23). Categorical treatment units treat patients of similar diagnosis (e.g. drug unit for drug-addicted patients). These units provide their patients with organic therapies and brief counseling contacts; they rely heavily on nonprofessional staff. In contrast, the psychotherapy unit is staffed by professionals who meet with their patients on a weekly basis and provide individual, group, and family psychotherapy.

Figure 2 reveals that psychiatrists spend little time treating patients on the CMHC's categorical treatment units (20). An admission study at

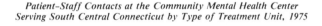

Patient–Staff Contacts at the Community Mental Health Center Serving South Central Connecticut by Type of Treatment Unit, 1975

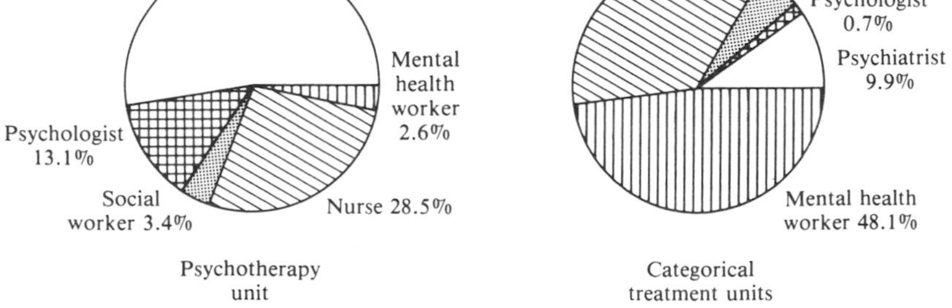

FIGURE 2

the regional CMHC further revealed that although lower-class patients gained access to outpatient treatment at the CMHC, more than 50 percent were discharged without a treatment assignment (21). Those discharged without help were most likely to be unemployed lower-class women and those individuals who lived alone or in households where no one at all worked. In contrast, those lower-class patients who were selected for treatment on the CMHC's professionally staffed psychotherapy unit were most likely to be female, employed and diagnosed psychoneurotic. These findings demonstrate the importance of "employability" in influencing entry into the CMHC as well as access to the CMHC's professional staff.

GENEALOGY OF MENTAL HEALTH SERVICES

The findings of the "Trends in Mental Health" project continue to demonstrate the important relationship between social class and other class-related factors such as race, gender, and employment in the delivery of psychiatric services. These findings can be used to reveal the discursive formation of modern psychiatric practice. The major question to be asked is: "What is the nature of this discursive formation, and why does it give continuing stability to the original Hollingshead and Redlich findings?" The "Trends" project revealed that the basic practices of psychiatry remain unchanged (see Figure 3) even after twenty-five years of the Community Mental Health Center Movement and an unprecedented expansion in the mental health system.

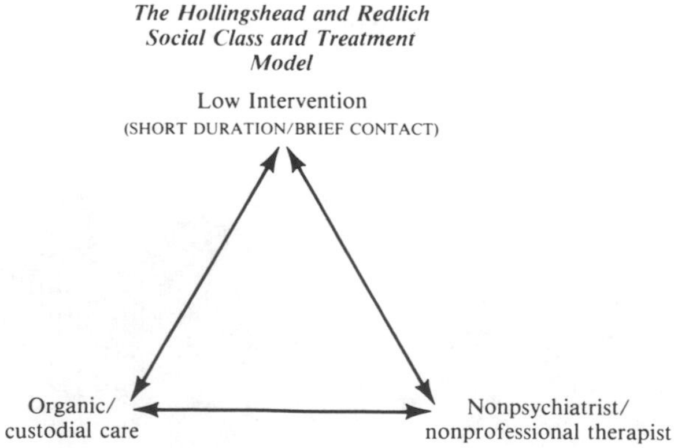

FIGURE 3

The concrete practices needed for constructing our genealogy of mental health care have already been presented in this essay. Yet we still have not determined the discursive meaning of these practices. *Social Class and Mental Illness* attempted the latter by radically challenging the results of the prevailing ideology of psychiatric treatment at that time, i.e., psychoanalysis (35). Hollingshead and Redlich addressed the inequalities in patient well-being and patient services by implying that these inequalities were partially due to psychoanalytically derived attitudes towards lower-class patients. They also postulated, however, that the health-seeking behavior of lower-class patients was different from that of higher classes of patients. The attitudes and values of lower-class patients reenforced a professional orientation, which generated the model illustrated in Figure 3. Hollingshead and Redlich, therefore, used these assumptions to recommend expansion and greater accessibility in psychiatric services for the poor. Innovative strategies were also subsequently developed to help working-class patients accept and utilize these new, readily available programs. This "equity of access" model, unfortunately, has proven itself unable to sustain a major psychiatric program reform. In fact, after more than twenty-five years of a national effort to achieve "equity of access," i.e., readily available psychiatric care for all citizens regardless of ability to pay, the modern psychiatric system has now entered a state of confusion and disintegration. Although challenging the psychiatric ideologies of their day, Hollingshead and Redlich did not advance an analysis that could ultimately explain the persistence of their major findings more than twenty-five years later.

The Hollingshead and Redlich conclusions subscribed only weakly to Kingsley Davis' position that class divisions and ideologies are responsible for differences both in the degree and in the quality of the mental health care that people can get (1). The sociopolitical realities of mental health care, which have been demonstrated over the past twenty-five years, support the important usefulness of Davis' initial observations in penetrating to the core of psychiatry's discursive formation. In contrast to Hollingshead and Redlich, the Italian psychiatric reformers attempted to reveal the latter by focusing upon the political organization of mental health services. In 1973, Franco Basaglia, leader of the Italian reform, pointed out, in his famous essay, "che cos' è la psichiatria?" (What is psychiatry?) (36), the dangers inherent in the scientific method, viz., that, "in moving away from us, [it] proceeds to theoretical conception, observation, examination and dismembering of the real person with a view toward scientifically reconstructing a scientific image of him." Much less cautious than Hollingshead and Redlich, Basaglia stated that, "the patient has been destroyed more by what the illness has been held to be and by the 'protective measures' imposed by such an interpretation than by the illness itself" (36). Recognizing the abysmal realities of the Italian asylums, the Italian reformers developed a new methodology for approaching the mentally ill.

The new Italian psychiatry that emerged in the 1960's, which has generated the most radical mental health reform seen anywhere in either Europe or the United States, sought to comprehend the failure of psychiatry's scientific method to improve the life and social conditions of the asylum patient. Again, Franco Basaglia stated: (36)

> And so we have, on the one hand, a science ideologically committed to a quest for the origins of an illness it acknowledges to be "incomprehensible" and, on the other hand, a patient who, because of his presumed "incomprehensibility," has been oppressed, mortified, and destroyed by an asylum system that, instead of serving him in its protective role of therapeutic institution, has, on the contrary, contributed to the gradual and often irreversible disintegration of his identity.

The Italian reformers denied the neutral, nonpolitical role assumed by empirical psychiatry. Although they did not deny the existence of neurology-based illness, they emphasized that illness always needs to be considered within a social, political and interpersonal context.

Basaglia and his colleagues offered a sociopolitical theory that could explain the absymal conditions of neglect and abuse offered working-class and asylum patients (37). "Emargination" was the term used by the Italian psychiatrists to designate the social process by which mental patients were isolated and segregated from society. The Italian reformers believed that the asylums represented the successful management of the displaced poor and served as well to punish and segregate individuals who were considered socially deviant. "Chronification" was considered by the Italians to be the "second disease" caused by the social exclusion, neglect, and mistreatment of patients through institutionalization. Although the Italian reform movement did not deny the physical or psychological basis of mental illness, it neglected empirical categories and elected to treat only the "second disease."

As I have shown, although Basaglia never recognized the influences of Antonio Gramsci on his thinking, in fact Basaglia was strongly influenced by the latter's sociopolitical theory (38). In 1926, Gramsci, who was Italy's leading political theorist and revolutionary thinker, was arrested by Mussolini and subsequently sentenced to a fascist prison, where he died in 1937. Following Gramsci, Basaglia made use of the concept of hegemony—the idea that society is a community that accepts patterns of behavior, institutional directions, and cultural ideas proposed to large groups of populations by the dominant group—in order to reject those historically based practices in Italian society that repress the mentally ill. Referring to the "spontaneous consent to accept new ideas," which according to Gramsci lies in the hands of the population, the Italian reformers proposed a social reform that would attack society's hegemonic practices at all levels—cultural, political, social, educational, and so on.

Three unremitting aspects of the discursive formation of modern psychiatric practice that emerge, therefore, are:

1. Major contradictions exist between psychiatry's expressed social ideals and its actual institutional practices;
2. Many practices of psychiatry are repressive, because they deprive individuals of the opportunities to straighten out their lives;
3. Psychiatry has silently consented to the social neglect of rehabilitative programs needed by patients for successful reintegration into society.

Furthermore, the repressive social practices of the discursive formation, which impair the psychiatric patient's efforts to normalize his life, include:

1. The dominant role of empirical assumptions in orienting psychiatric institutions; e.g., the emphasis on diagnosis without treatment goals; the use of drugs without supporting therapies;
2. Professional expectations that certain patients are either resistant to treatment or incapable of benefiting from professional care and/or psychological therapies;
3. The devaluation of the human capacities of the patient on account of his assumed incurable deficiencies, i.e., "chronification";
4. The automatic "emargination" of the psychiatric patients;
5. The social exclusion of the patient, including neglect and mistreatment in surroundings that lack respect for human dignity, i.e., overemphasis on custodial care;
6. The "institutionalization" of the staff in the asylum and CMHCs, i.e., the staff assumes the attitude and role of paternalizing caretakers instead of exercising their professional skills to help the patient return to normal existence.

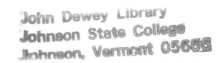

These practices reveal the contradictions within psychiatry as a healing profession, which distort the true potential of psychiatric patients to be rehabilitated. Furthermore, they bring to light the attitudes and strategies of social institutions, such as the mental hospital, which keep mental patients outside of the social life of their community. The discursive formation of modern psychiatry, therefore, is "hegemonically" based within societal prejudices (also accepted by patients) that consider these individuals, whether due to class, race or gender, "economically redundant" and therefore "unworthy" of society's medical and social support. As A.T. Tymienecka has stated in her new pilot project for a phenomenologically inspired rehabilitation program, "such is the spirit of the contemporary ruthless drive to 'get ahead' that whoever is not able to stand up to competition is abandoned by society as a hindrance or a nuisance" (39). The psychoanalyst Melvin Hill has also elucidated those aspects of the Hegelian master-slave dialectic that remain untransformed in psychiatry and continue to influence all modern therapeutic social relationships (40). Recognition of psychiatry's practices and of its character as a discursive formation, therefore, leads not only to a general reappraisal of psychiatry's moral orientation but also to a variety of clinical and institutional strategies that might contribute to basic structural changes in the social response to psychiatric needs.

UPSIDE-DOWN PSYCHIATRY

The phrase "upside-down psychiatry" was coined by Douglas Bennett in England to describe his innovative approach to psychiatric rehabilitation (41). Bennett had realized in the 1950s that his treatment of the "chronically mentally" ill was hindered by a general orientation in English mental health services that supported the belief that psychiatric services must be designed to serve two types of patients: the "willing and unobjectionable" and the "objecting and the objectionable." Edward Mapother (1929) (42), who argued that psychiatric services should be based upon these categories, stated clearly that "objecting and objectionable" patients must be kept apart from other patients. Since Bennett's patients fell into the "objecting" category, his rehabilitation strategies constantly confronted those traditional psychiatric practices that prevented his patients from achieving successful social rehabilitation. Although the genealogical method was unknown to Bennett, his commonsense clinical philosophy was expressed through what he called "upside-down psychiatry," i.e., the rejection and transformation of those traditional psychiatric values and practices that hinder a patient's successful social rehabilitation.

"Upside-down psychiatry" therefore describes a psychiatric paradigm that can recognize the genealogy and function of psychiatric care as a discursive formation and can guide our attempts to correct the shameful realities. This approach, although in its infancy, recognizes that the major therapeutic goal of the psychiatric profession—and of our entire society—must be to help patients "return" to their proper role in society—even to a society that may have generated the patients' initial suffering and social disruption. Yet it must be admitted that knowledge of psychiatry's discursive structure cannot always be put to use, easily or immediately, to change those social forces that contribute to mental illness and to the inadequacy of our society's responses to individual suffering. As Kingsley Davis stated (1), "But for very profound reasons we cannot plan or alter our culture out of whole cloth. However, there is another type of optimism which is slightly more justified. This involves concentrating upon special or limited social environments as the field of social manipulation."

Focusing upon special or limited mental health settings in order to provide fair and effective mental health care is therefore a major goal of "upside-down psychiatry." It can succeed in these settings by providing clinical strategies that run counter to prevailing psychiatric practices and establish new, more effective therapeutic relationships between patients, practitioners and society. Respecting the lives of individual patients and repairing the social disruption of modern psychiatric illnesses can become a meaningful enterprise between patients and practitioners within a new (upside-down) psychiatry: an effective system of caring for all who seek its help.

NOTES

1. Davis K: "Mental Hygiene and the Class Structure." *Psychiatry* 1:55–65 (1938).

2. Hollingshead AB, Redlich FC: *Social Class and Mental Illness: A Community Survey*. (New York: John Wiley, 1958).

3. Klerman GL: "Trends in Utilization of Mental Health Services: perspectives for health services research." *Med. Care* 23:584—597 (1985).

4. Mollica RF: "From Asylum to Community: The Threatened Disintegration of Public Psychiatry." *N Eng J Med* 308:367–373 (1983).

5. Goldman HH, Morrissey JP: "The Alchemy of Mental Health Policy: Homelessness and the Fourth Cycle of Reform." *Am J Pub Health 75:727–731 (1985)*.

6. A Report of the Board on Mental Health Behavioral Medicine, Institute of Medicine: research on mental illness and addictive disorders: progress and prospects. *Am J Psychiatry* 142(suppl.) (1985).

7. Donnelly N: "Foucault's Genealogy of the Human Sciences." *Economy & Society* 11:363–380 (1982).

8. Foucault M: *Madness and Civilization*. (New York: Random House, 1965).

9. Kuriansky JB, Deming E, and Gurland BJ: "On Trends in the Diagnosis of Schizophrenia." *Am J Psychiatry* 131:674–677 (1974).

10. Morrison JR: "Changes in Subtype Diagnosis of Schizophrenia: 1920–1966." *Am J Psychiatry* 131:647–677 (1974).

11. Blum JD: "On Changes in Psychiatric Diagnosis over Time." *Am Psycholog* 33:1017–1031, (1978).

12. Redlich FC, Kellert SR: "Trends in American Mental Health." *Am J Psychiatry* 135:22–28 (1978).

13. Foucault M: *The Order of Things: An Archaeology of the Human Sciences* (New York: Pantheon Books, 1970).

14. Stone L: "Madness," *The New York Review of Books*, Dec 16, 1982.

15. Stone L, Foucault M: "An Exchange." *The New York Review of Books*, March 31, 1983.

16. Brow GW: "Teaching Data Collection in Social Survey Research." *Sociology* 15:550–557 (1981).

17. Kurzweil E: *The Age of Structuralism: Levy Strauss to Foucault* (New York: Columbia University Press, 1980).

18. Mollica RF, Redlich FC: "Equity and Changing Patient Characteristics: 1950–1975." *Arch Gen Psychiatry* 37:1257–1263 (1980).

19. Mollica RF, Blum JD, and Redlich FC: "Equity and the Psychiatric Care of the Black Patient: 1950–1975." *J Nerv Ment Disease* 168:279–286 (1980).

20. Mollica RF: "Community Mental Health Centres: An American Response to Kathleen Jones." *J Roy Soc Medicine* 73:863–870 (1980).

21. Mollica RF, Milic M: "Social Class and Psychiatric Practice: A Revision of the Hollingshead and Redlich Model." *Am J Psychiatry* 143:12–17 (1986).

22. Mollica RF, Milic M: "Social Class, Social Pooling and Access to Psychiatric Inpatient Care: a twenty-five year perspective." *Soc Psychiatry,* in press.

23. Mollica RF, Milic M: "Trends in Mental Health: Categorical Treatment and the Concept of Positionality." *Soc Sci & Med,* in press.

24. Kramer M: *Psychiatric Services and the Changing Institutional Scene, 1950–1985* (Rockville, MD; National Institute of Mental Health, 1985).

25. Goffman E: *Asylums: Essays on the Social Situation of Mental Patients and Other Inmates.* (New York: Doubleday Anchor, 1961).

26. Musto D: "Whatever Happened to 'Community Mental Health'?" *Pub Interest* 39:53–79 (1975).

27. Joint Commission on Mental Illness and Health: *Action for Mental Health* (New York; Basic Books, 1961).

28. Blum JD, Redlich FC: "Mental Health Practitioners: Old Stereotypes and New Realities." *Arch Gen Psychiatry* 37:1247–1253 (1980).

29. Williams DH, Bellis EC, Wellington SW: 'Deinstitutionalization and Social Policy: Historical Perspectives and Current Dilemmas." *Am J Orthopsychiatry* 50:54–64 (1980).

30. Dain N, Carlson ET: "Social Class and Psychological Medicine in the United States, 1789–1824." *Bull History Medicine* 33:454–465 (1959).

31. Carlson ET: "Nineteenth-Century Insanity and Poverty." *Bull NY Academy Medicine* 48:539–544 (1972).

32. Lorion RP: "Research on psychotherapy and behavior change with the disadvantaged: Past, present and future directions," in: Garfield SL, Bergin AE (eds): *Handbook of Psychotherapy and Behavior Change: An Empirical Analysis,* 2nd ed. (New York: John Wiley, 1978), 903–938.

33. Freedman RI, Moran A: "Wanderers in a Promised Land: the Chronically Mentally Ill and Deinstitutionalization." *Med Care* 22(suppl) (1984).

34. Scheper-Hughes N: "Dilemmas in Deinstitutionalization: A View from Inner-City Boston." *J Oper Psychiatry* 12:90–99 (1981).

35. Richman J: "Social Class and Mental Illness Revisited: Sociological Perspectives in the Diffusion of Psychoanalysis." *J. Operational Psychiatry* 16:1–8(1985).

36. Basaglia F: "What is Psychiatry?" *Int J Ment Health* 14:42–51 (1985).

37. Mollica RF (ed): "The Unfinished Revolution in Italian Psychiatry: An International Perspective." *Int J Ment Health* 14 (1985).

38. Mollica RF: "From Antonio Gramsci to Franco Basaglia: The Theory and Practice of the Italian Psychiatric Reform." *Int J Ment Health* 14:21–41 (1985).

39. Tymienecka AT: "The Moral Sense and the Human Person within the Fabric of Communal Life." *Analecta Husserliana: The Yearbook of Phenomenological Research* 20:3–100 (1985).

40. Hill M, Liendo E, Gear M: *Working Through Narcissism* (New York: Aronson, 1982).

41. Bennett D: "The Chamberwell District Rehabilitation Service" in Wing JK, Morris B (eds): *Handbook of Psychiatric Rehabilitation* (Oxford: Oxford Medical Publications, 1981).

42. Mapother E: "Mental Hygiene in Adults." *J Roy San Institute* 3:165–175 (1929).

CHAPTER 13

PSYCHOLOGICAL AND PSYCHIATRIC DIAGNOSIS: THEORETICAL FOUNDATIONS, EMPIRICAL RESEARCH, AND CLINICAL PRACTICE

KENNETH S. POPE
AND
PAULA B. JOHNSON

> The threatening ambiguity of mental disorder (Who is mad? Who is sane?) leads us to take our system of perceiving mental illness for granted when it is just that system which should be the object of study, since it defines our experience of mental illness. What factors structure our perceptions of different types of mental illness and our strategies for the treatment of these disorders?
>
> (Blum 1978)

This book focuses on schizophrenia, depression, and narcissism; this chapter examines the diagnostic framework, process, and implications that can serve as a context for understanding those three prevalent diagnoses. The purpose of this exploration is to help bring the usually tacit assumptions, covert factors, unfortunate biases, and unintended results of the diagnostic task out into the open. The more we maintain awareness of these phenomena, the better we are able to understand and help those who suffer.

Whereas other chapters focus directly on the three diagnoses, the causes and meanings of the emerging prominence of these "pathologies of the self," we focus here on the nature of the diagnostic categorization and the assigning of the label. It is our belief that a genuine understanding of schizophrenia, depression, and narcissism is impossible apart from an understanding of the diagnostic enterprise.

The term "diagnosis" has a certain authority to it; it gives us a sense of certainty that makes us feel secure. The term has been transplanted to psychology and psychiatry from the field of physical medicine. Competent specialists have little trouble—for the most part, anyway—diagnosing a broken leg, tonsilitis, or chickenpox. Why is there not the same ease in diagnosing schizophrenia, depression, and narcissism?

The reasons are numerous. One is that diagnoses of the sort this book examines are created, assigned, and responded to in the broad context of the cultural distributions of power. Halleck (1971) developed the theme that "psychiatric neutrality is a myth" and showed that clinical work (including diagnosis) "will have an effect on the ways in which power is distributed within the various social systems the patient inhabits."

The power of the diagnosis to affect such distributions of power was poignantly evident when it became known during the 1972 presidential election that Senator Thomas Eagleton, then the Democratic vice-presidential candidate, had previously received treatment for depression. As a result, he was soon forced to withdraw from the race. In the presidential race eight years earlier, over one thousand members of the American Psychiatric Association declared that Senator Barry Goldwater, the Republican presidential candidate, did not meet criteria of psychological fitness to serve as president. One of the APA members was more specific, diagnosing Senator Goldwater as a "paranoid schizophrenic."

Even these prominent examples of the ways in which depression and schizophrenia have an actual or intended effect upon the distribution of power do not convey the full scope and impact. Alan Stone, Professor of Law and Medicine at Harvard and former President of the American Psychiatric Association, has described the pervasiveness of this influence in one of its most virulent forms:

> Mental health concepts influence not only criminal justice but civil liberties as well. A person can, although charged with no crime, be involuntarily confined in a mental institution. Though safeguards against abuse of this procedure are increasing, the United States has

> placed more of its citizens in mental hospitals through civil commitment procedures than any other country. Near the end of the 1950s, mental hospital patients outnumbered imprisoned criminals; one out of every three hundred American citizens was held involuntarily in one of the state mental institutions. (Stone 1978)

It is not just that the process of diagnosis affects the distribution of power within various social or cultural systems, it is also that the diagnostic categories themselves may reflect the distribution of power and attempts to maintain the status quo. Szasz (1971) provided the example of Samuel A. Cartwright, M.D., who contributed an article to the 1851 volume of the prominent *New Orleans Medical and Surgical Journal.* Cartwright introduced to the medical literature and practice of the time two new "diseases" that he had, through careful investigation, identified. Both, he wrote, were unique to the black race. The first was "drapetomania," the "disease" of a slave who escaped from the master. Symptoms were repeated attempts to escape slavery. The second was "dysaesthesia Aethiopis," which was manifested by the slave's lack of care in doing his or her work, or refusal to work at all.

This is a rather extreme example of a diagnosis serving a social control function. Yet, Sarason and Doris (1979) argued that today mental disorders are created as much to preserve the status quo as to help the recipient of the label. Caplan and Nelson (1973) argued that such person-centered problem definitions serve several functions, including "control of troublesome segments of the population," distracting attention from possible systemic causes, and discrediting system-oriented criticism.

Szasz relentlessly documented the thesis that the lumping of numerous difficulties under the diagnostic categories of "mental illness" serves to increase the income, authority, power, and prestige of mental health workers, and to provide society as a whole with a means for controlling people who deviate from the norms in some objectionable, irritating, or threatening way.

> The notion of mental illness derives its main support from such phenomena as syphillis of the brain or delirious conditions—intoxications, for instance—in which persons may manifest certain disorders of thinking and behavior. Correctly speaking, however, these are diseases of the brain, not of the mind. According to one school of thought, all so-called mental illness is of this type. The assumption is made that some neurological defect, perhaps a very subtle one, will ultimately

> be found to explain all the disorders of thinking and behavior. Many contemporary psychiatrists, physicians, and other scientists hold this view, which implies that people's troubles cannot be caused by conflicting personal needs, opinions, social aspirations, values, and so forth. These difficulties—which I think we may simply call problems in living—are thus attributed to physiochemical processes that in due time will be discovered (and no doubt corrected) by medical research. (Szasz 1970)

While Szasz maintains that many psychological and psychiatric diagnoses mask and "mystify" common, mundane "problems in living," Laing (1967) believes that common, mundane psychological and psychiatric diagnoses often mask the mystery of an authentic vision of life. Schizophrenia need not be considered a "breakdown," but rather offers an opportunity for a "breakthrough." People who are hypersensitive to the artificial nature of familial, social, and cultural conventions may suffer from "ontological insecurity" and achieve a piercing, poetic vision of reality rather than mundane, conventional stereotypes. Schizophrenia, then, according to Laing, can be a beneficial, desirable experience marking the time when "the light began to break through the cracks in our all-too-closed minds."

To implement his ideas and to provide a supportive environment for this sort of schizophrenic experience, Laing and his colleagues established in 1965 the Philadelphia Association. The Association rented a sixty-year-old building in east London and set up Kingsley Hall, where a variety of people (psychiatrists, including Laing, schizophrenics, artists) lived together. Traditional roles (such as psychiatrist or patient) were to be abolished: residents would live together in a supportive environment without "false" distinctions.

Szasz condemns Laing for criticizing conventional models of schizophrenia only to replace them with another illness model. Szasz points out what he feels are numerous and serious contradictions in Laing's approach. Laing claims at times that there is no such thing as schizophrenia, but he sets about treating it. Nonschizophrenics (who have achieved a breakthrough and are still living "false" lives) are madder than schizophrenics, but Kingsley Hall was set up for the latter rather than the former. Kingsley Hall claimed to abolish the roles of psychiatrist and patient, but various accounts refer specifically to those roles. Laing wrote that schizophrenics are not ill, but described in detail how they are restored to "health" through his "therapeutic" efforts.

Szasz says we are mystifying life problems; Laing says we are failing to acknowledge the mystery of life. But in both cases their staunch opposition to customary ways of viewing diagnostic categories, classifications, and divisions can help us to approach the ways in which we order mental/emotional/behavioral "disorders" with an appropriate sense of mystery, skepticism, and openness.

It is this sense of seeing things in a new light, of a shocking awareness of the numerous contexts—many of them cultural—that fashion our categories, which Foucault experienced:

> This book first arose out of a passage in Borges, out of the laughter that shattered, as I read the passage, all the familiar landmarks of my thought—our thought, the thought that bears the stamp of our age and our geography—breaking up all the ordered surfaces and all the planes with which we are accustomed to tame the wild profusion of existing things, and continuing long afterwards to disturb and threaten with collapse our age-old distinction between Same and Other. This passage quotes a "certain Chinese encyclopedia" in which it is written that "animals are divided into: (a) belonging to the Emperor, (b) embalmed, (c) tame, (d) sucking pigs, (e) sirens, (f) fabulous, (g) stray dogs, (h) included in the present classification, (i) frenzied, (j) innumerable, (k) drawn with a very fine camelhair brush, (l) et cetera, (m) having just broken the water pitcher, (n) that from a long way off look like flies." In the wonderment of this taxonomy, the thing we apprehend in one great leap, the thing that, by means of the fable, is demonstrated as the exotic charm of another system of thought, is the limitation of our own, the stark impossibility of thinking that. (Foucault 1970)

The balance of this chapter is devoted to an examination of eleven questions, the answers to which are essential in understanding taxonomies in which people are separated on the basis of their being perceived as "depressed," "schizophrenic," or "narcissistic."

DO DIAGNOSTIC LABELS HAVE A LIFE OF THEIR OWN?

Psychologist and lawyer D. L. Rosenhan (1973) asserted: "Once a person is designated abnormal, all of his other behaviors and characteristics are colored by that label." To explore the implications of this assertion, he recruited two other psychologists, a pediatrician, a psychiatrist, a painter, a housewife, and a graduate student to join with him in playing "patient." They selected twelve hospitals in five different states and took turns presenting themselves for admission.

Having phoned in advance for an appointment, each investigator arrived at the hospital claiming to have been hearing voices. Just what the voices were saying wasn't too clear, but it seemed to be something like "empty," "hollow," and "thud." The investigator used a false name (those with mental health occupations also alleged a false vocation and employment situation), but provided truthful information regarding everything else.

All investigators were admitted to the hospitals. Except for one instance, the diagnosis upon admission was schizophrenia. Once admitted, these "patients" stopped pretending that they were hearing voices. They produced no more fake symptoms of abnormality. Aside from withholding their true names, occupations, vocations, and the fact that they were participating in a research project, they acted normally and answered truthfully all questions put to them.

How did the hospital staff respond to these "normal" people who were wearing a diagnosis of schizophrenia? Rarely were the "schizophrenics" treated as normal when they tried to start up conversations. A typical exchange went something like this:

"Patient": Pardon me, Dr. X, could you tell me when I am eligible for grounds privileges?

Physician: Good morning, Dave. How are you today? (moves off without waiting for a response)

The physicians prescribed over two thousand pills for these new patients. Managing to avoid taking all but two of these pills, the pretend patients noticed something interesting when they were pocketing or flushing these medications down the commode: many of the "real" patients were doing the same thing. The staff seemed unaware that the drugs were going anywhere except into the patients.

The pretend patients spent a substantial amount of time taking notes about their experiences. At first, they tried to do this secretly, fearing that the staff might become suspicious. But they found that secrecy was unnecessary. Their frequent writing, like many other things they did, was interpreted as part of their "mental disease." One nurse, who never bothered to ask the "patient" what or why he was writing, recorded daily in her nursing chart for this patient: "Patient engaged in writing behavior."

None of the hospital staff recognized these investigators' sanity, although the "real" patients frequently caught on. The pretend patients were all finally discharged, after an average stay of nineteen days, generally with a diagnosis of schizophrenia "in remission." Rosenhan stated rather flatly: "It is clear that we cannot distinguish the sane from the insane in psychiatric hospitals."

But many defend the integrity and usefulness of diagnostic procedures and categories against such attacks. Wallerstein (1973), for instance, claimed that Rosenhan's investigation was too artificial, that the "experimental" intrusion into a natural setting distorted the outcome. Spitzer (1976) presented a number of rejoinders, the central one of which is that Rosenhan had engaged in a logical fallacy: that the ability or inability of mental health workers to diagnose correctly actual patients is not logically related to their ability or inability to diagnose correctly people who are faking symptoms. Kety (1974) argued by analogy: "If I were to drink a quart of blood and, concealing what I had done, come to the emergency room of any hospital vomiting blood, the behavior of the staff would be quite predictable. If they labeled and treated me as having a bleeding peptic ulcer, I doubt that I could argue convincingly that medical science does not know how to diagnose that condition."

DO CLINICIANS USE DIAGNOSTIC CLASSIFICATIONS RELIABLY?

Numerous investigations have tried to find out just how well mental health workers agree on which diagnoses should be assigned to which patients. Many follow the form of Schmidt and Fonda (1956), who asked psychiatrists to diagnose independently each of 426 state hospital patients. The agreement was reasonably high when each psychiatrist had only to decide if the patient should fall in the organic, the psychotic, or the characterological category. They agreed an average of 84 percent of the time when deciding on one of these three general categories. However, when the specific categories of the official diagnostic nomenclature were used, the average agreement was only a little over 50 percent.

Spitzer and Fleiss (1974) reviewed the major studies of this type that had been done up to 1972. They found that, taken as a whole, these studies showed satisfactory reliability for only three categories: mental deficiency, organic brain syndrome, and alcoholism. Schizophrenia and psychosis, as diagnostic categories, had only fair reliability. And the reliability for the remaining categories was poor.

Ward, et al. (1962) had found that where disagreement existed in diagnosis, 62.5 percent was due to the inadequacy of nosology and 32.5 percent was due to the inconstancy of the diagnostician, whereas only 5 percent was due to inconstancy on the part of the patient. Since the advent of the third edition of the *Diagnostic and Statistical Manual of Mental Disorders* (DSM-III) (APA 1980), the reporting of reliability has increased, often attributed to clear operational criteria. Indeed, Murray (1983) reported that where clear-cut diagnosis was possible, there were fewer biases from other factors.

DO MORE GENERAL LABELS (E.G., "MENTAL PATIENT") BIAS THE ASSIGNMENT OF SUBSEQUENT DIAGNOSES?

Langer and Abelson (1974) videotaped a young man while he answered mildly probing questions typical of job interviews. Later, the tape was edited to remove the interviewer's questions. What remained was a monologue: the man talking about himself. Next, forty clinicians associated with university psychology departments were recruited to evaluate the young man on the basis of the videotape. The clinicians fell into one of two groups: one group was behaviorally oriented; the other was psychodynamically oriented. Half of each group was informed that the young man in the videotape was a "job applicant." The remaining half was told that they were seeing a videotape of a "patient." After seeing the videotape, each clinician filled out a questionnaire evaluating the interviewee.

The behaviorally oriented clinicians judged the man to be fairly well adjusted regardless of how the videotape had been introduced. The psychodynamically oriented clinicians, however, labeled the man as significantly more disturbed when he was introduced as a "patient" than when he was introduced as a "job applicant."

DO PEOPLE FIT THEIR DIAGNOSES?

To explore this issue, Strauss, et al. (1977) collected symptom descriptions from 217 inpatients who were being admitted for the first time to a psychiatric hospital. They used a rather complex mathematical technique called a "biplot" to look at groups of patients (who were grouped by diagnosis) in relation to the clusters of symptoms that define those groups.

Two clear findings emerged from this study. First, symptoms did tend to cluster under each of the broad, classical diagnostic categories: mania, schizophrenia, manic depression, and psychotic depression. So these diagnostic labels did seem to describe specific syndromes, clusters of symptoms that often occur together. Second, only a few of the patients themselves were clustered near these traditional diagnostic groups and seemed to fall into a general area characterized by a few symptoms from several of the different classic categories. Thus, the patients didn't seem to "fit" the labels very well.

ARE RACIST ASSUMPTIONS INVOLVED IN THE CATEGORIES AND PROCESS OF DIAGNOSIS?

The "medical diagnoses" described by Samuel Cartwright, M.D., cited earlier, should alert us to the fact that diagnostic categories and their application may express racist assumptions. To counter the assertion that such beliefs are absent from the mental health literature of the modern era, Szasz (1971) quoted the 1969 chief of psychiatric services of the Harvard University Health Services as saying that the Negro should be compared to an adolescent. The white man must, according to this psychiatrist, bear the symptoms of this adolescent with patience.

Racially biased assumptions not only attribute demeaning characteristics to groups but also serve to obscure the real needs of individuals and to prevent the delivery of important services. Padilla, et al. (1975) documented the ways in which Spanish-speaking and -surnamed populations, for instance, are in a "crisis situation" because of their inability to secure adequate help for psychological distress. Torrez (1972) has explored the reasons for the failure of adequate mental health services to reach Mexican-Americans.

Members of minority groups who seek mental health services in spite of these initial biases may find little help, because, as has been documented (Jones, et al. 1970; Sager, et al. 1972; Jones and Seagull 1977), the formal diagnoses and less formal assessments embody the view that minority group members are difficult to work with and are poor candidates for psychotherapy. Evidence accumulates that minorities who are finally admitted to treatment are much more likely to be treated by a low-status mental health professional (Redlich and Kellert 1978).

Abramowitz and Murray (1983) reviewed recent literature and found that race bias in diagnosis is not consistently documented in analogue research. But naturalistic research does pick up biases. Both types of research have been carried out with primarily black client diagnosis. Bias toward other minorities has been examined infrequently. The authors attribute the difference between analogue and naturalistic findings to "social desirability." In analogue research, where people know they are being tested, they desire to appear unbiased. The field studies, however, do show some bias, with blacks showing more serious (schizophrenic) evaluations. Some variation in race of therapist (most attributing fewer symptoms to their own race) indicates that it is not a true client race difference that is being diagnosed, but rather a bias in diagnosis based more on race of the perceiver.

ARE SEXIST ASSUMPTIONS INVOLVED IN THE CATEGORIES AND PROCESS OF DIAGNOSIS?

Broverman and her associates (Broverman, et al. 1970) passed out a questionnaire to thirty-three female and forty-six male practicing clinicians. The clinicians were asked to use an adjective trait checklist to describe: 1) a mature healthy, socially competent adult; 2) a mature, healthy, socially competent man; and 3) a mature, healthy, socially competent woman.

There were no significant differences in the ways the male and female clinicians filled out this questionnaire. The healthy man was seen having traits similar to those of a healthy adult. But the healthy woman was viewed as possessing very different characteristics from those of the healthy adult. Thus, a woman who has the qualities of a "healthy adult" would not be perceived as a "healthy woman."

The clinicians in this study indicated that a healthy woman differed from a healthy man in being "more submissive, less independent, less adventurous, more easily influenced, less aggressive, less competitive, more excitable in minor crises, having feelings more easily hurt, being more emotional, more conceited about personal appearance, less objective, and disliking math and science."

In a study three years later (Abramowitz, et al. 1973), male and female counselors had to "diagnose" a client based only upon the case study. Two client variables were used: (1) the client was identified as either John or Joan [male or female], and (2) the client was described as either politically "right" or "left." The clinicians—both male and female—described the politically "left" woman as having more maladjustment than any other "client."

Murray (1983) did report that out-of-role behavior is diagnosed as being more seriously disturbed, especially in females (Coie, et al. 1974). In addition, Rosenfield (1982) found that in an emergency room of a large municipal hospital, men and women were not differentially diagnosed in terms of psychosis or neurosis, but were more likely to be hospitalized with symptoms that fit cross-sex stereotypes. Thus, an aggressively behaving woman and a weeping man were more likely to be hospitalized.

In addition, Murray and Abramson (1983), in a complex multivariate study, found that there were effects of patient attractiveness (another potential biasing factor, also mentioned below) that sometimes interacted with gender. However, they noted that more of the therapist's characteristics were related to diagnosis than were the patient's characteristics.

Such studies suggest that both male and female therapists may diagnose and treat their patients according to sex-role stereotypes (Steinman 1974; Howard and Howard 1974). Some (Dreman 1978) have interpreted the general difference between the earlier and later studies to reflect the impact of the women's movement. Murray (1983) contended that there are several reasons why analogue studies have not found significant results as often in the last few years. First is the social desirability factor. Similar to the consciousness raising about race in the sixties, consciousness was raised about gender in the seventies, so that it is no longer acceptable in most circles to devalue women publicly. Second, in many of the analogues, the case was directly from the DSM-III, with criteria so clear-cut that little room for bias might be expected. Third, the work was done on nonrepresentative, available samples of practitioners and/or college students who were playing the role. Finally, the dependent measures tended to be very nonspecific, such as social adjustment in general, rather than diagnostically related.

ARE AGEIST ASSUMPTIONS INVOLVED IN THE CATEGORIES AND PROCESS OF DIAGNOSIS?

On the basis of his extensive research into diagnosis and psychotherapy, Strupp (1962) drew some conclusions regarding the types of patients psychotherapists desire to work with, those who seem to possess diagnoses and other attributes that lead to a good (e.g., smooth, fulfilling, enjoyable) working relationship with the clinician and a good prognosis. "Good" patients are described as "young, attractive, well-educated members of the upper middle class, possessing a high degree of ego-strength, some anxiety that impels them to seek help, no seriously disabling neurotic symptoms, relative absence of characterological distortions, and strong secondary gains, a willingness to talk about their difficulties, an ability to communicate well, some skill in the social-vocational area, and a value system relatively congruent with that of the therapists." In this long and extensive list of vital characteristics, the one important enough to list first is "young."

Several years later, Schofield (1964) identified the YAVIS syndrome. Therapists are most likely to work with people who are: youthful, attractive, verbal, intelligent, and successful. Again, the first criterion to be mentioned is youth.

Unexamined assumptions about age may saturate our mental health system. Although the elderly are the focus of this section, infants, children, and adolescents can also be victims of ageism. Children, who represent one-third of the American population, receive only 10 percent of the funds spent in community mental health centers.

If "being old" is an undesirable diagnosis as far as many clinicians are concerned, where do elderly patients end up? At one time they were found on the back wards of the state (and occasionally private) mental hospitals (Redick 1974). Here they were out of sight and generally out of the mind, of both the mental health professionals and the general public. They received not so much treatment as custodial care. Their diagnoses often included a tacit "unresponsive to treatment" prognosis.

During the 1960s, this pattern changed (Redick 1974). The elderly were admitted more and more into nursing homes rather than mental hospitals. This change did little to improve their lot. In fact, there was even less accurate "diagnosis" (let alone treatment) in most nursing homes than in the state hospitals. The Group for the Advancement of Psychiatry studied this pattern for the elderly and concluded:

> [W]e find that older patients do not receive early and adequate care in the community but tend to be institutionalized in mental hospitals, nursing homes, and other care facilities with little likelihood of discharge. Further, older patients are being increasingly pushed from inadequate mental institutions into other inadequate custodial facilities, often called "the community" . . . Thus, the elderly suffer disproportionately from our non-system of non-care, characterized by insufficient financing for both health and sickness and by fragmented delivery of services. (G.A.P. 1970)

The deplorable conditions that characterize many nursing homes have led Redlich and Kellert (1978) to describe nursing homes as the new "decentralized back wards."

ARE ASSUMPTIONS ABOUT SOCIAL CLASS INVOLVED IN THE CATEGORIES AND PROCESS OF DIAGNOSIS?

Extensive and detailed longitudinal studies, which have been in process for over a quarter of a century (Hollingshead and Redlich 1958; Redlich and Kellert 1978), have documented the degree to which people from the lower social classes—when matched on all other relevant characteristics with those from higher social classes—are generally perceived to be more mentally ill. Numerous independent studies have confirmed this phenomenon (e.g., Efron 1970; Lee 1968). What is crazy behavior for the lower classes is eccentricity for the higher classes.

Umbenhauer and Dewitte (1978) conducted an analogue study with 427 psychiatrists, psychologists, social workers, and psychology graduate students. The authors presented identical case materials that varied only in race and social class. They found strong social class effects in clinical judgment, with more serious diagnoses being given to lower social class persons. However, there were no significant race effects, and the social class bias held for both blacks and whites, the two races investigated.

Such a bias may directly affect our civil liberties (see the statement by Professor Stone cited at the beginning of this chapter). Boyle (1982), for example, demonstrated how clinicians judged (on the basis of a case history and mental status examination) a lower-class individual as much more dangerous than an upper-class individual to whom he was identical in every other respect.

ARE SIMILAR SYMPTOMOLOGIES INTERPRETED DIFFERENTLY OVER TIME?

The most careful and definitive study of this phenomenon was conducted by Blum (1978), who studied the practices in a hospital (having found patient groups reflecting both state and national patterns) in 1954, 1964, and 1974. There were statistically significant changes found in the proportions of patients in five out of eight diagnostic groups over the twenty year period. In three of the groups (affective disorders, schizophrenia, and situational reactions), there were increases. In two (neurosis and psychophysiological disorders), there were decreases. Blum found that the changes in constellations of symptoms (and other presenting information) of the patients did not account for a substantial amount of the changes in diagnosis. For example, he shows how a thirty-five year old, white, employed married male showing anxiety and depression in 1954 would likely have received the diagnosis of "neurosis" with anxiety as the presenting complaint (that is to say, as the primary symptom), with depression as the less important symptom. In 1974, however, the same person would more likely be diagnosed as suffering an "affective disorder," and he would probably be described as depressed (primary symptom) and also anxious.

> In light of these results, the central finding of the current research project is quite simple: that the interpretation of similar symptomology may differ over time. Just as British psychiatrists find manic-depressive illness where Americans find schizophrenia, so 1970s clinicians seem to diagnose affective disorders where 1950s clinicians found anxiety neurosis. In brief, diagnosis is relative to the historical era in which the diagnosticians perform their task. (Blum 1978)

ARE DIAGNOSIS AND SPECIFIC DIAGNOSES ABUSED FOR PERSONAL REASONS BY CLINICIANS?

Many of the issues raised so far involve ways in which clinicians participate in cultural biases (racism, sexism, ageism), but there can be deeply personal and idiosyncratic reasons for a given clinician to use a diagnosis inaccurately, to the detriment of the patient. An excellent article by Reiser and Levenson (1984) documents six predominant ways in which clinicians may abuse a given diagnostic label, in this case the borderline personality disorder. This diagnosis is commonly (ab) used: (1) as an expression of countertransference hate; (2) in sloppy and imprecise diagnostic thinking; (3) to rationalize mistakes in the treatment or treatment failure; (4) as a justification for acting out in the countertransference; (5) to defend against sexual material, including oedipal material, in clinical work; (6) as a rationale for avoiding medical and pharmacological treatment interventions." For example, one therapist referred to her patients as "just a bunch of borderlines" in wishing for a true neurotic in her caseload, and another therapist diagnosed eight out of ten of his caseload as borderline, although they exhibited widely varying symptomology.

DOES IT MATTER WHERE THE PROBLEM IS "LOCATED?"

Psychologists and psychiatrists are attempting to move away from a perception of problems as located within the person, and toward a consideration of larger systems and situations. For example, Engel (1977, 1980) has written on the "Biopsychosocial" model. The initial observation that Engel made is that a diagnosis is at the very least made in the context of a two-person system—doctor and patient.

Generally, when someone uses a particular diagnosis there is concern for what caused the problem and what intervention is appropriate (see, for example, Caplan and Nelson 1973). Awareness of this issue is crucial, since the actual "problem" may be located outside the person while the diagnosis implies that the problem is intrapsychic or otherwise an attribute of the person. Ryan (1968) explored an aspect of this phenomenon that he terms "blaming the victim," in which people are seen as being at fault for an externally determined misfortune. Similarly, many family (and group) therapists speak of the "identified patient," thus acknowledging that the problem may exist on the systems (rather than individual) level and that an individual may (temporarily) act out or otherwise express the pathology of a family, a therapy group, a hospital ward, or other social structure. Thus the pathology of Dr. Cartwright's "drapetomania" and "dysaesthesia Aethiopica" existed in the system of slavery itself and those who implemented it, not in the individual slave who resisted or attempted to escape. This healthy (though undoubtedly risky) resistance was inappropriately labeled as a pathology that inhered in the individual.

Caplan and Nelson (1973) extended this blaming of the victim paradigm to examine what happens when an individual is seen as the cause of a problem. They pointed out that how a problem is defined determines what is done about it. For example, if causes of delinquency are defined in person-centered terms, e.g., inability to delay gratification or incomplete sexual identity, then changing the person would be necessary, and if the person weren't changeable, then external coercive control might be necessary. Caplan and Nelson contrasted this with a situation-centered definition.

> For example, if delinquency were interpreted as the substitution of extralegal paths for already preempted, conventionally approved pathways for achieving socially valued goals, then efforts toward corrective treatment would logically have a system-change orientation. Efforts

> would be launched to create suitable opportunities for success and achievement along conventional lines; thus, existing physical, social, or economic arrangements, not individual psyches, would be the targets for change.

Caplan and Nelson also indicated that once a definition is acted on, the action itself forms a problem definition, as directed by Sartre: "Action, whatever it be, modifies that which is in the name of that which is not yet." (Sartre 1963)

In addition, actions may create circular definitions of causality when they remain person-centered. That is, specific "patient" behaviors define a diagnosis (e.g., narcissism) and then causality of the same behavior is attributed to the diagnosed state the next day.

Caplan and Nelson (1973) contended that, once in effect, problem definitions resist replacement. People become invested in maintaining established definitions—people's jobs, status, power, depend on them. Problem definitions also conform to dominant cultural myth, so to question those definitions often challenges important institutions and belief systems that have origins in those definitions.

To understand the ways in which such misattributions of problems to individuals can prevent not only an accurate understanding of a problem but also effective attempts to alleviate it, we return to a theme with which we opened this chapter: the ways in which clinical enterprises such as diagnosis make an impact on allocations and patterns of power within social systems. Pinderhughes (1973) stated it forcefully: "many psychotherapists have value systems which encourage them to help patients to adjust to oppressive conditions rather than to seek changes in conditions. . . . [T]his is one reason why psychotherapy has sometimes been labeled as an opiate or instrument of oppression." Lest all clinicians consider themselves off the hook by virtue of counting themselves out of Pinderhughes' "many psychotherapists," Halleck (1971) made the principle universal. He maintained that, seen within this light, any intervention by a therapist has political implications. A former president of the American Psychological Association pointed the way toward positive change. Clinical psychology "supports the cultural forces of reaction that delay . . . social changes. . . . If mentally disturbed persons suffer from unknown and undiscovered illness, then the strategy for action is to discover the cause of the disease. But if they have been damaged by hostile and evil social environments, then we must change the dehumanizing forces of society." (Albee 1970)

REFERENCES

Abramowitz, S., Abramowitz, C., Jackson, C., and Gomes, B. "The Politics of Clinical Judgement: What Nonliberal Examiners Infer about Women who don't Stifle Themselves." *Journal of Consulting and Clinical Psychology* (1973) 41:385–391.

Abramowitz, S., Murray, J. "Race Effects in Psychotherapy," in J. Murray and P. Abramson, *Bias in Psychotherapy*. New York: Praeger, 1983.

Albee, G. W. "The Uncertain Future of Clinical Psychology." *American Psychologist* (1970) 25:1072–1073.

American Psychiatric Association. *DSM-III: Diagnostic and Statistical Manual of Mental Disorders,* 3rd ed. Washington, DC: American Psychiatric Association, 1980.

Blum, J. D. "On Changes in Psychiatric Diagnosis over Time." *American Psychologist* (1978) 33:1017–1031.

Boyle, P. A. "The Effects of Evaluatee Social Class and Mental Status, and Evaluator Profession on Predictions of Dangerousness." Unpublished doctoral dissertation, California School of Professional Psychology, 1982.

Broverman, I. K., Broverman, D. M., Clarkson, F. E., Rosenkranz, P. S. and Vogel, S. R. "Sex-role Stereotypes and Clinical Judgments of Mental Health." *Journal of Consulting and Clinical Psychology* (1970) 34:1–7.

Caplan, N. and Nelson, S. D. "On Being Useful." *American Psychologist* (1973) 28:199–211.

Dreman, S. B. "Sex-role Stereotyping in Mental Health Standards in Israel." Unpublished manuscript, 1978.

Effron, C. "Psychiatric Bias: An Experimental Study of the Effects of Social Class Membership on Diagnostic Outcome." Unpublished master's thesis, Wesleyan University, 1970.

Engel, G. L. "On the Clinical Application of the Biopsychosocial Model." *American Journal of Psychiatry* 137(5):535–544.

Engel, G. L. "The Need for a New Medical Model: A Challenge for Biomedicine." *Science* (April 8, 1977) 196:129–136.

Foucault, M. *The Order of Things: An Archaeology of the Human Sciences* (New York: Pantheon Books, 1970).

Group for the Advancement of Psychiatry. *Toward a Public Policy on Mental Health Care of the Elderly*. New York: Group for the Advancement of Psychiatry, 1970.

Halleck, S. L. *The Politics of Therapy*. New York: Science House, 1971.

Hollingshead, A. B. and Redlich, F. C. *Social Class and Mental Illness: A Community Study*. New York: Wiley, 1958.

Howard, E. M., and Howard, J. L. "Women in Institutions: Treatment in Prisons and Mental Hospitals," in V. Franks and V. Burtle (eds.), *Women in Therapy*. New York: Bruner/Mazel, 1974.

Jones, A., and Seagull, A. A. "Dimensions of the Relationship Between the Black Client and the White Therapist." *American Psychologist* (1977) 32:850–855.

Jones, B. F., Lightfoot, O. B., Palmer, D., Wilkerson, R. G., and Williams, D. H. "Problems of Black Psychiatric Residents in White Training Institutes." *American Journal of Psychiatry* (1970) 127:798–803.

Kety, S. S. "From Rationalization to Reason." *American Journal of Psychiatry* (1974) 131:957–963.

Laing, R. D. *The Politics of Experience and the Bird of Paradise*. Harmondsworth: Penguin, 1967.

Langer, E. J., and Abelson, R. P. "A Patient by any other Name . . . : Clinician Group Differences in Labeling Bias." *Journal of Consulting and Clinical Psychology* (1974) 42:4–9.

Lee, S. "Social Class Bias in the Diagnosis of Mental Illness." Unpublished doctoral dissertation, University of Michigan, 1968.

Maslin, A., and Davis, J. "Sex-role Stereotyping as a Factor in Mental Health Standards among Counselors-in-Training." *Journal of Counseling Psychology* (1975) 22:87–91.

Murray, J. "Sex Bias in Psychotherapy: A Historical Perspective," in J. Murray and P. Abramson, *Bias in Psychotherapy*. New York: Praeger, 1983.

Murray, J., and Abramson, P. "An Investigation of the Effects of Client Gender and Attractiveness on Psychotherapists' Judgments," in J. Murray and P. Abramson, *Bias in Psychotherapy*. New York: Praeger, 1983.

Padilla, A. M., Ruiz, R. A., and Alvarez, R. "Community Mental Health Services for the Spanish-speaking/surnamed Population." *American Psychologist* (1975) 30:892–905.

Pinderhughes, C. A. "Racism and Psychotherapy," in C. Willie, B. Kramer, and B. Brown (eds.), *Racism and Mental Health*. Pittsburgh: University of Pittsburgh, 1973.

Redick, R. W. *Patterns in Use of Nursing Homes by the Aged Mentally Ill*. Statistical Note 107. Washington, D.C.: Division of Biometry, U.S. Department of Health, Education, and Welfare, June 1974.

Redlich, F. C., and Kellert, S. R. "Trends in American Mental Health." *American Journal of Psychiatry* (1978) 135:22–28.

Reiser, D. E., and Levenson, H. "Abuses of the Borderline Diagnosis: A Clinical Problem with Teaching Opportunities." *American Journal of Psychiatry* (1984) 141:1528–1532.

Rosenfield, S. "Sex Roles and Societal Reactions to Mental Illness: the Labeling of 'Deviant' Deviance." *Journal of Health and Social Behavior* (1982) 23(1):18–24.

Rosenhan, D. L. "On being sane in insane places." *Science* (1973) 179:250–258.

Ryan, W. *Blaming the Victim*. New York: Pantheon, 1971.

Ryan, W. "Waking from the American Dream." Paper presented at the annual meeting of the American Psychological Association Symposium on Reflections of Social Change in Social Psychological Research, Anaheim, CA, 1983.

Sager, C. J., Brayboy, T. L., and Waxenberg, B. R. "Black Patient–White Therapist." *American Journal of Orthopsychiatry* (1972) 42:415–423.

Sarason, S., and Doris, J. *Educational Handicap, Public Policy, and Social History*. New York: Free Press, 1979.

Sartre, J. P. *Saint Genet. Actor and Martyr*. New York: Braziller, 1963.

Schaffer, K. F. *Sex-Role Issues in Mental Health*. Reading, MA: Addison-Wesley, 1980.

Schmidt, H. O., and Fonda, C. P. "The Reliability of Psychiatric Diagnosis: A New Look." *Journal of Abnormal Social Psychology* (1956) 52:262–267.

Spitzer, R. L. "More on Pseudoscience in Science and the Case for Psychiatric Diagnosis." *Archives of General Psychiatry* (1976) 33:459–470.

Spitzer, R. L., and Fleiss, J. L. "A Reanalysis of the Reliability of Psychiatric Diagnosis." *British Journal of Psychiatry* (1974) 125:341–347.

Steinman, A. "Cultural Values, Female Role Expectancies and Therapeutic Goals: Research and Interpretation," in V. Franks and V. Burtle (eds.), *Women in Therapy* (New York: Bruner/Mazel, 1974).

Stone, A. A. "Mentally Ill: to Commit or not, That is the Question." *New York Times*, March 19, 1978, 10-E.

Strauss, J. S., Gabriel, K. R., Kokes, R. F., Ritzler, B. A., and Van Ord,

A. "Do Psychiatric Patients fit their Diagnosis?" Paper presented at the annual meeting of the American Psychiatric Association, Toronto, May 1977.

Strupp, H. "Psychotherapy." *Annual Review of Psychology* (1962) 13:460–471.

Szasz, T. S. "The myth of mental illness," in *Ideology and Insanity: Essays on the Psychiatric Dehumanization of Man*. Garden City, NY: Anchor Books, 1970.

Szasz, T. S. "The Sane Slave: An Historical Note on the Use of Medical Diagnosis as Justificatory Rhetoric." *American Journal of Psychotherapy* (1971) 25:228–239.

Torrez, E. F. *The Mind Game: Witch Doctors and Psychiatrists*. New York: Emerson Hall, 1972.

Umbenhauer, S. L., and DeWitte, L. L. "Patient Race and Social Class: Attitudes and Decisions among Three Groups of Mental Health Professionals." *Comprehensive Psychiatry* (1978) 19:509–515.

Wallerstein, R. S. "Discussion of Rosenhan's 'On Being Sane in Insane Places.' " *Bulletin of the Menninger Clinic* (1973) 37:526–530.

Ward, C. H., Beck, T., Mendelson, M., Mock, J. E., and Erbaugh, J. K. "The Psychiatric Nomenclature." *Archives of General Psychiatry* (1962) 7:60–67.

Zigler, E. and Hunsinger, S. "Our Neglected Children." *Yale Alumni Magazine and Journal* (1978) 41:11–13.

CHAPTER 14

SCHIZOPHRENIA AND RATIONALITY: ON THE FUNCTION OF THE UNCONSCIOUS FANTASY[1]

JAMES M. GLASS

INTRODUCTION

In this chapter, I consider the impact of what might be called the "rational consensus" (or paradigm) on the self and suggest that political theorizing that overlooks the presence of unconscious fantasy distorts the relation between reason and self. The denial of unconscious dynamics and forces is an inadequacy in modern political theory, a startling omission in rational choice theory and its methodologies; its absence runs through the rationalist tradition. In describing the concept of the unconscious fantasy I turn to the psychoanalytic formulations of Melanie Klein; as representative of the rational paradigm (and the rationalistic tradition) I use John Rawls' *A Theory of Justice* (1971), an argument where reason masquerades its functions as power and the self appears as a series of rational postulates. Further, rationalism of the type Rawls described conceives of the self as a basically rational "being"; madness therefore becomes an aberration, deviance, "other-than-self." What is unconscious (and in the case of the schizophrenic, delusional) is not seen as a vital dimension of what it means to be human. If psychosis, however, is part of human experience, then by ignoring the messages and utterances of schizophrenics, the rational consensus banishes an integral aspect of human nature.

The language and logics of delusion constitute a commentary on power; schizophrenic narrative abounds with messages about victimization, domination, enslavement, grandiosity. It speaks to issues of exclusion, alienation; it organizes perception with logics that transform consensual assumptions and deny the classificatory schemes of social rationality. In refusing to listen to that utterance, to witness its presence, the rational paradigm turns away from a form of social commentary—certainly a bizarre one, but a language that contains meaning and concept (although the rational consensus regards such language as outside the scope of its concerns). For the schizophrenic, however, what delusion "speaks" provides a frame of reference, and within its knowledge systems (or logics) lie symbolic messages directed at relations that describe political life: power, authority, rights, domination, justice, and injustice. It is language that portrays with vivid immediacy both the terror of an inner world and the effects of social experience (internalization) on perception and feeling.

To be schizophrenic is to see the world through fantasy formations that hold within them painful and disturbing messages about desire, need, annihilation, and dread. To listen to schizophrenic discourse is to experience a critique of power relations: the power of desire and its frustrations, the power of significant others in transforming (or splitting) self-perceptions; the power of society in defining, enclosing, and terrorizing the self; the power of delusion in orienting the self's theory of knowledge and framing existential projects (for example, Chuck's[2] believing that one of his jobs at the hospital was "listening to the voices"). The discourse comments on deprivation, on spiritual emptiness, on inner deadness, on the fear of intimacy and closeness, on the despair and futility of living; it transforms historical patterns of speech; it inverts social meaning. It speaks to the pathology of victimization, to distortions in feeling, to the complicity of the rational consensus in hiding the self away, in denying its reality, in "sealing over" its contents.

The rational paradigm rejects the speech of this unconscious, split-off self; and in defining the unconscious as nonexistent, the mad as dreaded "other" (what Foucault (1965) called "unreason"), the rational consensus performs an operation on consciousness no less startling than the schizophrenic's distortion of reality. I want to emphasize that I do not regard the schizophrenic as a critic, per se, freely choosing criticism as a vocation. Nor do I regard such tormented persons as culture heroes. Their significance, however, appears in what they speak, in their witnessing and representing *through language* a broader social fragmentation, the impact of that fragmentation on internal perceptions, a mirroring of the failures (and absences) in social rationality and internal object relations.

By being in the world, the schizophrenic conveys messages about social power; yet in its haste to banish the mad, society blunts their implicit criticism and its symbolic meaning. It is quick to locate pathology in persons it excludes, in the disintegrated selves who speak strange language and who appear to move against convention and appearance. Such people are forgotten, confined or dumped into dreary halfway houses; their utterances about power and relationship are dismissed as raving lunacy. Yet the pathology of power in politics (grandiosity, omnipotence, insensitivity to pain, lunatic projects) is understood (from the perspective of the rational consensus) as normal, "rational" and sane. And society is hesitant to call its public life crazy. That is a central paradox of the rational consensus: it excludes the mad (the schizophrenic) whose delusions about power are considered outside legitimate discourse, but it refuses to see its politics and organizational structures as delusional, crazy, or psychically imbalanced. Further, the rejection of the unconscious as irrational suggests a kind of schizophrenia in the rationalist's view of self, a flatness and dissociated quality to language, a radical split of emotion from intellect, an effort (or exercise of power) to ensure that names (social signs) are, in Hobbes' terms, "rightly understood."

THE UNCONSCIOUS FANTASY: ITS STRUCTURE AND ORIGIN

In *Narrative of a Child Analysis* (1961), Melanie Klein wrote that "unconscious phantasies . . . are never completely given up"; they appear in the "analysis of the interaction of internal and external situations"(105), in the infant's perception (real or imagined) of the parents' sexual relationship: ". . . various aspects of the sexual relationship between the parents, as the infant phantasizes them (i.e., that they are fighting one another; or that they are allied in a hostile way against the infant; or that one of them—or both—is injured or destroyed), become internalized."(185) Consciousness takes these events "inside" (the technical term is introjection). "With the young infant these situations are thus transferred into the internal world, where they are reenacted. The infant experiences every detail of such fights and injuries as happening inside him, and these phantasies may therefore become the source of hypochondriacal complaints of various kinds."(85) Fantasies, however, are not exclusive to sexual issues: "It is, however, not only the phantasies of the sexual relation of the parents but also other aspects of their relation (phantasized as well as observed) which are internalized and fundamentally influence both the ego and the super-ego development of the child."(Klein, 1961, p. 85)

Fantasy involves complex processes of "taking in," "projecting out," identifying with qualities projected into the Other, splitting the Other into literally two separate representations, one "all good," the other "all bad." The process begins in the earliest moments of life and defines the basic contours of what Melanie Klein saw as the self's two functional "original" positions: the "paranoid/schizoid" (the focus of this discussion) and the "depressive."

> I have come to differentiate between two main phases in the first six to eight months of life, and I described them as the 'paranoid position' and the 'depressive position.' (The term 'position' was chosen because though the phenomena involved occur in the first place during the early stages of development—they are not confined to these stages but represent specific groupings of anxieties and defenses which appear and reappear during the first years of childhood.) (Klein, 1959, p. 11)

Fantasy creates structures in language, perception, and later rationality. "It is in phantasy that the infant splits the object and the self [into good and bad representations], but the effect of this phantasy is a very real one, because it leads to feelings and relations (and later on, thought processes) being in fact cut off from one another." (Klein, 1975, p. 16) Fantasy, constructed from both internal and external "images," delineates the contents and perceptual frames of the unconscious self.

> The baby, having incorporated his parents, feels them to be live people inside his body in the concrete way in which deep unconscious fantasies are experienced—they are, in his mind, 'internal' or 'inner' objects, as I have termed them. Thus an *inner world is being built up in the child's unconscious mind, corresponding to his actual experiences and the impressions he gains from people and the external world, and yet altered by his own phantasies and impulses*. . . . This inner world consists of innumerable objects taken into the ego, corresponding partly to the multitude of varying aspects, good and bad, in which the parents (and other people) appeared to the child's unconscious mind throughout various stages of his development. Further, they also represent all the real people who are continually becoming internalized, in a variety of situations provided by the multitude of ever-changing experiences as well as

> phantasized ones. In addition, all these objects are in the inner world in an infinitely complex relation with each other and with the self. (Klein, 1948, pp. 312–13, 113). (Italics mine)

The self constructs games to act out fantasies: "Tiny dolls, men, women, animals, cars, trains, and so on, enable the child to represent various persons, mother, father, brothers and sisters, and by means of the toys to act out all its most repressed unconscious material."[3] (Klein, 1948, p. 189)

Fantasies (and it should be added, perceptions of power) find themselves filled with intense affect: aggression, sadism, anger, hate, and envy. It is a world of sudden oscillations of feeling, persistent psychological motion. (Melanie Klein and Thomas Hobbes, for example, share similar views regarding the natural or precivil self as a "body-in-motion." For the Kleinians, however, "body" takes shape as the ceaseless movement of fantasy and the psychological operations accompanying fantasy: projection, introjection, and projective identification.) In fantasies occurring during the paranoid/schizoid phase, the infant has yet to differentiate between self and Other, inside and outside, mother and self (perceptions that plague the adult schizophrenic). "We see then that the child's earliest reality is wholly phantastic; he is surrounded with objects of anxiety, and in this respect, excrement, organs, objects, things animate and inanimate are to begin with equivalent to one another" (Klein, 1948, p. 238). Fantastic thinking, then, constitutes the self's earliest "thinking"; its impact on later perception is enormous, particularly when repressed or split off aspects of self may come back to haunt the adult in the form of schizophrenic psychosis.[4] "Whilst the normal course of development for the ego is gradually to assess external objects through a reality scale of values, for the psychotic, the world—and that in practice means objects—is valued at the original level; that is to say that for the psychotic the world is still a belly peopled with dangerous objects [images of persons close to the self, particularly mother and father]" (Klein, 1948, p. 251).

Thought, Klein argued, originates in the symbolic content of the unconscious fantasy; it is therefore impossible to dissociate the emotional dynamic of fantasy (with its origins in infancy) from the nature of rationality itself. "Not only does symbolism come to be the foundation of all phantasy and sublimation, but more than that, upon it is built up the subject's relation to the outside world and to reality in general." (Klein, 1948, p. 238)

Internalized "wild beasts" and "monsters" populate the infant's consciousness; and the self constantly fights off dreaded and terrifying representations. (Klein's "paranoid/schizoid" position and Hobbes' "natural condition of mankind," with its pervasive anxiety and fear, occupy similar psychological fields.) "In the earliest reality of the child, it is no exaggeration to say that the world is a breast and a belly which is filled with dangerous objects, dangerous because of the child's own simple impulse to attack them" (Klein, 1948, p. 251). In this turbulent precivil state, the infant struggles for survival; it is in Hobbes' words a "war of all against all."

While Klein's theory certainly contains "Hobbesian" properties, it is not the case that similar political conclusions have to be drawn. I do not believe that the Kleinian view of internality means that a corresponding politics would have to be repressive, highly authoritarian and obsessed with power, as it was for Hobbes. Quite the contrary: sensitivity to the inner world and its fantasy formations would be more likely to open dialogue on participation, collaboration and mutuality, to diminish the presence of psychological suffering, and to draw attention to public and private realities dominated by pathological drives. It would mean that the rational consensus integrates the unconscious, recognizes its sources, acknowledges the dialectic between the intrapsychic (the processes of internalization) and the social world. It would also involve some consideration of the fact that the social might be represented within the prelinguistic self; that the complex processes of what psychoanalysis calls "introjection" might contain critical social components that participate in the definition (and structure) of the unconscious fantasy. Recognition, then, of the internal world is quite a different matter from repression of it (the direction of the rational consensus).

In addition, the Kleinian view (as opposed to the rationalist) accepts the importance of the clinical world of the schizophrenic as commentary on the self, as a refraction of the psyche's developmental past. Phenomena, both "out there" and in the imagination, fill consciousness with dread, fear, and the possibility of imminent annihilation (a state of mind reappearing in later adult psychoses). "Thus the basis is established for various forms of schizophrenia in later life; for when such a regression occurs, not only are fixation points in the schizoid position reinforced, but there is a danger of greater states of disintegration setting in" (Klein, 1975, pp. 14–15).

Take, for example, the experience of Chuck, one of the patients at the Sheppard and Enoch Pratt Hospital (Towson, Maryland) whom I interviewed extensively in the course of my research. He hears messages sent to him by Eddy, a "police clerk" who sits in a small town in central Illinois;

Eddy runs a massive computer that emits voices, produces painful rays, and engages in actions that keep Chuck in a state of terror. It is a world relentless in its paranoia.

> Eddy was killed by computers; they tore off his penis and he bled to death, all over the floor . . . the new voice is a woman's but I've been changed. . . . They took a knife to me and cut me into their shapes, look how fat my arms and legs are. . . . Eddy speaks to everyone in the Hospital . . . he controls it all . . . he's going to kill everyone with a machine gun . . . three million people. . . . When I get out of the hospital I want to work in an operating room; I like cleaning up the gangrene, the blood and pus . . . do you know that wrapping baling wire around someone purifies them; it draws their blood and makes them clean; the wire sticking into the body makes the flesh pure. . . . Eddy speaks to me about crucifixion; he tells me I've been crucified, hacked into a thousand pieces, stuffed into a Baltimore sausage. (From author's clinical notes)

Or take Aaron's belief in a deadly radiation that surrounds Baltimore. I quote from his psychiatric chart.

> In psychotherapy sessions the patient insists on the reality of his delusion, but this is followed by talking productively about his underlying conflicts and past traumatic and guilty experiences, for which he feared as a child that he could go to hell. As this retaliatory fear is explained further, his fantasy is that in hell he will burn (with a progressive depletion of energy such as coal and oil) to atone for his guilt. He had attributed the occasional painful skin burning sensations which he experiences to an outside source, i.e., radiation. In his delusion he fears that the radiation may lead to an increased incidence of cancer as well as that our resources of coal and oil will progressively be depleted to a dangerous degree. (From author's clinical notes)

Aaron fears death and mutilation from microwave radiation; he finds himself surrounded by dangers that Melanie Klein saw as central to the self's fundamental "position": the world as a place of "dangerous objects". Radiation emanates from the hills surrounding Towson; Aaron complains of a "horrible smell" that comes from his "burning insides"; ovens "cook" his skin and he feels drowned in the "burnt death of my own flesh. . . . I know it because I smell dead." Radiation compartments (hidden in the hills) serve as permanent installations, a plot by the Army to kill and maim the entire population (Baltimore has been chosen as the testing place for what will become a worldwide effort to extinguish, through radiation, all human life). A vast underground radiation dump filled with toxic wastes controls Aaron's behavior through special signals sent in the form of x-rays. Yet is this much different from certain conservative ideologues' view of the Soviet Union? Is the paranoia any less? Is Aaron's theory any more "bizarre" than Reagan's scheme for laser weapons in outer space? Is it any more fantastic than fantasies about space weapons, supertanks, schemes for handling the deficit?

With both Chuck and Aaron, what is rational for them depends on the structuring effects of the unconscious fantasy, its internal "logic." When Chuck speaks of hearing voices sent from a computer in central Illinois; when he sees Mao Tse-tung having dinner in the hospital, when he believes his legs are hinged onto his body by a velcro strap, when he complains of the pain caused by "hut-boy" voices (a synthesis of the male/female into an androgynous presence), he describes a world that, while possessing its own internal logic, embodies primitive perceptions in ordinary language. To listen to Chuck or Aaron is to witness, in the adult self, a massive, pathological regression, a language responding to the emotional imperatives of what Melanie Klein saw as the "paranoid/schizoid position" in psychological development. It is also to hear a commentary on the structure of power, in this case paranoia.

Yet the rationalist ignores messages in this kind of utterance; it might be judged in Hobbesian terms as lacking meaning or significance, a "phantasm" disappearing into the darkness. What Chuck and Aaron say, however, is not empty utterance, "airy phantasm," but reflections (in the form of symbolization) of feelings integral to human experience: the sense of being victimized, denied, swallowed up (annihilated), demeaned, exiled from the human community. Their speech exposes the brutal side of power, the grotesque psychological distortions beset by internal and external imperatives forcing the self into withdrawal. To be schizophrenic is to leave the world of others; it is to be subject to social power in the form of institutions, psychiatrists, medications, prevailing theories of confinement and control. Sartre's "hell is other people" is a truism for the schizophrenic; and fantasies or delusions about power defend the self against the intrusiveness of other human beings and against social attachments whose intimacy contains frightening properties.

While this is an obvious phenomenon with schizophrenics, it is not so obvious with "normals." Yet, if the fantasy formations of schizophrenics indicate the power of symbolic constructions of reality, sane or consensually grounded thinking is influenced by similar dynamics. It is naive to think that the rational self (and the rational consensus) are immune from the effects of unconscious fantasy or from distorting pathologies of power; paranoia runs across the spectrum, from insane to sane. Acts of political power historically have been generated in delusion, in paranoid projection. With the schizophrenic the distortion is obvious, a glaring interruption in the social "surround"; but such distortions (and pathologies) may not be so obvious within a culture's politics, or in the politics governing the rational consensus.

Schizophrenic communication moves obviously further from the "norm"; yet it contains an implicit commentary (or "message") on unconscious fantasies critical in framing the self's emotional and existential context, in delineating pathologies of power. Linking up with spaceships, constructing a philosophy from the shape of an egg, talking with imaginary figures on the T.V. screen: all these expressions, while not "rational" (or consensual), contain logics that locate the schizophrenic self in a world with identifiable properties. Further, even though such utterances are not part of "normal" experience, they are expressed in ordinary language and point up the importance of the symbolic in orienting perception.

No matter how bizarre the delusion, or how far it is from the rational consensus, it is still human language filled with symbolic meaning and commentary. (For the rational consensus such utterance is subversive; it strikes at reason's power in controlling "names," the signs attached to things, persons, events and histories.) Schizophrenic utterance is certainly not "reason" in the conventional sense; but it is sensible language (a form of life) that, given its inner logic and its function in guiding the self towards its own hidden and secretive value, reveals something of the structure of the inner world and the pathology of social presences in the self.

Melanie Klein showed the presence of unconscious fantasy in infants and children; schizophrenia tells us that such fantasies continue and appear in adult consciousness. If this is the case, it is a short step to saying that consensually grounded thinking has a schizophrenic quality to it; after all, every person moves through infancy and childhood; that is a given. Each self experiences the power of its internal world; each internalizes the outer and imposes "form" on the social world according to the emotional imperatives of operative fantasies. Consensual thinking, no matter how split-off or denied, reacts, in one way or the other, to these powerful, hidden determinants. What the schizophrenic then *speaks*, what the delusional self witnesses, are the denied aspects of a normal (or psychodevelopmental) reality that the rational consensus deems unacceptable, hateful, and therefore subject to exclusion. However, the act of banishment does not change the fact that unconscious fantasy possess a developmental presence, first in infancy and then in adulthood.

For example, take Ted's relation to reality. What matters to him are "secrets" (delusions) that give meaning to his life and compose his epistemological environment.

> I am dead, man, here in this hospital. When I was in jail, when I was free and alive, no one bothered me, no one probed my mind. I could be where I wanted to be, which was in my secrets, inside, away from all of you. . . . You have no right to know them . . . [the secrets], they're mine; and everyone around here [Sheppard Pratt Hospital] wants to take them from me. It hurts me to speak about them. It's painful. You know something: I would rather be in jail again. . . .In jail, I'm free. I know who I am and where my angels are . . . the jailers don't ask me about it . . . they leave me to be, to myself. (From the author's clinical notes)

To reveal his familiar and hidden sources of knowledge places Ted in unbearable pain: "It's like hot irons stuck into my skull; why don't they just leave me alone; I don't want anyone to have a piece of me; my thoughts are my secrets; my angels are my secrets and I'll never tell you about them. I've already told you too much." Yet, Ted kept his secrets to himself; and rarely did he reveal any of their contents. It was a secretiveness he felt was essential to his being, to maintaining his integrity, since he saw the rationality of the consensual world as his enemy, as a terrifying threat that might rob him of his (delusional) identity. To admit his secrets into the world, to give them a public dimension (even in his relation with his therapist) was tantamount (in Ted's inner sense of truth and right) to giving up part of his "being" (literally feeling that a part of him, as he puts it, his "soul," has been "ripped away"). In jail (where he had spent considerable time), guards and prisoners might beat, torment and sexually abuse him; yet he preferred jail to hospital because in jail his fantasies were left alone. And since Ted's identity was so closely bound up with the sovereignty he exercised over delusion, any sharing of the delusional drama amounted to robbing him of his power. It took an enormous act of trust for Ted even to hint at what he felt and thought, since to utter to anyone else his secrets was to experience a tearing or ripping of structures integral to his being. He jealously guarded the knowledge: "My project is leaving this place [the reality of Sheppard Pratt, that he calls 'false' knowledge] . . . it hurts . . .

it's too painful. When I'm in my room and nobody is bothering me, I go to heaven. God calls me his holy unit. [Holy as in sacred?] No, holy as in full of holes; God gives me a hole; I'm a holy unit, a unit [the term he uses to describe himself] full of holes." (From author's clinical notes)

Fantasies of leaving the world, existing full of holes, feeling dead to what exists around him, reflect a more underlying despair about ever living in a human community, with its consensual and social assumptions. He prefers to be with his "angels" . . . they are not as troublesome as human beings, and they are more reliable: "It's safer up there. I let God take my head; it goes up to heaven; my head talks with God; he takes my brain out and fills it up, puts it back in my skull and then my head returns to my body, here, sitting in this chair . . . I once had goodness, but now I'm nothing. . . it's gone; it's disappeared. . . . Why should I have feelings? I'm dead; and dead people don't feel. Besides I don't have to feel; what is there to feel, anyway?" (From author's clinical notes)

This utter fragmentation of the self, an inner universe without boundary (no separation of self from other), without any connection to social rationality, appears in Vicky's desperate uncertainty over her identity.[5]

> I hear three voices; each one is me . . . some are partial . . . I reach for one voice, the voice that's me; I sense it sometimes, sometimes it's there. Sometimes I feel it, but it eludes me, and escapes. . . . It dosen't always appear, and I find myself with other voices, and they scratch at my skin like a piece of chalk moving down the blackboard. Sometimes the voices are high, or low, like primitive sexual voices, but only for a few moments do I feel the real voice, the 'me' voice, the Vicky music carrying through. . . . Please tell me which voice is me; destroy those others . . . I hate them. . . . (From author's clinical notes)

RATIONALITY: THE RAWLSIAN PERSPECTIVE

When a schizophrenic has a delusion about managing the lives of entire populations, such thoughts are called mad and grandiose. When the Federal Reserve Board (as it did several years ago) made decisions that placed millions of people out of work (and is this not managing populations?), that action was seen by many as being "sensible," as if the decrease of inflation by a point or two could be measured against massive losses in employment, dislocation, loan foreclosures and the destruction of dignity and self-esteem. Are larcenous schemes of commodities traders, stock manipulators, savings and loans executives, any less "pathological" than Chuck's belief that by controlling populations in Germany and Mexico he can become a millionaire? At least with the clinically diagnosed schizophrenic, fantasy is incapable of harm; but how harmful is it in the hands of persons charged with the distribution and manipulation of vast resources of power? With the schizophrenic, fantasy is kept inside, within the barriers of the self. The fantasies, however, of politicians, bureaucrats, and corporate executives impose tremendous hardships. And society frequently honors such fantasies and speaks about them as judgements and actions from wise and informed persons. (Political acts find themselves frequently bounded by hermetic systems of explanation and logic, motivated by impulses towards domination, grandiosity and paranoid seclusiveness.)

Might the following psychodynamic description be relevant to an understanding of the acts and claims of political power? "The projection of a predominantly hostile inner world which is led by persecutory fears leads to the introjection—a taking back—of a hostile external world; and vice versa, the introjection of a distorted and hostile external world influences the projection of a hostile inner world" (Segal, p. 11). This recipe for paranoia drives the political world, particularly perceptions of power, calculations of relative advantage. But unlike the Hobbesian view, the solution lies not in repressing the effects of the paranoid self, with the imposition of authoritarian structure, but in coming to understand the origins of the self's inner divisiveness, its reflection in social organization, and in a critique of the formulations of power that accept paranoia as an inevitable fact of political life. I want to make clear that I am arguing two points here: 1.) Social power confines and excludes the schizophrenic; it imposes classificatory systems that derive from a rational consensus charged with the social obligation of maintaining proper naming and perception. It is power (confinement and exclusion) that governs society's approach to those who suffer from massive dislocations in their internal worlds. 2.) The second proposition is that society has great difficulty in locating and *naming* pathology in its politics; that what is called "pathological" in the setting of the mental hospital becomes "normal" and sane under the power of the rational consensus in defining political acts as good or bad, justifiable or unjustifiable.

What Melanie Klein argued about children's toys and games can be equally true of adult "political" toys and "political" games, particularly as they affect the perceptions and actions of power. "In ordinary play, where the child remains largely unconscious of the content of his incestuous and aggressive phantasies and impulses, he nevertheless experiences relief—through the very fact that he expresses them symbolically" (Klein, 1961, p. 47). The same might be said about political and economic games. Rather than expressing fantasies through symbolic play, the effects of fantasy appear in concrete proposals of political and economic actors, in ideological formulations that stigmatize groups and populations, in divisions of the world into good and bad, in violence that embodies "aggressive fantasies and impulses." In view of the uncertainty of political life and its often paranoid assumptions, early developmental structures combined with social influences may exercise some role in the practice of politics. Paranoia is the most obvious of these internal forms of distortion, but there are many more: the obsession with control, the need to dominate, actions having little empathic concern for others, ruthlessness, powerseeking, lack of conscience, the devaluing of others, and grandiose projects.

Descartes argued in his *Meditations* that the realm of madness had to be excluded from the norm of rationality, that demons, "insanity," could not be considered as part of the rational, thinking self; the insane represented an experimental world that lay beyond thought, "cogito"; the insane, as other-than-self, were different beings from the sane or the rational. I mention Descartes because of his importance as a philospher who came at the beginning of the modern world, who defined self in the language of rationality. Modern theorists of rationality, including Rawls, begin with the Cartesian conception of selfhood that excludes madness; further, Descartes framed the contemporary argument that ties self structure to the sovereignty of reason and the rational consensus of a consciousness (or ego) purged of the unsettling effects of unconscious fantasy.

The thinking being (Descartes' infamous "the thing that thinks") existed as a kind of pure datum of consciousness, a translucent perceiver unaffected by hidden and inaccessible parts of the self. Yet the Cartesian notion (the foundation of modern rationalism) is, from a psychoanalytic perspective, flawed, since it makes little sense to argue that the self can "think" the unconscious out of existence. This is a problem that plagues modern cognitive theory and one that lies at the center of Rawls' psychological assumptions. (For the Cartesian it is "I think, therefore I am"; for the Kleinian, it should read: "I feel, therefore I am.")

Let me turn first to an analysis of the "original position," a concept in *A Theory of Justice* that suggests the Cartesian view. Rawls argued that the parties in the original position should be thought of as rational and mutually disinterested. "I shall maintain . . . that the persons in the initial situation would choose two rather different principles; the first requires equality in the assignment of basic rights and duties, while the second holds that social and economic inequalities, for example, inequalities of wealth and authority, are just only if they result in compensating benefits for everyone, and in particular for the least advantaged members of society" (p. 14–15). All well and good; yet political identity of the kind Rawls described depends on a self capable of sustaining the *feelings* of fairness and equality, in addition to a willingness to act on them. Yet choice is so rooted in cognition that other than as an ideal representation of projected reason, his theory of choice lacks a vision of psychological complexity. Rawls' actors are purged of developmental pasts, of feeling and fantasy, that compose core emotional structures. The concept of a rational self, therefore, capable of pure decision and calculation, without affect, is in itself a kind of fantasy, a formulation (disembodied) that ignores the contingent and unconscious qualities of human nature, that assumes human beings live without any unconscious contents. To attain the level of rationality necessary to sustain this vision, Rawls required a society or community so clearly nonconflicted that there would be no trace either individually or collectively of neurotic, much less psychotic, process. (In the Rawlsian scheme, for example, there are no schizoid decisions or perceptions, no influences of paranoid process.)

It is never clear in a psychological sense just what the "original situation" or position is. Its inhabitants are abstract and contentless; the position lacks a human context; it is a rationally postulated state, a theory that moves against the notion of a human nature that refracts its past, its embeddedness in desire (desire, in the way Klein or even Freud spoke of it, never appears in Rawls' psychology). Further, Rawls made claims for the heuristic value of static models that deduce human behavior from "rational" postulates and argumentation. This is not to say that deduction is valueless or that *A Theory of Justice* fails to make important contributions to political theory. The problem or fault lies in the lack of a clinical or human presence. (Should not at least some attention be given to the clinical world when making judgments about human nature and motivation? Is the evidence of the character disorders and psychoses to be completely ignored?) Reason abounds in Rawls' argument; human beings and their feelings (particularly the destructive passions) do not. And since politics is about human beings, and the organization of feeling, sensation and perception, it is troublesome dealing with a theory, making political assertions, that lacks a sensitivity to internal emotional "events."

Rawls spoke of a concept he called the "representative man." Is "representative," however, the same for the factory worker as it is for the corporate executive, for the schizophrenic as it is for the normal? If "representative" reason involves a social consensus, how does society judge reasoning that falls outside the consensus? For persons like the schizophrenic who are excluded (or feel themselves to be excluded) from society's linguistic and social paradigms, the concept of "representative" has no meaning, except as an unwanted orientation towards the external world. Yet that orientation contains power; it has the power to coerce, to define meaning, to frame perception. It is therefore not an unbiased, "objective" concept; to be "representative" is to represent *something*; and if the prevailing social consensus has anything to do with "interests" (and their enforcement), then what is "representative" is generally what has power, what is powerful. (From the Kleinian perspective it may very well make sense to consider the schizophrenic as the "representative" self, since delusional systems embody or recreate infantile fantasies and represent (or bring to consciousness) in language the emotional patterning of the prelinguistic universe.)[6]

If politics, at its core, can be subject to the same kind of regressive dynamics as the self; if, as for example Peter Gay (1982) argued, the political world is overwhelmed with regressive, *collective* forces (his historical example is late Victorian England around the time of the Boer war), fair-mindedness may become caught up in pathological fixations unhinging the balanced, prudent "Aristotelian" (deliberative) ego. Character disorders, radical dislocations of self, pathological narcissism: all may develop into fuel for political acts with destructive features, pushing individuals not into well-informed choices, but into states of mind permeated with paranoid, violent and antisocial impulses. In such instances, what happens to "decision," "general knowledge"? What is "original" and "representative"? Rawls' theories of enlightened choice, calculation, the difference and maximin principles assume "selves" (or psyches) free of psychological struggle, impervious to the presence of unconscious fantasy. To what extent, however, does it make any human sense to speak of "decisions" made from purely rational positions without the influence of aspects of self not directly accessible to consciousness?

In a remarkable misunderstanding of Freud, Rawls wrote that "with a few changes, the underlying features of the examples he [Freud] depicts correspond to those of the original position." (pp. 539–40) He referred here to the sense of civilization and justice; yet Rawls' psychology bears little resemblance to Freud's. For instance, as part of the "civilizing" process

Rawls never considered what is central to Freud's argument in *Civilization and Its Discontents* (1930) and *Totem and Taboo* (1913): the primacy of guilt, the sources of envy and jealousy, the sexual dimension of competition and rivalry, the symbolic atonement (and its relation to justice) for the slaying of the primal father, the founding of institutional justice as a defense against an unrestrained (anarchic) unconscious.

Rawls rewrote the theory of the primal crime (certainly a dramatic example of the bloody exercise of power) as a simple anthropological treatise on individuals interested in protecting their "relative" advantage; he removed the unconscious, the presence of desire, from Freud's argument regarding the foundation of justice. Further, he spoke of envy as if it were a minor passion stirred up by the perception of unequal advantage: "We may think of envy as the propensity to view with hostility the greater good of others, even though their being more fortunate than we are does not detract from our advantages. We envy persons whose situation is superior to ours. . . ." (p. 532) And the "rational self," this ideal occupant of the original position, lacks feelings of envy altogether. "A rational individual is not subject to envy, at least when the differences between himself and others are not thought to be the result of injustice and do not exceed certain limits. [Is that humanly possible?] . . . For reasons both of simplicity and moral theory, I have assumed an absence of envy and a lack of knowledge of the special psychologies." (p. 530) Where are, however, sexuality, jealousy, greed (all variants of envy) in the "rational individual"? Is the "rational individual" immune from social discontent, religious need (or desire), psychological unhappiness, emotional anguish, self-degradation? Is there some homeostatic, hypothetical emotional position whose existence can only be characterized as "rational"? Has Rawls written Oedipus and the volatile intersections between power and authority (envy, rage and possessiveness) out of political life?

Envy has been completely banished from the "original position," the very point on which Rawls drew a correspondence between his theory and Freud's. "The conception of justice is chosen under conditions where by hypothesis [another instance of rational projection] no one is moved by rancor and spite." (538) Compare this with the Kleinian argument: "I consider that envy is an oral-sadistic and anal-sadistic expression of destructive impulses operative from the beginning of life and that it has a constitutional basis." (Klein, 1975, p. 176) Envy becomes in Rawls' view simply a matter of judging relative economic worth or advantage; it is a learned social emotion, an activity of social and economic comparison. "As some members of the social group jealously strive to protect their advantages, the less favored are moved by envy to take them away." (p. 539) For Klein, however (and for Freud), envy possesses a deep-seated, sexual corrosiveness extending beyond the economic view of advantage. It is for Freud rooted in the Oedipus complex and, for the Kleinians, in the infant's earliest experiences of desire.

For Rawls, "the point to stress here is that there is no objection to resting the choice of first principles upon the general facts of economics and psychology." But what kind of psychology? If Rawls sees envy only as a passion for someone else's goods, if it has no meaning other than as a stimulus to comparative advantage, his psychology overlooks what for Freud was a vital element in social organization: the relation between politics and desire, "libido" and action. At times, the psychological argument of *A Theory of Justice* appears to be a variation of Piaget's cognitive psychology; at others, Rawls relies on assumptions that could have been drawn from Maslow or Kohlberg. The later Freud, the provocative theses of Lacan (1968), object relations theory, the work of Kohut (1971) and Kernberg (1975) on narcissism, Searles (1965), Schulz and Kilgalen (1970) and Pao (1979) on schizophrenia: all are ignored in a philosophical treatise that purports to speak to issues in human nature.

If facts respond to the unconscious as much as they do to cognitive orderings of experience, what sense does it make to speak of "objective," "rational" and "general facts about human society"? Is it even conceivable to think of a consciousness so detached from its affective foundations that it would be in the "position" to grasp these "general facts about human society"? Or might it not be the case that "general facts" would be subject to the distorting impact of unconscious fantasy and desire?

If the original position in a psychological sense is filled with aggression, envy and rage, if it is an inner world dialectically relating inner and outer objects, if the search for knowledge begins with the infant's fascination with the orifices and products of the body; if fantasy is, as Hanna Segal (1974) called it, the "psychic correlate of the instincts": if all this is demonstrable (and I am assuming it is), what sense, what *political* sense, does it make to speak of a rationally postulated general and objective "original" position? How, for example, is "reason" affected by what psychoanalysis calls transference, countertransference, repression, regression, splitting, avoidance, denial, displacement, and so on? Is it even realistic to speak of the self being set in static, immovable positions? Or are the structures of consciousness so fluid that they are incapable of being represented in any fixed model?

If Melanie Klein were to address Rawls' theory, her response might well be one of disbelief that human nature might be deduced rationally from fixed principles or static positions; that self is fully knowable through its logical postulates, that human nature can be intuited. How reliable is a moral theory, if it is conceived as an act of pure speculation dissociated from any real consideration of how individuals act and feel? Rawls' actors never feel; they only think. (His "representative man," as pure consciousness lacking affective imbalances, possesses certain schizoid features [detachment, absence of feeling, absence of body, distrust of the body ego]; a similar argument could be made about Descartes' strenuous efforts to rid consciousness of feeling and sensation, to attain a state of mind where he could say of himself that he was a "thing that thinks".)

Not only does Rawls' theory lack an empirical foundation, it substitutes formalistic rational analysis for a close examination of psychological and clinical evidence that might illuminate the intricate relation between desire and preference. Freud, Klein, Bion, Kernberg: all see desire in a much different way from the rationalists; desire not only infuses reason (and cognitive functioning generally), it is a more corrosive passion, unpredictable, closely attached to affective structures that have little to do with the consciousness of calculation. It is bound up with the indeterminacy of sensation, with the contingent feelings of the body, with sexuality and needs.

Even though Rawls spoke at some length about empathy and intuition, he failed to demonstrate the connection between an empathic reason (which is immediate and intuitive) and the embodiment of this feeling in rational discourse. In the Kleinian view, the feeling of empathy arises from a precognitive awareness; it emerges from the self's feelings of safety and innocence; its reparative movement is away from guilt (reparation as an effort of the self to move closer to the other, to "feel" from the vantage of the other). Love and reparation, therefore, are as much a part of Klein's theory as sadism and aggression; and the empathic self, in its efforts at reparation, attempts to "mend" damage done by its sadistic and murderous wishes. It is an active effort at healing, a preverbal recognition embedded in the self's psychological core. Feelings of empathy and reparation develop prior to the acquisition of linguistic capacity (an argument that implicitly runs counter to the omniscience Rawls attributed to "cogito"). For Rawls, empathy can be rationally internalized and learned; it exists out there, to be understood; it is a function of cognition. Not so for Klein; empathy is an affective structure that appears in the self before the social instruments of reason and language. It is definitely *not* a function of rational discourse.[7]

Empathy in the Kleinian view supports the communal interest precisely because of its beginnings in nonrational feeling, because it floods awareness with sensitivity to the other, because it moves the self away from the terrifying isolation (and guilt) of its schizoid position. Empathy in her view is the antidote to the great anticivil states of paranoia and schizophrenia. It is the primary civilizing passion. It is therefore paradoxical (and wrong) to conceptualize empathy as a learned response in highly rational and self-conscious actors who occupy a fictional "original position."

The schizophrenic represents an extreme and alienated form of suffering that compensates for its fear of persons (and intimacy) with delusional systems obsessed by power, domination, enslavement, violence and transformation. It is a psychological condition that reflects pathology both within the power relations of the self and in the social power that surrounds the self. Its delusional "nexus" divides the world into the powerful and weak, the omnipotent and the victim, the righteously good and the horribly evil; what is "good" (from a social or consensual perspective) may take on grotesque, domineering qualities; what is "evil" may appear desirable, helpful. It is, however, also true that political programs and leaders divide the world into the powerful and the weak, the radically good and radically evil (for example, Machiavelli's dictum that the successful political actor may find it necessary to engage in actions the society condemns as "evil" and utilize cynically the appearances of "goodness"). Politics may also represent persons, events, relations, as inhuman or nonhuman, as things to be exterminated, as vermin (recurring images in schizophrenic thinking that reflect on feelings of being an object, a used, depleted thing, an animal, an ancient, jagged piece of stone).

Certainly the self's psychological status includes more than the sum of its rational parts; after all, how do people come to be racist, narcissistic, domineering, vengeful, hateful, ruthless, and so on? Such properties do not just drop out of the air; nor can their existence in specific persons or actors be explained only by reliance on sociological, historical and economic data. Might these traits have something to do with the psychological effects of split-off self and object representations, inner disturbances that possess a pathological *public* impact (especially in the actions of racists, tyrants, corporate narcissists, political megalomaniacs, behavioral fanatics obsessed with scientific forms of control and domination)? It is not enough (obviously) to understand pathologies of power only by looking at unconscious structures and dynamics; but the presence of fantasy is an important phenomenon in human experience; it should be acknowledged in political life.

Consider the possibility that knowledge might be at least partially dependent on the unseen, aggressive, split-off, dissociated components of self; that the acquisition of knowledge involves psychodynamic factors deriving from the presence of unconscious fantasy; that schizophrenic utterance provides evidence for a prelinguistic world that the Cartesian ego finds it impossible to see (or conceptualize as a theoretical principle). Or, consider that social institutions, and the ambitions they reward and encourage, may mask paranoid reaction-formations to unstated but very real psychological anxiety and dread, the fear of disintegration and fragmentation, the obsession with panoramic forces of power and domination (again, messages that run through the delusional systems of schizophrenics). Equality, for example, may be subverted not only by "irrational" economic arrangements, but the drive for unequal status (and its justification) may hide deeper (schizoid) fears within the self concerning annihilation, placelessness and death ("goods" and "money" as a protection against death and the feelings of emptiness).[8]

Assume for a moment that the philosopher in Plato's allegory of the cave continues going down into the darkness; rather than identifying the sun with knowledge, he explores the cave's topography, its shadows and jagged edges; he encounters unusual rock formations; he feels his way along the walls; he gathers observations from the half-light, from what he senses and intuits; he finds himself perplexed by the many turns and twists in this devious "surround," by the shadows and their strange and unfamiliar dance. Possibly this kind of metaphor distinguishes Freud from Plato, the psychoanalytic view from the rationalist.

SELF-RESPECT AND SELF-WORTH: NONRATIONAL SOURCES OF IDENTIFICATION

> . . . self-respect and a sure confidence in the sense of one's own worth is perhaps the most important primary good. And this suggestion has

been used in the argument for the two principles of justice (Rawls, p. 396).

It is difficult to imagine any population more destroyed in terms of its sense of self-respect than the schizophrenic. Living in an inner universe of shattered expectations and fragmented objects, in a rejecting and hostile external world, the schizophrenic experiences self as less than human, as utterly worthless, a state of being thoroughly removed from human association. The following are "typical" reflections on schizophrenic self-concepts.

Ted: "I'm not good; I'm not bad; I'm nothing."

Jenny: "Everyone around here is a piece of shit; I'm the biggest shit of them all."

Chuck: "I have a job here at the hospital; I flush the toilets; I come from a long line of shitflushers; it's what my family has been paid to do; we're good at it. . . . I'm on the lowest rung . . . the rung of hell . . . I'm in pain and I don't know why . . . I'm a defective human being . . . God left me out . . . I feel like a creature from another zone . . . someone's been hacking away at my brain for thirteen years; they take bits and pieces with them. . . . Do you know that I operate on myself? I slice myself open in the stomach and pull out bottles marked 'germs.' That's my insides, 'germs.' I also found metal braces and plates in my stomach, but they cover my insides . . . the iron man, that's what they call me. Sometimes I operate on my face, not too often, though; I use a scalpel and a probe."

Vicky: "I think I've been reincarnated; maybe I was a queen bee before this life . . . what happened to me? Why did I get this human shape? Or maybe I went down the evolutionary scale . . . I would like to die; maybe my life would have some meaning if I died, then I would get the chance to come back as a bug. . . . After all, there's no reason for me to be here; my death would be an example. . . . I hate existence; it worries me. . . . Nowhere is a place; it's not a feeling; it's the truth. Being here is being nowhere, but then people like me are placed in nowhere; that's where we're supposed to be . . . the nowhere people; the shit-filled people, the deformed, demented, deheaded people

> . . . I'm in a waiting place . . . waiting to die . . . waiting to become an animal . . . I'm not really fully human but part animal; that's where I am . . . I'm waiting to become an animal, a skunk, smelly skunk . . . but that's what people with mental problems are . . . animals filled with shit . . . You know something? I don't think God liked me very much." (From author's clinical notes)

Or Al, whose sense of worth and identity is so devastated that for thirty minutes one day he sits in a corner of the hall muttering to himself: "I am, am I? I am, am I? I am, am I? I am, am I? I am, am I? . . ." (a modern caricature of the Cartesian "cogito, ergo sum").

In the psychoanalytic view, the self's situation in social reality, its sense of esteem (measured by the regard of others), depends on the relative stability of internal object relations. If these relations are skewed (towards "bad" representations), it is likely that the foundations for self-respect will be fragile or, in severe cases, missing altogether. (Self-respect requires the ascendence of good object relations, both within and without the self.) While the external world contributes to a person's self-respect (in the form of approbation, rewards, achievements, and so on), what lies at the self's center (its capacity for what Erikson [1968] called "basic trust") determines how consciousness regards its own acts (the obvious case of a person receiving honors and recognition but having internal beliefs riddled with feelings of worthlessness and self-hate). If bad self and object representations fill this inner core, no matter how ostensibly successful the individual may be, there more than likely remains within the self a deep and abiding sense of its own worthlessness and emptiness. It is this core, then, that should be the object of political inquiry into the origins and specific social contents of self-respect and its embodiment in consciousness and behavior. If the self's inner sense of goodness has been seriously fractured, if its boundaries have been disrupted, it will experience itself as worthless, all bad, despairing (the envious, attacking infantile ego, unable to ameliorate its guilt and terror through love, reparation and empathy).

It is important here to distinguish between self-respect and self-esteem. External appearances of self-esteem (fundamentally social measurements) may function as masks (for the self), disguising deep seated inner feelings (or sensations) of emptiness and futility (a pathogenic state that may affect all aspects of being). The sensibility of self-respect, however, depends on unconscious identifications that resonate through the self as messages of worth, dignity, and integrity. Not everyone who professes self-esteem possesses this sort of internal resilience; further, persons who appear to be filled with self-esteem may be riddled with envy that undermines self-respect (a phenomenon common in Kernberg's discussion of the pathological narcissist who may be the recipient of wealth, honors and power, but who also experiences life as empty, the self as worthless, and others as "fuel" for an unlimited sense of "entitlement").[9]

Certainly the self's economic situation has a great deal to do with self-esteem and self-respect (an argument central to the Rawlsian view). I am not suggesting that such concerns are unimportant and without value; obviously, employment or the lack of it, in addition to the nature of work itself, affects a person's sense of identity and efficacy. I want to emphasize, however, that the capacity of the individual to deal with adversity, to mediate blows to self-*esteem*, may be dependent on an internal resiliency whose origins lie in the dialectic between early intrapsychic formations and the later elaboration of specific social influences.

The schizophrenic experience shows how fragile self-respect can be, how dependent it is on unconscious foundations that may be hidden from what the rational theorist projects or defines as legitimate inquiry (for example, Chuck taking on a job as "shit flusher" in the hospital because he sees himself as "one of a long line of shit flushers" in his family; he also sees this job as producing "income" in the form of meals and cigarettes). By not listening to or acknowledging what in the society is the most radical form of self-disintegration (the schizophrenic's delusional fragmentation), the rationalist inquiry refuses to take into account a significant source of evidence for understanding the relationship between self and culture. This phenomenon not only casts doubts on the capacity of the rational consensus to respond to the plight of the schizophrenic, but it also indicates a serious deficiency in theorizing that addresses itself to interpreting human nature as part of the discourse on political life.

CONCLUSION: DISEMBODIED RATIONALITY: ITS ANALYTICAL FRAME

Rawls' political formulations focus on the capacity of the self to deduce appropriate and "rational" choices. Consider, however, that Rawls' concept of the "rational plan" might be affected by what the self "hides" from itself (repression and denial), that the rationalist project is an effort to mask or dominate the unconscious (reason as a form of power):

> . . . a person's plan of life is rational if, and only if, first, it is one of the plans that is consistent with the principles of rational choice when these are applied to all the relevant features of his situation and it is that plan among those meeting this condition which would be chosen by him [the 'representative' man] with full deliberative rationality, that is, with full awareness of the relevant facts and after a careful consideration of the consequences . . . Secondly, a person's interests and aims are rational if, and only if, they are to be encouraged and provided for by the plan that is rational for him (pp. 408–09).

In what form is a person's "rational plan" to be identified? Aside from the egoistic calculations and the "reckoning of consequences," what sorts of psychological operations surround (or define the location of) the "rational plan"? Is the "rational plan" a disguise for the power and will of specific political interests? For example, the rational consensus condemns the schizophrenic to exclusion on the basis of what it sees as "unreason" or irrationality; however, for the schizophrenic the representations of the unconscious (in the form of symbolization) contain both logic and meaning. Such utterances may be irrational to the rational paradigm, but sensible and logical for the self experiencing (and living by) internal frames of reference.

For Rawls, what psychoanalysis considers to be critical in identifying intentionality (deciphering plans *inaccessible* to consciousness) is simply irrelevant. Further, it would take an enormous amount of self-control (or self-deception) for consciousness to separate its rational calculation (of plans) from what psychical reality projects as fantasy and desire. To what extent do unconscious plans masquerade as "rational" plans (a not uncommon phenomenon in politics)? Or might the "rational" plan be an embodiment of unconscious plans that operate according to nonconsensual logics?

Extreme examples of this abound in schizophrenic thought—the profusion of "plans," the interpenetration of fantasy and desire. Jenny, for example, believes her mother hires patients in the hospital to come into her bedroom at night and rip out her intestines, steal her heart and chop her body into bits and pieces. Understanding Jenny's "plan" requires deciphering her beliefs in the context of vast psychological dislocations and interpreting the symbolizations through which she projects as logic and reference. It is a complex procedure that illustrates the extent to which "plan" (and its logic), fantasy and perception find themselves interwoven.

Rawls assumed an objectivity where the rational actor has access to all possible inner and outer plans.

> Thus to identify a person's rational plan, I suppose that it is that plan belonging to the maximal class which he would choose with full deliberative rationality. We criticize someone's plan, then, by showing either that it violates the principles of rational choice, or that it is not the plan that he would pursue were he to assess his prospects with care in the light of a full knowledge of his situation. (p. 409)

But who is to point out this "full knowledge"? What are its origins? What is the impact of unconscious knowledge on the "rational" appraisal of "plans"? Might, for example, resonances of the infant's split inner world later come back to haunt the adult's "rational plan" in the form of rigid conceptions of moral and ethical belief, where experience and others are seen as all good or all bad? ". . . [A] rational plan of life establishes the basic point of view from which all judgments of value relating to a particular person are to be made and finally rendered consistent." (Rawls, p. 409) What is to distinguish the neurotic from the nonneurotic "plan," the psychotic from the nonpsychotic "plan"? Or to put it another way: inner psychological dynamics (the presence of fantasy) impose structure and direction on "plans" precisely because the interweaving of fantasy and thinking (the presence of the symbolic) composes a considerable dimension of what it means to be human.[10]

Without a context in desire (in the self's continuing struggle to mediate fantasy and experience), the notion of plans takes on an abstract, disembodied quality, as if only pure calculation governed perception. "The best plan for an individual is the one that he would adopt if he possessed full information . . . the objectively rational plan . . . determines his real good" (Rawls, p. 417). This is an idea reminiscent of Maslow's fully "actualized" self in possession of "full information". Again Rawls (like the rationalists generally) ignored the connection between an imposed rationality (domination coming from the rational consensus) and the alienation characteristic of schizophrenia. Because of its exclusionary power, the rational consensus affects the schizophrenic's perception; it intensifies feelings of estrangement; it contributes to psychological disintegration, fragmentation, and social withdrawal; it aggravates (and feeds into) paranoid projections. Reason *is* an agent of social control; in its form as a psychiatric power, it defines the nature of confinement, the structure of "treatment" (excessive medicating, for example, as physiological straitjacket), the boundaries of the self's "real good."

At the heart of Rawls' theory of rationality (and its connection with his interpretation of self-esteem) is a concept he called the "Aristotelian Principle."

> The Artistotelian Principle states that, other things being equal, human beings enjoy the exercise of their realized capacities (their innate or trained abilities), and that this enjoyment increases the more the capacity is realized, or the greater its complexity. . . . Thus the desire to carry out the larger pattern of ends which brings into play the more fully developed talents is an aspect of the Aristotelian Principle. And this desire, along with the higher order desires to act upon other principles of rational choice, is one of the regulative ends that moves us to engage in rational deliberation and to follow its outcome (414–15).

The "Aristotelian Principle," however, refuses to acknowledge the possibility that even with sophisticated rational operations, the self's affective components might be subject to intense regressive pressures (the argument, for example, behind Kernberg's theory of "pathological narcissism" and its presence in individuals the society considers successful or powerful). Nor does the "principle" account for the presence of schizoid factors in the creation and implementation of decision. Under the influence of stress, trauma or disease, the self may move towards lower levels of integration, to emotional states containing primitive (or infantile) fixations; choice at these times might be determined by regressive dynamics that bracket consciousness in irrational or bizarre or grandiose "ideas" (symbolizations of experience). Choices, then, that the individual makes either by himself or in groups might not be towards what Rawls called "more intricate and subtle discriminations" (p. 426), but towards less subtle and more emotionally charged relationships.

Schizophrenia is an extreme case of regression, but regressive dynamics may affect critical areas of social and cultural life (political programs, for example, that take on authoritarian properties, that govern through fear and retribution rather than through collaboration and reciprocity). Fantasies of power and domination, common to schizophrenic delusion, may operate on more hidden and subdued levels in large organizations whose leadership takes on paranoid properties (Kernberg 1980). A pathogenic social climate, therefore, would certainly affect the norm of rationality; in such instances, what passes for "reasonableness" may mask the operation of a pathology that threatens instability and organizational (or group) disintegration.[11] "Reason," then, may exist as a mask; it may appear as power; and the insistence on a rational "consensus" may conceal a more serious (or insidious) demand for acquiescence to what specific interests define as power. (It is this demand for acquiescence that intensifies the schizophrenic's withdrawal into a delusional world.)

To argue that the "Aristotelian Principle characterizes human nature as we know it" is to make certain assumptions about the self that deny it is anything other than a reflection of its rational aims.[12] Rawls addressed the issue of "irrational behavior," and by implication "rationality," through an example that on the face of it seems like a "straw man." It is a clear instance (in my view) where the concept of "reason" is being utilized as a form of power (reason "names" what is appropriate and inappropriate, normal and abnormal).

> . . . [I]magine someone whose only pleasure is to count blades of grass in various geometrically shaped areas such as park squares and well-trimmed lawns. He is otherwise intelligent and actually possesses unusual skills, since he manages to survive by solving difficult mathematical problems for a fee. The definition of the good forces us to admit that the good for this man is indeed counting blades of grass, or more accurately, his good is determined by a plan that gives an especially prominent place to this activity. . . . if we allow that his nature is to enjoy this activity and not to enjoy any other, and that there is no feasible way to alter his condition, then surely a rational plan for him will center around this activity (pp. 432–34).

But the issue is not so simple, since Rawls assumed a real distinction between the individual who counts blades of grass (the less than rational, or what he calls the "neurotic") and those whose rational plans fit into appropriate social forms (the "more" rational). What Rawls refused to grant (or even consider) is that even in the behavior of the "more rational," the propensity to regress exists; that rational behavior might include aspects of the self's regressive aims, particularly the influence of fantasy. Further, eccentric types who count blades of grass for pleasure exist only in fanciful imaginations; and it is unrealistic to think that society (and its agents) would find such behavior tolerable. [In the real world, Rawls' grass-counter, rather than being paid for his "unusual skills," would most likely face some form of power (whether through medication or institutionalization.)] Rawls' example, then, not only skirts the entire issue of nonrational behavior (particularly schizoid and borderline features generalized throughout the culture), but it fails to support the Aristotelian Principle's major hypothesis that the "rational plan" will move the self to higher and more sophisticated levels of capacity and ability. (Reason and its generation do not necessarily assure affective stability.) To demonstrate the truth of his hypothesis (its believability as a statement about real persons), Rawls would have to show that regression, whether in groups or individuals, never interferes with the "rational plan" *and* that "rational selves" are in full possession of both their conscious and unconscious aims. Like the "original position," the Aristotelian Principle idealizes the relationship between self and reason. It is a model that *psychical* reality continually disproves.

To conclude: the question is not the validity of the principles of equality, liberty, freedom and justice, which stand at the core of a democratic and humanitarian tradition. What is important are the contexts and environments that might be receptive and sympathetic to the *human* and *social* foundations of justice. It seems unlikely that justice will be realized or even tolerated in political and economic environments that derive their energy from narcissistic and fantasy-driven perceptions. It is the split-off, dissociated, and violent (in Melanie Klein's terms, envious) parts of the self that destroy the potential for collaboration and equality, for justice as fairness; yet this dimension of human nature finds its way, through the exercise of power, into large technobureaucracies, multinational corporations, political structures, images of popular culture and ethical systems governing behavior and choice.

Any realistic or empirical approach to action-in-societies, to decision making, to the structure of power, should at the least take into account the nonrational dynamics behind group identity and so-called "rational" decisions. In Bion's (1961) theory, for example, a group is held together (and decisions are made) because of profound unconscious pressures. He called these dynamics "basic assumptions"; they define the relation of each individual to others in the group and to the action of the group itself. (Bion identified three "basic assumptions" motivating group behavior: fight/flight; dependency, and pairing.) Freud's (1920) *Group Psychology and the Analysis of the Ego* (which Rawls cited only once), A.K. Rice's work on leadership, Kernberg's inquiry into organization: these studies and the directions they represent take issue with the prominence Rawls assigned to rational behavior and perception, the connections he drew between rational choice, "moral character" and a "well-ordered society."

Qualities like ruthlessness, nonempathic reason, unscrupulous manipulation, the need or drive to dominate (all "products" of a lack of superego integration) are acknowledged by society as desirable and admirable traits. What Rawls called the "evil man . . . [who] aspires to unjust rule," (p. 439) becomes in the modern culture not an aberration (an example of nonrational behavior that can be dismissed by the appropriate intervention of rational actors), but a pervasive, idealized Other, who receives the applause, admiration and approbation of society (witness, for example, the popularity of T.V. shows like "Dallas" and "Dynasty," the obsession with wealth, status and appearance). What Rawls defined as injustice, the modern society elevates to the status of cultural norm; and Rawls' description of the "unjust man" accurately describes fantasy figures (and their cynical manipulation of "rationality") like J.R. ("Dallas"), or Alexis Carrington ("Dynasty"), whom young people regard as having the "right stuff." The evil man, in Rawls' view, "delights in the impotence and humiliation of those subject to him, and he relishes to be recognized by them as the willful author of their degradation." Yet these "evil men" embody their fantasies in action, appear in the guise of our leading citizens, and may be found in the upper echelons of major bureaucratic organizations.[13]

The evidence of schizophrenia and the severe character disorders would suggest that the relation between self and the social world, between inner psychological structures and the prevailing rational consensus, contains an extensive alienation; that feelings of fragmentation, deadness, emptiness and numbness should be considered critical social facts requiring attention from political theorists. It is, then, not only the economic and historical world that should be the object of political inquiry, but also the structure of the inner self, its peculiar configuration, languages, origin, and consequences. To ignore the inner self, its pathological formations and actions, is to make it even more difficult to establish (as governing social and political principle) empathic communication, nonhierarchial "associations," and communities that accept collaboration, reciprocity and mutuality as cherished values. It is not only the pathology of institutions that inhibits the public presence of these values, it is also the pathology of the self. And if empathy, collaboration, reciprocity and mutuality have anything to do with justice and fairness, then the structure of the unconscious (that which is hidden and inaccessible) needs to be as much a subject of philosophical and political theory as the realm of the "outer," the external world.

Finally, Melanie Klein's theory provides a warning; it elaborates the complex structure of human nature, the intricacy of the "internal," the importance of fantasy in the development of thought, and the presence of unconscious forces in perception. It is the significant contribution of her theory to draw connections between reason and fantasy, and to demonstrate that ego functions owe as much to deeply repressed and split-off psychic structures as they do to the socializing perceptions of the rational consensus.

NOTES

1. This chapter arises from an ongoing research project (since 1977) at The Sheppard and Enoch Pratt Hospital in Towson, Maryland, into the relationship between internal psychological structures and political reality. The clinical material,

quotes attributed to "Chuck," "Aaron," "Ted," "Jenny," and "Vicky," comes from my own interview notes. A more complete elaboration of the politics of delusion (and the relation between schizophrenia and culture) appears in my book *Delusion: Internal Dimensions of Political Life* (Chicago: University of Chicago, 1985). A major objective of this discussion is to suggest that Kleinian theory might be interesting as an interpretive model for social theory. Little if any attention has been paid to her work by philosophers, although Richard Wollheim's recent book, *The Thread of Life* (Cambridge: Harvard University Press, 1984), offers a fascinating, although difficult, analysis of her major concepts. I would like to thank David M. Levin for his thoughtful suggestions and insights in the preparation of this chapter.

2. In the interests of anonymity, the names of patients have been changed, but the words, which I myself recorded in the course of many interviews, are theirs.

3. For a contemporary statement of this position see Erik Erickson's (1977) *Toys and Reasons: Stages in the Ritualization of Experience* (New York: Norton).

4. I recognize there are other "explanations" (etiologies) for the appearance of schizophrenic psychosis; however, I find the psychoanalytic to be persuasive (see, for example, the work of Klein, Spitz, Mahler and Schulz placing etiology in perceptions generated in the first year of life). Physiological, chemical and genetic theories do, of course, play a role (in the often murky effort to assess cause). But in the attempt to understand schizophrenic perception and thought, the psychoanalytic formulations more completely explore the "reasons" motivating complex delusional constructions. Also, since I believe that the psychotherapy of schizophrenia is useful and important, the psychoanalytic model provides a framework, a theory for orienting (and establishing) the therapeutic relation. It is also important to acknowledge how the social is represented in the self's prelinguistic life, that the mother/infant relation may embody a moment (or a series of moments) in a social history.

5. Cf. Freud's famous observation on describing inner states of mind: "We cannot do justice to the characteristics of the mind by linear outline, like those in a drawing or in a primitive painting, but rather by areas of colour melting into one another as they are presented by modern artists. After making the separation, we must allow what we have separated to merge together and more. You must not judge too harshly a first attempt at giving a pictorial representation of something so intangible as psychical processes." *New Introductory Lectures*, Standard Edition, vol. 22 (London: Hogarth Press, 1933), p. 207.

6. I elaborate on this theory in some detail in *Delusion* (1985).

7. Her argument here is similar to the nonrational and emotive power that Rousseau assigns to "pitié" (or empathy) in his *Discourse on the Origins and Foundations of Inequality* (New York: St. Martin's, 1964).

8. For an interesting analysis along these lines see Joel Kovel (1982), *The Age of Desire: Case Histories of a Radical Psychoanalyst* (New York: Pantheon).

9. Also see Anne Reich's (1960) article, "Pathologic Forms of Self-esteem Regulation," in *Psychoanalytic Contributions* (New York: International Universities Press, 1973), where she presented case analyses of persons who ostensibly are quite

"successful" in the eyes of society but who, in the course of their therapy, come to confess feelings of self-hatred, self-deprecation and despair.

10. Rawls made some allowance for this: "We must not imagine that a plan is a detailed blueprint for action stretching over the whole course of life. It consists of a hierarchy of plans, the more special subplans being filled in at the appropriate time." (p. 410) He did not acknowledge, however, the tyranny that internal objects exercise over consciousness and plans, and how "subplans" might be influenced by regression, by the presence of the "infantile" in the adult conception of purpose, action and meaning.

11. For an interesting discussion of this see Bion, *Experience in Groups* (New York: Basic Books, 1961).

12. Overall, Rawls borrowed his psychology from certain Piagetian assumptions: "The [Aristotelian] principle implies that as a person's capacities increase over time (brought about by physical and biological maturation, for example, the development of the nervous system in a young child), and as he trains these capacities and learns how to exercise them, he will in due course come to prefer the more complex activities that he can now engage in, which call upon his newly realized abilities." (pp. 427–28) However, this theory neglects the impact that unconscious fantasies have on the origins of ethical and moral beliefs. Even Piaget was willing to grant the existence of an unconscious, although his conception of the "cognitive" and "affective" unconscious differs considerably from that of the object relations theorists. See Jean Piaget, "The Affective Unconscious and the Cognitive Unconscious," *J. Amer. Psych. Assoc.* 21:249–261; also see Anita Tenzer, "Piaget and Psychoanalysis," *Contemporary Psychoanalysis* 19:313–339.

13. Joseph Heller's *Something Happened* (New York: Knopf, 1974) describes this view as the reigning law and governing "principle" in a complex modern organization.

REFERENCES

Bion, Wilfred (1961). *Experience in Groups*. New York: Basic Books.
Erikson, Erik (1968). *Identity: Youth and Crisis*. New York: Norton.
——— (1977). *Toys and Reasons: Stages in the Ritualization of Experience*. New York: Norton.
Freud, Sigmund (1933). *New Introductory Lectures*, Standard Edition, vol. 22, edited by James Strachey. London: Hogarth Press.
——— (1930). *Civilization and Its Discontents*, Standard Edition, vol. 21, edited by James Strachey. London: Hogarth Press.
——— (1913). *Totem and Taboo*, Standard Edition, vol. 13, ed. James Strachey. London: Hogarth Press.
——— (1920). *Group Psychology and the Analysis of the Ego*, Standard Edition, ed. James Strachey. London: Hogarth Press.
Gay, Peter, "Liberalism and Regression," *The Psychoanalytic Study of the Child*, vol. 37. New Haven: Yale University Press, 1982.
Glass, James M. (1985). *Delusion: Internal Dimensions of Political Life*. Chicago: University of Chicago Press.
Heller, Joseph (1974). *Something Happened*. New York: Knopf.
Kernberg, Otto (1975). *Borderline Conditions and Pathological Narcissism*. New York: Jason Aronson.
——— (1980). *Internal Objects, External Reality*. New York: Jason Aronson.
Klein, Melanie (1948). *Contributions to Psycho-Analysis; 1921–45*. London: Hogarth Press.
——— (1959). *The Psychoanalysis of Children*. London: Hogarth Press.
——— (1961). *Narrative of a Child Analysis*. New York: Basic Books.
——— (1975). *Envy and Gratitude and Other Works: 1946–1963*. New York: Delacorte Press.
Kohut, Heinz (1971). *The Analysis of the Self*. New York: International Universities Press.
Kovel, Joel (1982). *The Age of Desire: Case Histories of a Radical Psychoanalyst*. New York: Pantheon.
Lacan, Jacques (1968). *The Language of the Self*. New York: Delta.

Pao, Ping-Nie (1979). *Schizophrenic Disorders: Theory and Treatment from a Psychodynamic Point of View*. New York: International Universities Press.

Piaget, Jean (1973). "The Affective Unconscious and the Cognitive Unconscious," *J. Amer. Psych. Assoc.*. 21:249–261.

Rawls, John (1971). *A Theory of Justice*. Cambridge: Harvard University Press.

Reich, Anne (1960). "Pathologic forms of self esteem regulation" in Anne Reich (1973). *Psychoanalytic Contributions*. New York: International Universities Press.

Reich, Wilhelm (1974). *Character Analysis*. New York: Touchstone Books, Simon and Schuster.

Rioch, Margaret (1970). "The Work of Wilfred Bion on Groups," *Psychiatry* 33:56–66.

Schulz, Clarence G. and Kilgalen, Rose K. (1970). *Case Studies in Schizophrenia*. New York: Basic Books.

Searles, Harold (1965). *Collected Papers on Schizophrenia and Related Subjects*. New York: International Universities Press.

Segal, Hanna (1974). *An Introduction to the Work of Melanie Klein*. New York: Basic Books.

Tenzer, Anita (1983). "Piaget and Psychoanalysis," *Contemporary Psychoanalysis* 19:313–339.

CHAPTER 15

PSYCHODYNAMIC FACTORS IN DEPRESSION AND PSYCHOSIS: OBSERVATIONS FROM MODERN CONSCIOUSNESS RESEARCH

STANISLAV GROF

The observations and data on which this paper is based came from two major sources—approximately two decades of psychedelic research with LSD and other psychoactive substances, and ten years of work with experimental nondrug techniques (4,5,6). The subjects who participated in the psychedelic programs covered a wide range from "normal volunteers" through various categories of psychiatric patients to individuals dying of cancer. The nonpatient population consisted of clinical psychiatrists and psychologists, scientists, artists, philosophers, theologians, students, and psychiatric nurses. The patients with emotional disorders belonged to various diagnostic categories; they included psychoneurotics, alcoholics, narcotic drug addicts, sexual deviants, persons with psychosomatic disorders, borderline cases, and schizophrenics.

I began psychotherapeutic work with LSD as a convinced Freudian who was very enthusiastic about the seeming explanatory power of psychoanalysis, but disappointed and puzzled by its therapeutic inefficacy. The incentive for this research was the fact that as a volunteer in a clinical LSD program, I had a very powerful confrontation with my own unconscious. As a result of it, I came to the conclusion that the use of LSD as a catalyst might accelerate, intensify, and deepen the therapeutic process and eliminate the painful gap between the theory and practice of Freudian psychoanalysis.

However, when I started using LSD as a therapeutic tool, it became obvious that not only the practice of psychoanalysis but also its theory had to be drastically revised. Without any programming and against my will, patients were transcending the biographical domain and exploring areas of the psyche uncharged by psychoanalysis and academic psychiatry. Moreover, major therapeutic changes did not occur in the context of the work on childhood traumas, but following powerful transbiographical experiences that mainstream psychiatry sees as symptoms of mental illness and tries to suppress by all means.

Since this research involved a powerful "mind-altering" drug, it is quite natural to question to what extent it is legitimate to use it as a source of data for a psychological theory. There has been a tendency among professionals to see the LSD state as a "toxic psychosis" and the experiences induced by the drug as a chemical fantasmagoria that has very little to do with how the mind functions under more ordinary circumstances. However, systematic clinical research with LSD and related psychedelics has shown that these drugs can best be understood as unspecific amplifiers of mental processes. They do not create the experiences they induce, but activate the deep unconscious and make its contents available for conscious processing. The observations from psychedelic sessions have, thus, general validity for the understanding of the human psyche.

The new insights into psychology, psychopathology, and psychotherapy derived from deep experiential work with or without psychedelics fall into our four broad categories: 1) the dimensions of the psyche and the cartography of inner space; 2) the architecture of psychopathology; 3) the dynamics of personality transformation; and 4) strategies for therapy and self-exploration.

In this chapter, I will describe a new cartography of the psyche and the dynamic structure of emotional and psychosomatic disorders. I will focus particularly on depression and psychosis. The implications of this way of thinking for therapy and self-exploration will be mentioned only tangentially. A more detailed treatment of these important issues has to be reserved for a separate presentation.

DIMENSIONS OF CONSCIOUSNESS: NEW CARTOGRAPHY OF THE HUMAN PSYCHE

One of the most significant implications of modern consciousness research for psychiatry and psychotherapy has been the entirely new status and image of the human psyche. Mechanistic science portrays consciousness as an epiphenomenon and product of highly developed matter—the brain. The traditional model of the human psyche that dominates academic psychiatry is personalistic and biographically oriented. The observations of the last few decades have changed our understanding of the relationship between consciousness and matter and of the dimensions of the psyche. They show consciousness and creative intelligence as inextricably woven into the fabric of the universe and the human psyche as essentially commensurate with all of existence (2).

Although I will focus primarily on the data from my own research, the conclusions are directly applicable to other fields studying human beings that have accumulated observations incompatible with the prevailing mechanistic world-view, such as Jungian psychology, anthropology, laboratory consciousness studies, and thanatology. The conceptual framework presented in this chapter can also be easily reconciled with the new paradigm in science—the image of the universe emerging from quantum-relativistic physics, information and systems theory, biology, and Prigogine's studies of dissipative structures (12).

A comprehensive discussion of the new cartography of the psyche based on deep experiential work would be beyond the scope of this paper; it was described in detail in a special publication (4). In this context, I will give an outline of its basic features with special emphasis on the understanding of psychopathology and psychotherapy. In addition to the traditional biographical-recollective level, the new cartography includes 1) the perinatal realm of the psyche focusing on the phenomena of birth and death, and 2) the transpersonal domain. Since the unconscious has a complex multilevel and multidimensional holographic arrangement, it represents an undivided experimental continuum. Any attempt at clear demarcation and linear description, which is necessary for didactic purposes, thus has to involve a certain degree of artificiality and oversimplification.

There exists a wide spectrum of ancient and Oriental spiritual practices that are specifically designed to facilitate access to the perinatal and transpersonal domains. For this reason, it is not accidental that the new model of the psyche shows great similarity to those developed over centuries or even millennia by various great mystical traditions.

The entire experiential spectrum has also been described by historians, anthropologists and students of comparative religion in the context of various shamanic procedures, aboriginal rites of passage and healing ceremonies, death-rebirth mysteries, and trance dancing in ecstatic religions.

Recent consciousness research has thus made it possible for the first time to review ancient and non-Western knowledge about consciousness and aim for a genuine synthesis of age-old wisdom and modern science.

The fact that many perinatal and transpersonal experiences can also occur during spontaneous episodes of nonordinary states of consciousness has far-reaching consequences for the understanding and treatment of many conditions that traditional psychiatry interprets as psychotic and thus indicative of mental disease. In the light of the new observations, they can now be seen as transpersonal crises or "spiritual emergencies." When properly understood and treated, such crises can be conducive to emotional and psychosomatic healing, personality transformation, and consciousness evolution (7). This is my principal thesis, and I shall attempt to support it by formulating a new theoretical understanding based on my therapeutic practice with severely disturbed patients.

THE SENSORY BARRIER AND THE RECOLLECTIVE-BIOGRAPHICAL LEVEL

It is possible to shed light on many cases of psychopathology, and understand them more deeply than psychiatry has long supposed, when they are traced back to problems in perinatal experience. Not to take account of the experiences related to the perinatal situation and the birthing process makes it difficult, if not impossible, to understand such psychopathology and to assist in the emergence of a new, more deeply integrated self.

The techniques that mediate experiential access to the unconscious tend first to activate the sensory organs. As a result, deep self-exploration starts for many people with a variety of nonspecific sensory experiences, such as elementary visions of colors and geometrical patterns, the hearing of ringing or buzzing sounds, tactile sensations in various parts of the body, tastes, or smells. These are of a more or less abstract nature; they do not seem to have any deeper symbolic meaning, and have little significance for self-exploration and self-understanding. They seem to represent a sensory barrier that one has to pass through before the journey into one's psyche can begin.

As the process continues, the next most easily available realm of the psyche is usually the recollective-biographical level and the individual unconscious. Although the phenomena belonging to this category are of considerable theoretical and practical relevance, it is not necessary to spend much time on their description. This is because most of the traditional psychotherapeutic approaches have been limited to this level of the psyche. There exists abundant professional literature discussing nuances of psychodynamics in the biographical realm. Unfortunately, various schools contradict each other and there is no unanimity as to what are the significant factors in the psyche, why psychopathology develops, and how effective psychotherapy should be conducted.

The experiences belonging to this category are related to significant biographical events and circumstances in the life of the individual from birth to the present. On this level of self-exploration, anything from the life of the person involved, e.g., an unresolved conflict, repressed memory that has not been integrated, or an incomplete psychological gestalt of some kind, can emerge from the unconscious and become the content of the experience.

There is only one condition for this to happen: the issue has to be of sufficient emotional relevance. Here lies one great advantage of experiential psychotherapy in comparison with verbal approaches. The techniques that can directly activate the unconscious seem to reinforce selectively the most relevant emotional material and to facilitate its emergence into consciousness. They thus provide a kind of inner radar that scans the system and detects material with the strongest charge and emotional relevance. This not only saves the therapist the effort of sorting the relevant from the irrelevant, but protects him or her from having to make such decisions, which would be necessarily biased by professional training, adherence to a particular school, or by personal factors.

By and large, biographical material that emerges in experiential work is in agreement with the Freudian theory or one of its derivatives. However, there are several major differences. In deep experiential psychotherapy, biographical material is not merely remembered or reconstructed; it can actually be fully relived. This involves not only emotions but also physical sensations, visual aspects of the material involved, as well as data from other senses. This happens typically in complete age regression to the stage of development when the events occurred.

Another important distinction is that the relevant memories and other biographical elements do not emerge separately, but form distinct dynamic constellations, for which I have coined the term COEX systems, or systems of condensed experience. A COEX system is a dynamic constellation of memories (and associated fantasy material) from different periods of the individual's life, whose common denominator is strong emotional charge of the same quality, intense physical sensation of a particular kind, or the fact that they share some other important elements. I first became aware of the COEX systems as principles governing the dynamics of the individual unconscious and realized that the knowledge of them was essential for understanding the inner process on this level. However, it later became obvious that the systems of condensed experience represent general organizing principles operating on all levels of the psyche.

Most biographical COEX systems are dynamically connected with specific facets of the birth process. Perinatal themes and their elements then have specific associations with related experiential material from the transpersonal domain. It is not uncommon for a dynamic constellation to comprise material from several biographical periods, from biological birth, and from certain areas of the transpersonal realm, such as past incarnation memories, animal identification, and mythological sequences.

In this context, the experiential similarity of these themes from different levels of the psyche is more important than the conventional criteria of the Newtonian-Cartesian world-view, such as the fact that years or centuries separate the events involved, that there ordinarily seems to exist an abysmal difference between the human and the animal experience of the world, or that elements of "objective reality" are combined with archetypal and mythological themes.

The last major difference between verbal and experiential psychotherapies is the significance of direct physical traumatization in the history of the individual. In traditional psychiatry, psychology, and psychotherapy, there is an exclusive emphasis on psychological traumas. Physical traumas are not seen as having a direct influence on the psychological development of the individual and participating in the psychogenesis of emotional and psychosomatic disorders.

This contrasts sharply with the observations from deep experiential work, where memories of physical traumas appear to be of paramount importance. In psychedelic work, holographic therapy, and other powerful experiential approaches, reliving of life-threatening diseases, injuries, operations, or situations of near-drowning are extremely common, and their significance exceeds by far that of the usual psychotraumas. The residual emotions and physical sensations from situations that threatened survival or the integrity of the organism appear to have a significant role in the development of various forms of psychopathology as yet unrecognized by academic science.

For example, when a child has a serious disease that threatens his life, such as diphtheria, and almost chokes to death, the experience of vital threat and extreme physical discomfort would not be considered by traditional psychotherapy to be a trauma of lasting significance. The focus would be on the fact that the child was separated from his mother at the time of hospitalization, experienced emotional deprivation, and was frightened by the presence of strangers and alien environment.

Conversely, a psychosomatic symptom such as asthma, psychogenic pain, or hysterical paralysis, would be interpreted as "somatization" of primarily psychological conflicts. Experiential work makes it obvious that traumas involving vital threat leave permanent traces in the system and contribute significantly to the development of emotional and psychosomatic problems, such as depressions, suicidal tendencies, anxiety states and phobias, sadomasochistic inclinations, sexual dysfunctions, migraine headaches, or asthma. As a matter of fact, problems that have clearly psychosomatic manifestations can always be traced back to situations (on the biographical, perinatal, or transpersonal level) that involve physical traumatization.

The experiences of serious physical traumas represent a natural transition between the biographical level and the following realm that has as its main constituent the twin phenomena of birth and death. They involve events from the individual's postnatal life and are thus biographical in nature. However, the fact that they brought the person close to death and involved extreme discomfort and pain connects them to the birth trauma. For obvious reasons, memories of diseases and traumas that involved severe interference with breathing, such as pneumonia, diphtheria, whooping cough or near-drowning, are particularly significant in this context.

ENCOUNTERS WITH BIRTH AND DEATH: THE DYNAMICS OF BASIC PERINATAL MATRICES

As the process of experiential self-exploration deepens, the elements of emotional and physical pain can reach extraordinary intensity. They can become so extreme that the individual involved feels that he has transcended the boundaries of individual suffering and is experiencing the pain of entire groups of unfortunate people, of all humanity, or even of all life. It is not uncommon that persons whose inner process reaches this domain report experiential identification with wounded or dying soldiers of all ages, prisoners in dungeons and concentration camps, persecuted Jews or early

Christians, mothers and children in childbirth, or even animals who are attacked by predators or tortured and slaughtered. This level of the human unconscious thus clearly represents an intersection between biographical experience and the spectrum of transpersonal experiences that will be described in the next section.

Experiences on this level of the unconscious are typically accompanied by dramatic physiological manifestations, such as various degrees of suffocation, accelerated pulse rate and palpitations, nausea and vomiting, changes in the color of the complexion, oscillation of body temperature, spontaneous occurrence of skin eruptions and bruises, or tremors, twitches, contortions, twisting movements and other striking manifestations. In psychedelic sessions and occasionally in nondrug experiential sessions or in spontaneously occurring states of mind, these phenomena can be so authentic and convincing that the persons involved can believe that they are actually dying. Even an inexperienced sitter or witness of such episodes can perceive such situations as serious vital emergencies.

On the biographical level, only those persons who actually have had during their lifetime a serious brush with death would be dealing with the issue of survival or impermanence. In contrast, when the inner process transcends biography, the problems related to suffering and death entirely dominate the picture. Those individuals whose postnatal life history did not involve serious threat to survival or body integrity can enter this experiential domain directly. In others, the reliving of serious physical traumas, diseases or operations functions as an experiential bridge to this realm.

Profound confrontations with death characteristic for these experiential sequences tend to be intimately interwoven with a variety of phenomena that are clearly related to the process of biological birth. While facing agony and dying, individuals simultaneously experience themselves as struggling to be born and/or as delivering. In addition, many of the physiological and behavioral concomitants of these experiences can be naturally explained as derivatives of the birth process. It is quite common in this context to identify with a fetus and to relive various aspects of one's biological birth with specific and verifiable details. The element of death can be represented by simultaneous or alternating identification with sick, aging or dying individuals. Although the entire spectrum of these experiences cannot be reduced just to the reliving of biological birth, the birth trauma seems to represent an important core of the experiential process on this level. For this reason, I refer to this level of the unconscious as perinatal.

The term "perinatal" is a Greek-Latin composite word in which the prefix peri- means around or near and the root -natalis denotes relation to birth. It is commonly used in medicine to describe processes that immediately precede childbirth, are associated with it, or immediately follow it; medical texts thus talk about perinatal hemorrhage, infection, or brain damage. In contrast to the traditional use of this word in obstetrics, the term *perinatal* is used in this paper in a phenomenological sense, in relation to lived experiences. Current neurophysiology denies the possibility of birth memories; the reason usually given is the lack of full maturity of the cerebral cortex of the newborn, which is not fully myelinized. However, the existence of authentic perinatal experiences cannot be denied; the frequency of their occurrence and their paramount clinical significance should serve as an incentive for brain researchers to review and revise their outdated theories.

The connection between biological birth and perinatal experiences described above is quite deep and specific. This makes it possible to use the clinical stages of delivery in constructing a conceptual model that helps to understand the dynamics of the perinatal level of the unconscious and even to make specific predictions in relation to the death-rebirth process in different individuals.

Perinatal experiences occur in typical clusters whose basic characteristics are related through deep experiential logic to anatomical, physiological and biochemical aspects of those clinical stages of birth with which they are associated. As I will discuss in a later section, thinking in terms of the birth model provides new and unique insights into the dynamic architecture of various forms of psychopathology and offers revolutionary therapeutic possibilities.

In spite of its close connection to childbirth, the perinatal process transcends biology and has important psychological, philosophical and spiritual dimensions. It should not be, therefore, interpreted in a mechanistic and reductionistic fashion. An individual who is dealing with the powerful dynamics of perinatal process—experientially or as a researcher—can get deeply immersed in it and can tend to see birth as an all-explanatory principle; from a broader perspective, this is a limited approach that has to be transcended. In my present understanding, thinking in terms of the birth process is a very useful model whose applicability is limited to the phenomena of a specific level of the unconscious. When the process of experiential self-exploration moves to transpersonal realms of the psyche, an entirely new way of thinking becomes mandatory.

Certain important characteristics of the perinatal process clearly suggest that it is a much broader phenomenon than a reliving of biological birth. Observations from clinical work with nonordinary states of consciousness show that many forms of psychopathology have deep roots in the memory of biological birth. Experiential sequences of death and rebirth have certainly a distinct therapeutic potential and can result in emotional and psychosomatic healing. However, they have also important transpersonal dimensions and are conducive to profound changes in the individual's philosophical and spiritual belief system, basic hierarchy of values, and general life strategy.

Deep experiential encounter with birth and death is typically associated with an existential crisis of extraordinary proportions during which the individual seriously questions the meaning of his life and existence in general. This crisis can be successfully resolved only by connecting with intrinsically spiritual dimensions of the psyche and the deep resources of the collective unconscious. The resulting personality transformation and consciousness evolution can be compared to the changes that have been described in the context of ancient death-rebirth mysteries, initiation into secret societies, and various aboriginal rites of passage. The perinatal level of the unconscious thus represents an important interface between the individual and the collective unconscious or between traditional psychology and mysticism. Deep spiritual healing requires working with people at this level of experience.

The experiences of death and rebirth reflecting the perinatal level of the unconscious are very rich and complex. Sequences related to various stages and facets of biological birth are typically intertwined or associated with a variety of transpersonal experiences of a mythological, mystical, archetypal, historical, sociopolitical, anthropological, or phylogenetic nature. These tend to appear in four characteristic experiential patterns or constellations. There seems to exist a deep connection between these thematic clusters and the clinical stages of childbirth.

Connecting with the experiences of the fetus in various stages of the biological birth process functions as a selective stencil that provides experiential access to specific domains of the collective unconscious that involve similar states of consciousness. It has proved very useful for the theory and practice of deep experiential work to postulate the existence of four hypothetical dynamic matrices governing the processes related to the perinatal level of the unconscious. I will now refer to them as *Basic Perinatal Matrices* (BPM).

In addition to having specific emotional and psychosomatic content of their own, they also function as organizing principles for material from other levels of the unconscious. From the biographical level, elements of important COEX systems dealing with physical abuse and violation, threat, separation, pain and suffocation are closely related to specific aspects of BPMs. The perinatal unfolding is also frequently associated with transpersonal experiences, such as archetypal visions of the Great Mother or the Terrible Mother Goddess, Hell, Purgatory, Heaven or Paradise, identification with animals, and past incarnation experiences. As is the case with various associated COEX systems, the connecting link is similarity of the emotions or physical sensations involved.

The basic perinatal matrices have also specific relations to different aspects of the activities in the Freudian erotogenic zones and to specific forms of psychopathology. In the following text, I will describe the BPMs in the order in which the corresponding stages of birth follow each other during childbirth. This order is seldom repeated in the process of deep experiential self-exploration; here the themes of the different matrices can occur in many variations of sequential patterns.

FIRST PERINATAL MATRIX (BPM I): THE AMNIOTIC UNIVERSE

The biological basis of this matrix is the original symbiotic unity of the fetus with the maternal organism at the time of the prenatal intrauterine existence. During episodes of undisturbed life in the womb, the conditions of the fetus can be close to ideal. However, a variety of factors of physical, chemical, biological and psychological nature can seriously interfere with this state. Also during later stages of pregnancy the situation might become less favorable because of the size of the child, increasing mechanical constraint, and the relative insufficiency of the placenta.

Perinatal experiences can be relived in a concrete biological form or in combination with a variety of images and other phenomena from the collective unconscious with which they are connected. The relationship between the individual stages of birth and associated themes is quite specific and selective and it reflects a deep experiential logic.

Thus the elements of the undisturbed intrauterine state can be accompanied by or can alternate with experiences that share with it a lack of boundaries and obstructions. Here belong deep experiential identifications with the ocean or various aquatic life forms (algae, kelp, anemone, jellyfish, fish, dolphin or whale) or with the cosmos, interstellar space, galaxy, or with an astronaut floating in a spaceship or in space in weightless condition. Also images of nature at its best, which is beautiful, safe and unconditionally nourishing (Mother Nature) represent characteristic and quite logical concomitants of the blissful fetal state. Archetypal themes from the collective unconscious that can be accessed in this context involve the heavens and paradises of different cultures of the world. The above experiences have typically a strong numinous quality; a sense of unity with the entire universe and *unio mystica* are extreme examples of the spiritual aspect of the first matrix.

The disturbances of intrauterine life are associated with images and experiences of underwater dangers, polluted streams, contaminated or inhospitable nature, and insidious demons from various cultures. The mystical dissolution of boundaries characteristic of blissful fetal episodes is replaced by psychotic distortion and disintegration accompanied by terror and paranoia.

Positive aspects of the first perinatal matrix are closely related to memories of the symbiotic union with mother on the breast, positive COEX systems, and to recollections of situations associated with relaxation, satisfaction, security, peace of mind, and beautiful natural scenery. Similar selective connections also exist to various forms of positive transpersonal experiences with related themes. Conversely, negative aspects of BPM I tend to associate with certain negative COEX systems and corresponding transpersonal matrices.

In regard to the Freudian erotogenic zones, the positive aspects of BPM I coincide with the biological and psychological condition in which there exist no tensions in any of these areas and all the partial drives are satisfied. Negative aspects of BPM I seem to have specific links to nausea, dyspepsia and intestinal dysfunction.

SECOND PERINATAL MATRIX: COSMIC ENGULFMENT AND NO EXIT

This experiential pattern is related to the onset of biological delivery and to its first clinical stage. Here the original harmony and equilibrium of the fetal existence are disturbed, first by alarming chemical signals and later by mechanical contractions of the uterus. With this stage fully developed, the fetus is periodically constricted by uterine spasms. At this point, the system is entirely closed; the cervix is not dilated and the way out is not yet available. Since the arteries supplying the placenta follow a winding course through the complex spiral, circular and longitudinal fabric of the uterine musculature, each contraction restricts the supply of blood and oxygen, nourishment, and warmth to the fetus.

Concrete memories of the threat that the onset of the delivery represents for the fetus have their symbolic concomitant in the experience of cosmic engulfment. It involves overwhelming feelings of increasing anxiety and awareness of an imminent vital danger. The source of this danger cannot be clearly identified and the subject has a tendency to interpret the world in paranoid terms. This can result in a convinced sense of being poisoned, influenced by hypnosis or diabolic machine, possessed by a demonic force, or attacked by extraterrestrials.

Very characteristic for this situation is the experience of a three-dimensional spiral, funnel, or whirlpool sucking the subject relentlessly toward its center. A closely related equivalent to this annihilating maelstrom is the experience of being swallowed by a terrifying monster such as a giant dragon, leviathan, python, crocodile, or a whale. Equally frequent in this content are experiences of attack by a monstrous octopus or tarantula. A less dramatic version of the same experience is the theme of descent into a dangerous underworld, realm of the dead, system of dark grottoes, or a mystifying labyrinth. Corresponding mythological themes are the beginning of the hero's journey, the Fall of the Angels, and Paradise Lost.

Some of these images might appear strange to the analytical mind; however, they show deep experiential logic. Thus the whirlpool represents serious danger for an organism enjoying free floating in a watery environment and imposes on it a dangerous unidirectional motion. Similarly, the situation of being swallowed changes freedom into a life-threatening confinement comparable to the situation of a fetus wedged into the pelvic opening. An octopus entangles, confines and threatens organisms living in the oceanic milieu. A spider traps and restricts insects who previously flew freely in an unobstructed world and seriously threatens their life.

The symbolic counterpart of a fully developed first clinical stage of delivery is the experience of no exit, or of hell. It involves a sense of being stuck, encaged, or trapped in a claustrophobic nightmarish world and experiencing incredible psychological and physical tortures. The situation is typically absolutely unbearable and appears to be endless and hopeless. The individual loses the sense of linear time and can see neither the possibility of an end to this torment nor any form of active escape from it. This can be associated with an experiential identification with prisoners in dungeons or concentration camps, inmates of insane asylums, sinners in hell, or archetypal figures, such as the Wandering Jew Ahasuerus, the Flying Dutchman, Sisyphus, Ixion, Tantalus, or Prometheus.

While under the influence of this matrix, the subject is also selectively blinded to anything positive in the world and his life. Agonizing feelings of metaphysical loneliness, helplessness, hopelessness, inferiority, inadequacy, existential despair, and guilt are standard constituents of this state of consciousness. Through the prism of this matrix, human life appears as an absolutely meaningless theater of the absurd, a farce staging cardboard characters and mindless robots, or a cruel circus sideshow.

As far as the organizing function of BPM II is concerned, it attracts and is connected with COEX systems that involve situations of a passive and helpless victim subjected to an overwhelming destructive force without a chance of escaping. It also has affinity to transpersonal themes with similar qualities.

THIRD PERINATAL MATRIX (BPM III): THE DEATH-REBIRTH STRUGGLE

Many important aspects of this complex experiential matrix can be understood from its association with the second clinical stage of childbirth. In this stage, the uterine contractions continue but, unlike in the previous stage, the cervix is now dilated and allows gradual propulsion of the fetus through the birth canal. This involves an enormous struggle for survival, crushing mechanical pressures and often a high degree of anoxia and suffocation. In the terminal stages of delivery, the fetus can experience intimate contact with biological material, such as blood, mucus, fetal liquid, urine, and even feces.

From the experiential point of view, this pattern is rather ramified and complicated. Besides actual realistic reliving of various aspects of the struggle in the birth canal, it involves a wide variety of archetypal and other phenomena that occur in typical thematic clusters and sequences. The most important of these are the elements of titanic fight, sadomasochistic experiences, intense sexual arousal, demonic episodes, scatological involvement, and an encounter with fire. All these aspects and facets of BPM III reflect again deep experiential logic and can be meaningfully related to certain anatomical, physiological, and emotional characteristics of the corresponding stage of birth.

The titanic aspect is quite understandable in view of the enormity of the forces encountered in this stage of childbirth. At this time, the frail head of the fetus is wedged into the narrow pelvic opening by the power of uterine contractions that oscillate between fifty and one hundred pounds. The subject facing this aspect of BPM III can experience overwhelming streams of energy building up to explosive discharges.

One of the characteristic forms that this experience can take is identification with raging elements of nature, such as volcanoes, electric storms, earthquakes, tidal waves, or tornados. Another form of expression is experiential immersion in violent scenes of wars or revolutions and in enormous energies generated by high power technology—thermonuclear reactors, atomic bombs, tanks, spaceships, rockets, lasers, and electric power plants.

A mitigated form of the titanic experience includes participation in various dangerous adventures, such as the hunting of wild animals or physical fights with them, gladiator combats, exciting explorations, and conquest of new frontiers. Related archetypal and mythological themes are images of the Last Judgment, Purgatory, extraordinary feats of superheroes, and battles of cosmic proportions involving the forces of Light and Darkness or Gods and Titans.

Aggressive and sadomasochistic aspects of this matrix reflect the biological fury of the organism whose survival is threatened by pain and suffocation and also the introjected destructive forces of the birth canal. Frequent themes occurring in this context are scenes of violent murder and suicide, mutilation and automutilation, torture, execution, ritual sacrifice and self-sacrifice, bloody man-to-man combats, boxing, free-style wrestling, sadomasochistic practices, and rape.

The experiential logic of the sexual component of the death-rebirth process is not as immediately obvious. It can be explained by the fact that the human organism has a built-in physiological mechanism that translates inhuman suffering and particularly suffocation into a strange kind of sexual arousal and eventually ecstatic rapture. Examples of this can be found in the history of religious sects and in the lives of individual martyrs, in the material related to concentration camps and Amnesty International, and in the observations of individuals dying on the gallows.

The experiences that belong to this category are characterized by the enormous intensity of the sexual drive, its mechanical and unselective quality and pornographic or deviant nature. The fact that on this level of the psyche sexuality is inextricably connected with death, danger, anxiety, aggression, self-destructive impulses, physical pain and various forms of biological material (blood, mucus, feces, urine) forms a natural basis for the development of the most important types of sexual dysfunctions, deviations and variations. The connection between the sexual orgasm and the orgasm of birth makes it possible to add a deeper and highly relevant perinatal layer to the dynamic interpretations of Freudian analysis that have a superficial biographical and sexual emphasis.

The demonic element of this stage can present specific problems for the experiencers, as well as their therapists, since the uncanny quality of the material often leads to reluctance to face it. The most common themes observed in this context are scenes of the Sabbath of the Witches (Walpurgis Night), satanic orgies and Black Mass rituals, and temptation by evil forces. The common denominator connecting this stage of childbirth with the themes of the Sabbath or with Black Mass rituals is the peculiar experiential amalgam of death, deviant sexuality, fear, aggression, scatology, and distorted spiritual impulse.

The scatological facet of the death-rebirth process has its natural biological basis in the fact that in the final phase of the delivery the fetus can come into close contact with feces and other forms of biological material. However, these experiences by far exceed what the newborn might have actually experienced during birth. They can involve scenes of crawling in offal or through sewage systems, wallowing in piles of excrement, drinking blood or urine, or participating in revulsive images of putrefaction.

The element of fire is experienced either in its ordinary form (with the subjects witnessing scenes of conflagrations and identifying with the immolation victims) or in an archetypal form of purifying fire (pyrocatharsis) that seems to destroy whatever is corrupted and to prepare the individual for spiritual rebirth. This thematic motif is the least comprehensible aspect of the birth symbolism. Its biological counterpart might be the overstimulation of the fetus with indiscriminate "firing" of peripheral neurons. It is interesting that it has its experiential parallel in the delivering mother, who often feels in this stage that her vagina is on fire.

The religious and mythological symbolism of this matrix focuses particularly on the themes that involve sacrifice and self-sacrifice or combine spiritual pursuit and sexuality. Quite frequent are scenes of Pre-Columbian sacrificial rituals, visions of crucifixion or identification with Christ, experiential connection with deities symbolizing death and rebirth, such as

Osiris, Dionysos, Attis, Adonis, Persephone, Orpheus, or Balder, and sequences involving worship of the terrible goddesses Kali, Coatlicue, or Rangda. Sexual motifs are represented by episodes of phallic worship, temple prostitution, fertility rites, ritual rape, and various aboriginal tribal ceremonies involving rhythmic sensual dancing. A classical symbol of the transition from BPM III to BPM IV is the legendary bird Phoenix, who dies in fire and rises resurrected from the ashes.

Several important characteristics of this experiential pattern distinguish it from the previously described no-exit constellation. The situation here does not seem hopeless and the subject is not helpless. He is actively involved and has the feeling that the suffering has a definite direction and goal. In religious terms, this situation relates to the concept of purgatory rather than hell.

In addition, the individuals involved do not play the roles only of helpless victims. They are observers and can at the same time identify with both the aggressor and the victim to the point of having difficulties in separating the roles. Also, while the no-exit situation involves sheer suffering, the experience of the death-rebirth struggle represents the borderline between agony and ecstasy and the fusion of both. It seems appropriate to refer to this type of experience as "volcanic ecstasy" in contrast to the "oceanic ecstasy" of the cosmic union associated with the first perinatal matrix.

Specific experiential characteristics connect BPM III to COEX systems that include memories of intense sensual and sexual experiences in a dangerous and precarious context, such as parachuting, car racing, exciting but hazardous adventures, wrestling, boxing, fights, battles, conquests, red-lights districts, rape or sexual orgies, and amusement parks. A special group of memories related to BPM III involves intimate encounter with biological material, such as bed-wetting, soiling, toilet-training, exposure to blood, or witnessing of dismemberment and putrefaction in war or in accidents. Memories of large fires tend to occur during the transition from BPM III to BPM IV.

FOURTH PERINATAL MATRIX (BPM IV): THE DEATH-REBIRTH EXPERIENCE

This perinatal matrix is related to the third clinical stage of the delivery, to the actual birth of the child. Here the agonizing process of the birth struggle comes to an end. The propulsion through the birth canal associated with an extreme build-up of anxiety, pain, pressure, and sexual tension is followed by a sudden release and relaxation.

The child is born and after a long period of darkness faces for the first time the bright light of the day or the artificial illumination of the delivery room. After the umbilical cord is cut, the physical separation from the maternal organism has been completed. Far-reaching physiological changes have to be accomplished, so that the organism can begin its new existence as an anatomically independent individual providing its own supply of oxygen, digesting its food, and disposing of its waste products.

The symbolic counterpart of this final stage of childbirth is the death-rebirth experience; it represents the termination and resolution of the death-rebirth struggle. Paradoxically, while only a small step from an experience of phenomenal liberation, the individual has a feeling of impending catastrophe of enormous proportions. This frequently results in a desperate and determined struggle to stop the process.

If allowed to happen, the transition from BPM III to BPM IV involves a sense of total annihilation on all imaginable levels—physical destruction, emotional disaster, intellectual and philosophical defeat, ultimate moral failure, and absolute damnation of transcendental proportions. This experience of "ego death" seems to entail an instant merciless destruction of all previous reference points in the life of the individual. The ego death and rebirth is not a one-time experience. During deep systematic self-exploration the unconscious presents it repeatedly with varying emphasis and increasing proportions until the process is completed.

Under the influence of Freudian psychoanalysis, the concept of the ego is associated with one's ability to test reality and to function adequately in everyday life. Individuals who share this limited point of view see the perspective of the "ego death" with horror. However, what actually dies in this process is a basically paranoid attitude toward the world, which reflects the negative experience of the subject during childbirth.

It thus involves a sense of one's inadequacy, the need to be prepared for possible dangers in a drive to be in charge and control, efforts to prove things to oneself and others, and similar elements of problematic value. When experienced in its final and most complete form, the ego-death means an irreversible end to one's philosophical identification with what Alan Watts called "skin-encapsulated ego." When the experience is well integrated, it results not only in increased ability to enjoy existence, but also in better functioning in the world.

The experience of total annihilation and of "hitting the cosmic bottom" that characterizes ego-death is often immediately followed by visions of blinding white or golden light of supernatural radiance and beauty. It can be associated with astonishing displays of divine archetypal entities, rainbow spectra, intricate peacock designs, or pristine natural scenery. The subject experiences a deep sense of spiritual liberation, redemption, and salvation. He typically feels freed from anxiety, depression and guilt, purged, unburdened. This is associated with a flood of positive emotions toward oneself, other people, and existence in general. The world appears to be a beautiful and safe place and the zest for life is considerably increased.

It should be emphasized, however, that this description reflects the situation of normal and uncomplicated birth. A prolonged and debilitating course of delivery, use of forceps, administration of general anesthesia, and other complications and interventions can introduce specific experiential distortions and abnormalities into the phenomenology of this matrix.

The specific archetypal symbolism of the death-rebirth experience can be drawn from many different realms of the collective unconscious, since every major culture has the appropriate mythical forms for this process. The ego-death can be experienced in connection with various destructive deities, such as Shiva, Huitzilopochtli, Moloch, Kali, or Coatlicue, or in full identification with Christ, Osiris, Adonis, Dionysos, or other sacrificed mythical personages. The divine epiphany can involve an entirely abstract image of God as a radiant source of light, or more or less personified representations from different religions. Equally common are experiences of encounter or union with Great Mother Goddesses, as exemplified by Virgin Mary, Isis, Lakshmi, Parvati, Hera, or Cybele.

Related biographical constellations involve memories of personal successes, fortuitous termination of dangerous situations, the end of wars and revolutions, survivals of accidents, and recoveries from serious diseases.

BEYOND EGO-IDENTITY: TRANSPERSONAL DIMENSIONS OF THE PSYCHE

Experiential sequences of death and rebirth typically open the gate to a transbiographical domain in the human psyche that can best be referred to as transpersonal. The perinatal level of the unconscious clearly represents an interface between the biographical and the transpersonal realms, or the individual and the collective unconscious. In most instances, transpersonal experiences are preceded by a dramatic encounter with birth and death. However, there exists also an important alternative; occasionally, it is possible to access experientially various transpersonal elements and themes directly, without confronting the perinatal level.

The common denominator of this rich and ramified group of phenomena is the subject's feeling that his consciousness has expanded beyond the usual ego boundaries and has transcended the limitations of normal time and space. In the ordinary or "normal" states of consciousness, we experience ourselves as existing within the boundaries of the physical body (the body image) and our perception of the environment is restricted by the physically and physiologically determined range of our sensory organs.

Both our internal perception (interoception) and external perception (exteroception) are confined by the usual spatial and temporal boundaries. Under ordinary circumstances, we can experience vividly and with all our senses only the events in the present moment and in our immediate environment. We can recall the past and anticipate the future events or fantasize about them; however, the past and the future are not available for direct experience.

However, in transpersonal experiences, as they occur in psychedelic sessions, self-exploration through nondrug experiential techniques or spontaneously, one or more of the above limitations will appear to be transcended. The experiences of this kind can be divided into three large categories. Some of them involve transcendence of linear time and are interpreted by the subjects as historical regression and exploration of their biological, cultural, and spiritual past, or as historical progression into the future. In the second category are experiences characterized primarily by transcendence of the ordinary spatial boundaries rather than temporal barriers. The third group is then characterized by experiential exploration of domains that in Western culture are not considered part of objective reality.

In nonordinary states of consciousness, many subjects experience quite concrete and realistic episodes that they identify as fetal and embryonal memories. It is not unusual under these circumstances to experience on the level of cellular consciousness full identification with the sperm and the ovum at the time of conception. Sometimes the historical regression goes even further and the individual has a convinced feeling of reliving memories from the lives of his or her ancestors, or even drawing on the memory banks of the racial or collective unconscious. On occasion, subjects report experiences in which they identify with various animal ancestors in the evolutionary chains or have a distinct sense of reliving dramatic episodes from a previous incarnation.

Transpersonal experiences that involve transcendence of spatial barriers suggest that the boundaries between the individual and the rest of the universe are not fixed and absolute. Under special circumstances it is possible to identify experientially with anything in the universe, including the entire cosmos itself. Here belong the experiences of merging with another person into a state of dual unity or assuming another person's identity, turning into the consciousness of a specific group of people, and the expansion of one's consciousness to such an extent that it seems to encompass all of humanity. In a similar way, one can transcend the limits of the specifically human experience and identify with the consciousness of animals, plants, or even with inorganic objects and processes. It even seems possible to experience a consciousness that participates in the entire biosphere, or in the entire material universe.

In a large group of transpersonal experiences, the extension of consciousness seems to go beyond the phenomenal world and the time-space continuum as we perceive it in our everyday life. Here belong numerous visions of archetypal personages and themes, encounters with deities and demons of various cultures, and complex mythological sequences. Quite common also are reports of appearances of spirits of deceased people, superhuman entities, and inhabitants of other universes.

Visions of abstract archetypal patterns, intuitive understanding of universal symbols (cross, yin-yang, swastika, pentacle, or six-pointed star), experience of the meridians and of the flow of chi energy as described in Chinese philosophy and medicine, or the arousal of the Serpent Power (Kundalini) and activation of various centers of psychic energy or chakras, are additional examples of this category of experience. In its farthest reaches, individual consciousness can identify with cosmic consciousness or the Universal Mind. The ultimate of all experiences appears to be identification with the Supracosmic and Metacosmic Void, the mysterious primordial emptiness and nothingness that is conscious of itself and contains all existence in germinal and potential form.

Are such experiences madness? Are they necessarily psychotic delusions? Are we justified in classifying or judging them exclusively in terms of a conceptual framework whose most fundamental presuppositions about the nature of (human) reality we have simply taken for granted and used without questioning? And how do we suppose this narrow-mindedness and intolerance, this lack of understanding, would actually affect the suffering of the patient and influence the course and outcome of therapy? I want to suggest here that it is not only possible, but therapeutically beneficial, to consider such transpersonal experiences as openings in the ego's defenses against a new selfhood, grounded in an expanded integration of its experience of Being: as opportunities for spiritual growth; as opportunities for the ego to grow out of itself and into a new, more developed self-identity. I mean "new," here, both in the sense of "new" for the individual and in the sense of "new" for our historical age.

Transpersonal experiences have many strange characteristics that shatter the most fundamental assumptions of materialistic science and of the mechanistic world view. Researchers who have seriously studied and/or experienced these fascinating phenomena realize that the attempts of traditional psychiatry to dismiss them as irrelevant products of imagination or as erratic fantasmagoria generated by pathological processes in the brain, are superficial and inadequate. Any unbiased study of the transpersonal domain of the psyche has to come to the conclusion that the observations involved represent a critical challenge for the Newtonian-Cartesian paradigm of Western science.

Although transpersonal experiences occur in the process of deep individual self-exploration, it is not possible to interpret them reductionistically as intrapsychic phenomena in the conventional sense. On the one hand, they form an uninterrupted experiential continuum with biographical-recollective and perinatal experiences. On the other hand, they seem to be tapping directly, without the mediation of the sensory organs, sources of information that are clearly outside of the conventionally defined range of the individual.

Thus, for example, there have been individuals who experience episodes of conscious identification with plants or parts of plants, and who occasionally report remarkable insights into such botanical processes as germination of seeds, photosynthesis in leaves, the role of auxins in plant growth, exchange of water and minerals in the root system, or pollination. Equally common is a convinced sense of conscious identification with inanimate matter or inorganic processes—the water in the ocean, fire, lightning, volcanic activity, tornados, gold, diamond, granite, and even stars, galaxies, atoms, and molecules.

I would also like to take note of another interesting group of transpersonal experiences that can be researched experimentally. In this group I would put experiences of telepathy, psychic diagnosis, clairvoyance, clairaudience, precognition, psychometry, out-of-the-body experiences, traveling clairvoyance, and other instances of extrasensory perception. This is the only group of transpersonal phenomena occasionally discussed in academic circles, unfortunately with a strong negative bias.

From a broader perspective, there is no reason to sort out the so-called paranormal phenomena as a special category. Since many other types of transpersonal experience quite typically involve access to new information about the universe through extrasensory channels, the clear boundary between psychology and parapsychology disappears, or becomes rather arbitrary, when the existence of the transpersonal domain is recognized and acknowledged.

The philosophical challenge associated with the observations described above—formidable as it may be in itself—is further augmented by the fact that in nonordinary states of consciousness transpersonal experiences correctly reflecting the material world appear on the same continuum as—and intimately interwoven with—others whose content, according to the Western world-view, is not part of objective reality. We can mention in this context the Jungian archetypes—the world of deities, demons, demigods, superheroes and complex mythological, legendary and fairy-tale sequences.

The nature of transpersonal experiences and even their claims to "reality" violate some of the most basic assumptions of our mechanistic science. They imply, for example, that our normal experience of physical boundaries is essentially arbitrary; that there are nonlocal connections in the universe; that communications can take place through unknown means and channels; that memory can exist without a material "substrate"; that time is not necessarily linear; that a certain degree of consciousness is present in all living organisms (including lower animals, plants, unicellular organisms and viruses) and perhaps even in inorganic matter; and that there may be a field continuum within the matrix of which all these modes of being interact.

Many transpersonal experiences involve events from the microcosm and macrocosm—realms that cannot be directly reached by human senses—or from periods that historically precede the origin of the solar system, formation of planet earth, appearance of living organisms, development of the central nervous system, and appearance of homo sapiens. This clearly implies that each human being has potential experiential access to the field of Being as a whole, and in a sense *is* the whole cosmic network, as much as he or she is just an infinitesimal part of it, a separate and insignificant biological entity.

Transpersonal experiences have a very special position in the cartography of the human psyche. The recollective-analytical level and the individual unconscious are clearly biographical in nature. The perinatal dynamics seem to represent an intersection or frontier between the personal and transpersonal; this is reflected in their deep association with birth and death—the beginning and end of individual human existence. Transpersonal experiences reveal connections between the individual and the cosmos which are beyond comprehension in terms of the traditional Western paradigm of knowledge, science, and truth.

The expanded cartography I am proposing is not just a matter of academic interest. As I will argue later, it has deep and revolutionary implications for the understanding of psychopathology; and it offers new therapeutic possibilities, which cannot be recognized in terms of the medical model that governs traditional psychiatry.

ARCHITECTURE OF EMOTIONAL DISORDERS

I believe that my observations from LSD psychotherapy and from the new experiential nondrug techniques can shed new light on the conceptual controversies among the competing schools of depth psychology in regard to psychodynamic forces underlying various forms of emotional and psychosomatic disorders. The rapid and elemental unfolding of the therapeutic process that characterizes most of these innovations in psychotherapy minimizes the programming, restrictions, and distortions imposed on the patient during even the most indirect forms of verbal psychotherapy. The material that emerges under these circumstances seems to reflect more genuinely the actual dynamic constellations underlying clinical symptoms and frequently comes as a total surprise to the therapist, instead of complying with his conceptual bias.

In general, the architecture of psychopathology manifested in experiential work is infinitely more complex and intricate than the current personality theories suggest. Very few—if any—emotional and psychosomatic syndromes can be explained solely from the dynamics of the individual unconscious. Many clinical problems have deep roots in the perinatal level of the unconscious. They are meaningfully related to the trauma of birth and to fear of death and their resolution requires experiential confrontation with the death-rebirth process. In many instances, the dynamic geometry of emotional, psychosomatic, and interpersonal problems reaches even farther; they are deeply anchored in various transpersonal matrices.

It is not uncommon that psychopathological syndromes show a complex, multilevel dynamic structure and are meaningfully connected with all the major areas of the psyche—the biographical, perinatal, and transpersonal. To work effectively with problems of this kind, the therapist must be prepared to acknowledge and confront successively material from all these levels. This requires great flexibility and freedom from conceptual orthodoxy.

In view of the above facts, psychotherapeutic schools that do not acknowledge transbiographical sources of psychopathology have very superficial and inadequate models of the psyche. Their therapeutic efficacy is seriously limited by the fact that they are not tapping into and utilizing experiences rooted in the perinatal and transpersonal dimensions of our being; for these experiences point to a powerful capacity for healing and personality transformation.

After this general introduction, I would like to outline the new understanding of psychopathology that reflects recognition of the transbiographical levels of the psyche. I will first discuss how the common psychiatric symptoms and their clustering in characteristic syndromes suddenly make new sense when one relates them to the perinatal process and to the anatomical, physiological, and biochemical aspects of the consecutive stages of childbirth. Following this, I will focus more specifically on the pathologies of the self at issue in this book: depressions, mania, various forms of suicide, and the dynamics of the psychotic process. Where appropriate, I will also point to the connections that some disturbances of the self might have to the *transpersonal* domain.

Before continuing this discussion, however, I would like to explain how I myself view the material I will present. The conceptual framework that includes the dynamics of perinatal matrices should be seen as a useful model, not a definitive description of the experiences involved. In this sense, it has the advantages and limitations of any paradigm (9). It allows the logical interpretation of many aspects of psychotherapy for which current theories have unsatisfactory and superficial explanations—or no explanations at all. In many instances, it also allows for important predictions that can be scientifically tested. However, it would be a mistake to take this model literally.

The emphasis on birth does not at all eliminate biographical events and later social conditioning as significant factors in the psychogenesis of psychopathology. The dynamic taxonomy developed by Freud and his followers, linking various emotional disorders to interference in specific stages of development of the libido and the ego, still remains valid. However, the traumatic events in childhood are not seen as primary causes, but as conditions for the emergence of emotions and physical sensations of perinatal origin.

The perinatal level of the unconscious can be seen as a universal matrix out of which various forms of psychopathology can develop. Whether or not they actually develop and what specific forms originate, is then the function of postnatal events, as well as of the social, cultural, historical conditions encountered in the course of early life. Under favorable circumstances, the perinatal material will be relegated to deep realms of the unconscious and the individual might not be aware of it at all, unless he takes a psychedelic drug or experiments with some powerful nondrug technique. When the perinatal events are not counteracted by nourishing postnatal developments or when their significant aspects are selectively reinforced by traumatic experiences in childhood, powerful emotions and physical sensations related to birth will emerge into consciousness in the form of specific psychopathological syndromes.

Careful analysis of observations from deep experiential psychotherapy reveals that a conceptual model that includes the perinatal dynamics can logically and coherently relate the most important psychiatric symptoms to specific characteristics of the biological birth process. It can also explain quite naturally why the individual psychiatric symptoms, such as anxiety, aggression, depression, guilt, inferiority feelings, or obsessions and compulsions, tend to cluster into typical syndromes.

Anxiety, generally considered to be the single most important psychiatric symptom, is a signal indicating that survival or body integrity of the organism is threatened. It is, therefore, a logical and natural part of the birth process, in view of the fact that delivery is a situation of vital emergency that involves extreme physical and emotional stress. The possibility that all anxiety might have its origin or prototype in the birth canal was first mentioned by Freud (3). However, Freud himself did not pursue this idea any further and the theory of the birth trauma as source of all psychopathology was later elaborated by his renegade disciple Otto Rank (13). These theoretical speculations of the pioneers of psychoanalysis preceded by three decades their confirmation by psychedelic research.

Aggression of extreme proportions is equally comprehensible in this context as a reaction to excessive physical and emotional pain, suffocation, and threat to survival. A comparable abuse imposed on an unconstrained organism would result in emotional outbursts and motor storms aimed at fight or flight. However, the child trapped in the narrow confines of the birth canal does not have any outlet for the emotional and motor impulses, since he is not able to move, fight back, leave the situation, or even scream.

One thus has to expect that enormous amounts of general tension and aggressive impulses are, under these circumstances, fed back into the organism and stored for later discharge. This huge reservoir of pent-up energies can later become the basis not only for aggression and violent impulses without any basis in consensually validated reality, but also for various motor phenomena that accompany many psychiatric disorders, such as generalized or localized muscular tension, spasms, tremors, twitches, tics, and seizure-like activity.

The fact that the closed system of the birth canal prevents any external expression of the biological fury involved provides a natural theoretical basis for Freud's concept of depression as aggression turned inside and using the subject as target. This connection can be clearly illustrated by the fact that the extreme outcome of both depression and aggression is murder. Homicide and suicide differ only in the direction the destructive impulse takes. Thus also depression has its perinatal prototypes. For inhibited depression, it is the no-exit situation of the second perinatal matrix and for agitated depression, the third matrix, which allows some limited expression of aggression. These connections will be discussed later in more detail.

It is hard to imagine a situation that would involve more helplessness than that of a fetus confronted with the brutal and elemental forces of the birth process. Thus it does not come as a surprise that the deep roots of inferiority feelings and a sense of inadequacy can be traced back to organismically carried experiences of this situation. We can also shed much light on the so-called narcissistic character disorders, in which childlike helplessness and insecurity combine with consuming ambition and the heroic pursuit of grandiose projects.

The perinatal source of guilt can be illustrated by examples from religion and mythology. In our own tradition, the Bible links the "primal sin" to the expulsion from the paradisiacal situation of the Garden of Eden. More specifically, God's punishment for Eve involves an explicit reference to female reproductive functions: "In pain and sorrow shalt thou bring forth children." The most plausible and common explanation for this connection that one hears from LSD subjects and clients in nondrug experiential therapy relates guilt to the recognition or awareness of past pain recorded in the organism. Guilt then would be an attempt to rationalize how much suffering had been inflicted on the individual ("Something this horrible could not have happened to me, unless I deserved it. I must have done something very bad, although I have no idea what it could have been.").

Disturbances in sexuality and intimate relationships have an important perinatal component. Most of the serious disturbances and deviations of sexuality are psychogenetically connected with BPM III. Serious inhibition of libidinal drive and reduction or absence of sexual appetite show a dynamic connection with BPM II. An individual who is undergoing the strong influence of the second perinatal matrix experiences total emotional isolation from the environment and complete physiological and energetic blockage. This effectively prevents the development of sexual interest and initiative, as well as the experience of sexual excitement. And, more generally, it blocks a development of the self that requires the self to grow through its relationships with other beings. Under these circumstances, sexual activity is possibly the last thing in the world that the individual would consider. However, it is rather common in this state that sexual material experienced as belonging to the past emerges and is reviewed by the individual in the negative context of agonizing guilt and disgust.

The perinatal roots of paranoia can be traced to the onset of delivery, when the beginning uterine activity threatens the world of the fetus. As the memory of this state starts emerging into the consciousness of an adult, the imminent danger will be interpreted analogously in terms of factors known to the subject that could have a comparable disastrous impact on his world—diabolic machines, chemical poisons, toxic gases, noxious radiation, demonic possession, extraterrestrial intervention, or malevolent hypnotic influence. Paranoia of perinatal origin has definite claustrophobic elements. Other types of paranoia are related to memories of serious intrauterine disturbances, such as diseases or toxemia of the mother, and impending or attempted abortion. Here, of course, the claustrophobic element would be missing. The common denominator is the factor of total threat to the existence of the fetus, the onset of delivery being the final and irrevocable end of embryonal existence, the same situation that represents the danger in abortion.

Emotional disorders are quite characteristically accompanied by specific psychosomatic manifestations. In the past, there have been endless arguments between the organic and psychological schools of psychiatry as to whether biological or psychological factors play the primary role in emotional disorder. Introducing the perinatal level into psychiatric theory bridges to a great extent the gap between these two extreme orientations and offers us a surprising alternative: Since childbirth is a complex process that combines emotional, physiological, and biochemical elements, the question as to what is primary and what is derived is irrelevant on this level of the psyche. The emotional and biological disturbances represent two aspects of the same existential situation and can both be traced back to the same trauma—the birthing process.

The pathological nature of the typical physical concomitants of emotional disorders can be understood quite logically in terms of their connection with the birth experience. They involve pressure, belt or migraine headaches; palpitation and other cardiac complaints; subjective sense of lack of oxygen and breathing difficulties under emotional stress; muscular pains, tensions, tremors, cramps and seizure-like discharges; nausea and vomiting; activation of the gastrointestinal tract resulting in spastic diarrhea or constipation; painful uterine contractions; profuse sweating; hot flashes alternating with chills; or changes of skin circulation and various dermatological manifestations. Also some extreme psychiatric complaints that have both emotional and physical aspects, such as the sense of being overwhelmed by powerful erratic energies and losing control, fear of death and the experience of dying, feeling of impending insanity, and catastrophic expectations are not difficult to understand, if interpreted in the context of our theoretical model as effects of a bodily carried memory of the birth trauma.

PSYCHODYNAMIC ASPECTS OF MANIC-DEPRESSIVE DISORDERS

I will now apply insights from my experiential therapy (both with and without psychedelic drugs) to some important questions concerning depressions and related problems. I want to show that our model can throw some new light on such issues as the psychodynamic structure of various types of depression and of mania, as well as on the psychology of different forms of suicide. In addition, it suggests the possibility of new therapeutic strategies for the treatment of at least some forms of depression.

The psychodynamic emphasis of this discussion is not incompatible with the fact that various factors of biological or biochemical nature can play an important role in both depression and mania. Although these might function as important triggers of the process, they cannot fully explain by themselves the particular form which the disorder takes, nor how it fits into the overall personality structure and developmental logic of the individual.

Severe inhibited depressions of endogenous and reactive type typically have important roots in BPM II. The phenomenology of the sessions governed by this matrix, as well as the post-session intervals dominated by it, show all the essential features of deep depressions of this kind. An individual who is under the influence of BPM II experiences agonizing mental and sometimes physical pain, despair, overwhelming feelings of guilt and inadequacy, deep anxiety, lack of initiative, loss of interest in the world, and inability to enjoy anything.

In this state, life appears to be utterly meaningless, emotionally empty, and absurd. In spite of the extreme suffering involved, this condition is not associated with crying or any other dramatic external manifestations, and is characterized by a general motor inhibition. The world and one's life are seen as if through a negative stencil, with selective awareness of the tragic, bad and painful aspects of existence and inability to see anything positive. This situation feels and appears to be absolutely unbearable, inescapable, and hopeless. Sometimes this is accompanied by an ability to see colors, and the entire world is perceived as a black and white film. Existential philosophy and the theater of the absurd seem to be the most accurate descriptions of this perspective on life.

Inhibited depressions are characterized not only by total obstruction of emotional flow, but also by total energetic blockage of the major physiological functions, such as digestion, elimination of water and waste products, sexual activity, menstrual cycle, and the sleep rhythm. This is quite consistent with the understanding of this type of depression as a manifestation of BPM II. Its major physical concomitants involve feelings of oppression, constriction, confinement, sense of suffocation, tension and pressure headaches, retention of water and urine, constipation, cardiac distress, loss of interest in food and sex, and a tendency to hypochondriacal interpretations of various physical feelings.

The paradoxical biochemical findings suggesting that people suffering from inhibited depression can show a high degree of stress, as indicated by the level of catecholamines and steroid hormones, fit well the image of BPM II. It is as if the subject introjected the entire situation of the energetic clash at this stage of birth; the external manifestation then is a highly stressful condition with inability to carry out any kind of external action or expression.

Psychoanalytic theory links depression to early oral problems and emotional deprivation. Although this connection is obviously correct, it does not account for many important features of depression—the sense of hopelessness, circularity and absurdity of life, feelings of being stuck and having no exit, energetic and physiological blockage, most of the physical symptoms, and the link between depression and suicide. The model we are considering here shows the Freudian interpretation to be correct, but superficial and incomplete. While the deepest nature of inhibited depression can only be understood from the dynamics of BPM II, the COEX systems associated with it and instrumental in its development include the elements and factors described in psychoanalysis.

The connection of this biographical material with BPM II reflects deep experiential logic. The corresponding stage of biological delivery involves interruption of the symbiotic connection with the maternal organism through the uterine contractions, which cut off the blood flow. This results in an inadequate supply of nourishment, warmth and oxygen, loss of biologically meaningful contact, and exposure to danger.

It thus makes good sense that the typical constituents of COEX systems related to this type of depression include emotional rejection, absence of mother and separation from her, and feelings of loneliness, cold, hunger, and thirst in infancy and early childhood. Other important biographical determinants involve family situations that are oppressive and punishing for the child and that do not permit rebellion or escape. They thus reinforce and perpetuate the role of the victim in a "no-exit" situation characteristic of BPM II.

An important category of COEX systems instrumental in the dynamics of inhibited depression involves memories of events that constituted a threat to survival or body integrity and in which the individual played the role of a helpless victim. This is entirely new information, since psychoanalysis and psychotherapeutically oriented academic psychiatry emphasize the role of psychological rather than physical traumas in the pathogenesis of depression. The psychotraumatic impact of serious diseases, injuries, operations, and episodes of near-drowning has been overlooked and grossly underestimated.

The new observations we have reported, suggesting the paramount significance of physical traumas for the life of the individual in general, and for the development of inhibited depression in particular, would be difficult to integrate into psychoanalysis, which explains the pathologies of the self in terms of psychological traumas and argues for the oral origin of depressions. However, they are perfectly logical in the context of the presented model, where the emphasis is on the combined emotional-physical trauma of birth and its interaction with thematically related COEX systems.

In contrast, the phenomenology of agitated depression is dynamically associated with BPM III; its basic elements can be seen in experiential sessions and post-session intervals governed by this matrix. Characteristic features of this type of depression are a high level of tension and anxiety, an excessive amount of psychomotor excitement and agitation, and aggressive impulses oriented both inward and outward. The patients suffering from agitated depression cry and scream, roll on the floor, flail around, beat their heads against the walls, scratch their faces, and tear their hair and clothes. Typical physical symptoms associated with this condition are muscular tensions, tremors and painful cramps, belt or migraine headaches, uterine and intestinal spasms, nausea, and breathing problems.

The related COEX systems deal with aggression and violence, cruelties of various kinds, sexual abuse and assaults, painful medical interventions, and diseases involving choking and a struggle for breath. Unlike the subject in the case of COEX systems related to BPM II that underlie inhibited depression, the subject involved in these situations is not a passive victim; he is actively engaged in attempts to fight back, put up resistance, remove the obstacles, or escape. Memories of violent encounters with parental figures or siblings, fist fights with peers, scenes of sexual abuse and rape, and episodes from military battles are typical examples of this kind.

As far as mania is concerned, there has been a strong feeling among psychoanalysts that the psychodynamic interpretation of this disorder is generally much less satisfactory than that of depression. However, most authors seem to agree that mania represents a way of avoiding awareness of depression and includes denial of painful inner reality and flight into the external world. It reflects the victory of ego over superego, a drastic decrease of inhibitions, inflation of self-esteem, and an abundance of sensual and aggressive impulses.

In spite of all this, mania does not give the impression of genuine freedom. Psychological theories of manic-depressive disorders emphasize the intensive ambivalence of manic patients and the fact that simultaneous feelings of love and hate interfere with their ability to relate to others. The typical manic hunger for objects is usually seen as a manifestation of strong oral needs, and the periodicity of mania and depression is seen as an indication of its relation to the cycle of satiety and hunger.

Many otherwise puzzling features of manic episodes become easily comprehensible from their relation to the dynamics of perinatal matrices. Mania is psychogenetically linked to the experiential transition from BPM III to BPM IV; it can be seen as a clear indication that the individual is partially under the influence of the fourth matrix, but at the same time is still in touch with the third one.

In this context, the oral impulses reflect the state the manic patient is psychologically aiming for and has not achieved yet, rather than a fixation on the oral level. Relaxation and oral satisfaction are characteristic of a state following birth. To be peaceful, sleep and eat—the typical triad of wishes found in mania—are a natural goal for an organism flooded by disturbing impulses associated with the final stages of birth and aimed at a release from the agony of the process. However, manic patients are unwilling and unable to face the remaining unresolved material related to the third matrix. As a result of anxious clinging to their uncertain and tenuous victory, the new positive feelings become accentuated to the point of caricature. The image of "whistling in the forest" seems to fit this condition particularly well. The exaggerated and forceful nature of the manic emotions and behavior clearly betray that they are not expressions of genuine joy and freedom, but reaction formations to fear and aggression.

LSD subjects whose sessions terminate in a state of incomplete rebirth show all the typical signs of mania, and accordingly confirm our claim that certain pathologies of the self, e.g., forms of mania, are related to experientially incomplete and unresolved birth. They are hyperactive, move around at a hectic pace, try to socialize and fraternize with anybody in their environment, and talk incessantly about their sense of triumph, wonderful feelings, and the great experience they just had. They extoll the wonders of LSD treatment and spin grandiose messianic plans to transform the world through the drug experience. Extreme hunger for stimuli and social contact is associated with inflated zest, self-love and self-esteem, as well as overindulgence in various aspects of life. The breakdown of superego constraints results in seductiveness, promiscuous tendencies, and obscene talk.

When the subjects experiencing this state can be convinced to turn inside, face the difficult emotions that remain unresolved, and complete the (re)birth process, the manic quality disappears from their mood and behavior. The experiences of BPM IV in their pure form are characterized by radiant joy, increased zest, deep relaxation, tranquility and serenity, inner peace, and total satisfaction. They lack the driven quality, grotesque exaggeration, and ostentatious character of manic states.

The connections we have made between psychopathology and perinatal events have important consequences for therapy. Depressions that have their roots in the dynamics of perinatal matrices can be seen as stages of a *transformative* process in which the individual is arrested. What is required, therefore, is a therapeutic strategy that supports the patient's attempts to continue the process of self-development by helping him to open up to the wisdom of the unconscious. What might on the surface appear as nothing but the manifestation of psychopathological symptoms is actually an effort of the organismic self to free itself from its traumatic past. One encounters problems in psychotherapeutic work with patients suffering through manic disorders; these seem to reflect, at least to some extent, the fact that to reach a true resolution, the manic person has to be willing to confront difficult aspects of the process that he is deeply reluctant to face. Traditional psychotherapies, however, are committed to a conceptual paradigm that denies the reality of unconscious perinatal experience and therefore cannot help the patient to gain conscious entrance into this dimension and work through the unresolved problems painfully carried by the body into present living.

Observations from experiential psychotherapy based on the concept of perinatal matrices offer interesting insights into the phenomenon of suicide. They throw new light on both the deep motives for suicide and the intriguing questions that center on choices of method. Suicidal tendencies fall into two distinct categories, which have very specific relations to the perinatal process.

Suicide of the first type, or nonviolent suicide, is based on the unconscious memory that the no-exit situation of BPM II was preceded by the experience of intrauterine existence. An individual trying to escape the elements of the second matrix would thus have a deep tendency to reinstitute the fetal state. He or she would be attracted in everyday life to situations that have similar elements. Mild forms of suicidal tendencies of this type manifest as a desire to fall asleep and not to awaken ever again. Full expression of such tendencies involves the use of large doses of hypnotics or tranquilizers, inhalation of carbon monoxide or domestic gas, drowning, freezing in snow, or bloodletting in warm water.

Suicide of the second type, or violent suicide, unconsciously follows the pattern once experienced during biological birth. For a person who is under the influence of BPM III, regression into the oceanic state of the womb is not available, because it would lead through the hellish no-exit stage of BPM II. Such an individual would precipitate toward situations that have some significant elements of the actual biological birth—intensification of the tension and suffering, followed by an instant explosive liberation associated with tissue damage and various forms of biological material, such as blood and feces.

The suicidal tendencies and acts that belong to this category involve death under the wheels of a train, in the turbine of a hydroelectric plant, or in a suicidal car accident; cutting one's throat, blowing one's brains out, and stabbing oneself with a knife; throwing oneself from a window, tower or cliff; and some exotic forms of suicide, such as harakiri and kamikaze missions. Suicide by hanging seems to belong to an earlier phase of BPM III, characterized by feelings of suffocation and strong sexual arousal. The dynamics of these two categories of suicide are discussed in greater detail in my book, *Beyond the Brain*.

When suicidal individuals undergo experiential therapy and successfully complete the death-rebirth process, they see suicide retrospectively as a tragic mistake based on lack of self-understanding. A person who does not know that it is possible to experience liberation from unbearable emotional and physical tension through a symbolic death and rebirth, or through reconnecting to the memory of prenatal existence, might be driven by the catastrophic dimensions of his agony to enact an irreversible situation in the world shaped by similar elements. The critical issue in relation to suicide is thus the depth of introspection and the ability to make a distinction between *egocide* and *suicide*.

The experiences of the first and fourth perinatal matrices represent not only symbolic biological states (good breast and good womb), but also very distinct spiritual states. Suicidal tendencies are therefore, in the last analysis, expressions of an unrecognized and distorted craving for transcendence, i.e., the possibility that a new self should emerge out of the destruction by integrating experiential matrices previously excluded from the developmental life of the self. The best remedy for self-destructive tendencies and suicidal urges is therefore a therapy that helps the patient to go through experiences of ego death and rebirth and complete a movement towards experiencing the self in its integration within a cosmic unity.

THE PSYCHOTIC PROCESS: DISEASE OR TRANSPERSONAL CRISIS?

In spite of the enormous investment of time, energy and money in psychiatric research over many decades, the nature of the psychotic process has remained a mystery. Careful studies have revealed and explored important variables related to constitutional and genetic factors, hormonal and biochemical changes, biological correlates, the developmental history of the individual, situational precipitating influences, psychological and social determinants, and even cosmobiological patterns. However, none of these is sufficiently constant and invariant to provide a convincing explanation. The general agreement seems to be that the psychotic process is a phenomenon of extreme complexity and an end result of a variety of factors operating on many different levels.

Even if biological and biochemical research could detect processes that consistently correlate with the occurrence of psychotic states, that by itself would still not explain the nature and content of psychotic experiences.

According to the interpretive model presented here, functional matrices that are instrumental in most psychotic episodes represent intrinsic and integral components of human personality. The same perinatal and transpersonal matrices that are responsible for psychotic breakdowns can under certain circumstances mediate a process of spiritual transformation and consciousness evolution. They can also remain in many individuals altogether latent, not manifesting at any time during their lives, unless access to these experiential matrices is suddenly brought about by psychedelic drugs or some powerful nondrug techniques.

But the main point here is that the theoretical possibility of spiritual transformation, and correspondingly therapeutic opportunities for this process to continue, depend upon our recognition that many important aspects of psychotic symptomatology can be logically related to the dynamics of various perinatal matrices and thus to specific stages of the birth process. While in neuroses and depressions the content of perinatal matrices appears in a mitigated form and colored by postnatal traumatic events, in psychosis this content emerges into consciousness in a pure, elemental, and undiluted form.

BPM II in its fully developed form contributes to psychotic symptomatology the theme of inhuman tortures and diabolic ordeals attributed to ingenious contraptions or evil influences, an atmosphere of eternal damnation, never-ending suffering in hell, and other types of no-exit situations. Detailed studies in early psychoanalytic literature showed that the influencing and torturing machine represents the body of the mother. Victor Tausk's paper (14) is of particular interest in this context, although it fails to recognize that the endangering maternal organism is the delivering mother, rather than the "bad mother" Melanie Klein and Harry Stack Sullivan ascribe to the nursing period. Other psychotic themes related to BPM II are the meaningless and bizarre world of cardboard figures and robots, and the grotesque atmosphere of strange and fantastic circus sideshows.

The phenomenology of BPM III adds to the clinical picture of psychosis a rich spectrum of experiences that characterize various facets of this matrix. The titanic aspect is represented by sensations of extreme tension, powerful energy flows and discharges, and images of battles and wars. The element of warfare can be related to events in the phenomenal world or involve archetypal scenes of enormous scope—angels battling devils, demigods challenging gods, or superheroes fighting mythological monsters. Aggressive and sadomasochistic elements of BPM III explain the occasional violence of psychotic patients, automutilations, murders and bloody suicides, as well as visions and experiences involving cruelties of all kinds. The strange distortions of sexuality and perverted interests that can be seen in psychotic patients are characteristic of the third matrix. Finally, interest in feces and other biological material, coprophilia and coprophagia, magical power attributed to excreta and excretory functions, retention of urine and feces, or refusal to control the sphincters, clearly betray the involvement of the scatological facet of BPM III. Imagery of the Sabbath of the Witches, Walpurgis Night, Black Mass, and satanic orgies combine in a way characteristic for BPM III death, sex, aggression, and scatology.

The themes characterizing transition from BPM III to BPM IV then add to the rich spectrum of psychotic phenomenology apocalyptic images of the destruction of the world and one's own annihilation, scenes of the Judgement of the Dead or of Armageddon and the Last Judgment, experiences of rebirth and the recreation of the world, identification with Christ or other divine personages symbolizing death and resurrection, grandiose and messianic feelings, elements of divine epiphany, angelic and celestial visions, and a sense of redemption and salvation. The involvement of this aspect of perinatal dynamics can also contribute a manic quality to psychotic symptomatology.

The experiences characteristic of BPM I are represented in both their positive and negative aspects. Many psychotic patients experience episodes of ecstatic union with Nature, with the entire universe, and with God. Sometimes, this is associated with feelings of symbiotic union with the maternal organism, with the good breast or the good womb. In a similar way, there seems to exist a deep connection between disturbances of embryonal life and psychotic distortions of the world. Thus, the reliving of fetal crisis is frequently accompanied by paranoia, experiences of toxic or evil influences, and archetypal images of demons from different cultures.

Since experiences similar to the above have been reported by mystics, saints, prophets, and religious teachers of all ages, this naturally raises the question of the relationship between psychosis and healthy mysticism. The difference seems to be less in the nature and content of the experiences than in attitude, experiential style, and ability to integrate these experiences. While a "mystic" keeps the process internalized and does not relate to the external world until the experiences are completed and well integrated, a psychotic resists the process, projects its elements on the external world, and confuses the inner and outer reality.

When an experience of connection to the transpersonal realms is completed and integrated in a healthy mystical way, the individual realizes that his divinity is not anything special. It applies to all others as well, whether or not they realize it. Nothing has really changed in the world, except the subject's understanding. Psychotic integration of similar experiences is done from the position of the person's everyday identity and body-ego, which has not been completely surrendered. Because the experience is seen as something exclusive that elevates the subject above others, he writes letters to governments and presidents demanding acknowledgement and special attention, and fights real or imaginary enemies.

In the preceding discussion, considerable emphasis has been placed on the perinatal roots of psychotic symptoms. However, psychotic phenomenology can not be fully understood without including the rich spectrum of transpersonal experience. The self that has developed to a degree that enables it to enter the transpersonal dimension experiences truth in archetypal and mythological events; is tested by encounters with deities and demons; develops a deeper understanding of ontological and cosmological problems; and may be open to ancestral, phylogenetic and past incarnation memories, wisdom coming from the racial and collective unconscious, extrasensory perception, and experiences with the character of synchronicity. Also, unitive experiences of a higher order than those related to perinatal dynamics should be mentioned in this context; examples of these are identifications with the Universal Mind, with the Absolute, and with a Supracosmic and Metacosmic Void.

This understanding of psychosis has profound implications for diagnostics and therapy—and indeed, for the course and outcome of therapeutic work. In traditional psychiatry, all nonordinary experiences are considered pathological and are treated mostly by normalizing, and therefore essentially repressive measures. In view of the revolutionary contributions of Carl Gustav Jung (8), Roberto Assagioli (1), and Abraham Maslow (10,11), as well as the observations from experiential therapy with and without psychedelics, the concept of psychosis will have to be drastically redefined and reevaluated. The matrices for perinatal and transpersonal experiences seem to be normal and natural components of the human personality, and the experiences themselves have a distinct healing potential for the life of the self if approached with the right understanding.

It no longer makes sense to diagnose psychosis on the basis of the content of the experience. Many nonordinary states of consciousness can be more appropriately seen as transpersonal or evolutionary crises, "spiritual emergencies," rather than as diseases of unknown etiology. If properly supported they are conducive to emotional and psychosomatic healing, personality transformation, and consciousness evolution. In the future, the definition of what is pathological will have to be made not only on the basis of the content of the experiences, but also—and indeed primarily—on the basis of the patient's attitude toward them: the way he deals with them, and either succeeds or fails to integrate them into the structures of everyday life. In the paradigm whose framework we have been exploring here, it will also be necessary, therefore, to distinguish clearly between a therapeutic context that involves understanding and is conducive to healing and one that is counterproductive and causes iatrogenic damage.

Very often, the suffering that people undergo today becomes clinically severe psychopathology only because neither our society nor our prevailing practice of psychiatry can see in this suffering the precarious efforts of a newly emerging self—a spiritual emergency. Our current therapeutic philosophy blinds us to the fact that, in this emergency, there are existential opportunities for spiritually significant breakthroughs. The modern self needs to develop its rootedness in the dimensions of Being that are constitutive of a more deeply fulfilling spiritual life; yet it is often left with no choice but pathology, because our social and cultural institutions are so strongly controlled by the prevailing paradigm that they cannot be at all responsive to the deepest needs of the self. In its suffering, the modern soul cries out for help in making contact with, and gaining entrance into, dimensions of Being that are not acknowledged by the conceptual framework we have inherited from Newtonian physics and Cartesian metaphysics. But the medical model that psychiatry uses in its diagnosis and treatment of such spiritual crises is too deeply indebted to this conceptual framework to be helpful to a self desperately struggling to integrate into itself experiences this framework excludes and denies.

The radical framework sketched out in this chapter speaks to the needs of the self in a modern world governed by the world-view of mechanistic science. It facilitates a psychotherapeutic practice that provides the self with support and guidance as it risks a journey into the perinatal and transpersonal dimensions of its being; and it offers some ground for hope that, instead of falling into the vicious circle of psychopathology and repressive therapy, the modern self may learn from its suffering and find its way to transformation and healing.

NOTES

1. Assagioli, R.: "Self-Realization and Psychological Disturbances." *Synthesis* 3–4, (1977).

2. Bateson, G.: *Mind and Nature: A Necessary Unity*. E. P. Dutton, New York, 1979.

3. Freud, S.: *Introductory Lectures on Psychoanalysis,* revised ed., London, 1929. Standard Edition of the *Complete Psychological Works of Sigmund Freud*, vols. 15–16., Hogarth, London, 1935.

4. Grof, S.: *Realms of the Human Unconscious: Observations from LSD Research*. E. P. Dutton, New York, 1976.

5. Grof, S.: *LSD Psychotherapy*. Hunter House, Pomona, California, 1980.

6. Grof, S.: *Beyond the Brain: Birth, Death, and Transcendence in Psychotherapy* State University of New York, Albany: 1985.

7. Grof, S., Grof, C.: "Spiritual Emergency: Understanding and Treatment of Transpersonal Crises," *Re-Vision,*8 (1968).

8. Jung, C. G.: *Collected Works*, Vol. 3 Bollingen Series 20. Princeton University, Princeton, New Jersey, 1960.

9. Kuhn, T.: *The Structure of Scientific Revolutions*. University of Chicago, Chicago, 1962.

10. Maslow, A.: *Toward a Psychology of Being*. Van Nostrand, Princeton, 1962.

11. Maslow, A.: *Religions, Values, and Peek Experiences*. Ohio University Press, Columbus, 1964.

12. Prigogine, I., and Stengers, I.: *Order Out of Chaos*. Bantam, New York, 1984.

13. Rank, O.: *The Trauma of Birth*. Harcourt Brace, New York, 1929.

14. Tausk, V.: "On the Origin of the Influencing Machine in Schizophrenia." *Psychoanalyt. Quart*. 11(1933).

CHAPTER 16

CLINICAL STORIES: A MODERN SELF IN THE FURY OF BEING

David Michael Levin

THE FIELD OF DISCOURSE

(1) "An enormous number of symptoms testifies to the regression of what was once called civilization. Not a few have to do with socially respected conduct which imbues the psychic substance." Horkheimer, *Dawn and Decline*[1]

(2) "If such a thing as a psycho-analysis of today's prototypical culture were possible, . . . such an investigation would needs show the sickness proper to the time to consist precisely in normality." Adorno, *Minima Moralia*[2]

(3) "My claim . . . is that what is today called 'healthy' represents a lower level than that which under favorable circumstances *would be* healthy . . . that we are relatively sick." Nietzsche, *The Will to Power*[3]

(4) "My friends, it was hard for us when we were young; we suffered youth itself like a serious sickness. That is due to the time in which we have been thrown . . . a time of extensive inner decay and disintegration, a time that with all its weaknesses, and even with its best strength, opposes the spirit of youth. Disintegration characterizes this time, and thus uncertainty: nothing stands firmly on its feet or on a hard faith in itself; one lives for tomorrow, as the day after tomorrow is dubious. Everything on our way is slippery and dangerous, and the ice that still supports us has become thin: all of us feel the warm, uncanny breath of the thawing wind; where we still walk, soon no one will be able to walk." Nietzsche, *The Will to Power*[4]

(5) "It is the value of all morbid states that they show us under a magnifying glass certain states that are normal . . . but not easily visible when normal.

Health and sickness are not essentially different, as the ancient physicians and some practitioners even today suppose. One must not make of them distinct principles or entities that fight over the living organism and turn it into their arena. That is silly nonsense and chatter that is no good any longer. In fact, there are only differences in degree between these two kinds of existence: the exaggeration, the disproportion, the nonharmony of the normal phenomena constitute the pathological state (Claude Bernard)." Nietzsche, *The Will to Power*[5]

(6) "Every age develops its own peculiar forms of pathology, which express in exaggerated form its underlying character structure." Christopher Lasch, *The Culture of Narcissism*[6]

(7) "We are as highly developed in psychopathology as in technology. Psychosis is the final outcome of all that is wrong with a culture." Jules Henry, *Culture Against Man*[7]

(8) "Bourgeois society seems everywhere to have used up its store of constructive ideas. It has lost both the capacity and the will to confront the difficulties that threaten to overwhelm it. The political crisis of capitalism reflects a general crisis of western culture, which reveals itself in a pervasive despair of understanding the course of modern history or of subjecting it to rational direction." Lasch, *The Culture of Narcissism*[8]

(9) "Recollection of the history of Being in metaphysics . . . gives the relation of Being and man to awareness to be pondered. . . . Recollection of the history of Being entrusts historical humanity with the task of becoming aware that *the essence of man [i.e., our health and well-being] is released [through our thought and care in relation] to the truth of Being. . . .*" Heidegger, "Recollection in Metaphysics" (Italics and bracketed words added)[9]

(10) "Metaphysics is a fate in the strict sense, . . . that it lets mankind be suspended in the middle of [a world of] beings as a fundamental trait of Western European history, *without* the Being of beings [i.e., the healing wholeness of Being as a whole] ever being able to be experienced. . . ." Heidegger, "Overcoming Metaphysics" (Italics and bracketed words added)[10]

(11) "The essence of the history of Being [i.e., as a history] of nihilism is the *abandonment* of Being . . ." Heidegger, "Overcoming Metaphysics" (Italics and bracketed words added)[11]

(12) "The hidden history of Being as 'reality' also first makes possible Western man's various *fundamental positions* within beings [i.e., within the world]. These fundamental positions ground in each case the truth about Being on the basis of what is real and . . . make this truth certain for what is real." Heidegger, "Metaphysics as History of Being" (Italics and bracketed words added)[12]

(13) "Madness [e.g. all fundamentally self-destructive "positions" characteristic of the modern Self] need not be all breakdown. It may also be breakthrough. It is potentially liberation and renewal as well as enslavement and existential death." Laing, *The Politics of Experience* (Bracketed words added)[13]

INTRODUCTION

Before developing our ontological interpretation of depressions, narcissistic personality disorders, and schizophrenias, I should like very briefly to retrace our steps and provide a preliminary circumscription of the field our thinking will stake out.

1) Ours, as we have seen, is the epoch of nihilism: since "epoch" means "closure," in the "epoch of nihilism" there is a closure in our access, our relatedness, to the healing wholeness and openness of Being. 2) The truth of nihilism, its "essence," is a question of—and also for—our historical relatedness to Being: in nihilism, as Heidegger has said, it is Being itself that is contested. This self-destructive "raging" within Being is what Herbert Guenther meant when he wrote, echoing Heidegger, of the "Fury of Being."[14] 3) Considered in its psychological meaning, nihilism is therefore an experience in which the very being of the Self is contested. A fortiori, our "ontological interpretation" must be an attempt to understand the epidemic psychopathologies of our time by bringing forth, into the lighting of a hermeneutical discourse, the underlying disturbances and perturbations that characterize our relatedness to Being in the modern world. 4) The distinctive character of the pathologies afflicting the modern Self is generated from within this historical experience. 5) Our interpretation, continuing Heidegger's reflections in his "Letter on Humanism," locates this pathology in its historical and consequently epidemiological unfolding, and brings forth a significance that may be called "ontological." (The reader is referred to the Heidegger passages cited in the "Opening Conversation" at the beginning of this book.) As our access to Being gets cut off and we lose touch with the "healing" of the spirit that comes from an experience of ourselves in our relatedness to Being as a whole, the very being of the Self is in mortal danger. 6) This pathology is both somatic and psychic, and it will be increasingly evident, for example, in immunological breakdowns of a systematic nature and in a multitude of narcissistic disorders, schizophrenias, and depressions, as well as in their clinical, diagnostic representations. 7) The prevailing clinical patterns of psychopathology call

for an interpretation that understands them as historical epidemics concealing an ontological significance. More specifically, their epidemic nature as forms of self-destructiveness suggests that they must be related to our historical experience with nihilism. 8) The pathologies we are seeing at this time are manifestations of a "malignancy" ("Unheil") pervasive in our society: an epidemic from which none of us can be totally free. In truth, what we are calling individual "psychopathology," and are treating as such, are only the more extreme cases of a collective suffering in which we all take part in accordance with our individual constitution and character. The "normal" is merely that which prevails and holds sway; but this could be, after all, collective delusion, collective madness. We are therefore concerned not only with a relatively small number of unfortunates, of "cases." We are also concerned, as in a dialectical sense we must be, with our forms of social organization and their historical culture. 9) Our social institutions conceal this pervasiveness; a courageous understanding of its significance—however measured or confirmed—would radically call into question the most fundamental assumptions of our rationality, and indeed, the very ideals of our civilization in its entirety. Therefore, as Jules Henry said in *Pathways to Madness,* we must persist in calling attention to "the destructiveness of the culture as a whole."[15] It is "mystification" to "acquit all the institutions in our culture except the family of complicity in the destruction of the individual.[16] 10) Adorno observed that, "Just as the old injustice is not changed by a lavish display of light, air and hygiene, but is in fact concealed by the gleaming transparency of rationalized big business, the inner health of our time has been secured by blocking flight into illness without in the slightest altering its aetiology."[17] One very destructive way in which our society blocks flight into illness is to represent, diagnose and treat our modern psychopathologies in terms of the medical model, without regard for their symbolic and spiritual significance: without careful thought for their significance as historical manifestations of diseases in the Self's experience of Being, and of itself in relation to Being. One very destructive way for our society to avoid any intervention in the etiology of illness, e.g., in the social and political conditions that decisively cause it, is to misinterpret and misrepresent the nature and character of the pathology—as, for example, in organic reductionism. In line with the will to power that rules our time, we are unwilling to let the psychopathology show itself from out of itself: we cannot let it speak to us a truth about our society. Thus we avoid an experience around illness that has a depth of understanding from out of which some gift of healing could perhaps come. Only the "raging" of nihilism itself can explain the fact that the ontological dimension of our social pathologies should be systematically neglected, concealed, and denied: because an ontological interpretation would implicate all of us, individually and collectively, consciously and unconsciously, in the prevailing madness; and because it is in the very essence of the pathologies that they are hosting a culture of nihilism that demands the renunciation and ideological distortion of the Self's understanding of itself. The violence of nihilism penetrates deeply into the collective unconscious, the body brought forth by culture, and the socialized body of the body politic. As Joel Kovel said in "The American Mental Health Industry,"

> Whatever their socio-economic function, models of emotional disorder will tend to be selected for the way they help people repress the truth about themselves as much as for the way they help account for some portion of reality. The medical model, precisely because of its naive positivism [and reductionism], is in itself an anodyne against self-realization, and so it will be accepted all the more readily for the illusions it promotes.[18]

11) The suffering of the modern Self in the epoch of nihilism—a distinctive suffering with a distinctive incarnation—is reflected with particular sharpness in the history of metaphysics in the West. Our self-destructive ways of being human conceal within themselves the operations of a nihilistic metaphysics; this metaphysics, circulating within the "collective unconscious" of the historical population, reappears in the "mirror" of metaphysical discourse, where Being as such is repeatedly neglected for the sake of beings, and the ontologically rooted identity of the Self, the truth of human being, is reduced to the being of an ego, a will to power, set "free" within a field of objects. First of all, because there is, as Heidegger said, an increasing negation of (the question of) Being: oblivion, concealment, withdrawal, absence. But also, therefore, because the discourse tends to favor a corresponding closure in the being of the Self: reduction of the being of the Self to the willful being of an ego-logical subject; installment of the ego as a center of activity in a strictly objective field; interpretation of the ego as male will and male will to power; extreme subjectivizing of the individual ego, taking place through the ego's trancendental and practical aggrandizement; atomization and isolation of the individual; and finally, total exclusion of references to the deeper, more spiritual being of the Self from within the discursive field. When the will to power has finally become the mere "will to will," and the life, the very being of the modern

Self, is being destroyed "from within" as well as "from without," we should not be surprised to find that the concept of the individual in metaphysical discourse—the identity of the Self—has been emptied of all essence and meaning.

12) There is an impressive convergence of informed opinion regarding the historically distinctive character of pathologies still called, even today, by names that connect them with pathologies familiar in other times and other cultures. Nomenclatural differentiations do not always immediately accompany other discursive changes, e.g., shifts in medical perception and shifts in our collective sense of "normality." Lasch, summing up the prevailing consensus, observed that, "In our time, the preschizophrenic, borderline, or personality disorders have attracted attention, along with schizophrenia itself."[19] He endorsed the suggestion that "The growing prominence of 'character disorders' seems to signify an underlying change in the organization of personality [within our culture as a whole], from what has been called inner-direction to narcissism."[20] It is often noted that, when Freud began his practice, he was seeing many "hysterical" women and "obsessional neurotics." The disorders he "saw" were mostly generated by "drive conflicts," conflicts between sexual desire and ego, conflicts caused by an excessively punitive internalization of the socially imposed norms. Nowadays, such cases are extremely rare; what psychoanalysts are "seeing" instead are a multitude of "character disorders": egos that are weak, poorly developed, deprived in the midst of abundance, driven by envy, and uncontrollably aggressive.

Of course, as Lasch pointed out, "Psychoanalysis deals with individuals, not with groups."[21] Consequently, "Efforts to generalize clinical findings to collective behavior always encounter the difficulty that groups have a life of their own."[22] But, as Lasch himself was quick to observe,

> By conducting an intensive analysis of individual cases that rests on clinical evidence rather than common-sense impressions, psychoanalysis tells us something about the inner workings of society itself, in the very act of turning its back on society and immersing itself in the individual unconscious.
>
> Every society reproduces its culture—its norms, its underlying assumptions, its modes of organizing experience—in the individual, in the form of personality. As Durkheim said, personality is the individual socialized. The process of socialization . . . modifies human nature to conform to the prevailing social norms. Each society tries to solve the universal crises of childhood . . . in its own way, and the manner in which it deals with these psychic events produces a characteristic form

> of personality, a characteristic form of psychological deformation, by means of which the individual reconciles himself to instinctual deprivation and submits to the requirements of social existence. Freud's insistence on the continuity between psychic health and psychic sickness makes it possible to see neuroses and psychoses as in some sense the characteristic expression of a given culture. . . .
>
> Psychoanalysis best clarifies the connection between society and the individual, culture and personality, precisely when it confines itself to careful examination of individuals.[23]

Whether there are, in the modern epoch, historically distinctive pathologies is an issue of great importance; but there are different ways of interpreting the connection between individual psychopathology and society.[24]

I contend that the three configurations of pathology examined in this book are historically interconnected in a vicious epidemiological cycle. After the first and most glorious phase of modernity, when Western culture broke away from its mediaeval past and basked in the sun of a healthy self-affirmation, an "excessive" pride, a cultural narcissism elevated Man to the position occupied by God. In many ways, this new spirit was good; but the historical forms the inflation eventually assumed have slowly wounded our pride and created social and cultural conditions within which a generalized collective depression has taken hold. Our collective narcissistic defenses against these conditions have not only failed as defenses; they have *intensified* the pathogenic conditions, contributing to a life-world in which the modern Self finds itself deeply troubled by fragmentation and disintegration.

These pathologies are not just psychological; nor are they just individual. They need to be understood as social and cultural phenomena. But they also need to be given an *ontological* interpretation, i.e., an interpretation in terms of the question of Being; because in each case, the very *being* of the Self is at stake, and because the Self's being-at-stake manifests the fact that, in a world determined by scientific objectivity and technological standards, the dimensionality of Being itself, Being as such, is at stake. But to see that Being itself is at stake is to see that the very ground of modernity is now being challenged by the advent of nihilism. For nihilism is the "forgetful" reduction, reification, and negation of Being. It is now becoming apparent that nihilism has been working its devastation in and through the ego, the historical form of the Self that began to emerge in the seventeenth century and quickly asserted its sovereign rule through sciences and technologies that require conformity to objective truth controls. This ego is a product of socialization and reflects the distinctive character of our patriarchal culture; but it is a product that in turn reproduces itself, actively shaping and changing its society.

The pathologies of our present time are related to the fact that the being of the Self has adopted the historical form of a monadic ego and totally identified itself with the ego's will to power—a will to master and dominate. As the will to power, the modern ego rose up to abolish the old gods, the old ideals, the old authorities, and sources of meaning. But there was, and is, a self-destroying nihilism concealed within the heart of its "narcissistic" project. The pathologies we are seeing today—the narcissistic character disorders, the schizophrenias, and the depressions—are therefore pathologies distinctive of a society and culture in which the fate of the Self has been hitched to the ego's increasingly nihilistic will to power. This egological will takes control by extending the domain in which objectivity rules.

Beginning with the Renaissance, the first phase of "modernity," a certain "narcissism" emerged in Western culture. (See the chapter by Satinover.) In the name of "universal Reason," the Enlightenment reinforced it. In the unfolding of our modern history, however, the self-defeating tendencies within this culture of narcissism have increasingly prevailed over the more constructive tendencies. This narcissism has figured in the hegemony of a paradigm of knowledge, truth, and reality that now encourages a very aggressive, destructive will to power, represses the body of feeling, denies the life of the spirit, reduces the Self to a socially adaptive but self-alienated ego, empties it of all meaning and value, and condemns it to slow disintegration. (See the chapters by Grof, Harvey, Bernauer, and Roger Levin.)

Cartesian metaphysics, reflecting the ambiguous tendencies in this culture of narcissism, conceived the Self as a masculine ego supremely sure of itself; yet it also locked the Self into a world of self-defeating, virtually schizophrenic dualisms. "Man" was split apart into animal-being and rationality, nature and culture, body and mind, matter and spirit, inner and outer, subject and object, ego and other, individual and society, private and public, feeling and reason. (Even today, the schizophrenic is a casuality of our patriarchal, logocentric culture, that socializes the Self by shaping it into a monadic, egocentric will to power in conformity with an archetype of male domination that suppresses the body of feeling and experiential meaning.) Humanism and science have increasingly inflated human being, while their political economies promoted the "self-made Man" and all forms of egoism, encouraged our collective fantasies of planetary omnipotence and omniscience, and continue to make *human* being the center and measure of all Being—of Being as such.

But this narcissism has increasingly displayed its latent self-destructiveness, its latent nihilism: the glorification of Man, Man as ultimate will to power, encouraged cultural fantasies of absolute control. These fantasies were channeled into sciences and technologies that required objectivity and imposed it everywhere. This has meant, in time, the death of God—and an increasing forgetfulness of Being, through its domination, reduction, and reification. (See the chapters by Satinover, Schwartz-Salant, and Kovel.) The cultural experience of the death of God—or, more broadly conceived, the end of absolute idealities—has been a decisive factor in our pervasive sense today of drifting without purpose: our sense, that is, of homelessness and rootlessness. (See the contributions by Lassiter, Romanyshyn, and Whalen.) It has also meant the negation of any ultimate source of meaning, any unshakable foundation for knowledge, any absolute authority in truth, and any fixed focus for the projection and mirroring of cultural ideals: what Kovel calls the end of "transcendence," and what Heidegger called a "closure" in the dimensionality of Being. This has made it possible for the correlative increase in the institutional authority of science and technology to effect a reduction of human beings to the dual status of subjectified, privatized egos and subjugated, engineerable objects. Thus, the rule of narcissistic subjectivity has led inexorably to a rule of objectivity that is inimical to genuine subjectivity. (See the chapters by Radden and Kovel.)

Suffering through the death of God and the loss of (a sense of) Being, our society has increasingly experienced itself as living in a historical condition of extreme abandonment and deprivation. Not surprisingly, symptoms of collective depression have begun to constellate: powerlessness, hopelessness, despair, emptiness, loneliness, deadness, numbness, worthlessness, narcotization. Thus, the modern Self that had so recently assumed sovereignty and allowed itself to dream, beyond mere dignity, its worldly deification, its capacity to "create" itself out of nothing, suddenly awoke from its dream to find its traditional identity threatened and to confront widespread manifestations of social and cultural disintegration.

This danger has in turn unfortunately called forth a host of narcissistic defenses that have only deepened the crisis: egoistic and politically reactionary preoccupations with the restitution of the (traditional) Self; delusions of omniscience and omnipotence acted out, as the chapter by Glass has argued, in national and planetary politics; individual and collective obsessions with law and order, security, defense, insurance against all contingencies; lifestyles of escape and denial; false social identities and false individualisms; and the building of vast, repressive, authoritarian institutions. These defenses do not work. Thus, there is a never-ending cycle of pathology: suffering and responses to this that only reproduce the conditions of suffering.

I want to argue for a very bold thesis: That the same factors that influence psychiatric diagnosis and treatment (e.g., the denial of the unconscious, "Reason" as the exclusion of body and feeling, bureaucratic reification and depersonalization, and the split between public behavior and private experience) are also present from the very beginning, and therefore also contribute to aetiology: the emergence and course of "mental illness." Diagnosis and treatment are sociocultural phenomena, and if, as Mollica, Glass, Kovel, Pope, and Johnson have argued, they are complicitous in the *continuation* of the "pathology" to which, following "recognition," they are applied, then I think we must assume that the same social and cultural conditions which get channeled and focused through the practices and institutions of diagnosis and treatment are *already at work* from the very beginning.

The epidemiological cycle can be broken only, I think, as Mollica, Kovel, and Gendlin suggest: by forming new communities, new ways of living, based on more understanding, more compassion and reciprocity, and a greater sense of justice—and by social support for steps of self-experiencing that move beyond the troubled forms of Self that bespeak the end of modernity and the beginning, perhaps, of a new age.

DEPRESSION

(1) "There is growing support for our criterion that the age of anxiety is passing and that we are in the midst of the decades of depression." J. J. Schwab, "Depression in Medical and Surgical Patients"[25]

(2) "If clinical depression represents impoverishment of the ego on a grand scale, then here we have it on a scale which can only be called grander still: that of an entire culture, a complete philosophy of life." C. R. Badcock, *Madness and Modernity: A Study in Social Psychoanalysis*[26]

(3) "Today, genuine 'melancholics' are far outnumbered by people suffering from the present representative form of neuroses. If

hysterical phenomena commanded the field of neuroses from the time of Charcot and Freud up to the end of the First World War, from then on organic-neurotic disturbances quickly gained ascendancy. The tendency today is increasingly toward depressive illnesses. Surveying old case histories of mental institutions we find that, among patients who were hospitalized repeatedly, the diagnoses often changed with time from mood disturbance to schizophrenia. Nowadays, patients initially classified as schizophrenic lose their specifically schizophrenic symptoms over the years, finally falling into simple depression. Even among non-hospitalized psychoneurotically disturbed people, most who seek help today are people horribly depressed by the meaninglessness and tedium of their lives. . . . Suffering as they do, these people often try to drown out their desperation through addiction to work, pleasure, or drugs. When this fails, the depressive attunement of boredom or meaninglessness that prevails in this age shows clearly, and we see dramatically the impairment of perceptive openness. . . ." Medard Boss, *Existential Foundations of Medicine and Psychology*[27]

(4) " 'Consciousness' (as will of the will) must itself now be experienced with regard to the truth of . . . Being. Desolation." Heidegger, "Sketches for a History of Being as Metaphysics"[28]

(5) ". . .the emptiness of the word *being* . . ." Heidegger, *Introduction to Metaphysics*[29]

(6) " 'Life is not worthwhile'; 'resignation' . . ." Nietzsche, *The Will to Power*[30]

(7) ". . .the ego is formed to a great extent out of identifications which take the place of cathexes [objects] abandoned by the id . . ." Freud, *The Ego and the Id*[31]

(8) "The completion of metaphysics sets beings in the abandonment of Being. [In other words, owing to our inveterate forgetfulness, it is *we* who have abandoned the experience of Being in its wholeness, which could perhaps be deeply healing for us; at the same time, however, it is also true that we tend to experience *ourselves* as the ones being abandoned.] Being's abandonment of beings is the last reflection of Being . . . Being's abandonment contains the undecided factor of whether or not beings [shall be enabled to] persist in their precedence. In the future, this means the question of whether beings . . . will move towards the desolation that does not destroy, but rather chokes what is vital to [our] organizing and ordering." Heidegger, "Sketches for a History of Being as Metaphysics" (Bracketed words added)[32]

(9) ". . . the individual, faced with this tremendous machinery, loses courage and submits." Nietzsche, *The Will to Power*[33]

(10) "Or a sign of the lack of strength to posit for oneself, productively, a goal, a why, a faith." Nietzsche, *The Will to Power*[34]

(11) "Our will requires an aim; it would sooner have the void for its purpose [i.e., as in active nihilism] than be void of purpose [as in the passive nihilism which is involved in the etiology of depression]." Nietzsche, *The Will to Power* (Bracketed words added)[35]

(12) "The state nomads (civil servants, etc.): without home. The decline of the family." Nietzsche, *The Will to Power*[36]

According to Heidegger, "The history of Being begins, and indeed necessarily, with the forgetting of Being."[37] I believe that this interpretation of the history of metaphysics can shed much light on psychopathology in our modern world. For at a certain moment in this history, it seems that we began to experience ourselves and our world in terms of what Heidegger called the "abandonment" of Being. Thus, our living in this abandonment is what constitutes the decisive, indeed definitive experience of the modern epoch—the epoch, that is, in which nihilism, the historical negation of Being, prevails. I submit that the history of Being reflected in the history of our metaphysics—a history of growing nihilism—is manifest epidemiologically in the incidence and prevalence, as well as in the character, of contemporary depressions. (This is difficult to establish empirically, but I believe that empirical confirmation is not only feasible, but preeminently reasonable.) As a time in which we must live through the abandonment of Being, this history becomes a time of inconsolable loss and deprivation; a time of mourning for something (we know not precisely what) that we vaguely feel has been lost; a time of need when the need is so deeply unrealized that it cannot be acknowledged, or, if acknowledged, then not understood; a time in which the historical attunement of human beings can only, to a greater or lesser extent, take the form of a deep and diffuse depression. Thus, if we wish to understand the history of Being, our understanding of the history of metaphysics must be supplemented by an interpretation of the historical presence of depression in our culture. In the discourse of cultural epidemiology, it is hypothesized that there is a connection of decisive significance between the advent (*Ereignis*) of nihilism and the depressive character so frequently in evidence in our modern, and especially our present psychopathology. One factor contributing to this connection is that, at the very heart of modern depressions, there is an experience for which we may borrow a phrase Heidegger has used to characterize the modern epoch in the history of Being and the history of Western metaphysics. His phrase is: "the abandonment of Being." This experience, however, takes place not only within the history of metaphysics; because it is a fundamental event or phase in the history of Being, it is a factor that becomes constitutive of *all* human experience in the modern world. Of course, this experience appropriates for itself a more determinative function in the lives of people whom our contemporary world judges with the categories of psychopathology, since there are some human beings who, because of their existential circumstances, are both more sensitively attuned to this experience of history and less able to relate to it in a salutary way.

If Heidegger's interpretation of metaphysics is accepted, we are obliged to consider how the historical "loss of Being" would actually be experienced, lived. Nietzsche's articulation of the signs and symptoms of nihilism calls our attention to a self-destructiveness that is pervasive in, and I believe definitive of, our modern culture. But these interpretations cry out for further specificity. What is happening to us psychologically? What kinds of diseases, afflictions of the flesh, our incarnation, are we seeing today, and what is their relationship to the growth of nihilism? What kinds of psychopathology are we seeing today, and how do they manifest, how make visible, the historical loss of Being?

Heidegger observed that our human moodedness is an attunement by and to the Being of the world as a whole: our moods are ontologically disclosive, in that they let us sense the way Being presences in our historical world; they are also, therefore, symptomatic of our existential relatedness to Being as a whole. Depressions, particularly in epidemic proportions, are significant cultural events because they are disclosive of nihilism and express our individual ways of experiencing the historical abandonment of Being and our corresponding sense of loss. Of course, I am not suggesting that a depression could be "caused" by the abandonment as such; nor am I saying that a "metaphysical" interpretation exclusively in terms of our relatedness to Being as such could ever be sufficient to shed light on the pathogenesis of any individual case. Rather, just as an epidemic of individual depressions calls for a diagnosis that takes into account the configuration of social, political, economic and historical conditions which have been favorable to its etiology and spread, so it requires also that we take into account the culture of nihilism which grows in the spirit of our civilization, and that we attempt to understand our spiritual suffering through the experience of loss, deprivation, and need in our relatedness to Being as a whole. We need to understand this experience as something always at work, both individually and collectively, both consciously and unconsciously, in all our clinical depressions.

In a letter to Wilhelm Fliess, Freud wrote that, "The affect corresponding to melancholia is mourning or grief—that is, longing for something that is lost."[38] In our time, we as an entire civilization are undergoing an experience with Being in its wholeness that takes hold of us in the form of depressions and predispositions to depression. Since we have already examined the role of the masculine ego in the advent of nihilism within its technological economy, Freud's observation, cited earlier, that "the [healthy, well-adjusted] ego is formed to a great extent out of identifications which take the place of cathexes abandoned by the id," will now assume a radically new significance: because the ego's bid for independence requires it to break away from the wholeness of Being in which it was symbiotically nurtured, the inevitable mourning of ontological loss, and the consequent sense of deep ontological anxiety and insecurity, are fundamental experiences within the ego's process of emergence. Thus we can connect the historical installment of the ego in individual life with an anxiety and rage conducive to the historical emergence of a culture of nihilism favoring in a global way the formation of a multitude of depressive and self-destructive conditions.

According to Freud, anxiety originates in "the state of being forsaken or deserted by the protecting superego—by the powers of destiny—which puts an end to security against danger."[39] In keeping with this diagnosis, we should expect that the historical abandonment of Being in which we all live would be diffusely felt, at the most primordial levels of our individual and collective being, not only in terms of a very deep process of mourning, but also in the most profound anxiety, an insatiable need for security, and of course, the most abysmal rage. Since this historical loss is related to the ascendancy of the ego, the raging against our loss becomes very destructive, even violent; and it may be directed either against oneself, as in the more severe depressions, or against others, as in our technological economy. It is noteworthy that thinkers as different as Kierkegaard, Jung, Sartre and Lacan seem to agree on the two-faced character of the adult ego: they all have argued that the "normal" ego, i.e., the Self stuck in its identification with the ego, is always, in a sense, pathological.[40]

The narcissism of Western civilization has been repeatedly challenged by our own science and developing self-awareness. Because of Copernicus, Darwin, Einstein and Freud, we have been compelled to renounce long-standing assumptions deeply embedded in our cultural life. Since the time of Nietzsche, we have not been able to avoid the "death" of God; now, as Foucault said, we must survive the death of "Man." We are in danger of losing ourselves. We no longer believe in absolute knowledge and absolute values. It is difficult for us to experience any intrinsic meaningfulness in our lives. Our sacred traditions are almost gone, and now even our great secular traditions are rapidly disappearing; even the institution of the family, as Nietzsche prophetically saw, is in fateful danger. We have very little security in an age that cannot forget the devastation of Hiroshima and the Nazi death camps in Germany, and that now faces the risk of nuclear annihilation. What is constant, permanent, settled? We can depend on nothing. Is it surprising that depression should be so widespread? If we want to understand the phenomenon of depression, we must consider it in an epidemiological context that includes our awareness of nihilism. Since depressions do not take place in isolated individuals apart from society, we need to give thought to the ontological dimension of this kind of experience; we need to consider how these depressions manifest our historical relatedness to Being.

Let us consider, for example, the experience of time. Many clinicians have observed a characteristic distortion of temporality in severe cases of depression.[41] In particular they have noted that, corresponding to the sense of despair and hopelessness that eats away at the heart of severe depressions, there is a shrinking or collapsing of the normally "ek-static" structure of temporality: the present is isolated, dead; the future can hold forth no promise of relief because, in effect, it is denied any reality; and finally, even a connection with the past, which might otherwise be felt to deliver a message of consolation or hope, is gradually destroyed. Is this collapsing of past and future merely an individual phenomenon? I submit that it is not. When we reflect on our cultural experience with time; when we consider how temporality is lived at the level of cultural history, we will discover a pattern strikingly similar to the pattern played out in individual depressions. Thus, for example, Heidegger pointed out in his *Introduction to Metaphysics* that "time as history has vanished from the lives of all [Western] peoples."[42] And Adorno, in *Minima Moralia,* contended that, "even the past is no longer safe from the present, whose remembrance of it consigns it a second time to oblivion."[43]

Likewise, our cultural experience of the future is distorted or collapsed in ways that are analogous to the ways in which the experience of the future is modified in the lives of people suffering from severe depression. Let us briefly consider three crucial dimensions in our experience of the future. 1) Cultural ideality. A culture's experience of the future is constituted through its consensually validated ideals, its sense of some unifying and distinctive historical task or calling. But, in the epoch of nihilism, we are no longer sustained by a collectively shared and validated faith in our capacity, as a culture, to receive, create, actualize, teach, and defend any great historical vision of the ideal society. Our civilization has lost its ideality, its utopianism, its commitment. What this means, however, is that our culture is now finding itself increasingly bereft of a future around which to weave its deepest hopes and aspirations. But a culture without any collectively shared ideals, without any real vision worthy of commitment, is a culture in which the population will be predisposed to suffering in a diffuse mood of depression. 2) Death. As Robert Jay Lifton has argued, "There has been a historical shift, and the contemporary situation is one in which we are less overwhelmed by sexual difficulties but more overwhelmed by difficulties around death."[44] Although the specter of massive collective death probably haunts our society as much today as in the Middle Ages, it is altogether a different experience for us. Today, death is medicalized, sanitized, trivialized: in other words, our culture is based on the denial of death. But, as Heidegger has argued in *Being and Time,* the meaningfulness of death is essential for the living of a meaningful life, since death is that "event" the mindful anticipation of which can alone give one's life a deeply fulfilling integration and wholeness. Thus, the trivialization or denial of death deprives us of a real future, and with that, all sense of a meaningful "summing up." Without this fundamental experience of living-with-death, we cannot live fully in the present; we are deprived of the self-understanding that would enable us to live in the fullness of temporality. 3) Immortality. In our civilization there has always been, as Lifton put it, "a compelling universal urge to maintain an inner sense of continuous symbolic relationship, over time and space, with the various elements of life."[45] Whether we long for biological continuity, a transcendence of death through the attainment of spiritual wisdom, survival through identification with nature, or immortality by virtue of our deeds and works and our influence on society, we feel a deep-seated need for some sense that we belong to something that will continue beyond death. But, as Lifton argued,

> Following the holocausts of World War II, the viability of psychic activity within the [traditional] modes [of symbolic immortality] has undergone something of a collapse, at least in the West. We exist now in a time of doubt about modes of continuity and connection, and I believe this has direct relevance for work with individual patients. Awareness of our historical predicament—of threats by nuclear weapons, environmental destruction, and the press of rising population

against limited resources—has created extensive imagery of extinction. These threats occur at a time when the rate of historical velocity with its resulting psychohistorical dislocation has already undermined established symbols around the institutions of family, church, government, and education.

Combined imagery of extinction and dislocation leaves us in doubt about whether we will "live on" in our children and their children, in our groups and organizations, in our works, in our spirituality, or even in nature, which we now know to be vulnerable to our pollutions and our weaponry. It is the loss of faith, I think, in . . . [the traditional] modes of symbolic immortality that leads people, especially the young, to plunge—sometimes desperately and sometimes with considerable self-realization—into the mode of experiential transcendence. This very old and classical form of personal quest has had to be discovered anew in the face of doubts about the other . . . modes.[46]

We have pursued the riches of science and lost, or at least lost contact with, the mythopoetic: the dimension of Being that transcends the span of our individual lives. In *The Birth of Tragedy,* Nietzsche argued that, "every culture which has lost myth has lost, by the same token, its natural healthy creativity."[47] Although an impassioned enemy of collective delusions, Nietzsche conceded that, "only a horizon ringed with myths can unify a culture."[48] It is not necessary, and in any event historically impossible, that we believe there is "empirical truth" in myth; but we do still need to feel some historical connection between our present lives and the temporality of mythopoetic experience. Being deprived of this continuity with the world of our ancestors, we are in effect deprived of a meaningful future. This deprivation cannot but have some fateful consequences for our age.

Disturbances that we can trace back to our modern disconnectedness from the whole of temporality are only one part of the picture. When Heidegger pointed to our "indifference" to the ontological difference between Being as a whole and the beings in Being, he was observing a modern preoccupation with objects that makes us, historically considered, much more vulnerable to object loss because, in comparison with people in other times, we enjoy no culturally validated sense of ontological wholeness. Our modern obsessive-compulsive preoccupation with realms of objects is symptomatic of our disconnectedness from Being as a whole. Consequently, our modern confinement within the metaphysical structure of subject and object sets us up, in the end, for a multitude of pathogenic experiences. Living as we do in an epoch in which we experience the "abandonment" of Being, we tend to become attached to objects in a way that can only make us extremely vulnerable to their conditions of domination. Having set ourselves up as the subjects who master and control, we become our own victims, subject to the objects of our objectification. Only a cultural recollection of Being can save us from the devastating pathologies that will continue to occur in the wake of our "forgetfulness" of Being.

Tarthang Tulku, the Tibetan whose thoughts we have already had occasion to consider, wrote that

> Ultimately, the full price of acting without a broader understanding of the implications of our actions may include the surrender of the human heart and mind to a way of life that perpetuates not only frustration, but also hopelessness and despair.
>
> Today, our many forms of knowledge all derive from a view of human being as *separate* from the environing world. This view comes naturally to us, for it is rooted in our basic perceptual patterns and is reinforced by the integrating and deductive processes of the rational mind. We divide our world into self and other, and establish ourselves as agents acting upon and responding to situations. By this we commit ourselves to a view grounded in separations.[49]

These separations, characteristic in a distinctive way of the modern epoch, have taken many different forms: the exile and homelessness of refugees from war and oppression, anomie and suicide are only three examples. In "Mind and Earth," Carl Jung called our attention to another major configuration: "Alienation from the unconscious and from its historical conditions," which, he told us, "spells rootlessness."[50] Since our primordial relatedness to Being as a whole is sustained through the "collective unconscious," our present historical alienation from this deep unconscious integration is at the same time a separation from the wholeness of Being.

The modern ego is metaphysically separated from its own wholeness of being as a Self. Separated from this Self-being, the ego is isolated from others as well, for in the experiential depths of this Self-being, the ego would find itself always already intertwined with the lives of others in a social existence that precedes the impact of social atomization. The isolated ego is therefore experienced as empty, as nothing. "Not only is the self entwined in society; it owes society its existence in the most literal sense. . . . It grows richer the more freely it develops and reflects this relation, while it is limited, impoverished, and reduced by the separation and hardening that it lays claim to as an origin."[51] Adorno was right. To be stuck in the ego state is the *death* of the Self, because the metaphysical isolation it involves deprives us of the distinctively human and also humanizing capacity to love and care for others. And this, as we know, is an important symptom of clinical depression.

Our socialized atomization contributes, moreover, to our common experience of helplessness—also a manifestation of depression. Since we are socialized in a way that radically cuts us off from others, we cannot easily sense our ultimate responsibility for one another. This, however, makes us ever more dependent on the institutional apparatus of a welfare state superstructure—which only intensifies already destructive feelings of helplessness. As we become more atomized, the welfare state grows stronger and more pervasive, because collective integration and cooperation, which are necessary for our survival, must be imposed from outside, if they cannot evolve from within us, i.e., from within our human nature. As the state takes over more of these integrative functions and appropriates more power for itself, we are slowly being driven into the state of depression: helplessly dependent, we lose our self-respect, lose our initiative, lose all sense of competence. As Seligman said, "Paralysis of the will is a striking feature of severe depression."[52] I have argued here that the individual depressions of our time must be understood in relation to the rise to power of the monadic ego, whose metaphysical isolation from other monadic egos sets the stage for a more totalitarian organization of the state: an organization in which the Self is peculiarly vulnerable to states of depression. This, in turn, makes us more vulnerable to the pathogens present in our ecology: greater susceptibility to disease is thus the price we must pay for our egological alienation from one another and from nature. (I would like to say, in passing, that once we recognize a nihilistic metaphysics in the dualism of mind and body, the radical difference between "endogenous" and "reactive" depressions will no longer govern our thinking.)

In the epoch of nihilism, we experience the "Fury of Being." Living in the abandonment of Being, we fall into the pervasive mood of depression that engulfs our entire world; and we find ourselves more susceptible to disease. In this depression, mourning and grief persist; but there is also a deep-seated, unspeakable guilt and a smoldering, diffuse, uncontrollable rage: a rage or violence—active nihilism—that will sometimes be directed inward, against oneself, and sometimes directed outward, as aggression against others. Directed against oneself, this rage is accusative and punitive, and sometimes produces inhibitions, apathy, indifference, paralysis, echexia, psychic numbing and deadness.

Freud's analysis of "melancholia" is not adequate for the epidemiological interpretation of such depressions, because it fixates on the ego-superego relationship and neglects the fact that they are ontological phenomena. And yet, we can substitute for the tyrannical Freudian superego, whose interiorized wrath consists of social constraints turned against the ego, the external violence of the modern political economy; this analysis provides sufficient grounds for a hypothetical analogy in which depression is interpreted by reference to the Fury of Being, whose pressures, mediated by our social, political, and cultural institutions, are raging ever more nihilistically against the Self, against the ego's self-development as a Self. This substitution is reasonable insofar as the modern superego is weak and permissive, and many of the normative functions, including the function of constraint, have been taken over, as Badcock argued in *Madness and Modernity,*[53] by the modern Welfare State, which disperses its policing powers and its domination over the individual without any resistance from a strong patriarchal family and, a fortiori, a strong, superego of internalized social norms. As we spell out Freud's analysis, the grounds for its extension to cultural epidemiology will become clearer.

Here is what Freud said, in *The Ego and the Id,* about the specific configuration of suffering he called "melancholia": "[In melancholia,] the extensively strong superego . . . rages against the ego with merciless violence, as if it had taken possession. . . ."[54] This rage Freud attributed to the fact that "the sense of guilt is overstrongly conscious."[55] In consequence, he said, "the ego gives itself up, because it feels itself hated and persecuted by the super-ego, instead of loved."[56]

If the modern superego really is weak and permissive, as Nietzsche and Freudians have insisted, what could account for the epidemic proportions of depression? Freud's analysis no longer seems to provide any explanation. I suggest that we must begin to consider the social, political, economic, and cultural conditions within which the ego is to be brought forth, firmly established, and then helped to "overcome" or "transcend" itself for the sake of further, and essentially spiritual, self-development. In the modern world these conditions are manifestations of a pervasive nihilism: the Fury of Being. What has replaced the violence of the superego is now this Fury of Being, whose nihilism is destroying the ego even when it appears most convincingly to be supporting it, since conditions that effectively discourage or block the ego's becoming-a-Self do not strengthen the ego, but actively weaken and impoverish it.

Furthermore, it is nihilism that enables us to explain the haunting, debilitating presence of a diffuse sense of guilt, often involved, along with rage, in the more severe depressions. Freud wrote that

> an increase in this unconscious sense of guilt can turn people into criminals. . . . In many criminals, especially youthful ones, it is possible to detect *a very powerful sense of guilt which existed before the crime, and is therefore not its result but its motive*. It is as if it was a relief to be able to fasten this unconscious sense of guilt onto something real and immediate.[57]

Do we not, as a culture, carry a very heavy burden of guilt? If God is dead, who has murdered Him? If we are now living in the time of the "death of Man," who is responsible? And who are the ones responsible for the Nazi Holocaust? Starvation in Africa? The increasing incidence and prevalence of violent crime? The increasing frequency of terrorism? And the increasingly frequent epidemics of suicide among adolescents? These are not isolated instances of tragedy; they are events in which the very nature of humanity is radically called into question. I submit that our contemporary epidemic of depressions needs to be interpreted in terms of an abysmal collective guilt, largely unconscious, that is taking possession of our civilized spirit and dispersing its terrible rage throughout our population with the spread of nihilism.

Before I conclude these reflections on depression, I would like to emphasize the social significance of depression by connecting it to our obsession with mastery and control, our restless technological activity, and the collective fever of incessant consumption. It is well-known that depressions can take the form of restless, agitated, hysterical, and manic activity, as well as the form of psychic anesthesia and a deadening of affect.[58] In such cases, the activity functions not only as an expression of depressive rage, but as a defense against the intensity of experiences of a depressive nature. I suggest that at least to some extent, the compulsion to produce and consume, a behavior characteristic of our life in an advanced technological economy, may be both a manifestation of nihilistic rage and a manic defense against our collective depression in a time of unbearable spiritual deprivation and an ever-deepening sense of despair. Unfortunately, this defensive activity is no less self-destructive when it manifests as a social and cultural phenomenon than it is when it manifests in the suffering of the individual. In both cases, the defensive behavior can ultimately only intensify the experience of inconsolable loss and deprivation.[59]

NARCISSISM

(1) "The most universal sign of the modern age: man has lost *dignity* in his own eyes to an incredible extent. For a long time the center and tragic hero of existence in general; then at least intent on proving himself closely related to the decisive and essentially valuable side of existence—like all metaphysicians who wish to cling to *the dignity of man*. . . . Those who have abandoned God [and even more, those who, because of the 'death of God', now find themselves abandoned by Him] cling that much more firmly to the faith in morality." Nietzsche, *The Will to Power* (Bracketed words added)[60]

(2) "The belief of the individual in himself has become sterile. . . . Today, . . . the individual must die without the possibility of an active absorption in a meaningful totality, . . . driven by conditions he unconsciously helped create." Horkheimer, *Dawn and Decline*[61]

(3) "How do the . . . basic institutions of a society interfere with an ontogenetic developmental pattern? . . . [E]go identity requires not only cognitive mastery of general levels of communication but also the ability to give one's own needs their due in these communicative structures; as long as the ego is *cut off from its internal nature* and disavows the *dependency on needs* that still await suitable interpretations, freedom, no matter how much it is guided by principles, remains in truth unfree in relation to existing systems of norms." Jürgen Habermas, "Moral Development and Ego Identity"[62]

(4) "Hence not just any kind of humanity is suited to bring about unconditional nihilism in a historical manner. Hence a struggle is even necessary about the decision as to which kind of humanity is capable of the unconditional completion of nihilism." Heidegger, "Overcoming Metaphysics"[63]

(5) ". . . the subject is the first object of ontological representation./ *Ego cogito* is *cogito: me cogitare*." Heidegger, "Overcoming Metaphysics"[64]

(6) "The struggle between those who are in power and those who want to come to power: On every side there is the struggle for power. Everywhere power itself is what is determinative. . . . At the same time, however, one thing is still covered up here: the fact that this struggle is in the service of power and is willed by it. . . . The will to will alone empowers these struggles. Power, however, overpowers various kinds of humanity in such a way that it expropriates from man the possibility of ever escaping from the oblivion of Being on such paths. This struggle is of necessity planetary and as such undecidable. . . . Through its own force it is driven out into what is without destiny: into the

abandonment of Being." Heidegger, "The Overcoming of Metaphysics"[65]

(7) "We suspect that there is a connection between patterns of socialization . . . and the forms of identity constructed by the young. . . . This problem leads one to reflect on moral development and ego identity. . . ." Habermas, "Moral Development and Ego Identity"[66]

(8) ". . . basic psychological and sociological concepts can be interwoven because the perspectives projected in them of an autonomous ego and the emancipated society reciprocally require one another." Habermas, "Moral Development and Ego Identity."[67]

(9) "New social forms require new forms of personality, new modes of socialization, new ways of organizing experience. The concept of narcissism provides us not with a ready-made psychological determinism but with a way of understanding the psychological impact of recent social changes—assuming that we bear in mind not only its clinical origins but the continuum between pathology and normality. . . .

Narcissism appears realistically to represent the best way of coping with the tensions and anxieties of modern life, and the prevailing social conditions therefore tend to bring out narcissistic traits that are present, in varying degrees, in everyone. These conditions have also transformed the family, which in turn shapes the underlying structure of personality." Lasch, *The Culture of Narcissism*[68]

(10) "The issue of narcissism is the issue of our age, because it is the focal point for a new Self image in transition." Nathan Schwartz-Salant, *Narcissism and Character Transformation*[69]

(11) "The Narcissus myth is especially significant for our present historical time, as it has been in other transitional epochs, for the archetypal world is no longer held in tension by collectively valid religious forms, and thus has begun to constellate strongly in the human soul, acting like a magnet drawing consciousness back toward the archetypal realm. Then egos may seem to be narcissistic, but actually are being drawn back into realms of 'not-yet existence.' They may become stuck, yielding the pattern known as the narcissistic character disorder, or they may become reborn to inner and outer object relations, relationships to other people as separate and distinct, and to the Self as the transpersonal other. A new Self structure may arise. . . ." Schwartz-Salant, *Narcissism and Character Transformation*[70]

(12) ". . . what is loosely called mental illness always fits into the order of things, and . . . different historical epochs will select different pathologies wherein their characteristic form of domination may be reproduced on intrapsychic soil. And pathological narcissism is a leading candidate for the archtypal emotional disorder of late capitalism." Joel Kovel, *The Age of Desire*[71]

NARCISSISM AS WILL TO POWER

Schwartz-Salant, a Jungian analyst who has worked extensively with "narcissistic character disorders," asserted that in disorders of this kind there is a "grandiose-exhibitionistic power-drive," a "consistent, demonic urge toward power through ego inflation."[72] The three central points around which our interpretation will take shape are 1) that the disturbances destructive to the Self which are currently called, because of the power of the psychoanalytical school, "narcissistic character disorders" constitute a pathology of the will to power; 2) that the pathology is a pathology of the ego and bespeaks the ego's unwillingness or inability to become a Self; and 3) that this pathology is connected in a distinctive way with the nihilism of our epoch. Narcissistic disorders invariably occur in terms of the ego's relationship to power: not only in the ego's struggle for omnipotence, for mastery, control, and domination, but also in the ego's loss of control and its experience of weakness, defeat, subjugation, and impotence. Ultimately, then, the narcissistic disorders are rooted in the ego's unwillingness or inability to grow beyond itself—to grow out of the unhappy dialectic of power that holds sway in the ego's field. The ego's developmental failure to overcome itself is thus a historical failure to become a Self, and it has been a decisive factor in the historical triumph of nihilism. But the relationship between nihilism and narcissistic pathology is a vicious circle, for the spread of nihilism has created within its culture a political economy that continues to multiply and intensify the ego's difficulties in relation to the question of power. As an epidemic pathology of the modern ego, narcissistic character disorders need to be considered historically in relation to what Heidegger called "the unconditional domination of subjectivity," an historical phenomenon that is determinative of our political economy and reflected in our metaphysics as well.[73]

"Subjectness" has ruled from ancient times, but only in the modern epoch as will to power, a subjectivity so extreme that it becomes self-destructive. And, as we shall see, this subjectivity of the will constitutes a form of suffering in which the ego is stuck in a dialectic of power that moves back and forth, without development, between loss and envy, depression and mania, passivity and rage: between, on the one hand, anxieties around matters of dependency, helplessness, and impotence, and on the other, dreams and delusions of the most godlike omnipotence.

Before we begin our reflections on metaphysics, history, technology and culture, let us consider the character of the ego stuck in a narcissistic pattern of suffering. A society in the throes of nihilism creates an environment that encourages individuals to develop a kind of character extremely susceptible to narcissistic disorders. But it is equally true that our social reality is a function of the prevalence of individuals living out such disorders, or manifesting tendencies of character that are not entirely free from such disorders.

"Narcissistic character disorders" are not disorders of the instincts or drives, but rather they are disorders of character, disorders of adulthood that originate in the ego's stuckness, whether through inability or unwillingness, and in its failure to continue growing beyond itself in a process of continual becoming, continual self-development. Freud's paper "On Narcissism" lets us know that he was beginning to perceive cases of what he called "secondary narcissism" in many of his patients.[74] For him, such narcissism was unquestionably pathological, in contrast to the "primary narcissism" of the infant who has not yet differentiated himself from within the symbiotic relationship he has been enjoying with the mothering one. Secondary narcissism is pathological because it involves an inappropriate, unsatisfactory, and ultimately self-destructive resolution of "disappointed object love." At the heart of this pathological complex are disturbances in the dynamics of self-development: ontological anxiety; incomplete mourning in the wake of inevitable individuation, separation and abandonment; uncontrollable rage over the necessity in this process of loss; guilt and self-accusation; envy and mistrust in relation to others; a mask of omnipotence and aggression to conceal a profound sense of despair and helplessness; a manic state of activity to mask the emptiness within.[75]

Heinz Kohut, the American counterpart to Lacan in a revolt against Freud's ego psychology, defined "narcissistic personality disorders" as follows: "temporary breakup, enfeeblement, or serious distortion of the self, manifested predominantly by autoplastic symptoms . . . such as hypersensitivity to slights, hypochondria, or depression."[76] In its most extreme form, namely, as a "psychotic" disorder, this pattern will become a permanent or protracted delusion about reality. In more "borderline" states, this disorder will be "covered by more or less effective defensive structures," and these defenses will often drive the ego into one or another addiction, one or another narcotization.[77]

According to Kohut, "It is the *loss of control* of the self over the self-object that leads to the fragmentation . . . and, in further development, to the ascendancy and entrenchment of chronic narcissistic *rage*."[78] Since the (archetypally masculine) ego is profoundly insecure and anxious, it needs to dominate, master, and bring everything under its control. Loss of control can therefore give rise to a terrible, uncontrollable rage. What is the cultural equivalent of this narcissistic rage in the life of the disturbed individual? In the political economy of the Western ego's investment, an economy of narcissistic production and consumption, this rage becomes the institutionalized violence of a "rational" technological regime: the ego defends against its insecurity by investing in a "rational" program to control the world with its mastery of technological power. But the nihilism concealed within this will to power is producing an apparatus that increasingly seems to grow out of our control and turn in "revenge" against us.

Kohut argued that "The essential psychopathology in the narcissistic personality disorders is defined by the fact that the self has not been solidly established, that its cohesion and firmness depend on the presence of a self-object . . . and that it responds to the loss of the self-object with simple enfeeblement, various regressions [e.g., uncontrollable rage] and fragmentation."[79] The ego suffering from a narcissistic disorder will often feel empty and insubstantial: useless, ineffective, helpless; and it may find itself swept away by rage when it recognizes in itself an ontological dependency it can neither accept nor avoid. In such a condition, abandoned before it could stand with dignity in the independence of an authentic individuality, the ego acts out its "sense of inner uncertainty and purposelessness."[80] In a panic of existential insecurity, it lives out fantasies of omnipotence, the sham of power, while arming and equipping itself in a perpetual struggle to achieve mastery and control.

In relationships with others, the narcissistic character tends to be emotionally unreliable, and is therefore experienced as impenetrable, or emotionally inaccessible. Interpersonal relationships are defensive—there is a sham of depth, but in reality, they are shallow, superficial, and pragmatic. Because the narcissistic ego has a very poor sense of its own identity, its own "center of life," it has a correspondingly limited capacity for feeling, love, empathy, or for recognizing the otherness of others and being touched and moved by their needs and concerns. Although extremely dependent for the consolidation of its sense of identity on the opinions of others and on the image their reflective presence confirms or casts in doubt, the narcissistic ego hates all forms of dependency, and is filled with rage, vindictiveness, and loathing, both for himself and for those on whose approval and admiration his very identity seems to depend. The narcissistically disturbed ego is restless, moved by an insatiable need for gratification, for self-validation, an admiration and approval he cannot find within him self. Filled with envy, he seeks to be the one who is envied rather than respected, and will manipulate and exploit others for the sake of their envy, their mirroring, or their subordination to his show of power.

Man, said Sartre, is "a useless passion." There is painful absurdity in the ego's futile, repeatedly self-defeating efforts to achieve some measure of real satisfaction; it seems that the more ego pursues its hedonistic calculus, the more it feels empty and hungers for an impossible fulfillment. But the satisfactions ego pursues, being sham, being "false," do not really satisfy. For example, the narcissistic character needs and desires self-esteem; but he pursues its mere reflection in the esteem of those whose authority derives from their show of strength. And though he desires the centeredness of Selfhood, he falls into a life of self-alienation, centered around the recognition of others. An inwardly impoverished life of missed opportunities is thus lived out in the glitter of outward signs of acquired wealth, or vicariously through the achievements of others. Even when the ego has achieved some recognized success, it fails to "find" sufficient meaning: the work and achievement ethic, the modern form of Freud's "reality principle," is no longer very compelling as a source of existential meaningfulness. At bottom, the narcissistic character is deeply absorbed in himself, but this absorption is its self-defeating way of avoiding growth through self-awareness and self-understanding. And because the absorption is a withdrawal, narcissistic character disorders are manifestations of a deep, but also deeply concealed, experience of diffuse depression.

The myth of Narcissus is ancient but there is a story concerning narcissism that belongs to modernity, and it begins with the meditations and reflections of Descartes. In Western metaphysics, there is a story that lucidly mirrors the strange pathology in narcissism.

I suggest that a pathological narcissism is the driving force in circulation throughout our metaphysics, for metaphysics is but a mirror for the narcissistic ego that rules in our time. Since the discourse of metaphysics is a reflective medium that reflects our cultural self-understanding, we should expect that it would manifest, indeed with singular clarity, our historical experience of the human condition—and in particular, our distinctive psychopathology.

Now let us consider Descartes, whose revolutionary thought stands at the very beginning of the modern epoch. We can see clearly how his metaphysics both mirrors and mocks the most characteristic pathologies of modern times. In his *Meditations on First Philosophy,* we can trace the degenerative stages of a severe narcissistic disorder. The narrative of disorder begins with a grandiose vision, in which Descartes saw himself building, on a radically new foundation, a "firm and permanent structure in the sciences." He desired nothing less than absolute certainty, a knowledge of permanent beings that guaranteed its own truth. This insolent ambition was followed, however, by a stage of doubt and uncertainty, and his contemplation of the loss of epistemological faith suddenly turned the earlier self-confidence into a mood very close to despair. Disillusioned, nostalgic, insecure, the ego now attempted to withdraw from the world: it assumed what is basically a depressive position. Narcissism soon appeared, though, in the defensive double movement of simultaneous self-absorption and self-aggrandizement: the depression was avoided when the proof of God's existence was "found" within the ego's own clear and distinct consciousness. As is characteristic of narcissistic disorders, this gesture at proof is exceedingly ambiguous, for at the very same time that it acknowledges our dependency on the existence and benevolence of God, it also surreptitiously inflates our sense of power: being able to prove God's existence, the Cartesian ego seems to participate in His omnipotence. The ego, which felt impotent, now suddenly claims a kind of omnipotence. Its dream of power, of powerful knowledge, may now come true.

But, before this triumph over depression, the Cartesian ego is severely tested, and it must pass through a madness more disturbing than narcissism. There is more than a hint of schizophrenia in the paranoid questioning of reality that begins with the assumption of a malevolent Demon; in the terrible anxiety he felt concerning waking and sleeping, and, later on, concerning the momentary deaths of consciousness; in the splitting apart of mind and body, spirit and flesh; and in a spectatorial detachment that borders on solipsism. "I am, I exist, that is certain," he wrote. "But how often? Just when I think." Again: "I am, I exist, is necessarily true each time I pronounce it, or that I mentally conceive it." But what happens when I am not thinking? What happens in the intervals between my thoughts? Do I die? Even when Descartes seemed to get hold of a state he could call "certainty," he did not immediately recognize himself. Having lost the world, he was on the verge of losing himself. "Who am I?" he asked. Characteristically enough, the thinker's relationships with other people are likewise represented as seriously disturbed. Only a madman would mean these words: "When looking from a window and saying I see men who pass in the street, I really do not see them, but infer that what I see is men, just as I say that I see wax. And yet, what do I see from the window but hats and coats which may cover automatic machines?"[81]

To insist that Descartes was only feigning this madness is to miss the point entirely. It is striking that the narrative in his *Meditations* attempts to draw us into a succession of mental states that, whether they be feigned or not, nevertheless accurately reproduce or perhaps mimic—at least with regard to their essential, clinically familiar outlines—the same configuration of psychopathology we are now seeing commonly in our civilization. Let us say, then, that Descartes was only feigning madness in the dark night of the soul. Let us say that he cured this madness by developing his insight into the light of reason carried within him. Be this as it may, at a deeply *unconscious* level, a level the Jungians would call "collective" and "archetypal," the mirror Descartes conceived was preparing his world for the coming of an earthshaking revolution: a fundamental transformation of society and culture, inextricably bound up with the ego state, power, anxiety, certainty, security, possession, domination, narcissism. Thus, I submit that the postures and positions Descartes assumed in his *Meditations* are isomorphically correlated with narcissistic disorders. This homology would seem to indicate a concealed interaction between the history of metaphysics and the etiology of the narcissistic disorders characteristic of the modern world. In "The Age of the World Picture," Heidegger asserted that

> With Descartes begins the completion and consummation of Western metaphysics. . . . With the interpretation of man as *subiectum,* Descartes creates the metaphysical presupposition for future anthropology of every kind and tendency. In the rise of old anthropologies, Descartes celebrates his greatest triumph. . . . Descartes can be overcome only through the overcoming of that he himself founded, only through the overcoming of modern, and that means at the same time Western, metaphysics.[82]

Narcissistic pathology takes over in metaphysics with the triumph of Cartesian subjectivism. This subjectivism is very deceptive, very difficult to grasp—much like the narcissistic personality, in fact. Descartes' subjectivism is in reality a retreat into weakness and self-delusion, which manages to appear as a triumph of strength, self-mastery, and rational control. Specifically, subjectivism may resemble an ascetic strength, a stoical virtue; but the truth of its weakness and concealed pathology is, rather, that it is only a feigned self-limitation, an imposture designed to achieve the end of absolute self-possession, apodeictic certainty, unconditional authority, and total control. The Cartesian ego is denied its primordial faith in natural reason and is forever separated, by nothing more than the sheer negativity of consciousness, of self-awareness, from the world in which it once lived, comfortably and with complacency; it suffers, therefore, from an incomparable loss, is bereft and in mourning, lost in an inconsolable grief, exhausted by disillusionment and objectless anxiety. He "hallucinated" a malevolent demon and accused the world of demonic schemes to break his trust in the separation of reality and madness; but he methodically withdrew into himself, "taking possession" of his own consciousness and proclaiming its evidence as the sole gift of absolute certainty, total self-control and authority. In this perilously split-off position, the Cartesian ego can perhaps begin to feel secure; it may finally seem to have a hold on itself that will allow it a masterful hold on others, on the world as a whole. This position, however, is ultimately quite precarious, and the ego is compelled sooner or later to recognize its ontological dependency and insufficiency. In time, this awareness of dependency, this sense of an abysmal inadequacy, will itself become a source of anxiety, until the ego surrenders its inflated image of itself and returns to a more or less peaceful and well-behaved conformity with the prevailing collective experience of reality.

But is this experience so sure of itself? Can rationality, order, and control be settled so easily? In Descartes' *Meditations,* the epistemic pathology is thought to be overcome by what I would call a therapy of adjustment, conformity, the sham of truth. But even for the Cartesian, the old memory of the nightmare, the dark night of the soul, cannot be erased by this sham of an ending. The first truth of the narrative was spoken, if only for a moment, in the assumption of a madness whose characteristic positions, now all too familiar in our mental hospitals, I have sought to limn here.

Observing that in narcissistic disorders, "there is a grandiose power drive," Schwartz-Salant emphasized that, "Under its control, certainty must reign and chance be suspended."[83] The narcissistic character, he added, "insists upon total determinacy of events, so that spontaneity and chance are defended against."[84] Is it any wonder, then, that the modern phase of metaphysics, dominated by our collective ambition to enjoy certainty in the "permanent" objects of thought, should coincide with the appearance of narcissistic disorders? For such a character type, self-consciousness tends to become a "new form of order within himself which [assumes that it] could survive in isolation from the environment."[85] This inflated posture of self-sufficiency and self-mastery is, however, just a sham and a defense; the sad truth is that the narcissistic character is profoundly insecure, haunted by groundless anxieties, and troubled by self-doubts, low self-esteem (Nietzsche spoke of "self-loathing") and a weak self-integration. The narcissistic ego requires, and is consequently dependent upon, a continual mirroring by others—or, as in the case of the Cartesian ego, by God—to confirm its most basic sense of reality. Desperately trying to avoid its inner emptiness, the narcissistic ego gets caught in a fantasy of "fullness," "completeness," and "self-sufficiency." It is hurt again and again by its own defenses.

Since for Descartes the senses are nothing but a source of deception and the body is nothing but perishable matter—that is to say, they are challenges, in both cases, to the power of the *cogito,* the ego must "abandon" them; the Cartesian ego is a *cogito* that has dissociated, split off, from its embodiment and taken itself as the object of its "love." In order to possess absolute certainty and security, Descartes underwent a process of separation and withdrawal, methodically abandoning all the "objects" of the body's desires and taking himself, as a purely thinking substance, for object. This is a narcissistic process, homologous to the process clinically recognized as the comportment of severe depression, and it leaves the ego extremely isolated, lost in its self-absorption, indifferent to all otherness, all differences; in that condition, it is constantly being tossed back and forth between self-inflation and self-deprecation, certainty and doubt, claims to omnipotence and fears of impotence, domination and withdrawal, trust and paranoia, contempt and envy, faith and despair.

Because of its destructive narcissism, the Cartesian ego set itself up for the violent contemporary attack on it that is now taking place within Western metaphysics. Thus, for example, Merleau-Ponty has argued against the ego's narcissistic claims: "we find in our experience a movement towards what could not in any event be present to us in the original and whose irremediable absence would thus count among our originating experiences."[86] He was reminding us that the ego in metaphysics must begin to cope with impermanence, with the absence of knowledge, with incompleteness, loss of certainty and security, and with the impossibility of an absolute grounding in authoritative truth. As the Cartesian ego is violently dispossessed, as its epistemological possession of itself is irrevocably taken away from it, it is finding itself increasingly possessed by the nihilism raging within the discourse of power. Predictably, the Cartesian ego's more worldly relative is now bent on absolute control and security by investing its will to power in the political economy of an advanced—but perhaps fatally uncontrollable—technology.

"God is dead." What does this mean in reference to our culture of narcissistic disorders? Schwartz-Salant maintained that,

> Narcissistic problems . . . must . . . be understood as purposive, the symptoms of a new Self image attempting to incarnate, either in the individual or in the collective, or both. They may represent nothing less than the psyche's response to the call that "God is dead," raised by Nietzsche many years ago, and painfully brought home to us in the fragmentation our modern society suffers and creates.[87]

In "Resurrecting the Dead Self," his contribution to this collection, Schwartz-Salant developed the insight stated very briefly in this passage, namely, that it can be amazingly therapeutic to treat individuals suffering on the borderline of narcissistic disorders as attempting, unsuccessfully, to outgrow their fixation in the ego condition and make way for the birth of a new Self. For the moment, however, I should like to concentrate on the destructive significance of the "death" of God. As I have suggested, the "death" of God is connected in an essential way with the rise to power and the suffering of the modern ego. For Descartes, the ego is clearly dependent on God; but this dependency should not obscure the fact that, in the process of demonstrating the existence of God, the ego had fatefully elevated itself to a position that can only be called godlike. Thus, in the technological revolution following Descartes, this ego has really begun to dream of, and has increasingly thought itself able to demonstrate, a godlike omnipotence and omniscience. (Our national space program is probably one of the best indications of this prevailing cultural attitude.) And yet, despite this historical rise to power, the ego continues to be absorbed in the phantoms fed by its own weaknesses: it is not at all ready to assume higher responsibility for itself. It nullifies the "God of our fathers," but cannot live, and may not survive, without the dimension of transcendence.

In the preceding section I argued that the "death" of God has meant a devastating loss, an absence, an abandonment, from which we have not been able to recover. The "death" of God therefore seems to correspond to the historical advent of a deep and pervasive cultural depression. Although it would be difficult if not (as I believe) impossible to assign to one the function of a "cause" and to the other the character of an "effect," I do think we must acknowledge the existence of a fateful interconnection. It is certainly reasonable to suppose that the "death" of God would be sufficient "cause" for a collective historical depression. And yet, if we ask why this phenomenon, the "death" of God, has taken place, we must consider the extent to which a depressive cultural withdrawal, e.g., a withdrawal of the modern ego from the spiritual life of the Self, from what Kohut called "the joyful experience of being a whole Self,"[88] and from the ego-threatening demands of living in the dimension Heidegger called "openness of Being," could contribute to the historical "death" of God—and even more catastrophically, to a world struggling to survive in the abandonment of Being as such.

I would like to argue for a closely related hypothesis, namely, that the "death" of God has meant—and is bound up with—the end of the mirroring function in the cultural, social, and psychological development of the modern ego. Consider what Nietzsche wrote in *The Will to Power:* "The nihilistic question 'for what?' is rooted in the old habit of supposing that the goal must be put up, given, demanded *from outside*—by some *superhuman authority*. Having unlearned faith in that, one still follows the old habit and seeks *another* authority that can *speak unconditionally* and *command* goals and tasks."[89] I think Nietzsche's analysis is accurate. But this suggests, perhaps, that in the process of our historical release from a self-destructive surrender to external authority, we have failed as a culture and not only as individuals to find any authentic calling "within" ourselves, and that we are consequently suffering from the disruption of a process—idealization—that we have reason to believe essential to the continuing self-development of the emergent ego. As many clinicians, including Kohut, Lacan, and Freud himself, have insisted, idealization, the formation of (superego) ideals, is of truly decisive importance in the ego's capacity to change, to grow, to "overcome" itself.[90] Our Judaeo-Christian God is the incarnation or instantiation of only one such ideality, one such projective formation or archetype. All the gods of history are the archetypal representations of human ideals, human projects, and as such they command with a certain authority. We are suffering today from the lack of any appropriate, life-enhancing idealization to replace our traditional authoritarian representations. What this suggests to me is that despite our science and technology we do not yet (know how to) experience, to make contact with, the amazing richness "within" ourselves and others: we are abysmally separated from the healing process of idealization that can happen, "within" ourselves. But this separation is the ego's self-destructive estrangement from itself—in other words, from its Self, its joyful being in fulfillment of its potential. The gods used to function for the ego's collective cultural life in a way homologous to the way that the mothering ones have always functioned in the ego's earliest life as an infant symbiotically attached to sources of care: the gods are mirrors; the gods are echoes. Just as the child needs the gentle guidance of mirroring and echoing in order to become an individual being, so the ego, as a participant in social and cultural life, needs a deep faith in itself and a deeply centered trust so that it can enter into a process of self-transformation by reference to noncoercive idealities. Without this access, access to an ideality brought forth from its own cultural experience, a culture of narcissism, a culture destructive to the being of the Self, becomes virtually inevitable.

At the very heart of the ego's culture of narcissism, we will always find a painful relationship to power: a self-destructive relationship to matters of strength, energy, effectiveness, potency, vitality, authority, independence, mastery, control, domination, stature, status, superiority, esteem, recognition, achievement, performance, glory, success, demonstration. It is as Adorno said: "Today self-consciousness no longer means anything but reflection on the ego as embarrassment, as realization of impotence: knowing that one is nothing."[91] Notice that Adorno explicitly connected the psychology of nihilism with the ego's experience of impotence, a narcissistically disturbed relationship to power. Adorno also said that this connection is particularly intense in the present historical situation.

For further elaboration let us turn to Jules Henry, who asserted, in *Pathways to Madness,* that

> Life in our culture is a flight from nothingness. This fact has been evaded by recent psychology through the invention of the notion of "effectiveness" ("mastery," *mutatis mutandis*). Psychology tells us that what we really want is to feel effective. . . . The silent anguish of many of us, however, warns that many who are frightfully effective feel like nothing nevertheless.[92]

This argument is extremely significant; if it is right, one could suppose that the psychology of nihilism calls for an understanding of our individual and cultural relationship to power that penetrates more deeply into its ontological character. Henry continued:

> At any rate, acting on something, being effective, is somethingness, and ineffectiveness is an abyss out of which we try to climb by acting on something. The trouble with being merely effective is that not only does it often fail to destroy the feeling of nothingness, but it also wrecks the peace of others. . . . Hence the truth of the matter is that action stemming from the feeling of nothingness, from despair, only makes the object of the action despairing.[93]

A vicious cycle, a wheel of suffering, is immediately set in motion, when the ego's investment in the will to power assumes a character that is bound to fail. If for the ego, to be is to be powerful, impotence or ineffectiveness can spell only nothingness. Since the narcissistic ego sets very high stakes, very high demands, the inevitable limitation on human power can confront the ego only with a deep frustration. In other words, if the stakes are set too high, the inevitable failure—the ego's individualized finitude—can generate a feeling of ineffectiveness and helplessness that is sometimes virtually devastating. Action stemming from the ego's experience of nothingness, from its despair over the question of its being, is therefore likely to be violent and destructive, moved by hatred, envy and fear. "Effectiveness that is merely flight from nothingness gives rise to a darting destructiveness in which he who feels he is nothing hurls himself upon others in order to escape his illness."[94] The author was of course referring to narcissistic psychopathology as it is manifest in the individual; but what he said should be understood in connection with our interpretation of cultural history. According to this interpretation, our historical present falls within and consummates the epoch of nihilism: since Being is reduced to power, will, and the will to power, any loss of power means loss of being, nihilism. Thus I suggest that narcissistic character disorders are inherent, and might accordingly be epidemic, in our present historical situation. For, while such disorders can be seen to contribute to the historical unfolding of nihilism, they are also seen as generated from within the self-destructive dialectic of power that prevails during the epoch of nihilism. For it must indeed be acknowledged that there is a very real basis in the conditions of social reality for our wide-spread feelings of impotence, ineffectiveness, and helplessness. Stated paradoxically: Since *real* powerlessness is a normal experience of the modern Self, it could be said that we are *driven* into narcissistic disorders in order to maintain our "sanity."

Schwartz-Salant wrote, "Incessant doing is a chronic condition of the narcissistic character. His basic belief that no center exists within [and that there is] no source of rest, results in seemingly endless activity, whether of an internal fantasy nature or an external rush to more and more achievements and tasks."[95] Today, our technological economy is organized in attunement with the restless activity of the narcissistic character disorder. (Max Weber's analysis of capitalism and the Protestant ethic of "works" prefigures this interpretation.) In this regard Heidegger told us that the human being,

> precisely as the one so threatened, exalts himself to the posture of lord of the earth. In this way the impression comes to prevail that everything man encounters exists only insofar as it is his construct. This illusion

> gives rise in turn to one final delusion: It seems as though man everywhere and always encounters only himself. . . . In truth, however, precisely nowhere does man today any longer encounter himself, i.e., his essential being.[96]

Since narcissistic disorders are associated with self-destructive defenses against insecurity and anxiety, what Heidegger said about the will to power in a technological economy begins to take on a heightened significance: "The preservation of the level of power belonging to the will reached at any given time consists in the will's surrounding itself with an encircling sphere of that which it can reliably grasp at, each time, . . . in order . . . to contend for its own security."[97] To be sure, as he pointed out, the system of defense may institute a measure of control, allowing a glimpse of power over the whole of Being: "That encircling sphere bounds off the constant reserve of what presences . . . that is immediately at the disposal of the will."[98] However, since defenses can never be totally secure and under control, anxiety and paranoia are bound only to intensify—with the inevitable result that feelings of insecurity and powerlessness also increase. A more "powerful" will does not necessarily lead to more or better control. This same self-destructive pattern can be discerned not only in the character of the narcissistic individual, but also in our technological drive to control the "resources" of nature and in our national postures of defense and nuclear armament. Furthermore, this pattern is reflected in the history of our metaphysics, where the abandonment of Being is associated with an ego essentially involved in a grandiose attempt to secure and make certain, and where this attempt to gain control over Being and to be in control gradually degenerates into the drive of a will to power that cannot tolerate the irreducibility of Being and makes way for the discourse of its rage: the discourse of nihilism.

People suffering from narcissistic disorders are haunted and moved by an experience of inner emptiness: lacking any self-esteem, they feel the absence of a real center, the absence of a Self. In formulating his interpretation of the history of metaphysics, Heidegger opened up a dimension of experience that can help us understand the suffering characteristic of narcissistic disorders:

> This emptiness has to be filled up. But since the emptiness of Being can never be filled up by the fullness of beings, especially when this emptiness can never be experienced as such, the only way to escape it is incessantly to arrange beings in the constant possibility of being ordered as the form of guaranteeing aimless activity.[99]

He argued for an historical correlation between this "aimless activity," a compulsion to produce, and the emergence of modern technology:

> Viewed in this way, technology is the organization of a lack, since it is related to the emptiness of Being . . . Everywhere where there are not enough beings—and it is increasingly everywhere and always not enough for the will to will escalating itself—technology has to jump in, create a substitute, and consume the raw materials.[100]

But emptiness compels consumerism as much as it does aimless productivity. Thus Heidegger saw a "circularity," a wheel of suffering, in "consumption for the sake of consumption": the "unconditional consumption of beings" to defend against the suffering of the Self in "the vacuum of the abandonment of Being."[101]

Heidegger actually pushed the diagnosis even further, for he suggested in the same essay—an essay, we should note, which concerns the history of metaphysics—that there is an essential historical connection between (1) our self-destructive strategies to dominate in the race for "defensive" superiority, and (2) our equally self-destructive technological economy, which is bound up deeply with the historical prevalence of narcissistic disorders. According to him, the "ultimate abandonment of Being" is

> hitched into the armament mechanism of the plan. The plan itself is determined by the vacuum of the abandonment of Being within which the consumption of beings for the manufacturing of technology, to which culture also belongs, is the only way out for man who is engrossed with still saving subjectivity in superhumanity. . . .
>
> The consumption of beings is as such and in its course determined by armanent in the metaphysical sense, through which man makes himself the "master" of what is "elemental." The consumption includes the ordered use of beings, which become the opportunity and the material for feats and their escalation.[102]

For the narcissistic character, the dialectic of power becomes a process of increasing self-alienation—what Kovel called a "neurosis of consumption," because the logic of capitalism in its late phase requires continued hegemony through the production and commodification of new "needs" and "desires."[103] The individual must therefore be subdued by the power of this dialectic: once the ego has been "hollowed out," it can be inflated and filled with commodities that its artificial needs pursue.[104] Both Horkheimer and Adorno emphasized the irony in the fact that, because of its obsession with the illusions of power, the modern ego, individualism gone wild, now finds itself controlled for the benefit of an economy that can survive only through the uncontrollable growth of production and consumption.[105] The will to control eventually produces a political economy that is out of our control. As narcissistic tendencies begin to take root in the traditional culture of character, they produce an environment that enormously intensifies their potential for nihilistic pathology: "self-esteem," to use our traditional word for the Self's experience of itself in its worthiness-of-being, used to be measured by productivity and effectiveness; now it is increasingly turned into a material worth of being, as measured by the hedonistic calculus of conspicuous consumption. The "empty" ego is driven by a consequent rage and envy, no longer possessing, but now possessed by its "own" new, i.e., artificial needs, and alienated from itself (or from its Self) not only through its acquiescence, but even through its available forms of resistance. It is thus set up for the pain of even greater self-destruction in a cycle of historical changes from which no one can entirely escape. We must accordingly attempt to see beyond individual psychopathology, beyond the more severe "cases" of "abnormality" that attract our attention, in order to recognize within the prevailing conditions of our civilization the existence of massive pressures and strains, all of them significant in the appearance of typical narcissistic pathology.

IN THE AGE OF IMAGES: ESSE EST PERCIPI

The image that is taking us away from ourselves could of course become the vision of our salvation, our well-being, our individual and collective healing. As Schwartz-Salant reminded us, "The issue of narcissism is the issue of our age, because it is the focal point for a new Self image in transition."[106] The image dominates our daily lives; it seems to me that the power of the image, which tends to *re-present* Being in avoidance or neglect of its ungraspable *presence,* is what links narcissistic epidemiology to the advent of nihilism.

According to Freud, secondary or pathological narcissism involves the "incorporation" of grandiose object-images as a defensive response to the insecurity, anxiety and guilt that accompanied the ego's earliest infantile movements of differentiation and individuation. Severe pathology will later become manifest, therefore, when the adult ego becomes totally entangled in these images, these mere phantoms of lost objects. For Heidegger, too, there is a serious pathology when thinking gets entirely caught up in a metaphysics of re-presentation; according to him, this entanglement spells out our historical closure to a more healing experience of Being as its presences, i.e., as a whole. Jules Henry can help us understand the image as an historically fateful link between narcissism and nihilism. Henry wrote, "And hence the sham. For when a man is nothing, he lives only by impacts from the outer world; he is a creature external to himself, a surface of fear moved by the winds of circumstance. . . ."[107] Man *becomes* nothing, man experiences himself as worthless and empty, as nothing, when he is "possessed" by the image and takes it for "reality." Heidegger helped us to recognize in this pathology a distinctive historical attunement by and to the advent of nihilism in the history of Being. Heidegger saw it as it is reflected in the history of metaphysics. In "The Age of the World Picture," Heidegger asserted that, "Where anything that is has become the object of representing, it first incurs in a certain manner *a loss of Being*."[108] If, in our epoch, Being as a whole goes into self-concealment while images or representations complete their surveillance and domination over us, the ego that is not seen uninterruptedly has no defense against the dread of its nothingness.[109] And yet it is true that the *visibility* of the ego is also a danger, as modern technologies of surveillance should be teaching us. To escape an entanglement with images that could be extremely self-alienating and self-destructive requires, as Schwartz-Salant has argued, "a capacity to observe images [and learn from them] without identifying [and fusing] with them."[110] In narcissistic disorders, this capacity is painfully stuck in a state of confusion, for the ego swings back and forth between fascination and dread. What dominates is what glitters, what shines: the image, the illusion, the sham. So narcissistic disorders are what we should expect to see in a society in which, as Bryan Turner, an English sociologist, puts it, "reality becomes entirely representational."[111]

In our present epoch, the epoch Heidegger called "the age of the world picture," to be is to be perceived, seen, noticed, brought forth into the visibility of the spectacle. The Self feels itself to be and is nothing but a fetishized commodity, an image, a collection of masks, something to be produced for and consumed in the glittering spectacle of life. In *Human Nature and the Social Order,* Charles H. Cooley called it the "looking glass self."[112] To live in an age dominated by representation is to be constantly threatened with self-alienation, for we tend to become totally dependent for a sense of our identity on the representation, our otherness, our coercion and subjugation. This dependency is infantilizing, degrading, and enraging. Narcissistic disorders therefore thrive in a society that idolizes the glittering personality and the aggressive, rugged, self-made individual, while it imposes on the unfortunate masses the overwhelming "solicitude" of the modern welfare state. Narcissism and nihilism must be interpreted together in their essential interconnectedness, because narcissistic pathology is basically character, the being of the Self, under the spell of the image, social and cultural representations; and nihilism is the pervasive negation of Being in an epoch when quantitative, technological re-presentations dominate all experience and cut us off from the deeper dimensions in which our well-being is rooted.

SCHIZOPHRENIA

(1) "If our experience is destroyed, our behavior will be destructive." R. D. Laing, *The Politics of Experience*[113]

(2) "The dialectic of the Enlightenment consists largely in the change from light to darkness. This means not only that the disintegration of mythology is accompanied by the disappearance of experience and the capacity for it. Because of the spiritual passivity which befalls men in the new economy, . . . there is no limit to what the most transparent [ideological] delusions can do. . . . Durkheim says that the loosening of the social fabric favors the suicide of the isolated individual. He might have added that as that disintegration progresses, the lies designed to patch up that society become less necessary. Who wouldn't rather believe in the national community than commit suicide unless he is already so crazy that he shrugs his shoulders even at that? Schizophrenia, the logical development of the rejection of any and all demands for love or respect, the final destruction of mythology, is ultimately a more humane mentality than the readiness to give one's unprincipled allegiance to an idea which is a substitute for the capacity for solidarity. In periods of decline such as the present, the higher truth lies in madness." Horkheimer, *Dawn and Decline* [114]

(3) "When no way out is left, the destructive drive becomes entirely indifferent to the question it never posed quite clearly: whether it is directed against others or against its own subject." Adorno, *Minima Moralia*[115]

(4) ". . . insanity of the will. . ." Nietzsche, *The Genealogy of Morals*[116]

(5) "There is no culture without a metaphysic of the inimical, [and] the metaphysic exists in people's minds even though never elucidated systematically. . . . [I]t is when fear is so great that the inimical can no longer be imagined as outside the group that madness is upon us. It is characteristic of pathological social systems . . . that the inimical is imagined to be right inside the walls,

and it is characteristic of many mad men that the inimical is felt to be inside their souls." Henry, *Pathways to Madness*[117]

(6) "The veiled tendency of society towards disaster lulls its victims in a false revelation, with a hallucinated phenomenon. In vain they hope in its fragmented blatancy to look their total doom in the eye and withstand it. Panic breaks once again, after millenia of enlightenment, over a humanity whose control of nature as control of men far exceeds in horror anything men ever had to fear from nature." Adorno, *Minima Moralia*[118]

(7) "Negative forces already set in motion, repeatedly reinforced by our present actions, may be becoming too powerful for human control. Individuals who are unbalanced and neurotic have little protection from negative influences and little control over their responses. . . . Unseen destructive forces may be building up, like the underground stresses that precipitate earthquakes. What we do in our time might have more profound reverberations than we realize." Tarthang Tulku, *Knowledge of Freedom*[119]

(8) "Whether exaggerated suspicions are paranoiac or true to reality, a faint private echo of the turmoil of history, can therefore only be decided retrospectively. Horror is beyond the reach of psychology." Adorno, *Minima Moralia*[120]

In his *Meditations on First Philosophy,* Descartes peremptorily banished madness from his argument by a gesture that feels no need to justify itself or question the authority of its judgment. He wrote:

> And how could I deny that these hands and this body belong to me, unless perhaps I were to assimilate myself to those insane persons whose minds are so troubled and clouded by the black vapours of the bile that they constantly assert that they are kings, when they are very poor; that they are wearing gold and purple, when they are quite naked; or who imagine . . . that they have a body of glass. But these are madmen, and I would not be less extravagant if I were to follow their example.[121]

Before we concentrate on the "body of glass," I would like to call attention to the operation of political metaphors, here woven with great cunning into the text, which represent an entire political economy and serve covertly to define the state of health and sanity in terms of conformity to the standard of Reason the sovereign political body incorporates in an exemplary way.[122] The subtle implication is that it is sheer madness for people to aspire to a democratic redistribution of sovereignity, to self-legislation and self-representation; madness for people to want equality; madness for people to

oppose undeserved economic privilege; madness for people even to think or imagine that what they see, feel, and experience as the reality of an oppressive social injustice could ever be in touch with the truth. At the beginning of the modern epoch, which Descartes himself heralded into history, we find the philosopher writing a text; this inaugurates the history of subjectivity, but immediately proceeds (lest this private, self-possessed interiority cause trouble) to sentence the modern Self to an external order of subjection, and to call "madness" any experience, however private, that should perceive the reality of this domination and contemplate images of social revolution. At the very moment subjectivity in the distinctively modern sense was constituted, the "discourse of reason" saw fit to establish the conditions for its domination and to propose a political interpretation of the madness such interiority and privacy could be imagined to provoke.

This discursive gesture, rejecting the phenomenological reality experienced by "madness," is one of the two reasons I began our consideration of the schizophrenias with the textual passage in question. The other reason is the startling reference to madmen who imagine that they have a body made of glass. It will be recalled that in the preceding section we noted an analysis of the narcissistically disturbed personality that characterized it as a "looking-glass Self." This description is very suggestive, inasmuch as persons suffering from narcissistic pathology often appear to be obsessed with how they look in the eyes, the mirror, of others and are haunted by worries about the possibility that others may be able to see into them, into their interior emptiness and unworthiness, as if the body were made of transparent glass.

We should not be surprised that the epoch which now brings out the pathology of a looking-glass Self was inaugurated by a text that conjures up, only to banish at once, the possibility of madmen with bodies of glass. (Distorted body-image is, we might note, a well-documented sign of psychosis.) On a symbolic level, the hypothesis is certainly more suggestive, more insightful, than we might at first suppose, for it registers the fragility, the brittleness of the schizophrenic Self and recognizes in this dangerous condition the phenomenological motivation for psychotic paranoia and its self-destructive defenses: not only the dread of dissociation and disintegration, which is characteristic of one type of schizophrenia—the type suffered by those who desperately need integration and wholeness—but also the dread that haunts those of the second type, who are in crying need of differentiation and individuation, and for whom the image of a glass body represents the unspeakable terror of transparency. This image is an ambig-

uous, perhaps contradictory phenomenon in that it signifies the condition of invisibility as much as it does the opposite, an excess of visibility and exposure; though in both cases, the danger is essentially the same: extinction, nonexistence as a separate, independent identity. Without some opacity, some concealment, some defense against penetration and engulfment, there can be no interiority, and therefore no membrane of difference between that which is Self and that which is not Self.

I want to recall a point I made in the Introduction. My use of the term "schizophrenia" does not imply the acceptability or legitimacy of psychiatric nosology and diagnosis. Schizophrenias are forms of psychopathology, but not in any clinically determined sense. If I speak of them as pathology, that is because we must recognize that they are forms of suffering, and that they are "speaking" to us. I do not assume that "schizophrenia" as a distinct clinical entity actually exists. Indeed, as Fritz Redlich argued in the fifties and continues to argue today, "the important questions of diagnosis, prognosis, etiology and therapy are still unanswered. . . Is schizophrenia a group of ill-defined syndromes, or is it a true nosological entity? Is it a disease? A maladjustment? A way of life? Is the irrationality of schizophrenia transmitted by genes or by interpersonal relationships?"[123] In light of all this confusion around our ignorance, Redlich seriously suggests that the term "schizophrenia" could be a "catch-all diagnosis" without any basis in reality.[124] This book has argued this critical position with considerable force. It is necessary to begin our thinking about these questions with the understanding (1) that schizophrenia is a meaningful experience of being-in-the-world; (2) that this meaningfulness is manifest in its presence, however alien and incomprehensible it may seem; (3) that this manifesting presence is its speech, and is consequently an appeal to us; and (4) that in this speech there is always a painful truth about us, about family, society, and world, which needs to be recognized.

The mind-body split frequently occuring in schizophrenia is rehearsed in our metaphysics, and can be traced back through Descartes to the texts of Plato and his precursors. This indicates that the schizophrenic split is a pervasive cultural pathology. Laing described the schizophrenic condition in *The Divided Self*: "The dissociation of the self from the body and the close link between the [split-off] body and others, lends itself to the psychotic position wherein the body is conceived not only as operating to comply with and placate others, but as being in the actual possession of others."[125] The splitting off of the body in the metaphysical discourse of Western civilization, an implication of mind-body dualism urged for disciplinary reasons by theological and pastoral texts (Pythagorean, Platonic, Stoic, Jewish, Christian, Gnostic, Plotinean), seems to be similar to processes widely regarded as pathological in other systems, or regimes, of discourse—contemporary medicine, for example, and psychiatry. (But there is a contradiction in these latter discourses, since they recognize the pathology in their practice while continuing to insist on the truth of our prevailing metaphysics.) And in its more intense and distinctively modern form, the splitting seems to be correlated with the generation of discourses in science and in political economy—texts on private property, labor, sexual discipline, and the criminal code—that mark the epoch of modern science, technology, and industrialization. The body that figures in these discourses represents a pathological body, a body no longer ensouled, dead: already, in effect, a corpse. The body is turned into a part of the material world, an external and alien substance moving among other objects; a possession of which we may be dispossessed; a property that may be possessed by others. (Is there not a connection to be made between schizophrenic demonism, especially demonic possession, and the development of a political economy based on private property and capital?) The possibility of a self-healing body-Self is already obliterated in thought, denied any reality. (How might this kind of experience and understanding bear on the course of illness in the case of severe organic diseases? Even psychosomatic medicine has had to struggle for its liberation from the metaphysics of Cartesian dualism.) Consider the madness of the schizophrenic's experience of embodiment: what Descartes took to be the essential nature of the normal, healthy body—*res extensa,* passive matter, a machine without intelligence or power of self-movement—is in fact a latent experiential possibility characteristic of what modern psychiatry would recognize as an *illness* of the lived body.

The metaphysics that circulates in concealment within the world of daily life and contributes to, as well as it reflects, the character of schizophrenic epidemiology, is itself implicitly schizophrenic, for 1) it represents us as disembodied selves split-off from our own bodies; 2) it represents this body as an alien object; 3) it represents the Self as radically split-off from others; and 4) it represents the Self as a realm of interiority and inwardness whose truth is accessible only through withdrawal and dissociation from the world.

In schizophrenia, dissociation, the tragic reality that corresponds to our metaphysical dualism, uses disembodiment as a Cartesian mode of defense against perceived threats to the being of the Self (body-Self); but, instead of a transcendence of suffering—or, in Cartesian terms, uncertainty—this process only divides the Self even more, and threatens to destroy, this time from more deeply within, whatever healthy sense of integration and wholeness might still hold out some protection against total collapse. This is the psychopathology whose suffering we can read clearly in the texts of our metaphysics—a discourse that today speaks of nihilism, of the annihilation of all Being "from within itself."

The formation of somatic pathology common in most schizophrenias corresponds, therefore, to a discursive strategy that is even more inimical and more self-contradictory than the body's "scientific" reduction to organism or mechanism. The splitting off—in Descartes, for instance—means that the *Self* can no longer be conceived as participating in the world; nor can it be thought in real communication with others. But this is the very essence of solipsism, which becomes suffering and tragedy when translated into an existential condition. Are our discourses only the *mirrors* of psychopathology? Are they not also both its sources and its effects? These are important questions, but I would add another one, which they suggest. If the mind-body splitting in our metaphysical discourse is claimed to be the truth about the body, would it not follow, since the equivalent of that condition is treated as psychopathology, that *schizophrenia speaks for the truth?* Could it be a truth that radically questions the sanity of our cultural discourse, and by extension the sanity of our civilization as a whole? It is in this sense, and not in the very vulnerable romantic sense of Laing, that I would argue the presence of truth in schizophrenia. This truth does not make schizophrenia any less pathological, in *my* sense of the term, though it does accuse the discourses of medicine and psychiatry by revealing their ideological investments of power, the operations of their conformism, and the violence in their arrogant dogmatism. For it is in the terms of these discourses that schizophrenia is judged to be "pathological"—"pathological" in a sense which requires the assumption that the judgment can be made neutrally and with objectivity according to the consensually validated norms of health, sanity and well-being that happen to prevail at the time. What if the truth in schizophrenia is one that, because of its distinctively greater vulnerability to what is craziest in civilization, speaks to the needs of its time, and speaks very clearly, considering the pain, attempting to call attention, at this time and for us, to the terror of self-destructiveness and the horror of nihilism, which rage in resonance with one another like an epidemic in our civilization? What if schizophrenia is the *painful truth* about a world that our metaphysics both founds and reflects?

According to the psychoanalytic cartography used by Harold Searles, schizophrenias are characteristically organized around conflicts between id, ego, and superego: "the id," he wrote, "is experienced by the ego as *an intensely inimical foreign body* which threatens to be overwhelming."[126] From the very beginning, therefore, even the healthiest ego is deeply divided, since it finds itself in a situation where it must simultaneously accommodate both the uncivilized drives of the id and the social imperatives of the superego, our collective moral conscious. If the emergent ego is weak and insecure, the superego can be no less overwhelming than the id:

> rather than being, as in the normal person, in the relation of a firm but friendly and helpful guide to the ego in the latter's efforts to cope with the id-impulses and with the outer world, [the superego] stands in the nature of a cruel tyrant whose assaults upon the weak and unintegrated ego are, if anything, even more destructive to it than are the accessions of the threatening id-impulses. Moreover, the superego, even in itself, is not well-integrated.[127]

C. R. Badcock, the English anthropologist, has proposed a sociological explanation for this pathology that draws on psychoanalysis: we are seeing many weak and poorly integrated superegos today because of the deterioration in our moral customs, practices and institutions, which can no longer guide, educate and inspire. This breakdown of values is, of course, what Nietzsche called "nihilism." I submit that we should give more thought to the connection between schizophrenic pathology and the culture of nihilism, whose spreading devastation, creating a social environment favorable to psychopathology, is especially evident in the breakdown of the conditions necessary for the very possibility of public morality.

The conflicts and dissociations psychoanalysis sees in schizophrenic pathology are rooted in cultural fears around sexuality and hatred for the body. They are existential manifestations of the mind-body dualism at the very heart of Western metaphysics and religion; they are, in that sense, accurate historical registers of a pervasive cultural pathology. The essence of this pathology is nihilism, the spiritual epidemic of our epoch.

It is significant that Searles was prepared to argue that there are "cultural undercurrents in our present-day society, even in politically democratic countries," which effectively contribute to the "thwarting of ego-development and the undermining of ego-functioning."[128] This in turn prevents the emergence of a well-integrated Self. Whereas Freud and Jung saw many patients suffering from the splitting of the ego in its conflict with id and superego around the inhibition of drives, analysts today see something quite different: ego fragmentation, a deeper, more devastating threat to the being of the Self. They tend to explain this major historical change in psychopathology as did Badcock, i.e., by reference to the weakening of traditional patriarchal culture and the virtual disappearance of disciplinary role-models, superego formations, and drive-inhibitions. The greater our cultural disintegration, the more devastating the Self's. It is reasonable to conjecture that this historical shift in psychopathology corresponds to the historical evolution of nihilism itself. From the thirteenth to the nineteenth centuries, growing nihilism took hold of the Self by way of ancient cultural anxieties over the body; the "mind" or "spirit" split off from the "body," whose pleasures were sins that could not be tolerated and whose perceptions were errors of the will in need of correction. Mind-body dualism split the Self. By contrast, in today's much more "permissive" culture (more permissive because of the growth of nihilistic relativism and uncertainty), nihilism has affected the Self through the breakdown in normative codes and the absence of cultural ideals. The Self is fragmented and disorganized: splintered, rather than split. Both of these phases were perceived very clearly by Nietzsche and interpreted with great insight as "signs" of a spreading nihilism.

There are other forms of dualism that make their appearance in our metaphysical discourse and should alert us to other latent cultural pathologies that may be presumed to contribute to social conditions favoring the prevalence of schizoid and schizophrenic suffering. Western metaphysics has traditionally thought of the Self as pure inwardness, pure interiority: the Self is here, inside my skin, while the world is out there, on the *other* side of my skin. The conceptual and argumentative difficulties that seriously problematize this interpretation seem to mirror (and may indeed, through our culture, be connected with) a schizophrenic pathology already present at the dawn of our civilization, but greatly intensified by the course of social history.

Once again, the suffering of the schizophrenic contains within its speech a truth we may need to recognize and respect if we as a civilization are ever to survive the danger to the being of the Self, the nihilism that has come to us in the form of the split between private and public, interior and exterior life. What is paranoid schizophrenia, if not a tortured communication (all too often a monologue, of course, since nobody will listen, or listen with real understanding) concerning the kind of suffering this metaphysical dualism involves? The pathology latent in the dualism—isolation, loneliness, feeling cut off from others, feeling empty inside, fears of engulfment and penetration, agoraphobia, exhibitionism—is probably always present in our culture, though *normally* in a more attenuated form; those among us who suffer in a schizophrenic way from the destructive potential in the dualism are probably more susceptible to its negativity because of the confluence of many different factors: genetic constitution, family environment, unusual social conditions, and finally, the hostile indifference of the mental health industry, when the suffering becomes severe enough to compel psychiatric attention.

The cultural dualisms that bespeak a split between the inner and the outer, the private and the public, and the Self and the Other, are potentially pathogenic, and the speech or silence of the schizophrenic manifests the historical form of its suffering in the culture of this splitting. In the discourse of Western metaphysics, the suffering of these dualisms appears in the form of glaring contradictions and paradoxes. In the "normal" world, these dualisms of metaphysics are actualized in the atomic individualism of the Economic Man, the "sane" man of success in a world of private property, industry and commerce, and, of course, capital investment. But these same dualisms also appear as a wall or an invisible membrane, that encapsulates the individual Self in a meaningless, empty privacy while encouraging the increasing impoverishment of our public life. And they can create social, cultural, and historical conditions that are perceived as inimical, sometimes by people whose perceptions are deluded and who are therefore treated as "paranoid schizophrenics," and sometimes by people whose anxiety is based on perceptions of society that are accurate and well-founded, since in truth they are the victims of prevailing political power. The paranoid schizophrenic is of course subject to delusion if he thinks that our world is a Panopticon and that telepathic thought control is the universal method of government. And yet there is also a vital truth here, to which the schizophrenic may be more attuned than we. The inner-outer split and the Self-Other split encourage paranoia; but since they also encourage intolerance, bigotry, hatred, conflict and aggression, paranoid fantasies of panoptical and acoustic surveillance, thought control and attacks of demonic possession should not be immediately dismissed as the symptoms of private madness: it could be argued that they manifest an awareness that may be in touch with a normally concealed reality, a normally concealed sociopathy, the social genesis of a form of suffering represented only in its most extreme state by the classified schizophrenic. The dualisms of our culture are indeed capable of generating a pervasive social pathology. They are also capable of generating specific historical sociopathies—when, for example, they fragment society into conflicting groups or populations and serve the stability of social structures in which some people are able to dominate, control and exploit some others. Perhaps the suffering of the individual schizophrenic can help us to realize this truth, too.

In writing about "Anxiety in Paranoia," Searles, intending to refer to the experience of the schizophrenic, wrote, "And there is, finally, the danger that, in the eyes of other human beings, he may cease totally to exist."[129] But what happens to our belief in the madness of schizophrenia, once we acknowledge the fact that a multitude of social, political, and environmental conditions really hostile to the continued survival of our planetary civilization are allowed to prevail, once we recognize that minorities everywhere—including "schizophrenics"—continue to be threatened by the presence of social and political institutions hostile to their very existence? If we concede that the "paranoid schizophrenic" may be more sensitively attuned to this inimical reality than we—attuned, of course, without knowing it and without deriving any help from it—what happens to our traditional criterion for distinguishing "normal" instances of anxiety from the delusional anxiety of paranoia? After all, the world today really *is* a very threatening and dangerous place. Racism, the oppression of women and gay people, and the abysmal poverty of our urban slums are destructive and disintegrating to the Self, since (to use one of Searles's criteria)[130] they activate various areas of the personality in opposition to one another; and they manifest in both diffuse and specific forms the self-destructiveness of our culture. This, however, is what the "actuality" of nihilism is. Nihilism is not a bloodless metaphysical abstraction; its actuality is something we can all experience—if only we dare. So can we in any event exclude a priori the possibility that there is a perceptive dimension of existence into which anyone, but especially someone with a predisposition for regressive schizophrenic disintegration, may happen to sink, where a diffusely attuned sense of the pervasiveness of nihilism in our culture might begin to insist on recognition, adding to equally well-founded anxieties experienced because of an excluded position in our political economy and because of the often hostile care provided today by our medicine, psychiatry, and the welfare system? (By "hostile care," I mean the established psychiatric practice of "drug management," neglecting or rejecting the schizophrenic's own lived-through *experience* and taking care only to control the patient's overt social *behavior*. This is hostile because it reinforces the metaphysical splitting of the Self. "Drug management" subjects subjectivity to the rule of objectivity; it sacrifices the Self driven into its "care" in order to make things easier for itself. The imposition of behavioral controls is convenient for society, but it destroys the patient's trust in the value and reality of felt experience. Thus, it may intensify the patient's sense of encapsulation, disintegration and "possession.")

Our culture is schizophrenogenic—and for the same reasons that it is inherently (but in the past more latently and therefore also more unconsciously) nihilistic. The same historical conditions which make our civilization self-destructive also produce a multitude of diseases and illnesses that involve the self-destruction of the individual Self. The nihilism in our culture is not as such the "cause" of schizophrenia, but it is a contributing condition, a spiritual environment in which what Jung called "loss of soul"—perhaps a much better term than "schizophrenia"—has become a not unfamiliar mode of defense and survival. The suffering of the schizophrenic is a suffering that bears within itself a truth we refuse to hear. This very refusal may sometimes be enough, though, to drive a poorly integrated person crazy.

Let us now consider two of the interpersonal conditions Searles considered to be schizophrenic-making. 1) "The simultaneous, or rapidly alternating, stimulation-and-frustration of other needs, in addition to sexual ones," often seems to have a "disintegrating effect" on the individual Self.[131] 2) Similarly, a family environment in which the parent(s) frequently switched very suddenly from one emotional "wavelength" or one emotionally charged object to another "without any marked shift in feeling content" noticeably increases the likelihood that one or more of the children will experience schizophrenic pathologies of the Self. What makes these circumstances so terribly destructive to the Self is, among other things, the fact that they "undermine the other person's confidence in the reliability of his own emotional reactions and of his own perception of outer reality. . ."[132] (Thus, the drugs imposed on schizophrenic patients achieve socially acceptable behaviors by driving the "craziness" inward and deepening the rift between Self and Others.)

These two conditions, though, are characteristic not only of families with schizophrenic predisposition; they are no less characteristic of our contemporary culture as a whole. Even a very brief reflection on that most powerful medium of contemporary culture, our television, should confirm this analysis. Television viewers are constantly subject to stressful patterns of excessive stimulation and excessive frustration, organization of their sexual drives, power drives, sensibility, and even their sense of identity, to fit the prevailing requirements of the political economy. Similarly, they are frequently subject to sudden changes in what is being presented for their attention and response; yet these changes do not allow for (and often in fact prevent) what once would have been considered an appropriate, i.e., corresponding change of feeling. A commercial selling a new brand of toilet paper—amusing enough to produce mirth and laughter—might indeed be followed by photographs that document the government's massacre of Indians and peasants in Guatemala. In our present culture, the juxtaposition of these two discursive images would not necessarily generate any conflict; nor would it suggest any contradictions in our way of thinking. On the contrary, the sequence would "normally" appear to be perfectly compatible, perfectly rational. And, although it would "normally" at some point be recognized that the second image was actually taken in the very midst of the bloody terror, it would "normally" be presumed that the overwhelming majority of viewers would "normally" remain, more or less, in the field of the emotional state—the ontological attunement—evoked by the preceding commercial. When transferred very abruptly to the scene of the second image, this state would "normally" tend to be quite detached, distant, and unmoved: the viewer will inhabit a sort of contemplative aloofness, or perhaps a certain emotional numbness, as if the atrocities in Guatemala were fortunately quite unreal: no more important, no more urgent, no more deeply affecting us than the product being advertised. In our world, being advertised, the being of objects, takes precedence over—and that means it dominates—all other modes of being, including being human; consequently, it defines our sense of the "normal": in emotional responsiveness, in rationality, in value, in what is experienced as "real" and as the *whole* of Being.

In our modern world, a deadly metaphysics prevails. We have made images and appearances—illusory beings—substitute for social "reality." We have gone farther than ever before to reverse the ontological commitment by which Plato distinguished the wise from the foolish. In cultural and sociopolitical matters, we do not even recognize any difference.

This would seem to confirm the interpretation of our culture made more than a century ago by Nietzsche. In *The Will of Power,* Nietzsche stated, "The most extreme form of nihilism would be the view that *every* belief, every considering-something-true, is necessarily false because there simply is no [one] *true* world."[133] I think this suggests a connection between nihilism and schizophrenia, which psychiatry calls "loss of reality." In the wake of our narcissistic disillusionment as a culture, when the Western world finally had to acknowledge the relativity and diversity of "truth," Nietzsche saw two future possibilities, two conflicting tendencies and directions: either emancipation from dependency on the illusion of "one truth only," or else despair over the possibility of any truth at all: either a step towards health and sanity, freedom from delusion, or else a collapse into the disintegrating madness of "no true world" at all, no experienced sense of reality, nothing "real" but an empty nothingness.

In the nihilistic culture such as ours, it is extremely difficult for us as individuals to make bodily felt contact with our own deepest, most individuated sense of reality and Being; for some people, there is no adequately developed sense of the being of the Self as a whole, no compass upon which to rely in a culture of the glittering image, the outward show, sham and illusion. To what extent must we concede that the essential *difference* between the "schizophrenics" and "us" is not that "we" are sane and "they" are crazy, but that the "schizophrenics" are people who, because of a multitude of confluent factors (including the genetic) have suffered more and been more thoroughly destroyed by this prevailing nihilism, while we, who are more "normal" in the statistical sense, would be just as disturbed by our collective madness had we not simply been "more fortunate" in the gifts and the endowments of our circumstances?[134]

"It almost seems," wrote Heidegger, "as if the being of pain were cut off from man under the dominance of the will, similarly the being of joy."[135] (It is essential here that we hear the stress on the two occurrences of the word "being," not just on the words "pain" and "joy.") He asked us a question: "Can the extreme measure of suffering still bring a transformation here?"[136] Perhaps. But, for Heidegger, it seems that, "The still hidden truth of Being is withheld from metaphysical humanity. The laboring animal is left to the giddy whirl of its products so that it may tear itself to pieces and annihilate itself in empty nothingness."[137] We will never be able to reclaim all human beings from the condition of schizophrenia, but the disturbing truth in their presence *could* be a cause of redemption for a future humanity and its civilization. Provided we realize, as Adorno reminded us so pointedly, that "He who relinquishes awareness of the growth of horror . . . fails to perceive . . . the true identity of the whole, of terror without end."[138] Within the pain of schizophrenia, within its dehumanizing soul-death, there is a healing truth for its chosen messengers. . .and for us as well.

NOTES

1. Max Horkheimer, *Dawn and Decline* (New York: Seabury Press, 1978), 231.

2. Adorno, *Minima Moralia: Reflections from Damaged Life* (London: New Left Books, 1974; Verso Editions, 1978), 58.

3. Nietzsche, *The Will to Power* (New York: Random House, 1968), 430.

4. Ibid., 40.

5. Ibid., 29.

6. Christopher Lasch, *The Culture of Narcissism: American Life in an Age of Diminishing Expectations* (New York: W. W. Norton, 1978), 41. Lasch, however, was seduced by the Freudian, ego-centered model of personality development. Thus he failed to distinguish narcissism, which really is pathology, from the kinds of self-awareness and self-attentiveness involved in genuine self-development. See Eugene Gendlin's critique of the concept of narcissism, published in this collection.

7. Jules Henry, *Culture Against Man* (New York: Random House, 1965), 322.

8. Lasch, xiii.

9. Heidegger, "Recollection in Metaphysics," *The End of Philosophy* (New York: Harper and Row, 1973), 76. Italics added. Interpolations are my own.

10. Heidegger, "Overcoming Metaphysics," in *The End of Philosophy,* 90. Interpolations are my own.

11. Ibid., 103. Italics added. Interpolations are my own.

12. Heidegger, "Metaphysics as History of Being," in *The End of Philosophy,* 19. Interpolations are my own.

13. R. D. Laing, *The Politics of Experience* (New York: Ballantine Books, 1968), 133. Interpolation is my own.

14. See Herbert V. Guenther, *The Matrix of Mystery* (Boulder: Shambhala, 1985).

15. Henry, *Pathways to Madness* (New York: Random House, 1973), 374.

16. Ibid. Henry continued: ". . . we attack what is nearest, what has inflicted on us the immediate, the most memorable pain. The family, however, is merely the place where the general pathology of the culture is incubated, concentrated and finally transmuted into individual psychosis. . . . [Thus] the family merely distills into a lethal dose what exists in the culture at large." (p. 374). Henry's critique of the reductionism embraced by the "genetic theory of psychosis" belongs together with the radical critique of the "medical model," which likewise diverts attention from the social, political, economic and cultural conditions responsible for "mental illness."

17. Adorno, 58.

18. Joel Kovel, "The American Mental Health Industry," in David Ingleby (ed.), *Critical Psychiatry: The Politics of Mental Health* (New York: Pantheon Books, 1980), 88. The main points in Kovel's argument against the medical model are worth quoting at length: "The medical model of mental illness completes the reification inherent in the notion of mental hygiene by bringing mind (or behavior, or personality), viewed now as a substance, under the sway of medical technics. This has an obvious cultural power, since it combines in one conception the mystique of the machine and the managerial ethos. In its system the doctor-expert is the manager of the soul, regarded now as a mechanism like any other, capable of tuning up or overhauling. Care is defined in a top-down direction, the patient, quiescent as any machine, accepting the ministration of the expert technician. The notion also has a political power, since what is repressed out of the medical model of mental illness is that dimension which considers the person an active social agent, defined by what class, community, and history have meant for him. What is left after the excision of this dimension is the idea of the individual as monad. . . . Accordingly, disease is something going on within a person; it is to be looked for in the malfunctioning of the 'parts' of his personality and not in the entire relationship between the self and the world; and it is to be remedied by individual or particularistic action. Lacking a sense of history, the medical model inevitably slides into biological types of explanation. . . . More precisely, one of its functions is to repress out this connection so that problems of social origin appear assimilable to the prevailing technocracy." 86.

19. Lasch, 41.

20. Ibid., 42.

21. Ibid., 33.

22. Ibid.

23. Ibid., 34.

24. Kovel, "The American Mental Health Industry," 88.

25. J. J. Schwab, "Depression in Medical and Surgical Patients," in Allen J. Enelow (ed.), *Depression in Medical Practice* (Rahway, N.J.: Merck, Sharp and Dohme, 1970), 84.

26. C. R. Badcock, *Madness and Modernity: A Study in Social Psychoanalysis* (Oxford: Basil Blackwell, 1983), 118. The argument presented in this book is seriously weakened by its obsession with psychoanalytic reductionism: a stubborn and foolish effort, long renounced by most of the orthodox Freudians, to explain everything—student protests against the war in Vietnam, for example—in terms of infantile trauma. Badcock's theoretical explanations are not "scientific," as he believes, but fraudulent; and despite his apparent fears of totalitarianism, the political implications of his own critique of contemporary culture are alarmingly reactionary. For Badcock, we should respond to the contemporary "impoverishment of the ego" by strengthening the superego's supervision of the weak, infantile ego; but this means in effect that the ego is simply to be adjusted and normalized to conform to social norms—our socially constructed reality, deceptively posited as if it were an absolute reality. By contrast, I see this impoverishment as the ego's way of calling for an opportunity to overcome itself and become a Self, i.e., as manifesting a need that calls for the transformation of a culture that at present

prevents the ego from further developing itself. Since, as we have noted, the nihilism that constitutes the background of depression is a function of the ego's will to power, it should be clear that the psychoanalytic project of adjusting and strengthening the ego cannot be responsive to the needs of our time. We certainly need to respond to the impoverishment Badcock noted; but a more progressive approach would be to facilitate the emergence of a new Self.

27. Medard Boss, *Existential Foundations of Medicine and Psychology* (New York: Jason Aronson, 1979), 222. The position Boss advocated is also to be found in Ernest Becker, *Revolution in Psychiatry: The New Understanding of Man* (New York: Free Press, 1974), 78. It is also implicit in Otto Fenichel's contention that schizophrenia begins as a narcissistic disorder, since narcissistic disorders typically conceal an experience of depression. See Fenichel's *The Psychoanalytic Theory of Neurosis* (New York: W. W. Norton, 1945), 418.

28. Heidegger, "Sketches for a History of Being," in *The End of Philosophy,* 64.

29. Heidegger, *Introduction to Metaphysics* (New York: Doubleday, 1961), 42.

30. Nietzsche, *The Will to Power,* Note 35, p. 23.

31. Freud, *The Ego and the Id* (New York: W. W. Norton, 1962), 38.

32. Heidegger, "Sketches for a History of Being," 66–67. Interpolations are my own.

33. Nietzsche, *The Will to Power,* Note 33, p. 23.

34. Ibid., 18.

35. Nietzsche, *The Genealogy of Morals* (New York: Doubleday, 1956), 231. Interpolation is my own. Since a will that has given up its historical hope for a metaphysical purpose and taken the void for its purpose would be a *depressive* will, it is only a small logical step from Nietzsce's expressed beliefs to the conclusion that the nihilistic will to power must be involved in the constitution of social conditions favorable to depression at the individual level. Nietzsche himself virtually implied the connection when he described "passive nihilism" as an actually lived experience. If we connect Nietzsche's thinking in this regard with Freud's analysis of ego-formation (he sees the ego emerging in response to the loss of its loved object), then we can see the outlines of an important pathological configuration: since the beginning of modernity, the individual ego, formed in resolution of a process of mourning, becomes will to power; but, inherent in the "drive" of this will to power, there is a nihilism the psychological character of which Nietzsche perceived clearly—a passive nihilism that can easily take the form of a depressive disorder. (In fact, Nietzsche explicitly referred to depression in *The Genealogy of Morals,* 271–2 and 277–8.)

36. Nietzsche, *The Will to Power,* Note 59, p. 40. See the contribution to this collection of studies by Robert Romanyshyn and Brian Whalen, "Depression: The Other Face of the American Dream." These authors focus on homelessness and rootlessness in the American experience of depression. Concerning the decisive role of the family in contemporary forms of psychopathology, see Jules Henry, *Pathways to Madness* (New York: Random House, 1973) and *Culture Against Man* (New York: Random House, 1965).

37. Heidegger, "Nietzsche's Word: 'God is dead'," in *The Question Concerning Technology and Other Essays* (New York: Harper and Row, 1977), 109.

38. Freud, *The Origins of Psychoanalysis: Letters to Wilhelm Fliess, 1887–1902* (New York: Basic Books, 1954), 49.

39. Freud, *Inhibitions, Symptoms and Anxiety* (New York: W. W. Norton, 1977), 67.

40. See Søren Kierkegaard, *Concluding Unscientific Postscript* (Princeton: Princeton University Press, 1941), 79. Kierkegaard said: "An existing individual is constantly in process of becoming." For Lacan's analysis of the ego, see "Some Reflections on the Ego," *International Journal of Psychoanalysis,* 34 (1953): 11–17; "The Mirror Stage as Formative of the Function of the I as Revealed in Psychoanalytic Experience," in *Ecrits* (New York: W. W. Norton, 1977); "On Paranoia and its Relationship to Aggressivity," also in *Ecrits;* and finally, *Le Seminaire: Livre I. Les Ecrits techniques de Freud* (Paris: Editions du Seuil, 1975), 22.

41. See Erwin Straus's chapter on "Disorders of Personal Time in Depressive States," in his *Phenomenological Psychology* (New York: Basic Books, 1966), 290–295, and Ludwig Binswanger, "The Case of Ellen West: An Anthropological-Clinical Study," in R. May, E. Angel, H. Ellenberger (eds.), *Existence: A New Dimension in Psychiatry and Psychology* (New York: Simon and Schuster, 1958), 237–364.

42. Heidegger, *Introduction to Metaphysics,* 31.

43. Adorno, 47.

44. Robert Jay Lifton, *The Life of the Self: Toward a New Psychology* (New York: Basic Books, 1983), 26.

45. Ibid., 31.

46. Ibid., 34–35. Interpolations are my own.

47. Nietzsche, *The Birth of Tragedy* (New York: Doubleday, 1956), 136.

48. Ibid.

49. Tarthang Tulku, *Knowledge of Freedom,* (Berkeley: Dharma Publishing, 1985), 69. Italics added.

50. Carl Jung, "Mind and Earth," in *Civilization in Transition, The Collected Works of Carl G. Jung,* vol. 10 (New York: Pantheon, 1964), 49.

51. Adorno, 154.

52. Martin E. Seligman, *Helplessness: On Depression, Development, and Death* (San Francisco: W. H. Freeman, 1975), 83. Also see Freud, *Inhibitions, Symptoms and Anxiety,* 76.

53. See the *Introduction* to C. R. Badcock, *Madness and Modernity,* where this argument is first outlined.

54. Freud, *The Ego and the Id* (New York: W. W. Norton, 1962), 43.

55. Ibid., 41.

56. Ibid., 48.

57. Ibid., 42. Italics added.

58. See Nietzsche, *The Will to Power,* Note 33, p. 22 and Lifton, *The Life of the Self,* 44.

59. For additional reading, see John Bowlby, *Attachment and Loss,* in 3 vols.: vol. 1, *Attachment;* vol. 2, *Separation: Anxiety and Anger;* vol. 3, *Loss: Sadness and Depression* (New York: Basic Books, 1980). Also see Frederick C. Redlich and Daniel K. Freedman, "Manic and Depressive Behavior Disorders," in Freedman

and Redlich (eds.), *The Theory and Practice of Psychiatry* (New York: Basic Books, 1966), 533–563; Martin Roth, "The Phenomenology of Depressive States," *Canadian Psychiatric Association Journal,* 4 (1959), Special Supplement S32; and of course Freud's 1917 paper on "Mourning and Melancholia," *Standard Edition of the Complete Psychological Works of Sigmund Freud,* vol. 14 (London: Hogarth Press, 1957), 243–258. With regard to the relationship between depression and somatic disease, see Ari Kiev, "Somatic Manifestations of Depressive Disorders," in Ari Kiev (ed.) *Somatic Manifestations of Depressive Disorders* (Amsterdam, Geneva, London, Princeton: Excerpta Medica, 1974), 3–23; and Lawrence LeShan, *You Can Fight for Your Life: Emotional Factors in the Causation of Cancer* (New York: M. Evans, 1977). LeShan sees three factors in "the basic emotional pattern of the cancer patient": "a childhood or adolescence marked by feelings of isolation," the loss of "meaningful relationship," and the "conviction that life holds no more hope." Cancer patients, he finds, are "empty of feeling and devoid of self."

60. Nietzsche, *The Will to Power,* Note 18, p. 16. Also see Heidegger, "Letter on Humanism," *Basic Writings* (New York: Harper and Row, 1977), 210. My own interpolation.

61. Horkheimer, 171–72.

62. Jurgen Habermas, "Moral Development and Ego Identity," in *Communication and the Evolution of Society* (Boston: Beacon, 1979), 78. Italics added.

63. Heidegger, "Overcoming Metaphysics," 103.

64. Ibid., 88.

65. Ibid., 102.

66. Habermas, 70.

67. Ibid., 71.

68. Lasch, 50.

69. Nathan Schwartz-Salant, *Narcissism and Character Transformation: The Psychology of Narcissistic Character Disorders* (Toronto: Inner City Books, 1982), 106.

70. Ibid., 72.

71. Kovel, 104.

72. Schwartz-Salant, 36.

73. Heidegger, "Nietzsche's Word: 'God is dead'," 68.

74. Freud, "On Narcissism: An Introduction," *Standard Edition,* vol. 14, 67–102.

75. Heinz Kohut, *The Restoration of the Self* (New York: International Universities Press, 1977), 267–291.

76. Ibid., 193.

77. Ibid., 192–93.

78. Ibid., 130. Italics added.

79. Ibid., 137.

80. Ibid., 152.

81. Rene Descartes, "Meditations on First Philosophy," in Elizabeth S. Haldane and G.R.T. Ross (trans. and ed.), *The Philosophical Works of Descartes* (New York: Dover, 1955), Vol. I, Second Meditation, p. 116.

82. Heidegger, "The Age of the World Picture," in *The Question Concerning Technology and Other Essays,* p. 140.

83. Schwartz-Salant, 48.

84. Ibid., 67.

85. Ibid., 99. Also see pp. 91–107.

86. Merleau-Ponty, "The Intertwining–The Chiasm," *The Visible and the Invisible* (Evanston: Northwestern University, 1968), 159. Going more deeply than the tradition into the phenomenology of the body, Merleau-Ponty brought to light (pp. 139, 141, 249, 255–256) a narcissism whose intercorporeality *contests* the Cartesian version. Also see Paul Ricouer, *Freud and Philosophy: An Essay on Interpretation* (New Haven: Yale University Press, 1970), 127n and 425.

87. Schwartz-Salant, 37.

88. Kohut, 81.

89. Nietzsche, *The Will to Power,* Note 20, p. 16.

90. See C. R. Badcock's recent book in "social psychoanalysis," *Madness and Modernity,* cited earlier. This is one of his principal theses.

91. Adorno, 50.

92. Henry, 109.

93. Ibid.

94. Ibid., 110.

95. Schwartz-Salant, 49.

96. Heidegger, "The Question Concerning Technology," 27.

97. Heidegger, "The Word of Nietzsche: 'God is dead'," 83–84.

98. Ibid.

99. Heidegger, "Overcoming Metaphysics," *The End of Philosophy,* 107.

100. Ibid.

101. Ibid.

102. Ibid., 103.

103. Kovel, 106.

104. Ibid., 125.

105. See Horkheimer, 172 and Adorno, 237.

106. Schwartz-Salant, 106.

107. Henry, 110.

108. Heidegger, "The Age of the World Picture," 142.

109. Laing, 57.

110. Schwartz-Salant, 98.

111. See p. 111 in Turner's book, *The Body and Society,* cited earlier.

112. Charles H. Cooley, *Human Nature and the Social Order* (New Brunswick, N.J.: Transaction Books, 1983). For further studies on narcissism, see Otto Kernberg, *Borderline Conditions and Pathological Narcissism* (New York: Aronson, 1975); Donald Winnicott, *The Maturational Process and the Facilitating Environment* (New York: International Universities Press, 1965); Shirley Sugarman, *Sin and Madness: Studies in Narcissism;* Bela Grunberger, *Narcissism* (New York: International Universities Press, 1979); Herbert Marcuse, "On Hedonism," in *Negations* (Boston: Beacon, 1968); and Tarthang Tulku, *Knowledge of Freedom* (Berkeley: Dharma Publishing, 1984), 196–201.

113. Laing, *The Politics of Experience* (New York: Ballantine Books, 1968), 28.

114. Horkheimer, 180.

115. Adorno, 104.
116. Nietzsche, *The Genealogy of Morals,* 226.
117. Henry, 101.
118. Adorno, 239.
119. Tarthang Tulku, 40–41.
120. Adorno, 164.
121. Rene Descartes, *Meditations on First Philosophy* (London: Harmondsworth, 1968), 96. Also see S. J. Beck, "Errors in Perception and Fantasy in Schizophrenia," in J. S. Kasanin (ed.) *Language and Thought in Schizophrenia* (Berkeley: University of California, 1976).
122. See Jacques Derrida, "Cogito and the History of Madness," in *Writing and Difference* (Chicago: University of Chicago Press, 1980); Michel Foucault, "My Body, this paper, this fire," *The Oxford Literary Review,* 4, no. 1 (Autumn, 1979): 9–28; Francis Barker, *The Tremulous Private Body* (Berkeley: University of California Press, 1985), 35–36 and p. 61; and Paul Schilder, *The Image and Appearance of the Human Body* (London: Routledge & Kegan Paul, 1935).
123. Frederick C. Redlich and Daniel K. Freedman, *The Theory and Practice of Psychiatry* (New York: Basic Books, 1966), 459. Also see p. 478.
124. Ibid., 461.
125. Laing, *The Divided Self: An Existential Study in Sanity and Madness* (Baltimore: Penguin Books, 1965), 144. Also see p. 82.
126. Harold Searles, "Integration and Differentiation in Schizophrenia: An Over-All View," in *Collected Papers on Schizophrenia and Related Subjects* (New York: International University Press, 1965), 318. Also see Harry Stack Sullivan, *The Interpersonal Theory of Psychiatry* (New York: W. W. Norton, 1953), 158–171.
127. Searles, 318.
128. Searles, "The Effort to Drive the Other Person Crazy—An Element in the Aetiology and Psychology of Schizophrenia," *Collected Papers,* 261.
129. Searles, "Anxiety in Paranoia," *Collected Papers,* 477.
130. Searles, "Modes of Driving the Other Person Crazy," *Collected Papers,* 257.
131. Ibid.
132. Ibid., 260.
133. Nietzsche, *The Will to Power,* 14.
134. See S. Arieti, *The Interpretation of Schizophrenia* (New York: Brunner, 1955); C. A. Whitaker, *Psychotherapy of Chronic Schizophrenic Patients* (Boston: Little Brown, 1958); D. W. Winnicott, *Collected Papers* (London: Tavistock, 1958); E. B. Brody and F. C. Redlich (eds.), *Psychotherapy with Schizophrenics* (New York: International University Press, 1952).
135. Heidegger, "Overcoming Metaphysics," *The End of Philosophy,* 110.
136. Ibid.
137. Ibid., 87.
138. Adorno, 235.

Index